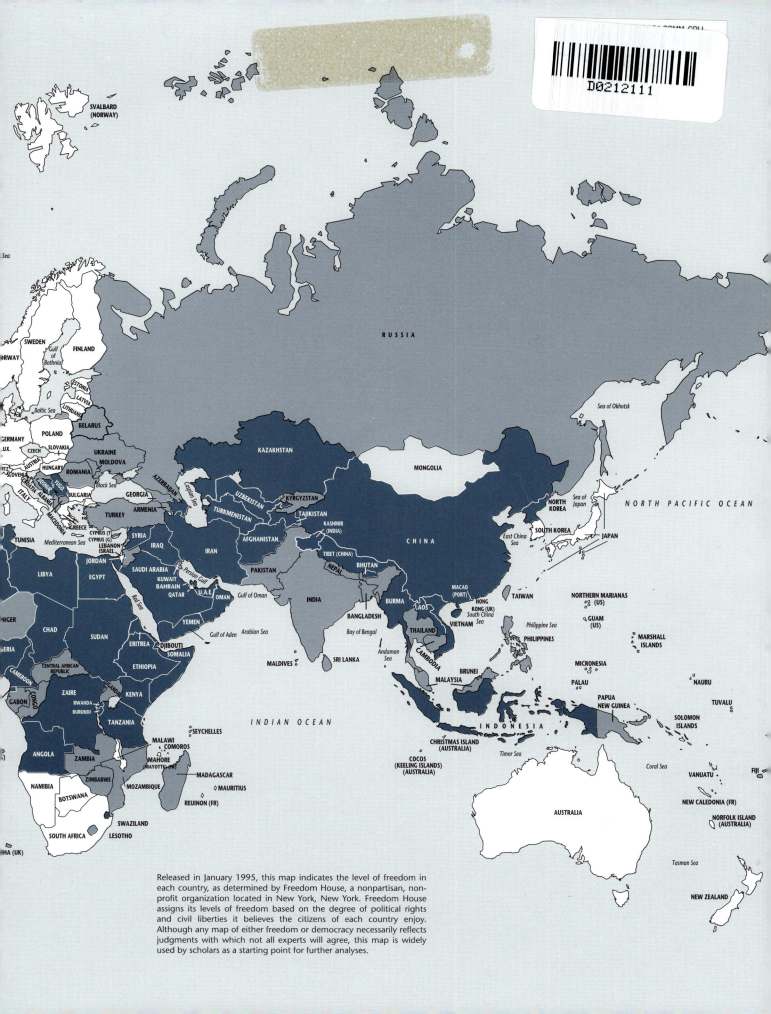

Released in January 1995, this map indicates the level of freedom in each country, as determined by Freedom House, a nonpartisan, non-profit organization located in New York, New York. Freedom House assigns its levels of freedom based on the degree of political rights and civil liberties it believes the citizens of each country enjoy. Although any map of either freedom or democracy necessarily reflects judgments with which not all experts will agree, this map is widely used by scholars as a starting point for further analyses.

THE ENCYCLOPEDIA OF DEMOCRACY

THE ENCYCLOPEDIA OF DEMOCRACY

S E Y M O U R   M A R T I N   L I P S E T
Editor in Chief

V O L U M E   I V

C O N G R E S S I O N A L   Q U A R T E R L Y   I N C .
Washington, D.C.

Book design and production by Kachergis Book Design,
Pittsboro, North Carolina

Printed and bound in the United States of America

The paper used in this publication meets the minimum requirements
of the American National Standard for Information Sciences—Permanence of Paper for Printed Library Materials, ANSI z39.48-1984.

Photo credits and permissions for copyrighted material begin on page
1553, which is to be considered an extension of the copyright page.

Endpapers Map of Freedom courtesy of Freedom House, New York,
New York

Pericles' funeral oration reprinted by permission from *Thucydides History of the Peloponnesian War*, translated by Rex Warner (Penguin Classics,
1954). Translation copyright © Rex Warner, 1954.

African Charter on Human and Peoples' Rights copyright © Amnesty
International Publications. Reprinted by permission.

LIBRARY OF CONGRESS CATALOGING-IN-PUBLICATION DATA
The encyclopedia of democracy / Seymour Martin Lipset, editor in chief.
    p.   cm.
  Includes bibliographical references (p.   ) and index.
  ISBN 0-87187-675-2 (set : alk. paper)
  ISBN 0-87187-886-0 (v.1 : alk. paper)
  ISBN 0-87187-887-9 (v.2 : alk. paper)
  ISBN 0-87187-888-7 (v.3 : alk. paper)
  ISBN 0-87187-889-5 (v.4 : alk. paper)

  1. Democracy—Encyclopedias.   I. Lipset, Seymour Martin.
JC423.E53   1995
321.8'03—dc20
                        95-34217
                          CIP

ABOUT THE EDITORS

EDITOR IN CHIEF

SEYMOUR MARTIN LIPSET is the Virginia E. Hazel and John T. Hazel, Jr. Professor of Public Policy and Professor of Sociology at the Institute of Public Policy at George Mason University. He is also the Caroline S. G. Munro Professor in the Departments of Political Science and Sociology, and Senior Fellow at the Hoover Institution on War, Revolution, and Peace, Stanford University. He received his Ph.D. from Columbia University.

Professor Lipset is the vice chair of the Center for Peace in the Middle East and is a past president of the American Political Science Association. He is coeditor of the *International Journal of Public Opinion Research* and is the author of many books, articles, and monographs, including *Political Man: The Social Bases of Politics; Revolution and Counterrevolution; Continental Divide: Values and Institutions of the United States and Canada;* and *Distinctive Cultures: Canada and the United States.*

EDITORIAL BOARD

LARRY DIAMOND is senior research fellow at the Hoover Institution on War, Revolution, and Peace, Stanford University, and coeditor of the *Journal of Democracy.* He received his Ph.D. from Stanford University. He is the author of several articles and books, including *Class, Ethnicity and Democracy in Nigeria: The Failure of the First Republic,* and is coeditor of *Democracy in Developing Countries.*

ADA W. FINIFTER is professor in the Department of Political Science at Michigan State University and managing editor of *American Political Science Review.* She received her Ph.D. from the University of Wisconsin—Madison. She is the author of several books and monographs and the editor of *Political Science: The State of the Discipline* and *Alienation and the Social System.*

GAIL W. LAPIDUS is senior fellow at the Institute for International Studies, Stanford University, and professor emeritus of political science at the University of California, Berkeley. She received her Ph.D. from Harvard University. She is the author of *State and Society in the USSR* and *Women in Soviet Society: Equality, Development and Social Change.*

AREND LIJPHART is professor of political science at the University of California, San Diego, and president of the American Political Science Association. He received his Ph.D. from Yale University. Among his many publications is *Electoral Laws and Party Systems in Western Democracies, 1945–1990.*

JUAN J. LINZ is Sterling Professor of Political and Social Science at Yale University. He received his Ph.D. from Columbia University. He is the author or coeditor of several books, including *The Breakdown of Democratic Regimes: Crisis, Breakdown, and Reequilibrium.*

THOMAS L. PANGLE is professor of political science at the University of Toronto and a fellow at St. Michael's College. He received his Ph.D. from the University of Chicago. He is the author of several books, including *The Ennobling of Democracy as the Challenge of the Postmodern Age* and *The Spirit of Modern Republicanism: The Moral Vision of the American Founders and the Philosophy of Locke.*

LUCIAN W. PYE is Ford Professor of Political Science at the Massachusetts Institute of Technology. He received his Ph.D. from Yale University. He is a past president of the American Political Science Association. His many publications include *The Mandarin and the Cadre: The Political Culture of Confucian Leninism* and *Asian Power and Politics.*

GEORGE H. QUESTER is professor and chairman of the Department of Government and Politics at the University of Maryland. He received his Ph.D. from Harvard University. He is the author of *Deterrence before Hiroshima* as well as many other books, articles, and monographs.

PHILIPPE C. SCHMITTER is professor in the Department of Political Science at Stanford University. He received his Ph.D. from the University of California, Berkeley. He is coeditor of *Transitions from Authoritarian Rule: Prospects for Democracy* and *Private Interest Government and Public Policy.*

CONTENTS

THE ENCYCLOPEDIA OF DEMOCRACY

S

Sakharov, Andrei Dmitrievich

Renowned Russian physicist who became still better known as the most distinguished Russian political dissident from the 1960s until the 1980s. Sakharov (1921–1989) was awarded the Nobel Peace Prize in 1975. Born in Moscow, the son of a physics teacher, he became one of the most important theoretical and nuclear physicists of his generation. Having played a vital role in the development of the first Soviet hydrogen bomb, he became acutely concerned about the harmful effects of testing nuclear weapons. That anxiety brought him into conflict with the Soviet authorities in the era of Nikita Khrushchev, who was first secretary from 1953 to 1964.

Later Sakharov broadened his areas of concern to embrace the cause of human rights within the Soviet Union. He was constantly harassed by the secret police (the KGB), with the direct approval of the Communist Party leadership. Although Sakharov's fame provided some measure of protection, it did not prevent the leadership under Leonid Brezhnev from exiling him from Moscow to the provincial city of Gorky (now Nizhny Novgorod) in 1980, following his outspoken criticism of the Soviet military intervention in Afghanistan in December 1979. Although communication from Gorky was difficult, Sakharov continued to criticize the Soviet government and to campaign for human rights with the help of his indefatigable wife, Yelena Bonner.

Under a different Soviet leadership, Sakharov was allowed to return to Moscow—following a telephone call from Mikhail Gorbachev in December 1986—and he at once resumed his dissident activities. He called for more resolute democratization and proposed that a new union treaty be drawn up to put the association of nations of the Soviet Union on a new, voluntary basis.

Andrei Dmitrievich Sakharov

When elections were introduced for a new legislature, the Congress of People's Deputies of the USSR, in 1989, Sakharov was elected from the Academy of Sciences (a third of the deputies having been chosen by "social organizations" and two-thirds from territorial districts). He became an exceptionally active deputy, although persecution over the years by the KGB had taken its toll on his physical strength. He clashed repeatedly with conservative Communist deputies and also at times with Gorbachev, to whom he had offered "conditional support." Sakharov remained unafraid of courting unpopularity (as when he claimed that Soviet troops in Afghanistan had committed atrocities).

Although long revered by the intelligentsia in the Soviet Union as a beacon of moral rectitude, Sakharov began to gain popularity with a broader Soviet public only in the last year of his life—and, still more, as a martyr after his death. The most inspirational of dissidents, whose campaigns had at last been accorded political legitimacy, died on December 14, 1989, while preparing for the next day's struggle at the Second Congress of People's Deputies.

See also *Dissidents; Union of Soviet Socialist Republics.*

Archie Brown

Julio María Sanguinetti

Sanguinetti, Julio María

First democratic president of Uruguay after the country spent twelve years under military rule. Sanguinetti (1936–) was elected president in 1984 after a negotiated transition from authoritarian rule. During his first administration (1985–1989), he had to reach some form of agreement concerning past human rights violations and to consolidate the restoration of democracy.

A lawyer, journalist, and writer, Sanguinetti began his political career in the Batllista faction of the Colorado Party under the leadership of Luis Batlle Berres. He was elected to the Uruguayan Congress in 1963 and reelected in 1966 and 1971. In 1966 he helped draft the document that became the 1967 constitution. He also served as minister of industry and energy (1966–1971) and as minister of education and culture (1973). After a military coup in 1973, he was forbidden to engage in political activity.

In 1980 Sanguinetti opposed the constitutional reform advocated by the armed forces then in power. During the transitional period, he was one of the major negotiators in the talks with the military. In the 1984 election the Colorado Party won with 41 percent of the votes. Under Uruguay's system of double simultaneous vote, Sanguinetti, who was the Colorado Party's presidential candidate, was elected by 31 percent of the votes.

The early years of Sanguinetti's administration were marked by the consensus of political factions that wanted to protect the country's fragile democracy. But the divisive issue of human rights violations had to be dealt with. During the Sanguinetti administration a law was passed that allowed the state to refrain from prosecuting human rights abuses committed by the military and police forces during the authoritarian period. The law was widely opposed. In April 1989 it was the subject of a plebiscite, which the Sanguinetti government won with 56 percent of the votes.

In November 1994 Sanguinetti ran as the principal candidate of the Colorado Party for a second term as president and won a very tight race over the National Party and the Broad Front, a leftist coalition. After this difficult victory, Sanguinetti began building a government of coalition.

Juan Rial

São Tomé and Principe

See *Africa, Lusophone*

Saudi Arabia

See *Middle East*

Scandinavia

Five countries—Denmark, Finland, Iceland, Norway, and Sweden—that stretch from the borders of Russia and Germany to the North Atlantic. The Scandinavian (also called Nordic) countries make up a singular geographic, socioeconomic, and political region within western Europe. A largely evolutionary pattern of political development has yielded constitutional monarchies in Denmark, Norway, and Sweden and republics with elected heads of state in Finland and Iceland. Despite these nominal differences, all the Scandinavian countries are characterized by parliamentary forms of government, working multiparty systems, and a political culture in which decisions are usually reached by consensus rather than through conflict.

Since the 1930s the Scandinavian states have maintained stable political democracies while achieving economic prosperity and establishing comprehensive welfare systems. Sweden, in particular, has been in the forefront of Western nations in seeking to supplement political democracy with innovative forms of industrial and economic democracy. At the same time, the Nordic states face multiple domestic and regional challenges to their continued economic and political stability.

Factors of Scandinavian Singularity

The distinctive political, social, and economic achievements of the Scandinavian states can be attributed to several factors. One is the region's relative insularity in the far northern reaches of western Europe. Denmark is a geo-graphical extension of the European continent, thrusting northward from Germany into the North Sea to the west and separated by a narrow sound from Sweden to the east. Physically separated from, but constitutionally part of, Denmark are the self-governing territories of Greenland (situated off the coast of Canada) and the Faroe Islands (located north of the United Kingdom). Finland shares a long eastern border with Russia and shorter northern and western borders with Sweden and Norway. The remainder of Scandinavia consists of the Swedish-Norwegian peninsula and Iceland in the North Atlantic.

The insulating effects of geography have made the region culturally and socially homogeneous. Denmark, Norway, and Sweden were settled between 14,000 and 4000 B.C. by Germanic tribes that moved northward from the Baltic regions. Norwegians and Danes later claimed and settled the Faroe Islands, Iceland, and Greenland. Finland is a more complex case involving successive migrations by Germanic tribes, Swedes, Lapps, and a Finno-Ugrian tribe from central Russia whose southern branches moved into Estonia and Hungary. After national kingdoms were established in the early Middle Ages, relatively little migration took place.

Ethnic homogeneity in Scandinavia is reinforced by the unifying effects of language and religion. Originally, the Danes, Norwegians, and Swedes spoke much the same language. Substantial national and regional differences in speech and grammar evolved over the centuries, but the three languages remain closely related. Because of their geographical isolation in the North Atlantic, the Icelanders continue to speak and write an ancient form of Scandinavian. Finnish is linguistically distinctive, but a minority of Finns speak Swedish as their first language.

Even more pervasive is religious homogeneity. The region as a whole became Christianized from about A.D. 800, and during the sixteenth century the Scandinavian kingdoms converted uniformly to Lutheran Protestantism. Minority faiths (including various Protestant sects, Roman Catholicism, and Judaism) exist, but the "majority culture" remains overwhelmingly Lutheran.

Additional factors in Scandinavia's regional singularity are the countries' closely intertwined national histories and a diffuse sense of a shared Nordic identity. Denmark and Norway (along with more remote Iceland) were originally a single kingdom, as were Sweden and Finland. Danish rulers united the region in 1397 to form the Kalmar Union, but the Swedes rebelled during the 1520s to reestablish Sweden and Finland as a separate kingdom. In the course and aftermath of the Napoleonic Wars, Russia annexed Finland in 1808–1809, and the victorious anti-French coalition forced Denmark, which had been allied with France, to cede Norway to Sweden in 1814. Full national autonomy was achieved throughout Scandinavia only in the twentieth century. Norway declared its independence from Sweden in 1905, Finland seceded from the Russian empire during the throes of the Revolution of 1917, and Iceland severed constitutional ties from Denmark in 1944.

Transitions to Democracy

Scandinavia's intertwined history and other regional singularities made for parallel patterns of successful democratization during the latter half of the nineteenth century and the early part of the twentieth. Comparable to the evolutionary course of constitutional and political change in England following the Glorious Revolution of 1688, democratization in Scandinavia proceeded in a largely peaceful fashion. Democratization occurred first in Norway, followed by Denmark, Finland, Sweden, and Iceland.

Various historical and systemic factors distinctive to Scandinavia contributed to the ultimate success and stability of democracy in the Nordic states. They include a deeply rooted tradition of rule by law and strategic collaboration among reform-minded political parties and socioeconomic organizations. Nationalism also contributed to the democratization process, particularly in Norway, Finland, and Iceland, where opposition to outside rule served as a unifying force in a simultaneous struggle for national independence.

Codified rules governing interpersonal relations as well as the rights and obligations of elected kings were present in Sweden as early as the first century after Christ. The precedent of formal legal codes binding on rulers and citizens alike served as the basis for national constitutions promulgated in 1282 in Denmark-Norway and in 1682 in Sweden-Finland. Alongside formal legal codes and written constitutions, representative institutions emerged during the medieval period in the form of regional assemblies of freemen and a national assembly of nobles in Denmark; a general assembly (*Althing*) in Iceland; and a four-estate parliament (*Riksdag*) representing the nobility, the clergy, urban citizens, and farmers in Sweden-Finland. The powers of these representative bodies were subsequently eclipsed by the advent of monarchical supremacy in 1681

in Denmark-Norway and periods of absolutism in Sweden-Finland (1682–1718 and 1771–1809), but historical memories of a Scandinavian tradition of constitutionalism inspired later generations of reformers to seek to restore a system of rule by law.

Such aspirations were partially fulfilled in 1809 in Sweden following the kingdom's loss of Finland to Russia. A coalition of disgruntled nobles and military officers deposed the last of Sweden's absolute monarchs, and a parliamentary committee crafted a new constitution that established a balance of political power between the king and the Riksdag. To prevent the potential abuse of bureaucratic power, the founders of 1809 created a new office of parliamentary ombudsman with autonomous legal authority to ensure that the civil service (including the military) performed its duties in strict accordance with the law. The Riksdag invited a French marshal and former confidant of Napoleon, Jean-Baptiste-Jules Bernadotte, to become crown prince in 1810. Bernadotte subsequently ruled as King Charles XIV John.

These events set into motion an evolutionary process of constitutional and political change that culminated a century later in the advent of modern Swedish parliamentarianism. Bernadotte—like the British kings George I and II before him—never learned the native tongue of his adopted country and therefore depended for counsel on his parliamentary advisers. For this reason, an incipient form of cabinet government began to emerge from the outset of Bernadotte's reign.

Democratic breakthroughs occurred in Norway and Denmark for strikingly different reasons. A delegation of Norwegian nationalists drew up a liberal constitution at Eidsvoll in 1814 in an attempt to declare Norwegian independence after centuries of Danish domination. That effort failed when the victorious anti-Napoleonic coalition transferred authority over Norway from Denmark to Sweden in compensation for Sweden's earlier loss of Finland to Russia. Sweden nonetheless recognized the substance of the Eidsvoll constitution, including its provisions for a separate Norwegian parliament (the *Storting.*)

During subsequent decades, pro-independence forces in the form of a Liberal Left Party and the Agrarians gained increased popular support. The introduction of annual legislative sessions in 1866 enhanced the parliament's role as the principal institutional source of opposition to Swedish rule, and in 1884 the Liberals and Agrarians compelled the Swedish king to accept the principle of cabinet government in Norway. By 1887 Norway's incipi-

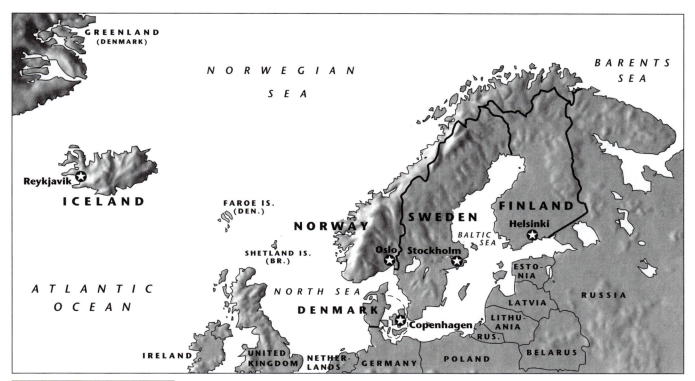

ent industrialization encouraged the formation of a third reformist group—the Norwegian Labor (Social Democratic) Party—whose leaders joined with the Liberals and Agrarians to press for suffrage reform as the next step toward full democracy. Increasingly assertive in regard to Sweden, a majority in the Storting introduced manhood suffrage in 1898 and declared full independence in 1905. The right to vote was extended to women between 1907 and 1913. Primarily because of the intensity of the independence movement, Norway became the first of the Nordic countries to achieve parliamentary government on the basis of universal suffrage.

Denmark's transition to democracy followed quickly. The Continental revolutions of 1848 had inspired an ostensibly liberal constitution based on manhood suffrage (adopted in 1849), but conservative elites sustained the system of monarchical absolutism through the remainder of the century. Advocates of reform included an agrarian-based Left Party, urban radicals, and, after 1871, the Social Democrats. Yielding to increased electoral support for

pro-democracy groups in the wake of industrialization and urbanization, the Danish king, in 1901, appointed a cabinet responsible to the parliamentary majority in the lower house of the bicameral *Rigsdag*. A governing coalition dominated by the agrarian and urban Liberals introduced universal suffrage (based on proportional representation) in 1915 to complete Denmark's political democratization. A new constitution adopted in 1953 transformed the Rigsdag into a unicameral parliament known as the *Folketing*.

Democratization was slower in Sweden. The abolition of the four-estate parliament in favor of a bicameral Riksdag in 1866–1867 encouraged the formation of a Ruralist Party representing smaller farmers in the lower house, but the Ruralists lacked a coherent program of reform and proved no match for the nobility that dominated the indirectly elected upper house. The initiative for democratic reform fell instead to Sweden's nascent liberal movement and the Social Democrats. Significantly, at their founding congress in 1889, the Social Democrats disavowed Marxist notions of class conflict and violent revolution in favor of strategic collaboration with the Liberals on behalf of common minimum objectives—notably suffrage reform and the introduction of the principle of parliamentary government. With continuing industrialization and the proliferation of trade unions from the 1890s onward, both parties increased their electoral strength. In a series of constitutional reforms implemented in 1907–1909, the Liberals and the Social Democrats struck a historic compromise with the Conservatives to introduce manhood suffrage and proportional representation. Under the duress of World War I, the Swedish king appointed a majority Liberal–Social Democratic cabinet in 1917. The Liberal–Social Democratic coalition enacted universal suffrage in 1919–1921, thereby completing the democratization process.

Swedish democracy has been modified through the creation in 1970 of a unicameral parliament (still known as the Riksdag), whose members are elected for three-year terms, and the adoption of a new constitution in 1973–1974, which transformed the monarchy into a strictly ceremonial office. The new constitution formally codifies principles of popular sovereignty and parliamentary government and provides for the election of the prime minister by members of the Riksdag.

In Finland the Russian revolutions of 1905 and 1917 directly affected the attainment of democratization and national independence. Even after it was incorporated into the Russian empire as a semiautonomous grand duchy in 1809, Finland retained its own constitution and administrative-legal structures. An embryonic parliament existed in the form of a four-estate diet known as the *Eduskunta,* which met in 1809 to sanction Russia's annexation of Finland but otherwise did not convene again until 1863. Through the latter part of the nineteenth century, efforts by czarist officials to Russify Finnish society and politics met with increasingly vocal opposition. A Finnish Party and a Swedish People's Party were established during the 1860s and 1870s to defend the majority and minority cultures and languages, respectively. By the 1890s a Finnish Social Democratic Party (which was ideologically more radical than its counterparts in neighboring Sweden and Denmark) joined them in opposition to Russian dominance. Russia's first revolution of 1905 offered the reformers an unexpected opportunity to press their political demands during a brief period of liberalization. The four-estate parliament was replaced by a unicameral legislature, and Finland enacted universal suffrage in 1906. The czarist government sought to reverse liberalization by resorting once again to a concerted program of Russification. This effort ended in 1917, when Russia experienced two revolutions, withdrew from World War I, and overthrew its monarchy. A Socialist-led majority government was

formed in Finland in March, and the Finnish parliament proclaimed independence on December 6, 1917.

A tragic interlude of civil war followed, in which the Finnish Social Democrats—increasingly the captives of revolutionary leaders inspired by V. I. Lenin's example—sought with the support of the fledgling Bolshevik regime in Moscow to seize power and establish a Marxist state of their own. Beginning in January 1918, Finland was convulsed for four months by a savage military-political struggle between revolutionary "Red Guards" and a nationalist "White Army" under the command of Gen. Carl Gustav Emil Mannerheim, a former czarist officer. In contrast to the outcome of the Russian civil war across the border, the Finnish Whites won. General Mannerheim's forces captured and disarmed Russian garrisons in central-western and northern Finland and then defeated the Finnish Reds to the south. The war ended after a German expeditionary force captured the capital, Helsinki. Following national elections in March 1919, the Eduskunta adopted a new republican constitution. The constitution established a dual executive consisting of an indirectly elected president and a cabinet responsible to a parliamentary majority. At long last independent, Finland became the fourth Scandinavian country to attain democracy.

Iceland, too, defined its national identity in opposition to external rule. For centuries a Danish colony, Iceland began its struggle for independence during the 1830s. A new generation of nationalist poets helped awaken consciousness of a distinctive Icelandic culture and rekindled historical memories of a distant independent past. In 1848 the Danish king allowed the reestablishment of an Icelandic parliament (the *Althing)* on a consultative basis. Legislative factions, which began to appear during the remainder of the century as advocates of home rule, eventually evolved into modern political parties consisting of the Progressives, the Independence Party, and a Farmers' Party. Because industrialization did not commence until the early part of the twentieth century, the Social Democratic Party was founded only in 1916.

Following its own transition to parliamentary government in 1901, Denmark sanctioned the introduction of universal suffrage in Iceland in 1903. In 1918 the Danish government proclaimed an Act of Union recognizing Icelandic home rule in all but foreign affairs. Iceland achieved full independence (endorsed by a national plebiscite) in June 1944, at a time when Denmark itself was occupied by

German troops. The new constitution provided for a directly elected president with the authority to appoint a prime minister, who in turn was politically accountable to a majority of the members of the unicameral Icelandic parliament. Both the president and legislative deputies are elected for four-year terms.

Sweden, Norway, and Denmark pursued policies of neutrality during World War I and cooperated closely both among themselves (and with newly independent Finland) within the League of Nations during the interwar period. They sought—vainly, as events proved—to remain neutral during World War II as well. Joseph Stalin attacked Finland in 1939 in a fruitless attempt to reincorporate the country into the Russian empire, and Germany invaded and occupied Denmark and Norway in 1940. Neutrality worked only for Sweden, which alone among the Nordic states escaped direct involvement in the war. As a result of these divergent wartime experiences, postwar leaders in Denmark, Norway, and Iceland decided to join the North Atlantic Treaty Organization (NATO) in 1949, whereas Sweden retained its traditional policy of nonalignment. Under terms of a state treaty signed in 1948 with the Soviet Union, Finland, too, embraced a foreign policy of neutrality.

After World War II, the Scandinavian states intensified regional public and private ties by promoting cultural, social, and political cooperation through the Nordic Council (established in 1952) and implementing a common labor market and passport union. Postwar efforts to establish a full-fledged Scandinavian common market foundered when Denmark opted to join the European Economic Community (now the European Union) in 1972. With the end of the cold war, Sweden and Finland became members of the European Union in 1995, while Norway rejected membership.

Modern Scandinavian Democracy

The evolutionary nature of Scandinavia's democratic transitions—with the exception of Finland's civil war of 1918—helps explain the emergence of national political cultures characterized by pragmatism and ideological moderation. An important constant over time has been Scandinavia's deeply rooted tradition of constitutionalism, which legitimized rule by law and accorded respect to opposing points of view. Traditional aristocratic-bureaucratic elites initially resisted demands for reform, but they ultimately accepted political change when it became inevitable. That they did so was due in no small measure to the responsible behavior of the Liberals, Social Democrats, Agrarians, and other reformist parties that sought democratization and—in the case of Norway and Iceland—national independence. Only in Finland were constitutional democrats compelled to resort to arms in order to ensure a successful democratic transition.

Support for constitutional norms among the general population and elites has developed into a democratic political culture in which consensus plays an important role. A key measure of that democratic consensus was weak popular support for radical right movements during the height of fascist power in Central and Eastern Europe. Norwegian National Socialists (Nazis) captured a minuscule average of 2 percent support in the two national elections preceding the German invasion in 1940, and their Danish counterparts mobilized only 2.1 percent in the 1943 election (which was held under German occupation). In Sweden, Nazi sympathizers received less than 1 percent of the vote in elections held between 1932 and 1940. Because of the perceived threat of a possible Soviet invasion, the corresponding percentage was higher in Finland, peaking at 7 percent in 1936.

In contrast, support for radical left movements in Scandinavia has proved somewhat stronger—as events in 1918 in Finland dramatically indicated. The Norwegian Labor Party also became radicalized early in the interwar period when its leaders temporarily joined the Soviet-dominated Third International, prompting dissident moderates to form a separate Social Democratic Workers' Party. The Labor Party quit the Third International several years later, and the two factions reunited in 1927. Radical socialists throughout Scandinavia formed communist parties during the early 1920s in support of a Marxist path to socialism. None, however, has actively pursued revolutionary methods. Communist strength increased to an average of 11.6 percent in the first elections after World War II in Denmark, Norway, and Sweden but dropped to 4 percent or less in subsequent decades. A communist-dominated electoral alliance known as the Finnish People's League fared somewhat better in successive postwar elections to the Eduskunta, but the league began to lose votes in the early 1970s, and the communist component has since split into feuding Stalinist and Eurocommunist factions. In recent years, most radical left support has gone to maverick non-Marxist "people's parties" in Denmark and Norway or to environmentalist movements.

Much of the explanation for the relative weakness of leftist radicalism and fascism in Scandinavia lies in the organizational strength and policy effectiveness of the Social Democrats, the largest party throughout most of the region. Affiliated with powerful national federations of organized labor, which provide the bulk of their electoral support, the Social Democrats rose to power during the late 1920s and mid-1930s and dominated national politics throughout central Scandinavia for most of the next fifty years. Governing variously in coalition with the Liberals and the Radical Liberals (as in Denmark), the Agrarians (as in Sweden), or alone (as was generally the case in Norway), Scandinavia's Social Democrats served as the main architects of expansionist economic policies and comprehensive social reforms that earned for Scandinavia a collective reputation as a "model for the world."

The Social Democrats acted on their ideological affirmation of material progress and social security to help engineer Scandinavia's recovery from the debilitating effects of the Great Depression, implement comprehensive welfare services, and manage unprecedented economic expansion after World War II. Social legislation sponsored by the Social Democrats included universal retirement benefits, disability and unemployment insurance, national health care, financial assistance to low-income families and single parents, and cash allowances for all children regardless of household income. The Social Democrats also implemented supplementary pension systems in Sweden and Norway during the 1950s and 1960s to benefit middle-class wage earners. Their long-term success in office throughout Scandinavia was by no means due to partisan efforts alone. The Social Democrats cooperated closely with the private sector to promote economic growth while benefiting from an extraordinary expansion of world trade during much of the postwar era.

During the 1970s and early 1980s Sweden's Social Democrats embarked on an ambitious course to promote industrial and economic democracy. Under the leadership of Prime Minister Olof Palme, they initiated legislation to expand the consultative rights of unions in managerial decisions and introduced a controversial system of "wage earner funds" (financed through a tax on company profits) whose purpose was to purchase company shares on the stock market. Palme's assassination by an unknown assailant in 1986, however, marked a temporary end to Swedish efforts to extend democratic principles from the political system to individual enterprises and the economy at large.

Despite their impressive economic and social achievements, the Social Democrats gradually lost electoral support during the 1980s and 1990s. In part, they were victims of their own success; voters wearied of familiar faces and policies. More important, bureaucratization and the high costs of the welfare state—which have resulted in some of the highest tax rates in the world—created an electoral backlash in favor of various nonsocialist parties and new protest movements such as tax-revolt Progress Parties in Denmark and Norway and a populist New Democracy party in Sweden. Recurrent international economic crises have also contributed to a general process of electoral dealignment throughout the region. As a result of these trends, the Social Democrats have been compelled periodically to relinquish cabinet posts to nonsocialist coalition governments. Nonetheless, they remain the largest party throughout Scandinavia (except in Iceland), and they continue to play a major political role whether in opposition or as leaders of minority governments.

By virtue of their history, constitutional traditions, and political culture, the Scandinavian countries remain firmly committed to modern democratic values, institutions, and procedures. This commitment will guide continuing efforts by Nordic leaders to ensure the region's future economic and political viability as they seek closer ties with the European Union and respond to domestic challenges.

See also *Europe, Western; Russia, Pre-Soviet; Social democracy; Tax revolts; Welfare, Promotion of.*

M. Donald Hancock

BIBLIOGRAPHY

Castles, Francis. *The Social Democratic Image of Society: A Study of the Achievements and Origins of Scandinavian Social Democracy in Comparative Perspective.* London: Routledge and Kegan Paul, 1978.

Derry, Thomas K. *A History of Modern Norway, 1814–1972.* London: Oxford University Press, 1973.

Einhorn, Eric S., and John Logue. *Modern Welfare States: Politics and Policies in Social Democratic Scandinavia.* New York and London: Praeger, 1989.

Lauwerys, J. A., ed. *Scandinavian Democracy: Development of Democratic Thought and Institutions in Denmark, Norway, and Sweden.* Copenhagen: Danish Institute, Norwegian Office of Cultural Relations, and Swedish Institute, 1958.

Rustow, Dankwart A. *The Politics of Compromise: A Study of Parties and Cabinet Government in Sweden.* Princeton: Princeton University Press, 1955.

Scott, Franklin D. *Scandinavia.* Cambridge, Mass., and London: Harvard University Press, 1975.

———. *Sweden: The Nation's History.* Minneapolis: University of Minnesota Press, 1977.

Storing, James A. *Norwegian Democracy.* Oslo: Universitetsforlaget, 1963.

Tomason, Richard F. *Iceland: The First New Society.* Minneapolis: University of Minnesota Press, 1980.

Wuorinen, John H. *A History of Finland.* New York and London: Columbia University Press, 1965.

Schumpeter, Joseph

One of the great economists of the twentieth century, best known for his theory of the entrepreneur. Schumpeter (1883–1950) was born in the Austro-Hungarian Empire, in a small town that today is situated in Slovenia and called Trest. In 1906 he received a doctorate from the University of Vienna. He later worked as an economist at various universities in Austria and Germany. After immigrating to the United States in 1932, he worked at Harvard University until his death.

From early on Schumpeter was passionately interested in politics as well as economics; he served as the Austrian finance minister in 1919. Throughout his life he wrote and commented on various political topics, but he is primarily known to political scientists today for his brilliant discussion of democracy in *Capitalism, Socialism, and Democracy,* published in 1942. In this book Schumpeter presented democracy as a method (primarily for the selection of political leaders) rather than as a goal in itself—an approach inspired by the work of the German sociologist Max Weber.

The Schumpeter-Weber theory of democracy influenced several of the major political scientists in the United States, such as Robert Dahl and Seymour Martin Lipset. A certain affinity also exists between Schumpeter's view of the political process as a competition for votes and the approach of the public choice school, in the sense that both assume that self-interest, rather than idealism, is what really matters in politics.

In chapters 20–23 of *Capitalism, Socialism, and Democracy,* Schumpeter presented his own theory of democracy as a method in contrast to what he termed the classical doctrine of democracy. The classical doctrine, he said, defined democracy as an institutional arrangement for making political decisions that realizes the common good by making the people decide issues. They do so by electing

Joseph Schumpeter

individuals who then assemble to carry out the will of the people. The classical doctrine had its roots in eighteenth-century political thought as well as in utilitarian philosophy. Schumpeter noted that it was still extremely popular with the electorate and was often referred to in political propaganda. He believed, however, that this doctrine was totally at odds with reality. For example, Schumpeter maintained, it is impossible to establish the common good, and even if it were possible to do so, this common good would be so general that it would be of no help in deciding particular questions.

Schumpeter also rejected the concept of individual volition, which he saw as central to the classical doctrine of democracy. This concept holds that individual citizens know exactly what they want in each and every question. On the contrary, Schumpeter viewed the average citizen as indecisive, irrational, and irresponsible in political questions.

Such elitist overtones should not be allowed to detract from the great originality and power of Schumpeter's argument, especially his concept of democracy as a method. Instead of viewing politicians as secondary to the political process and as mere channels for the wishes of the electorate, Schumpeter saw them as key actors in the democratic process. Following this line of thought to its logical conclusion, he came up with an alternative definition of democracy. He defined democracy as an institutional arrangement for making political decisions in which individuals acquire the power to decide by means of a competitive struggle for votes. In this view, democracy is a form of political system in which politicians have to appeal to the electorate in order to be elected. As a result, one can dispense with notions such as the common good and the belief that individual citizens always know what they want. Schumpeter's theory of democracy as a method is far more realistic than the classical doctrine.

Schumpeter's discussion of democracy is part of a larger argument about the relationship between socialism and democracy. Although he personally detested all forms of socialism, Schumpeter believed that it would in principle be possible to have democracy in a socialist society. This could happen, however, only if socialism had been introduced in a peaceful manner and if capitalism had reached a very high level of development—two conditions that immediately ruled out the Soviet Union. But even if a genuinely democratic type of socialism could conceivably come into being some day, Schumpeter said, it would be extremely fragile. The reason for this fragility—and here again Schumpeter echoed Weber—was that socialist politicians would sooner or later be tempted to extend their power to running the economy, and when this happened, their power would soon become dictatorial.

See also *Dahl, Robert A.; Lipset, Seymour Martin; Socialism; Weber, Max.*

Richard Swedberg

BIBLIOGRAPHY

Downs, Anthony. *An Economic Theory of Democracy.* New York: Harper and Row, 1957.

Mitchell, William C. "Schumpeter and Public Choice (Parts I–II)." *Public Choice* 42 (1984): 73–88, 161–174.

Schumpeter, Joseph A. *Capitalism, Socialism, and Democracy.* 3d ed. New York: Harper Colophon, 1975.

———. *Politische Reden.* Edited by Christian Seidl and Wolfgang Stolper. Tübingen: Mohr, 1992.

Swedberg, Richard. *Schumpeter: A Biography.* Princeton: Princeton University Press, 1991.

Xenos, Nicholas. "Democracy as a Method: Joseph A. Schumpeter." *Democracy* 1 (1981): 110–123.

Science

The methodical observation, description, and theoretical explanation of natural phenomena. As the basis of modern technology, science is an important prerequisite for the rise and endurance of democracy.

We often think that the intimate relation between science and democratic politics developed only with the Second World War, the atomic bomb and the cold war, and, more recently, the advent of environmentalism. Certainly these great events made the sciences—especially the natural sciences—matters of essential importance to the survival of democratic government. World War II might not have been won by the Allies had it not been for the development of radar. The regime of nuclear deterrence put physics, nuclear engineering, and ballistic rocketry at the center of nations' concerns. And the environmental challenge puts the biological and chemical sciences at the heart of many policy questions.

The environmental challenge is a result of modern technology, which is based on natural science and crucial for the material prosperity on which democracy in large part depends. It is thus true that in our time the interests of science—its financial support and its freedom and protection from interference—are bound closely to the interests of democracy.

Greek Science and Politics

But in fact the question of science and politics is very old, going back to the ancient Greeks and the beginnings of reflection about justice and the best regime. The first works on these topics—the plays and dialogues written about Socrates (c. 470–399 B.C.), the first important political philosopher—could without exaggeration be said to concern the relation between science and politics. In his comedy *The Clouds,* Aristophanes ridiculed Socrates for being both a sophist and a student of natural philosophy. As a natural philosopher, Socrates was accused of teaching that human beings were lumps of charcoal and that Zeus, the supreme deity, did not exist. As a sophist, he was accused of teaching his students how to make the weaker argument appear to be the stronger and thus how to evade justice and the law. In the play the connection between these two vocations is obvious: one who does not believe in the gods has no good reason, other than fear of punishment, to obey the law and respect justice. The knowledge that comes from science leads to atheism and enables the knower to speak well and thus influence the law and avoid punishment.

The same charges are at stake in Plato's *Apology of Socrates,* in which Socrates presents his defense against charges of atheism and corrupting the young. As is well known, Socrates lost his case and was put to death. As is less often noticed, it was a democratic regime before which he appeared.

For the Greeks, it was not at all clear that natural science was good for political life in general or democracy in particular, precisely for the reasons made clear in the accounts of Socrates' trial: justice and obedience to the laws depend on belief in the gods, and natural philosophy casts their being into doubt.

Socrates denied being a natural philosopher. It was later said that he brought philosophy down to earth from the heavens and invented political philosophy as opposed to natural philosophy. Unlike natural philosophy, political philosophy claimed to be a science of justice. Aristotle makes it clear that political philosophy seeks the truth about the just and the noble—what is by nature just and noble, as opposed to what is considered so by mere convention—even though he is careful to note that justice and nobility, because they are changeable, differ from the objects of the deductive sciences, which treat of unchangeable things.

But taking justice and nobility as genuine objects of knowledge did not mean that political philosophy and democracy—or political philosophy and any other kind of regime, for that matter—would necessarily get along. For in distinguishing between natural and conventional justice, political philosophy cast doubt on the goodness of most regimes and condemned democracy as one of the bad ones. Moreover, the distinction between nature and convention opened the way to an understanding of the good—hedonism—that was justly frowned on by anyone, including democrats, who believed in the superior moral status of the common good. It was thus not clear that political philosophy could be at peace with those who love the laws of their time and believe them to be divine.

Christianity

This situation changed with the coming of Christianity. Although sometimes quite hostile to science, especially in its earliest period, Christianity was in important ways compatible with the scientific understanding of nature. St. Augustine (A.D. 354–430), for example, argued that science and knowledge did not threaten true religion. On the contrary, in his view, natural science disproved the basic tenet of paganism—the idea that the stars and planets are gods—and thus paved the way for the Christian Gospel.

Likewise, Thomas Aquinas (1225–1274) argued that reason, including natural and political philosophy, is compatible with divine law and that the idea of a knowable, rational universe is compatible with divine power and creation. From this point of view, it would not be an exaggeration or distortion to say that the advent of Christianity helped pave the way for the idea that science and morality—and hence science and politics—can work together harmoniously.

The modern case for basing politics on science, however, was made in large part against the claims of Christianity. When Augustine and Aquinas spoke of science, they referred to knowledge that could discover the purposes of nature; they meant a teleological science, one that could comprehend some overall divine plan. Such knowledge, they believed, would disclose by reason alone what our place in nature is and what is good for us as occupants of that place. Science, then, would culminate in natural law, which prescribes what is just and unjust in human affairs. Natural law points to and is completed by divine law.

It is true that the doctrine that the universe reflects God's unfathomable will, and not some universal reason that determines God's will (known as theological voluntarism), and the later Protestant doctrine of justification by faith alone, both led to another concept of nature—a nonteleological one. It is likewise true that such a concept of nature is more in the spirit of modern science than is Augustinianism or Thomism. But modern science rejected both the teleological concept of nature—which was the basis of Thomism—and the idea, common to both Thomism and Protestantism alike, that human beings must live encumbered by sin and its wages, death.

Nothing could better reflect this modern attitude than the astonishing claim made by the English philosopher Francis Bacon (1561–1626) that when human learning is properly understood and empowered, its "noblest work" could be the conquest of death itself. In order to make such a claim, Bacon had to reject the possibility of divine miracles, including and especially the miracles of revelation and resurrection.

The Scientific Method

With the rise of modern science, especially as it was understood by thinkers such as Bacon, René Descartes, Thomas Hobbes, and John Locke, the situation once again resembled that in Socrates' Athens: science could well be hated by the people and their rulers because it challenged the divine basis of law. But the similarity did not mean that the prospects for science were the same as they were for the Greeks. The modern thinkers argued that modern natural science was different from its ancient counterpart. As Bacon explained, modern science was unique in being based on method.

By method, Bacon meant that scientific knowing should consist of regular and repeatable ways of forcing nature out of its forms and courses as we perceive them through mere common sense. When this system was followed, it would then be possible to transform the things of nature with an eye to making them useful for human ends. We discover nature by doing things to unravel the given forms of things, not by contemplating such forms as a world of unchangeable essences, as was the case with teleological natural science. And when we possess knowledge in this way, we can do more—both for life's practical needs and for further knowing. Thus modern science—science governed by method—was essentially technological in its means, in its concept of what nature is, and in its ends. The end of knowledge is power, said Bacon, to be used for the "relief of man's estate."

With this power as its offering, modern science could be compatible with the hopes and aspirations of the people, among whom religious belief would be weakened as the promise of earthly satisfaction was expanded. The atheism of science, then, would be easy to hide because, unlike the Athenians who persecuted Socrates, people in modern times would not jump so quickly to the conclusion that to study nature as if it were not created by God, and human beings as if they were not made in God's image, was to be an atheist. This situation is depicted in Bacon's famous fable *New Atlantis,* which presents a society organized around the thinking of the new modern science: the people are religious, but in an easygoing, superficial way, and they never worry that what is done by the scientists (who work largely out of sight) ignores or denies God or breaks divine law.

This concept of science was inherently democratic, because the interests of the gifted few—the scientists—were to discover the means for producing the material things desired by the people. Not everyone can study science, but everyone can enjoy its products. The scientists' real allies would thus be the people, not a privileged aristocracy interested in some contemplative perfection of the soul. Moreover, according to Bacon and his followers, such as Hobbes and Locke, a world dedicated to the scientific conquest of nature would be able to forget the conflicts that had fractured and bloodied Christendom. The scientific war against nature would replace the war of sect against sect. Indeed, science would make it possible to eliminate the scarcity that is at the root of all disputes about justice and political rule. Not only could the problem of religious conflict be settled, but the age-old disputes among regimes could be ended as well—and necessarily in favor of democracy because of the egalitarian character of modern science.

Science and Modern Public Policy

A glance at the history of the twentieth century must cast some doubt on this hopeful expectation. In the cases of fascism and communism, science appeared to be as good for tyranny as for democracy. In fact, the combination of modern science and tyranny produced an unprecedented political monstrosity: totalitarianism. Totalitarianism would not have been possible without the technology of mass communications and propaganda and without the vast power of the weapons made possible by modern science.

But it is worth remembering that modern totalitarianism was a popular, mass phenomenon that grew in response to the acquisitive, secular, and "bourgeois" democracy imagined by the first architects of the scientific project. Fascism was in large part a reaction to the blandness, softness, and banality of such a political culture, and communism was in large part a reaction to its apparent moral crassness and failure to solve quickly enough the problem of inequality.

Science has not proved incompatible with modern totalitarianism, although in the case of communism it now seems clear that socialism, not capitalism, fetters the means of production when these are informed by fast-moving developments in science and technology. Outside the Western world, modern science has in general been a force for liberalization. But it remains to be seen whether the full-fledged project of science as it developed in the West—the Baconian conquest of nature—necessarily secularizes society and obliterates traditional culture and politics. Likewise, it remains to be seen whether this project will spread to the entire world.

So although we cannot conclude that science always leads to democracy, it is fair to say that modern science is a powerful impetus to democracy and that democracy as we know it—which depends on an ever rising standard of living—cannot long endure without freedom for scientific progress. But we should not take this to mean that there are no tensions between science and democracy, or that progress in science does not pose challenges that have to be met by democratic institutions. Scientific technology differs from the traditional productive arts and crafts in many complicated respects, but perhaps the most important is its power to transform its host society in profound and often unexpected ways.

Consider the videocassette recorder, the fax machine, the cellular phone, and the fiber optic cable. Taken individually and as a whole, these inventions have important effects on civic and political life. Their combined effect is to erode the separation between public and private life as entertainment, work, and political communication enter the confines of the home and the automobile. Blurring the line between public and private life has important implications for our understanding of political and civil rights and for our conception of the scope of private liberty and its personal immunity from interference by the state.

Or take the development of safe contraception and the rapidly expanding technologies of birth and fertility. These have freed women from the constraints of biology and thus have led to transformations in the structure of the family and the place of women in business and public life. And these changes have generated such questions as the morality of abortion, the role of the state in advancing the equality of women, and the political relevance of sex (yet another erosion of the difference between public and private life).

Thus not only does scientific progress generate new problems to be solved by democratic polities (such as who controls and gets the benefits of some new device or technique), but it also puts pressure on assumptions and distinctions thought fundamental to democratic life.

On a more mundane level, conflicts can arise between scientific elites and a democratic electorate. In modern democracies the people rule, but only indirectly through representatives and not as a collective body that actually deliberates and then makes and executes the laws. The people choose those who rule and then judge the outcome. And so there is room in government and public life for those who are professional—who answer first to the standards of their expertise and only later to the desires and opinions of the many.

Most science today is practiced in universities and in large business firms and corporations, fairly well away from the institutions of government. But scientists act as professional public servants in many of the regulatory agencies of government, as advisers to various legislative bodies, and of course as petitioners for government support for their institutions and projects. In all these ways, scientists act politically on behalf of citizens who wish to be safe from disease and to live as long and as comfortably as possible.

As scientists and the voters come into closer proximity, conflict between scientific standards and public interests can occur. First, it is hard for scientists in a democracy to keep their activities from the people, and so it is not always possible for them to avoid generating unwarranted hopes, which are soon disappointed, or exaggerated fears, which are not always so soon dispelled. The short-range reputation of science is thus not guaranteed, even though modern democracies assume its benefits as a foregone conclusion. Moreover, since they often depend on public funds, a temptation can arise for scientists—especially in the fields that bear on medicine—to exaggerate what they can do or even to cheat in their experiments or descriptions of results.

As science becomes more important in formulating public policy, there are inevitable questions about the scope and legitimacy of democratic control: should scientists decide a matter, such as what to do about acid rain or global warming, or must they only advise those who can never appreciate fully the scientific nuances of a problem? The standards of science are not the same as those of public choice, if only because science must wait for all the evidence while the public may not be willing or able to tarry for so long. The difference can lead to frustration and misunderstanding on both sides—and to bad public policy.

Questions and Problems

It is safe to say that the prospects for democracy are closely bound to the course of modern science. In general, scientific progress is good for democracy. But modern science is essentially technological, which means not only that it produces practical results but also that it informs society as a whole. It produces a people more tolerant of change and novelty, more skeptical about religion and moral values, and—because they live in ever greater comfort and good health—less able to endure suffering and exhibit self-discipline and self-restraint.

Questions could be and have been raised as to whether these resulting traits of character are good or bad for a people's capacity for self-government. The issue is complicated, because a technological culture not only creates dependency but also makes demands of its own for responsibility, discipline, and self-restraint. It takes hard work to become a scientist, of course, and the technological complexity of work in general requires greater initiative on the part of individuals than is the case for older, more crudely mechanical forms of production. But if we assume that, on balance, a society informed by science and technology does not necessarily undermine the democratic character of those affected by it, there remains a question of what happens to those who are not.

For as work and economic life are ever more broadly transformed by the spirit and techniques of science, education in science—especially in the technologies that basic science constantly generates—becomes the key to the individual's material success and place in the social order. But that education is not easy, and it is possible that a relatively large number of individuals in any society will be unable to succeed at it. It is thus possible that as science and technology make all better off in fact (in the United States, for instance, one-half of the homes occupied by those legally defined as poor have air conditioning), the divide between the relatively rich and the relatively poor might grow and become rooted in differences in ability, rather than in the accidental injustices of social class and family background.

Democratic societies may have to face difficult and altogether new problems of social and political integration, caused by the very force—scientific progress—that formerly was thought to be beneficial in all ways. In a scientific culture the dream of meritocracy—long held out as an obvious prize of democratic justice—could turn out to be less wholesome for democratic government and values than expected. As science progresses, understanding the moral foundations of individual human dignity may become more important than ever before. About such foundations, science has little, if anything, to say.

See also *Education; Environmentalism; Technology.*

Jerry Weinberger

BIBLIOGRAPHY

Bacon, Francis. *New Atlantis and Great Instauration.* Edited by Jerry Weinberger. Rev. ed. Arlington Heights, Ill.: Harlan Davidson, 1989.

Bronowski, Jacob. *Science and Human Values.* New York: Harper and Row, 1965.

Ellul, Jacques. *The Technological Society.* Translated by John Wilkinson. New York: Knopf, 1964.

Ezrahi, Yaron. *The Descent of Icarus: Science and the Transformation of Contemporary Democracy.* Cambridge, Mass., and London: Harvard University Press, 1990.

Heidegger, Martin. "Science and Reflection." In *The Question concerning Technology and Other Essays.* Translated by William Lovitt. New York: Harper Colophon, 1977.

Price, Don K. *Government and Science: Their Dynamic Relation in American Democracy.* Oxford: Oxford University Press, 1962.

———. *The Scientific Estate.* Cambridge: Harvard University Press, Belknap Press, 1965.

Young, Michael. *The Rise of the Meritocracy, 1870–2033: An Essay on Education and Equality.* Harmondsworth: Penguin Books, 1965.

Scotland

See *United Kingdom*

Secession

Secession of territory, the most radical form of separatism, is an effort to dismember an independent state, by forcible or nonforcible means, into two or more internationally recognized countries. With the end of the cold war and the collapse of the Soviet Union, the glue holding together many ethnically pluralistic societies in Eastern Europe and the developing countries began to crack, allowing long-submerged groups to arise again and demand self-determination. An explosion of identities became apparent, with formerly suppressed groups reflecting on which ethnic group they belonged to and which political unit they wished to be associated with. New state units and national formulas emerged, sometimes followed by terrible destruction, violence, and civil wars. A post–World War II global community that had come to know a reasonably stable international state system now witnessed tumultuous transitions—including partition and secession.

Partition and Secession

Partition and secession can be very close in structural terms. Partition involves the division of a functioning state into two or more parts in response to the initiative of internal or external sources. Such a partitioned state allows for the exercise of partial or full powers by the territorial authorities, but the breakup of the state does not follow automatically. Where separation takes the form of partition (Cyprus, Israel, Northern Ireland) or de facto autonomy (Angola, Kurdistan, Sudan), the political and economic costs of delinkage are often high but the possibility of reintegration remains.

Territorial secession occurs at the initiative of an administrative or ethnoregional unit that seeks, by military or other means, to detach itself fully from the core country and to gain international recognition for itself as a sovereign entity. Secession is the most extreme strategy of isolation, for the connections between the contending state and ethnoregional entities are broken into distinct political systems. A political memory of past differences is likely to endure, and the potential for conflict remains high for a considerable time.

Societal interests call for secession when they regard reformist measures within the state (the internalist solution) to be inadequate. Presented as a nonnegotiable demand, the call for secession not surprisingly brings on a sharp counterdemand from state authorities, leading in many instances to antagonistic relations, civil conflict, and war. The peaceful breakup of Czechoslovakia into two countries (the Slovak Republic and the Czech Republic) on January 1, 1993, was an exception in this respect. This peaceful transition is explained in part by the calming influence that Czechoslovak federal legislators exerted during the country's dissolution.

Secessionist movements are most likely to arise in a context of deepening scarcity where sizable ethnic groups have a history of grievances and have keen political memories of conflictual relations. Ethnic fractionalization by itself is not a significant predictor of discord. Discord arises when such pluralism is combined with a sense of relative deprivation and a history of past conflict. A weak state also facilitates the emergence of powerful ethnoregional claims. Sometimes such a state lashes out in a brutal or repressive manner. (For example, former president Mohamed Siad Barre overreacted in the face of regional opposition in Somalia.) In other cases, the weak state may stand to the side while local groups act assertively or provocatively.

Secessionist demands reflect the desire both to narrow the definition of the core identity group and to align nationhood with sovereign statehood. Secessionist leaders may call for self-determination, seeking thereby to restore valid state-society relations and to foster citizen participation, community cohesion, and unity of purpose. For such leaders, the urge for a separate political existence has a symbolic significance that may well override such questions as economic viability. As a consequence, the breakup of large states can result in the emergence of small territorial entities that disappoint citizens' aspirations for a better quality of life.

Secessionist Methods and International Responses

In mobilizing their constituents to press for full self-determination, ethnic and national leaders use a variety of means to champion their separatist cause. In organizing their members to resist state control, they may weaken the power of central state institutions in their region. At times, these opposition elites may attempt to foster a situation of ungovernability—using boycotts, work stoppages, sabotage, insurrection, and armed violence to create a political environment conducive to decisive change. Despite heavy odds against them, secessionist movements in Kashmir, Kurdistan, southern Sudan, and Sri Lanka have waged long guerrilla struggles against well-entrenched government forces, but with little success so far. In 1991 northern Somali authorities, motivated largely by the Issaq clan's anger over harsh treatment by the Siad Barre regime, used the opening provided by the disintegration of the Somali state to declare their own independence. Thus far, the international community has reacted very cautiously to this declaration.

Not all efforts to alter boundaries and achieve national self-determination have failed, however. In Armenia, Bosnia-Herzegovina, and Croatia, highly destructive insurgencies have wrested enclaves away from state defense forces. In Eritrea, where the Eritrean People's Liberation Front fought a thirty-year war against Ethiopia to regain territorial autonomy, an overwhelming majority of 99.8 percent of the voters endorsed independence in the 1993 referendum. The international community seems likely to resist further state realignment and fragmentation wherever feasible, but when presented with reasonably clear cases of mutually agreed upon change, it seems likely to accept the inevitable.

How the international community responds to secessionist claims in the post–cold war period is likely to prove critical. On the one hand, external states and international organizations can provide secessionist movements with indispensable support. This support has taken a variety of forms, including safe sanctuary (Ethiopia's provision of access to southern Sudanese insurgents); assistance to refugees (Sudan's help to the Eritreans); military assistance (Belgian aid to Katanga; the provision of French arms to Biafra); calls for recognition (West German appeals for a conciliatory Soviet approach); recognition (Eastern Europe; Eritrea); a UN-supervised referendum (Eritrea); sanctions (UN initiatives in Bosnia-Herzegovina); and mediatory activities (the Organization of African Unity, or OAU, in Biafra; India in Sri Lanka).

On the other hand, the international community has frequently given strong backing to the principle of the territorial integrity of states and has defended existing international boundaries. Thus, while declaring that "all peoples" have a right to self-determination, the UN Charter asserts that attempts to disrupt existing boundaries violate the charter. A number of regional organizations are equally emphatic about shoring up the contemporary state order. On various occasions, for example, the OAU has been loath to allow secessionists to plead their cases before it, fearing that they might offend a member state and legitimize secession. In the late 1960s the Nigerian government resisted mediatory efforts by intergovernmental bodies that it deemed unsympathetic to its claims and made sure that the OAU Consultative Mission to Nigeria would take no action that would implicitly raise Biafra to the status of a diplomatic equal with the Nigerian state.

In the contemporary world the state has endured and can be expected to play an important role because it is important to the survival and well-being of its citizens. Nevertheless, with many countries mired in recession and exhibiting declining capabilities, it is not surprising that ethnoregional leaders increasingly question the existing order and demand autonomous powers, even recognition of new sovereign states. Although the elites at the political center can be expected to resist these appeals, the counterelites may be able to achieve their goals in whole or in part—provided they can enlist international support for their claims. Success in creating a new sovereign entity will prove to be a positive and meaningful change only if it leads to a reduction in internal conflict in the successor state and assures its society of increased economic development, a new sense of community, security, and some form of democratic governance. In time, the spread of such democratic practices and institutions should lead to a reduction in regional and global tensions; the political science literature shows that democratic states are less likely than authoritarian states to fight with each other. This reduction in tension may also enable new forms of interterritorial connection among diverse peoples to flourish.

See also *Nationalism; Popular sovereignty.*

Donald Rothchild

BIBLIOGRAPHY

Buchheit, Lee C. *Secession: The Legitimacy of Self-Determination.* New Haven: Yale University Press, 1978.

Heraclides, Alexis. *The Self-Determination of Minorities in International Politics.* London: Frank Cass, 1991.

Hill, Stuart, and Donald Rothchild. "The Impact of Regime on the Diffusion of Political Conflict." In *The Internationalization of Communal Strife,* edited by Manus I. Midlarsky. London and New York: Routledge Chapman and Hall, 1992.

Horowitz, Donald L. *Ethnic Groups in Conflict.* Berkeley: University of California Press, 1985.

Lijphart, Arend. *Power Sharing in South Africa.* Berkeley: University of California Institute of International Studies, 1985.

Ronen, Dov. *The Quest for Self-Determination.* New Haven and London: Yale University Press, 1979.

Rothchild, Donald, and Victor A. Olorunsola, eds. *State versus Ethnic Claims: African Policy Dilemmas.* Boulder, Colo.: Westview Press, 1983.

Senegal

A democracy in West Africa dominated by a single party, now the Socialist Party. The French colony of Senegal emerged in the mid-nineteenth century from a handful of trading posts on the Atlantic shoreline: St. Louis, Dakar, Rufisque, and Gorée. Before then the area was dominated by powerful chiefs and Muslim religious leaders, especially of the Wolof or Fulani groups. The Wolof now account for 44 percent of Senegal's population; Fulani speakers, 23 percent; and the Serer, 15 percent, according to the 1988 census. Muslims account for 85 percent of the population; Catholics, 5 percent; and African traditional religions, 5 to 10 percent. Senegal became independent in 1960, about the same time most of the states of France's African empire gained their independence.

Historical Background

Electoral democracy in Senegal dates to 1848, when the inhabitants of the French colony in this West African territory were awarded the right to elect a deputy to the French National Assembly. This was a year of revolutionary enthusiasm in France. Senegal's electoral right was withdrawn by Napoleon III in 1851, but it was restored under the French Third Republic in 1875. From then on Senegal had not only an elected deputy in Paris but also elected municipal governments in the coastal communes. A legacy of 1848 was suffrage for all adult males born in the communes, regardless of race, making Senegal a pioneer of voting rights in black Africa.

Democratic politics in the colonial communes was, to be sure, a corrupt enough tradition, dominated by the money of the French trading companies and the political weight of the colonial administration. The ordinary voter was usually glad to sell his vote at a very modest price. The deputies were all white Frenchmen until 1902, and the Senegalese seat was seen as being in the gift of the French government of the day. In 1902 a Senegalese trader of mixed race, François Carpot, was elected deputy, and from 1914 to 1934 Blaise Diagne, the first black African to serve in the French Parliament, was regularly reelected deputy. Diagne was the master politician of the commune tradition, corrupt on a grand scale but also a man with enough independent power to bring about the nomination of a colonial governor of Senegal in 1930.

The revival of democratic politics in Senegal after World War II extended the electorate beyond the coastal towns into the rural hinterland. The dominant Senegalese politician in this postwar period was Léopold Sédar Senghor. In 1948 Senghor created the Senegalese Democratic Bloc, a political party that was based on his recognition of the indispensable role of rural notables in reaching a rural electorate. The notables in question, particularly the leaders of the country's Sufi Muslim brotherhoods, were often in a position to deliver the votes of their clienteles: this system was democracy based on the patronage principle.

Thanks to the support of these rural notables, who in turn enjoyed the support of their own clienteles, the Senegalese Democratic Bloc won the elections of 1951 and 1952, assuring its lasting hegemony. Since that time the dominant party has changed its name three times and its leader once, but it has never failed to win an election.

The First Years of Independence

Léopold Senghor's presidency during the first twenty years of Senegalese independence (1960–1980), and the domination of his party, were contested at first (1960–1966) by politicians and parties of the left or extreme left. These parties were in general based in urban areas, and Senghor's strategy was to portray them as representatives of urban privilege. (He relied on his own excellent connections with the rural Muslim aristocracy.) Senghor's tactic was also to work toward the incorporation of political opposition within his own party, picking out particular opposition leaders and offering them cabinet positions. This tactic appeared to have reached its logical conclusion in 1966, when the last legally recognized opposition party, the African Congress Party, joined the governing party, then called the Senegalese Progressive Union; three leaders of the African Congress Party then joined the government. Within this process of incorporation, a mediated democracy was at work: politicians usually did not receive an offer from the government unless they enjoyed substantial popular support and thus had something of value to contribute to the governing coalition.

The gentle art of coalition building was accompanied by occasional measures of severity against opponents who were considered to be dangerous. For example, Mamadou Dia, Senghor's first prime minister, spent thirteen years in detention after allegedly leading a coup d'état in 1962. When severe action by the president was needed (during this attempted coup in 1962 or the general strike in 1968), it was more than useful to be able to call on support from the French army, which since independence has maintained a base in the Senegalese capital and elsewhere in valued former colonies in Africa. A French armed presence has helped to ensure the survival of civilian regimes in Côte d'Ivoire and Cameroon as well as Senegal.

The decade from 1966 to 1976 was a period of de facto single-party government in Senegal, although clandestine opposition survived, notably in the capital city of Dakar. This opposition, in general coming from the left, was centered at the University of Dakar. Although sometimes derisively labeled the politics of the "little groups," or *groupuscules,* the opposition could assume threatening proportions, as in June 1968 when protesting students and striking trade unions nearly brought down the Senghor regime. Supplementary patronage expenditures together with a hint of coercion saw the regime through that particular crisis.

A form of electoral democracy survived even under these single-party conditions. The governing Senegalese Progressive Union held elections to choose the party candidates for the National Assembly (or municipal council). These internal elections were contested by factional groupings—"clans" in local parlance. Clan politics focus on personalities rather than on ideologies or political programs. Elections are often bitterly contested, with all eyes fixed on the prize of office and the expected rewards of victory. The sale of party cards in an annual membership drive to known supporters is fundamental to building a winning clan, together, of course, with the denial of cards to the enemy. This style of factional politics has a genuinely adversarial quality; violence is deployed as well as supernatural sanctions (the semi-Muslim magic of *maraboutage*).

Multiparty Politics

Beginning in 1974, multiparty politics revived in Senegal, perhaps because Senghor wanted to prepare the political conditions for his own retirement. A 1976 constitutional revision specified the creation of a tripartite political structure, with one party to the left (Marxist-Leninist or communist), another party to the right (liberal and democratic), and a third party in the center (socialist and democratic). Suitable candidates then declared themselves for these ideological slots: Mahjmout Diop's African Independence Party, banned since 1961 as a subversive communist organization, took up the position to the left; Abdoulaye Wade's Senegalese Democratic Party under some ideological protest took up the position to the right; and the gov-

erning party, soon to be renamed the Socialist Party, took the strategic center ground.

The first elections to be held under this new dispensation came in 1978 and gave the Socialist Party its expected majority (82 seats out of 100), with the Senegalese Democratic Party taking the remaining seats (18). Since that time the Democratic Party has consistently been the principal challenger to the governing party. When Senghor resigned as president at the end of 1980, the constitution designated the prime minister, Abdou Diouf, his successor. One of Diouf's first important initiatives, in April 1981, was to open up the field of multiparty electoral competition. Henceforward there was to be no ideological restriction to the registration of political parties, and any number could be legally recognized provided that they were not based on primordial identifications such as language, region, or religion. The early years of Diouf's presidency were marked by general popular approval of this youthful leader of apparent integrity and energy.

The rest of the story of Senegalese democracy thus far is above all the rise and fall of Abdoulaye Wade. Many other aspiring political leaders came forward after Diouf unblocked party registration, but most of the new parties were university based, the *groupuscules* in legal form. Marxism, in effect, went legal and appeared to have little audience outside the capital city, indeed beyond the university precinct. But Wade's Democratic Party was another matter, with branches throughout most of the country, even in regions previously considered to be part of the governing party's heartland. This party could present itself as a viable reformist alternative to the governing Socialist Party, with new faces if not such strikingly new policies, and with a flair for the effective electoral campaign.

Prospects for Change

The Senegalese Democratic Party distilled its message to a single telling word in the 1988 campaign, the word *change,* taken up by the party's supporters in the streets. These elections appear to have marked the high point for the party and its leader, although the officially declared results gave little indication of the party's surge: 103 National Assembly seats went to the Socialist Party, and the remaining 17 seats to the Senegalese Democratic Party, while Diouf received 74 percent of the vote for president and Wade received 26 percent. Serious rioting followed the declaration of these results. Cars were burned and buildings looted. Wade and his principal associates were jailed for several days.

The Senegalese Democratic Party vehemently denounced the following examples of electoral malpractice in the 1988 campaign: the secret ballot was no more than "optional"; the polling card came with no photograph attached (allowing multiple voting); and the vote was counted in the capital city by civil servants behind doors that were closed to all observers from the opposition parties. Most of those civil servants were members of the governing party, and they were in a position to make up their own electoral result. It would appear in this case that the Senegalese Democratic Party did very much better than the official results indicated and may even have won in some of the cities.

Wade lost much of his crowd appeal when he accepted a position in the Diouf government (April 1991–October 1992), a position he said was essential to win reform of electoral procedures. The next elections, in February 1993, were for the presidency, with Wade and Diouf as the main candidates. Although the principal defects of the electoral system appeared to have been eliminated, the result was the usual crushing victory for the government candidate (Diouf received 58 percent; Wade received 32 percent). Protests this time were lame enough, and it appeared that the opposition had run out of belief in its principal candidate. In addition, the patronage resources of the governing party were, as usual, formidable at election time.

Senegalese democracy thus remains without an opposition electoral victory. Although the country's economic stagnation has made the government unpopular, most evidently in the capital city, its downfall at the polls appears unlikely. Senegal remains fortunate in being able to call on substantial foreign economic assistance, particularly from France, while living under the tightened financial discipline of structural adjustment policies since 1979–1980. And the country's democratic reputation appears to stimulate the generosity of international donors. Because its agricultural sector is stagnant, and local industry is hopelessly uncompetitive, democracy may have become the country's most reliable source of foreign exchange.

See also *Senghor, Léopold Sédar*.

D. B. Cruise O'Brien

BIBLIOGRAPHY

Coulon, Christian. "Senegal: The Development and Fragility of Semidemocracy." In *Politics in Developing Countries: Comparing Experiences with Democracy*, edited by Larry Diamond et al. Boulder, Colo.: Lynne Rienner, 1995.

Cruise O'Brien, D. B. *Saints and Politicians: Essays in the Organisation of a Senegalese Peasant Society*. Cambridge: Cambridge University Press, 1976.

———, and C. Coulon. "Senegal." In *Contemporary West African States*, edited by D. B. Cruise O'Brien, J. Dunn, and R. Rathbone. Cambridge and New York: Cambridge University Press, 1989.

Diop, M.C., ed. *Sénégal: Trajectoires d'un état*. Dakar/Paris: Codesria/Karthala, 1992.

Fatton, Robert, Jr. *The Making of a Liberal Democracy: Senegal's Passive Revolution, 1975–1985*. Boulder, Colo.: Lynne Rienner, 1987.

Gellar, Sheldon. *Senegal: An African Nation between Islam and the West*. Aldershot: Gower; Boulder, Colo.: Westview Press, 1986.

Kanté, Babacar. "Senegal's Empty Election." *Journal of Democracy* 5 (January 1994): 96–108.

Vaillant, Janet G. *Black, French, and African: A Life of Léopold Sédar Senghor*. Cambridge, Mass., and London: Harvard University Press, 1990.

Senghor, Léopold Sédar

First president of the West African Republic of Senegal (from 1960 to 1980). Senghor (1906–) has been the architect of the Senegalese state and the protagonist of democracy in a style adapted to African social and historical conditions. A poet and scholar in the French language and member of the French Academy, he has turned his cultural attainments to political advantage over a long and remarkable career.

Senghor was born in Joal, Senegal, and educated by Catholic missionaries before he went to study in Paris. He was chosen by the French Socialist Party in 1945 for one of the two Senegalese seats in the French National Assembly. He broke away from the Socialist Party three years later, in 1948, in protest against the party's defense of a relatively privileged urban electorate (the coastal communes). He saw himself as the defender of Senegal's rural hinterland and quickly recognized the likely consequences of extending the right to vote to the country's rural areas. His new political party, the Sengelese Democratic Bloc, won two decisive elections, in 1951 and 1952, which provided the basis for a party hegemony that has lasted (under various names) until the present time.

Senghor's electoral success was based above all on his co-optation of rural notables, most importantly the leaders of the country's Sufi Muslim brotherhoods. These leaders could call on the unconstrained allegiance of hun-

Léopold Sédar Senghor

glect the important political realities of patronage and factionalism within the governing party—realities that have never corresponded to a French-style politics of ideology. His political mastery lay in straddling the politics of ideology and the politics of patronage.

In 1980 Senghor retired as president in favor of his prime minister, Abdou Diouf. A resident of Senegal for part of each year, he is applauded when he goes out in the streets.

D. B. Cruise O'Brien

BIBLIOGRAPHY

Vaillant, Janet G. *Black, French, and African: A Life of Léopold Sédar Senghor.* Cambridge, Mass., and London: Harvard University Press, 1990.

dreds of thousands of disciples. Thus their approval provided a very important element in any election campaign. Senghor made an impression by doing what no coastal politician had done before: he went to the local Muslim holy places and asked the leaders what they wanted. His Roman Catholicism, rather than being an obstacle in his political career, may even have been an advantage in giving him a proper appreciation of the principle of religious hierarchy.

This campaigning strategy carried over into the style of government in independent Senegal. Under President Senghor the governing party tolerated political opposition, with multiparty elections from 1960 to 1966 and from 1976 to the present. Senghor was indeed responsible for the revival of multiparty democracy in 1976, in a style modeled on the ideological divisions of French politics (left, right, and center). At the same time he did not ne-

Separation of powers

The assignment of different powers (legislative, executive, judicial) to distinct branches of government in order to protect liberty. The principle of separation of powers grew out of—but is essentially distinct from—the theory of the mixed regime, which can be traced back to classical Greek political thought. Plato and Aristotle employed the concept, but it was probably best known in the work of the Greek historian Polybius. The mixed regime was an attempt to provide a balanced, stable constitution by combining the principles of different forms of government, which provided a place in the regime for the major social classes. The Roman Republic, for example, combined the principles of monarchy (in the consulate), aristocracy (in the Senate), and democracy (in the tribunes and the assembly).

Modern separation of powers theory shared the concern of mixed regime theory for a kind of balance in the constitution, but the balance took a different form. Rather than seeking to represent different social classes, separation of powers theory distinguished certain political functions (legislative, executive, judicial) and divided them among different sets of personnel.

Early modern political philosophers such as Thomas Hobbes and John Locke argued that the purpose of government is to protect fundamental natural rights, above all the right to self-preservation. Hobbes thought that absolute government could secure these rights better than other forms of government.

Locke agreed with Hobbes about the ends of government but considered absolute government a threat to these same rights. He opted, therefore, for a system in which the essential functions of government (legislative and executive) would be separated. The legislative institution (parliament) would be the supreme power, and its control of taxation was particularly important. At the same time, it would be restrained, especially by the requirement of acting only by general laws (not particular decrees). The executive, a monarch, would have the duties of carrying out the laws and of wielding the force of society in foreign affairs. The king also would have the power to veto legislation, would regulate the times and duration of parliaments, and would exercise the prerogative power (under ultimate legislative control) to act with discretion for the public good in matters unforeseen by the legislature. (In Locke's formulation the judiciary was subsumed under the executive power.)

Montesquieu, a French political thinker who was to be very influential with early Americans, followed Locke in praising the English system for dividing the different powers of government. With Montesquieu the judicial power emerges as one of the distinct powers. The judiciary is especially important for liberty, which consists in the citizen's sense of security, and is associated especially with ad hoc bodies such as juries.

In Montesquieu's description of English government, the legislature is composed of one house for the hereditary nobility (the House of Lords) and another representing the people (the House of Commons). Parliament enacts laws and oversees their execution, but otherwise has no power over the executive. The monarch can act with the necessary dispatch to execute laws. He supervises the army and has veto power. His person is sacred, but the ministers he needs to act can be examined and punished by the legislature.

The American Founding

To the American Founders, the need for separation of powers was a nearly universal political maxim, associated with the great authority of Montesquieu. State constitutions written after 1776 often carefully specified that there would be a strict separation of powers in the new state governments. But these simple declarations were, in the words of James Madison (a member of the Continental Congress and later president of the United States), mere "parchment barriers."

Paradoxically, Madison argued, in *Federalist* No. 51, preserving the separation of powers required a qualified rather than an absolute separation. The enforcement of the principle depended on checks and balances based on a partial blending of powers. For example, while it would be inadmissible for the executive to exercise the entire legislative power, it was necessary and desirable for the executive to have a share in that power, in the form of the veto, whereby to check the legislature.

The great security against a concentration of powers was to give to each department the necessary constitutional means and the personal motives to resist encroachments by the others. Ambition must be made to counteract ambition.

The executive branch had once been viewed as the chief threat to separation of powers (especially in light of Americans' experience with the British monarch). But experience with the new state constitutions and reflection on the principles of republicanism caused the Framers of the Constitution to shift their attention to the legislature, the branch closest to the people and therefore the dominant branch.

To prevent legislative violations of the separation of powers, the Framers first adopted the principle of bicameralism. The legislature was divided into two houses, the Senate and the House of Representatives, and the differences between them were magnified in several ways to make the check more effective. The houses were given different modes of election, the Senate being elected by state legislatures and the House by the people. They also had what Madison called different principles of action, based on their different sizes and powers (the special role in revenue measures for the House and the share in the appointment and treaty powers for the Senate). The sharing of executive powers by the Senate—together with the likelihood that the Senate would contain members ambitious for executive office—fostered a similarity in viewpoints, the basis for a limited alliance between what was supposed to be the weaker legislative branch and the executive.

The second means of preventing legislative encroachment was to strengthen the other branches of government. Congress was denied a role in selecting the president, and its legislation was made subject to a qualified executive veto. The judiciary, though selected by the president with the advice and consent of the Senate, was independent by virtue of its tenure during good behavior. It also had the key power of judicial review. Congress was, moreover, generally denied the power to manipulate the salaries of members of the other branches.

By contriving the interior structure of the federal government in this way, the Framers believed that it would be possible to maintain the division of powers among the different branches. The purpose of separation of powers was, above all, to preserve the rule of law and to prevent tyranny by government officials. The nation was not to be subjected to legislation based on the preferences of the rulers but was to be governed by impartial laws that applied to all citizens (the lawmakers themselves included). No one branch would be likely to become predominant, since the checks and balances, reinforced by the self-interest of the members of the various branches, would prevent that.

In addition, separation of powers was viewed as an auxiliary aid against tyranny of the majority, since the executive veto and the independence of the judiciary could slow down an overbearing popular majority acting through the legislature. (In this regard, it is worth noting the invocation of the classical mixed-regime analysis by John Adams, later the second president of the United States, in his *Defence of the American Constitutions* [1787]. Adams thought that different parts of the government should be viewed as representing different classes—for example, the Senate provided a special place where the rich could be both represented and closely watched.) The chief focus of separation of powers undoubtedly was to limit government in order to preserve liberty, but it had another dimension as well: by making possible a strong and independent executive and judiciary, separation of powers contributed to the strength and efficiency of the government.

The American model of presidential government has been imitated elsewhere, most notably in Latin America. But differences of political culture have led to different results (often very strong presidents and weak parties).

Parliamentary Government

Even as the American Founders were imitating Britain, British government was evolving into a new form. The monarch's powers became more attenuated and executive power shifted to a cabinet of ministers responsible to the House of Commons. Walter Bagehot, a mid-nineteenth-century writer, described the British arrangement as a "fusion of powers," superior to governments (such as the American) based on the separation of powers. But even in

parliamentary government there is still a separation of function and personnel and some ideal of balance. The Commons discusses and approves legislation, while the cabinet supervises its preparation and execution, with the assistance of a nonpolitical civil service. There is an overlap here between the older distinction of legislative from executive functions and two new distinctions: first, the distinction between government (the power to direct public policy) and control of the government (the power to support or dismiss those who exercise governing power—for example, the prime minister and cabinet); and, second, the distinction between politics (making the decisions that direct public policy) and administration (the actual implementation of policy decisions).

The French Third Republic (1870–1940) and Fourth Republic (1946–1958) exemplified another form of parliamentary government. The French system arose in the context of a very different history (having oscillated since 1789 between republicanism and authoritarianism) and a different party system. (The deeper divisions in French society led to the existence of many parties, in contrast to the two-party system of Great Britain.) In general, the result was that the executive power was weaker and governments much more unstable in the French republics than in Great Britain. But the very depth of differences in French politics helped to maintain at least the ideals of balance in government and of the separation of powers.

Historical Development

As one might expect in a government with a strong separation of powers, like the United States, the separation has been variable, depending on the circumstances of the nation (domestic and foreign) and the personal attributes of those who have held various offices. The nineteenth century, for example, was generally a period of legislative dominance, although the executive dominated during the Civil War. By the end of the century, separation of powers was being subjected to sharp criticism. Woodrow Wilson, who would be elected president in 1912, in his *Congressional Government* (1885), followed Bagehot in arguing that the separation of powers (with federalism) was the chief institutional defect of the Constitution. This diffusion of power, he argued, led to incoherence and inefficiency in legislation and made genuine accountability impossible. Wilson was among the first in a long line of such critics, which later included scholars James MacGregor Burns and James Sundquist.

The same forces that led to this critique—above all, the vastly expanded expectations placed on government in the twentieth century—have led to a long-term trend of shifting power from the legislature to the other two branches. (Keep in mind that the scope of the federal government has broadened dramatically in the twentieth century.) Power that once would have been considered legislative is now exercised routinely by the president and the executive branch, under broad delegations of rule-making power, and by the judicial branch, in the form of a more expansive concept of the power of judicial review. Moreover, the very existence of independent regulatory agencies, with quasi-legislative and quasi-judicial powers, can be viewed as an anomaly in a system of separation of powers.

This same trend has been powerful in other nations. In Great Britain, there has been a substantial shift of power from the cabinet to the prime minister. In France, the instability of the Third and Fourth Republics led to the creation of a hybrid form of presidential-parliamentary government in the Fifth Republic, in which a separate and sometimes powerful president (directly elected since 1962) coexists with a premier and cabinet responsible to the popular assembly. (In earlier hybrids, where elected presidents had replaced monarchs, the president's powers generally had been more limited.) This combination of presidential and parliamentary government has become more common, having been adopted in countries such as Portugal, Poland, and Peru, with the relative strength of president and premier varying somewhat.

Thus, in both presidential and parliamentary governments, and in mixtures of the two, separation of powers is a permanent feature in the landscape of modern representative democracies.

See also *Bagehot, Walter; Checks and balances; Federalists; Hobbes, Thomas; Locke, John; Madison, James; Montesquieu; Representation; United States Constitution; Wilson, Woodrow.* In Documents section, see *Constitution of the United States (1787).*

Christopher Wolfe

BIBLIOGRAPHY

Diamond, Martin. "Separation of Powers and the Mixed Regime." *Publius* 8 (summer 1978): 33–43.

The Federalist. Edited, with introduction and notes, by Jacob E. Cooke. Middletown, Conn.: Wesleyan University Press, 1961.

Goldwin, Robert A., and Art Kaufman, eds. *Separation of Powers: Does It Still Work?* Washington, D.C.: American Enterprise Institute, 1986.

Gwyn, W. B. *The Meaning of the Separation of Powers.* New Orleans: Tulane University Press, 1965.

Scigliano, Robert. *The Supreme Court and the Presidency.* New York: Free Press, 1971.

Shugart, Matthew, and John Carey. *Presidents and Assemblies: Constitutional Design and Electoral Dynamics.* Cambridge: Cambridge University Press, 1992.

Vile, M. J. C. *Constitutionalism and the Separation of Powers.* Oxford: Clarendon Press, 1967.

Serbia

See *Europe, East Central*

Seychelles

See *Africa, Subsaharan*

Sierra Leone

See *Africa, Subsaharan*

Sieyès, Emmanuel-Joseph

French cleric, pamphleteer, ardent nationalist, and democrat, who was prominent in the French Revolution. When his ecclesiastical career foundered because of his common birth, Sieyès (1748–1836) turned his talents to opposing the monarchy and nobility.

In January 1789 Sieyès wrote four pamphlets, including the *Essay on Privileges* and *What Is the Third Estate?* He attacked social and political inequality while eloquently defending the interests of the middle class and the need for a

Emmanuel-Joseph Sieyès

representative government steered by the "general will." Elected as a delegate to the Estates General, he proposed that the third estate (those not of the clergy or nobility) should form the National Assembly, thereby identifying it alone as the sovereign French nation and as the origin of all legality and justice, with the exclusive prerogative to declare a new constitution. His passionate address to the Assembly on June 10, 1789, is credited with launching the French Revolution.

In 1789, as a member of the Committee on the Constitution, Sieyès proposed a plan to reorganize France into departments; he also proposed a declaration of rights, the suspension of tithes, and a jury system. As a member of the Committee on Public Instruction, he published a journal (with the Marquis de Condorcet and Georges Duhamel) proposing a national education system. Although initially a constitutional royalist, in 1793 Sieyès voted in favor of the execution of Louis XVI. He played no role, however, during the Reign of Terror and opposed Jacobinism, the most radical of the revolutionary groups.

In May 1799 Sieyès was made one of the five directors who held executive power, but in November he participated in the successful overthrow of the Directory. He cooperated with Napoleon Bonaparte in the Senate, but he also drafted a constitution limiting the power of the executive. Restrictions on executive power were rejected when Napoleon declared himself supreme ruler of France.

Sieyès is praised by many political historians for the importance he placed on a declaration of rights, his ideas on the separation of the executive and legislative powers, and his constitutional theory on popular sovereignty.

See also *Revolution, French.*

Peter C. Emberley

Singapore

An island city-state in Southeast Asia at the southern end of the Malay Peninsula, which gained independence in 1965 and has undergone rapid modernization. Singapore's principal resource is its people. The 3.1 million citizens are about 77 percent Chinese, 14 percent Malay, 7 percent Indian, and 2 percent other ethnic groups. Singaporeans, who live in a densely populated city, are the wealthiest, best housed, and healthiest people in Southeast Asia. They also enjoy the most Westernized conveniences and public services of the region.

In the 1960s Singapore was still little more than a swampy port facility for the British, who had begun colonizing the area in the early 1800s. Sir Stamford Raffles, an agent for the British East India Company, first established British control over Singapore in 1819.

Occupied by the Japanese during World War II, Singapore became a British Crown Colony in 1946. It attained self-rule in internal affairs in 1959 and in 1963 joined Malaya, Sarawak, and Sabah in the Federation of Malaysia. The incorporation of Singapore into Malaysia was intended to ensure economic stability by providing an agricultural base and to ensure national security against perceived communist advances. Malaysia ousted Singapore in 1965, however, because it feared Chinese dominance over politics in the new federation.

Lee Kuan Yew, who had been educated at the British universities of Oxford and Cambridge, became prime minister of Singapore in 1957. He led his country to complete independence in 1965, amid much concern on the part of the nation's leaders that Singapore would not be able to cope on its own. Lee led Singapore to economic heights unparalleled in the rest of Southeast Asia. He stepped down as prime minister in 1990, allowing his deputy, Goh Chok Tong, to become prime minister, while

Lee became the "senior minister." Goh emphasized Lee's style of consultation and consensus and remained in Lee's shadow.

A One-Party State

Politics in Singapore is based on the British parliamentary model, although the parliament is unicameral rather than bicameral. Legislators are elected to five-year terms, and almost all are members of Lee's People's Action Party. From the late 1950s on, the People's Action Party continually won parliamentary election victories every four years. Until 1991 only an occasional, single seat was won by opposition-party candidates; in that year the opposition won four seats.

The People's Action Party has continued to win large majorities in parliamentary elections both because the opposition is fragmented and because the party controls the entire bureaucracy, including the lowest levels of precincts. In addition, most voters see the dominance of the People's Action Party as the best chance for Singapore's continued political and economic stability and growth. The opposition has been co-opted by Singapore's economic growth, passage of popular social-welfare legislation, low level of unemployment, and noncorrupt government. From a Western perspective, a one-party state is neither competitive nor democratic. From the perspective of Singaporeans, paternalistic government provides law and order and achieves economic growth.

The People's Action Party has kept potential opposition parties from mounting effective campaigns. The leaders accept in principle the concept of a critical, competitive opposition—they do so as long as that opposition remains weak. The party has mobilized the civil service to carry out its programs and thus consolidate its rule. To many citizens of Singapore, the party is synonymous with the state. Singaporeans saw the phenomenal economic growth that touched virtually every person during the postindependence period as an accomplishment of the People's Action Party. With its clean sweep of every election, the party has been transformed into a state institution.

The dominance of the People's Action Party also results to a great extent from the leadership of Lee Kuan Yew. Brilliant, energetic, and motivated, Lee appeared as the consummate pragmatist, concerned with efficiency and results. He showed himself to be ruthless upon occasion, as when he ordered political adversaries to be imprisoned. At the same time, he took credit for the high standard of living that Singaporeans enjoy.

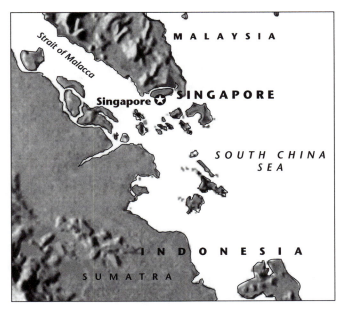

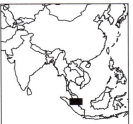

The case of Singapore raises the question of whether a one-party state can be democratic. The governmental system of Singapore does not meet the criteria of full civil liberties and competitive choices of leaders. From the Chinese perspective, however, Western-style majority rule leads to chaos, instability, dissension, and inefficiency.

Prime Minister Lee argued that in the Chinese tradition there is no concept of a loyal opposition. For example, it is not possible for people to support an opposition candidate without withdrawing their total support from the government. This tradition is based on Confucian philosophy, which stresses the principles of centralized authority. Obedience to those in authority was the cement of the Confucian order. As long as the authorities met the needs of the people and led them according to moral principles, the ruler was considered to have the mandate of heaven and was therefore deemed legitimate by the public. Given this cultural perspective, a strong one-party system is most conducive to effective rule. As might be expected, Singaporeans do not swing back and forth from opposition to support for the People's Action Party.

One-party systems can provide policy alternatives in the case of differences in opinion among the party leaders. Moreover, if two-way communication between the government and the people is established, the citizenry can influence public policy. In Singapore, intraparty factionalism is prevalent, and varying points of view are aired publicly. In addition, the People's Action Party has established various grassroots organizations, including Citizens' Consultative Committees designed to elicit ideas from the public. Singapore's semidemocracy has provided the republic with effective and accountable government, consistent with its traditions and history and supportive of the goals of development, order, and merit.

Communitarianism Versus Individualism

Singaporeans do not enjoy the kind of civil liberties expected by citizens in Western democracies. Indeed, Lee Kuan Yew has expressed disdain for the Western value of "individualism," which he contrasts with Singaporean "communitarianism." He consistently has criticized the absence of discipline in Western societies (as well as in developing countries) and has noted Singapore's excellent record of public safety as compared with the dangers of crime-ridden U.S. cities. Tight controls have made it possible for Singaporeans to walk the streets in any place and at any time; graffiti, gangs, and criminals are almost unknown. Furthermore, Singapore has a superb educational system and has achieved a 99 percent literacy rate. The high standard of living and the low level of homelessness compare favorably with the high levels of poverty and homelessness in "democratic" societies.

Lee's critics have complained about censorship and other constraints on individual freedoms. Lee himself emphasizes the advantages of a country that is free from pornography; free from corrupting influences, such as prostitution, gross materialism, and drug abuse; and free from foreign ideas that are contrary to Confucian values and that undermine the people's respect for authority.

Most Singaporeans have been willing to accept the tight discipline because the state has achieved such high levels of economic growth. Nevertheless, Singapore faces significant problems. Worldwide protectionism could undermine the economic growth of countries, like Singapore, that depend on exports. Moreover, wage increases have reduced the number of cheap local laborers available. Multinational corporations increasingly are turning to nations with cheaper labor than Singapore.

More important, the rapid modernization of Singapore has undermined the traditional values of its people. Housing projects, for example, have subverted the former emphasis on the extended family, in which several generations lived together in housing compounds. Once characterized by spirit, heart, and vitality, Singapore seems cold and materialistic to many. The extraordinary cleanliness of the city seems sterile, and even the perfect landscaping appears antiseptic rather than lush. For tourists, shopping is the main attraction.

The standard of living in Singapore is equal to those of New Zealand, Ireland, and Spain; Singapore has an income of more than $10,000 per capita. There is virtually no unemployment, and with few exceptions poverty has been eliminated. A public housing scheme, cheap health care, and universal public education have enhanced the living standards of Singaporeans. Perhaps no other city in the world can claim as high a degree of modernization as Singapore.

Singapore has achieved such a high level of economic development because the interventionist state is involved in all aspects of the national economy. By structuring the economy toward high-technology industries, emphasizing exports, and establishing conservative fiscal policies, the government achieved a phenomenally high growth rate of 8 percent in the 1980s and early 1990s. Many of the exports are products of multinational corporations. Foreign capital plays a major role in the domestic economy as well.

The unique aspects of Singapore make it difficult to compare it with developing countries. Its status as a city-state with virtually no agricultural base, its small population, and its remarkably high standard of living make Singapore an anomaly among its Southeast Asian neighbors. Thus the urban island-state is not a useful model for other nations to emulate because its conditions are so unusual.

Yet despite Singapore's uniqueness, many leaders of developing countries have looked with favor at the "Asian style of democracy" found there. Singapore, Taiwan, and South Korea are Asia's most successful developing nations in terms of economic growth. All three adopted a pattern of government featuring one-party dominance, hierarchical and centralized rule, emphasis on communitarian values rather than individualism, strong state intervention, and discipline. Such a system may not meet Western criteria for democracy, but it is appropriate for the cultures and traditions of the citizens of Singapore.

See also *Abdul Rahman, Tunku; Asia, Southeast; Confucianism; Dominant party democracies in Asia; Malaysia.*

Clark D. Neher

BIBLIOGRAPHY

Bellows, Thomas J. *The People's Action Party of Singapore: Emergence of a Dominant Party System.* New Haven: Yale University, Southeast Asian Studies, 1970.

Chan, Heng Chee. *The Dynamics of One-Party Dominance: The PAP at the Grassroots.* Singapore: Singapore University Press, 1976.

George, T. J. S. *Lee Kuan Yew's Singapore.* London: Andre Deutsch, 1973.

Josey, Alex. *Lee Kuan Yew.* Singapore: Asia Pacific Press, 1968.

Rodan, Garry. *The Political Economy of Singapore's Industrialization: National, State, and International Capital.* New York: St. Martin's; London: Macmillan, 1989.

Slavery

A form of coerced labor involving the exploitation of individuals or groups over whom some or all of the powers of ownership are exercised. We learn from the Bible that the Jewish people were held in bondage by the Egyptians. We also learn that slavery was a feature of the Jews' own society, as it was of most societies in the ancient world. Indeed, until relatively recent times, it was to be found in most societies of which we have record, although the extent of dependence on slavery and the forms it took varied widely.

Given the many advantages to be derived from employing a wholly subservient labor force, some forms of slavery have persisted right up to the present, and new types continue to appear. In the twentieth century the exploitation of the labor of prison and concentration camp inmates by Nazi Germany, the Soviet Union, and other totalitarian powers has been seen as a modern variant. But whatever its character, most people today would regard slavery as a wholly illegitimate violation of basic human rights.

It might well be supposed, therefore, that no practice could be more at odds with democracy than slavery. How could an institution based on the total subordination of one individual to another be reconciled with a system claiming to derive its legitimacy from notions of freedom and equality? And, indeed, the two often have been seen as polar opposites: slavery has served as a convenient synonym for tyranny, the employment of brute force and denial of human rights; democracy, as a synonym for liberty, self-determination, and respect for the individual.

In modern times the qualities popularly associated with democracy have been so generally celebrated that even regimes patently undemocratic in their use of power have included the word in their titles. Slavery, on the other hand, has always had derogatory associations, not only as a condition to be avoided but as implying a degree of moral and material degradation on the part of the enslaved. No good connotations are attached to slavishness, certainly none that can be readily associated with the effective operation of a democratic political order.

Yet, as history shows, democracy and slavery have not only coexisted at times but have been seen as mutually supportive. In such instances the essential prerequisite has always been the drawing of a distinction between citizens, whom the laws embrace, and outsiders, to whom quite different principles apply. Two examples will serve to illustrate the strengths and weaknesses of this strategy: Periclean Athens and the Old South of the United States.

Ancient Athens

The distinction between slaves and citizens was never more marked than in the case of the first full-fledged democratic society of which we have record, Periclean Athens. From 461 B.C. until Athens was conquered by the Macedonians in 338 B.C., Athenians practiced a form of popular government more closely approximating modern democratic ideals than anything that was to emerge for the next 2,000 years. (A revolt against Macedonian rule was suppressed in 322 B.C.) In some respects Athenians carried the idea of popular sovereignty further than is commonly the case today. Being smaller than modern nation-states, the city-states of antiquity, of which Athens was perhaps the most notable, were able to practice forms of participatory democracy that allowed citizens to engage in discussions, decision making, and office holding to an extent nowadays possible only at the local level and seldom practiced even there.

All Athenian citizens were entitled to attend the *Ecclesia,* the general assembly, held ten times a year, at which final decisions on important matters were made. Although estimates vary, the number of participants probably did not exceed 50,000, of whom presumably only a minority would be present on any given occasion. More important, however, in the context of the present discussion, is the fact that not all adults were citizens. The privilege did not extend to women, foreigners, or slaves. It would be wrong to conclude, as some have done, that citizenship was confined to the idle rich. Cobblers, blacksmiths, and other humble folk were included and were paid an expense allowance to compensate for what they had lost by not working.

Meanwhile, however, busily at work in Athens's shops,

factories, and mines while their masters discussed the political issues of the day was a slave labor force whose members nobody thought of as belonging to Athens's body politic or even as being Athenians. But the prosperity and defense of the state depended in no small measure on their labors. Many were, in fact, foreigners, either captives taken in war or their descendants. How numerous they were is a matter of debate—estimates vary from 20,000 to 100,000, and doubtless the numbers fluctuated over time—but it is generally agreed that Athens was, in the full sense of the term, a slave society rather than simply a society that happened to have slaves. In other words, slavery was an integral and essential part of the Athenian economic and social system.

By associating democratic rights with citizenship, Athenians could pride themselves on their civil liberties while enjoying the benefits derived from employing a labor force whose members enjoyed no rights at all. As far as we know, Greek philosophers did not go out of their way to argue, as others were later to do, that Athens's slaves materially assisted the democratic process by relieving those responsible for its workings of some of the time-consuming tasks that might otherwise have fallen to them. Nor, apparently, was much made of the fact that citizens and their families were spared many of the menial duties that society required but that might have been thought unfitting for those entitled at other times to act as officials and lawmakers—although that, too, was presumably true.

In fact, the philosophers of the ancient world largely took the existence of slavery for granted. Plato had no compunction about making slavery part of his ideal republic, so long as it was confined to those of foreign stock, for whom he thought it well suited because they, unlike Greeks, were accustomed to living under tyrannical regimes. His concern was to increase the powers of masters rather than to expose the injustices of slavery. Even when freed, he argued, slaves should be required to leave the state, a recommendation reminiscent of policies later adopted in the Old South of the United States.

Plato, needless to say, was no democrat. Nor was his pupil Aristotle, who similarly based his justification of slavery on an assumption of the slaves' inherent inferiority. His self-assurance on this point is striking, considering the fact that slaves were racially indistinguishable from Athenians and the haphazard way in which misfortune overtook individuals in the often unstable political circumstances of the time. How he could be so sure that it was those best suited to enslavement who wound up as slaves, he neglected to explain. Whether as critics of slavery or informed observers, the Athenian philosophers are disappointing. Even the Cynics and Stoics, who did admit that there might be a very considerable gap between what was theoretically desirable and the practices of their own day, stopped well short of any suggestion that slavery was either illegitimate or irreconcilable with the requirements of a free society. Servitude was too much part of Greek culture to be questioned seriously.

Other societies of the ancient world, having never aspired to democratic values, found little difficulty in justifying slavery. This they did, as others were to do later, in terms of what they saw as a natural hierarchy, evident at the most basic level in the family and manifested in all social institutions. When, in due course, Christianity became a dominant influence, it found ways of shaping its message to accommodate the social practices of the time. Granted, the Golden Rule enjoined people to treat their neighbors as they themselves would want to be treated, but it did not need to be construed in ways that failed to make allowance for the very different stations in life in which God had placed them. In any case, what mattered was not what happened in this life but what would happen in the life to come, when all would be judged according to their merits. Crucial though the influence of Christian teaching was in the eventual overthrow of slavery, the emphasis up to the Reformation was on accommodation.

Colonial Slavery

The voyages of discovery in the fifteenth and sixteenth centuries and the settlement of the Americas opened a new chapter in Europe's experiences with slavery. By that time, slavery had largely disappeared from Western Europe, although it persisted in parts of the Mediterranean world and on Europe's eastern fringes. The new forms of slavery that developed as a result of Europe's expansion, however, were different from those that had been practiced before. Most obviously, those whom Europeans now encountered were men and women so different from themselves in appearance and culture as effectively to rule out any possibility of their being accepted as equals. The notion that enslavement should be reserved for foreigners and unbelievers, as taught by the ancient philosophers and in the Bible, thus took on a new meaning. Those whom Europeans now encountered were not only unfamiliar with Christian teaching but so alien in other respects as to make some people question whether they were, properly speaking, fellow human beings at all.

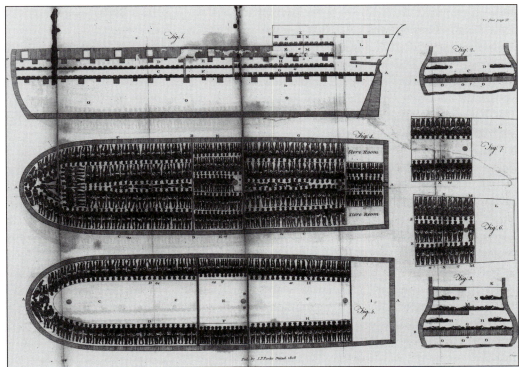

Slaves taken from Africa to the New World were transported under appallingly inhumane conditions. The drawing of a slave ship is from 1808, the year the slave trade ended in the United States.

Racial distinctiveness thus became, from the outset, one of the principal characteristics of, and justifications for, modern slavery. Another was the fact that the slaves were obtained and mostly employed in faraway places. Such reservations as Europeans had about subjecting fellow Christians to forced labor were readily suspended when it came to dealing with heathens in places where quite different rules of conduct pertained. Much went on in Europe's colonies that would not have been permitted at home.

Moreover, these events were occurring at a time when even at home the prevailing ideology was unashamedly authoritarian and autocratic. Signs of emerging democratic institutions are hard to detect, except possibly in England's North American colonies, where representative government had early taken root. In England parliamentary authority was proving more resilient than elsewhere.

In neither case, however, is there much to suggest that these democratic tendencies gave rise to doubts concerning the legitimacy of slavery. British traders had engaged in the Atlantic slave trade from its outset, and by the late seventeenth century had established themselves as the New World's principal suppliers. Barbados was the first New World colony to fully exploit African gang labor, which was employed in the production of sugar. On the

North American mainland the demand for labor was largely met by indentured workers, immigrants brought over from England who had agreed to work for a stated number of years in return for their passage.

By the 1660s Virginia had adopted a slave code that removed such doubts as had previously existed concerning the relative standing of indentured workers and slaves. Europeans were to serve only for the terms for which they had contracted and were entitled to appeal to the courts for redress should they believe the agreements into which they had entered had been broken. Africans, on the other hand, had no contracts, were obliged to serve for life—as were their descendants—and were susceptible to being sold, moved about, put to work, punished, used as financial collateral, or otherwise disposed of in any way their owners saw fit. This law was enacted at a time when blacks constituted not more than 3 percent of Virginia's work force and so could hardly have been deemed essential for the colony's well-being. In a society that prided itself on its English liberties and was far advanced for its day in its commitment to representative government and the rule of law, imported Africans were categorized as persons with no rights whatever.

Nor was the situation noticeably different elsewhere. The northern colonies, with their shorter growing seasons, did not develop export staples of the kind on which their southern counterparts came to depend and so never came to rely on slave labor to the same extent. Yet there, too, from the earliest days, blacks were distinguished from other workers. Despite their highly intellectualized view of the world and their belief in the binding nature of contractual relationships, Puritan New Englanders, influenced perhaps by their close links with Barbados, were no less willing than Virginians to embrace chattel slavery. As John Saffin, a wealthy Boston merchant and slave owner, noted in 1701, it was not God's intention to impose social equality. Some were chosen to be kings and princes, others to be slaves. This was the traditional defense of slavery unsullied by notions of English liberty or a belief that belonging to society was a form of social contract that conferred rights as well as obligations on individuals.

Meanwhile, in England, John Locke, who based his entire social philosophy on just such notions of liberty, struggled to reconcile political theory and contemporary practice. On the one hand, he argued that there was no justification for the view that slavery was a natural extension of the social order. Attacking the claims of royalist political writer Robert Filmer, who saw slavery as deriving from the need to preserve monarchical power, Locke even went so far as to declare that slavery was so vile an institution that no true-born Englishman could defend it. Yet Locke himself invested in the Royal African Company, which received most of its wealth from slave trading, and assisted in the drafting of a proslavery constitution for the Carolinas, apparently without qualms.

There can be no question that Locke regarded American slavery as a necessary institution. Like other defenders of slavery, he saw slaves as a group apart, whose condition was unaffected by the social contract. For just as a murderer forfeited his life by his action, so too did those taken captive in a just war. If their captors chose to spare their lives and enslave them, it could be construed as an act of mercy. Whether this circumstance bore any resemblance to the way in which slaves were actually acquired, or to the normal treatment of prisoners of war, or why, supposing enslavement justifiable on these grounds, it should extend to the progeny of war captives are questions not considered. Had the slaves in the American colonies been English, or simply white, presumably very different considerations would have applied. That so articulate an exponent of human rights could dismiss basic issues in such a perfunctory manner is indicative of the unthinking way in which Locke's contemporaries accepted the enslavement of Africans.

The Development of Antislavery Sentiment

With the rise of Enlightenment thought in the eighteenth century, the assumptions on which slavery was based came under scrutiny. The fact that slavery had been accepted over the ages was no longer seen as proof that it was justified. Views of the kind expressed by Locke were shown to be riddled with contradictions. There was no correspondence between the claims of those who defended the institution and what was known about how slaves were obtained and treated. How could it be assumed that they were any less susceptible to pain and hardship than Europeans would be? The suffering slave, as depicted in countless paintings, poems, and tales, became a familiar figure by the late eighteenth century.

Enlightenment thinkers cast doubt on the notion that slaves were, for whatever reason—ancestry, race, crime, barbarous condition—outside civil society. Once that assumption was set aside, the issue acquired a new relevance. What concerned leading Enlightenment thinkers, in fact, was not slavery as such but the question of human rights to which slavery was now seen as linked. "Man was born free," wrote French philosopher and political theorist Jean-Jacques Rousseau, "but everywhere he is in chains." Rousseau was speaking figuratively, but implicit in his argument was the idea that the actual chains worn by slaves in Europe's colonies were part and parcel of the same system that kept Europeans at home in bondage to outdated beliefs and practices. In Rousseau's writings, and, although generally in a less radical form, in the writings of his contemporaries Montesquieu, Guillaume-Thomas François Raynal, and Denis Diderot, slavery became a symbol of man's subjection to a corrupt social order. If society was to rid itself of the tyranny of kings and princes, it also would have to free itself from slavery.

These ideas were familiar to the leaders of the American War of Independence. The United States was the first modern nation to put democratic theory into practice by casting off monarchical authority and replacing it with a government deriving its powers from the consent of the governed. The Declaration of Independence was a classic piece of Enlightenment polemics in its denunciation of King George III and its invocation of the principles of liberty, equality, and representative government.

Its Framers, to be sure, were hardly democrats in the

modern sense. Most were planters or merchants, members of the colonial upper class, well aware of the privileged positions they occupied and accustomed to being treated with a measure of social deference. Property qualifications were still generally imposed for voting or holding office. Nevertheless, the United States had moved appreciably closer to being a democracy than any other nation at that time.

Not surprisingly, commentators had been quick to note the contradictions between the revolutionaries' demands for liberty and their continuing support of slaveholding. The point was not lost upon the revolutionaries themselves, many of whom made no bones about expressing their detestation of the institution. Some, like Benjamin Franklin, had long been on record as opposing slavery. Others were spurred to action by the idealism of the moment. A group of citizens in Darien, Georgia, drew up a testimonial calling on their fellow countrymen to prove their good faith by declaring to the world their abhorrence of slavery.

A passage in Thomas Jefferson's initial draft of the Declaration of Independence, which later was deleted, described the slave trade as cruel and contrary to human nature, while making it plain that the culprit in this instance was George III and not slave-importing planters. Some of Jefferson's fellow slaveholders expressed unease over the possible implications of what was being said around them. In May 1776 the Virginia Convention, discussing the adoption of a bill of rights, ruled that its provisions did not extend to slaves. It was all very well to invoke a general principle to prove that Americans were the equals of Englishmen, as long as all recognized that slaves were not constituent members of society and therefore were not entitled to liberty. As always, where slavery was concerned, special rules applied.

Nevertheless, it was no coincidence that during the war and in the years immediately following, northern legislatures, beginning with Vermont in 1777, embarked on programs of emancipation. As was to be expected, the first to free their slaves were those least dependent on them. Vermont had virtually no slaves. New York and New Jersey had more and took longer. It was not until 1799 that New York got around to freeing its slaves.

Meanwhile, in those states where large numbers of slaves resided, other considerations prevailed. Given the intellectual ethos of the times, those who defended slavery did so principally on pragmatic grounds. It was, as Jefferson had been keen to point out, a problem that Americans of his generation had inherited. The key decisions had been made in earlier and less enlightened times. The choice was not whether to have slavery, because slavery already existed, but whether to abolish it, bearing in mind that the cure might well prove worse than the disease.

That this would prove the case few southerners doubted. Some did free their slaves, but for the majority the prospect of mass emancipation challenged their whole concept of America as a white society, conjuring up images of genocidal struggles such as occurred in Haiti when the French first abolished slavery and then attempted to restore it in the 1790s. Held to labor, slaves were useful and harmless, but once freed what would become of them? They were unprepared for freedom and if they were freed, whites would be unwilling to live alongside them. Regardless of abstract principles, the prospect of any general freeing of slaves evoked alarm.

The claim later made by Abraham Lincoln and others, that the Founders believed they had placed slavery on the road to destruction, is open to question. It is true that they had scrupulously avoided using the word *slavery* in the Constitution; on the other hand, they had known that anything likely to weaken the institution would prevent ratification, and they were even persuaded on that account to insert provisions guaranteeing the continuation of the slave trade for twenty years.

It is also worth noting that concerns about the appropriateness of slavery in a nation dedicated to extending human rights had not lessened the demand for slaves. During the twenty years prior to the ending of the slave trade in 1808, more slaves were imported into North America than in any equivalent period, and almost as many as during the entire previous history of the traffic. While northerners were freeing their bondservants, southerners were busily increasing their stake in the institution.

The subsequent course of events is too familiar to need rehearsing. The polarization of opinion regarding slavery led to political conflict and ultimately to civil war. Meanwhile, overseas observers expressed astonishment at the incongruity of the spectacle presented. As the Irish poet Thomas Moore noted on his visit to the city of Washington in 1804, the contrast between American ideals and practices—between charters and rights on the one hand and whips and manacles on the other—could not have been more striking. His conclusion was that Americans' claims to virtue were a sham. Their nation, young in years, was old in sin.

The Relationship Between Slavery and Democracy

What has intrigued some commentators, however, is the question of whether it was entirely a coincidence that in modern times, as in the ancient world, it was a slave society that pioneered the development of democracy; for there is no question that by the second quarter of the nineteenth century the United States was emerging as a democracy in the full modern sense. In other words, was there something about having slaves that actually encouraged the adoption of democratic beliefs and practices?

Antebellum southerners would have had little difficulty answering this question in the affirmative. It was a fact too self-evident to require demonstration that democracy flourished more readily in a society composed of planters and small farmers than in capitalist societies of the kind found in the North and Europe. So-called free society was an illusion created by the exploiters of labor to conceal the methods used in what was in effect a struggle of man against man and class against class. Only in an agrarian setting, southerners argued, could a truly democratic society, necessarily based on the support of hard-working yeomen farmers, be achieved and the evils associated with urban living, wage labor, and class warfare avoided. To this argument was commonly added the observation that all truly civilized societies required that certain routine and menial tasks be performed. These tasks were not befitting free citizens but were ideally suited to imported Africans by virtue of their innate abilities and training. Thanks to the labors of their black bondmen—who, it was noted, were assured of a measure of care and security not accorded free workers—southern whites, it was claimed, enjoyed the freedom and leisure to develop their democratic ideals and institutions in ways not otherwise possible.

Patently self-serving though these claims were, they have received some support from modern scholars to the extent that slavery is shown as creating common bonds of interest among southern whites. Edmund Morgan, writing of colonial Virginia, has noted that, following Bacon's Rebellion of 1676, planters switched from employing potentially insurrectionary whites brought over from England to buying imported Africans, whose inferior status as slaves allowed owners to exercise a greater degree of control. Maintaining white supremacy was a policy on which all whites could agree. George Fredrickson, commenting on the nineteenth-century South as a whole and observing

parallels between it and South Africa, has drawn attention to what he terms the *Herrenvolk democracy* that united whites, regardless of wealth or social status, in defense of southern institutions. Others have noted the disproportionate contribution made by southerners of the revolutionary generation to the theory and practice of democracy.

Common to all these accounts is the notion that shared views on race and slavery spared southern whites the class antagonisms that have made ruling elites elsewhere so reluctant to share their privileges. What else could have made the southern gentry so much more democratic in outlook than their English counterparts?

It should be noted, however, that the development of America's democratic institutions was a national rather than a regional achievement. Northerners were no less egalitarian in their attitudes than southerners. It is altogether more plausible to suppose that slavery and democracy developed in tandem than that one caused the other. Without denying, therefore, that slavery helped reconcile southern whites to the striking differences in wealth and status for which their region was noted, it should be asked whether there were other factors at work that fostered the development of both democracy and slavery.

The answer, it has been suggested, lies in the ready availability of land. This encouraged the proliferation of family farms, which, in turn, promoted egalitarian attitudes and a sturdy independence not found among rural populations elsewhere.

It also meant that few Americans were prepared to work as wage laborers. The English gentry, owning land and living in a small, well-populated island, were never short of workers. In America, by contrast, the problem was not obtaining land but finding laborers to work it. The labor pool in most cases was limited to the farmer's own family, with the result that small-scale farming was the norm. However, the raising of export staples in some parts of the South required large-scale farming and a sizable labor force. Producers turned to coercion as the solution to their labor problem. This they were able to do thanks to the export value of their crops and the ready availability first of white indentured laborers and subsequently of black slaves from Africa.

Thus the same circumstances, namely the shortage of labor and the plentifulness of land, that fostered the growth of those agrarian communities that are commonly seen as providing the necessary social basis for the development of democratic institutions also favored the development of slavery in the export-producing regions of the South. Viewed in this light, American slavery and American freedom are revealed as two sides of the same coin. The conditions that contributed to the liberty of some encouraged the enslavement of others.

The U.S. experience may be cited either as proof that democracy and slavery can coexist, as they did in the South for many years, or as proof that they are fundamentally incompatible, as illustrated by the struggles between North and South culminating in the Civil War (1861–1865). At issue in this conflict was the very meaning of America, in particular the question whether the universal truths on which it claimed to base its political system were either true or universal. Impressive though the southern defense of slavery was in its deployment of arguments drawn from history, Scripture, philosophy, and anthropology, no effective way was ever found of countering the charge of intellectual inconsistency.

An Uneasy Coexistence

The Athenian and American experiences are crucial to our understanding of democracy and slavery because they illustrate how two fundamentally incompatible ideologies can coexist within a single body politic. Depending on the definition used and how the demarcation lines are drawn, democracy might appear to be compatible with virtually anything. Democracy and slavery can appear to be compatible if a limited definition of *democracy* is used, if the groups concerned are well defined, and if the different laws applying to them are clearly delineated and generally accepted.

In practice the coexistence of democracy and slavery is bound to present problems. An important point in the case made by American abolitionists against slavery was that its defense necessitated restricting the freedom of northern white citizens by impeding their free use of the mails and imposing limits on what it was permissible to discuss in Congress. It also confronted them with the torturing dilemma of whether to deny the dictates of their consciences or, by speaking out, to endanger the Union.

Slaveholders, in turn, expressed concern not only about the threat to their interests posed by the abolitionists but also about the way the beliefs and practices of the wider community impinged on their efforts to keep their bondservants docile by ensuring that they remained in a state of ignorance, illiteracy, and dependence. Even where distinctions of race are involved, the practical difficulties of maintaining parallel systems remain formidable—as illustrated by the demise of apartheid in South Africa.

It also should be noted that the two examples discussed, Athens and America, were highly atypical slaveholding societies and highly atypical democracies by virtue of their being both at the same time. In the case of Athens, what was unusual was not slavery but democracy, for slavery in various forms existed throughout the ancient world. In modern times the first societies to abolish slavery were among the most democratically advanced of the age, namely the northern states of the United States.

Elsewhere slavery similarly gave way in response to liberal pressures. Britain abolished slavery in its empire in 1834, and France in 1848, in each case at a time of liberal fervor, although well before either nation could claim to have adopted democracy in the full sense of the term. The North's victory in the Civil War effectively sounded the death knell for black chattel slavery in the New World, even though Brazil did not formally abolish it until 1888.

Few today defend slavery. Nevertheless, predictions that it would soon disappear from the world have proved to be ill-founded. Old forms linger in parts of Africa and Asia, and new variants are apt to appear wherever law enforcement is weak and vulnerable groups can be exploited for economic advantage. Often slavery is associated with destitution, and occasionally some forms of the institution are defended on the grounds of religion or local custom.

But by far the most important and disquieting contribution of the twentieth century to human bondage has been the use of forced labor by totalitarian powers, most notably exemplified by the Nazi attempt to create a slave empire stretching from the Atlantic Ocean to the Ural Mountains. Such forms of slavery as still exist attract the attention of Antislavery International and the United Nations, and states routinely pursue policies to ensure slavery's elimination, some more energetically than others. No state today admits to sanctioning slavery; were one to do so, it would be regarded as emphatically not democratic.

See also *Abolitionism; Aristotle; City-states, communes, and republics; Classical Greece and Rome; Consent; Declaration of Independence; Human rights; Jefferson, Thomas; Lincoln, Abraham; Locke, John; Montesquieu; Plato; Popular sovereignty; Racism; Revolution, American; Rousseau, Jean-Jacques; States' rights in the United States; War and civil conflict.* In Documents section, see *American Declaration of Independence (1776); Constitution of the United States (1787).*

Howard Temperley

BIBLIOGRAPHY

Davis, David Brion. *The Problem of Slavery in the Age of Revolution, 1770–1823*. Ithaca, N.Y.: Cornell University Press, 1975.

————. *The Problem of Slavery in Western Culture*. New York: Oxford University Press, 1988.

Fredrickson, George M. *The Black Image in the White Mind: The Debate on Afro-American Character and Destiny, 1817–1914*. Hanover, N.H.: University Press of New England, 1987.

Jordan, Winthrop D. *White over Black: American Attitudes toward the Negro, 1550–1812*. Chapel Hill: University of North Carolina Press, 1968; London: Norton, 1980.

Morgan, Edmund S. *American Slavery, American Freedom: The Ordeal of Colonial Virginia*. New York and London: Norton, 1976.

Slovak Republic

See *Czechoslovakia*

Slovenia

See *Europe, East Central*

Small island states

Small independent island states range from Tuvalu, which has 9,000 inhabitants, to Jamaica, with a population of 2.4 million. Many other small islands have autonomous democratic institutions in association with larger states. Of the thirty-one independent small island countries, twenty-seven are functioning democracies, two have democratic institutions without enjoying fully democratic politics, one is a constitutional monarchy whose hereditary nobility has special parliamentary rights (Tonga), and one is an absolute monarchy (Bahrain).

Geographically, the biggest cluster of democratic insular states is in the English-speaking Caribbean, where, with the exception of Grenada, all the island states have enjoyed uninterrupted democratic politics since independence in the 1960s. The second largest cluster is in the Pacific Ocean, where democratic institutions often cohabit more or less successfully with traditionalist ones, typically assemblies of chiefs. (See Table 1.)

All of Europe's three small island states—Cyprus, Iceland, and Malta—are democratic. There are three African island states, the Cape Verde Islands, São Tomé and Principe, and the Comoro Islands. In 1991 the Cape Verde Islands and São Tomé and Principe inaugurated a wave of African democratic transitions by holding free elections in which newly founded opposition parties defeated the former single parties. The Comoro Islands, however, are plagued by political instability.

In the Indian Ocean, Mauritius has remained democratic since independence in 1968. In the Seychelles a single-party system was set up by a coup d'état in 1977, one year after independence, but multiparty democracy was reinstituted in 1992. The Middle East's sole island state, Bahrain, while not democratic, has sustained the most liberal political climate of all the Persian Gulf monarchies; the nation had a brief spell of constitutional government between 1973 and 1975.

Advantages of Insularity

In view of the commonly observed correlation between level of economic development and democracy, the prevalence of democratic governance on small island states is astonishing, since, with few exceptions, they are poor. Remoteness and isolation (hence high transport costs to markets), small economies, limited natural resources, high birth rates coupled with limited space, trade deficits, economic dependence on single products, and, in the case of archipelago states, territorial fragmentation limit the prospects of socioeconomic development. Does insularity then entail political advantages that mitigate its negative economic consequences?

One who thought so was the French political philosopher Montesquieu. In *The Spirit of the Laws* (1748), Montesquieu wrote approvingly of the independence of islanders. Yet he mistakenly believed that islands were naturally protected from outsiders and from tyrants. History shows that the sea has not stopped conquerors (all thirty-one small island states have a colonial history), and one of the worst tyrannies the world has ever seen, that of Francisco Macías Nguema, was for many years centered on the small island of Fernando Póo (Bioko), part of Equatorial Guinea on Africa's west coast. The fact remains, however,

TABLE 1. Independent Small Island States

Country	Political system	Former colonizer	Date of independence	Population
AFRICA				
Cape Verde Islands	Parliamentary democracy	Portugal	1975	390,000
Comoro Islands[a]	Semipresidential democracy	France	1975	51,000
São Tomé and Principe	Semipresidential democracy	Portugal	1975	121,000
CARIBBEAN				
Antigua and Barbuda	Parliamentary democracy	Great Britain	1981	66,000
Bahamas	Parliamentary democracy	Great Britain	1973	260,000
Barbados	Parliamentary democracy	Great Britain	1966	260,000
Dominica	Parliamentary democracy	Great Britain	1978	72,000
Grenada	Parliamentary democracy	Great Britain	1974	95,000
Jamaica	Parliamentary democracy	Great Britain	1962	2,400,000
St. Kitts and Nevis[b]	Parliamentary democracy	Great Britain	1983	42,000
St. Lucia	Parliamentary democracy	Great Britain	1979	155,000
St. Vincent and the Grenadines	Parliamentary democracy	Great Britain	1979	109,000
Trinidad and Tobago	Parliamentary democracy	Great Britain	1962	1,200,000
EUROPE				
Cyprus	Presidential democracy	Great Britain	1960	725,000
Iceland	Parliamentary democracy	Denmark	1944	262,000
Malta	Parliamentary democracy	Great Britain	1964	360,000
INDIAN OCEAN				
Maldives[a]	Presidential democracy	Great Britain	1965	230,000
Mauritius	Parliamentary democracy	Great Britain	1968	1,000,000
Seychelles	Presidential democracy	Great Britain	1976	69,000
MIDDLE EAST				
Bahrain	Traditional monarchy	Great Britain	1971	530,000
PACIFIC OCEAN				
Fiji	Parliamentary democracy	Great Britain	1970	750,000
Kiribati	Presidential democracy	Great Britain	1979	75,000
Marshall Islands	Parliamentary democracy	United States	1990	50,000
Micronesia, Federated States of	Presidential democracy	United States	1990	108,000
Nauru	Presidential democracy	Great Britain	1968	10,000
Palau	Presidential democracy	United States	1994	16,000
Solomon Islands	Parliamentary democracy	Great Britain	1978	335,000
Tonga	Constitutional monarchy	Great Britain	1970	92,000
Tuvalu	Parliamentary democracy	Great Britain	1978	9,000
Vanuatu	Parliamentary democracy	Great Britain/France	1980	156,000
Western Samoa	Parliamentary democracy	New Zealand	1962	162,000

a. Political instability in the Comoros and the Maldives has impeded the functioning of formal democratic institutions.
b. St. Christopher and Nevis is another official name for the federation.

that three islands vie for the honor of having Europe's oldest parliaments: Iceland, the Isle of Man, and Sicily. Although insularity is conducive to strong feelings of local identity, the reasons for the relative prevalence of democracy must be sought elsewhere.

Of the thirty-one independent small island states, twenty-three were at one point part of the British Empire. They fit the pattern, observed in Asia and Africa, that former British colonies have a more successful democratic record than do former colonies of other European nations. That so many island states were British colonies is, of course, no coincidence. Britain reigned supreme as a sea power in the heyday of European imperialism, when islands and other territories around the world were occupied. Many islands are still British possessions (including Bermuda, the Falklands, and St. Helena).

The French colonial empire also included many islands, but most of these were legally integrated with France after World War II: Martinique and Guadeloupe in the Caribbean; Réunion in the Indian Ocean; Tahiti, New Caledonia, and assorted other islands in the Pacific Ocean; and St. Pierre and Miquelon off the coast of Newfoundland in Canada. The high subsidies granted the islands by France have led to a level of prosperity that, together with their participation in the democratic politics of France, makes independence a relatively unattractive option.

The political legacy of British colonialism includes a history of limited self-government before independence (especially in the Caribbean), a political class imbued with the values of British parliamentary government, civilian supremacy over the military, and parliamentarism rather than presidentialism. These attributes give credence to the views of those who argue that parliamentarism is more conducive to stable democracy than presidentialism. However, this legacy was also bequeathed to other parts of the world, where democracy has fared considerably less well than it has in the islands.

Because of their small size, most islands have a relatively homogeneous population and thus are spared the disruptive influence on democracy of ethnic cleavages. Malta and Iceland are Europe's only true nation-states: there are no national minorities in Iceland and Malta, and there are no Maltese or Icelandic minorities outside these islands. With the notable exception of Trinidad and Tobago, all English-speaking Caribbean states are largely peopled by descendants of African slaves. Among former Portuguese colonies, the Cape Verde Islands and São Tomé and Principe have relatively homogeneous Creole populations, in stark contrast to Angola and Mozambique, whose ethnic diversity has led to civil war. The same is true of the Seychelles. In the Pacific, most states other than Fiji are overwhelmingly Micronesian, Melanesian, or Polynesian.

Where cultural cleavages exist, democracy has indeed come under strain. In Fiji, where immigrants from India slightly outnumbered the indigenous population by the 1980s, an electoral victory by a predominantly Indian party triggered two military coups in 1987 that restored Melanesian supremacy. That supremacy was enshrined in a new democratic constitution in 1990. Similarly, New Caledonia's population is split into two groups of almost equal size: native Melanesians, who favor independence, and French settlers, who wish to remain part of France. Self-determination and democracy have thereby come into conflict in New Caledonia. In Cyprus, arrangements made to safeguard the interests of the Turkish minority did not work satisfactorily after independence in 1960. Ultimately Turkey invaded the northern part of the island in 1974, and later a separate state was established. But in Trinidad and Tobago the cleavage between Afro-Trinidadians and descendants of East Indians, while affecting politics deeply, has not undermined democracy, and Mauritius is a shining example of how to handle cultural and racial pluralism satisfactorily.

The second advantage of insularity is that island states have no land neighbors. This absence means that they need not maintain standing armies and hence have only small military establishments, sometimes none at all. Civilian supremacy, a necessity in a democratic state, is thereby facilitated.

Relations Between Islands

An important feature of small island politics is the strength of localist feeling bred by the unambiguous boundedness of physical space and the consequently palpable "otherness" of other islanders. These attitudes often make political unity between islands difficult to achieve, and where it exists it is threatened by centrifugal tendencies, as individual islands attempt to assert their independence. The Federation of the West Indies broke apart in 1962 over Jamaica's and Trinidad's fears of being dominated by the other. The Gilbert and Ellis Islands became independent as two separate states, Kiribati and Tuvalu, in the late 1970s. The U.S. Trust Territory of the Pacific Islands fragmented into four states in the course of its constitutional development: three sovereign states—the Marshall Islands, the Federated States of Micronesia, and Palau—and one state associated with the United States—the Commonwealth of the Northern Marianas. In the Netherlands Antilles in the Caribbean, Aruba seceded from the five other islands in 1986 and is slated to become independent separately.

At times individual islands in island groups have preferred to remain under colonial rule rather than be submerged in larger states. Anguilla (in the Caribbean) and Mayotte (in the Indian Ocean) succeeded in not joining the Federation of St. Kitts and Nevis and the Comoros, respectively, but Abaco, Banaba, and Espiritu Santo failed in their attempt not to become part of the independent Bahamas, Kiribati, and Vanuatu, respectively.

Once constituted as states, multi-island democracies often reflect this centrifugal tendency in their territorial organization. In states where one island clearly dominates demographically, some delegation of power to the smaller islands has often maintained national unity. Such cases are Banaba, Barbuda, Rodrigues, Rotuma, and Tobago, in relation to Kiribati, Antigua, Mauritius, Fiji, and Trinidad, respectively. In some other cases, federations have been established. Examples are the Federated States of Micronesia, which comprise the four states of Yap, Chuuk, Pohnpei, and Kosrae; the Federal Islamic Republic of the Comoros, which consists of the three islands of Njazidja, Nzwani, and Mwali; the Federation of St. Kitts and Nevis; and the Netherlands Antilles, which consist of Curaçao, Bonaire, and three small islands, and are associated with the Netherlands.

Except on the dominant islands in each group, voting in these polities is usually along island lines. Presumably to prevent such an outcome, the constitution of the Republic of Cape Verde forbids the formation of parties on a geographical basis. The only case where island separatism has led to intractable conflict is on Bougainville, part of Papua New Guinea.

Autonomy Without Independence

Islanders' desire to be masters of their own destiny has led to the maintenance or establishment of autonomous political structures in many insular regions for which outright independence was not desired or was impractical. The Isle of Man and the Channel Islands are direct Crown dependencies of the British monarch and have never joined the United Kingdom (or the European Union). In northern Europe, Finland's Aaland Islands and Denmark's Faroe Islands have been granted large measures of autonomy, as have Portugal's Azores and Madeira in southern Europe. In the Mediterranean, Italy's Sicily and Sardinia are two of the country's five "special regions," which enjoy greater autonomy than do other regions of the country. Traditionally centralist France granted Corsica special status in 1981; it has its own assembly. In the Pacific, the Cook Islands, Niue, and Tokelau have similar arrangements with New Zealand, as does the Commonwealth of the Northern Marianas with the United States. With the partial exception of certain Channel Islands, where Europe's last feudal structures survive, all these small territories enjoy democratic politics within an institutional framework that safeguards islanders' specificity without exposing them to the vagaries of full independence.

Somewhat related to the situation of autonomous islands is the case of island states in federations. Islanders may identify more with their state than inhabitants of continental states do with theirs. This feeling often gives rise to independence movements, which remain, however, very weak. Australia's Tasmania, Canada's Newfoundland, and the United States' Hawaii and quasi-insular (in relation to the continental states) Alaska fall into this category. In a nondemocratic setting, the same pattern obtains in Zanzibar's relations with Tanzania.

See also *Caribbean, English; Caribbean, Spanish; Colonialism; Commonwealth, British; Parliamentarism and presidentialism.*

H. E. Chehabi

BIBLIOGRAPHY

Chehabi, H. E. "Self-Determination, Territorial Integrity, and the Falkland Islands." *Political Science Quarterly* 100 (summer 1985): 215–224.

Connell, John. "Island Microstates: The Mirage of Development." *Contemporary Pacific* 3 (fall 1991): 251–288.

Domínguez, Jorge I., Robert A. Pastor, and R. Delisle Worrell, eds. *Democracy in the Caribbean: Political, Economic, and Social Perspectives.* Baltimore: Johns Hopkins University Press, 1993.

LaFlamme, Alan G. "The Archipelago State as a Societal Subtype." *Current Anthropology* 24 (June 1983): 361–362.

Lowenthal, David, and Colin G. Clark. "Island Orphans: Barbuda and the Rest." *Journal of Commonwealth and Comparative Politics* 18 (November 1980): 293–307.

Meller, Norman. "The Pacific Island Microstates." *Journal of International Affairs* 41 (1987): 109–134.

Richards, Jeffrey. "Politics in Small Communities: Conflict and Consensus." *Journal of Commonwealth and Comparative Politics* 20 (July 1982): 155–171.

Sobukwe, Robert

Founding president of the Pan-Africanist Congress (PAC) and a leader in the struggle against apartheid in South Africa. Sobukwe (1924–1978) was born in a small town in the Eastern Cape. With Nelson Mandela and others, he founded the African National Congress (ANC) Youth League in 1944, while studying at Fort Hare University. African nationalism became his guiding philosophy in the struggle against apartheid.

The Africanists within the ANC trace their origins to the birth of the Youth League and to the ideas of two intellectual leaders in the league, Anton Lembede and A. P. Mada. Known as the African-minded bloc, this group operated openly within the ANC in the 1950s. It believed that only black Africans should participate in organizations that purported to represent Africans, and it particularly disliked whites holding leadership positions within anti-apartheid organizations. By contrast, other rising young leaders of the ANC, such as Mandela and Oliver Tambo, believed a nonracialist perspective was consistent with the tenets of African nationalism.

The philosophical cleavage within the ANC continued to widen until April 1959, when Sobukwe led a breakaway faction in forming the Pan-Africanist Congress of Azania (the organization's preferred name for South Africa). Sobukwe became the first president of the PAC and re-tained this position, even in detention, until his death. The catalyst for the Africanists' break with the ANC was its adoption of the Freedom Charter, which asserted: "South Africa belongs to all who live in it, black and white, and no government can justly claim authority unless it is based on the will of all the people." Sobukwe and his fellow Africanists in the PAC believed that South Africa belonged to African people and not to white settlers.

In early March 1960 Sobukwe launched his first major campaign as president of the PAC—a protest against the pass system, a linchpin of apartheid. Although the campaign professed and practiced nonviolence, the white police opened fire on anti-pass demonstrators in Sharpeville two weeks later, killing nearly 70 Africans and wounding almost 190. The Sharpeville massacre dramatically escalated protest and repression in South Africa and galvanized the anti-apartheid movement. During the protests, Sobukwe was arrested in Soweto. The Sharpeville killings were instrumental in turning the ANC and PAC away from nonviolence and toward armed struggle. The ban on both organizations on April 8, 1960, damaged in particular the PAC, which was barely a year old and left leaderless after Sobukwe's arrest. Most of its key members were jailed or forced into exile. As an illegal organization, the PAC continued to work against apartheid, but the organization was not as successful or internationally well supported as the ANC.

Sobukwe was tried in 1960 and sentenced to three years in prison. After serving his full sentence, he was detained on Robben Island and kept separate from other prisoners for another six years. He was released in 1969 but continued to be detained under house arrest in Kimberley, where he died of cancer in March 1978.

Although the PAC was overshadowed by the ANC and never recovered from the setbacks of 1960, under Sobukwe's leadership it played a major role in mobilizing protest against apartheid. A decade later its influence was felt again in the rise of the black consciousness movement.

See also *Biko, Bantu Stephen; Mandela, Nelson.* In Documents section, see *African National Congress Freedom Charter (1955).*

Khehla Shubane

BIBLIOGRAPHY

Pogrund, Benjamin. *Sobukwe and Apartheid.* Johannesburg: Jonathan Ball, 1990; New Brunswick, N.J.: Rutgers University Press, 1991.

Social democracy

An egalitarian politics that includes a strong commitment to the modern welfare state and to the redistributive function of the state. Social democrats affirm the classic liberal principles associated with representative democracy and the mixed economy, embrace political reformism (as opposed to the revolutionary tradition stemming from Karl Marx), and give allegiance to the moral ideal of social justice. Although it is impossible to situate social democracy on the liberal-socialist continuum with any precision, it is located roughly to the left of liberalism and to the right of socialism.

It is considerably easier, however, to define social democracy in relation to more extreme political alternatives—for example, libertarian liberalism and Marxist socialism. Whereas libertarians uphold an uncompromising vision of the rights of individuals to resist the welfare state in its aspirations to redistribute wealth, social democrats emphasize notions of social responsibility and the duty of the state to aid less privileged members of the community. Social democrats see the power of the state as a legitimate agent of these collective responsibilities.

On the other side of the spectrum, Marxists hold that capitalism must be overthrown, whereas social democrats look to find the solution to social ills within the free market economy (suitably modified). One might say that Marxism seeks to "economize" the idea of social justice, that is, to identify the moral claims of disadvantaged social classes with the advance of a fully rational (postcapitalist) economy. Social democracy, on the other hand, seeks to "remoralize" political economy, that is, to phrase the question of social justice as a problem of morality rather than one of economics.

Evolution of the Movement

Social democracy arose at the beginning of the twentieth century, when Eduard Bernstein, a German Marxist, presented his version of socialism. Bernstein acknowledged that Marx's predictions—presumed to be scientific—of the demise of capitalism and the consequent triumph of working-class revolutionism were little more than false prophecies. This acknowledgement of Marxism's spurious promise gave rise to Bernstein's revisionist socialism, which emphasized a parliamentary and reformist pursuit of socialist aims. A comparable political development, begetting social democracy as a middle position between socialism and liberalism, took place in Britain in the late nineteenth and early twentieth centuries through the vehicle of the Fabian movement. (Beatrice and Sidney Webb, Graham Wallas, George Bernard Shaw, and H. G. Wells were notable Fabians.) This Fabian revisionist-socialist tradition in Britain extends to C. A. R. Crosland's book *The Future of Socialism* (1956).

Viewing social democracy historically as a process of political accommodation with capitalism, or with the quasi-capitalist mixed economy, an unchastened Marxist no doubt would object that socialism is watered-down Marxism and social democracy is watered-down socialism—a double dilution. To address such a challenge, with its implicit charge that social democracy retains no theoretical integrity of its own, but simply defines itself by its half-heartedness in relation to the social ideals from which it borrows its real substance, it might be helpful to put aside the question of the historical genesis of the social democratic movement and of its century-long course of development (a development that in practice shades off into welfarist liberalism). Let us inquire instead at the level of principles, asking whether social democracy does indeed name a coherent set of ideas possessing a moral core with its own distinctive identity.

Justifications

The basic rationale underlying any version of socialism or social democracy is that it is offensive for certain members of society to earn incomes that are grossly out of relation to their real contribution to the welfare of society. (Such disparities in earnings arise because of arbitrary aspects of the social system.) When one reflects on the wealth accumulated today by sports stars, celebrities in the entertainment industry, and opportunistic speculators, this perception seems well founded. And if one considers the social power commanded by wealth and ownership in an even moderately or benignly capitalist society, the case mounts for social democratic redistribution, that is, for direct state intervention in the web of economic relationships to promote moral purposes.

A variety of arguments can be made to justify social democratic policies. One strategy is to argue that all individuals in a liberal society should receive an equitable share of social resources in order to explore and give play to each individual's unique visions of his or her life purpose or plan of life (whatever it happens to be). Moreover, there should be no lack of moral and material encouragement for individuals to make of their lives something that confers self-respect and wins the respect of others and to grasp the opportunities for self-development that a liberal regime puts in their hands. This argument is, roughly speaking, the form of social theory associated with welfarist liberals such as John Rawls and Ronald Dworkin. The authoritative statement of this liberal-individualist version of social democracy is Rawls's towering work *A Theory of Justice* (1971).

It may be helpful to contrast the idea of distributive justice, which defines this kind of theory, with the libertarian doctrines formulated by Robert Nozick and Friedrich von Hayek. Nozick and Hayek allow no legitimate place for state economic intervention or redistributive social policies. An egalitarian liberal like Rawls believes that a just society must engage its citizens in an agreement, at least hypothetically, as to a fair distribution of all the goods and benefits that the society makes available for consumption. That is, social justice requires, and social theory attempts to clarify, what Nozick labels, in order to reject it, a "patterned principle" of distributive justice.

A libertarian thinker like Hayek, by contrast, does not allow some kind of supercontract somehow negotiated by the society as a whole. Rather, he maintains, procedural justice extends no further than the imperative that the multiplicity of discrete contracts entered into by consenting individuals must be honored by those who have promised to do so. For Hayek, Rawls promises something that is necessarily out of reach—namely, the vision of an overarching social order that legislates specific distributive outcomes. As Hayek sees it, Rawls's appeal to substantive principles of macrojustice cannot help but coercively invade and overturn acts of microconsent, and therefore one would be better off abandoning altogether the search for a general theory of distributive justice.

Another argument to justify social democratic policies has a collectivist orientation. Michael Walzer, for instance, defends a robustly egalitarian liberal regime. In *Spheres of Justice* (1983), he argues that the standard for judging questions of distributive justice is not based on individuals' rights to design for themselves an autonomous plan of life but rather is a communal standard, arising from the shared experiences and collective self-understanding of a given society. Walzer wants to show that sometimes a society is implicitly committed, according to the logic of its shared practices and self-conception, to ideals that are insufficiently realized in its existing institutions and policies.

Such an account, he believes, applies in particular to the American welfare state. If Americans had a clear grasp of their own identity, of the underlying commitment to provide for reciprocal needs implicit in their historical community, they would embrace more expansive collective provision for health care than their social and political system currently offers. They would empower less privileged groups in the society to seize greater control over their own social and economic destiny (for instance, by encouraging the formation of workers' cooperatives). And they would strive to lessen the domination of money and market power in shaping power and opportunities across the whole fabric of social and political life—or so Walzer argues. In any case, the comparison of Rawls and Walzer shows that one can argue from either individualist or collectivist premises in the direction of more or less convergent policy commitments.

Characteristics

Social democracy, then, admits of alternative routes to a common destination. Yet there is an irony in appealing to American theorists to defend social democratic conclusions, whether one prefers the more liberal or more socialist version, for in an important sense, social democracy is the outgrowth of an authentically European social consciousness (and, in this sense, is remote from the categories of thought of American liberalism). The social democratic idea is sometimes conceived in terms of social rights, characteristic of twentieth-century liberal democracies, which are thought to offer a supplement to the nineteenth-century political rights and eighteenth-century civil rights associated with earlier incarnations of liberalism. (The original, and still most famous and influential, source of this conception is T. H. Marshall's work on citizenship and social class.)

The problem with this formulation is that it favors the notion of rights held by individuals at the expense of notions of social duty and obligation. In this regard it seems alien to the collectivist traditions upon which European social democracy historically draws. According to the definition of socialism that Mikhail Gorbachev, then leader of the Soviet Union, offered in his address to the Twenty-seventh Communist Party Congress in 1986, citizens' rights must be tied to their duties. Moreover, as Morris Janowitz has pointed out, it may well be that Marshall himself meant to affirm a reciprocity of rights and duties, rather than intending any one-sided primacy of individual rights and entitlements. For these reasons, a more promising idiom to express the idea of social democracy is offered by the vocabulary of citizenship (where citizenship is not taken to be exhausted by a rights-based concept).

The idea here is that social democracy specifies a certain concept of citizenship, of the social conditions that must be met in order for individuals to consider themselves full members of the political community. Social democracy, on this understanding, presupposes at least a minimal core of social membership: no one starves, no one goes homeless, no one lacks for essential medical needs; the elderly are cared for; and no child is denied the opportunities necessary for eventual full participation in the life of the society. It seems reasonable to draw from the logic of the social democratic idea a further corollary: all people should have the opportunity for employment and the sense of dignity that goes with the knowledge that they are making a productive contribution to the needs of society.

Admittedly, this last requirement looks impossibly ambitious, given the onerous public debts and the huge structural unemployment being suffered at present by most liberal-capitalist countries (even those ruled by nominally socialist or social democratic governments). For that matter, the other items on our list defining social democratic citizenship are also far from being realized in contemporary liberal democracies. Of this social democratic vision, some intimations can be detected in the muted idealism expressed by U.S. president Bill Clinton in his inaugural address in 1993. Clinton voiced the conviction that the nation, conceived as a moral community, cannot be indifferent to whether its members, as individuals and as whole classes, thrive or are crushed in the marketplace of everyday life. He said the state must ensure that the perils of life in civil society are not so overwhelming that certain members of the society are effectively denied the conditions of meaningful citizenship.

The Meaning of Social Democracy

What does it mean, then, to embrace social democratic commitments? Typical of the social democrat is a sympathy for the underdogs in society, whether workers, women, or cultural minorities or the elderly, sick, or disabled. Social democracy implies a principled commitment to the welfare state, as opposed to a merely instrumental acceptance of it. Social democrats tend to be the ones who mobilize political support for progressive social legislation—welfare and unemployment benefits, labor legislation favorable to trade unions, expanded educational opportuni-

ties, provisions for health care and child care, guaranteed pension plans, public housing, and so on—prodding the rest of the population to adopt creative means to ameliorate the social condition. In this respect, the cause of social democracy has made notable advances with the postwar achievements of the welfare state in most Western democracies.

As a species of democratic theory, social democracy may be construed as an ambitious interpretation of what full democracy requires. Defining the social democratic synthesis in relation to its two components—socialism and democracy—we might say that social democracy is more than democracy but less than socialism. A social democrat believes that a set of fair and reasonable mechanisms for electoral representation does not sufficiently qualify a society as a genuine democracy. Real democracy depends on shaping a more robustly egalitarian web of social relationships. As the Canadian political theorist C. B. Macpherson has argued, democratic theory falls short of its mandate if it limits itself to the question of how to democratize government; rather, democratic theory in its fullest sense must concern itself with how to democratize society. That is, it must address the problem of how to institute a more egalitarian government throughout economic and social life. This challenge to the standard liberal understanding of democracy has been given a sharp formulation in the claim by Gorbachev (in *Perestroika*, 1987, 127–128) that the democratic claims of Western societies would be more credible if workers and office employees started electing the owners of factories and plants, bank presidents, and so on.

Accordingly, efforts by various democratic theorists such as Carole Pateman and Robert Dahl to investigate possibilities of democratizing the workplace are entirely in the spirit of social democratic ideals. In this sense, social democracy means more democracy; but it means less socialism insofar as social democrats do not necessarily share a faith, or perhaps have shed their faith, in the economic prescriptions of classic socialism (as regards, for example, the nationalization of industry). When one has given up on any magic solutions supposedly forthcoming from the economic doctrines of socialism, what remains is a demanding egalitarian morality that is common to social democrats and old-style socialists.

In the 1980s the energies of Marxism expired in the debacle of Eastern European command economies. At the same time, the attack on the welfare state during the administrations of President Ronald Reagan in the United

States and Prime Minister Margaret Thatcher in Great Britain revealed itself to many as another, and opposing, false promise, exposing the social and moral bankruptcy of libertarian ideals. As the extremes come to be discredited, social democratic morality and politics gain a renewed legitimacy.

Social democracy, one is tempted to say, is the moral residue that is left when socialists lose their confidence about how to organize a modern economy. But even if this definition of social democracy seems ungenerous, the power of this moral residue should not be underestimated. Indeed, in the 1990s social democratic ideas may be winning back a bit of their former luster (to the extent that we have not yet reached the stage where all social doctrines and ideologies yield to universal cynicism).

See also *Bernstein, Eduard; Industrial democracy; Macpherson, C.B.; Marxism; Socialism; Welfare, Promotion of.*

Ronald Beiner

BIBLIOGRAPHY

Beiner, Ronald. *What's the Matter with Liberalism?* Berkeley: University of California Press, 1992, chap. 6.

Dahl, Robert A. *A Preface to Economic Democracy.* Berkeley: University of California Press; Oxford: Polity Press, 1985.

Macpherson, C. B. *Democratic Theory: Essays in Retrieval.* Oxford and New York: Oxford University Press, 1973.

Marshall, T. H. *Class, Citizenship, and Social Development.* Garden City, N.Y.: Anchor Books, 1965.

Pateman, Carole. *Participation and Democratic Theory.* Cambridge and New York: Cambridge University Press, 1970.

Plant, Raymond. *Citizenship, Rights, and Socialism.* Fabian Tract 531. London: Fabian Society, 1988.

———. "Social democracy." In *The Blackwell Encyclopaedia of Political Thought,* edited by David Miller. Oxford: Blackwell, 1987.

Rawls, John. *A Theory of Justice.* Cambridge: Harvard University Press, Belknap Press, 1971; Oxford; Oxford University Press, 1973.

Walzer, Michael. *Spheres of Justice: A Defense of Pluralism and Equality.* New York: Basic Books, 1983; Oxford: Blackwell, 1985.

Social movements

Social movements are loosely organized sequences of collective action on the part of unrepresented groups—or those who claim to represent them—in sustained interaction with elites, authorities, or other groups. At its dawn in Western Europe and North America, modern democracy was unquestionably a social movement. The first activists of modern democracy regarded themselves—and were widely seen—as agents of a new creed and political vision. Like activists in modern social movements, they used concerted forms of collective action against their opponents. It is therefore puzzling that so little attention has been given to the relationship between movements and democratic development. Most scholars of democratic development either ignore social movements or regard them as inherently hostile to democracy.

This lack of attention has resulted, first, from the traditions of discourse in social movement studies and, second, from the viciously antidemocratic behavior of the totalitarian movements between the two world wars. As we shall see later, another reason for scholarly suspicion was the unusual "surplus" of organizational control in the movements of the interwar period—a characteristic that is, happily, atypical of social movements in general. When we turn to the authoritarian collapses of the 1970s and 1980s, we will see that mass movements of a less structured type have converged with elite consensus to produce successful democratic transitions.

Traditions of Discourse

Theory and research on social movements have had two main historical sources: first, the conservative reaction to the French Revolution and the Industrial Revolution and, second, the rise of the socialist movements of the late nineteenth century. Neither strand of theory has helped very much in relating movements to democratic development. The first fostered the idea that movements were the vehicles of the mob, while the second associated movements and social class. Both missed the fact that the protagonists in the most successful movements were neither mobs nor organized proletarians but contingent coalitions of networks and groups united around collective action. This is the typical form of the social movement today: informal organizational networks within broader constituencies without formal links between leaders and followers.

As the nineteenth century proceeded, the decline of bomb-throwing anarchism and the pacification of the working class began to combat the negative presumptions of early theorists. But the great cataclysms of the twentieth century—fascism, Nazism, and the Russian Revolution—revived and intensified the earlier view. This tendency was particularly strong in the United States, where European exiles from fascism brought with them nightmarish memories of the "mob" and a bitter predilection against extremism. Reinforced by this new source of energy, American social science was particularly vulnerable to the persuasion that movements were an expression of dysfunction. Moreover, the cold war revived the earlier linkage of class and movement and identified both with organized communism.

The movements of the 1960s contested these dark visions, reviving the idea that movements could be positively related to democratic development. As the student, antiwar, women's, gay, and environmental movements involved hundreds of thousands of people in largely peaceful collective action, movements were "normalized." The amount of social movement activity increased, but the goals and forms became absorbed into the repertoire of democratic politics.

This outcome was especially true of the civil rights movement in the United States. With its ideology and tactics of nonviolence, the civil rights movement could not easily be construed as a threat to democratic practice, and through its representation of formerly unrepresented African Americans, it helped to bring social movements into the mainstream of American democracy. Not only that: as David Snow and Robert Benford have shown (in *Frontiers of Social Movement Theory,* edited by Aldon Morris and Carol McClurg Mueller, chap. 6, 1992), the movement provided a "master" ideological frame for social activism stressing rights and nonviolent collective action. The same forms and frames were adopted by movements of Hispanic Americans, Native Americans, and gays, among others. The feminist movement—in many ways the most successful heir to the civil rights legacy in the United States—was also born within a rights framework, although in the early 1990s its emphasis on rights has been contested by those stressing "difference."

This incorporation of American movements into democratic practice in the 1960s had little effect on theorists' understanding of democratic development. Most of the movements of the 1960s—the democratic movement in Czechoslovakia being a notable exception—sprang up in already mature liberal democracies. They reveal, however, the double-edged nature of social movements. On the one hand, these movements were sometimes violent and always expressive; and they frequently posed demands that, if fully realized, would have undercut the rights of other groups of citizens. On the other hand, most of their participants proved not to be advocates of anarchy or underminers of democratic politics. On the contrary, as Samuel

Barnes points out (in his article on protest movements in this encyclopedia), they were predominantly participants in conventional political activity with high levels of political consciousness and support for democracy.

The most positive aspect of the 1960s movements for democratic development was their capacity to place issues on the agenda that the existing parties had ignored and to act as tribunes for social groups that felt themselves to be unrepresented. In opposing the Vietnam War, in championing the rights of African Americans and other minorities, and in advancing the cause of women, gays, and people with disabilities, these movements expanded democratic representation, while only occasionally providing political space for advocates of violence and intolerance. In some cases, such as that of the German environmental party, the Greens, the new movements eventually were transformed into constructive and conventional members of the polity.

Democratic Theory and Antidemocratic Movements

But not all challengers seek to widen the polity. Some movements seek to curtail others' rights and even imply their exclusion or liquidation. The goal of the Italian fascists and German National Socialists was to exclude Socialists and Communists from the polity and, ultimately, to destroy entire religious and racial groups.

The political history of Eastern and Central Europe in the first half of the 1990s also shows how movements can threaten democracy. After the collapse of communism in this region in 1989, a wave of racist, skinhead, and protofascist violence erupted, mainly against immigrant workers performing menial jobs. The campaign of Serbian militias against Bosnian Muslims in the former Yugoslavia can properly be seen as the work of a nationalist movement that was loosed by the collapse of social control after the fall of communism in the region. Like the movements of the 1920s and 1930s, this and other outbursts in the region were the byproducts of episodes of democratization.

Not only in the tumultuous aftermath of communism, but also in the relative calm of U.S. politics, social movements have arisen that attack the rights of others and even threaten democracy itself. From the militant antiabortion movement, which has sometimes targeted abortion clinics, to the anti-Semitic utterings of leaders of the Nation of Islam, some American movements resemble—at least superficially—the antidemocratic movements of Europe. This should serve as a caution that advocates of democracy have much to fear—if they often have much to hope for—from the presence and activism of social movements.

It would be mistaken, however, to look on ordinary participants in social movements as if they were necessarily opposed to liberal democracy. A potential for mobilization does not translate automatically into collective action. A social movement will coalesce only in the presence of political opportunity and only if leaders arise to mobilize consensus and channel it into sustained sequences of collective action against elites or opponents. These occurrences not only condition mobilization in general but also affect the type of movement that results. History shows that the character of movements—whether they be democratic or antidemocratic—is not an automatic reflection of the character of constituencies or of their social demands.

For example, the first fascist movement, launched in Italy after World War I, was able to gain the consent of millions of Italians, not because Italians have an authoritarian character, but because of political opportunities afforded Benito Mussolini by the collapse of the old liberal coalition, the split on the left between moderates, "maximalists," and Communists, and the inability of the country's Catholic majority to produce a governing coalition. The 1919 expansion of the suffrage, as well as the economic devastation that had been caused by Italy's wartime mobilization, also helped Mussolini to come to power. The fear and confusion of the postwar years and the excesses of parts of the labor movement produced a political opportunity for a supreme opportunist to undermine Italy's fragile democracy.

The same was true in Yugoslavia after the collapse of communism. Although journalists have pointed to the age-old hostility among Muslims, Serbs, and Croats, they often neglect to acknowledge that these groups lived in peace for many years prior to 1989. It was domestic and international opportunities that gave Slobodan Milošević, the prime minister of Serbia, the chance to establish a hegemonic Serbian state in the region, triggering a violent spiral of nationalist outbidding and giving local political entrepreneurs the opportunity to grab land for themselves and their followers.

Thus there can be no a priori answer to the question of whether and how social movements contribute to democracy, but only a set of answers rooted in history, politics, and political strategy. During some phases of political change, movements have contributed to democratic development, while at other times they have proved inimical to democracy. The potential for mass mobilization can be directed toward or away from democratic development, and only in rare cases does a single organization control the movement entirely. This takes us to the role of organization in social movements.

Movements and Movement Organizations

Collective action has characterized human society for as long as there has been social conflict—which is to say, from whenever human society can be said to have begun. But such actions usually expressed the claims of ordinary people directly, locally, and narrowly responding to immediate grievances, attacking opponents, and almost never seeking allies among other groups or political elites. The result was a series of explosions—seldom organized and usually brief—punctuating periods of passivity. These explosions constituted contentious collective action, but they were not national social movements.

Sometime in the course of the eighteenth century a new and more general repertoire of collective action developed in Western Europe and North America. Unlike the older forms, which expressed people's immediate grievances directly against antagonists, the new repertoire was national, autonomous, and modular: that is, it consisted of forms of organization and action that could be used by many different actors in pursuit of many different claims and serve as a bridge among groups. The effect of such coalitions was to broaden social movements and formalize their organizational structure. The demands of the new organizations became increasingly proactive.

The new breadth and modularity of collective action could be seen in the antislavery movement that swept England in the 1780s before reaching the European continent and eventually the United States. Petitions, demonstrations, and newspaper campaigns distinguished the movement from earlier forms of collective action. Broad and modular collective action could be found in the American Revolution, which developed the tactic of the boycott of imported goods, and in the barricades of the French Revolution, which were employed both for corporate group objectives and as an instrument of social insurrection. What is important to note is that these episodes preceded the invention of the organized mass party or movement and in no way depended on it. The associations that underlay these movements were generally informal networks of activists that never organized more than a fraction of those who occasionally took part in their petitions, marches, demonstrations, and strikes.

Fueled by print and association, coalitions of people with overlapping claims focused sustained sequences of collective action against elites and opponents. Rude, often violent, and seldom self-consciously democratic, the new movements in Britain, France, and North America forced open the gates of participation to new challengers and expanded claims against old elites. From the late eighteenth century on, once these conventions and resources became available to ordinary people, movements could spread to entire societies, producing cycles of protest and reform.

These cycles illustrate the multifaceted and internally contradictory nature of social movements. For although leaders and organizations were at their core, these were usually no more than networks of loosely linked activists that controlled collective action for brief periods and were often in conflict with one another. Seldom possessing formal membership or rules, they owed their very strength to their capacity to mobilize people over whom they exercised no control. Movement organizations, then as now, were usually no more than the most visible summits of the potential icebergs of participation that lay hidden beneath the surface of public life.

The degree of organizational control over social movements has varied throughout history. Two classic examples of democratic episodes that illustrate these differences are the revolutions of 1848 and the wave of mobilization in Europe after World War I. Although these two watersheds were similar in many ways, they were different in at least one sense. The semispontaneous nature of the 1848 revolutions contrasts with the much more highly organized character of the movements following World War I. Whereas temporary networks and organizations were pivotal in the 1848 conflagration, the 1918–1921 cycle was piloted by centralized organizations.

In one sense, the new forms of movement only added greater cohesion and ideological clarity to the patterns of the past. But in another sense, they changed the relationship between movement and state and between movement and followers. For once an organization takes over the leadership of an inchoate and many-stranded social movement, it has a vested interest in the continuation of collective action—even once the popular "demand" for it has declined.

Thus, in 1848, unorganized masses of people rose up and then subsided when the "springtime of peoples" had passed. But in the cycle that followed World War I, movement leaders using collective action for organizational ends attempted to organize followers permanently and continued to mount collective action long after mass demand for it had subsided. The result was to exacerbate social conflict and to fuel a countermovement of elites, the lower middle class, and the military—the shock force of fascism.

This process of organizational encapsulation of social movements has obvious and negative implications for democratic development. To the extent that protest cycles come under the control of organizers who use collective action to maintain a following, cycles no longer follow the natural parabola of mass mobilization but respond to the organizational needs of their leaders. Protest becomes professionalized, and the satisfaction of a particular demand does not necessarily lead to the withdrawal of collective action. The question for students of democracy is whether and to what extent the organizational pattern of the interwar period is repeated in other democratic social movements.

Recent research on the "new" social movements from the 1960s on in the United States and Western Europe suggests that the interwar pattern was atypical. The movements that bubbled up during the decline of state socialism in Eastern and Central Europe in 1989 also did not take the centralized, militant form familiar from the European past, perhaps because of the odium in which the concept of party organization was held in the former Soviet bloc.

With some important exceptions, such as movements of militant Muslim fundamentalists, social movements in contemporary industrial societies are more likely to crystallize around informal and shifting organizational networks that do not control their supporters than around centralized bureaucratic organizations with dedicated cadres of militants. If this supposition is true, the potential for exploitation of social movement claims for organizational ends is not as great as it was in the interwar period. It remains to be seen, however, whether this will be true of movements in rapidly industrializing, non-Western societies, such as those of Latin America and Southeast Asia.

Elites and Recent Democratizations

The excesses of the movements of the interwar period, and the spiral of violence and reaction that they triggered, led many to the conclusion that mass politics had to be kept in check if democracy was to flourish. Others believe that it was the particular movements of the interwar period—extreme socialism, fascism, and Stalinist communism—that were antidemocratic. For the first group, the danger of unfettered mass participation is genetic; for the latter it is contingent.

Prescriptions about the role of social movements in democracy are opposed along the same lines. Unless mass movements are kept under control, one view goes, they will produce chaos and lead invariably to reaction. In the second view, the nature of particular movement organizations and the particular conditions under which they operate will determine whether democratic breakthroughs will be successfully consolidated.

The failure of the Spanish Republic in the interwar years provides support for both theses: one could find in it evidence of uncontrolled mass violence to support the first view and of a struggle for power among elites with little dedication to democracy to support the second. More recent democratic episodes—for example, those of southern Europe and Latin America in the 1970s and 1980s—also lend themselves to both interpretations. On the one hand, these transitions were guided by elites (but, happily, the elites wanted a liberal democratic outcome). Those who feared a recurrence of the excesses of the interwar period therefore found in the elite democratizations of Spain and Brazil a welcome relief. But those who took a more contingent view pointed to the essentially democratic vocation of the particular groups who empowered these transitions—at both the elite and the mass levels. For it was not only elites who were determined to manage peaceful transitions to democracy, in this view, but also the union leaders, military men, and ordinary workers and soldiers who used the political opportunities afforded by these transitions with restraint.

The Spanish transition in the 1970s was the watershed in which both kinds of interpretation find support. On the one hand, the transition from the fascist regime of Francisco Franco to democracy was carefully managed by elites who came from the Franquist camp and by the major forces of the opposition; on the other hand, there was a great deal of mass mobilization—especially of organized labor—helping to drive it to completion. In contrast to the 1930s, when the Spanish left was radical, divided, and associated with international Stalinism, the labor and opposition movement in Spain in the 1970s was moderate, unified, and working for democracy in the context of a Western Europe that was solidly in the democratic fold.

Political Learning and Democratization

The democratic transitions of the 1970s and 1980s underscore the importance of political learning in the rela-
tionship between social movements and democratic development. Both the elites who guided those transitions and the citizens who lived through them learned about the strategies that are likely to lead to successful democratic transitions and those that are likely to fail.

The democratization movements in East Central Europe in the early 1990s show even more clearly the joint effects of elites, mass movements, and open opportunity structures in bringing about successful transitions. Because those transitions are not yet complete, we cannot offer any sweeping generalization, but if we look at the moment of transition in 1989–1990, it is clear that entrenched elites converged on minimal projects of transition that would leave their lives—if not their statuses—intact. Mass movements were mainly united around the goal of democratic succession and showed little inclination for retribution or violence. And—in contrast to the interwar period, when fascism and Stalinism competed for hegemony—democracy had no ideological competitors; it guided the strategies of both elites and the mass public.

The relationship between social movements and democracy must therefore be analyzed in terms of the opportunity structure of each historical period, the mobilization potential of the citizenry, and the dispositions and strategies of both elites and movement supporters. Taking advantage of emerging political opportunities, early democratic movements expanded the scope and the arenas of participation. When permanent movement organizations developed, they learned to use collective action to advance their organizational goals and competed with each other in ways that led to escalating spirals of violence and radicalization. These fed a reaction against mass politics on the part of the citizenry that culminated in the democratic breakdowns and authoritarian inversions of the interwar period.

The protest movements of the 1960s, the democratic movements of the 1970s, and the democratic breakthroughs of 1989 in East Central Europe appear to have restored the positive linkage between democracy and social movements. But the racist and ethnic nationalist movements of the early to mid-1990s represent both a new spiral of violence and a risk of the return of earlier forms of authoritarianism. If movements are contingent developments that depend upon mobilization potentials, leadership inclinations, and political opportunities, then democracy itself may be a contingent outcome of conflict.

See also *Abolitionism; Civil rights; Fascism; Feminism; Protest movements.*

Sidney Tarrow

BIBLIOGRAPHY

McAdam, Doug. *The Political Process and the Rise of Black Insurgency.* Chicago: University of Chicago Press, 1982.

Morris, Aldon, and Carol McClurg Mueller. *Frontiers of Social Movement Theory.* New Haven and London: Yale University Press, 1992.

Olson, Mancur. *The Logic of Collective Action.* Cambridge: Harvard University Press, 1965.

Przeworski, Adam. "Democracy as a Contingent Outcome of Conflict." In *Transitions from Authoritarian Rule: Comparative Perspectives,* edited by Guillermo O'Donnell, Philippe Schmitter, and Lawrence Whitehead. Baltimore and London: Johns Hopkins University Press, 1986.

Tarrow, Sidney. *Power in Movement: Collective Action, Social Movements and Politics.* New York and London: Cambridge University Press, 1994.

Tilly, Charles. *From Mobilization to Revolution.* Reading, Mass: Addison-Wesley, 1978.

Traugott, Marc, ed. *Cycles and Repertoires of Collective Action.* Durham, N.C.: Duke University Press, 1995.

Zald, Mayer N., and Roberta Ash. "Social Movement Organizations: Growth, Decay, and Change." In *Social Movements in an Organizational Society,* edited by Mayer N. Zald and John D. McCarthy. New Brunswick, N.J.: Transaction, 1987.

Social security, Promotion of

See *Welfare, Promotion of*

Socialism

An alternative to capitalist profit-driven and competitive economies, in which such measures as constraints on economic inequalities and control of labor or capital markets are undertaken in order to achieve substantial social equality and cooperation. During the nineteenth and early twentieth centuries, socialism was considered linked with democracy in the broad sense of self-government both by theorists and in the popular consciousness. From the mid-twentieth century through the collapse of communist regimes beginning in 1989, however, socialism and democracy came to be generally considered antithetical. The chief causes of this shift were the autocratic behavior of socialist states and the resilient combination of liberal-democratic political institutions with capitalist economies in the wealthier countries.

These developments create a problem for contemporary socialists. Like their predecessors, socialists in the 1990s believe that the vicissitudes of a capitalist market and the ability of private owners to dispose of profits and to manage labor perpetuate inequalities of wealth and power. These inequalities in turn at least impede and at worst render impossible an otherwise attainable level of democracy. Accordingly, socialists who resist the view that a socialist alternative to capitalism is doomed to be even less friendly to democracy are divided. Some claim that liberalizing reforms—such as those attempted by Alexander Dubček in Czechoslovakia in the 1960s or by Mikhail Gorbachev in the Soviet Union in the 1980s—could in principle have succeeded. Others argue that the socialism in such countries was not of the right sort or was not socialism at all.

Contemporary socialists also disagree about several other important issues: whether capitalism can be reformed or must be replaced; whether the chief constraint on democracy is located in a division between capitalist owners and propertyless workers, in an anti-cooperative competitive market, or in unequal distribution of goods; and what alternative forms of production or principles of distribution are to be preferred. The answers to these questions involve such fundamental issues as how to define socialism and democracy themselves. These debates, like the unfulfilled democratic promises of socialism that prompted them, have historical roots, well summarized by G. D. H. Cole and Leszek Kolakowski in their histories of socialism and Marxism.

The Early Nineteenth Century

Socialism was named in the early nineteenth century by followers of the French social theorist Claude-Henri Saint-Simon and the British social reformer Robert Owen. Both men advocated education of workers and capitalists alike to achieve reforms leading to a society in which people would cooperatively produce and equitably distribute goods. Other early socialists had somewhat different visions of social reform. Louis Blanc advocated what today is called a welfare state. Blanc was less speculative and utopian than Saint-Simon and Owen. But Charles Fourier projected a radical change of societies to "phalanxes" in which the constraints of a division of labor and of mores such as monogamy had been overcome. Pierre-Joseph Proudhon, who coined the phrase "property is theft," favored industrial democracy and "mutualist" federations of manufacturing and agricultural communities.

These early socialists shared a belief in the power of education and experimental communities to win converts from all classes who would work toward these goals. This belief distinguished them from other socialists of the time, such as Louis-Auguste Blanqui. The Blanquists were inspired by the French agitator François-Noël Babeuf. He and his followers saw the French Revolution as a forerunner of a more radically egalitarian revolution. The Blanquists in turn participated in militant and insurrectional activities that led in 1871 to the short-lived Paris Commune, when workers occupied part of that city. Blanqui saw revolution as essentially a working-class affair. Like Babeuf before him, he thought that revolutionary conspirators would initially be obliged to employ dictatorial methods.

These were by no means the only socialist tendencies in the early nineteenth century. In France, Etienne Cabet saw in early Christianity examples of egalitarian and communal societies. In England in 1838–1839 a campaign for passage of a bill called the People's Charter sparked a working-class movement, the Chartists. This group demanded universal manhood suffrage and democratic parliamentary reform. The views of Owen and the Chartists also merged with English utilitarianism, which sometimes took on a socialist flavor, especially in the work of John Stuart Mill. The seeds of most later socialist trends, organizational disputes, and debates about the relation of socialism to democracy can be found in these early socialist thinkers and movements.

The Late Nineteenth and Early Twentieth Centuries

In the late nineteenth and early twentieth centuries, socialist parties and coalitions formed in nearly all countries of Europe. Each of these groups included a wide variety of orientations toward socialism and toward democracy. This was especially true of the two main international organizations: the International Workingman's Association (First International), founded in London in 1864, and the Second International, founded in Paris in 1889. Of the many positions that emerged in the complex politics of these organizations, three broad streams bearing on the relation of socialism to democracy can be identified: reformist, Marxist-revolutionary, and anarchist.

The reformist stream was the forerunner of later twentieth-century social democracy. (The term is historically confusing, since the nineteenth-century revolutionaries also called their parties social democratic.) The Marxist stream yielded revolutionary political organizations—mainly communist parties—and also influenced generations of independent socialists and movements. The more militant anarchist trend gave rise to relatively few organizations of anarchists and to the ideas of a variety of radicals.

The differences between the reformist and the Marxist-revolutionary streams began to clarify at a conference held in Gotha, Germany, in 1875, when Germany's two socialist parties merged to form the Socialist Workers' Party. The reformist group was the former Social Democratic Party. Its members were called Lassalleans after Ferdinand Lassalle, who, though deceased by that time, had been an influential founder of this group. Lassalleans favored parliamentary activity to achieve democratic political and egalitarian economic reforms and workers' cooperatives. Against them stood August Bebel and Wilhelm Liebknecht, leaders of the former Social-Democratic Workers Party, together with Karl Marx and Friedrich Engels. Although they were not completely opposed to reform activity, this group looked primarily to political organization of the industrial working class to achieve radical transformation of existing political and economic structures, eventually producing a conflict-free, collectivist society.

Similar differences emerged in France between the Socialist Party of France, whose dominant figure was the revolutionary Blanquist, Jules Guesde, and the French Socialist Party, which followed the reformist thinking of Jean Jaurès.

In Russia, V. I. Lenin polemicized against those whom he called "legalists," notably Peter Struve, for trying to achieve social change by strictly parliamentary and legal means. Like its Western European counterparts, the Russian Social Democratic Party was divided into wings. After a party congress in 1902 the members of these wings were called Bolsheviks and Mensheviks (respectively, those who were in the majority and in the minority of a crucial vote). Lenin and the Bolsheviks pushed for largely extraparliamentary activity and minimal cooperation with nonsocialist anti-czarists. The Mensheviks charged the Bolsheviks with Blanquism; Lenin retorted by associating his critics with the views of Louis Blanc.

The First International was founded in London because of the presence there of exiled revolutionaries, like Marx. The main line of British socialist thinking, however, was more in the tradition of Robert Owen. The playwright George Bernard Shaw, Sidney Webb, and Beatrice Webb campaigned for educational reform and economic welfare achieved by parliamentary means. In 1883–1884 some British socialists founded the Fabian Society with this aim. The group took its name from the Roman general Fabius Cunctator, who was known for military tactics that avoided direct confrontation. Democracy for the Fabians meant electoral politics and parliamentary government, and they came increasingly to be affiliated with Britain's Labour Party.

On the Continent, socialistic ideas were popularized by the French writer Victor Hugo, as they were in Britain by writers such as Shaw and William Morris. In Germany, Eduard Bernstein, whom some regard as the theoretical founder of social democracy, championed the Fabian views in his debates with Marxists in the Second International.

Before and just after World War I, influential Austrian and German liberal socialists were concerning themselves with parliamentary and legal reform. One of these, Hugo Preuss, drafted the constitution of the German Weimar Republic. British socialist G. D. H. Cole shared Preuss's liberal values, but thought that these would be best served if national associations of manual and professional workers coordinated industry in the service of the public good. Cole led the movement called *guild socialism* to promote this end and founded the National Guilds League in 1915.

The furthest removed from the Fabians and other reformers were the anarchists. Notable anarchists included the Russians Pyotr Kropotkin (a prince who renounced his title) and Mikhail Bakunin (also an aristocrat) and the Italian Enrico Malatesta. Like the Marxist revolutionaries, anarchists were attracted to radical critiques of existing society in the style of the Blanquists. Although the Marxists wished to temper the Blanquist refusal to work within the existing system, the anarchists rejected any accommodations to the status quo. As to their goals, they were influenced by Proudhon and thought of socialism as self-managed communities. This made socialism and democracy identical in their eyes, since in these communities people governed themselves cooperatively and directly.

Formal institutions of the state are unnecessary in self-governed societies and actually form a major obstacle to their attainment. Although a loose association of anarchists, informally called the Black International, was founded in 1881, anarchists extended their critique of institutions to political parties. Contrary to the popular image of anarchism, they also opposed organized conspiratorial groups of the sort Babeuf and Blanqui thought necessary. In this and in their Proudhonist emphasis on communities of workers, the anarchists resembled the syndicalist movements of France, Italy, and Spain. The chief advocate of syndicalism, Georges Sorel, believed that spontaneous uprisings of workers, as in general strikes, would bring into existence mutualist societies of the sort Proudhon favored. Syndicalism came to be known as anarcho-syndicalism.

Socialist ideas were less sharply defined and socialist organizations less prominent in North America than in Europe, though populism and Jeffersonian democracy to some extent shared the socialists' antipathy to capitalist inequalities of power and wealth and favored local self-government. More explicitly socialistic were members of the social gospel movement, who advocated equality and democracy on Christian grounds. The chief exponents of these views were the German exile Walter Rauchenbusch in the United States and James Shaver Woodsworth in Canada. Eugene Debs drew on various strands of populist, Jeffersonian, and egalitarian thought to participate in founding the Socialist Party (called the Social Democratic Party of America at its founding in 1897). Although Debs was not a member of the social gospel movement, both he and Norman Thomas, who later headed the Socialist Party, shared its secular values and were influenced by it.

Attempts were made in North America to put into practice the visions of some of the early socialists—Saint-Simon, Owen, Fourier, Cabet—by constructing utopian communities. Since there were few of these experiments, and they were short lived, they had little effect on popular thinking. Workers' and farmers' cooperatives, designed on lines recommended by Proudhon, met with more success. Canada's Cooperative Commonwealth Federation (forerunner of its current social democratic New Democratic Party) was founded on the basis of such cooperatives; its first leader was the social gospelist Woodsworth. In the United States populism proved fertile ground for anarcho-syndicalist movements, which found their most colorful leader in William "Big Bill" Haywood. A militant miner, Haywood was a prominent leader in both the Socialist

Party and the International Workers of the World (called the Wobblies). He and other populists came into conflict with Marxist-inspired workers' movements, such as the Socialist Labor Party of Daniel De Leon.

Dictatorship of the Proletariat

Controversies over the relationship between reform and revolution in the late nineteenth and early twentieth centuries largely concerned strategies for achieving socialism. They also involved some far-reaching differences about the nature of socialism and democracy. Until the debates of the First and Second Internationals, it was assumed that socialism had to do with social cooperation and equality, but socialists differed over the meaning of these concepts. For Saint-Simon a cooperativist society maintained social hierarchies based on merit. People should make contributions appropriate to their abilities while being rewarded according to their contribution to society. Blanc advocated distribution in accord with people's needs. Fourier wished to overcome divisions of labor, so that each person would be able to perform a variety of tasks.

Marx and Engels complicated this debate. In their writings they divided communism into two stages. The first of these, which they called socialism, would prepare society's economy and culture for the higher stage of communism proper. Saint-Simon's principle of distribution in accord with work was to prevail under socialism. Under communism the more thoroughgoing egalitarian principle of distribution by need would be achieved. In addition, the division of labor would be overcome, and people would acquire completely cooperative values. Another Marxist intervention was to have profound effects on later socialist practice related to democracy. At the meeting of German socialists in Gotha, Marx and Engels took issue with the central place the Lassalleans accorded equality. They insisted instead that the first stage of communism should be regarded exclusively in revolutionary working-class terms.

Basing their argument on economic and historical theory, they claimed that socialist revolutions, whether achieved by electoral means (as they thought possible in England, Holland, and the United States) or by armed insurrection, had to be undertaken by the industrial working class, or proletariat. Having achieved state power, this class would deploy state means, including force and the threat of force, to achieve a transition to full communism. All previous states had maintained armies, police, and other institutions of coercion, and to this extent they were dictatorial. The working-class state would differ from them because the "dictatorship of the proletariat," as Marx and Engels called it, would act in the interests of the majority working class. Socialism, then, should be identified with the dictatorship of the proletariat.

Later debates about this notion threw into sharp relief the major differences among reform, Marxist-revolutionary, and anarchist strains of socialist theory and practice. Rather than suggesting a bridge between pre- and post-communist societies, as the Marxists intended, the idea highlighted the difference between Marxists and the reformists, who saw socialism as the extension of existing economic and democratic gains attainable within reformed political structures. Anarchists shared the Marxist vision of higher communism, but they saw institutions of state coercion as the main impediment to such a future. Thus they regarded a revolutionary workers' state as a contradiction in terms.

Marx and Engels thought that socialist revolutions would begin in the industrialized countries and would then spread within a few decades to the entire world. When it appeared that this would not happen, but that there was a real possibility of socialist revolution in economically backward Russia, the Marxist debate over the dictatorship of the proletariat intensified. To Lenin, the dictatorship of the proletariat really meant the dictatorship of a political organization, the Bolsheviks, claiming to represent the proletariat. He accordingly devoted much attention to questions of party composition and organization.

Lenin's focus on revolutionary political organization sharpened his differences with the Mensheviks, who concluded from the adverse circumstances of Russia that the only realistic course was patience and reform in alliance with the bourgeoisie. It also brought him into conflict with other Marxist revolutionaries, such as Rosa Luxemburg and Karl Kautsky. Luxemburg, though a strong critic of reformists like Bernstein, also criticized Lenin. She feared that the dictatorship of the Bolsheviks would replace working-class revolutionary activity and become oppressively antidemocratic. Kautsky, known as a leading defender of Marxist orthodoxy, charged Lenin with being out of accord with Marxism. He observed that Marx and Engels had modeled the dictatorship of the proletariat after the Paris Commune, which included political parties and liberal freedoms and in any case was intended to be of short duration.

Lenin responded to these criticisms that the dictatorship of the proletariat—regarded as the political hegemony of the Bolsheviks, if necessary in a single-party state—was itself a form of democracy, superior to other forms. He further asserted that one should never talk of democracy without asking whose class interests are served by institutions called democratic. These views constituted a departure from previous socialist thinking about democracy. The socialist tradition had included elitist (Saint-Simon) and dictatorial (Blanqui) strains, but these were seen as necessary constraints on democracy and not as exercises in democracy. At the same time, Lenin introduced an instrumental concept of democracy; he saw democracy as a means to the goal of socialist revolution rather than as a goal of socialism.

A Dark Interlude

The Russian Revolution was seen for several decades as a triumph of popular self-determination. But its democratic credentials disappeared as the grossly oppressive nature of its government, especially in the 1930s and 1940s under Joseph Stalin, began coming to light. In this period and beyond, the worst fears of Lenin's critics were realized. Blatant state oppression was excused as necessary for a revolutionary cause more important than democracy; at the same time it was rationalized as identical with a higher form of democracy.

These problems did not attend social democracy, though it languished somewhat before and during World War II. In this period those who might have pursued specifically socialist politics either involved themselves in governments limited to welfare measures, such as the New Deal in the United States, or else became embroiled in constraining political coalitions, like the socialist-led government of Léon Blum in France. After World War II both reformist and revolutionary socialists found it difficult to develop theories or engage in socialist politics because of cold war repression.

Within the communist movement during this time, two events stand out as potentially innovative from a democratic point of view: the revolution in China, based on its large peasant majority, and an attempt in Yugoslavia to combine workers' self-managed enterprises with a noncapitalist market. Viewed as democratic experiments, these are inconclusive, since both were subject to autocratic Communist Party policies similar to those of the Soviet Union. China in addition suffered the brutal and anti-intellectual Cultural Revolution.

From the 1960s Onward

In the late twentieth century, established socialist theory and practice has twice been surprised by democratic upheavals. First, there was the explosion of extraparliamentary democratic activity in the 1960s, giving rise to the civil rights, women's, students', and national liberation movements. Second, there was the collapse of communist governments in the name of democracy in the Soviet Union and Eastern Europe. The Eastern European collapse, dramatically marked by the fall of the Berlin Wall in 1989, was explicitly antisocialist, at least as socialism had been known in the affected countries.

The student-led demonstrations and university occupations in France, the United States, and nearly every other developed country beginning in 1968 included anticapitalist and sometimes anarchist rhetoric and demands. Still, most participants in what were called the new left movements viewed them as generally liberating rather than as specifically socialist.

Socialists of the old schools awakened to new democratic possibilities, and socialists born of the democratic movements soon accommodated themselves to these events. Humanist socialists, such as the English historian E. P. Thompson, criticized a previous socialist emphasis on impersonal economic and historical forces. In a similar spirit, authors of the new left revived early writings of Marx, in which he had discussed personal alienation.

The civil rights movement led socialists to reevaluate traditional disparagements of civil liberties. Some socialists, notably the Canadian political theorist C. B. Macpherson, developed more balanced appraisals of liberal democracy. The women's liberation movement gave rise to a school of Marxist feminists who retrieved interpretations of the oppression of women by Engels, Bebel, and other early socialists as expressions of class struggle. In reaction against this class reductionism a variety of non-Marxist socialist feminist writers sought alternative explanations.

Very few socialists in the earlier twentieth century had addressed the question of national self-determination. With the exception of largely pragmatic discussions by Lenin, only Max Adler, Bruno Bauer, and other members of an Austrian school of thought called Austro-Marxism had treated this subject in any depth. National liberation movements in the developing world led socialists to return to this earlier work and to develop new approaches to the relationships among nationalism, socialism, and democracy.

In the post–cold war period a variety of approaches called democratic socialist emerged to challenge both Marxism and social democracy. After the Russian Revolution the Second International coalition of revolutionaries and reformists had largely broken down. Communism on a world scale came under strict Soviet control—first in the Comintern, or Third International, established by Lenin in 1919 and then under the Cominform imposed by Stalin in 1947. Although the Cominform was dissolved in 1956, because of discontent on the part of Yugoslav and other communists with Soviet domination, its member parties continued to rationalize authoritarianism as a special form of democracy.

The Second International continued to exist as a forum for exchange of opinion among social democratic parties. However, its socialist wing, represented by leaders such as Willy Brandt in Germany and Olof Palme in Sweden, continued to weaken until by the mid-1980s social democratic politics was content to accommodate to capitalism. Democratic socialism thus emerged as an effort to find a "third way" between communist authoritarianism and social democratic capitalist accommodation.

For the most part, democratic socialist views found organizational expression within specific social movements instead of political parties. One exception was the Green Party in Germany, which included socialist planks in an ecological platform. Another was the Democratic Socialists of America, a coalition of leftist groups founded by Michael Harrington and others in 1983. This party has attempted to define a leftist social democratic position that had been elusive in U.S. politics.

On a grander scale were the efforts in the 1970s and early 1980s of people in the democratic wings of communist parties to break ranks with the Soviet approach to democracy. These efforts succeeded, at least for a time, in Italy, Spain, France, England, and Japan. Labeled *Eurocommunism* by the press, this movement was strongest and most consistently anti-Leninist under the leadership of Enrico Berlinguer in Italy. Like many other democratic socialists, the Eurocommunists drew on the work of Antonio Gramsci, a founder of the Italian Communist Party. Gramsci was unique among thinkers of the Second International in wishing to combine radical, revolutionary values with a reformist view about continuity between capitalism and socialism regarding democratic advances. Similarly, he adhered to a Marxist belief in the necessity of a revolutionary party, while sharing the anarchist emphasis on independent popular democratic struggles.

Some of the Eurocommunist parties, such as the one in France, reverted to more traditional Marxism. Others changed their names and adopted policies even further removed from Marxism. All these parties, along with non-Marxist socialist and social democratic organizations, suffered from the collapses of communist governments that began in 1989. In public consciousness the idea of socialism generally was tainted by communist autocracy, inefficiency, and corruption. Contemporary democratic socialists have thus devoted attention to explaining the fall of these regimes and have also begun to develop alternative concepts of socialism and its relation to democracy.

These efforts have been marked by pluralism in three senses. First, there has been a rapprochement between socialism and the theory called pluralist by political scientists in the 1950s, which focused on conflicts among interest groups. Socialist forerunners of these political scientists, such as the Russian legalists, Preuss, and Joseph Schumpeter, had been in the minority of socialist thought. Most socialists had defended a notion of democracy as popular sovereignty against pluralist concepts of conflict management and competition. Many democratic socialists now share the idea that democracy must accommodate conflict, while the leading U.S. pluralist, Robert Dahl, has adopted socialism.

Pluralism in a second sense refers to the toleration of people with life goals different from one's own. Nearly all democratic socialists now try to fit into their theories traditional, liberal democratic respect for different people's differing values. This attitude is in keeping with suspicion of the class reductionism and paternalism associated with the notion of the dictatorship of the proletariat, and it departs from an earlier socialist view that saw homogeneity of values as a necessary prerequisite for a cooperative, socialist society.

Finally, democratic socialist theory itself draws on a large diversity of theoretical perspectives. For example, some democratic socialists propose ethical views in the rationalist tradition of the eighteenth-century Enlightenment, while others favor anti-Enlightenment, postmodernist theory. The failure of communist command economies has sparked work by democratic socialists on market socialism, and some even borrow from traditionally procapitalist economic models. Both individualistic and communitarian approaches to democracy are used. Religious views, such as those of the liberation theologians in South America and elsewhere, supplement predominantly secular socialist thought. Many democratic socialists incorporate feminist or ecological ideas into their theories.

In a pluralist spirit, democratic socialists are for the most part open to yet more alternative perspectives. Moreover, the collapse of communism calls for imaginative thinking by socialists. For both these reasons, democratic socialist ideas will likely continue to proliferate. It remains to be seen, however, whether a viable third way between authoritarian socialism and capitalism can be found.

See also *Anarchism; Bernstein, Eduard; Capitalism; Communism; Dahl, Robert A.; Engels, Friedrich; Gramsci, Antonio; Leninism; Luxemburg, Rosa; Macpherson, C. B.; Marx, Karl; Marxism; Schumpeter, Joseph; Social democracy; Social movements; Welfare, Promotion of.*

Frank Cunningham

BIBLIOGRAPHY

Bobbio, Norberto. *The Future of Democracy.* Minneapolis: University of Minnesota Press, 1987.

Cole, G. D. H. *A History of Socialist Thought.* London: Macmillan, 1965.

Cunningham, Frank. *Democratic Theory and Socialism.* Cambridge and New York: Cambridge University Press, 1987.

Gould, Carol C. *Rethinking Democracy: Freedom and Social Cooperation in Politics, Economy, and Society.* Cambridge and New York: Cambridge University Press, 1988.

Habermas, Jürgen. *Legitimation Crisis.* Boston: Beacon Press, 1973.

Kolakowski, Leszek. *Main Currents of Marxism: Its Rise, Growth, and Dissolution.* 3 vols. Oxford and New York: Oxford University Press, 1981.

Laclau, Ernesto, and Chantal Mouffe. *Hegemony and Socialist Strategy: Towards a Radical Democratic Politics.* London: Verso; New York: Routledge Chapman and Hall, 1985.

Roemer, John E. *A Future for Socialism.* Cambridge: Harvard University Press; London, Verso, 1994.

Schweickart, David. *Against Capitalism.* Cambridge and New York: Cambridge University Press, 1994.

Young, Iris Marion. *Justice and the Politics of Difference.* Princeton: Princeton University Press, 1990.

Socialization, Political

Political socialization refers to the processes by which individuals learn the political norms, values, and behavior patterns of the nations, groups, or subgroups to which they belong. These characteristics can be thought of as each group's political culture. Political socialization means learning the enduring attitudes and ways of behaving that characterize a group over an extended period of time.

Learning Political Attitudes and Behaviors

Political socialization may include both formal teaching and informal learning; it may be either self-directed and self-motivated or influenced by other people, groups, or institutions. These others are often called *agents of socialization.* Political cultures tend to endure because their most important elements are reinforced by different institutions and agents of political socialization and are passed on from one generation to another.

Parents and other members of the family, teachers and schools, religious institutions, formal and informal groups, co-workers, professional colleagues, peers, and friends all have the potential to be agents of political socialization. Important events (war, economic depression, and the like) can also have long-term influences on political attitudes and behavior, especially among younger people, whose attitudes and behavior patterns tend to be more malleable than those of their elders.

The mass media are also considered to be an agent of socialization. In totalitarian societies the print and broadcast media typically present an official point of view. But in democratic societies, where information is seldom controlled, the mass media play an important role in informing the citizenry and helping to structure the way political issues and conflicts are viewed. The mass media are undoubtedly of extraordinary importance when societies make the transition to democracy because they can encourage the development of new values and behavior patterns consistent with democracy; many other agents of socialization foster traditional values that discourage individual participation and opinion holding.

Political attitudes and values help to shape individuals' political goals and the way and extent to which they participate in political life. In democracies, differences in voting rates and other types of political participation—such as talking to others about politics, donating money, campaigning, and running for office—reflect individuals' beliefs about appropriate political roles for citizens in general and for people like themselves in age, sex, educational level, social class, or ethnic group. These beliefs may be based on what they have observed of other people around them or what they have been taught is appropriate, two common processes of political socialization. Similarly, individuals' political goals—the issue positions they take, the party or candidates they vote for, the causes for which they work or to which they contribute, and the way in which they interact with others—reflect their political values. People differ in tolerance toward other ethnic or religious groups, in respect for the rights of others, and in their willingness to abide by the "rules of the game" in their society. All these attitudes are part of a political culture and are relevant to whether democratic political processes can be sustained.

Political participation is an important right of citizenship in all democracies, so attitudes that encourage voting and other forms of participation are important outcomes of political socialization processes. Especially important for electoral participation is a sense that a particular political party best represents one's own interests and beliefs. When people do not perceive differences between the parties in their political system, they are less likely to think their own participation is worthwhile.

Family Influences

Research in the United States shows that the party identification of children and adolescents is frequently the same as or close to that of their parents, but this pattern does not appear in all countries. Comparisons of the attitudes of parents and their children in five Western democracies are provided in a cross-national study of political participation headed by Samuel Barnes and Max Kaase. In Britain the pattern of parental influence on children's partisanship was similar to that observed in the United States. In Germany, Austria, and the Netherlands, however, parents had less effect on the partisanship of their children. On more diffuse attitudes, such as political trust or support for the political system, there was moderate family influence in European countries but virtually none in the United States. The authors speculate that trust may be easier to pass on in Europe because it is less likely to be associated with partisan affiliations there than in the United States.

With respect to attitudes toward governmental policies and programs, the picture is also mixed. For broad value priorities, there is no evidence of marked familial influence. Parental influence is variable with respect to an overall issue agenda concerning how extensive government involvement should be in a variety of social, economic, and civil rights initiatives. In Austria and Germany agreement within families was higher than in the other countries studied. However, public attitudes toward this particular issue agenda have changed dramatically since 1980, with a worldwide movement toward less governmental involve-

ment. This is a good example of how large-scale political events and trends can overtake familial influence in shaping attitudes of the younger generations.

For attitudes that relate to an individual's level of political participation—such as political efficacy, approval of political protest, protest potential, or even level of conventional participation—there is little evidence that parents have much effect on their children. Parents' and children's tolerance of protest and the perceived effectiveness of protest are somewhat more strongly correlated, but not by much.

Apart from the parents' own political attitudes and behavior, family relationships and child-rearing patterns may affect the attitudes that children form toward politics. In the United States research by Kent Jennings and Richard Niemi shows that parents who discuss politics among themselves and with their children are more likely to pass on their partisanship, whereas in homes with little political discussion, children are less likely to share their parents' partisanship and are more likely to develop no partisanship at all. Research in both the United States and Israel shows that children whose parents encourage them to participate in family discussions and to express their own opinions are more likely to feel politically efficacious, to seek out political information in the mass media, and to want to participate.

A multination study by Jennings of teenagers and their parents (in Austria, Britain, Finland, Germany, Italy, the Netherlands, Switzerland, and the United States) showed that in all countries, teenagers tended to talk more with their mothers than with their fathers about study or work, religion, and sex, but that in all countries except the United States, they talked more with their fathers about politics. The author points out that this pattern may perpetuate the greater political participation of men in these countries. In the United States mothers often share the political role, and some research even suggests that when the parents disagree, slightly more children adopt their mother's than their father's party identification.

During times of rapid political and social change, the influence of family on a child's political ideas will be weaker than usual. In such circumstances, political influences come from many sources, and children and adolescents often have greater opportunity for their own political experiences and firsthand observations. In such situations, especially among adolescents, who tend to want to be like their friends, peers may be quite influential. If a political attitude held by an adolescent's peers is also widespread in the society at large, familial influence may be very much weakened.

In general, familial influence weakens as people age and accumulate their own information and social and political experiences. In time, the perspectives of parents and children may increasingly diverge, especially with respect to issues or events for which social, political, and historical change causes parents and children to have very different experiences. With respect to party identification in the United States, however, the influence of parents generally persists even if it weakens over time.

Other Childhood Influences

Most children learn about and favor the symbols and rituals of their country at a young age. Even very young children can recognize the flag of their country, and most think it is prettier than other flags. This early learning lays the foundation for national loyalty and patriotism, which is reinforced in the elementary schools of most countries through observance of national rituals (salutes to the flag, pledges of allegiance, singing of the national anthem, celebrations of national holidays, and the like).

These early feelings of patriotism can influence adult behavior powerfully because they tend to make citizenship and national identification important parts of the self-concept. For example, many international migrants do not change their citizenship even when they expect to live permanently in the country to which they have migrated. Ada Finifter and Bernard Finifter found that among Americans who migrated to Australia and did change citizenship, this change often was found to be a difficult and emotional decision. Resistance to changing citizenship has been noted in many studies of international migrants of various nationalities.

Young children tend to personalize political ideas. For example, they may view a particular leader, such as a popular president or mayor, as a symbol of their political system. As children in democratic political systems age and develop cognitive skills, they become more aware that the means by which political decisions are made is a more important embodiment of their political system than any particular leader.

Many young children also think of political leaders in benevolent terms, for example, as being willing to help them. This attitude may reflect the positive way teachers or parents talk to children about politics. However, children tend to become less trusting and more cynical about politics as they grow up. If they live in a culture or subcul-

ture in which adults feel discriminated against or alienated from the political system, children may begin to develop similar attitudes at a relatively young age. This tendency has been shown not only for racial and ethnic minorities in the United States but also for other groups, including whites, who feel deprived or isolated from the economic and social mainstream.

Because people generally feel closer to their families than to unrelated people, imparting human or even familial status to national symbols is sometimes an effective means for the early development of patriotism, nationalism, and generally positive attitudes toward one's political system. Focusing on national heroes has a similar effect. Many nations have such symbols: Chairman Mao in China; Marianne in France; Uncle Sam, George Washington as the "father of our country," or the writers of the U.S. Constitution as "our forefathers" in the United States; Simón Bolívar, "the Liberator," in Venezuela, Columbia, and other South American countries; the royal families of many nations; and the presentation of the nation itself in family terms, as Mother Russia or "the motherland" or "the fatherland."

Although patriotism is widespread, consensus on more specific political attitudes, such as those relating to current political leaders or different political issues or programs, is more difficult to find. Adults in different social groups frequently differ in their political attitudes, and they pass on some of their attitudes to their children. Children's attitudes may also differ from group to group. For example, despite relatively similar feelings of loyalty and patriotism, groups nevertheless may differ in the degree of political trust or cynicism they feel toward those who are in charge of the current government. Or they may differ as to how fairly they think they are treated by the country's political institutions. The political attitudes of members of minority groups may differ from those of larger groups: minority groups may see the government more negatively if they perceive discrimination or more positively if they think that the government is trying to assist them. For example, most African Americans today are thought to be less trusting of government than most whites, but that was not so in the 1960s: at the height of the civil rights movement, blacks of all ages were more trusting of the national government than whites were. Conversely, members of majority groups may resent government efforts to aid minorities if those efforts are perceived as excessive or detrimental to their own interests.

Research is mixed on the effect of the school environment on political attitudes. Some research suggests that students are more likely to develop attitudes of political efficacy if they attend schools that encourage student participation, but other studies show no effect. One study found that public schools often emphasize "good citizenship," whereas private schools are more likely to focus on academic excellence and students' personal growth.

Changes Through the Life Cycle

School attendance, even through high school, may make children's and adolescents' attitudes appear relatively homogeneous. But once they leave school, their attitudes are likely to become more similar to those of adults in their social groups. For example, the expectations of girls and boys in school for their own future political participation do not differ as much as the actual participation of adult women and men. The same is probably true among different racial and ethnic groups.

Over time, children and adolescents may change their attitudes quite a bit—even attitudes like party identification, which may be an important part of a person's self-concept. As people age, however, their attitudes are increasingly less likely to change because most people act in ways that confirm and reinforce their political attitudes and are more receptive to ideas that agree with theirs while filtering out discordant information. Nevertheless, there is probably no period in life when political attitudes are absolutely fixed, and it is common to think of political socialization as a lifelong process. "Resocialization" can occur when a person experiences a significant change in attitudes or must adapt to new political roles or situations. In these cases the individual does not usually present a blank slate to the new situation; he or she is likely to adopt new attitudes that are consistent with those that were previously held.

Major political events can have influences on people's attitudes that persist over many years, although the influences may weaken. In the United States, for example, many people who first voted during the Great Depression of the 1930s, when the Democratic Party under President Franklin Delano Roosevelt was establishing its national political dominance, became Democrats. This generation can be distinguished from those both older and younger in its higher proportion of Democratic identifiers throughout the years. The dying out of this strongly Democratic cohort has contributed to the weakening of the Democratic Party. Conversely, many young people became Republicans during the 1980s, when the Republican Party controlled the presidency.

Sometimes important political events have a much stronger impact on one part of a generation than another. Jennings has shown that American college students who participated in protests against the Vietnam War were more liberal afterward than fellow students who did not protest. Although their liberalism has weakened as they have aged, they remain more liberal than those who did not protest. Similarly, men who spent more than a year in combat in Vietnam have experienced more political alienation than have other military personnel.

Processes of Socialization

Processes of political socialization in democracies differ in many ways from those in nondemocratic, and especially in totalitarian, societies. Totalitarian governments usually have formal systems of political socialization to ensure that as many members of the society as possible learn the norms, values, and behavior patterns that will tend to support their rule. When formal political socialization demands the learning of a particular system of thought or party line, perhaps in political education or "reeducation" classes or in party cell meetings, we may consider the process indoctrination rather than socialization. Because indoctrination also teaches a political culture, it may be seen as an extremely rigid, nonpermissive, and formal sort of political socialization.

The political cultures of democratic societies are likely to be less rigid and more tolerant of political diversity than those of totalitarian societies; thus their political socialization processes are usually less formal and sometimes even rather haphazard. Indeed, in a democracy like the United States where individual freedom is highly prized, any attempt by governments at formal methods of political socialization is likely to be strongly resisted.

The political cultures of democratic countries are often more heterogeneous than those of undemocratic or totalitarian systems. The heterogeneity has several sources: freedom of thought is a basic tenet of democracies, democracies are more tolerant of different ideas, and democracies are much less likely than totalitarian systems to engage in formal political socialization. These factors (as well as the greater economic success of democracies) also stimulate more immigration, which leads to more ethnically and culturally diverse societies.

Like other types of political systems, democracies socialize their members through patriotic celebrations and rituals. In addition, school textbooks may emphasize the positive aspects of national history. But these efforts will be much less pronounced than in totalitarian systems. Democracies are unlikely to sponsor and require attendance at political meetings at people's workplaces to reinforce the official ideology, as was done under the communist systems in China and the Soviet Union. They are unlikely to send dissidents to reindoctrination camps in order to rid them of deviant ideas and force them to accept the official ideology, as was done to many Chinese university students who participated in the political protests in Tiananmen Square in 1989. And they are unlikely to have large numbers of citizens spying on each other and reporting to the secret police on the attitudes and behavior of their neighbors and co-workers, as was done on a very large scale under the communist regime in the former East Germany.

Totalitarian systems typically prohibit the expression of political views that do not support the political rulers. Political protests by religious and ethnic minorities in Iraq and Syria have been suppressed violently. Under the current Islamic fundamentalist regime in Iran, appropriate dress for women is specified, Western music is outlawed, and a variety of rigid rules govern many other aspects of day-to-day life; harsh penalties are imposed for even minor infractions. Fundamentalist religious regimes may justify such repressive measures as expressions of moral codes or religious values. Nevertheless, their ultimate effect is to suppress dissent and forestall the development of political democracy and religious freedom.

Many examples of repression, murder, and attempts to "reeducate" dissidents in totalitarian societies could be cited. Even if these crude efforts at political control do not really change the basic attitudes of the people who are subjected to them, they are likely to change their behavior and discourage open dissent.

Even basically democratic systems sometimes lapse in their support for freedom of thought, as in the United States in the 1950s. For a time, anticommunist witch hunts rose to the level of congressional hearings, and people who were accused of being communists were denied employment in some industries. In some countries that are considered basically democratic, school textbooks may present such distorted images of particular historical periods that citizens are unaware of important aspects of their own political history, as in Japan with respect to the country's role in World War II.

International Effects

Many political and economic ideologies are based in different value systems and reflect different political cultures. These differences are among the factors that affect understanding and communication among the people and leaders of different countries and, therefore, their ability to achieve mutually beneficial and peaceful international relations. For example, conflicts between socialist and market or capitalist economies are grounded in disagreements about the appropriate role of the state in a nation's economic life. Beliefs about the appropriate role of the state may in turn be based on views of the relative importance of equality versus individual freedom of citizens. The pursuit of equality may impose limits on the individual freedoms of some citizens, while the pursuit of freedom may lead to important inequalities among citizens. Similarly, some people and nations will seek innovation and change in the pursuit of progress, while others value tradition and constancy above all. These kinds of differences tend to be bound up in larger systems of values that cohere into different political cultures.

There is no shortage of countries that are aligned with each other despite having very different political cultures. But if cultural differences overlap with other disagreements and nations begin to perceive each other as threats, their cultural differences can complicate the situation and hinder a rapprochement. Such differences were certainly part of the ideological cold war between the Western powers and the former Soviet bloc of nations. Many Americans, and to a lesser extent Western Europeans, feared the collectivism of the Soviet system, while Soviets feared the economic insecurity associated with capitalist systems. These cultural differences existed over and above the military threat each perceived from the other. Similarly, differences in beliefs about the role of religion in national life affect communication and understanding between some countries of the Islamic world and more secular nations that limit the role of religion in state affairs.

Countries with similar political cultures usually find it easier to communicate, and their shared values make it less likely that they will become opponents. The similarity of the political cultures of Canada, Britain, Australia, and the United States, for example, makes it relatively unlikely that they would be unable to solve their differences peacefully. Thus the political cultures of nations play a role in their interactions. Even within the most homogeneous nations, however, some widely held values will be inconsistent or will conflict with each other, and some groups will tend to hold opposing views. For example, the very same differences of opinion over the role of the state in the economy or the role of religion in public life that differentiate nations also may exist among significant groups within one nation.

It is sometimes very clear that one value or another dominates the political culture of a particular nation. Frequently, however, differences in basic values among citizens are at the root of the major ideological differences and political conflicts within a nation, and these may form the basis of the nation's political party system. Thus one can interpret differences between the Labour Party and the Conservatives in Britain, the Labor Party and the Liberal Party in Australia, the Democrats and Republicans in the United States, Socialists and Christian Democrats in many countries of Europe and Latin America, and hardline Communists versus reformers in the nations of the former Soviet Union as conflicts about the role of government in a nation. These differences may be largely based on disagreements about the importance of equality versus freedom.

Just as such value differences can affect relations between nations, severe conflict among groups within a nation can limit national integration, especially in the absence of shared commitments to other values. In extreme cases, disagreements within a nation about basic values can escalate to social and political strife and civil war. Value conflicts within nations are in many ways just as important as international value differences.

At its heart, then, political socialization is about political attitudes and values: how these differ among individuals, groups, and nations; how they are formed; and how they affect political actions and interactions. Thus political socialization is about the process, the substance, and the effects of political learning. It clearly is a major determinant of the political life of every nation and of the way nations interact.

See also *Education; Education, Civic; Media, Mass; Political culture; Public opinion; War and civil conflict.*

Ada W. Finifter

BIBLIOGRAPHY

Abramson, Paul R., and Ronald Inglehart. *Value Change in Global Perspective.* Ann Arbor: University of Michigan Press, 1995.

Barnes, Samuel H., Max Kaase, et al. *Political Action: Mass Participation in Five Western Democracies.* Beverly Hills, Calif.: Sage Publications, 1979.

Finifter, Ada W., and Bernard M. Finifter. "Party Identification and Political Adaptation of American Settlers in Australia." *Journal of Politics* 51 (1989): 599–630.

———. "Pledging Allegiance to a New Flag: Citizenship Change and its Psychological Aftermath among American Migrants in Australia." *Canadian Review of Studies in Nationalism* 22 (1995).

Fitzgerald, Frances. *America Revised.* New York: Vintage Books, 1980.

Jennings, M. Kent. "Gender Roles and Inequalities in Political Participation: Results from an Eight-Nation Study." *Western Political Quarterly* 36 (1983): 364–385.

———. "Residues of a Movement: The Aging of the American Protest Generation." *American Political Science Review* 81 (1987): 367–382.

———, and Richard Niemi. *Generations and Politics: A Panel Study of Young Adults and their Parents.* Princeton: Princeton University Press, 1981.

Renshon, Stanley Allen, ed. *Handbook of Political Socialization: Theory and Research.* New York: Free Press, 1977.

Sigel, Roberta S., ed. *Political Learning in Adulthood: A Sourcebook of Theory and Research.* Chicago: University of Chicago Press, 1989.

Solidarity

The first independent trade union in Soviet-dominated Eastern Europe. Solidarity played a critical role in unraveling the communist system in its native Poland and in other East European countries as well. It emerged from workers' strikes that erupted in the summer of 1980 in response to government attempts to raise food prices. The protest, which built on a tradition of workers' rebellions against the regime's economic policies, coalesced with the efforts of intellectuals who had begun spearheading democratic opposition movements after the 1976 workers' rebellion. Demands for economic concessions were soon combined with a wide range of political demands.

The extent of the 1980 strikes, which affected more than 4,000 enterprises by the end of August, and the determination of the strike committees that orchestrated the actions culminated in the Gdansk agreements (August 31, 1980). The Polish party-state was forced to accept the right of workers to form organizations independent of party and state control and to accept greater freedom of religious and political expression. This unprecedented agreement opened the door to the formation of the first independent trade union in the Soviet bloc, which became an umbrella organization uniting anticommunist opposition forces.

Solidarity, as the union came to be known, emerged gradually during the weeks following the Gdansk agreements. The interfactory strike committees that had represented all factories and institutions in a given region during the protests became a powerful driving force in establishing the union's structure. When the activists of some thirty-five new union organizations met in Gdansk on September 17 to discuss the problems of union structure, the decision was made to form one national union based on the Gdansk statutes and to adopt the name "Solidarity." After this decision was taken, union leaders started organizing the factory and regional branches of the unified movement across the country and began struggling for the union's legal recognition. The battle for government recognition, during which Solidarity called a one-hour warning strike and threatened to call a general strike, ended on November 10, when the Polish Supreme Court accepted Solidarity's charter.

The union was designed as a federation of largely autonomous regional chapters coordinated by the National Committee. The National Committee had a presidium of twelve members, headed by Lech Walesa, and was headquartered in Gdansk. It served as a consulting and mediating body and represented the entire union in its dealings with the state and with foreign organizations. The committee also controlled the organization's finances.

The union comprised thirty-eight regional committees and two smaller districts as well as enterprise committees in factories and institutions, which altogether employed nearly 40,000 full-time functionaries. Coordination committees, organized along professional lines, cut across the regional structure, and a network of enterprise committees representing the biggest companies in the Polish economy emerged in March 1981. This network—called Sieć—was a prime advocate of industrial self-management proposals. By September 1981 Solidarity had approximately 9.5 million members and represented most of the work force in Poland. The institutionalization of Solidarity provided the impetus for the independent organization of other social groups, including farmers, artisans, and students.

Despite its trade union formula, Solidarity was not a class movement; nor did it represent a single ideology. The movement developed a powerful identity based on the principle of self-organization of civil society, which blended trade unionist, democratic-liberal, and national and religious traditions and discourses. This identity included all segments of Polish society and all social classes. The

movement's actions and demands caused turmoil in Poland, threatened the survival of the communist regime, and destabilized political relations within the Soviet bloc.

After its first national congress in September 1981, Solidarity adopted a politically assertive agenda in response to the government's failure to comply with the Gdansk agreements. Pressured by the Soviet Union and unwilling to institute political reforms, the Polish regime decided to crush Solidarity by force. On the night of December 12, 1981, thousands of Solidarity's leaders and advisers were arrested, the union's headquarters were seized, the country's borders were closed, all communication networks were blocked, and troops entered cities and took control of all important installations in the country. The communist regime declared martial law the next day and suspended civil and political rights and shut down all organizations.

Militarized police crushed most strikes during the first days of martial law, and the parliament outlawed Solidarity on October 8, 1982. Despite the startling short-term success of martial law, it neither broke the Solidarity movement nor improved the state's capacity to deal with Poland's political and economic crises. After the military crackdown, conflict persisted, marked by political repression, street demonstrations, and the determined underground struggle of Solidarity.

The organization adopted a decentralized structure involving hundreds of groups and initiatives and maintained self-help, information, and publication networks that were supported by the Roman Catholic Church and international organizations. Despite its survival, however, Solidarity was not able to challenge effectively the post–martial law regime, and it experienced growing political and social fragmentation.

In the spring of 1988, after several years of relative social peace, strikes and protests again erupted in factories and universities across the country in response to the deteriorating economic situation and relaxation of the regime's repressive policies. During these strikes the restoration of Solidarity became the major demand. At the end of August, Polish authorities finally agreed to meet with representatives of the Solidarity-based opposition movement. The resulting "roundtable" negotiations ended in an agreement signed April 5, 1989, that provided for the relegalization of Solidarity, Farmers Solidarity, and the Independent Student Union. The opposition also gained access to the official political process through semidemocratic elections, which were scheduled for June 1989. The agreement set in motion a rapid process of democratization in which Solidarity leaders and advisers played a major role.

After the success of Solidarity-backed candidates in the June 1989 elections and the formation of a noncommunist government—Poland's first since World War II—the movement underwent a radical evolution. The grand coalition of opposition forces that had rallied under the Solidarity banner during the communist regime unraveled once the communists had been defeated at the polls. In the new political environment, many union members and leaders took positions in the parliament and government and founded political parties claiming Solidarity's heritage. Solidarity's chairman, Lech Walesa, was elected to the presidency in 1990.

As the cost of economic reform mounted, the new generation of union leaders gradually withdrew its support for economic reform and grew more hostile toward successive governments' economic policies. To emphasize their trade union identity and to distance themselves from the government's economic program, union leaders fielded their own candidates in the country's parliamentary elections. In the October 1991 elections Solidarity won twenty-seven seats in the parliament; in the September 1993 elections it failed to secure the necessary 5 percent of the vote to be represented. This defeat closed an important chapter in Poland's political history.

Solidarity was one of the most celebrated democratic movements of the second half of the twentieth century. It ushered in the democratic transition in Poland and contributed to the collapse of communist rule in Eastern Europe. Following the establishment of a democratic regime in Poland, Solidarity returned to its trade unionist roots. Since 1991 Solidarity has become a militant, protest-prone trade union, representing some 2.7 million members. Its new leaders staunchly defend troubled state industries and oppose ever more vocally the economic policies pursued by Poland's postcommunist governments.

See also *Poland; Walesa, Lech.*

Grzegorz Ekiert

BIBLIOGRAPHY

Ash, Timothy Garton. *The Polish Revolution: Solidarity.* New York: Vintage Books, 1985.

Bernhard, Michael H. *The Origins of Democratization in Poland.* New York: Columbia University Press, 1993.

Kennedy, Michael D. *Professionals, Power, and Solidarity in Poland: A Critical Sociology of Soviet-Type Society.* Cambridge: Cambridge University Press, 1991.

Kubik, Jan. *The Power of Symbols against the Symbols of Power.* University Park: Pennsylvania State University Press, 1994.

Laba, Roman. *The Roots of Solidarity.* Princeton: Princeton University Press, 1991.

Ost, David. *Solidarity and the Politics of Anti-Politics.* Philadelphia: Temple University Press, 1990.

Staniszkis, Jadwiga. *Poland's Self-Limiting Revolution.* Princeton: Princeton University Press, 1984.

Touraine, Alain. *Solidarity. The Analysis of a Social Movement: Poland 1980–1981.* Cambridge: Cambridge University Press, 1983.

Somalia

See *Africa, Horn of*

South Africa

A former white-ruled republic, situated on Africa's southern tip, that held its first nonracial elections in April 1994. Race had long polarized South Africa's 40 million people (30 million blacks, 5 million whites, 3.4 million "colored" people, and 1 million Asians), and the country was known for its system of apartheid, a form of racial segregation and minority rule. A decades-long ideological experiment had entrenched white dominance and sought to create separate "homelands" for black ethnic groups. The most populous were the 8 million Zulus, the 6.8 million Xhosa speakers, and 5.6 million Sotho speakers.

In February 1990 South Africa's white government, headed by Frederik W. de Klerk, had signaled its intention to negotiate a democracy with the hitherto outlawed black nationalist opposition. Although the government expressed willlingness to negotiate, the historical background against which this attempt was launched presented obstacles to democracy more formidable than those encountered by many democratizing societies.

South Africa, however, had an advantage denied some countries hoping to become democracies—a limited democratic tradition. Whites (13 percent of the population) had enjoyed regular competitive elections since 1910, when four white-ruled states agreed to form a union under

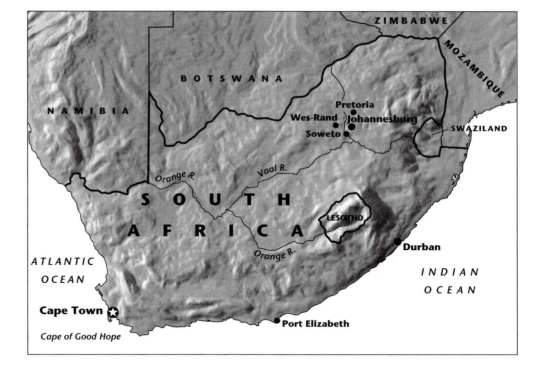

British colonial rule. The 1910 Union of South Africa was an attempt, imposed by British conquest, to incorporate into a common polity two hostile white blocs: Afrikaners (people of Dutch descent) and English speakers. Like other British colonies, they adopted the Westminster parliamentary system, and until the 1990s whites enjoyed the trappings of pluralist democracy. But the roots of union ensured that democracy remained oligarchic and that, even for the minority, it increasingly became a matter of form rather than content. The colored (mixed race) and Asian minorities (together 11 percent of the population) were granted a vote for separate and subordinate parliaments only in 1984; black Africans (76 percent of the population) were denied the franchise until 1994.

Seeds of Oligarchy and Resistance

In 1652 the Cape of Good Hope, Africa's southernmost shoreline, was colonized by the Dutch. After conquering the indigenous Khoi and San peoples, the Dutch penetrated into the interior. Great Britain formally established a colony at the Cape in 1806, and in 1820 the first British settlers landed on its shores. The settlers clashed repeatedly with the authoritarian colonial rulers. Those of Dutch descent, who proclaimed their attachment to their new continent by labeling themselves Afrikaners, were particularly resistant to colonial rule. But this resistance, which nurtured a democratic ethos within the settler community, was accompanied by a strong antipathy to the indigenous tribes and to Malay slaves imported to work in the colony. The strength of opposition to British rule and enthusiasm for white democracy usually coincided with support for racial dominance.

These tensions crystallized in the 1830s. Conflict with tribes on the Cape's eastern frontier and continued resentment of colonial rule prompted Afrikaner settlers to migrate. For the rest of the century, the Afrikaner, or Boer (farmer), settlers penetrated inland, subduing the resident black tribes. They established independent Boer republics that were governed democratically; however, for the conquered black inhabitants they proclaimed the principle of no equality with whites in church or state. The exclusivity of this policy contrasted with the paternalism of the Cape colony, whose authorities extended the franchise to a few blacks who met education and property qualifications.

Boer sovereignty ended in 1902, after a brutal three-year war between Britain and the Boer republics. When the Boer forces surrendered, British authorities sought to cement their victory with a campaign to suppress the Boer language (Afrikaans) and culture. This policy stiffened an Afrikaner nationalism with twin objectives: independence from colonial rule and hegemony over the black majority. When a whites-only national convention convened in 1909, the more compliant Afrikaner leaders dominated; even then the price of unity was agreement that the limited franchise for black Africans not be extended outside the Cape. Within three years the Union Parliament enacted the 1913 Land Acts, depriving Africans of land ownership rights outside some 7 percent of the country set aside as reserves.

Two issues dominated parliamentary politics for much of the rest of the century. The first was the attempt by the Afrikaner elite (60 percent of the white population) to wrest power from the economically dominant English speakers (40 percent of the white population). This effort culminated first in the victory of the National Party in 1948 and then in the establishment of a republic in 1960. The second was the means by which white supremacy was to be maintained: the paternalism that had created the limited Cape franchise clashed with the aggressive exclusivism that had developed in the Afrikaner republics. But the 1913 land ownership laws that consolidated white hegemony also triggered the other force in twentieth-century South African politics: organized black resistance to white rule.

By 1912 tribal units had been conquered, and white rule was consolidated. The political aspirations of blacks now hinged on inclusion in common representative institutions. Their vehicle was the South African Native National Congress, launched in 1912 to defend land rights and to press for political rights. Eight years later the group became the African National Congress (ANC), the chief organization of the African nationalist movement for the rest of the century.

The ANC initially was moderate in methods and goals. Its leadership was an African intelligentsia educated in the Christian liberal tradition brought by British missionaries. Their mission education nurtured a respect for liberal values and an abiding belief that moral appeals to the colonial power would ensure the extension of political rights to the disenfranchised. Among the first acts of the Congress was the sending of a delegation to London to urge the monarch to intervene on behalf of his loyal black subjects. For the next three decades the moral appeal was the ANC's primary weapon. The ANC elite did not seek the overthrow of the union but incorporation within its democratic institutions—gradually if need be. They cherished the hope that the extension of political rights to some would begin a process that would eventually extend to them all.

Route to Polarization

The ANC moderates were ignored. The Crown was concerned with developing the British Westminster model of democracy among the white settlers. Blacks' demands were irrelevant or inimical to this task. Concessions to local demands for political autonomy were made to the strong white lobbies, not the weak black ones. And the inexorable move of colonial policy toward white self-rule ensured an equally inevitable drift away from black enfranchisement.

White democracy produced two sorts of government. The first was an alliance of English speakers and Afrikaner leaders who had made their peace with the empire; it favored a paternal "trusteeship" over black Africans. The limited Cape franchise for blacks was abolished by such a government in 1936. An elected advisory body, the Native Representative Council, was established in its stead. (Evidence of the ANC's enthusiasm for even limited democratic institutions was its willingness to contest elections for, and serve in, this body.) But this type of government was less rigid in its insistence on social and economic segregation.

The second kind of government was based on Afrikaner nationalism. When Afrikaners first won power, in alliance with white labor in 1924, their government reserved skilled work for whites. When they triumphed in 1948, they abolished even advisory representation for black Africans and initiated a program of rigid racial segregation in pursuance of a proclaimed policy of "white mastery." The trend in white politics was toward this second, more racist form of government. Only twice in white democracy's eighty-four-year history (1910–1994) did power change hands at the polls; each time Afrikaner nationalism and stricter racial exclusivism triumphed.

These trends ensured the failure of ANC moderation, which by the 1940s was discredited among young African intellectuals. Control of the ANC's Youth League passed to militant nationalists such as Oliver Tambo and Nelson Mandela (both later to become presidents of the ANC). These nationalists were convinced that white goodwill was a scarce or fictional commodity. Their goal was not incorporation into the white-ruled polity but national liberation; their preferred method was mass mobilization. After the 1948 election, their argument became compelling to the older generation of ANC leaders.

Although at first hostile to white communists, the Youth Leaguers soon modified their attitude. The South African Communist Party, the only party with white members to associate itself unreservedly with black resistance in the preceding three decades, became a useful ally in the struggle against apartheid. By the late 1940s the ANC was committed to mass defiance of apartheid and had cemented an alliance with the communists. This bond was strengthened when that party was banned in 1950, and a Congress of Democrats formed largely by white communists forged an alliance with the ANC.

Even then prospects for accommodation did not seem irretrievably lost. Black mobilization in the 1950s was harassed but not banned. And, despite the ANC's new militancy, its Christian liberal tradition proved tenacious. The president of the ANC for much of the decade, Chief Albert Luthuli, was steeped in Christian social democracy. (He was awarded the Nobel Peace Prize in 1960.) Mandela, then head of the ANC in the Transvaal Province (the country's most populous province and its economic heartland), revealed later that he would have favored accepting limited African representation in Parliament as a stage on the route to universal franchise. The ANC mixed civil disobedience with calls on the government to negotiate. But whites' resistance to compromise stiffened, and the pleas were ignored.

By the late 1950s the contradiction between allowing blacks to mobilize and ignoring their demands ensured growing instability, culminating in the shooting deaths in March 1960 of nearly seventy Africans at the Sharpeville police station south of Johannesburg. The government reacted by banning the ANC and the more militant, black exclusivist Pan-Africanist Congress, which had broken away from the ANC the previous year under the leadership of Robert Sobukwe. In addition, the government implemented the first of a series of laws infringing on due process and individual liberties. Reestablished in exile, the ANC determined to destroy the white state by force.

If the ANC's response seemed to exclude the peaceful extension of democratic institutions, the strategy of the National Party, beginning in the 1960s, did so more forcefully. In its attempt to quell African resistance, the National Party enacted security laws that curbed the rights of individuals, freedom of expression, and political activity by the opposition. The state exercised unlimited power to detain individuals, to ban opponents from political and even social activity, and to outlaw publications that furthered communism, a term defined so widely that it sometimes encompassed liberal opinion. Opposition movements that did not participate in Parliament or in the separate institutions created for the majority were outlawed or subject to security action. The press, although it remained privately owned, was subject by the 1980s to more than a hundred laws restricting reportage and comment. Although the National Party was wedded to the form of parliamentary procedure, legislation increasingly transferred power from the judiciary and legislature to the "opinion" of the executive. Ironically, the British democratic tradition against which Afrikaner nationalists had fought helped them to secure political dominance: the Westminster doctrine of parliamentary supremacy prevented the judiciary from pronouncing on legislation. Only administrative acts could be challenged in the courts.

In its attempt to consolidate Afrikaner power, the National Party used ethnic patronage in the civil service, the judiciary, and parastatals (state-owned corporations). The Afrikaner Brotherhood, a secret society to which most cabinet ministers and National Party intellectuals belonged, was the prime vehicle; membership was essential for senior public appointments. Because a guaranteed Afrikaner majority ensured repeated reelection of the National Party, the response of English speakers was either to forgo politics for business and the professions or to regard parliamentary activity as a form of protest politics. The result was a "white democracy" in which the same party was routinely returned to power for more than four decades. In this white political culture, politics became the route to advancement for Afrikaner nationalists and an object of indifference for the remaining 40 percent of the white population.

But it was above all the National Party's racial program that militated against a peaceful expansion of democracy. The election of Hendrik Verwoerd as prime minister in 1958 transformed the policy of white mastery into a rigid ideology—apartheid. Verwoerd and his successors ostensibly rejected white domination. They insisted that self-determination would be extended to black South Africa—but not in a single polity. Verwoerd made 87 percent of the country "white South Africa." In the remaining 13 percent of the country, black Africans were encouraged to develop their own representative institutions and to establish independent states. But Africans were not, in this view, a homogeneous group: the tribal units that existed before white conquest were the authentic instruments of black national identity. Ten black "homelands" were therefore established, and in 1971 each black South African was assigned to one.

The ideology, ostensibly more egalitarian than its predecessor, precluded an expanded democracy. Black exclusion from central government became an article of ideo-logical faith. Because black people were now citizens of other "states," to which they would have to return to exercise their "citizenship," they were stripped of all rights and entitlements in the white 87 percent. Property ownership and the right to work in skilled positions and, in many cases, to live as a family were available in the ethnic homelands only; adequate education and health care were available nowhere. Urban black townships were starved of resources in order to induce their residents to return to their homelands. The government's policy not only radicalized blacks, the direct victims of apartheid prohibitions, but stunted their opportunities to participate in associations and democratic institutions.

The assignment of separate, ethnically based, political institutions to the majority, rationalized as a training in democracy, had precisely the reverse effect. These institutions—elected ethnic legislatures in the homelands and local (cross-ethnic) councils in the urban areas—were denied resources and effective powers and so were forced to act as agents of white rule. Black nationalists viewed them as a symbol of exclusion from the central polity and as major vehicles of white domination. To frustrate apartheid, black nationalists mobilized against its closest and most vulnerable manifestations—black elected councils and administrations. During the 1970s and 1980s the election boycott became a primary weapon of resistance. Persons who assumed elected office were vilified; in the 1980s they became victims of violence. Participation in representative institutions by blacks was transformed from a majority aspiration to an act of betrayal.

End of Oligarchy

From the late 1960s on, the unworkability of apartheid became increasingly evident. Economic and demographic pressures made it harder for the government to control the kind of work blacks did and where they lived. In 1973 industrial strikes in the port city of Durban signaled the end of workers' quiescence. Internal resistance was revived by the black consciousness movement. Its theorist, Stephen Biko (who died in police custody in 1977), stressed black assertiveness and self-sufficiency. In 1976 conflict in the Soweto township outside Johannesburg began a decade and a half of militant urban resistance. Almost imperceptibly at first, the National Party began to retreat from apartheid.

The ensuing reform period saw the increasing recognition of black urban permanence. As it became clear that

people who were not leaving the white heartland would voice political demands within it, the government began a series of tortuous experiments in "broadening democracy" while maintaining white supremacy. Changes were made only when necessary and if white political dominance was not threatened. Prime Minister Pieter W. Botha introduced a constitution bill (approved in 1983) that extended the franchise to the colored and Asian minorities but in a form that assigned them a subordinate role and excluded the African majority; the Africans were to be content with municipal government in segregated townships (itself a concession). These actions sparked the most aggressive protests yet, and in 1985 Botha was forced to concede the principle of African citizenship in a common polity for the first time. Even then the constitutional changes proposed by his government envisaged separate and subordinate black representation.

Government attempts to strengthen black political participation in subordinate forums merely heightened mobilization against those forums and their incumbents. In the absence of legitimate political channels, the foes of apartheid sought to render the country ungovernable by withholding participation in local councils and by boycotting schools and white-owned stores. The resistance, led by students who rejected their elders' passive acceptance of white domination, became increasingly coercive. The government responded with stringent security action, culminating in the 1986 declaration of a state of emergency, which was used to suppress domestic resistance movements in the hope that "moderate" black leaders would emerge to negotiate the political incorporation of blacks on white terms. The state of emergency stayed in effect until 1990.

A Fragile Settlement

Against this background, South Africa began to negotiate democracy. By 1990 apartheid, and economic sanctions imposed by most Western governments in reaction to it, had weakened South Africa's economy. Reform and repression had failed to produce a compliant majority leadership willing to negotiate on the government's terms. International developments (including the collapse of communist regimes) convinced the white government that a favorable settlement could be worked out. All these factors prompted de Klerk, who succeeded Botha in 1989, to lift the bans on the ANC, the Communist Party, and the Pan-Africanist Congress on February 2, 1990, and to invite them to negotiate a new order.

Black residents of a township near Johannesburg await their turn to vote during South Africa's first all-race elections held in April 1994.

Thus began a process that, despite repeated setbacks, moved almost inevitably to a settlement. But it also triggered the bloodiest political violence in the country's history. The prospect of democracy was resisted by white right-wingers and by blacks who had controlled homeland governments and who feared that majority rule would reduce them to impotence.

For both the white elite and the black resistance, a negotiated compromise was a second-best option. Throughout the reform period the National Party's strategy had been to yield only as much as was necessary to remain in power. By the 1990s the parameters of the possible had shifted, but the goal remained almost unchanged: de Klerk and his party stressed that they must have a guaranteed share in government once the vote was extended to all. Not until three years into the transition would they concede that apartheid was morally untenable; at this point they acknowledged only that it had not worked. White South Africa's leadership was not embracing a competitive democracy in a reconciled nation but attempting to concede universal franchise on terms that would secure them a share of power almost regardless of election results.

By the early 1990s the ANC had become the most pragmatic champion of majority liberation. Willing to negotiate a compromise, it faced considerable opposition within its own constituency. Three decades of exile and guerrilla activity had built a revolutionary culture intent on de-stroying minority power, not compromising with it. The youth activists who had led the internal resistance of the 1980s were more impatient with compromise than were the exiles. Economic stagnation and vast inequalities in access to social goods ensured that opponents of compromise would enjoy an audience among key sections of the ANC constituency.

The fact that a settlement was being attempted at all, however, confirmed the lack of alternatives to a compromise between the country's major power blocs. The costs of white rule had become unsustainable, yet the white government retained enough military force to make revolution impossible. The white government and the ANC had little option but to continue to move toward the settlement they had reached in November 1993. A five-year interim constitution provided for the election of a government of national unity in which the larger minority parties would be represented in proportion to their support. It also specified that a bicameral national legislature would draft the final constitution. The shared cabinet reflected an acknowledgment by the ANC that democracy was likely to survive only if the country's white rulers, whom it expected to defeat in an election, retained a role in government. Agreement on the interim constitution opened the way for an election in April 1994.

The prospects for democratic compromise looked bleak during the period before the country's first nonra-

On May 9, 1994, after South Africa's historic election, President-elect Nelson Mandela enters the Parliament chambers accompanied by former president F. W. de Klerk *(right)* and Vice President-elect Thabo Mbeki *(left).*

cial election. The Inkatha Freedom Party formed an alliance with white right-wingers and rejected participation in the election until its demand for vastly increased powers for the region in which it was strongest was met. The Inkatha controlled the homeland assigned to Zulu-speaking blacks, and it alone among the homeland parties commanded significant support. The Inkatha also demanded a constitutional role for the Zulu king, with whom it cooperated in rallying opposition to a settlement among Zulu speakers who felt more comfortable with traditional institutions than with democracy. The Inkatha's demands heightened violence and raised the prospect that the new democracy would begin without the participation of a significant minority party that had shown its ability to threaten stability.

The strength of the pressures that forced the country's politicians to resign themselves to compromise became evident a week before the April 26–28 election. At this eleventh hour the Inkatha, in negotiation with the ANC and the government, agreed to participate in the election. By then a significant section of the white right wing had already joined the democratic contest. Against all expectations, the country's first universal franchise election included the entire spectrum of opinion except for the most extreme elements of the white right wing.

The election was marred by significant administrative failures on the part of a newly created Independent Electoral Commission and by allegations of fraud by some competing parties. But flawed as the election clearly was, it vastly strengthened prospects for consolidating a fragile democracy. The country's new voters, despite being forced to wait as long as three days to cast their ballots in some cases, greeted the inconvenience with forbearance. Violence declined sharply during the election period. And the major competing parties, after loudly accusing each other of vote rigging, negotiated compromises that enabled a result to be declared with the support of all parties.

The outcome—whether serendipitously or as a result of interparty negotiation—was tailor-made for the power-sharing compromise that the election was meant to produce. As expected, the ANC won a comfortable majority (62 percent of the vote), but it failed to gain the two-thirds necessary to dominate drafting of the permanent constitution. The National Party achieved the 20 percent necessary, according to the agreed constitutional formula, for de Klerk to become one of two executive vice presidents. It also won control of one of the nine provinces created by the constitutional settlement. The Inkatha won control of the Kwazulu-Natal Province, where its support was concentrated, and 10 percent of the national vote, enough to appoint three cabinet ministers. In short, the main contenders won enough votes to ensure their commitment to the new order.

South Africa's new democratic rulers assumed office against a background of conflict that served as a reminder of democracy's fragility. The fact that the protagonists now shared power in the same executive did not mean that the potential for conflict had ended. Rather, the potential for conflict had been imported into the heart of government.

Although corrupted by decades of apartheid, a constitutional tradition nevertheless existed. This, together with international pressure for democratization, held out some prospect for the emergence of a democratic center. And, despite the legacy of the past four decades, a diverse and often vigorous civil society sometimes showed greater propensity for pragmatism and accommodation than did the political elites. Economic interdependence between blacks and whites also weakened support on both sides for extreme solutions.

The early years of the new government will determine whether South Africa can build a sufficient sense of common national purpose to sustain a democracy. But the post-1948 legacy of violence and racial polarization seems likely to ensure that a South African democracy will be partial, at least for the next decade. South Africa remains a divided society in which pluralism and compromise presented themselves to political leaders as an unavoidable necessity, not a preferred option. Its democratic experiment will demonstrate whether, for want of alternatives, its politicians will confound those who doubt the viability of democracy in divided societies.

See also *Biko, Bantu Stephen; de Klerk, Frederik Willem; Mandela, Nelson; Sobukwe, Robert.*

Steven Friedman

BIBLIOGRAPHY

Adam, Heribert, and Kogila Moodley. *The Negotiated Revolution: Society and Politics in Post-Apartheid South Africa.* Johannesburg: Jonathan Ball, 1993.

Davenport, T. R. H. *South Africa: A Modern History.* Johannesburg: Macmillan, 1987; London: Macmillan, 1991.

Du Toit, André, and Hermann Giliomee. *Afrikaner Political Thought, 1780–1850.*Vol. 1 of *Afrikaner Political Thought.* Berkeley: University of California Press, 1983.

Friedman, Steven, ed. *The Long Journey: South Africa's Quest for a Negotiated Settlement.* Johannesburg: Ravan Press; Athens: Ohio University Press, 1993.

———, and Doreen Atkinson, eds. *The Small Miracle: South Africa's Negotiated Settlement.* Johannesburg: Ravan Press, 1994.

Giliomee, Hermann, and Lawrence Schlemmer. *From Apartheid to Nation-Building.* Cape Town: Oxford University Press, 1989.

Horowitz, Donald. *A Democratic South Africa? Constitutional Engineering in a Divided Society.* Cape Town: Oxford University Press, 1991.

Lodge, Tom. *Black Politics in South Africa Since 1945.* London: Longman, 1983.

Roux, Edward. *Time Longer Than Rope: A History of the Black Man's Struggle for Freedom in South Africa.* Madison: University of Wisconsin Press, 1964.

Slabbert, Frederick van Zyl. *The Quest for Democracy: South Africa in Transition.* Harmondsworth, England: Penguin Forum Series, 1992.

South America

See *Andean countries; Argentina; Brazil; Caribbean, English; Caribbean, Spanish; Chile; Colombia; Uruguay; Venezuela*

South Korea

Independent East Asian country that was established in 1948. South Korea, officially known as the Republic of Korea, is a model of an authoritarian system that sponsored economic growth and development, thereby setting the stage for a transition to democracy in the late 1980s.

Historical Background

The last native Korean dynasty, the Yi, was overthrown in 1910, after more than five centuries of authoritarian rule based on Confucianism. From 1910 to 1945 the Japanese ruled Korea as a colony. After World War II Korea was divided by the Allies into two zones of occupation, with Soviet troops in the north and U.S. forces in the south. In 1948 Korea was officially divided into two states: the Republic of Korea (South Korea) and the Democratic People's Republic (North Korea). Syngman Rhee was elected the first president of South Korea by its unicameral National Assembly. His government initially attempted to establish a constitutional democracy but soon became increasingly authoritarian.

The Korean War began in June 1950. North Korea, with Soviet support, attacked South Korea, which had United

afford the luxury of democracy. By heavily promoting economic growth and development, Park attempted to win the support of students, intellectuals, and champions of human rights who strongly opposed his dictatorship. He believed that when the per capita GNP reached $2,000, a transition from authoritarianism to democracy would be possible.

But the Park regime sought legitimacy on the basis of economic and social development while denying political competition, participation, and civil and political liberties for the people. In the presidential election of 1971 Park was almost defeated by the opposition leader Kim Dae Jung, who received 46 percent of the popular vote. The next year Park instituted the so-called Yushin (revitalizing reform) Constitution by which, in the name of national security, all opposition political parties and democracy movements were disbanded. In 1979 Park was assassinated by his own security chief over disagreements about how to cope with increasing disorder and demands for democracy in South Korea.

One of several causes of the democratic movement in the 1970s was social and economic change. The economy was then beginning a transformation from an agrarian to a manufacturing base. More than 65 percent of the work force was engaged in industry, while less than 15 percent worked in the agricultural sector. Thus the Republic of Korea achieved the status of a newly industrializing country as measured by the proportion of gross domestic product attributable to industry (more than 60 percent). Furthermore, the country was becoming urbanized: in the 1970s more than half the population lived in cities.

By the end of the 1970s the level of literacy in rural areas had reached 85 percent, and compulsory education had been extended to middle school. There was effective mass communication by means of radio, television, and newspapers. In addition, despite the creation of *chaebol* (conglomerates of capital industries), the Republic of Korea had a rather equitable distribution of wealth—a factor widely considered to be strongly conducive to democracy.

After the assassination of President Park, however, martial law was instituted and all political activity was barred. During the transition from Park's government to a democratic regime, social and economic disorder erupted. Maj. Gen. Chun Doo Hwan, security chief in the capital city of Seoul, carried out a coup in December 1979 that overthrew the caretaker government and established a military regime. Chun's regime became the most repressive in modern Korean history, in large part because of its ruth-

Nations forces under the leadership of the United States. The North Korean forces were soon augmented by Chinese communist troops. Negotiations for a cease-fire began as early as 1951 but dragged on for almost two years. The war officially ended in July 1953.

In 1960 Rhee and his followers rigged the presidential election for his third term. This act led to student demonstrations against the dictatorship, which brought down the government. The parliamentary government of Chang Myon (John M. Chang), which followed Rhee's regime, was considered the most democratic government in South Korea's history. That government was overthrown in 1961 by a military coup led by Maj. Gen. Park Chung Hee.

Park, who assumed the presidency, ruled South Korea with an iron fist, turning it into a garrison state. His rationale for such repressive rule was twofold: the need to counter the constant threat from the communist regime in North Korea and the argument that South Korea, with a per capita gross national product of $87, could not

less suppression of the 1980 Kwangju uprising. Although there was widespread opposition to his regime, Chun's government lasted until 1987.

A New Movement for Democracy

In the late 1980s the Chun regime was finally forced to make concessions to a democratic movement led by students and intellectuals and including many members of the middle class. The movement's leaders demanded free and direct election of the president and an end to Chun's regime. South Korea was scheduled to host the 1988 summer Olympic games, and worldwide attention was focused on the country. After many weeks of escalating tension and violent confrontations between tear gas–wielding police and protesters, Chun's government finally yielded, and elections were scheduled.

Roh Tae Woo was the leader and presidential nominee of the ruling Democratic Justice Party, whose election was virtually assured. Roh, who had participated in the coup that brought Chun to power, had held numerous posts in Chun's government. In June 1987, at the peak of the violence and disorder, he announced a campaign pledge: his successor would be elected by popular vote in a free election under a democratic constitution. Roh won the election. The consequent constitutional amendment, approved by the National Assembly on October 12, 1987, by a vote of 254 to 4, changed the method of election from indirect to popular vote, balanced the executive and legislative powers, and provided for decentralization of government. In the October 27 referendum the constitution won resounding approval. Voter turnout was also high: more than three-fourths of eligible voters went to the polls.

The parliamentary election of 1988 brought an unexpected setback to the ruling Democratic Justice Party, which failed to secure a majority in the National Assembly. The Party for Peace and Democracy, led by Kim Dae Jung, became the largest opposition party; two other opposition parties also won a significant number of seats. Together, the three opposition parties held a substantial majority of seats. If they cooperated, they could reject presidential nominations, stall budget deliberations, and control the legislative process. As a consequence, in 1990 the Democratic Justice Party merged with two of the opposition parties to create the Democratic Liberal Party. Kim Dae Jung's reorganized Democratic Party was left as the only opposition party. Even so, there were no strong differences between the parties: both were basically conservative entities organized by political personalities. In

1992 Kim Young Sam, the Democratic Liberal Party candidate, was elected president; he was inaugurated in early 1993.

The process of democratization that began in 1987 made South Korean society more open, diverse, and decentralized than it had ever been before. The mass media were freed from government restrictions, thousands of political prisoners were released from prison, and long-suppressed labor unions were permitted to organize for better wages and improved working conditions. But the process also triggered explosions of long-suppressed issues. Social order deteriorated and crime increased. Economic discipline was less rigorous. As a result the balance of payments began to shift from surplus to deficit, and the rate of economic growth and development slowed.

Impediments to Democracy

The process of democratization in South Korea, though steady, suffered from several weaknesses. One problem was the relative underdevelopment of the political parties. The parties were never institutionalized; instead, they were organized and operated around political personalities with similar political ideologies and little commitment to the programs and policies set forth by the parties themselves. Party organizations were dissolved when their leaders lost an election or resigned from politics, in part because campaign financing depended heavily on the party leader's ability to bring in money, rather than on contributions from party members. In addition, since the parties were organized on the basis of personalities and regional ties, they did not really represent the views of voters.

Other problems included the political factionalism that denied a stable majority in parliament and undercut the president's support base, as well as the regionalism that tended to fragment South Korean society. The most serious problem in South Korea's democratic transition was the political culture of its leaders, who continued to invoke authoritarian loyalties and to support hierarchical structures in political and social organizations.

The traditional political ideology of Confucianism could not easily be eradicated or transmuted into a civic culture. A public opinion survey conducted in 1992, after five years' experience with democracy, showed that a large percentage of the South Korean population still supported an authoritarian political culture. Only half believed that democratic reform might be achieved by the late 1990s. One-fourth of the people expressed support for dictatorial rule and believed that it was good for South Korea.

New Stage in the Transition

On the positive side, almost two-thirds of the South Korean population was born after the Korean War. These generations learned about democratic values and institutions in school and resisted the authoritarian political culture of the 1970s and 1980s. Better educated and more urban than the older generation, they were firmly committed to democratic values.

Moreover, at least one important element of democratization was being put in place: the decentralization of authority and greater local autonomy. Under the authoritarian military regimes of Park and Chun, local self-government was nonexistent and could not even be discussed. The leaders feared that local autonomy would mean the end of their regimes.

After 1987 the democratization process directed attention to the relationship between democracy and local autonomy. Local self-government became a hot issue in political debates. Discussions were held between the ruling and opposition parties on when and how to revive local government. After a long delay, elections for local assemblies were held in 1991, and legislative activities were inaugurated. The election of provincial, municipal, and local officials, however, was postponed until 1995.

Prospects for democracy in South Korea are good if the Kim Young Sam government, inaugurated in 1993, succeeds in carrying out its planned democratic reforms. If it does, South Korea will likely achieve democratization as well as industrialization by the end of the twentieth century. However, if popular participation in political decision making through legitimate institutions is not achieved, and if decision-making power remains in the hands of a small group in the central government, there will likely be an ongoing struggle between the people and those who hold power.

See also *Confucianism; Roh Tae Woo.*

Ilpyong J. Kim

BIBLIOGRAPHY

Diamond, Larry, Juan J. Linz, and Seymour Martin Lipset, eds. *Democracy in Developing Countries: Asia.* Boulder, Colo.: Lynne Rienner; London: Adamantine Press, 1989.

Kim, Ilpyong J., and Young Whan Kihl, eds. *Political Change in South Korea.* New York: Paragon House, 1988.

Kim, Ilpyong J., and Jane Shapiro Zacek, eds. *Establishing Democratic Rule: The Emergence of Local Governments in Post-Authoritarian Systems.* Washington, D.C.: Washington Institute Press, 1993.

Linz, Juan J. *The Breakdown of Democratic Regimes: Crisis, Breakdown, and Reequilibration.* Baltimore: Johns Hopkins University Press, 1978.

———. "Transition to Democracy." *Washington Quarterly* 13 (summer 1990): 143–164.

Lipset, Seymour Martin. "Some Social Requisites of Democracy: Economic Development and Political Legitimacy." *American Political Science Review* 53 (1959): 75.

Macdonald, Donald S. "Korea's Transition to Democracy." In *Democracy in Korea: The Roh Tae Woo Years,* edited by Christopher J. Sigur. New York: Council on Ethics and International Affairs, 1992.

Sovereignty

See *Globalization*

Soviet Union

See *Union of Soviet Socialist Republics*

Spain

A country situated at the western end of the Mediterranean Sea on the Iberian peninsula. Spain's government became a parliamentary monarchy after the death of Francisco Franco in 1975 opened the way to democratic government.

Historical Background

The medieval Spanish kingdoms, like other western European kingdoms, developed representative institutions, whose emergence was fostered by the feudal order, the existence of cities under royal authority, and a church that

cooperated with the secular rulers but also enjoyed the autonomy characteristic of Western Christianity. Some of the representative bodies, which were called Cortes, were quite developed. The Cortes of the kingdom of Aragon had parallels only in Hungary and England. These Cortes survived formally until the advent of the modern unitary state (and in the case of the kingdom of Navarre until 1839).

Muslims occupied parts of Spain for almost eight centuries. After Queen Isabella of Castile and King Ferdinand of Aragon married in 1469, uniting their two kingdoms, they conquered Granada, the last Muslim kingdom, in 1492. Their grandson, Charles I of Spain, fought a coalition of the cities and nobles, who claimed traditional privileges, and won for himself the title of Holy Roman Emperor (as Emperor Charles V). Under Charles's Hapsburg dynasty the various kingdoms retained their traditional constitutions, but the kings limited the powers of the Cortes by convening them as infrequently as possible. The Bourbon dynasty, which came to power in 1700 after defeating the Hapsburgs, consolidated power into an absolute monarchy following the French model.

In many parts of Spain, feudalism was weak, and nowhere was there serfdom like that common in eastern Europe. A petty nobility (the *hidalgos),* an independent peasantry, and city dwellers constituted a large part of the population. In the south, large estates of the upper nobility dominated a countryside inhabited largely by descendants of the Islamic Moorish population. With increased royal power the idea of subjects' equality to the kings prevailed. The expulsions of the Jews in 1492 and of the *moriscos*—the descendants of Muslims whose conversion to Christianity was suspect—in 1609, and the persecution by the Catholic Inquisition of the small Protestant population, created a society that was religiously and ethnically homogeneous and later paved the way for citizenship for all Spaniards.

In the sixteenth and seventeenth centuries, theologians also formulated the idea of the basic equality of all human beings, rejecting the idea of a basic inequality between Spaniards and the Indians they had conquered in the New World. Writers like the Jesuit historian Juan de Mariana (1536–1624) developed the idea of resistance to arbitrary authority and the legitimacy of tyrannicide.

The kingdoms in the seventeenth century, and the more centralized and unified Bourbon monarchy in the eighteenth, like other European monarchies, weakened or destroyed the representative institutions. They also created a unified body of laws that royal officials enforced.

In 1808 the French under Napoleon Bonaparte invaded Spain and captured the king and his son, leaving the country bereft of its legitimate rulers. The French established Joseph Bonaparte, Napoleon's brother, as king and enacted a constitution. The Spanish people, including many officials and army officers, resisted French domination and created provincial representative bodies (juntas). In a return to tradition, the Cortes were convened in Cádiz, representing not the separate kingdoms but the whole realm, including Spain's overseas empire.

Although Spain was at war and communication was poor, the Cortes, which had only limited representativeness, assumed national sovereignty and wrote a constitution in 1812. Based on the historical tradition of representative bodies and the influence of the French revolutionary constitution of 1791, the constitution was a model of liberal concepts that would influence constitution makers in many other countries. Although—like other constitutions of this period—it does not fit the present view of democracy, its unicameral legislature, which did not distinguish between nobility, clergy, and the commoners, set the basis for equal representation of citizens.

Democracy in Spain emerged from the liberal heritage of the 1812 constitution and the popular struggle against Napoleon—which also generated a populist reactionary movement—through many conflicts in the nineteenth century that led to the enactment of several constitutions, the proclamation in 1873 of a short-lived First Republic, and two dictatorships in the twentieth century. Universal male suffrage was enacted in 1868 and, after another period of restricted suffrage with the restoration of the Bourbon monarchy in 1875 and the enactment of the constitution of 1876, was reenacted in 1890.

The early extension of suffrage was perhaps incongruent with the slow economic development and the persistence of traditional social structures in large parts of the country, which led to the perversion of democratic institutions. Among the many factors contributing to the failure of a smooth transition from constitutional liberalism to democracy were the country's economic underdevelopment, conflicts between church and state, a series of military defeats as Spain attempted to hold onto its overseas possessions and expanded into Morocco, the impact of European ideological conflicts, and an anarchist labor movement.

The Second Republic

In 1923 Gen. Miguel Primo de Rivera led a successful coup d'état and installed himself as dictator. When Primo de Rivera resigned in 1930, the king and the ministers he appointed, uncertain how best to reinstate constitutional government, opted for a plan of progressive steps starting with municipal elections in April 1931. In those elections the republican-socialist candidates defeated the monarchists in almost all major cities, and the Second Republic was proclaimed in Eibar and Barcelona. Popular enthusiasm and the unwillingness of the head of the Civil Guards to use force to uphold the monarchy compelled the king to renounce his powers and go into exile.

The Second Republic ushered in a period of democratization and profound social and cultural change. Women's suffrage was enacted after considerable debate, with the opposition coming from leftist bourgeois parties, who feared the influence of the clergy on women voters, and from conservatives. The republic was greeted with high hopes. But the enactment of a partisan rather than a consensual constitution, the constitution's anticlerical provisions, and other policies and reforms that alienated some groups without winning support from others, together with the local revolts of anarchists, eroded that enthusiasm. In 1933 the climate fostered a military putsch that failed. The government turned to the right, supported by an electoral law favoring the conservative coalition against a divided left.

When the largest party in the parliament—CEDA, the conservative Catholic Confederación Española de Derechas Antónomas (Confederation of Spanish Autonomous Rightists)—entered the cabinet in October 1934, the leftists, the socialists, and the Catalan nationalists started an uprising. It was quelled by government forces, but only after considerable bloodshed. The left distrusted the CEDA for its corporatist-authoritarian tendencies, and the socialists were divided by revolutionary rhetoric. The leftist Popular Front won the 1936 election, but the socialists were not ready to enter the minority left-bourgeois government. The right took advantage of the violence fomented by the left and by a small fascist party, and the resulting breakdown of order, to prepare for a military putsch.

The republic had initiated important reforms of the

military, educational institutions, and labor law; most important, agrarian reform was instituted. The constitution also provided for the autonomy of certain regions where nationalism based on distinctive languages, historical traditions, and nationalist parties demanded it. Those reforms, and particularly a hostile policy toward the Catholic Church, all generated strong opposition. Furthermore, by 1936 democracy had been destroyed in Italy, Portugal, Germany, Austria, and the Balkan and Baltic countries, and ideological polarization characterized interwar Europe.

Spain Under Franco and the Transition to Democracy

An uprising by a large part of the armed forces in July 1936 unleashed a latent social revolution. Although the republicans—often called loyalists—reorganized a democratic government, control had passed to the parties and the militia of the left, who represented only part of Spanish society. The uprising led to the mobilization of two groups: the leftist militias and trade unions, which supported the legal government, and the insurgent military rightists and Falangists. The civil war that ensued ended with the victory of the conservative-fascist-military coalition led by Gen. Francisco Franco. The "Nationalists" had the support of fascist Italy, Nazi Germany, and Portugal, while the Republicans had the half-hearted support of Western democracies, Mexico, and the Soviet Union. On one side, the Falangists-fascists and, on the other, the communists gained growing influence.

Franco became the head of the state and the government, leader of a single party formed by the fusion of the Falangists and the ultraconservative traditionalists. The regime that would last until his death in November 1975 would undergo many changes. Initially, totalitarian tendencies were strong. Later it became an authoritarian regime that underwent a certain economic and then cultural liberalization. Franco's "organic democracy," as he called his regime, excluded political freedoms and parties but was based on the representation of a variety of interests, organizations, and institutions in the legislature (the Cortes), some members of which were elected by heads of household. But Franco's government was never accountable either to the voters or to the legislature, even though he held two referendums on the creation of an authoritarian monarchy (1947) and on his constitution (1968) to give some legitimacy to his regime. Opposition grew in the lat-

er years of Franco's rule, although it was illegal and was persecuted.

The death of Franco initiated a process that led to free elections in Spain. The regime change took place peacefully. The Cortes, which had been largely appointed by Franco, approved a Law for Political Reform that made possible free competitive democratic elections. This law was subsequently approved in a popular referendum. The process has been described as a negotiated reform, reflecting the fact that King Juan Carlos I and Prime Minister Adolfo Suárez chose to institute reforms rather than to break with the past and establish a provisional government as the opposition demanded.

In 1977–1978 a new democracy was successfully established. The economic and social changes under Franco, the weakening of ideological conflicts, and the European context made possible the peaceful transition to democracy, the enactment of a consensual constitution, the institutionalization of a quasi-federal state to deal with nationalist sentiments, and the full consolidation of a parliamentary democratic monarchy.

In October 1978 the democratically elected legislature approved a constitution, which was voted on in a national referendum in December 1978. Supported by all major parties except the Basque Nationalists, it won the approval of 88 percent of the voters (with 67 percent voting). The constitution provided for two legislative chambers. The opposition in the lower chamber could effect a change in government by calling a vote of no confidence and putting forward an alternative government. The constitution established separation of church and state but provided for cooperation between the two as well as freedom for private education. It included an extensive declaration of civil, political, and social rights and also established a constitutional court and an independent judiciary. It provided for the rights of nationalities and regions by creating seventeen autonomous communities that were to enact their own statutes. Those would be approved in some cases by popular referendum and the national legislature, but regional parliaments and governments received wide powers in this quasi-federal state. The constitution also consolidated the monarchy, which was to play a decisive role in defeating a military insurrection in February 1981.

Broad support for democracy, the support of all major political parties for constitutional government, the development of patterns of negotiation between trade unions and employers, and subordination of the military to civil authority worked together to secure democratic institutions in Spain.

Political Parties

After Franco's death a large number of parties appealed to voters. But by the first national election in 1977, they were reduced to four nationwide parties: the Communist Party, the Socialist Workers' Party, the centrist Union of the Democratic Center, and the conservative Popular Alliance. Nationalist parties in Catalonia and in the Basque region also gained parliamentary representation. An internal crisis led to the disappearance of the Union of the Democratic Center in 1982, and many of its voters turned to the Socialist Workers' Party and later to the reorganized conservatives, renamed the Popular Party. A small centrist party, led by Adolfo Suárez, did not survive. A leadership and ideological crisis weakened the Communist Party, but as a result of its fusion with other minor groups to constitute the United Left and because of the economic crisis in the early 1990s, it has regained some votes. The antidemocratic extreme right has gained only one seat in the legislature since democracy took hold in Spain.

The party system today is based principally on competition between the moderate Socialist Workers' Party and the conservative Popular Party—basically a two-party system with a minor role for the Communist Party. However, the presence of an important Catalan center party, Convergence and Union, and of the Basque Nationalist Party means that governments are likely to be minority governments dependent on the support of at least one of these regional parties. This situation has not prevented considerable government stability, with Felipe González, the leader of the Socialist Workers' Party, in power for more than twelve years, facing the strong opposition of the Popular Party under the leadership of José María Aznar.

Spain has held free elections since 1977 to elect members of its congress and senate. In the elections of 1977 and 1979, the Union of the Democratic Center, led by Adolfo Suárez, won the largest plurality and formed a series of minority governments that carried the burden of institutionalizing democracy. Suárez's resignation in 1981 led to the appointment of fellow party member Leopoldo Calvo Sotelo, who assumed power after the coup attempt in February 1981. Under Calvo Sotelo's government, the military implicated in the putsch were tried and sentenced, and Spain joined NATO.

In 1982, faced with a crisis in the governing party and the electoral defeat in regional elections, Calvo Sotelo dissolved the two legislative houses and called anticipated elections. The Socialist Workers' Party won an absolute majority of seats. Although the party lost the majority in the 1993 election, it continued to govern with the support of Convergence and Union.

Accommodating Nationalism

The new democracy had the difficult task of responding to nationalist demands in the Basque country and Catalonia and of managing the country's multilingual character. In addition to the Castilian spoken throughout Spain, several regions—including the Basque country, Catalonia and the Balearic Islands, and Galicia—have their own languages. In the Basque country, where nationalist sentiment is especially strong, a terrorist movement (Basque Homeland and Liberty), formed under Franco, became more violent with democracy. Despite hopes that with autonomy and democratic representation of nationalist aspirations, the movement would disappear, it has continued claiming lives, though it has lost support among the Basque population.

Recognition of nationalist demands involved difficult negotiations and a complex democratic process. The 1978 constitution granted autonomy to the historic nationalities (Catalonia, the Basque country, and Galicia) and Navarra. Through an elaborate process involving local initiatives or legal enactment by the Cortes, autonomy could be extended to other regions.

The final result was the creation of seventeen autonomous regions. Each autonomous region has a popularly elected legislature and a government with a president who needs the support of that legislature to govern. The rules for reforming the laws governing these autonomous regions, the nationalist sentiments in the Basque country and Catalonia, and the constitutional guarantee of the rights of the historic nationalities mean that Spain will never again be a unitary centralized state.

See also *Authoritarianism; Europe, Western; Fascism; Multiethnic democracy; Suárez González, Adolfo.*

Juan J. Linz

BIBLIOGRAPHY

Carr, Raymond. *Spain, 1808–1939.* Oxford: Clarendon Press, 1966.
———, and Juan Pablo Fusi. *Spain from Dictatorship to Democracy.* London: Allen and Unwin, 1979.
Gunther, Richard, Giacomo Sani, and Goldie Shabad. *Spain after Franco: The Making of a Competitive Party System.* Berkeley: University of California Press, 1988.

Linz, Juan J. "Early State Building and Late Peripheral Nationalisms against the State: The Case of Spain." In *Building States and Nations,* edited by S. N. Eisenstadt and Stein Rokkan. Vol. 2. Beverly Hills, Calif.: Sage Publications, 1973.

———. "From Great Hopes to Civil War: The Breakdown of Democracy in Spain." In *The Breakdown of Democratic Regimes,* edited by Juan J. Linz and Alfred Stepan. Baltimore: Johns Hopkins University Press, 1978.

———. "The Party System of Spain: Past and Future." In *Party Systems and Voter Alignments,* edited by Seymour Martin Lipset and Stein Rokkan. New York: Free Press, 1967.

———. "Spanish Democracy and the estado de las autonomías." In *Forging Unity out of Diversity: The Approaches in Eight Nations,* edited by Robert A. Goldwin, Art Kaufman, and William A. Schambra. Washington, D.C.: American Enterprise Institute, 1989.

Malefakis, Edward E. *Agrarian Reform and Peasant Revolution in Spain: Origins of the Civil War.* New Haven: Yale University Press, 1970.

Payne, Stanley G. *The Franco Regime, 1936–1975.* Madison: University of Wisconsin Press, 1988.

———. *Spain's First Democracy: The Second Republic, 1931–1936.* Madison: University of Wisconsin Press, 1993.

Pérez-Díaz, Víctor. *The Return of Civil Society: The Emergence of Democratic Spain.* Cambridge, Mass., and London: Harvard University Press, 1993.

Benedict de Spinoza

Speech, Freedom of

See *Freedom of speech*

Spinoza, Benedict de

First theorist of liberal democracy. Baruch ("Benedict" in Latin) Spinoza (1632–1677) was born in Amsterdam, to parents who had fled the Inquisition in Spain and Portugal. He was educated in rabbinical schools and taught the trade of lens grinding, by which he supported himself after his excommunication from Jewish society in 1656.

Spinoza formulated the idea that the best government is one in which ultimate authority rests with the majority, who govern a society where all may think as they wish and say what they think. He was the first theorist to articulate a fundamental harmony between democracy and science, devoted to unfettered rational inquiry.

Before Spinoza, philosophic and political freedom were at odds. Both historical experience and theoretical reflection argued that healthy self-government depended on severe communal civic virtue and therefore on a legally enforced code of shared morals and beliefs. Particularly important were beliefs in divinities who enforce justice with rewards and punishments. As a result, a profound tension persisted between the closed character of republicanism at its best and the life of the inquisitive mind, which was seen as humanity's highest, if rarest, calling.

Classical political philosophy was keenly aware that democracy, because it entails rule by the unleisured poor, tends to let citizens live as they please, preoccupied with making a living and therefore careless of moral education and the common good. This democratic tendency to license, however favorable in the short run to freedom of thought (and hence philosophy), was seen as a grave long-run deficiency. Only if democracy were "mixed" with less permissive oligarchic, aristocratic, and monarchic constitutional elements was it likely to produce serious-minded youth, potentially alive to philosophy's disturbing challenge, and sober, educated statesmen and citizens who could oppose the drift toward mob rule, demagoguery, and class warfare. Left to itself, democracy tended to vibrate between moral laxity and periodic reactions of popular religious fanaticism. Such outbursts of popular religious fervor had been a principal factor in the trial and execution of Socrates in Athens in 399 B.C. and in persecutions of Aristotle and other philosophers, not only in other Greek city-states but in Roman, medieval, and modern republics as well.

Like his classical predecessors, Spinoza believed that the highest and most fulfilling human existence was the philosophic life. He recognized that misguided religious piety poses the gravest political threat (and most unsettling intellectual challenge) to philosophy and science. But he advocated disposing of the threat by advancing a new, scientific basis for religion and government. To enlighten both elites and masses, he devoted the greater part of his chief work of political philosophy, *The Theologico-Political Treatise* (1670), to a critical examination of the Bible. In the process, he founded the modern study of biblical textual criticism.

Spinoza claimed to demonstrate that the Scriptures, read literally and in the light of empirical reasoning, reveal themselves to be a record of intellectually primitive but highly imaginative attempts by leaders to instill obedience in the superstitious masses that composed prescientific tribal cultures. The core teaching to which obedience was sought was a simple notion of justice and charity that corresponds roughly to what reason teaches is the true ethics. There is thus nothing expressly taught in Scripture that cannot be seen as agreeing with science and philosophy, which have an independent and largely superior access to the nature of all things, including God and morality. Any attribution of the truly miraculous, or supernatural, to biblical theology is the result of misreadings that mistake the original context and character of prophecy.

The second part of the *Theologico-Political Treatise* outlines the new, scientific principles of justice. The doctrine is derived, with significant modifications, from Spinoza's great contemporary, Thomas Hobbes. The starting point is the undeniable necessity, and hence the inalienable "natural right," of every being (and therefore of every human being) to preserve itself in a competitive world. For humans, preservation means not only physical security but also rational self-governance to whatever degree is possible. The reasonable basis of political society is in the contract individuals make with one another to provide for their mutual preservation. Thus they transfer their natural rights to a "sovereign" government that will have the col-

lective force to ensure that individuals abide by the laws that promote the general welfare. Justice is nothing more and nothing less than strict fidelity to this contract.

The sovereign power can be placed in the hands of one (monarchy), a few (aristocracy), or the majority of the people (democracy). Democracy—and more particularly liberal democracy, which can allow a diverse populace to live in harmony—is the most natural and reasonable form of government. Its consensual character, grounded in free debate among conflicting points of view, promotes prudent policy making, while best preserving the original, natural equality and self-governing liberty implicit in the contract. Liberal democracy consequently is least likely to depart from the original purpose of government or to become oppressive. Because it is least likely to lose its legitimacy in the eyes of the multitude, it is the most stable form of government. What is more, liberal democracy can allow freedom for philosophy and in the process promote true virtue.

Although democracy does require some civic virtue, or patriotic and charitable transcendence of self-interest, that virtue can be grounded in the citizen's attachment to "liberal" virtue, or the sense of dignity afforded by loyalty to a free society. In a free society individuals are given a voice in public policy, and left free to think and speak as they wish, as long as they behave with justice and charity. Because most human beings, however, are neither very reasonable nor sufficiently attached to rational and liberal dignity, virtue continues to need the sanction of belief in a God who rewards and punishes. But true piety ought to be understood as rooted in uncoerced assent of the mind. Hence government, while supporting religion, should also support religious toleration. It ought not to police the thought or words of citizens but to judge everyone pious as long as their beliefs engender behavior that conforms to the rules of justice.

In his *Political Treatise* (1677), Spinoza examined the best version of each of the three forms of government. He died before writing the section on democracy. Scattered remarks suggest that he would have advocated a federation of commercial republics, centered on the urban entrepreneurial middle class.

Through his theory of a contractual democracy animated by a virtue centered on freedom and supported by a civil religion, Spinoza profoundly influenced Jean-Jacques Rousseau. Spinoza's synthesis of Hobbes's notion of individual natural rights and the older classical notion of virtue as the "highest good" inspired the German idealists from Immanuel Kant to G. W. F. Hegel and Karl Marx. His biblical criticism is the foundation of all modern liberal theology. But nearly all those who followed in his wake were forced to soften and mitigate his ruthlessly unsentimental vision of human psychology.

See also *Freedom of speech; Hobbes, Thomas; Idealism, German; Liberalism; Republics, Commercial; Rousseau, Jean-Jacques; Theory, Ancient; Virtue, Civic.*

Thomas L. Pangle

BIBLIOGRAPHY

Powell, Elmer. *Spinoza and Religion.* Boston: Chapman and Grimes, 1941.

Spinoza, Benedict de. *The Collected Works of Spinoza.* Edited and translated by Edwin Curley. Vol. 1 [others forthcoming]. Princeton: Princeton University Press, 1985.

———. *The Correspondence of Spinoza.* Edited by Abraham Wolf. London: Dial Press, 1928.

———. *The Political Works of Spinoza.* Edited and translated by A. G. Wernham. Oxford: Oxford University Press, 1965.

Strauss, Leo. "How to Study Spinoza's Theologico-Political Treatise." In *Persecution and the Art of Writing.* Glencoe, Ill.: Free Press, 1952.

Spoils system

The practice of awarding most public jobs to supporters of the winning political party. Many practices associated with the spoils system—including the purchase of office, nepotism, and the use of patronage to reward friends—have always been associated with government as well as with business and the church. The systematic use and acceptance of the practice, however, are associated primarily with nineteenth-century American politics.

The term *spoils* was first applied to American politics by Sen. William Marcy of New York in 1832. He defended President Andrew Jackson's appointment of Martin Van Buren as ambassador to London by saying "to the victor belong the spoils of the enemy." In using the language of warfare to defend the outcome of a peaceful democratic election, Marcy graphically acknowledged the emergence of a competitive party system in the United States. The practice, whereby the winners of a political battle rewarded their supporters with public employment, was already in use in New York and Pennsylvania. It was to become the

common practice at all levels of government during the remainder of the nineteenth century. In turn, it became a central issue in efforts to reform American politics.

Party and Bureaucracy

The spoils system itself, however, should be understood as a major political reform. It represented a break with an elitist past and an important advancement in an evolving democracy. The United States was the first nation to break with a hierarchical social structure that determined the staffing of public offices. It was also the first to spawn political parties organized around the need to reach out to a mass electorate. The spoils system emerged therefore as the answer to three questions generated by the new democracy: What control should elected officials have over the administrative bureaucracy? What, if any, special competence or personal background is needed for public office? And how should political parties, the engines of democratic competition, be staffed? Each question arose independently during the first forty years of the republic. But their answers taken together provided the rationale for what came to be called the spoils system.

The first question, about elective control of appointments, arose only with the end of the Federalist dynasty. Under the Constitution, presidents appointed all major officials, with the advice and consent of the Senate. The appointment of lesser officials was to be defined by law. The power to appoint was generally assumed to mean also the power to remove. The first two presidents, George Washington and John Adams, treated public positions as permanent appointments, to be held for life or during good behavior. Over a twelve-year period they removed only eighteen officials, none for political reasons. Since, within the developing party system, both men were Federalists, the potential conflict inherent in the policy of life tenure did not arise between a newly elected executive and his predecessors' appointed officials.

The conflict arose in 1800, when the Democratic-Republicans under Thomas Jefferson defeated John Adams in a bitter partisan contest. After his defeat, Adams, during his remaining days in office, appointed a large number of officials, including a group that came to be known as the "midnight judges." Jefferson chose to challenge Adams's appointments, and the Supreme Court under Chief Justice John Marshall supported Jefferson's power to remove the judges by declaring unconstitutional the act that had created the judgeships. The case of *Marbury v. Madison* (1803) is justly famous for setting the precedent of judicial review of legislative acts. At the same time the case called attention to the effect of electoral results on public appointments, although it did not definitively settle the substantive issue of a newly elected president's control over the previous administration's appointees.

The issue receded after 1800 because competition between the major parties, the Federalists and Democratic-Republicans, eroded. For the next twenty-four years the Democratic-Republicans and their Virginia dynasty dominated the presidency. It would be twenty-eight years before another incumbent president was defeated. It is true that many Federalists, having got used to the idea that office belonged to them by right, complained that they were being denied appointments. But their party was declining, and in 1820 the Federalists failed even to run a candidate for the presidency. The partisan concerns that had led Jefferson to attack the midnight judges dissipated for several decades after his election.

Control of Appointments

Concern, however, emerged within the dominant Democratic-Republican Party over how long federal executive appointments should last. Factionalism within the dominant party replaced two-party competition and produced new conflict over the control of appointments. The sentiment developed that appointments ought not to be permanent. In 1820, the year in which the incumbent president, James Monroe, was reelected without opposition, Congress, over the objections of Jefferson and James Madison, passed a tenure of office act setting the maximum term for major federal appointments at four years, terminating with the inauguration of the president. Although everyone was of the same party, differences emerged over the elected executive's control of public office.

Factionalism within the Democratic-Republican Party was also responsible for the second issue related to the emergence of the spoils system, the question of competence for public office. In the 1820s the grip of the Virginia dynasty on the party was broken. The egalitarian spirit that the contemporary observer Alexis de Tocqueville found dominant in American society brought forth a new kind of leader. Andrew Jackson was a war hero and a westerner; he directed his appeals to the common people, to all who felt disadvantaged by established political practices. These practices rested, among other things, on the assumption that the holding of public office required special skills, training, or experience. In 1829 Jackson challenged

this assumption in an address to Congress. Despite his rhetoric, Jackson did not greatly change policy. After his election, by most estimates, he replaced no more than one-fifth of the incumbent federal employees. Nevertheless, the sentiment he had endorsed, that any able-bodied citizen could fill any public job, constituted the second important component in the rationale for the spoils system.

Partisan Competition

Ultimately, the rationale for the spoils system came to depend on the reemergence of a competitive party system and the recognition that democracy depended on active partisan competition. The 1830s saw the demise of one-party politics. Free elections brought about a split in the Democratic-Republican Party: the opposition to Jackson emerged as the Whig Party and Jackson's successors became the Democrats. Competition between the two parties was lively throughout the country. From 1832 to 1856 four changes in party control of the presidency and five changes in party control of the House of Representatives took place. In 1856 the Republicans supplanted the Whigs as the second major party.

Competition created the need to staff the competing party organizations. The need for staff was made more urgent by the practice of universal white male suffrage, which required electoral campaigns to reach out to a broad population. The democratic impulse that turned more and more judicial and administrative positions into elective offices also added to the urgency. Increasingly, after 1830, states and localities subjected county clerks, state and local treasurers, auditors, superintendents of education, judges, attorneys, and sheriffs to periodic popular elections. Frequent elections for a multitude of offices under competitive conditions meant that candidates and their parties needed campaign workers. In turn, reliable campaign workers required a source of reward or support beyond the satisfaction of helping the party reach its goals.

Public offices were the most obvious rewards available to American political leaders. Election presumably conferred the right to control all subordinate places attached to a particular elective office. Whigs, Democrats, and later Republicans, therefore, were quick to fire their opponents' appointees and hire their supporters for public jobs ranging from street cleaner to high administrative office. Thus the premise that public offices were needed to sustain the parties, which were themselves essential to democracy, was the principal catalyst for the spoils system.

Because the U.S. government has a federal structure,

the spoils system became primarily the instrument for maintaining state and local political organizations. Most public offices, including federal posts appointed by the president, were turned over to state and local party leaders. The requirement that the Senate approve presidential appointments gave U.S. senators a major role in the distribution of federal patronage. The role was strengthened by the emergence of the practice of senatorial courtesy. This practice required that all appointments in a state—everything from customs inspectors and postmasters to federal marshals, attorneys, and judges—be cleared through the state's U.S. senators of the president's party. The widespread use of the spoils system at the federal level legitimized its use by state and local governments. It became one of the most conspicuous aspects of American politics, commented upon by two highly respected foreign observers, James Bryce and Moisei Ostrogorski. The spoils system was basic to their conclusion that American parties, although marvels of organizational strength, were not concerned with larger issues of politics. They had become "small" parties in the Tocquevillian sense rather than "large" parties competing over distinct views of government. The use of public jobs to reward party workers was also important in the growth and support of political machines, the disciplined organizations that were able to control many offices in local and some state governments.

Implications for Democracy

In effect, the rationale for the spoils system represented a new theory of American democracy. The priority of electoral decisions required that bureaucrats be subordinated to elected officials. The most effective way of accomplishing that requirement was to clear out bureaucrats beholden to the past. The egalitarian premise that public office required no special expertise made it easy to replace such officials. Moreover, such jobs were needed by the engines of democracy, competitive political parties. Ultimately, in theory at least, unelected officials were subdued and made to serve the party and therefore the voters.

Among the premises of this theory only the first has stood the test of time. In the United States as well as in other developed democracies it is assumed today that a newly elected executive should be able to appoint major policy-making subordinates. The numbers vary from about 100 in the United Kingdom to about 5,000 in the United States. The second premise, however, that any public office can be adequately filled by any competent citizen, has not survived. It was not entirely accepted even during the heyday of the spoils system. In many instances, people who held technical posts were retained because their skills were needed. With the rise of the administrative state, the United States has followed the lead of other industrialized nations and adopted procedures for hiring and promoting public personnel mostly on the basis of expertise.

The premise that public jobs should be used as a means of staffing political parties faced the greatest challenge. It opened the way for abuse, prompting reforms that undermined the premise. As long as a party's workers, and much of its electorate, owed their partisan attachment solely to direct personal benefits, the party's leadership was free to engage in any kind of behavior that ensured these benefits. Thus kickbacks from public contracts, electoral fraud, and the bribing of officials were widely reported as common practice in post–Civil War American politics. The scandals in President Ulysses S. Grant's administration helped fuel a reform movement whose central goal was to create a federal civil service. The assassination of President James Garfield in 1881 by a disappointed office seeker provided additional impetus for passage of the Pendleton Act of 1883, which created a merit system for many posts in the federal government. The act subsequently was expanded to cover most federal employees. During the twentieth century most state and local governments also adopted some form of merit system for employment. The introduction of the city manager was inspired also by the desire to professionalize public employment. Although the parties continued to control some public positions, primarily in a few northeastern states, they could no longer rely on the public payroll to secure their personnel and their electoral base. Thus reforms designed to deprive political parties of public patronage brought about the end of the spoils system.

See also *Bryce, James; Civil service; Corruption; Jackson, Andrew; Ostrogorski, Moisei Yakovlevich; Parties, Political; Patronage; Politics, Machine.*

Joseph A. Schlesinger

BIBLIOGRAPHY

Bryce, James. *The American Commonwealth.* New York: Macmillan, 1915.

Epstein, Leon. *Political Parties in the American Mold.* Madison: University of Wisconsin Press, 1986.

Fish, Carl R. *Civil Service and Patronage.* New York: Longmans, Green, 1905.

Ostrogorski, Moisei. *Democracy and the Organization of Political Parties.* Vol. 2. Edited and abridged with an introduction by S. M. Lipset. Garden City, N.Y.: Anchor Books, 1964.

White, Leonard D. *The Republican Era: A Study in Administrative History, 1869–1901.* New York: Macmillan, 1958.

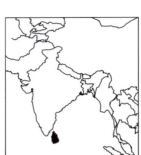

Sri Lanka

An island republic off the southern tip of India, once a British colony. Sri Lanka (formerly Ceylon) became independent in 1948, after more than 400 years under European colonial tutelage. The Portuguese first established themselves in the coastal areas in 1517. The Dutch displaced the Portuguese in 1655 and were ousted in 1795 by the British. In 1815 the British gained control of the whole island, including the Kandyan kingdom in the mountains.

From the 1930s on, Sri Lanka developed a strong tradition of constitutional, democratic practice. Between 1931 and 1993 eleven national elections were held. Two of these, based on a universal franchise, took place before independence. Between 1956 and 1977 governments changed hands peacefully in six successive elections. In every case, a government defeated at the polls relinquished power. There were no successful coups d'état; the military did not take control. Few countries have shown such a sustained high level of political participation as Sri Lanka. Until the 1980s electoral turnouts were often greater than 80 percent. In the 1980s and early 1990s, however, the Sri Lankan political system faced major challenges.

Sri Lanka's record of democratic practice is all the more remarkable because the country is a complex, multiethnic society. The Sinhala-speaking majority, mostly Buddhist, makes up more than 70 percent of the population. The principal minority is Sri Lankan Tamils; mostly Hindu and speaking Tamil, they represent 12 percent of the population. Although Sinhala is the official language, both Tamil and Sinhala are recognized as "national languages" in the constitution of 1978. Two-thirds of the Tamils have been concentrated in the Jaffna peninsula and northern and eastern provinces of the island. The Tamils played an important role in the country's growth; for example, in the 1950s more than 40 percent of clerical service recruits and more than 30 percent of university graduates were Sri Lankan Tamils. A smaller minority (5.5 percent) is the "estate Tamils," descendants of Tamil people brought from India in the nineteenth century to work British-owned tea estates in the central highlands. The rest of the population is Muslim and Christian (about 7 percent each). About 10 percent of the population speaks English. Within the principal communities caste distinctions are important and helped shape political identities.

The constitution introduced by the British in 1931 established universal adult franchise for the first time in a non-Western colony. There were no literacy requirements for voting, and Sri Lankan voters turned out in large numbers that year to elect members of the State Council, which had power and responsibility for all aspects of internal civil administration. Legislators used these powers to introduce far-reaching reforms in social welfare, education, health care, and land reform.

In 1947 the two principal communities were led by men of similar educational background, English speakers of anglicized culture, who were familiar with the restraints and conventions of contemporary British political practices. As spokesman for leading Sinhalese politicians, D. S. Senanayake negotiated the independence agreement with the British, which a number of Tamil leaders also agreed to. He became the country's first prime minister, and his party, the United National Party, formed the first independence government.

The 1948 independence constitution affirmed the principle of majority rule, but it also included protections for the minorities. For example, section 29(2) prohibited legislation discriminating against a community or followers of a religion. Moreover, areas in which minority groups were concentrated and less developed rural areas received more than their proportionate share of representatives in the new State Council, as a counterbalance to the power of the urban elite. Sinhalese and Tamil were both named national languages, although the language of government in effect remained English. The new state, called Ceylon, was secular; there was no official religion.

The Political Pendulum

Unlike many new democracies, where one-party rule quickly eliminated competition among parties, Sri Lanka retained political choice. Since 1948 the pendulum of politics has swung several times between the United National Party and the Sri Lanka Freedom Party.

After the death of Senanayake in 1952, his son Dudley took his place. In 1952, in a massive 70 percent turnout, voters once again favored the United National Party. In 1951, however, the independence coalition had split when S. W. R. D. Bandaranaike organized the Sri Lanka Freedom Party. That party won by a landslide in 1956. Actively supported by Buddhist priests and the educated, Sinhala-speaking middle class, the party emphasized the politics of cultural nationalism and the special character of Ceylon as a Sinhala-speaking, Buddhist country. It promised to make Sinhala the sole official language. The United National Party won only eight seats in 1956, and all but one cabinet minister were voted out. The majority of the population identified with the government more than before. The Freedom Party government was "socialist"; it encouraged the organization of labor and advocated a larger role for the government in the economy.

Bandaranaike was assassinated in 1959. An election in early 1960 gave the United National Party the most seats but not a majority, and Dudley Senanayake preferred to call a new election. In July, Bandaranaike's widow, Sirimavo Bandaranaike, won a sufficient majority for the Freedom Party to govern for the next four years. She became the world's first woman prime minister.

In late 1964 the United National Party engineered a vote of no confidence, bringing the Freedom Party government to a premature end. In the 1965 election, the United National Party narrowly returned to power for another five years under Dudley Senanayake's leadership. This time, however, the party shared power with the Tamil Federal Party, founded in 1951 to promote Tamil interests. Departing from the socialist policies of the Freedom Party, the new government successfully increased rice production.

In 1970 the pendulum swung once more, and the Freedom Party formed a government in coalition with three Marxist parties. A new constitution was adopted in 1972. It addressed Sinhalese grievances by reviving the country's ancient, pre-European name *Lanka* and adding the honorific *Sri* and by designating Sinhala as the sole official language. It strengthened the executive by eliminating the Senate and ending the judicial review of legislation. The new government adopted an economic policy that favored government controls and import substitution (a collection of policies designed to promote a country's self-sufficiency). It nationalized many enterprises, implemented a major land reform, and expanded government-managed industries.

The government faced a major challenge in 1971, when thousands of unemployed rural Sinhalese youths, led by the People's Liberation Front, attempted a one-night seizure of power. The insurrection was put down vigorously, resulting in more than 1,000 deaths. Some 14,000 youths were held for a year in rehabilitation camps. At the same time, the international increase in the price of oil, along with further deterioration of Sri Lanka's terms of trade and strengthening of government controls on trade, contributed to economic stagnation and widespread frustration.

In 1977 the United National Party returned to power, gaining a four-fifths majority, the largest ever achieved by a single party. Except for a few dissenting ministers, the government under President J. R. Jayewardene supported ethnic and caste inclusion, reversed many of the previous government's economic policies, and opened the economy with the help of the World Bank. It undertook major hydroelectric projects and encouraged foreign investment in export industries. Ranasinghe Premadasa, the prime minister, promoted rural housing and urban development. For a time the economy registered growth rates of 5–6 percent, though inflation sharpened contrasts between rich and poor. The government established another new constitution, this one giving more powers to a directly elected executive president. Proponents claimed the change was essential to ensure the political stability necessary to promote economic development like that of Singapore. The constitution also introduced proportional representation for parliamentary elections.

In 1982 a presidential election returned Jayewardene for a second term. Instead of calling a parliamentary election as expected, he organized a controversial referendum that approved prolonging the life of the existing parliament for another five years. Although the 1978 constitution permitted such a referendum, many voters resented being deprived of the time-honored opportunity to vote in an election.

Characteristics of the System, 1931–1983

By most criteria for assessing newly independent regimes, Sri Lanka for many years seemed a model democracy. Electoral turnouts remained high, and politicization went unusually far. Based on universal franchise, the political system of Sri Lanka had become a multiparty system in which two major parties—the United National Party and the Freedom Party—replaced each other periodically. Meanwhile smaller Marxist parties organized and utilized trade unions, and parties of the ethnic minorities continued to voice their growing sense of grievance.

Parties competed by outbidding each other in offering benefits to the voters. For many years the bureaucracy was reasonably effective. As a result, the people of Sri Lanka were better served by health clinics, nutrition programs, and elementary and secondary education than any others in South Asia. On the other hand, competing politicians often raised expectations beyond what the political economy could deliver and intensified local rivalries. Competition for leadership within the major communities induced rivals to accentuate ethnic differences between the communities.

In spite of brief periods of constraint, there was considerable public debate, much of it appearing in newspapers in the three main languages. At independence, more than half the population of Sri Lanka could read and write; by the 1980s the literacy rate had climbed to more than 90 percent.

An electoral commission oversaw the orderliness, secrecy, and fairness of elections, and the police generally protected voters from overly zealous party workers—except in the violence associated with the 1983 referendum and the 1988 and 1989 elections.

Whenever a party enjoyed a landslide victory, as in 1956 and 1977, minority parties, such as the Tamil ethnic parties, had little parliamentary leverage. When the major parties were more evenly matched, however, as in the 1960s, the Tamil ethnic parties could offer their support to whichever major party was most responsive to their interests.

From 1948 to 1993 Sri Lanka had three different constitutions. Both the Freedom Party and the United National Party governments manipulated the constitutions to their short-run political advantage, but they remained fundamentally within constitutional bounds, except during times of crisis.

Critics argued that "the people" were not well represented by the major parties. For example, neither party was internally democratic; each was led by wealthy members of the elite or highly placed professionals. Leadership of both parties remained within the founding families. This situation was especially so with the Freedom Party. Structurally, each party was a loose coalition of patron-client relationships or caste followings. By the 1977 election, however, other political figures, people of humble beginnings, had become prominent.

Political Challenges to the Establishment

Two major movements challenged the political establishment. The most protracted was the Tamil secessionist movement, which emerged in the Jaffna region in the mid-1970s. For a long time some Tamils had wanted to replace the highly centralized, "colonial" structure of government in Sri Lanka with some form of autonomy. Their demands had been consistently rejected by the majority.

The Tamils worried about their political future when they heard majority leaders emphasize the Sinhala character of Sri Lanka. At the same time, Sinhala zealots among priests and teachers depicted Tamils as their historic enemies. The Freedom Party, hard pressed by the People's Liberation Front in 1971, increased the number of university openings for unemployed Sinhalese youths by reducing the disproportionate number of university places that historically had been filled by Tamils. It also virtually ceased the recruitment of Tamils into the national police and military services. Anti-Tamil riots took place after each election. The excesses committed by the police and army in efforts to repress disorders in the north often drew new members to the Tamil secessionist movement.

The accumulation of cultural and career grievances released unexpected political energies. Tamils became more militant, and Tamil members of the parliament, seeking reelection and unable to ignore the impatient youths, increasingly advocated independence. Their secessionist rhetoric in turn increased Sinhalese anxieties.

The Tamil sense of grievance was further intensified by anti-Tamil riots following the 1977 election, when the United National Party returned to power. The government attempted to satisfy Tamil grievances by constitutional changes, by administrative order, and by protracted negotiations and hesitant implementation of district development councils. The measures were not sufficient to calm the Tamils' anger and relieve their fear. Radical Tamil groups, including the Tamil Liberation Tigers, blocked government efforts to restore order and organized terrorist incidents.

In 1983 Sri Lanka experienced the worst anti-Tamil riots ever. The event radicalized many Tamils who had kept hoping for a negotiated resolution to the situation. Thousands of Tamils fled to Madras, India, where competing politicians dramatized their support for one or another faction of Tamil militants. Indira Gandhi, prime minister of India, actively involved her government in the issue, with offers of mediation between the Sri Lankan capital, Colombo, and Jaffna. She also offered direct assistance to the militants in the form of training camps, communications, money, and arms.

Following a dual policy, President Jayewardene negotiated with the more moderate Tamil leaders and also strengthened defenses. He gradually tripled the size of the armed forces, and by 1988 he had increased defense spending from 1 percent of the gross domestic product (GDP) to more than 5 percent.

The radical Tamils made repeated attacks on government facilities. They intimidated and even assassinated Tamils who cooperated with the government, and they staged terrorist attacks in the south. As the conflict continued, the extremist Tamil Liberation Tigers came to dominate the movement.

In 1987 Jayewardene and Rajiv Gandhi, who succeeded Indira Gandhi as prime minister of India, negotiated the Indo–Sri Lanka Accord. The Sri Lankan government acknowledged that Sri Lanka was a multiethnic state where language and other rights of minorities would be duly protected. The agreement defined a devolution of government powers to provincial councils. For its part, the government of India agreed to send a peacekeeping force to reassure the militants and guarantee implementation of the accord.

The Tamil Liberation Tigers turned on the Indian peacekeepers. The initial 3,000 Indian troops grew to 60,000. By the time the Indian army was asked to withdraw by Sri Lankan president Ranasinghe Premadasa in 1990, it had lost more 1,200 men, and more than twice as many were seriously wounded.

Jayewardene's "invitation" to the Indian peacekeepers profoundly affected Sri Lankan domestic politics, precipitating a second major challenge, the reemergence of the People's Liberation Front.

The presence of Indian troops touched a sensitive Sinhalese nerve, providing a near perfect justification for the rebirth of the People's Liberation Front and its campaign to destroy the Sri Lankan political establishment. In 1988–1989 the People's Liberation Front tried to disrupt elections by assassinating political candidates and known supporters of the major parties. During the summer of 1988 it virtually brought Colombo, Kandy, and other cities to a halt through strikes, work stoppages, and assassinations. In the end, by directly threatening the lives of the families of military and police officers, the People's Liberation Front roused the army to action. The army demolished party cadres, captured and killed Front leaders, and eliminated known and suspected followers. In this atmosphere of suspicion and deadly violence, innocent people undoubtedly also "disappeared."

In 1988, toward the end of his term, Jayewardene passed leadership of the United National Party to his prime minister, Premadasa. Despite violent efforts by the People's Liberation Front to prevent elections in December 1988, Premadasa was narrowly—and, the opposition claimed, dubiously—elected executive president. In the face of threats from the People's Liberaton Front, only 55 percent of the electorate dared go to the polls. Parliamentary elections held in February 1989 under proportional representation confirmed the United National Party in power for five more years, but with a much narrower majority than before.

The years 1983–1989 were the worst ever for democracy in Sri Lanka, as the competitive ballot was replaced by violence. An estimated 30,000 people died; hundreds of thousands more became refugees, and thousands left the island permanently.

Return to Normalcy?

After the destruction of the People's Liberation Front in 1992, provincial council elections were held in 1993 under nearly normal conditions of public peace, except in the north and east, where the Tamil Liberation Tigers effectively blocked free elections. This time 77 percent of eligible voters cast ballots, suggesting that once again Sri Lanka was returning to orderly democratic processes. Indeed, in the next national election, in August 1994, the United National Party was replaced after seventeen years in power, when the Sri Lanka Freedom Party won a near majority on a platform of ending the war. Chandrika Bandaranaike Kumaratunga, the daughter of two former prime ministers, became prime minister. Her mother became president.

In spite of this positive sign, Sri Lanka had an army three times larger than before, weapons were readily available among the population, and communal differences remained acute. The Tamil Liberation Tigers, their membership concentrated largely in the Jaffna peninsula, remained intractable, unilaterally breaking a truce offered by the new government and rejecting a more generous offer of devolution of powers to Tamil areas.

See also *Buddhism; India; Multiethnic democracy.*

W. Howard Wriggins

BIBLIOGRAPHY

Coomeraswamy, Radikha. *Sri Lanka: The Crisis of the Anglo-American Constitutional Traditions in a Developing Society.* New Delhi: Vikas, 1984.

deSilva, K. M. *A History of Ceylon.* London: C. Hurst, 1981.

———. *Managing Ethnic Tensions in Multi-Ethnic Societies: Sri Lanka 1880–1985.* Lanham, Md.: University Press of America, 1986.

Manor, James. *Sri Lanka in Change and Crisis.* London: Croom Helm, 1984.

Obeyesekere, Gananath. "Sinhalese-Buddhist Identity in Ceylon." In *Ethnic Identity: Cultural Continuities and Change,* edited by George deVos and Lola Romanucci-Ross. Palo Alto, Calif.: Mayfield Publishing, 1982.

Ratnatunga, Sinha. *Politics of Terrorism: The Sri Lanka Experience.* Balconnen, Australia: International Fellowship for Social and Economic Development, 1986.

Roberts, Michael, ed. *Collective Identities, Nationalisms and Protest in Modern Sri Lanka.* Colombo, Sri Lanka: Marga Institute, 1979.

Tambiah, S. J. *Ethnic Fratricide and the Dismantling of Democracy.* Chicago: University of Chicago Press, 1986.

Wilson, A. Jayeratnam. *Politics in Sri Lanka: 1947–1973.* London: Macmillan, 1974.

Wriggins, W. Howard. *Ceylon, Dilemmas of a New Nation.* Princeton: Princeton University Press, 1960.

Elizabeth Cady Stanton

Stanton, Elizabeth Cady

Leader of the women's suffrage movement in the United States. Stanton (1815–1902) was born in Johnstown, New York. She married Henry Brewster Stanton, an abolitionist and lawyer who advocated social equality for women.

In 1840 the Stantons attended the World Antislavery Convention in London, where convention leaders excluded women delegates from the floor. After this experience, Stanton vowed to organize women in the United States to work for equal rights. Moving to Seneca Falls, New York, in 1847, she worked to pass the New York Married Women's Property Act, which allowed married women to control their own property.

With four other women, including Lucretia Mott, a Quaker minister and reformer she met at the antislavery convention, Stanton organized a women's rights convention in July 1848. Stanton's Declaration of Sentiments, modeled on the Declaration of Independence, was unanimously approved at the convention in Seneca Falls. Her resolution calling for women's enfranchisement passed narrowly after long and intense debate.

Stanton devoted her energy to temperance, abolition, and women's rights. In 1851 she began collaborating with Susan B. Anthony, who was known for her organizational and tactical skills. From 1852 to 1853 Stanton was president of the Woman's State Temperance Society. During the Civil War she and Anthony founded the Women's Loyal League and petitioned Congress to abolish slavery.

After the Civil War, Stanton and Anthony used their political skills to expand democratic rights to women. From 1868 to 1870 they published the suffragist newspaper *Revolution.* In 1869 they organized the National Woman

Suffrage Association over which Stanton presided until it merged with the American Woman Suffrage Association in 1890. She presided over the new organization until 1892.

In collaboration with Anthony and Matilda Gage, she worked on the six-volume *History of Woman Suffrage* and prepared a two-volume *Woman's Bible* (1895, 1898). Her autobiography, *Eighty Years and More: Reminiscences, 1815–1897*, was published in 1898.

Stanton lectured nationwide on behalf of women's rights. She championed social equality for women, especially more equitable divorce laws. She proposed a federal women's suffrage amendment on which the Nineteenth Amendment to the U.S. Constitution was based. She died in New York City in 1902.

See also *Anthony, Susan B.; Pankhurst, Emmeline; Women and democracy; Women's suffrage in the United States.* In Documents section, see *Declaration of Sentiments (1848).*

Susan Gluck Mezey

State growth and intervention

The expansion of state organization and personnel and the imposition of state interests and activities upon society. The state's performance of social and group-specific functions and its extraction of revenues, conscripts, and other resources from society are important features in the development of human history. The first interventions of the state into society accompanied the emergence of the state as a distinct institution.

As Charles Tilly wrote in his *Formation of Nation States in Western Europe* (1975), intervention began with the emergence of states as organizations that were able to control the population of definite territories, were distinct from other organizations, were sovereign entities, were centralized, and were composed of formally coordinated parts. Later extensions of the state into the lives of its subjects and citizens came with its modernization in the age of industrial, national, and democratic revolutions. The functions of the state proliferated in the twentieth century.

Premodern States

Before the great revolutions in communications, nationalism, democracy, and industry that marked the modern era, the high costs of territorial control relative to available resources limited the state's intervention in people's lives. Both social and technological means of control and subduing popular resistance to control were costly. A self-equipped army could maintain itself for only three days in the times of Alexander the Great and Julius Caesar. Beyond the third day, ancient armies had to turn to foraging and pillaging local lands and populations or to establishing long and extremely costly supply lines. Foraging and pillaging carried on within a state's territory risked the ruination and alienation of the state's subjects, while supply lines strained the surplus production capacity of societies in which most people lived close to subsistence. Sustained intimidation by distant armed forces might extract periodic tributes and command allegiance for future wars; however, it also decentralized power, saving semi-independent tributaries from becoming fully subject to the state. In most empires the activities of the state were essentially limited to the metropolitan core.

Despite the serious obstacles to state expansion, the ancient world did produce states that intervened in the lives of their populations. Such states emerged in the extraordinarily fertile river valleys of Egypt, the Levant, India, and China. In those places agriculture depended on irrigation, and centralized, coercive control of the necessary infrastructure both enhanced the power of the state and subsidized its operation.

In Greece and Rome unprecedented extensions of slavery released new wealth for financing state rule. At the same time, innovations in mass mobilization and military organization cut the costs of territorial control. The new institutions of political participation and legally encoded citizenship extended the reach of military conscription deep into domestic populations in republican Greece and Rome. In the Roman Empire, with its elaborate rule of law, extensive conscription persisted for a time, until it was largely replaced by reliance upon German mercenaries.

Extraordinary plunder could also sustain a state for a time. This was the case in sixteenth-century Spain, which reaped the wealth of its newfound colonies. State revenue extraction from plunder, tribute, customs duties, labor obligations, tax farming, rentals of public lands, and the like, however, seldom made up as much as 10 percent of the value of production within a given territory during the premodern era. The scarcity of surplus production beyond the subsistence needs of populations and inefficient premodern techniques of revenue extraction made any larger share for state coffers impracticable. Indeed, intrusions by invading foreign states may have had more of an effect on everyday life than state interventions did, at least until the modern era.

Modern States

Merchant, financial, and industrial capitalism emerged in the late Middle Ages and the Renaissance. In that era, monarchs and their allied "war parties" built up state administrations for financing and managing armed forces. These official structures were closely linked to the new class of capitalists. Aided by resources supplied by capitalists, monarchs were able to subordinate ethnic and linguistic minority groups, as well as less aggressive groups of nobles. The growing states were absolutist where their capitalist allies were duly subordinated; constitutionalist states developed where capitalists voiced their views by means of "estates" and parliamentary assemblies. In all cases, the growing states of the sixteenth through eighteenth centuries pursued both military and mercantile expansion.

The case of Great Britain provides an early and well-documented instance of state growth. The revenues of the British state tripled in about a century, between the reigns of Elizabeth I (1558–1607) and James II (1685–1688). Its expenditures then doubled from the reign of William and Mary (1689–1702) to the outbreak of the French Revolution (1789). In their pursuit of international military advantage, states nurtured productive enterprises by means of purchases of military goods, investment in the infrastructures of military manufacturers, and policing of colonial markets. Thus the British state's domestic and colonial spending, as well as military spending, rose throughout the period 1500–1785.

Revolutionary and Napoleonic France infused new ideals of nationalism and citizenship into this dynamic by fueling warfare with huge numbers of volunteers and conscripts. French mobilization for total war under the young Napoleon Bonaparte raised the levels of mobilization throughout Europe as various European nations instituted conscription and other institutions copied from the French. For example, passage of income and wealth taxes in France in 1793 and in the early Napoleonic era appears to have stimulated the Dutch, English, and Austrians to pass similar taxes in the last years of the eighteenth century. But the rise in military expenditures was the most direct and pronounced effect of the French model. From 1790 to 1815 British military expenditures grew by 700 percent, while total British state spending increased by 300 percent.

In the nineteenth and twentieth centuries similar dramatic expansions in state revenue extraction and spending followed each major escalation of warfare by newly industrialized and nationalistic states and peoples. With World War I, state expenditures for the first time began to exceed 10 percent of the national production of large nations. Between 1913 and 1917 spending as a percentage of gross national product (GNP) jumped from roughly 10 percent to 34 percent in France, from 7 percent to 57 percent in Great Britain, and from 2 percent to 24 percent in the United States.

These increases in national spending, buoyed by increases in nations' domestic incentives and compensation for war mobilization (in forms as varied as soldiers' compensation and general public pensions), did not return to prewar levels. By 1924 spending had settled at about 20 percent of GNP in France and at 16 percent in Great Britain, although it fell back to 4 percent in the United States.

Military spending as a percentage of national spending grew explosively during World War II, hitting peaks of 42 percent, 61 percent, and 64 percent of GNP, respectively, in the United States, Germany, and Great Britain. Moreover, domestic spending once more grew in tandem with military spending, and total postwar spending remained (once again) at levels well above those of the prewar period: at 25 percent of GNP in the United States and at more than 35 percent in Germany and Great Britain. U.S. spending had increased by 600 percent from comparable 1930 levels, while spending in Germany and Great Britain had increased 300 percent. Much of the growth in spending from 1930 to 1950 represented increased social spending, for such purposes as social insurance payments, education, job training, public works, and buoying up of consumer demand. The increase in social spending was a result of the rise of the welfare state.

The Multifunctional State

From their first appearance, states were involved in managing their relations with other states and regulating the relations of their subjects or citizens with other nations and their peoples. These activities included diplomatic relations, migration, war, war preparations, and deterrence of war. Early states also had to undertake the financing and administration of these international activities. By the early modern era some states were extensively involved in regulating their citizens' roles in property ownership, commerce, and so forth. They also made expenditures to improve the national infrastructure, building roads, schools, port facilities, and courts. They undertook other activities thought to be crucial to economic prosperity and military capability.

In the late nineteenth and early twentieth centuries the functions of the state proliferated. States began to address risks to health, income, and general welfare posed by the new industrial order. For example, early factories posed grave threats to life and limb; marketplace employers fired workers more freely than feudal patrons; and a slow shredding of the extended family tore up a traditional safety net. Fortunately, democratic movements and institutions opened up new avenues for the newly at-risk populations.

Varied philosophical and political orientations guided policy responses to the new risks: patriarchal and progressive-liberal, social Christian and communist, social democratic and Christian democratic. As diverse as they were, however, these orientations shared certain themes relating to the communitarian redirection, or revision, of the liberal-capitalist order. They also tended to focus on similar kinds of programs, such as child-labor laws, industrial accident insurance, and old-age and unemployment insurance, if not necessarily health insurance or child allowances. There was more divergence on other measures, such as those for fiscal and monetarist macroeconomic stabilization. Only some governments pursued full-employment goals and offered job-training assistance.

Capitalist economic development and democracy appear to have been important preconditions for the proliferation of government functions, especially social security measures. By the end of World War I, almost all substantially industrialized nations (except for a few marginal cases like Spain) had adopted a social insurance policy covering work accidents. In addition, the ten sovereign nations that adopted three out of four major types of social insurance programs—old age and disability insurance, sickness insurance, work accident insurance, and unemployment compensation insurance—were among the twenty most economically developed nations in the world. Moreover, nearly all the nations that underwent economic development early on (c. 1918) were political democracies. The exceptions were a few monarchies (Austria, Germany, and Spain) that could claim active and influential, though circumscribed, parliamentary and party politics.

Within the developed democratic nations, differences in particular aspects of democratic politics remained important for the adoption of social insurance measures and the development of social insurance policy. Partisan differences in governmental leadership became the driving force behind social reforms during the first half of the twentieth century. Before the Great Depression began in 1929, liberal parties, pressured and aided by labor unions and parties (the so-called lib-lab coalitions), led the way in countries where liberal parties were strong. In Belgium and the Netherlands, where liberals were weak, Catholic parties with ample labor constituencies pioneered reforms. During the 1930s social democratic governments took the lead in the Scandinavian nations and in Australia and New Zealand. These were paralleled by the reform-oriented governments of Franklin Delano Roosevelt in the United States and Mackenzie King in Canada. During and after World War II, social democratic governments, complemented by Christian democratic governments, enacted virtually all social insurance and related income and job security reforms.

The social insurance reforms of the capitalist democracies in the 1930s and 1940s were accompanied and followed by state interventions aimed at recovering or sustaining high levels of employment by means of public works, labor market training and job search policies, and, most important, fiscal stimulation of consumer demand and thus of production and employment. The stimulative fiscal policy was pursued under the influence of the macroeconomic theories of John Maynard Keynes. Indeed, the whole array of employment and social security policies that emerged after World War II was encouraged by Keynes's ideas, which reversed policymakers' attitude toward government spending. Earlier, policymakers' approach to relieving hard times had been to balance the budget; now their approach was to spend, even to engage in deficit spending.

During the Keynesian era from 1950 to 1980, government spending and taxation as a percentage of gross domestic product (GDP) in the most affluent capitalist democracies rose from an average of 25 percent to about 50 percent. The goals of the Keynesian welfare state with regard to employment, stabilization, and growth appear to have complemented the reduction of risks and inequalities sought by these policies. Between the 1930s and the 1960s average rates of unemployment in the sixteen most affluent capitalist democracies fell from more than 15 percent to less than 5 percent. The percentage of normal income that could be reclaimed from state social insurance programs everywhere increased dramatically. In many of the small democracies of western Europe, income-replacement levels approached 100 percent. In combination with effective "high employment" policies, this strategy virtually eliminated poverty in Scandinavia, the Netherlands, and Austria.

Among less developed nations, the rates of adoption and financing of social insurance programs have lagged behind those in affluent democracies. Yet adoption of such programs has spread widely, through a process of diffusion characterized by demonstration in developed countries and imitation in developing countries.

In communist countries, state command economies were put in place by midcentury. In such economies the state produced and distributed most of the goods and services and even consumed much of what was produced during the period 1950–1990. In these countries, even without considering intrusions of party agents and state police into private life, state penetration into the lives of subjects reached unprecedented levels. These countries lacked the aid of political democracy (that is, competitive election of government leaders by a wide franchise of citizens) to subject state intervention to a measure of institutionalized citizen control. Nonetheless, communist concepts of citizens' socioeconomic, if not civil or representative, rights were often lofty, encompassing rights to free medical care and gainful work. Before the economic and political exhaustion and unraveling of the communist system in the late 1980s, communist delivery of the material goods promised to the average citizen was substantial, though it never rivaled that of social democratic, capitalist nations.

Crisis and Reconsideration

Between 1973 and 1983 the long postwar economic expansion of the West and its high levels of consumer, entrepreneurial, and state economic confidence were severely shaken by events. In the early 1970s the system of fixed exchange rates that had prevailed since the late 1940s collapsed, undoing the ability of the massive U.S. economy (with its costly arsenal) to finance itself without risk to the value of the dollar and without increases in U.S. interest rates. The price of oil increased more than 300 percent, and the prices of wheat and other agricultural commodities doubled or tripled, driving up producer and consumer costs worldwide. Stagflation (simultaneous recession and inflation) handcuffed Keynesian policy instruments, such as governmental deficit spending to stimulate demand when productive resources were underutilized.

Keynesian techniques could not arrange trade-offs between inflation and unemployment once the two had exchanged their age-old negative correlation (more inflation, less unemployment, and vice versa) for the positive one (more inflation, more unemployment) of the stagflationary period. Keynesian policy making came under assault, and policymakers' favorable predisposition toward spending eroded, cutting off the expansion of programs and budgets. Moreover, increased U.S. military spending triggered a huge explosion in the U.S. public debt, and the increase in the long-term interest rates needed to finance the debt raised international interest rates, placing a high rent on the operations of an already sluggish international economy.

The events that undercut Keynesian rationales and material resources for state expansion in the affluent democracies hit the developing nations with a massive transfer of international loans and then with demands for debt repayment. Thus the economic strength and state expansion of these nations suffered especially severely.

The communist countries (in particular, those dominated by the Soviet Union) were by no means insulated from these events. Indeed, the transfer of international loans and, later, the burden of their repayment posed special difficulty for them. Moreover, the accelerating U.S. military spending posed a direct competitive challenge to the Soviet-dominated countries that sorely strained their adaptive capacities. The breakup of Soviet domination and of the Soviet Union itself in the late 1980s and early 1990s meant that the fullest state retrenchment occurred outside the Western sphere of initial economic (stagflationary) and ideological (Keynesian) crisis. The command economies disintegrated, while in Western democracies the expansion of the welfare state merely slowed, and developing states mainly retrenched their economic and welfare functions and outlays.

Although such leading welfare states as Sweden and the Netherlands were also retrenching in the early 1990s, the interventionist state still found supporters. The public industrial policies of Japan and Germany were still admired. As of the early 1990s the direction of movement in the public-private mix was unclear for the affluent democracies taken as a whole.

In the developing world, a resurgence of democracy has been accompanied by an inexorable debt burden and the continuing spread of laissez-faire, anti-Keynesian, and antiwelfare ideas. Yet democracy typically enhanced state intervention in social security during the twentieth century, although preferences for a substantially market-oriented, public-private mix remained influential. The late twentieth-century debt crisis strengthened the control of the International Monetary Fund (IMF), a transnational bank with great power over international credit. It reinforced IMF calls for international economic openness and domestic "restructuring." This meant a decided tilt toward the free market (for example, lowered tariff barriers and private purchase of formerly nationalized firms). Nonetheless, the sum of the forces acting on the public-private mix remains difficult to tally. Whether or to what extent an overall reversal in trends toward increased state intervention has taken place is an open question.

A decisive reversal of modern trends toward increased state intervention can be clearly seen in the emergent market-oriented economies of East Central Europe. Even in those countries, however, it is impossible to predict what type of transformation of Western political economic precedents will carry the day.

See also *Capitalism; Development, Economic; Laissez-faire economic theory; Republics, Commercial; Welfare, Promotion of.*

Alexander M. Hicks

BIBLIOGRAPHY

Bunce, Valerie, and Alexander Hicks. "Capitalisms, Socialisms and Democracy." *Political Power and Social Theory* 6 (1987): 89–132.

Collier, David, and Richard E. Messick. "Prerequisites versus Diffusion: Testing Alternative Explanations of Social Security Adoption." *American Political Science Review* 69 (1975): 1299–1315.

Kolberg, Jon Eivind. *The Study of Welfare State Regimes.* Armonk, N.Y.: M. E. Sharpe, 1992.

Maddison, Angus. *Dynamic Forces in Capitalist Development: A Long-run Comparative View.* Oxford and New York: Oxford University Press, 1991.

Mann, Michael. *The Sources of Social Power: A History of Power from the Beginning to* A.D. *1760.* Vol. 1. Cambridge and New York: Cambridge University Press, 1986.

Poggi, Gianfranco. *The State: Its Nature, Development, and Prospects.* Stanford, Calif.: Stanford University Press; Oxford: Polity, 1990.

Przworski, Adam. *Capitalism and Social Democracy.* Cambridge and New York: Cambridge University Press, 1985.

Scharpf, Fritz. *Crisis and Choice in European Social Democracy.* Ithaca, N.Y.: Cornell University Press, 1987.

Tilly, Charles, ed. *The Formation of Nation States in Western Europe.* Princeton: Princeton University Press, 1975.

Webber, Caroline, and Aaron Wildavsky. *A History of Taxation and Expenditures in the Western World.* New York: Simon and Schuster, 1986.

States' rights in the United States

States' rights in the United States refers to the principle that the national government arose from the consent of the state governments and thus state governments, which gave up some of their rights to a central government, retain other rights, powers, and responsibilities that the federal government cannot abolish or assume. States' rights as a principle associated with American democratic thought predates the U.S. Constitution. To understand the contemporary discussions related to the appropriate balance of power between the federal government and the states, it is useful to consider the preconstitutional as well as the constitutional debates that addressed this concern. Also relevant to an appreciation of the role of states' rights concerns is the historical evolution of the balance of power between the states and the federal government since 1789.

The Constitutional Debate

In the years preceding the ratification of the U.S. Constitution, the states were the primary power holders in the newly formed nation. Under the Articles of Confederation (1781) the central government was assigned relatively limited authority and power. Most power and governmental authority resided in the separate states, and people were citizens of the separate states. The confederation that was approved by the former colonies was a weak union of strong states.

The confederate arrangement was not successful, and so there was pressure to alter the system. The resulting changes were embodied in the Constitution in 1789. Although the central government in the new union was granted considerably more power than had been the case under the Articles of Confederation, the states retained considerable influence and power.

The debate that emerged between the Federalists and the Antifederalists shed considerable light on the issue of relative power to be granted to the state units and the central unit of government. Both the Antifederalists and the Federalists were advocates of republican government and popular government. What distinguished the two groups was the form of republicanism they preferred and the type of federal government they believed would best lead to the society they envisioned. The Antifederalists were against the Constitution as proposed; generally, they believed that republics had to be small to survive—not unlike the ancient Greek city-states. This position was for preserving the existing situation.

The Antifederalists could invoke Montesquieu, the French philosopher whose work influenced some of the intellectual elites of this era. Montesquieu had written that the basis of republican government is a small unit where citizens know each other, where they share habits and values, and where they are not likely to become too unequal in their fortunes. He believed that without these three conditions in place the citizens of a republic will not trust each other enough to agree on policies—including how to prevent tyranny.

The Federalists, in contrast, found the reasons for establishing a large and complex republic to be compelling. James Madison presented this position very clearly in *Federalist* No. 39 as well as in *Federalist* Nos. 10, 37, and 51. He maintained that the new constitution preserved the roles of the states. Along with the other Federalists, he wanted a union that was neither fully federal nor fully national but rather a melding of both forms. Madison assumed that the states would continue to play a major role and would remain the predominant partners in the new nation. Their position in the federal-state nexus was secure.

The drafters of the Constitution included protections for the states even as they granted the national government supremacy in cases of conflict between the states and the central government. In Article I, Section 8, seventeen specific grants of power were provided to the national government as well as the power "To make all Laws that shall be necessary and proper for carrying into Execution the foregoing Powers, and all other Powers vested by this Constitution in the Government of the United States or in any Department or Officer thereof." This provision, known as the necessary and proper clause, along with Article VI—the national supremacy clause, which declares the national law to supersede all others—has been the basis of extensive federal power.

However, numerous protections of states' rights as well as denials of federal actions are explicitly stated too. Moreover, just in case there was any ambiguity about the protection of the states' roles, the Tenth Amendment notes, "The powers not delegated to the United States by the Constitution, nor prohibited by it to the States, are reserved to the States respectively, or to the people."

Changing Balance

The balance of power between the states and the national government was reasonably clear in 1789. But in the years that followed the ratification of the Constitution, new issues arose and new questions were posed for the role of the states in the federal union. For example, John C. Calhoun in his 1831 Fort Hill Address endorsed the notion of states' rights or nullification as a fundamental principle of the American federal system. He believed that the states should be able to act unhampered by the national government in their own spheres of authority.

In the early years of the republic the need for cooperation between the federal government and the state governments did become apparent. Some activities were more appropriately carried out by the central government than by the many states. Thus the Bank of the United States was formed, state war debts were assumed by the central government, and some early coordination of transportation (in the building of canals, for example) was initiated. Also, the Supreme Court under the leadership of Chief Justice John Marshall helped to strengthen the central government in relation to the states. In *McCulloch v. Maryland* (1819), Marshall wrote that the union was not generally left dependent on the states "for the execution of the great powers assigned to it."

The appointment of Roger Taney to the Supreme Court acted as a check on the growth of federal power. Most notably, in *Dred Scott v. Sandford* (1857), Chief Justice Taney argued a states' rights position when he reasoned that the Missouri Compromise was unconstitutional and that state laws governing slavery were supreme. (The Missouri Compromise, passed by Congress in 1820, prohibited slavery in the Northwest Territory, while permitting the rest of the states to determine their own rules regarding the institution.)

In the years prior to the Civil War, despite some narrow national interventions in the activities of the states, questions regarding the appropriate balance of power between the jurisdictions were limited. The Tenth Amendment was seen as governing numerous relationships between the federal government and the states. In 1854, when President Franklin Pierce vetoed legislation providing land to the states for facilities for the mentally handicapped, he stated that public charity was the business of the states, not of the federal government.

The Civil War (1861–1865) led to a refocusing of power

relationships between the central government and the states. The secession of the southern states from the Union and the resultant mobilization of the northern states to maintain the Union strengthened the national government. During the Civil War, President Abraham Lincoln was careful not to end slavery in the states that remained in the Union. His Emancipation Proclamation ended slavery only in the states that had seceded from the Union. Not until 1866 and the ratification of the Thirteenth Amendment was slavery abolished. The ratification of the Fourteenth and Fifteenth Amendments led gradually to incursions by the federal government into the sovereignty of the states, as the federal government began to protect individual rights more aggressively. Since the Fourteenth Amendment was added to the Constitution in 1868, the federal government has extended the protections of the Bill of Rights to citizens in their relationships with the states.

In 1862 Congress had enacted the Morrill Act. This legislation provided that public lands be granted to the states. Public institutions of higher education (land-grant colleges) were supported with the profits from land sales. In return, Congress exacted some requirements from the states. Military instruction and training in agriculture and the mechanical arts must be offered at the land-grant institutions. In addition, the states had to make annual reports to Congress on the status of these institutions. The precedent was set for the federal government to demand minimum standards in exchange for resources granted to the states. This principle became the basis of federal oversight of state programs in the twentieth century, when more significant federal funds were made available to the states.

In the latter half of the nineteenth century the industrial base of the nation expanded rapidly, and Congress enacted legislation to control interstate commerce. The Sherman Antitrust Act of 1890 and the Clayton Act of 1914 were passed by Congress. In later years, Congress enacted further measures designed to control other facets of industry and commerce. Although commerce within a state was not affected by actions at the federal level, industry and commerce became steadily more national in scope.

The adoption of the Sixteenth Amendment to the Constitution (1913), which permitted the institution of a federal income tax, provided the national government with a new and powerful mechanism with which to limit and potentially control states' actions—money. By 1922 the federal government received 60 percent of its revenues from the income tax. This tax provided the basis for an increased sharing of revenues with the states and local government, which had much less elastic revenue sources at their disposal.

The Federal Aid Highway Act, which Congress enacted in 1916, established the grant-in-aid mechanism for the disbursal of some federal money to the states. For every dollar spent by a state on highways—up to a predetermined limit—the federal government would provide a dollar match for the program. A new sort of federal intervention into states' activities was institutionalized, and in the years that followed additional federal grant-in-aid programs were established. However, it took the economic dislocations of the Great Depression that began in 1929 for the grant mechanism to be understood and for the national government's power to control state activities to be appreciated. A more complete appreciation of the implications of this tool was not gained until the 1960s, when the War on Poverty legislation was enacted.

The states challenged the federal grant-in-aid mechanism. In 1923 the Supreme Court heard *Massachusetts v. Mellon* and *Frothingham v. Mellon.* In these two cases the states sought to prevent the secretary of the Treasury from spending federal funds to implement the Shepard-Towner Act (which from 1921 to 1929 provided maternal and child care). The Supreme Court held that it did not have jurisdiction. In so doing it let the act and the grants mechanism stand. In 1937 the Supreme Court considered the question of the constitutionality of federal grants again. In *Steward Machine Co. v. Davis,* the Court upheld the constitutionality of grants when it held the Social Security Act to be a cooperative attempt among public agencies.

The Contemporary Relationship

The United States today is a diversified and multiethnic nation. The various populations, with their various demands, are spread across the country. Increasingly, New York, California, Illinois, and Florida, for example, are becoming more alike in the problems they must confront. Ready access to modern communications, personal and mass transportation, and public education have all fostered a national culture. The states, however, are not equally able to cope with their problems because economic development and resources are not evenly distributed. Since the 1960s it has become clear to many people that a democratic nation cannot afford to have the equivalent of developed and less developed nations alongside each other. The national government has been pressured to develop programs and provide funding for social policies. This pressure has led to major federal interventions into areas once assumed to be the states' responsibilities. Thus federal involvement in public welfare, health care, food programs, and education have eclipsed the prerogatives of the states.

The funding for such programs has brought with it greater federal regulation, thus impinging on the rights of the states to set public policy. Regulations are developed to direct and standardize the implementation of specific laws; cross-cutting regulations (that is, those regulations with which all recipients of any federal monies must comply regardless of the specific nature of the program being funded) are developed to impose social and cultural standards on citizens in all states. For example, any agency—public or private—that receives federal funds must comply with regulations for affirmative action, freedom of information, and access for people with disabilities. All the states receive federal money, and thus all the states are affected by federal regulation.

There are still policy areas in which the states are autonomous and in which there is no significant national government involvement. For example, domestic relations, intrastate commerce, and property law are areas of almost exclusive state activity.

The mechanism used by the federal government to provide money to state and local governments remains the grant-in-aid. Formulas for distributing funds started to become more elaborate when Congress enacted the Highway Act of 1956, which gave states nine dollars for every dollar they spent in the construction of the interstate highway system. Most of the large grant programs such as Medicare and Aid to Families with Dependent Children distribute funds to the states on the basis of a congressionally determined formula. Many of the smaller programs distribute funds on the basis of a project grant mechanism, which requires that states apply for federal funding. The funding agency in the bureaucracy that administers the program in question establishes the procedures and the size of the grant.

The Great Society legislation of the 1960s provided for an expanded grant-in-aid mechanism to distribute money to the states for domestic service programs, such as Medicaid and compensatory education. Most of the grants distributed funds to the states and localities to help run programs that many people assumed were legitimately in the domain of states' powers and responsibilities. For example, education, training, and safety services all began to receive federal dollars. With the money came more rules and regulations regarding how the money could be spent. Also, cross-cutting regulations increased in number.

During President Richard M. Nixon's administration (1969–1974), some efforts were made to loosen the program-specific regulations by developing new grant mechanisms—block grants and general revenue sharing. Block grants provided the states with money to operate in a designated policy area as opposed to money for a specific program. Also, no matching funds had to be provided by the states in order to receive the block grant money. Block grants are still made, but most federal grants (more than 600) and most of the grant money ($205 billion in fiscal 1993) goes to the states through categorical grants-in-aid. Revenue sharing provided the states with money that could be used for any purpose (with no state matching funds needed). This program was phased out in the 1980s.

Federal grants provide the states with funds for a wide variety of domestic programs—including programs as diverse as housing, public welfare and services, education, highways, and the construction of firehouses. The methods that have been developed to fund the programs have become much more complicated than a simple 50-50 or 90-10 split. The use of computers makes it possible to develop very elaborate funding formulas that can include such criteria as population distribution, state income, state tax effort, degree of state industrial development, and extent of poverty.

Because members of Congress have to go home and win elections, every state seems to get its share of federal grants. The states do not object to the money coming in. In fact, state and local officials lobby Congress very diligently for federal money. They do object to all the rules and regulations that accompany the money. They also object to mandates that state and local governments comply with federal rules and regulations without getting assistance to cover the costs associated with compliance. In fact, the states and localities increasingly need federal money to run their programs and pay their bills, in part because the federal government has a greater capacity to raise money. Also, most states and localities are required by state law to balance their budgets; they cannot go into debt to fund important programs. The federal government does not face this restriction.

In some ways the states and localities are needy and dependent. Within the states there is conflict between the desire to benefit from the federal largesse and the desire to be less regulated and to develop and maintain programs without federal oversight. Nonetheless, in the United States the imposition of rules and regulations, as well as the issuance of mandates that go along with the necessary granting of federal funds for state and local programs, is part and parcel of being a unified nation.

The language of states' rights is sometimes used to justify federal budget cuts, easing of federal regulations, and privatization of services. It is not always clear that states' rights are the primary concern of people who invoke the concept. It sometimes appears that concerns with profit making are really driving the debate.

Daniel Elazar, a noted scholar of federalism, has argued that at all times in American history there have been cooperative programming and efforts between the federal government and the states. It seems that the federal actor has become the more dominant player and the states have seen their relative strength in the federal-state relationship diminish. The issue of states' rights in contemporary politics is still alive, but it does not seem as central to policy debates as it did 200 years ago.

See also *Antifederalists; Federalism; Federalists; Madison, James; Secession; United States Constitution.* In Documents section, see *Constitution of the United States (1787).*

Marian Lief Palley

BIBLIOGRAPHY

Beer, Samuel H. *To Make a Nation: The Rediscovery of American Federalism.* Cambridge: Harvard University Press, Belknap Press, 1993.

CSF Notebook. "A Guide to the Federalist." Philadelphia: Center for the Study of Federalism, Temple University, fall 1988.

Elazar, Daniel J. *The American Partnership: Intergovernmental Cooperation in the Nineteenth-Century United States.* Chicago: University of Chicago Press, 1962.

———. "Federalist-State Collaboration in the Nineteenth-Century United States." In *Cooperation and Conflict: Readings in American Federalism,* edited by Daniel J. Elazar et al. Itasca, Ill.: Peacock, 1969.

The Federalist Papers. Edited by Clinton Rossiter. New York: New American Library, 1961.

Goldwin, Robert A., ed. *A Nation of States.* Chicago: Rand McNally, 1963.

Hale, George E., and Marian Lief Palley. *The Politics of Federal Grants.* Washington, D.C.: CQ Press, 1981.

Robertson, David Brian. "The States in the Federal System." In *Policy Studies Encyclopedia.* 2d ed. Edited by Stuart Nagel. New York: Marcel Dekker, 1994.

Walker, David. *Toward a Functioning Federalism.* Cambridge, Mass.: Winthrop, 1981.

Wright, Deil. *Understanding Intergovernmental Relations.* Pacific Grove, Calif.: Brooks/Cole, 1988.

Suárez González, Adolfo

Prime minister of Spain from July 1976 through January 1981 and principal architect of the Spanish transition to democracy. Suárez (1932–   ), in his leadership role following the death of Gen. Francisco Franco in November 1975, contributed decisively to the processes of peacefully dismantling the former authoritarian regime, restructuring the Spanish state, and establishing a stable democratic regime.

Born into a lower-middle-class family in Avila, Suárez received a law degree from the University of Salamanca. After a series of minor positions within the Franco regime, he was appointed civil governor of the province of Segovia in 1969, then director of the state television system. He became vice–secretary general of Franco's National Movement, a post he held until June 1975. He was minister and secretary general of the National Movement in the first post-Franco government of Carlos Arias Navarro (December 1975–June 1976). His plans for political reform were frustrated by the lack of effective support from Arias. Suárez's fortunes changed with a speech he gave to the parliament calling for the establishment of political pluralism and a multiparty democracy in Spain. He so impressed King Juan Carlos (who succeeded Franco as head of state) that the king replaced Arias with Suárez as prime minister.

Suárez quickly began dismantling the Franquist regime, using the very institutions, procedures, and legal principles established under Franco. Thus the transition to democracy took place within a continuous legal framework and was supported by the legitimate authority of Juan Carlos, Franco's chosen successor. Other important features of this transition were steady progress toward liberalization, the convening of democratic elections prior to a stated deadline, constant dialogue between Suárez and leaders of the anti-Franco opposition (which took place in private so as to facilitate openness and insulate opposition leaders from pressures from more radical sectors of their clienteles), and demobilization of opposition forces.

Continued use of some of these procedures, especially private meetings among party leaders, facilitated the resolution of crucial and potentially divisive issues regarding the writing of a new constitution (1977–1978) and the enactment of autonomy statutes for the Basque and Catalan regions (in 1979). Perhaps the most important aspect of the politics of consensus involved abandonment of majoritarian, winner-take-all rules of the game and a commitment to enacting constitutional documents that would not be regarded as unacceptable by any significant political or social group.

But the politics of consensus took its toll on Suárez's political career. Important groups within his own party, the Union of the Democratic Center, felt that he had gone too far in making concessions to Socialist, Communist, and regional nationalist opposition forces. Some government ministers felt that Suárez devoted too little time to managing his cabinet, policy making, and participating in parliamentary debate. Thus, when his party suffered setbacks in a series of regional elections in 1980, many of the party's leaders concluded that he had become an electoral liability.

After much public squabbling and criticism, Suárez resigned as head of the Union of the Democratic Center in January 1981. Perhaps his finest hour occurred during the vote of investiture of his chosen successor as prime minister, Leopoldo Calvo Sotelo, when Suárez courageously stood up to rebellious soldiers who had invaded the parliament in a coup attempt. Continuing intraparty struggles led him to form the Democratic and Social Center on

the eve of the disastrous 1982 election. Although this party had some success in the 1986 and 1989 elections, a series of tactical blunders led to a devastating defeat in the May 1991 municipal and regional elections. Suárez resigned as leader of the party the day after the elections and subsequently retired from political life.

See also *Spain.*

Richard Gunther

BIBLIOGRAPHY

Gunther, Richard, Giacomo Sani, and Goldie Shabad. *Spain after Franco: The Making of a Competitive Party System.* Berkeley: University of California Press, 1986.

Linz, Juan J. "Innovative Leadership in the Transition to Democracy and a New Democracy: The Case of Spain." In *Innovative Leaders in International Politics,* edited by Gabriel Sheffer. Albany: State University of New York Press, 1993.

Morán, Gregorio. *Adolfo Suárez: Historia de una ambición.* Barcelona: Planeta, 1979.

Sudan

Independent country, located in Northeast Africa, that has had a troubled and violent political history since independence in 1956. The largest country in Africa, Sudan is split by severe social cleavages that have led to alternating periods of civilian and military rule. The most fundamental cleavage is that between the predominantly Islamic north and the culturally African south. Both regions also have ethnic and ideological divisions, and the north is divided along the lines of various Islamic sects.

Sudan's nearly 600 ethnic groups speak more than 400 languages and dialects, although Arabic and English are commonly spoken by the elite. People identifying themselves as Arabs are the largest single group, constituting nearly 40 percent of the total population and a majority in the north. Most of the residents of the south speak Nilotic languages; the Dinka, Nuer, and Shilluk are the major ethnic groups there.

Colonial Legacy

From 1821 to 1885 Egypt governed Sudan but viewed the region predominantly as a source of slaves. In the early 1880s a Sudanese religious leader known as the Mahdi led

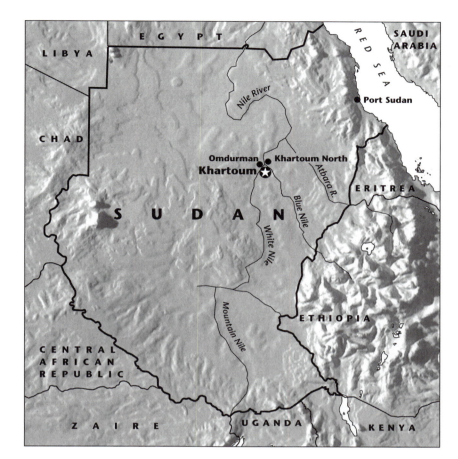

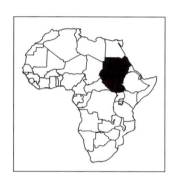

a *jihad* to expel the Egyptians. From 1885 to 1898 the Mahdist regime (known as the Mahdiyah) ruled Sudan. British forces destroyed the Mahdiyah and established joint Anglo-Egyptian control in 1899. Egypt's role in this joint administration was limited, and the British governor general acted as a de facto colonial authority.

The British generated economic activity, such as the Gezira cotton scheme along the Nile, but generally they governed indirectly through local elites, many of them members of the Ansar, the followers of the Mahdi. London closed the south to outsiders, including northern Sudanese, leaving the region isolated and with only limited social services provided by Christian missionaries. The British granted Sudan independence in 1956, after settling issues with Egypt and determining that the south would be part of the new state. The legacy of colonialism, notably the favoritism toward certain northern groups and the differential economic development that favored the north, widened the social cleavages that continue to plague independent Sudan.

Since independence a wide variety of leaders and regime types have sought the basis for stable power without enduring success. Sudan's society consists of a number of well-organized constituencies prone to factionalism. In the north many people have been divided into competing sects based on politically and economically powerful Islamic orders. The Ansar, led by the descendants of the Mahdi, are particularly strong in rural areas. They are organized politically in the Umma Party, led since the 1960s by Sadiq al-Mahdi. The Khatmiyah, a rival sect, is led by the Mirghani family. The Khatmiyah, along with other more secular and urbanized groups, form the core of the Democratic Unionist Party. The Sudanese Communist Party (based in the universities and labor unions) wielded significant political influence in the 1950s and 1960s. The Muslim Brotherhood, which developed in opposition to the communists and to the secularization of Sudanese society, began to cultivate important political support beginning in the mid-1970s and competed in the 1986 elections under the name of the National Islamic Front. The south has been united primarily by its shared apprehension of domination by northern Arabs. Armed insurgencies, led at first by the Anyanya (scorpion) guerrillas and since 1983 by the Sudanese People's Liberation Movement, have resisted the northern-based governments.

Sudan has had extensive if troubled experience with democratic politics. Relatively free multiparty elections were held in 1953 (under British rule), 1958, 1965, 1968, and 1986. Unfortunately, the highly divided nature of Sudanese society has prevented any party from winning a majority of seats. As a result, each parliamentary period has been marked by weak coalition governments, plagued by inter- and intraparty rivalries, corruption, and byzantine maneuvering for partisan or personal gain. The military intervened in 1958, 1969, 1985, and 1989—years when party defections and deadlock prevented effective action to manage Sudan's severe social and economic problems.

Early Years of Independence

The first postindependence government was formed on the basis of multiparty elections for a Constituent Assembly in 1953. These gave the National Unionist Party (the predecessor of the Democratic Unionist Party) the most seats, followed by Umma. Ismail al-Azhari, the first prime minister, lost his support in Parliament to Abdallah Khalil in July 1956. Khalil put together a coalition of Umma supporters and defectors from the National Unionist Party and won the next election in 1958. Southerners participated in the 1958 campaign in a loose association known as the southern liberal bloc. Khalil's governing coalition, however, suffered from factionalism and corruption. The weak regime drifted and threatened to splinter, while challenges mounted from the radical movement, trade unions, and general economic decline.

In November 1958 Khalil organized a "preemptive coup" in collaboration with the army's senior officers. The new regime, led by Maj. Gen. Ibrahim Abbud, banned all political parties but ruled for the next six years with the active support of significant parts of the old elite. In 1963 Abbud established locally elected councils that in turn selected delegates to provincial and central councils. Abbud succeeded in settling a longstanding dispute with Egypt over water rights, and he improved economic conditions. Over time, however, he became increasingly authoritarian and isolated. Opposition developed among radical dissidents in the armed forces and the Communist Party. Most important, Abbud's attempts to impose Arab and Islamic culture on the south escalated the armed resistance in that region.

A general strike and violent riots, known as the October Revolution, overthrew Abbud in November 1964. A transitional regime led by Sir al-Khatim Khalifa tried to create a government based on the new political forces involved in the demonstrations (professional groups and trade unions organized in the United National Front). Eventually, however, this regime proved unable to contain the power of the old establishment (religious leaders, large landowners, merchants). Elections in 1965 gave Umma and the National Unionist Party a majority of seats. No voting took place in the war-torn south until 1967.

The period from 1965 until 1969 saw a variety of weak governments in which leaders tried to build coalitions among the principal political parties. Divisions within Umma made the task of building a strong coalition extremely difficult. Throughout this period Sudan's problems, particularly the war in the south, resisted resolution.

Military Coup and Civil War

This chaotic democratic period ended on May 25, 1969, when a group of radical young officers led by Col. Jaafar Muhammed al-Numeiri seized power. Over the next sixteen years Numeiri experimented with a variety of political structures and made alliances with diverse social groups in an attempt to stabilize and institutionalize his power.

Immediately after the coup, Numeiri banned political parties and ruled through a Revolutionary Command Council. His first cabinet included a number of radical civilians with ties to the Sudanese Communist Party. Numeiri's first battles were against the Ansar sect, which fought government forces for control of Aba Island near Khartoum in March 1970. Next, Numeiri moved against the Communist Party, marginalizing its base until the Communists struck back, staging a nearly successful coup in July 1971. In an effort to establish a new basis for his power, Numeiri dissolved the Revolutionary Command Council and promulgated a new constitution that provided for a presidential form of government. A dubious October 1971 plebiscite endorsed Numeiri for a six-year term with 98.6 percent of the vote.

Following his move against the Communist Party, Numeiri looked to the south as a potential new base of support. In March 1972 Numeiri's government signed the Addis Ababa accords with the Anyanya guerrillas, ending the destructive civil war. This agreement provided the south autonomy with an appointed regional president and an elected Southern Regional Assembly. Elections for the assembly took place in 1973 and 1978. Widely hailed as an indication of Numeiri's leadership, the agreement gave him popular support both in the south and the north and won him international favor.

To further his hold on Sudanese politics, Numeiri organized the Sudan Socialist Union in January 1972 as an all-encompassing umbrella to channel political participation and penetrate the countryside. Numeiri constructed a variety of affiliated professional and mass organizations and a system of local councils that sent delegates to higher provincial councils. Elections in 1974 for a slate of candidates approved by the Sudan Socialist Union created a People's Assembly. The assembly had the authority to pass legislation, but the powerful presidency could veto and rule by decree.

After mending fences with the south, Numeiri's focus shifted to opposition from traditional Muslim groups in the north. The president survived a violent Ansar-inspired coup attempt in July 1976 and the following year opened talks with exiled Ansar leader Sadiq al-Mahdi (then heading the conservative National Front). Numeiri and al-Mahdi reached an agreement that allowed members of the traditional sectarian parties to participate as individuals in the 1978 People's Assembly elections. Although still technically a single-party system, the Sudan Socialist Union lost its coherence, and the People's Assembly broke down because of factionalism and corruption.

By 1983 Numeiri had become increasingly dependent on the traditional sectarian parties for support. As a result, he abandoned his greatest accomplishment, the peace agreement with the south. In June 1983 Numeiri unilaterally subdivided the south, effectively annulling the Addis Ababa agreements and unleashing renewed armed conflict. In September 1983, in an effort to undercut his fundamentalist opponents and consolidate his constituency in the north, Numeiri adopted *shari'a* (law based on the religious principles of Islam). In response, the Sudanese People's Liberation Movement began an insurgency in the south that quickly frustrated Khartoum's ability to govern.

Numeiri's political dominance withered in the face of a popular uprising (the *intifada*) provoked by spiraling inflation, corruption, and strikes that followed currency devaluations and removal of food subsidies. Pushed by mobilized urban groups of professionals, the military overthrew Numeiri on April 6, 1985, and formed a Transitional Military Council. Under the leadership of Lt. Gen. Abd al-Rahman Siwar al-Dahab, the military council dismantled the Sudan Socialist Union, legalized the old political parties, held elections, and turned over power after one year.

More than forty political parties competed in the generally free elections in April 1986. No voting took place in 37 of the 68 southern constituencies, however, because of continuing civil conflict. Southern insurgents in the Sudanese People's Liberation Movement under the leadership of John Garang demanded that the military give up power immediately and refused to participate in the elections.

Of the 264 constituencies where polling occurred in 1986, Umma won 99 seats, the Democratic Unionist Party won 63, the National Islamic Front (the political organization of the Muslim Brotherhood) won 51, and other regional parties (including several based among southerners) won the remainder. Umma leader Sadiq al-Mahdi formed a coalition government that included Umma, the Democratic Unionist Party, and several of the regional parties. It was opposed by the National Islamic Front and the Communist Party.

During the next three years, a continuous series of crises developed, leading to six successive coalition governments. Yet Prime Minister al-Mahdi and his coalition partners opened talks with Garang and the People's Liberation Movement and seemed to be near a peace agreement. The military stepped in again in June 1989, however, aborting both the peace process and the democratic experiment.

Gen. Umar Hassan Ahmad al-Bashir led the coup and established a Revolutionary Command Council of National Salvation. The military dissolved the elected legislature, arrested al-Mahdi and other leaders, and banned political parties again. Relying on the fundamentalist National Islamic Front for support, al-Bashir's government sharply limited political activity and pursued a brutal war against insurgents in the south. A constitutional conference in April 1991 failed to resolve the deep and bitter conflict between those who insisted on *shari'a* and those who demanded a secular constitution. Umma and the Democratic Unionist Party operated in exile and in 1990 formed an alliance with the People's Liberation Movement to create the National Democratic Alliance. The alliance has stated its commitment to democracy and a secular constitution.

Through the early 1990s Sudan suffered from an authoritarian form of government, extensive human rights violations, and a devastating civil war. The historical experience with democracy—most notably the parliamentary government established at independence in 1956 and the two parliamentary periods that followed military rule in 1964 and 1986—demonstrates the latent strength of the nation's democratic tradition. Elected government is a widely held aspiration of the Sudanese people. Despite its prevalence, military rule is regarded as an aberration, a temporary condition until new elections can be held. As its deeply rooted and powerful political movements indicate, the nation's civil society is well organized even if highly divided. Although elected governments have failed to endure in Sudan in the past, further efforts to build democracy are likely.

See also *Africa, Subsaharan; Fundamentalism; Secession.*

Terrence Lyons

BIBLIOGRAPHY

Bechtold, Peter. "More Turbulence in Sudan: A New Politics This Time?" *Middle East Journal* 44 (autumn 1990): 579–595.

Deng, Francis. *War of Visions: Conflict of Identities in the Sudan.* Washington, D.C.: Brookings Institution, 1995.

Holt, P. M., and M. W. Daly. *A History of the Sudan: from the Coming of Islam to the Present Day.* 4th ed. London: Longman, 1986.

Medani, Khalid. "Sudan's Human and Political Crisis." *Current History* 92 (May 1993): 203–207.

Niblock, Tim. *Class and Power in Sudan: The Dynamics of Sudanese Politics, 1898–1985.* Albany: State University of New York Press; London: Macmillan, 1987.

Woodward, Peter. *Sudan, 1898–1989: The Unstable State.* Boulder, Colo.: Lynne Rienner, 1990.

Sukarno

Sukarno

Leader of the struggle for Indonesian independence from Dutch rule and first president (1945–1967) of the resulting Republic of Indonesia. As a young man Sukarno (1901–1970) became the protégé of the leader of the Islamic Association, Indonesia's first mass national movement. In 1927, after studying engineering in Bandung, West Java, he founded what became the Indonesian National Party. The party sought full independence from Dutch rule. Using his talent for oratory, Sukarno cultivated national support for that goal across ethnic, religious, and class boundaries. The Dutch arrested him in 1929 and again in 1933.

Between 1942 and 1945 Sukarno cooperated with the Japanese, who occupied the Netherlands Indies as its "liberators." On August 18, 1945, acting in the vacuum between the defeat of Japan at the end of World War II and the return of Dutch forces, a committee to prepare independence named Sukarno president of the Republic of Indonesia; he had proclaimed its existence the previous day. During the following struggle against Dutch reoccupation, Sukarno tried to keep the new republic unified through alternating phases of fighting and negotiating. In 1949 the Dutch finally acknowledged Indonesian sovereignty.

During the ensuing period of parliamentary rule, Sukarno grew impatient with what he considered the inability of "fifty percent plus one democracy," as he called it, to sustain a nation increasingly divided along ethnoreligious and regional lines. He advocated a system of "guided democracy" in 1957 and implemented it two years later. In that authoritarian system he tried to balance and unite nationalist, religious, and communist organizations and beliefs. Meantime, the economy deteriorated and the balance of contending forces grew more precarious.

In 1965 the assassination of six anticommunist generals shattered the balance. Surviving army officers blamed the communists and destroyed them or tolerated their destruction in a bloodbath that helped General Suharto to elbow Sukarno out of power and replace him as acting president in 1967. Suharto became full president a year later. His movements restricted and his stirring voice silenced, Sukarno died in 1970.

Sukarno's name retained nationalist appeal. In 1993 his daughter, Megawati Sukarnoputri, was elected head of the opposition party into which her father's party had been folded more than twenty years before.

See also *Indonesia.*

Donald K. Emmerson

Sun Yat-sen

Chinese revolutionary leader and statesman who advocated democracy and envisioned the way democracy should develop in China. In 1921 Sun Yat-sen (1866–1925) became the provisional president of the first republic in Chinese history.

Sun (Sun Zhongshan in pinyin) was born in a village south of Guangzhou (Canton) two years after the devastating Taiping Rebellion against the Qing dynasty had ended. He grew up as the last Chinese empire was being dismembered by foreign states. Sun's early education was in his village and in Hawaii; he then studied medicine in Hong Kong. In 1894 he went to Tianjin to present a proposal for China's reform to Li Hongzhang, one of the most powerful officials in the empire. When Li refused to see him, Sun abandoned medicine and turned to revolution. He believed that only the violent overthrow of the Qing monarchy would save China and build new moral and political foundations. For the next fifteen years Sun lived abroad, devoting his life to revolution. He became the leader of the overseas revolutionary movement and organized the Chinese United League on April 6, 1906, in Japan.

Formation of the Republic

A military uprising erupted in Wuchang in Hubei Province on October 10, 1911. Sun's United League was instrumental in forcing the Qing emperor to abdicate. The league formed the new Republic of China, with Sun as provisional president. On February 13, 1912, he resigned, handing power over to the new president, Yuan Shikai, China's most powerful military leader. This act allowed

Sun Yat-sen

the power-hungry Yuan to try to become another emperor.

Yuan's grab for power in 1914 crippled the new republic. Regional military leaders expanded their power in various provinces. For the next two decades China was plunged into chaos as the warlords fought one another. From 1914 until his death in 1925, Sun devoted himself to building a new political party and a small, modern army to reunify China. He was assisted by young, loyal supporters such as Chiang Kai-shek, Hu Han-min, and Wang Ching-wei. Sun established the Chinese Nationalist Party, or Kuomintang, on October 10, 1919, and began carving out a small revolutionary base in Guangzhou City and its environs in 1920.

At first Sun sought financial and military support from the Western powers, but they rebuffed him, regarding him as weak and ineffectual. In desperation he turned for support to the Soviet Union, which sent advisers, such as Adolf Joffe and Mikhail Borodin, along with funds and military aid. With this assistance, Sun established a military academy outside Guangzhou to train officers who would develop a military force.

In the fall of 1924 Sun decided the time was right for launching a military expedition to attack and defeat the northern warlords and unify China under his political party. Meanwhile, the Chinese Communist Party, founded in 1921, had agreed to an alliance with the Nationalist Party. In December, however, Sun's health suddenly worsened. He visited Beijing to receive medical treatment and also to make one last effort to negotiate with the northern warlords to reestablish the republic. In January 1925 Sun underwent surgery for cancer of the gallbladder; he died on March 12.

The Three Principles of the People and the Four Rights

Sun's peripatetic life as a revolutionary allowed him to study Western history and reflect on why the West, and later Japan, had modernized their societies and developed democracy, while China had not. Sun first alluded to democracy on November 26, 1905, in an editorial in his organization's newspaper. He argued that Europe and America had achieved greatness by adopting the Three Principles of the People: nationalism, people's rights (sometimes translated as "democracy"), and people's livelihood. He elaborated these concepts in lectures that later were published.

In Sun's view of history, China, unlike the West, had evolved through only two great stages: a long period of struggle against nature, followed by thousands of years of autocratic rule in which individuals competed with each other to become emperor. Only in the early twentieth century had China finally entered the age of democracy by removing corrupt rulers. It needed now to become independent of foreign control by Western powers. Once the Chinese people had created their nation-state, China could begin to establish democracy as a natural development reflecting that worldwide trend.

Sun also observed that autocratic rule in Europe had produced a stratified society based on hereditary rights for a small, privileged group. This development had given rise to resentment and a powerful demand for personal liberty, supported by many levels of society. But Chinese society had had greater social mobility than Western societies, thus minimizing resentment, so the pursuit of liberty had never been a driving force in China. China's fundamental problem, according to Sun, was to free itself of foreign control and to acquire control over its trade, finances, and other activities so as to become a sovereign state.

The first republic of 1911 had failed, Sun argued, because the United League never established a military administrative rule to prepare the nation for a period of political tutelage. Political tutelage meant having a single party organize a new government and initiate economic policies for national reconstruction. Sun believed that after his party had established a constitutional government and elected new leaders, it would permit other political parties to compete in new elections.

Sun recognized that Western democracy had developed slowly and imperfectly. Women had been denied the vote until the early twentieth century, while minorities, workers, and farmers had not acquired enough power to have a political voice. Aware of such defects in Western democracies, Sun wanted to develop a perfect democracy for China that would give people their full rights and yet allow the country to be ruled by those of greatest ability. Democracy, in Sun's view, meant empowering the people to govern their country through an elected elite. Sun believed that the people must have sovereignty and that the machinery of government must have ability and power.

Sun borrowed four ideas from the U.S. political system to empower the Chinese people: the people should be able to elect their officials, recall officials if they are inadequate, initiate new laws when old ones function poorly, and hold referendums to gain popular approval for new laws. Through the exercise of these rights, Sun believed, the popular will could be realized effectively. If the government machinery operated poorly, it could be repaired by the people exercising their four rights.

Governmental Structure and Politics

The system of government that Sun envisaged for China's democracy was a five-power government comprising a legislative, judicial, executive, civil service examination, and censoring branch. Each power would check and balance the others. Sun realized that a constitution was necessary to provide rules for governing and to define the powers and duties of the five branches, but he never indicated which constitution he preferred. Instead, he concentrated on explaining the key principles that he believed would make democracy work in China.

Sun took an elitist view of government management, insisting that only individuals of great talent should be allowed to serve in government. He never thought deeply about the political process to select leaders and officials, and he seemed not to realize that elections could be fraudulent or that talented candidates might not win the most votes. He envisioned the role of the press as one of educating citizens and instructing officials and leaders, rather than of criticizing national leaders and political parties. Moreover, the press should speak with a single voice rather than expressing diverse views. Sun believed that a uniform opinion would represent the will of the people. He favored competition among political parties but on the condition that parties would hold power alternately and be monitored by those out of power. According to Sun, political parties should compete not to gain power but to promote justice.

Sun's many speeches and lectures about political life and democracy in China reflect a Confucian view of the world. Sun believed that Chinese democracy would succeed only if officials and citizens behaved in a moral and virtuous way. Both officials and citizens needed to cultivate certain Confucian ethics such as benevolence and magnanimity. The injustices and inequalities among people could be reduced only if leaders and citizens practiced the Confucian way of mutual understanding, consensus, and harmony.

The Division of China

Sun's death made it very doubtful that his democratic principles could take root in China. Chiang Kai-shek, his loyal military commander, fervently believed in Sun's ideology but lacked his vision, intelligence, and experience. As Chiang's power grew, he became chairman of the Nationalist Party and, in 1928, president of the government of the Republic of China in Nanjing. Although he used Sun's doctrine to formulate government political policies, his emphasis was on military and strategic concerns. Chiang neglected the programs that Sun had argued should first be applied at the county and village levels: local democratic governance, land to be owned by the one who tilled it, and government assistance to farmers and businesspeople.

In late summer 1937 Japan invaded China. The Nationalist Party and the Nanjing government still had not developed strong links between the villages and cities, not even in Zhejiang and Jiangsu provinces on the coast of the East China Sea, where their military power had been greatest. Superior Japanese military power forced the government of the Republic of China to move inland and resettle in poor provinces. By the end of World War II the Nationalist Party and the government of the Republic of China had lost their vitality and much of their popular support. The ill-fated civil war that followed pitted Communist Party military forces against the armed forces of the Republic of China. The Republic of China suffered a disastrous defeat, and the Nationalists and the central government retreated from the mainland to the island of Taiwan.

In 1949 China splintered into two competing states occupying different territories, each claiming to represent China. Chiang's government had drafted a constitution in 1947 based on Sun's Three Principles of the People. It had even held elections in war-ravaged China to produce a new leadership, which soon relocated to Taiwan. The new government hoped to make that island province a model of modernization and democracy that would win the respect of the people on the mainland and inspire the Chinese people to unite China under Sun's Three Principles. The great contest between the Communist Party and the Nationalist Party continues: which can create a democracy that will win the support of all the people of China?

See also *China; Confucianism; Taiwan; Three People's Principles.*

Ramon H. Myers

BIBLIOGRAPHY

Chang, Sidney H., and Leonard H. D. Gordon. *All under Heaven: Sun Yat-sen and His Revolutionary Thought.* Stanford, Calif.: Hoover Institution Press, 1991.

———. *Bibliography of Sun Yat-sen in China's Republican Revolution, 1885–1925.* Lanham, Md.: University Press of America, 1991.

Hsu, Leonard Shih-lien. *Sun Yat-sen: His Political and Social Ideals.* Los Angeles: University of Southern California Press, 1933.

Ling, Yu-long. "The Doctrine of Democracy and Human Rights." In *Sun Yat-sen's Doctrine in the Modern World,* edited by Chu-yuan Cheng. Boulder, Colo.: Westview Press, 1989.

Sun Yat-sen. *Prescriptions for Saving China: Selected Writings of Sun Yat-sen.* Translated by Julie Lee Wei, E-su Zen, and Linda Chao. Edited by Julie Lee Wei, Ramon H. Myers, and Donald G. Gillin. Stanford, Calif.: Hoover Institution Press, 1994.

———. *San Min Chu I: The Three Principles of the People.* Translated by Frank W. Price. Edited by L. T. Chen. Shanghai: China Committee, Institute of Pacific Relations, 1927.

Sweden

See *Scandinavia*

Switzerland

A landlocked federal republic located in the mountains at the center of western Europe, the world's oldest direct democracy. The Swiss Confederation, as it is formally known, is composed of twenty-three cantons. A constitution dating from 1291 afforded certain rights and privileges to the autonomous communes that established the early Swiss Confederation in the cantons of Uri, Schwyz, and Unterwalden. The present Swiss constitution was adopted in 1848 and revised in 1874. Switzerland has three official languages (German, French, and Italian) and four official nationalities (including Romansch). About half of the Swiss population are Protestants, the other half Roman Catholics.

Switzerland represents an alternative model of democracy to the familiar Anglo-American liberal democratic model, based on representative government and individual rights. Swiss democracy focuses instead on participatory government and communal responsibilities. The Swiss political system has been organized around a confederal system in which communes and cantons, rather than individuals, are the primary bearers of rights. Swiss citizens, embedded in a strongly decentralized form of governance, participate far more in the legislative process than do citizens in typical representative systems.

Distinctive Characteristics of the Swiss Confederation

Among democratic institutions that make Switzerland special, several are worth attention. First among these is its decentralized confederal political system, in which citizenship derives primarily from the commune, secondarily from the canton, and only in the third instance from the federal or central government at Bern. This characteristic manifests itself as a sense of communal and cantonal identity *(Kantönligeist)*, which impels many Swiss to identify themselves first in terms of their communal and cantonal origins and only then as Swiss. Ask a Swiss where she is

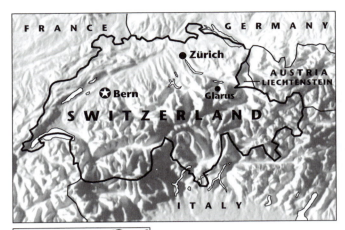

from, and she will first say Frauenkappeln (the commune), then Bern (the canton), and only last Switzerland.

The dispersion of power to the cantons and communes in crucial sectors—such as transportation, education, and welfare—creates a political system oriented toward local and regional politics rather than national politics. The commune, or *Gemeinde,* endows individuals with their civic identities. It also gives them their religious identities through the church commune, or *Kirchgemeinde.*

A system of town and cantonal assemblies exists in which the entire citizenry of a given region meets at least once a year to act as the supreme legislative body for the region. Although many of the cantonal assemblies (the so-called *Landesgemeinden* of German-speaking cantons, such as Uri, Schwyz, Unterwalden, and Glarus) have disappeared, local participatory assemblies are among the oldest and most widespread of Swiss political institutions. They establish citizenship and participation as crucial mediators of democratic politics and give direct democracy a literal sense equaled in few other systems. Nothing depicts democracy in its natural state more vividly than a picture of the entire citizenry of a Swiss town gathered in an open meadow to deliberate and vote on matters of common concern.

In the Swiss system, both constitutional and legislative initiatives and referendums play an extremely important role in the legislative process. Swiss law guarantees citizens a role in constitutional change as well as in legislation. That role has often appeared conservative to observers because it has been used to block rather than to effect

Since 1386, the Popular Assembly of Glarus has met at least once a year to vote. The assembly meets in the town square against the backdrop of the Swiss Alps.

change. Still, the referendum remains a powerful instrument of democracy. For example, in the 1980s a remarkable one-third of the Swiss voted to end obligatory military service, which, though it survived, was severely tested. And in 1993 the Swiss used the referendum to block a prospective application for membership in the European Community (now called the European Union).

Switzerland has a rotating presidency: executive leadership circulates among the seven members of a relatively anonymous federal council. This committee system diminishes the importance of executive authority and the kind of charismatic leadership that typifies presidential democracies such as France and the United States. At any given time, many Swiss may be uncertain who occupies the presidency. In so decentralized a system, with the political focus almost entirely on legislation, the executive has less power than in almost any other modern democracy.

The Citizen-Soldier and Armed Neutrality

The Swiss concept of citizenship is forged from the idea of the citizen-soldier, associated with the Germanic tribes from which feudal Switzerland's earliest democratic institutions arose. The idea of soldiers as citizens and citizens as soldiers animated direct democracy and gave citizenship a particularly robust character in early times. In the ancient world, civic virtue was linked to *virtù,* or virility—that is, the special abilities associated with soldiering and the martial arts. Switzerland gave new meaning to the ancient notion of civic republicanism in its reliance on citizen-soldiers (many of whom acted as mercenaries for other European countries in the early modern era).

More recent conceptions of the Swiss citizen derive from this ideal of the citizen-soldier. An example is the view of the citizen as an agent of active lawmaking with responsibility for executing policy, such as a declaration of war. This same idea has placed obstacles in the way of female suffrage, however, and has contributed to the traditional hegemony of men in Swiss society. Women did not gain the right to vote in national elections until 1971, long after other democratic nations had granted women the right to vote.

Linked to the ideal of the citizen-soldier is an insistence on Switzerland's political independence and armed neutrality in international relations. The mountainous Swiss nation occupies a strategically important location: its alpine passes provide access between north and south, east and west, between France and Austria, Germany and Italy. This fact has given added momentum to the Swiss policy of independence and neutrality, which arose from the ancient republican conviction that independence if not autarky (economic self-sufficiency) was a necessary condition of self-determination and democratic government.

In its earlier history, Switzerland was drawn into Europe's destructive wars; the Thirty Years' War of the seventeenth century was devastating to the old confederation. The Napoleonic invasion again disrupted Swiss democratic institutions. Thereafter Switzerland adhered scrupulously to a policy of armed neutrality, remaining neutral in both World War I and World War II. Similarly, Switzerland stayed clear of the North Atlantic Treaty Organization (NATO) and Europe's cold war defense strategies (although its sympathies were unquestionably pro-Western).

To the Swiss, democracy in a small, vulnerable nation seemed defensible only through neutrality. The Swiss have remained extremely well armed and self-consciously neutral, voting by referendum to stay out of the United Nations and the European Union.

The Structure of Confederation

The Swiss hold the belief that society is divided not only into communes but also into families. In the traditional Swiss view, citizens represent and are represented by their families. Historically, this belief served as another justification (along with the equation of citizenship and soldiering) for the longstanding and much criticized absence of female suffrage.

The primacy of the family, along with the sovereignty of the communes, through which the Swiss receive their sense of civic identity, helps explain the lack of a strong tradition of individual rights in Switzerland. Where society is seen as consisting of families and communes rather than just individuals, the idea of a bill of personal and private rights is unlikely to find favor.

The confederal structure of Switzerland corresponds to its religious, linguistic, and ethnic diversity. Switzerland offers one of the oldest examples of a genuinely multicultural society held together by common beliefs, shared civic ideals, and a mutually agreed-upon constitution. Switzerland's four official nationalities and two Christian confessions (Catholic and Protestant) have been held together by a web of civic and social relationships. That web has survived a brief religious civil war in 1847, and the French-German enmities of both world wars. The Swiss, however, have been less open in dealing with foreign immigration. The country closed its borders to Jewish and other refugee immigrants during World War II, and in the following decades it has been known for sometimes treating so-called guest workers less than hospitably. Switzerland's linguistic divisions have also played a crucial role, with the more progressive French cantons voting for membership in Europe and the German cantons voting overwhelmingly and successfully against membership. Some think these divisions may yet put the confederation in peril.

The political system that evolved out of Switzerland's distinctive characteristics offers a provocative contrast to democracies organized around individual rights, representation, and a more passive citizenry that limits its participation to watchdog. Some modern political scientists have used Switzerland as a model of a "consociational" democracy—that is, one built more on cooperation and consensus than on adversarial party politics. The absence of a bill of rights, for example, seems less of an issue for people who identify rights with communities rather than individuals, just as the absence of a strong president seems less important to people for whom legislation means direct involvement in an initiative and referendum process. In this sense, Switzerland has become a kind of test case for small nations organized largely around relatively participatory principles.

Critics have observed that its decentralized constitution and participatory practices have made Switzerland a relatively conservative country. The referendum more often has been used to block legislation than to encourage innovation. Similarly, even after the granting of female suffrage, the ideal of the citizen-soldier, which confined soldiering to males, remained an obstacle to full participation by women in the political system.

The example of Switzerland suggests that democracy is a plural phenomenon that takes many different forms, rather than a single universal system. It also suggests that the relationship between individuals and communities, rights and responsibilities, participation and representation may look very different depending on historical circumstances and political practices. Swiss democracy does not fit the model with which Americans and many Europeans are most familiar. Still, it appears to feature many of democracy's crucial institutions. It also gives the term *popular sovereignty* a direct meaning missing in many larger constitutional and representative democracies.

See also *Federalism; Multiethnic democracy; Popular sovereignty; Referendum and initiative; Virtue, Civic.*

Benjamin R. Barber

BIBLIOGRAPHY

Barber, Benjamin R. *The Death of Communal Liberty: Freedom in a Swiss Mountain Canton.* Princeton: Princeton University Press, 1974.

Bonjour, Edgar, H. S. Offler, and G. R. Potter. *A Short History of Switzerland.* Oxford: Clarendon Press, 1952.

Codding, George A. *The Federal Government of Switzerland.* Boston: Houghton Mifflin, 1961.

Hilowitz, Janet Eve. *Switzerland in Perspective.* Westport, Conn., and London: Greenwood, 1990.

Ionescu, G., ed. "Can the Confederatio Helvetica Be Imitated?" Special issue of *Government and Opposition* (winter 1988).

Kohn, Hans. *Nationalism and Liberty: The Swiss Example.* New York: Macmillan, 1956.

Steinberg, Jonathan. *Why Switzerland?* Cambridge and New York: Cambridge University Press, 1976.

Steiner, Jürg. *Amicable Agreement versus Majority Rule: Conflict Resolution in Switzerland.* Translated by Asger Braendgaard and Barbara Braendgaard. Chapel Hill: University of North Carolina Press, 1974.

Syria

See *Middle East*

T

Taiwan

A small, semitropical island about one hundred miles east of mainland China, the center of government of the Republic of China since 1949. The central government of the Republic of China and the Nationalist Party (the Kuomintang, or KMT) moved from the mainland to Taiwan in 1949, after being defeated in a civil war with the Communist Party and its armed forces. The Republic of China furnishes a rare example of an authoritarian state gradually letting go of power to promote a democratic political system.

Taiwan's population in the mid-1990s was about 21 million. About 85 percent of the population are native Taiwanese; the rest came from other provinces of mainland China.

Establishment of Authoritarian Rule

Imperial Japan occupied Taiwan between 1895 and the end of World War II. In 1943 the Cairo Conference mandated that Taiwan and other territories be restored to China, and on October 25, 1945, Japan formally returned Taiwan to the control of the central government of the Republic of China. The retreat of the government to Taiwan in 1949 divided China into two sovereign states: the People's Republic of China, which under Communist rule governed the mainland provinces, and the Republic of China, which governed Taiwan and its small offshore islands. The government of the Republic of China and the ruling Nationalist Party insisted that they represented the mainland provinces and that the regime of the Communist People's Republic was illegitimate.

To underscore that claim, the Republic of China in 1948 added to its 1947 constitution eleven amendments called

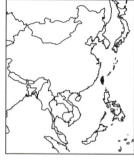

the Temporary Provisions, which were to be effective during the period of Communist rebellion. The Temporary Provisions nullified much of the constitution and granted the president's office great powers. On May 19, 1949, the Republic of China imposed martial law in Taiwan; this action allowed military courts to judge and sentence any individuals or groups threatening national security. It also guaranteed that no political party would organize to challenge the Nationalist Party.

The government continued to rule by martial law until July 15, 1987. The lifting of martial law permitted the rapid evolution of a political marketplace in which other parties competed with the Nationalist Party in elections to select leaders who represented the people of Taiwan rather than the mainland. This transition to democracy was not only permitted but encouraged by the government. The process of democratization in Taiwan was unique because the Nationalist-ruled authoritarian state initiated democratic reforms while still threatened by an external enemy, the People's Republic of China.

In addition, the state faced the threat of the Taiwanese nationalist movement, which sought to overthrow the government by peaceful or violent means. That nationalist movement began in February 1947 with an uprising in Taiwan; the government ruthlessly suppressed it. Many embittered Taiwanese fled to join opposition groups that were forming in Japan, the United States, and elsewhere.

The Nationalist Party and the government of the Republic of China controlled Taiwan's society rigidly and dealt harshly with individuals who threatened national security or undermined party and government rule. Security personnel, as well as the police, monitored the activities of intellectuals, journalists, educators, politicians, and professionals who were perceived as criticizing or opposing the regime. The government conducted a campaign of "white terror" in the 1950s, arresting anyone alleged to be a critic of or a threat to the government and the ruling party. It is estimated that tens of thousands of people were incarcerated for varying periods.

Unlike the communist parties and other despotic regimes that ruled many nations in the decades after World War II, the development-oriented, authoritarian Nationalist Party was committed to building a democracy. Its leadership adhered to the ideology of the political theorist and revolutionary Sun Yat-sen (1866–1925). Sun's doctrine encouraged a strong commitment to building a Chinese-style democracy in Taiwan—but only after the Nationalists decided when and under what conditions political reforms should be introduced. Because of the severity of external and internal threats, the Nationalist leadership waited until the spring of 1986 to decide to reform the polity.

Until then, Nationalist leaders and government officials had established a limited democracy by adhering to the 1947 constitution for governing Taiwan. That constitution provided for five branches, or Yuans: the Executive, Legislative, and Judicial Yuans; the Control Yuan, which monitored general administration; and the Examination Yuan, which oversaw civil service examinations. The constitution stipulated that elections must be held every six years to select a new National Assembly. This would have meant a new election in 1953 (the first election under the constitution had been held on the mainland in 1947), but an election was impossible in the divided nation. The Executive Yuan finally obtained a legal ruling in January 1954 allowing all first-term elected representatives of the central government to continue to serve and enjoy their rights beyond 1953. The National Assembly, made up of mainlanders elected in 1947, continued to elect a president and vice president every six years until March 1990, when this procedure was used for the last time. The Legislative Yuan, composed exclusively of mainlanders, rubber-stamped legislative bills submitted by the Nationalist Party and the Executive Yuan. In this way, the mainlander-dominated government and the Nationalists ruled the Republic of China.

Modernization and Reform

Between 1950 and 1955 the authoritarian government launched reforms to modernize and gradually democratize the economy and polity of the Republic of China. A land-reform program redistributed land to poor farmers and landless households by granting them low-interest loans to purchase land and compensating landowners with bonds. In 1950 regular elections began for town, city, and provincial councils, city mayors, and district chiefs. By 1952 primary school children received free education. These reforms set the stage for the people to prosper with equity, for more people to become educated, and for the people to participate in local government.

By 1970 about 70 percent of the people lived in towns and cities of more than 2,000 persons. Taiwan's citizens, though highly literate and reasonably well educated, still had an income of only $389 per capita. Local elections became a regular activity in people's lives. A new civil society took form, and more young people entered political life.

When mainlander representatives in the central government retired or died, resulting vacancies had to be filled. To that end the Nationalists and the government permitted supplementary national elections in 1969 in which competing candidates could be elected to fill vacancies in the Legislative Yuan, the Control Yuan, and the National Assembly. This reform allowed young politicians, especially those who opposed the Nationalist Party, to be elected to government positions. The ruling party, however, still held a majority and continued to control central government policies and to pass laws.

During the 1970s and early 1980s many politicians referred to themselves as "outside the Nationalist Party" and began to oppose the regime. They published magazines critical of the Nationalists and the government. Although the government banned these publications, others soon appeared. This upsurge of political discussion and election activity reflected a growing political opposition demanding greater democracy. As Taiwan's civil society grew, the nation also was becoming more isolated in the world. The People's Republic had replaced the Republic of China in the United Nations in 1972, and the United States broke diplomatic relations with the Republic of China in 1979.

In the midst of these events Chiang Ching-kuo, the son of Chiang Kai-shek (who was president of China from 1928 to 1949), came to power. Born in 1909, he had spent twelve years of his youth as a hostage in the Soviet Union. His father had groomed him to be his successor. Chiang Ching-kuo became the sixth president of the Republic of China in March 1978 and was reelected in 1984, after naming Lee Teng-hui, a brilliant economist, official, and native Taiwanese, to be his vice president. As early as the 1970s Chiang had recruited talented Taiwanese for party and government positions and considered how to expand democracy.

End of Martial Law

Preoccupied with Taiwan's increased international isolation, a growing political opposition, his own worsening health, and several major scandals within the KMT, Chiang did not undertake political reform until 1986. Like his father, he wanted to reestablish the 1947 constitution and the doctrine of Sun Yat-sen on the Chinese mainland. He finally believed that China could be unified only if a democracy was first built in Taiwan. No one but Chiang had the power to initiate political reform and make his party accept it.

Chiang decided that the Nationalist Party must lift martial law, allow a free press to develop and political parties to form, and amend the constitution to provide for election of all national officials and representatives. These political reforms were dangerous because the Taiwanese nationalist movement, the Communist People's Republic,

and KMT conservatives could intervene and cause turmoil, but time was running out on the seventy-seven-year-old president.

In late March 1986 Chiang established a reform committee made up of twelve people to study how to replace martial law with a new security law, establish a law to allow political parties to compete, and amend the constitution to hold national elections.

Before the committee completed its work, some of the "outside" politicians illegally established the Democratic Progressive Party. Chiang refused to outlaw the party and jail its leaders, even though they had defied martial law. Instead, he urged his party to press forward with reform and use the law and the constitution to promote democracy.

In January 1987 the government allowed newspapers to expand their daily editions and ended censorship. By July 15 the government had enacted a new security law and lifted martial law. The Nationalist Party and government then passed a law giving political parties the right to register and compete in elections. These legal reforms transformed Taiwan's political life. In November 1987 Chiang obtained party and government agreement to allow citizens who were not officials to visit their relatives on the mainland. In campaigning for the December 19, 1989, election, people publicly debated for the first time whether Taiwan should become the Republic of Taiwan, and the Democratic Progressive Party won six of the twenty mayoral/county magistrate seats—a major setback for the Nationalists.

Chiang died on January 13, 1988. A few hours later, in a smooth leadership succession, his vice president, Lee Teng-hui, became the first Taiwanese to be elected president of the Republic of China. At the Seventh Nationalist Party Congress in July, party members approved President Lee as party chairman. He was the first person to serve concurrently as the nation's president and Nationalist Party chairman since 1949. A major transfer of political power took place over the next five years, first within the Nationalist Party and then in the new political marketplace. The speed of democratization between 1986 and 1994 was unprecedented in the history of Chinese civilization.

Democratic Transition

Between 1990 and 1994 several major events threatened the democratic transition. First, in the March 20, 1990, presidential election, Lee defeated a group of mainland Nationalist Party politicians in the National Assembly who tried to replace him. His triumph was marred by widespread public protests against the National Assembly and demands that the senior representatives retire. In order to resolve this crisis, Lee promised the nation that within three years he would complete constitutional reform, broadening elections and making democracy a reality in Taiwan.

Few people believed the new president could keep his word. Meanwhile, the People's Republic pressured Taiwan to become a special province with great autonomy and to expand its economic links with the mainland. The Democratic Progressive Party demanded the elimination of the National Assembly and a redraft of the 1947 constitution, hoping to create a Republic of Taiwan without any links to the mainland.

Lee dealt with the threat of Taiwanese nationalism by convening a conference on national affairs in June and July 1990, at which 225 public figures and scholars from across the political spectrum met to discuss political reform. Lee even invited Taiwanese dissidents from abroad and representatives of other parties. The conference was a turning point in the political life of Taiwan. The Democratic Progressive Party and Nationalists achieved a political reconciliation and agreed to exchange information.

Opposition politicians had always blamed the Nationalists for their repression of the February 1947 uprising. The Office of the President and the Executive Yuan set up a commission of experts to review that tragic affair. In the spring of 1992 the commission issued a report in part blaming the government and recommending that a memorial be established and compensation paid to the victims. In May 1993 the government approved the commission's recommendations, thus putting the issue to rest.

In October 1990 President Lee assembled private citizens and leading politicians, including K'ang Ning-hsiang of the Democratic Progressive Party, in a commission to study the unification of China and to formulate a policy toward the People's Republic. In February 1991 the commission presented a three-stage plan for the unification of the Republic of China and the People's Republic in the distant future, provided the people of both states agreed. This blueprint became the basis for a new, pragmatic foreign policy toward the People's Republic.

In mid-1990 the Judicial Yuan had ruled that all senior representatives of the central government must retire by December 31, 1991. The president convened the National Assembly in April 1991 to annul the Temporary Provisions, end the war with the communists, and pass additional articles stipulating elections for a new National Assembly and Legislative Yuan. The National Assembly elections, held in late 1991, were peaceful; the KMT won three-quarters of the seats—a majority vote to amend the constitution.

The new National Assembly represented only the voters of Taiwan and its offshore islands, rather than claiming to represent the mainland. It convened in spring 1992. By May it had passed eight new articles, which called for election of a president and vice president by 1996 and presidential nomination of members of the Judicial, Examination, and Control Yuans, subject to approval by the National Assembly. In December 1992 elections for the Legislative Yuan were held, and the Democratic Progressives won 50 of the 161 seats.

By May 1993 Lee had fulfilled his promise to reform the 1947 constitution; the Nationalist Party, in cooperation with other political parties, had expanded central government elections for Taiwan and its offshore islands. The Democratic Progressive Party complied with the rules and competed in those elections. It gradually expanded its political power in the new Legislative Yuan and won appointments to the Control Yuan in February 1993. By working within the framework of the constitution and seeking voter support in the political marketplace, the Democratic Progressive Party demonstrated that it was a responsible opposition party.

During 1993–1994 the party elders of Chiang Ching-kuo's generation voluntarily retired from the government and party without trying to undermine the political reforms. The Nationalist Party began splitting in 1993, and in 1994 a faction of mainlanders left the party to form the New Party. In mid-August 1994 the Nationalists held their Fourteenth Party Congress, which elected four vice chairs, cast secret ballots for the party chairman (reelecting Lee Teng-hui) for the first time in party history, and elected younger Taiwanese to the central and standing committees. Lee had now neutralized his opponents in the KMT.

In the summer of 1994 the National Assembly again amended the constitution, to include rules for popular election of the president and vice president. In late November 1994 the nation held the first election for a provincial governor and for mayors of Kaohsiung and Taipei. The Nationalist Party candidates easily won the provincial governorship and Kaohsiung mayoral election, but the party lost the Taipei mayoral race to the Democratic Progressive candidate.

Taiwan began preparations in 1995 for the year's end

Legislative Yuan election and for the presidential and vice presidential elections in mid-1996. The rapid transition from a limited democracy to a full democracy in Taiwan between 1986 and 1996 was a political miracle in twentieth-century Chinese politics, making Taiwan the first Chinese democracy.

See also *China; Sun Yat-sen.*

Ramon H. Myers

BIBLIOGRAPHY

Chao, Linda, and Ramon H. Myers. "The First Chinese Democracy of the Republic of China on Taiwan, 1986–1994." *Asian Survey* 34 (March 1994): 213–230.

Cheng, Tun-jen, and Stephen Haggard, eds. *Political Change in Taiwan.* Boulder, Colo.: Lynne Rienner, 1992.

Chiu, Hungdah. *China and the Taiwan Issue.* New York: Praeger, 1979.

———. *Constitutional Development and Reform in the Republic of China on Taiwan (with Documents).* Occasional Papers/Reprints Series in Contemporary Asian Studies 2:61. College Park: University of Maryland, School of Law, 1993.

———, ed. *China and the Question of Taiwan: Documents and Analysis.* New York: Praeger, 1973.

Leng, Shao-chuan, ed. *Chiang Ching-kuo's Leadership in the Development of the Republic of China on Taiwan.* Lanham, Md.: University Press of America, 1993.

Tien, Hung-mao. *The Great Transition: Political and Social Change in the Republic of China.* Stanford: Hoover Institution Press, 1989.

Tsang, Steve, ed. *In the Shadow of China: Political Developments in Taiwan since 1948.* London: Hurst; Honolulu: University of Hawaii Press, 1993.

Tanzania

See *Africa, Subsaharan*

Tax revolts

Forms of collective resistance to the efforts of government to collect or increase taxes. Such protests have a long, often violent, history. Taxation converts private income into public resources. For any government, great undertakings require money, more money, and still more money. The general examination of who pays, how much, and for what reveals the anatomy of political and social power in a society.

The successful imposition of taxes by ruling groups seeking increased military might was fundamental to the construction of strong states in modern Europe. Although economic expansion facilitated taxation, the extension of the fiscal reach of the state was also closely connected with increased coercion. The drive to enlarge and centralize the state's taxation power regularly encountered bitter popular resistance. Religious conflicts aside, most of the rebellions in European states from the fourteenth through the eighteenth century were tax revolts, mainly in rural areas. These protests included murderous attacks on tax collectors and pitched battles with government troops.

Incidents of resistance to government efforts to extract taxes are by no means confined to European societies. For example, a wave of violent protests against the imposition of higher grain taxes and other surcharges and fees erupted in rural China in the mid-1840s. During the death throes of the Qing dynasty in the early twentieth century, hikes in a dizzying array of levies on wine, meat, the rice cauldron, and lumber prompted another wave of assaults against local gentry, tax collectors, and village leaders linked to the national authorities.

Similarly, the imposition, with little consultation, of a "poll" (or "head") tax on all adult males at the end of 1905 caused the Zulu rebellion against the government of Natal, a disturbance that has been called the last tribal revolt on South African soil. In Uganda and Kenya the attempt of the British colonial authorities to extract taxes led to evasion and resistance.

Hence managing hostile reactions against taxation without undermining the ability to collect is a persistent preoccupation of governing elites everywhere. The battle cry "no taxation without representation" proclaims the democratic imperative of basing fiscal power on popular consent. Yet soon after the American Revolution, George Washington's administration faced the Whiskey Rebellion, a violent uprising against the federal excise tax on liquor. This event had a strong ideological resemblance to earlier protests against the British monarchy. Securing national independence did not end the struggle between citizens and state over money.

In both Europe and the United States the incidence of violent protests against taxation declined in the nineteenth century. A greater degree of representation, more political participation, and rising feelings of national consciousness created a basis for obtaining mass assent to new levies. Taxes became more acceptable as they became more broadly based and more clearly linked to distributing benefits throughout the population. With the development of representative institutions, tax rebellions increasingly have taken the form of electoral uprisings.

Tax Revolts in Modern Democracies

Tax evasion is a private form of protest, a kind of covert exit from the prevailing regime. By contrast, the term *tax revolt* designates overt, collective acts of opposition. These range from verbal complaints to mass demonstrations and voting for proposals to reduce or limit taxes. As the sociologist Harold Wilensky shows (in *The "New Corporatism"*), differences in the intensity, durability, and scope of tax revolts can be gauged by comparing the electoral success and longevity of antitax candidates or parties, the organizational strength of antitax movements, and the actual changes in taxation.

In the economically advanced modern democracies the fiscal needs of the welfare state are a major catalyst for conflict over taxes. The twentieth century witnessed the spread of a conception of citizenship as entailing social as well as legal and political rights. This provided the basis for the welfare state—the gradual enactment of governmental standards of income, health, education, housing, and nutrition as a matter of entitlement.

Once entitlement programs are in place, demography and democracy generate tensions over taxation. For example, an aging population drives the cost of pensions and health care upward. Rising expectations about the acceptable minimum standards of income and care are another pressure for increased spending. Elected politicians have a strong incentive to accede to demands for more benefits, especially when confronted by well-organized constituencies of recipients. Finally, as the public sector expands, government employees themselves become a powerful interest group whose push for higher salaries and job security necessitates additional tax revenues.

The desire for more benefits and government services, however, is unaccompanied by a commensurate willingness on the part of ordinary citizens to pay for them. Among political activists, attitudes toward taxation might well be one element of a coherent ideology that encompasses beliefs about individual responsibility, the dangers of bureaucratic power, and the efficacy of state management of the economy. Surveys of mass opinion, however, reveal ambivalence and inconsistency in public thinking about the welfare state. The same people who complain that their taxes are too high frequently voice support for more rather than less government spending for virtually every entitlement program. The strategic problem for officeholders facing such conflicted voters is how to extract the revenues necessary to provide the services and benefits that are expected without precipitating political disruption and electoral defeat.

Tax Systems as Causes of Revolts

Historical experience suggests that economic, cultural, and institutional factors all contribute to the likelihood of a powerful tax revolt. During periods of recession, for example, demands for public assistance grow, while government revenues decline. Resentment against taxation to make up for lost revenues tends to increase at such times, if only because incomes are stagnant or shrinking. For similar reasons, high rates of inflation prepare the ground for antitax movements. In a progressive tax system, as people earn more money, they are subjected to a higher tax rate, and therefore they see less of an increase in their real income. Inflation accelerates this "bracket creep" while providing a windfall for government. When rising prices and higher income taxes squeeze real disposable income, antitax sentiments are likely to intensify.

The role of the taxation system itself in stimulating protest is complex. Wilensky's comparative study concluded that, within broad limits, the absolute level of the overall tax burden in a country is not consistently related to the strength of organized protest against taxes. Among the economically advanced democracies the United States has a relatively low tax burden and a low level of public social spending, yet it has experienced a high incidence of antitax activity. Sweden spends more than the United States and imposes higher taxes without having provoked a powerful popular backlash against the financing of the welfare state. The results of referendums proposing radical cuts in property taxes in the American states confirm that a relatively high tax burden is not a sufficient condition for a victorious tax revolt.

The main limit on the tax burden, then, is political rather than economic. The practical ceiling for taxation is determined by the intensity of political resistance to attempts to impose an additional burden. That there is such a limit, however, seems clear, and even the most generous welfare states must ultimately encounter opposition as they recycle an ever larger share of private income back to the taxpayer in the form of transfer payments.

A rapid and substantial increase in taxes is a more reliable predictor of rebellion than the absolute level of taxation. The success of the antitax Progress Party in Denmark in 1973 was stimulated by a rapid rise in income taxes. Abrupt and substantial increases in taxes also preceded the antitax movements in the American states in the late 1970s.

The visibility of higher taxes is particularly important in stimulating protest. Politically, the safest tax is one that is neither seen nor felt, just collected. Citizens also are more likely to tolerate taxes when the benefits they pay for are manifest and certain. Indirect taxes, such as the sales tax, user fees, and contributions to social security, come closest to meeting these criteria. Property taxes and income taxes, on the other hand, are highly visible levies that are extracted in several big bites and used for disparate purposes.

The countries that experienced intense tax revolts in the 1960s and 1970s—such as Denmark, the United States, Great Britain, and Switzerland—were those with a relatively greater reliance on property and income taxes. Municipal and regional governments typically use the property tax as their main source of revenue; this helps explain why those governments are so often a target of tax rebellions.

Two episodes in twentieth-century American history illustrate the distinctive unpopularity of the real estate property tax. In the 1920s state and local collections, overwhelmingly based on property taxes, grew rapidly. The economic collapse at the end of the decade sparked a widespread tax revolt. A number of states enacted overall limitations on the general property tax, hundreds of taxpayers leagues were created, and a well-organized tax strike persisted in Chicago from 1930 to 1933.

By contrast, the passage of Proposition 13 in California in 1978 occurred during a period of sharply rising rather than deflating real estate values. Property taxes surged while real incomes remained stagnant. The failure of state government to react to taxpayers' complaints resulted in the passage of several far-reaching tax-cutting initiatives with national political repercussions.

Political Factors

Political culture affects the incidence of tax revolts. The American ethos is characterized by suspicion of power and celebrates the rights of the citizen against the state. Americans' lack of deference to authority is conducive to a readiness to protest that is lacking in many other societies. The pervasive American image of economic success as an

accurate measure of one's personal effort and worth functions both as an ideological obstacle to the expansion of the welfare state and as a legitimating principle for antitax proposals.

Institutional arrangements affect the progress of tax revolts. Loosely structured political systems with fragmented decision-making processes and many points of electoral access for mobilized groups provide a relatively favorable battleground for the tax rebels. The ability of citizens to place measures on the ballot and vote on them directly enhances the impact of antitax feelings on public programs, either because the tax revolt wins at the polls or because legislators try to circumvent popular initiatives by cutting taxes on their own. Similarly, where electoral laws make it easy to convert votes into seats, new antitax parties and candidates have a greater chance of success.

On the other hand, corporatist processes diminish the strength of a backlash against taxation. When decisions about fiscal and social policies emerge from a negotiated settlement involving the central government and the major labor, employers, and professional organizations, the top leaders of interest groups appear better able to maintain the loyalty of their mass followings and ward off the electoral threat of parties opposed to higher taxes.

The successful tax revolt in California in the late 1970s illustrates the interplay of these institutional, cultural, and political factors. Proposition 13 was precipitated by the failure of a bitterly divided state legislature to produce a promised solution for the problem of escalating property taxes. The initiative process provided a ready vehicle for an angry and disenchanted electorate to reject the pleas of both established political parties and impose its own solution, a tax regime that has hindered the subsequent growth of government.

Who Votes for the Tax Revolt?

More than a century ago, Karl Marx described the tax struggle as the oldest form of class struggle. Although material self-interest plays an important role in determining electoral support for tax revolts, resistance is rarely organized along neat class lines. Taxpayers are a heterogeneous group, and tax issues often are seen as interest group or community conflicts, aligning suburbs against cities, rich regions against poor regions, and private-sector employees against government workers.

Voters are sensitive to the anticipated impact of proposed tax reforms on their fiscal burden, but specific proposals divide people in different ways. Home ownership rather than a voter's level of income predicted support for cutting property taxes in one study, while the reverse was true when it came to a proposal to reduce state income taxes.

More generally, electoral support for the tax revolt is unusually strong among middle-income voters from both blue-collar and white-collar occupations. As Terry Nichols Clark and Lorna Ferguson observe (in *City Money*), this broad group does not rely heavily on welfare state programs, but it is not wealthy enough to ignore the effect of the tax bite due to the expansion of government benefits. The political emergence of this "middle-mass" group in the 1970s helps explain the shift toward fiscal conservatism in the United States and other countries at that time.

The antistatist rhetoric of tax limitation movements attracts support from the political right; voting for tax-cutting proposals is associated with approval of a "smaller government that does less" and belief in market principles. However, it is the populist rather than the conservative content of modern tax revolts that widens their mass following. The leaders of tax revolts tend to appeal to voters directly rather than through existing parties or interest group organizations. They generally propose to cut the taxes of individual taxpayers and are less concerned about the burden imposed on large corporations. Most important, a powerful impulse underlying tax revolts is the desire to hold the governing elite—which is perceived as remote, profligate, and unresponsive—accountable to "the people."

A cynical image of politicians and officials contributes to the success of tax revolts. Polls consistently show that political alienation—a lack of faith in the trustworthiness of established authorities and institutions—predisposes people to vote for antitax propositions and candidates. A powerful tax revolt thus is a symbolic message to those in power, a warning about the shaky legitimacy of existing processes of reaching decisions about taxation and government spending.

Oliver Wendell Holmes once remarked that taxes are the price we pay for civilization. A shared willingness to pay this price indicates a sense of common political identity, while a tax revolt bespeaks public doubts about the boundaries of the political community and the mutual obligations of its members. One element in the late-twentieth-century backlash against the welfare state is anger at the waste, fraud, and abuse in expensive entitlement programs. Another is resentment at paying higher taxes in order to assist those perceived as undeserving or marginal members of the polity, such as the economic underclass, certain minority groups, or illegal immigrants. As demographic, technological, and economic trends continue to fragment existing nation-states and alter political loyalties, the contours of future tax revolts may shift, but the democratic problem of securing consent for fiscal power will endure.

See also *Accountability of public officials; Referendum and initiative; Taxation policy; Welfare, Promotion of.*

Jack Citrin

BIBLIOGRAPHY

Ardant, Gabriel. "Financial Policy and Economic Infrastructure of Modern States and Nations." In *The Formation of National States in Western Europe,* edited by Charles Tilly. Princeton: Princeton University Press, 1975.

Clark, Terry Nichols, and Lorna Ferguson. *City Money.* New York: Columbia University Press, 1983.

Sears, David O., and Jack Citrin. *Tax Revolt: Something for Nothing in California.* Enlarged ed. Cambridge, Mass., and London: Harvard University Press, 1985.

Wilensky, Harold. *The "New Corporatism," Centralization and the Welfare State.* Beverly Hills, Calif.: Sage Publications, 1976.

———. *The Welfare State and Equality: Structural and Ideological Roots of Public Expenditures.* Berkeley: University of California Press, 1975.

Taxation policy

A government's approach to collecting the revenues necessary to meet expenditure demands. Revenue collection—specifically, taxation—represents a policy problem for any government and a special difficulty for democratic governments. These governments must raise enough revenue to cover their expenditure needs without offending the public so much that the government is voted out of office.

Citizens make contradictory demands of democratic governments. They demand the full gamut of public services, ranging from defense through social welfare, but they do not want to pay high taxes to fund those services. Balancing such opposing political pressures represents a major challenge of governance for most contemporary democratic systems. Thus, although taxation is usually treated as the arcane province of economists, lawyers, and accountants, tax policy is also a central political question.

Paying for Government

Governments meet the challenge of contradictory signals from their citizens in a variety of ways. First, they can borrow heavily to cover revenue shortfalls. The level of public borrowing has increased for most democracies to the point that for many debt itself has become a significant political and economic issue. This is true even for countries, such as Germany and Japan, that have had a reputation for proper fiscal management.

Second, governments can reduce expenditures or at least reduce the rate of growth in expenditures. This strategy is risky politically, given the number of groups in a society that expect to have their demands addressed by government. Many politicians have campaigned in favor of reducing expenditures but have found themselves unable to do so once in office: citizens like the idea of cutting programs in general but do not want reductions in programs that benefit them personally.

The other means that governments have of making their books balance is to increase taxes and other forms of revenue collection, such as setting fees for government services. This approach may be at least as difficult politically as cutting expenditures, especially in the 1990s. Citizens are reluctant to provide any additional money to government, especially when many of them are having extraordinary difficulties in making their own family budgets balance. In the United States, Bill Clinton's presidential campaign in 1992 was successful in spite of his forthrightness about the possibility of increases in some taxes, but the distasteful prospect was palatable only in the context of an immense budget deficit and promises to cut government spending—especially "wasteful spending." Also, most of the tax increases were to be imposed on a small group of the very affluent, and taxes were to be cut for the "middle class." Even those factors did not save the president's budget proposals from intense criticism once he was elected to office.

This article examines tax systems in democratic states in the context of the political pressures on governments to balance their budgets while minimizing negative political reactions. We will first examine the sources of tax revenues in the countries of the Organization for Economic Cooperation and Development (OECD), an organization of industrial democracies, which promotes economic cooperation and the dissemination of information, as well as those of less wealthy democratic countries. We will then examine several special issues of tax policy, such as the use of "tax expenditures" that confer benefits on special groups in society and the impact of the "tax revolt" of citizens in several democratic regimes. Finally, we will look at some strategies that governments may adopt in order to increase their tax revenues while maintaining their legitimacy.

Tax Handles

Governments have in general three major tax "handles" they can pull to generate tax revenue. The most familiar of these handles is income. Most democratic governments rely heavily on taxes on income (including payroll taxes such as social security as well as taxes on corporate income) to fill their coffers. The second tax handle is consumption: governments have shown an increasing willingness to levy taxes on their citizens when they spend money. These taxes can be general—for example, sales and value added taxes—or they can be on specific commodities—for example, "sin taxes" on alcohol, tobacco, and gambling. Third, governments can levy taxes on the accumulated wealth of their citizens, held in the form of real estate, stocks and bonds, or other assets. Taxes on wealth tend to be the least commonly used, but for some local governments they may be the principal source of revenue. Although taxes are used primarily to raise revenue, they can also be used for a variety of other economic, social, and political reasons.

Table 1 provides some information about how tax revenues are raised in the OECD countries. Several points should be made about these data. First, all governments use almost all taxes available to them. The high-spending governments of these countries must try to tap all available resources if they want to finance their activities. Yet there are still marked differences between Denmark, which raises a very large proportion of its revenue from the personal income tax, and France, which instead relies on payroll and consumption taxes. Likewise, some countries, including the United States and Canada, use wealth taxes (in the form of local property taxes) rather heavily, while others barely use them. Governments of the political left tend to favor personal and corporate income taxes, and governments of the right tend to use more regressive consumption taxes. Regressive taxes take a larger percentage of resources from the poor than from the affluent.

Patterns of Taxation

We can identify four groups of countries based upon their tax policies. The most familiar of these are the Anglo-American democracies and their friends (Japan and

TABLE 1. Revenue Sources of OECD Countries, 1990 (percentage of total taxes)

Country	Personal income	Corporate income	Employees' social security	Employers' social security	Property	General consumption	Specific consumption
Australia	43.2	13.9	0.0	0.0	8.9	8.1	15.2
Austria	21.2	3.3	13.9	16.2	2.7	20.8	9.0
Belgium	30.7	6.4	11.6	20.7	2.6	16.1	7.4
Canada	40.8	6.8	4.3	9.7	9.0	13.9	9.9
Denmark	52.7	3.3	2.4	0.7	4.2	20.5	11.0
Finland	46.8	5.5	0.0	7.4	2.8	24.1	12.7
France	11.8	5.4	13.3	27.3	5.2	18.8	8.5
Germany	27.4	4.7	15.9	18.8	3.3	17.0	9.4
Greece	14.5	5.6	13.4	12.8	5.8	27.2	16.0
Iceland	26.5	2.8	0.3	2.9	8.5	32.4	17.0
Ireland	31.9	5.0	5.2	9.0	4.7	20.6	20.1
Italy	26.3	10.0	6.3	23.6	2.3	14.7	10.6
Japan	26.8	21.5	10.9	15.2	9.0	4.2	7.3
Luxembourg	24.1	16.2	10.7	13.5	8.5	13.9	9.1
Netherlands	24.7	7.6	23.5	7.9	3.7	16.5	7.5
New Zealand	46.5	6.5	0.0	0.0	6.2	22.6	9.2
Norway	25.9	8.9	8.4	16.6	2.9	18.3	15.6
Portugal	16.0	7.4	10.2	16.4	2.4	19.8	23.4
Spain	21.8	8.8	5.8	25.5	5.5	16.1	10.4
Sweden	37.9	3.1	0.0	25.4	3.5	14.6	9.0
Switzerland	34.6	6.5	10.4	10.3	7.8	10.0	7.1
United Kingdom	28.4	11.0	6.6	10.0	8.4	16.6	12.3
United States	35.8	7.3	11.6	16.6	10.8	7.6	6.8

SOURCE: Compiled by the author from figures in Organization for Economic Cooperation and Development, *Revenue Statistics of OECD Member Countries, 1965–1991* (Paris: OECD, 1992).
NOTE: All countries impose other small taxes that do not fit these categories; thus percentages will not equal 100.

Switzerland). Countries in this group depend rather heavily upon the personal income tax and the corporate income tax. They tend to impose social security taxes rather equally on employers and employees. These countries also tend to use consumption taxes, especially general consumption taxes, less than do most other countries. Perhaps the most distinctive feature of these countries is their reliance on property taxes at the provincial (state) and local levels. The taxation pattern has become traditional, and the governments have found little reason to change. When these governments do change their tax patterns, they often fail politically. After Margaret Thatcher's government imposed a per capita ("community charge") tax in place of the property tax in Britain in the early 1990s, the resulting discontent hastened Thatcher's fall from the leadership of the Conservative Party and the office of prime minister.

A second pattern of tax policy choices is found among the Scandinavian countries. This pattern appears more likely to produce significant socioeconomic redistribution than any other. First, taxes (and with them public expenditures) are high in total. Second, there is a heavy reliance on income taxes and on the employer's contribution to social security funds. Other taxes are used, and some, such as taxes on alcohol and tobacco, are levied at very high rates—as much to deter consumption as to raise revenue. This pattern is a function of a long period of domination of Scandinavian politics by social democratic parties as well as a political culture that stresses equality and the role of the state. It is not clear whether this pattern can be sustained in light of the changing political fortunes of the political left and the general questioning of the role of the state in these countries.

A third pattern of taxation is found among the Mediterranean countries (except Spain) as well as in the Republic of Ireland. These countries traditionally have encountered substantial difficulties in collecting tax revenues from citizens directly, so they must rely more on revenues from businesses and from consumption taxes and government monopolies. In some countries, governments have exclusive control of important businesses and use the profits to help fund other public services. These governments still manage to tax the incomes of their citizens, but they do so primarily through social security taxes rather than through direct income taxes. These taxes are, in reality, impositions on income but are paid on the basis of a company's payroll rather than on the basis of an individual's declared income. Likewise, everything else being equal, consumption (or expenditure) taxes tend to be easier and less expensive to collect, and to be a more reliable source of revenue, than income taxes. The evidence is that, unless charged at extraordinarily high rates, taxes on commodities such as alcohol and tobacco do not reduce consumption significantly; so governments can increase revenues by increasing these taxes. The combination of payroll taxes (which tend to have little effect on the earnings of the self-employed or on recipients of investment income) and high consumption taxes makes these revenue systems rather regressive.

The fourth pattern includes the remaining countries of continental Europe. This pattern is unusual because no particular taxes stand out. That is, countries in this group tend to use almost all taxes available to them, at about the average rate for the entire OECD. Such a pattern appears to make political sense for two reasons. First, the absence of distinctively high levels of any one tax tends to make the overall pattern of taxation less visible than it might otherwise be to citizens. Second, most of the countries in this group have had political patterns that could be labeled broadly as corporatist. The various interests in the society tend to have legitimate access to policy making, and they generally make their representations to government in an open forum. As a result, there are fewer special concessions to one group or another, and the tax burden is spread relatively equally.

We have substantially less complete information about tax revenues in developing political democracies than about those in the OECD countries, but we can still make several points about the tax policies of these systems. First, these countries attempt to use the tax handles available to them, but they are constrained by their lower level of economic development. They therefore tend to rely more on consumption taxes than on income taxes, with the exception of social security taxes on payrolls. These poorer countries also tend to concentrate on business taxes, in part because businesses keep better records than do individuals, especially poor farmers and workers. Finally, we must be aware that taxes make up a smaller portion of total revenues in these systems than in developed countries, and that these governments tend to support their activities through economic activities such as nationalized industries and charges for services. As the International Monetary Fund and the World Bank pressure the governments of the poorer democracies to privatize major industries, these countries will have to rely more on taxation to finance government operations.

Loopholes

In addition to influencing the economy and society through their tax-collecting methods, governments attempt to wield influence through the way they choose not to collect taxes. The preferences written into tax laws are referred to by academics as *tax expenditures*—and colloquially as *tax loopholes*. Most citizens in most countries take advantage of tax expenditures, such as deductions for the cost of buying a home or for contributions to charity. Most citizens like loopholes that reduce their own tax liabilities but resent those that are less widely available.

Tax politics often revolves as much around the adoption of loopholes as around the selection of one tax instrument or another. Tax legislation has been described as a Christmas tree surrounded by a number of presents for powerful special interests. Interest groups benefit from the relative obscurity of tax laws: because the advantages created are not easy for most citizens to see, interest groups can exert their influence without as much opposition as expenditure programs—even with the same result—would attract. The history of tax politics has been characterized by the gradual addition of hundreds of special benefits through the tax code, followed by tax reforms that attempt to create a simpler and fairer tax system. That simple tax system tends not to survive very long; it quickly becomes complicated by new loopholes.

Although the creation and preservation of loopholes are central features of tax politics, these have economic as well as political drawbacks. One criterion for a good tax system is that it is "fiscally neutral," that is, it does not divert resources. For example, giving special tax breaks for home ownership tends to direct a great deal of capital in the United States to that form of asset rather than to investments in more productive enterprises. Yet, by giving specific industries privileges through the tax system, loopholes shift the balance among potential uses of investments and may divert money to projects that do not have the greatest economic return.

Tax Revolts

Aside from participating in political activities directed at increasing the value of loopholes that favor them, citizens have other means of attempting to reduce their tax burden. The first is to engage in political activity that will reduce overall levels of taxation within the society. A number of movements of this type have been active in recent years. The most famous in the United States is Proposition 13, the successful 1978 ballot initiative in California that limited property taxes there. The California initiative was followed by a number of initiatives and referendums to limit taxes and spending in other states and localities. These continue to be proposed across the United States. In the 1992 elections there were more than a dozen local tax initiatives, more than half of which were adopted by the voters.

Most societies do not permit their citizens access to instruments of direct democracy; this includes the United States at the federal level. Citizens have nonetheless attempted to limit or reduce their tax bills through the political process. In several countries of Western Europe antitax parties have been organized, and some have enjoyed a good deal of political success. For example, for some years the rabidly antitax Progress Party in Denmark (led by the flamboyant Mogens Glistrup even while he was in jail for tax evasion) was the second largest party in parliament. The Progress Party in Norway, New Democracy in Sweden, and the Small Farmers' Party in Finland have also enjoyed some substantial political successes since the late 1970s. These parties have not been successful in significantly reducing the levels of taxation in these countries, as they had hoped. They have, however, pressured their governments to slow the growth of the public sector. The governing parties knew that if they allowed taxes to increase excessively, voters could turn to another party.

Citizens often despair of their ability to influence government taxing and spending directly through political actions. They sometimes believe that they have been let down by politicians who were elected on promises to reduce, or at least control, taxing and spending. The tax revolt then can go beyond political activity to more direct means. Disaffected citizens can attempt to evade taxes by underreporting the income they receive, overreporting their legally allowable deductions, or both. The ease or difficulty of practicing tax evasion depends on one's economic position. Self-employed people—including many doctors, lawyers, child care workers, domestics, and plumbers—can earn income without keeping complete records and therefore are in a much better position to evade taxes than are individuals who work for organizations.

Governments attempt to collect all the revenue that is legally due to them, but collecting can be difficult. By estimating the amount of cash in circulation or looking at the differences in reported incomes and expenditures, we can get some idea of the level of evasion. In some industrialized democracies the level of income evaded may amount to as much as 10 percent of gross national product. This adds up to a huge loss of revenue for government and an increased tax burden on those citizens who choose to, or who must, be honest about how much money they earn.

As distressing as the loss of revenue is for government, the political implications may be even more troublesome. Research concerning public feelings about taxation and tax evasion indicates that tax evasion is often politically rather than economically motivated. That is, people choose to evade less because they need the money than because they have little respect for the government's ability to spend the money properly. It appears that when conventional political actions are ineffective, citizens will engage in unconventional and illegal activities. Thus tax evasion represents the quiet loss of legitimacy for government as well as the loss of its money.

Making Taxation Palatable

Tax politics inevitably involves creating costs for most citizens by imposing new taxes or increasing the rates of existing taxes. To do this in a democratic government requires that officials making the policy decisions take into account public reaction to those taxes. This section briefly lays out some strategies by which governments can raise revenues while maintaining their democratic legitimacy. Of course, that democratic legitimacy may be closely associated with the probability that the government will be reelected.

First, in general it is easier to raise the rate of an existing tax than it is to add a new tax. It is even more desirable from the government's point of view if increased revenue yield can be gained without overt political action. Some taxes are more buoyant than others; that is, their yield tends to respond more directly to economic changes. The yield from a progressive income tax (one that takes a larger percentage of the resources of wealthier persons than of the poor), for example, will increase as either inflation or economic growth pushes more people into higher tax brackets. Governments rarely get the opportunity to reap windfalls like this any more, however, and one of the results of tax revolts in many countries has been to force the indexation of income tax brackets—that is, the adjustment of the brackets to keep them in line with inflation. Furthermore, tax reforms in the 1980s have often reduced the number of income tax brackets so that automatic revenue increases from inflation have become less common.

A highly visible new tax that falls on income or property is especially controversial. Governments sometimes attempt to play a game of "switch" with their citizens, substituting a new tax for an old tax. This strategy is likely to be unpopular, unless a noncontroversial tax, such as an earmarked tax on a nonessential commodity, is chosen. Even then, skeptical citizens will wonder why their government would go to the trouble of making the switch. The disadvantage of imposing a new tax was very evident when the British government imposed the new community charge tax to replace the familiar local property tax.

A second strategy for governments is to raise revenues by means other than taxes. Governments increasingly have attempted to impose fees and charges rather than taxes to increase their revenue. Many goods and services provided by governments can be sold to the public, even if they have been provided without additional charges in the past. Some services that most citizens consider an essential part of government, such as fire protection, actually can be sold.

In general, citizens would rather pay a charge for a specific service than a general tax that provides a range of services. They can recognize the direct connection between the fee paid and the service received and believe that they have greater control over a government that provides its services through a market mechanism. At least if they do not consume the service they will not have to pay for it, as they would if it were financed through a tax. Although they may be forced to pay the fee, as, for example, for garbage collection, they believe they have a better concept of the cost of producing the service and can react politically if the expense becomes unacceptable.

Even if a service is not marketed, taxes can be devised that allow citizens to see the connection between the tax and a particular service. Governments often earmark taxes for particular purposes, in part so that the users of a service finance that service. The most common example is the use of gasoline taxes to finance highways and other forms of transportation. Likewise, there are proposals in the United States to utilize increased tobacco taxes to finance health care, given the additional health costs imposed on society by tobacco use. Again, many citizens prefer this form of taxation, assuming they have to pay taxes at all. They often feel that general taxes go into some sort of endless void, whereas with an earmarked tax they can identify what is being bought with the tax revenue. Economists and government officials, on the other hand, generally do not like earmarked taxes because this type of taxation restricts freedom of action by governments; the government, for example, may be left with too much earmarked money for some purposes (such as highways) and not enough for others (such as mass transit).

If governments have reached the logical limits on the taxes they impose on specific commodities, they may decide to tax consumption generally. Citizens tend to prefer consumption taxes over income taxes. People generally sense that everyone has to pay the consumption tax, whereas some favored people can avoid income taxation through loopholes. Governments also like consumption taxes because, everything else being equal, these taxes are easier to collect than income taxes. It is easier to collect from a limited number of businesses who have some record-keeping capacity than it is to deal with millions of individual citizens who often keep inadequate financial records, if they keep any at all. Furthermore, consumption taxes are somewhat more reliable than income taxes. Even if their income goes down slightly, individuals may attempt to maintain their consumption of goods and services, especially of basics such as food, clothing, and shelter. Thus, although consumption taxes are sometimes criticized as being regressive, both average citizens (other than economists) and government officials may prefer this form of taxation.

It can be politically advantageous to rely largely on taxes that actually fall on someone other than the person or institution nominally paying the tax. Many taxes can be shifted to others. In general, personal taxes such as the income tax cannot be shifted, but most of those levied on businesses can be shifted to consumers, workers, or stockholders. Tax shifting is an especially useful strategy for ideologically conservative governments attempting to appease their business constituents. For example, although there is substantial academic debate about the details, it is clear that in most instances businesses do not really bear the burden of taxes. Taxes that are nominally imposed on businesses are actually passed along to consumers in the form of higher prices or to stockholders in the form of lower dividends. Likewise, the employer's share of social security taxes is less a charge on the business than a tax on the workers, who receive lower wages, or on consumers, who pay higher prices. This ability to shift the burden of taxes is one reason that governments that are heavily influenced by business interests may nonetheless have relatively high corporate taxes.

Avoiding Political Problems

Governments that must raise unpopular taxes can minimize the negative political fallout from doing so. One way is to create a "fiscal illusion." That is, successful politicians must find ways to make the total costs of government less apparent to the citizens who must pay the bill. The use of payroll withholding for the income tax in the United States, for example, makes the total impact of the income tax less apparent than it would be if the taxpayer had to write one big check on April 15 each year. Similarly, paying a property tax monthly along with the mortgage payment, so that the mortgage company sends the money to the government, makes this tax less visible than it might otherwise be.

Taxes seem less onerous in a fiscal system in which no single tax seems excessively high. Thus the last of the four tax patterns described earlier is becoming more common: governments are using all possible taxes at high enough levels to allow them to reduce their traditional dependence upon very high levels of few taxes. Because taxpayers do not pay all these taxes at the same time or in the same way, only the best informed know how much they are really paying. The apparent tax bite on citizens can be minimized further in federal systems and in other political systems with autonomous subnational governments. In those systems not only the central government but a variety of other authorities levy taxes. Individual citizens must be unusually vigilant and interested to be aware of how much of their money is going to the public sector.

Governments can often raise tax revenues while minimizing political difficulties by placing the principal burden of any new or increased taxes on the wealthy. Deficit reduction legislation proposed in the U.S. Senate in the mid-1990s was deemed to be politically acceptable (potentially at least) because more than three-quarters of the burden was projected to fall on people earning more than $100,000 per year—and more than two-thirds would fall on people earning more than $200,000. "Soaking the rich" is a good strategy politically, but it is not necessarily so good financially for a government that must raise very large sums. Although to the average citizen it appears that most of the income earned in the society goes to the wealthy, in contemporary industrial democracies that is not the case. Total income in the society is distributed roughly in a diamond, with the bulk being earned by people in the middle classes. For example, in the United States, according to Internal Revenue Service figures, more than one-third of total taxable income in 1989 was earned by people earning from $19,000 to $50,000 that year. Another one-fifth of the total was earned by people making from $50,000 to $75,000. Many other democratic governments have even more equal income distributions. Therefore, if governments want to generate enough revenue, they must go where the money is. That is, of course, also where the votes are, so the political risks encountered in tax policy become all the more obvious.

Quandaries for Democracies

In a democracy governments cannot always raise revenue in ways they favor. Furthermore, they may not be able to raise revenues in ways that are economically desirable. Political pressures often direct the burden of taxation away from industries and groups of individuals that have the influence to have their own special loopholes adopted. The existence of loopholes can make private economic choices dependent upon the tax policy of government rather than upon economic reality in the marketplace. The tax reforms adopted by a number of industrialized countries during the 1980s were an attempt to make their tax systems more fiscally neutral, but tax politics since then have restored many of the old concessions.

See also *Corporatism; Tax revolts.*

B. Guy Peters

BIBLIOGRAPHY

Conlan, Timothy, Margaret Wrightson, and David Beam. *Taxing Choices.* Washington, D.C.: CQ Press, 1989.

Haskel, Barbara. "Paying for the Welfare State." *Scandinavian Studies* 59 (1987): 221–253.

Kay, John, and Michael A. King. *The British Tax System.* 5th ed. Oxford: Oxford University Press, 1989.

Listhaug, O., and A. H. Miller. "Public Support for Tax Evasion: Self-Interest or Symbolic Politics?" *European Journal of Political Research* 13 (1985): 165–182.

McDaniel, P. R., and S. S. Surrey. *International Aspects of Tax Expenditures: A Comparative Survey.* Boston: Kluwer, 1985.

McQuaig, Linda. *Behind Closed Doors.* Toronto: Viking, 1987.

Murray, J. H., and A. S. Birnbaum. *Showdown at Gucci Gulch.* New York: Random House, 1987.

Page, Benjamin. *Who Gets What from Government?* Berkeley: University of California Press, 1983.

Peters, B. Guy. *The Politics of Taxation: A Comparative Perspective.* Oxford: Blackwell, 1991.

Radian, A. *Resource Mobilization in Poor Countries.* New Brunswick, N.J.: Transaction, 1980.

Rose, Richard, and Terence Karran. *Taxation by Political Inertia.* London: Macmillan, 1986.

Sears, David O., and Jack Citrin. *Tax Revolt: Something for Nothing in California.* Enlarged ed. Cambridge, Mass., and London: Harvard University Press, 1985.

Steinmo, Sven. *The Politics of Tax Reform.* New Haven: Yale University Press, 1993.

Weaver, K. *Automatic Government: The Politics of Indexation.* Washington, D.C.: Brookings Institution, 1988.

Witte, John. *The Politics and Development of the Federal Income Tax.* Madison: University of Wisconsin Press, 1987.

Technology

Technology—the application of natural science to practical uses—is widely thought to be an essential condition for the development and endurance of democracy. Today we take it for granted that democracy cannot arise or long endure in conditions of extreme poverty and without the promise of a steadily rising standard of living and that therefore it depends on technological progress. We assume a harmony between political health and innovation in natural science and especially in the technology based on that science.

But this position is relatively new. It was first broached by the English philosopher Francis Bacon and his followers in the seventeenth and eighteenth centuries and became widely accepted only after the French Revolution. It was not the position of the ancient Greeks or of the long tradition of political thought and practice influenced by Aristotle.

The Greek View

The Greeks would disagree about the need for technology for two reasons. First, they thought unbridled technical innovation (which they conceived of and well imagined) was incompatible with the requirements of political liberty; and, second, they rejected the concept of human nature at the root of our modern view. The Greeks re-

garded technical innovation as a mixed blessing. On the one hand it is needed in some degree for political liberty, simply because no one can be free without some degree of leisure, which is made possible by the developed productive arts. But, on the other hand, such innovation flatters the human love of power and novelty and hence threatens the political order that it underpins. We find this view expressed in the fifth century B.C. by the famous historian Thucydides, who begins his *Peloponnesian War* reflecting that the Greeks were superior to the barbarians as regards discoveries in the arts, but that the Athenians, who embodied Greek inventiveness to the highest degree, were propelled by this trait to a love of conquest and thus to a disastrous imperialism that threatened the entire Greek world.

Likewise, Aristotle argues that any healthy political order depends on the rule of law, which requires that the laws be revered and obeyed as primordial and unchangeable. For this reason the spirit of political health is at odds with the spirit of invention in the arts, for which the new is better than the old and innovation is a virtue. In Aristotle's view, no good political order can last for a long time because its very goodness requires two incompatible elements: technical invention and the rule of law. Law is required for the sake of freedom, and invention is required for the sake of military defense and leisure, without both of which freedom would be meaningless. Thus the Greeks believed that technology incorporated the tragic limits of all human endeavors. What we need for a good life is at the same time the cause of freedom's demise.

But the Greeks would also have rejected the modern view of technology because, for them, it is based on a distorted view of human needs. According to Aristotle, our material needs are limited to what is required for the good life. The end of political life is moral virtue, not endless material acquisition, which even if it were possible would distort the soul and constitute merely a false happiness. For Aristotle, one who believed that life is fulfilled by material acquisition would care more for riches than for freedom, more for fleeting pleasure than for genuine contentment and virtue. True human happiness requires the ability to rise above the material needs that assail us. Virtue thus requires us to spend money well rather than to busy ourselves with making it, to give rather than to take, to overcome the fear of death rather than to cling to life at all costs.

Aristotle thought such freedom from needs possible in rare circumstances and individuals, and he used this possibility—the gentleman—as the standard for measuring the moral worth of the various political regimes. Thus aristocracy is better than democracy because an aristocracy produces and is ruled by such virtuous men. A democracy that inclines in an aristocratic direction is better than a more egalitarian one. And in any good regime, excessive wealth should be avoided, and those engaged in the mechanical arts should not be considered citizens.

The Early Modern View

In holding this view, Aristotle rejected the concept of human nature at the root of modern politics: the idea that human needs are infinite. All the great theorists of modern politics—including Thomas Hobbes and John Locke, the American revolutionaries, the framers of the American Constitution and their Antifederalist opponents, the classical economists such as Adam Smith, and the great theorist of communism, Karl Marx—agreed about the character of human desire: people seek power in order to get more power; the end of government is not to produce rare virtue but to facilitate ever growing prosperity; our infinite needs and adaptability make the difference between ourselves and the animals; happiness, whatever it is, must take account of the fact that our wants become needs and multiply as fast as our ability to satisfy them.

The modern thinkers denied the ancient view of human nature for a number of reasons. First, they simply thought it to be false. What Aristotle called virtue was in reality a delusion: no human being was as independent and free from pressing needs as Aristotle said the virtuous individual would be. Second, they thought the ancient view ineffective and dangerous when applied to political affairs. This point was best made by the Florentine political philosopher Niccolò Machiavelli in the sixteenth century. Machiavelli argued that taking one's bearings from what might be possible in the rarest instances and best circumstances risked blindness and vulnerability to the real harshness and dangers of political life. Third, modern thinkers thought that a focus on moral virtue as the measure of the best regime could feed the terrible religious conflicts that raged in the Christian world. Fourth, they thought the ancient view to be patently unjust, since it denied the equality of human beings and accepted as inevitable the institution of slavery.

Finally, as Bacon said so forcefully, the ancient view was based on a false understanding of nature and a consequent failure to understand how far science could go in forcing nature to satisfy our desires. The ancients rejected the idea of our infinite neediness because, to their dim view, it would lead to despair: how cruel of nature to make us in such a way that we are condemned to inevitable dissatisfaction. But in Bacon's view the ancients came to this conclusion because they woefully underestimated the practical powers of the human mind. They did not understand the real possibilities of technology.

According to Bacon, the Greek intellectual legacy was a crippling burden to be jettisoned as soon as possible. In a world rent by religious strife, it would be far better to replace the war of sect against sect by the war of all humanity against nature than to preach vain lessons about moral virtue. Moreover, a proper understanding of natural science—one that focused on the material causes of things rather than on theological speculation and metaphysical abstractions—would help solve one of the most intractable of political problems: the difference between the talented and energetic few and the slower, less talented many. In the world he envisioned, the most exacting and exciting activity would be the conquest of nature, to which the gifted and ambitious would be attracted. But in this case, the results of unfettered ambition—technological progress—would redound to the benefit of all.

John Locke, the English philosopher, made this argument in an explicitly political and democratic way in his famous *Second Treatise of Civil Government* (1689). There he made it clear that a government founded on the consent of the governed would aim to secure the widest array of private liberty—that a government to which individuals would consent would be one that left them alone to attend to their private affairs and property as much as possible. The primary occupation of private liberty would be material acquisition, made ever more productive by advances in the mechanical arts and sciences. This pursuit would lead to inequality, to be sure. But according to Locke, such inequality would be healthy and no threat to political liberty. The poorest man in England, he said, would be better off than the king of the natives in America, and he surely meant that most Englishmen would be far better off than the aristocrats of Aristotle's supposedly good regime.

Locke, perhaps the most important theorist of modern democracy, assumed Bacon's argument about the egalitarian character of modern technology: the activities of the most ambitious and gifted—the scientists and the inventors and entrepreneurs—would produce goods that are usable by all and that enrich and improve the lives of all. In this way the age-old stumbling block to democracy—

the split between the rich and the poor—could be sufficiently eased. Under such conditions, government could be derived from the consent of the governed, and the people as a whole (both the rich and the poor) could be trusted with the right of revolution against any government that would oppress them.

The Contemporary World

Experience has proved Bacon and his followers to be correct at least in this regard: modern democracy is indeed dependent on technological progress. No one now thinks that prosperity is dangerous to democracy. On the contrary, both in theory and in practice we know that democracy is threatened by a stagnant or declining economy and that economic growth depends on scientific technology. When economic decline threatens, the social consensus—based on the shared hope for material improvement—is fragmented: the rich and the less well off mistrust each other, the old fear the young, the powerful look hungrily at the weak, and the fearful look to a tyrannical savior.

Political and cultural mechanisms can hold the democratic consensus together, but no one thinks that they can do so alone for a prolonged period of time or that they can do so if the material situation gets bad or chaotic enough—as was seen in the case of Germany during the late 1920s and early 1930s. Modern democracy is vulnerable to such threats precisely because it is rooted so firmly in the technological spirit. In rigidly traditional societies, where poverty is thought of as an inescapable fact of life, people can endure levels of hardship and deprivation unimaginable to the citizens of modern democracy, without demanding political change and often without a whimper.

As we saw with European fascism and Japanese militarism in the 1930s and 1940s, with the decades of communism in the former Soviet Union and Eastern Europe, and perhaps today less dramatically in quasi-authoritarian regimes such as Singapore and Hong Kong, the technological spirit, and even technological prowess and prosperity, do not by themselves ensure a democratic form of government. Modern totalitarianism would have been impossible without the powers of communication and control generated by scientific technology; in all its forms it has been dedicated to the technological project. We will never know whether imperial Japan and Nazi Germany, had they been victorious in World War II, would have evolved toward democracy because of the purportedly egalitarian character of technology. But certainly we know that communism collapsed in part because the Soviet Union and its satellites were unable to harness the powers of technology well enough to keep up with the democratic West—even though we cannot be sure that the results of this collapse will be democratic. It is at least plausible that when technologically driven economic development is successful, it becomes much harder to preserve dictatorial and extremely undemocratic forms of government. Modern democracy is impossible without technology, although we cannot be sure that technology guarantees democracy.

Moreover, technology can pose problems even when it does not falter and even where democracy is well established. Rapid technological change, such as robotics and other forms of automation, can cause social dislocations as the character of work and employment is transformed. The dependence of most citizens on technologies they do not understand can make it difficult for them to control those in command of these technologies, who often must be trusted in the making of public policy.

The computer and other electronic devices can make it easy to invade individual privacy. The extension of life spans poses new problems of intergenerational justice, as the young are compelled to work longer to support the old who are idle. The advent of the "media culture," especially television, at once changes the formation of public opinion and gives that opinion more direct and immediate influence on political life. The discovery of safe birth control, which made it possible for women to escape the confines of the family and the household, has caused lasting and important changes in the structure of the family and in our very understanding of individual rights, legal equality, and the boundary between public and private life. Many more examples of such challenges could be given or imagined as technology advances with ever greater speed.

But, in general, well-established democracies have been able to cope with such changes and seem likely to do so in the future. First, there are often technological solutions to the problems generated by technology, as we see in the case of the danger to the environment, the management of nuclear deterrence, and the rise of new kinds of work to replace those made obsolete. Second, there is a close kinship between the democratic and the technological spirits: when technology buffets a democratic people, it buffets a people formed in technology's own image. Believing that their needs are infinite, democratic peoples are filled with the restless spirit of innovation and are oriented to the promise of the future. Indifferent to the claims of tradition and the wisdom of the old, they seek always to be on the "cutting edge" of change. At the same time, they are as much dedicated to comfort, safety, and health as to the sheer power generated by technology. As a consequence, they are both adaptable to new circumstances and careful not to let the prospects of change get so far out of hand, or so inflame their passions, as to threaten the liberties that protect their steady enjoyment of material comfort.

Heidegger and Technological Society

There are some—often influenced by the German philosopher Martin Heidegger (1889–1976)—who think that the happy coexistence of democracy and technology is an illusion. According to this view, the technological frame of mind leads to what can best be described as mass culture. As expanding technology facilitates (and indeed requires) universal education and easy communication, the gap between the most and the least educated in society is narrowed. Culture becomes "popular," judged by the standard of taste and excellence held by the mass of people who benefit from technology.

The watchword of this standard is relativism, according to which nothing is better or worse than anything else. This standard is buttressed by the philosophy of scientific technology, according to which the only real things in the world are material bodies understood as bundles of stored energy. Thus in the technological world all things—human beings and their various activities, nature, works of art and culture, even objects of worship—are understood to be the same: all are alike as the sources of usable energy or raw material for an aimless will to power. In such a world, the differences among things disappear, and all things are taken to be the homogeneous products of an endless cycle of production and consumption.

The world is transformed into a kind of Disneyland, that wonder of the entertainment industry where entirely different and once profound experiences and ways of life can be reproduced, marketed, and then consumed, for the price of admission. Such a world is at best flat, banal, and lifeless, according to Heidegger, and at worst lacking in the moral and intellectual resources needed to recognize and resist the oppressions and horrors that become possible when the world and everything in it are conceived as a kind of giant gas tank or reservoir of useful energy. For

Heidegger, democracy is no remedy for these problems, since it is bound essentially to the project of modern technology and thus is not essentially different from fascism or communism.

It is not easy simply to dismiss Heidegger's argument, and one could point to recent signs that seem to bear out his dire account of technological society: a coarsening of civic culture in the advanced democracies; the rise of postmodernism, a philosophy and attitude that pushes moral relativism to an extreme degree and doubts the very goodness of reason and universal values as guides to political life; a weakening appreciation for individual responsibility and self-reliance; and the creeping violence and vulgarity of popular culture—all of which might undermine a people's capacity for democracy and self-government. There is no doubt that the world view of technology can and does contribute to such ills, and it is possible that, confronted with a disenchanted, technological world of soft satisfactions, the human heart may come to yearn for mystery and danger more than for freedom and equality.

But the Heideggerian view takes for granted that democracy has no spiritual resources that can resist the corrosive aspects of technology, and it assumes that technology is in fact inevitably as corrosive as he describes it. We can be sure of neither fact. Perhaps technology by itself calls forth new kinds of human excellence, strength, and self-reliance; perhaps democratic life by itself calls forth an openness to human dignity and moderation. When we reflect on the harshness and injustice of life before the great modern project of technology—when we remember, for instance, that Greek democracy did indeed depend on slavery—it becomes much easier to appreciate the partnership between democracy and technology. And when we reflect on the horrors of totalitarianism, where tyranny and technology came together, it becomes much easier to tell the difference between democratic and non-democratic regimes.

Doubts about the marriage of technology and democracy are likely to persist, even as technological democracy extends its reach around the globe and provides freedom and a decent life for more and more people and nations. In large part these doubts arise because technology opens up an often unpredictable future. But the uncertainty also arises because the promise of technology is so vast, amounting to nothing less than the permanent reign of justice and the complete conquest of nature. With such a high standard of accomplishment, we should not be surprised if we are disappointed when promises do not quite measure up.

See also *Education; Postmodernism; Relativism; Science.*

Jerry Weinberger

BIBLIOGRAPHY

Bacon, Francis. *New Atlantis and Great Instauration.* Edited by Jerry Weinberger. Rev. ed. Arlington Heights, Ill.: Harlan Davidson, 1989.

Borgmann, Albert. *Technology and the Character of Contemporary Life: A Philosophical Enquiry.* Chicago: University of Chicago Press, 1984.

Caton, Hiram. *The Politics of Progress: The Origins and Development of the Commercial Republic, 1600–1835.* Gainesville: University of Florida Press, 1988.

Ellul, Jacques. *The Technological Society.* Translated by John Wilkinson. New York: Knopf, 1964.

Habermas, Jürgen. *Toward a Rational Society: Student Protest, Science, and Politics.* Translated by Jeremy Shapiro. Boston: Beacon Press, 1970.

Heidegger, Martin. *The Question concerning Technology and Other Essays.* Translated by William Lovitt. New York: Harper Colophon, 1977.

Jonas, Hans. *The Imperative of Responsibility: In Search of an Ethics for the Technological Age.* Chicago: University of Chicago Press, 1984.

Marcuse, Herbert. *One-Dimensional Man.* Boston: Beacon Press, 1964.

Melzer, Arthur, Jerry Weinberger, and M. Richard Zinman, eds. *Technology in the Western Political Tradition.* Ithaca, N.Y.: Cornell University Press, 1993.

Winner, Langdon. *The Whale and the Reactor: A Search for Limits in the Technological Age.* Chicago: University of Chicago Press, 1986.

Terms of office

The periods of time served by elected officials. A term of office may be specified as a maximum time within which new elections may be called, or it may be established in the constitution. Most parliamentary systems establish a maximum term of office for members of parliament; either the prime minister's cabinet or parliament itself has the discretion to dissolve parliament and call early elections. Generally, the parliament chosen at the election following a dissolution begins a new full term of its own. Thus, in such systems, the dates of elections are not fixed and may not be known with certainty until a few months before the elections are held.

In presidential systems the terms of office for both the national legislature and the president are fixed. The constitution specifies a maximum term and does not permit early elections. (Some presidential constitutions make an exception in the case of death, resignation, or impeachment and dismissal of the president; if there is no vice presidency, one way of replacing the president is to set an early election.)

Terms vary in length, but terms of four and five years are the most common. In parliamentary systems the maximum term is most often four years. Terms in Australia, New Zealand, and Sweden are a maximum of three years. The parliaments of Great Britain, Canada, India, and Jamaica, among others, serve maximum terms of five years. In most democracies all the seats of the lower house—or the entire legislature if there is only one house—are renewed at each election. Argentina is very unusual among contemporary democracies in that the lower house continues to be elected to staggered terms: every two years one-half of the membership is renewed. It remains quite common for upper houses to be elected to staggered terms, following the principle that an upper house is to be more deliberative and therefore less immediately responsive to short-term fluctuations in the electorate's preferences. In Australia and Japan, one-half of the membership of the upper houses is renewed every three years. In India and the United States, one-third of the seats in the upper houses are up for election every two years.

Term lengths in presidential systems vary considerably more than those in parliamentary systems. Most presidential term lengths are four to five years. Probably no national constitution has ever mandated a shorter presidential term than four years; however, some chief executives, including the governors of some U.S. states, serve two-year terms. Several presidencies have longer terms. Six-year terms are currently the rule in Argentina, Finland, Mexico, Nicaragua, and the Philippines. The French Fifth Republic and Ireland have seven-year presidential terms; the 1980 constitution of Chile provides for an eight-year term, although a special agreement at the time of transition to competitive elections in 1989 limited the term of the first elected president to four years.

The provisions of several constitutions call for legislative elections to occur more frequently than presidential elections. For example, members of the U.S. House of Representatives serve two-year terms, but the president serves for four years. The pattern of more frequent legislative elections is also seen in Brazil, Chile, Finland, France, and Korea, as well as in some other countries.

Whenever a president and the legislature are elected at different times, and for terms of different length, it is common for divergent parties or blocs of parties to control the legislature and the presidency (a phenomenon known as divided government). Presidential systems are often criticized for this tendency to produce partisan incompatibility between the elected branches. Divided government, however, is far less common when presidents and legislatures are elected at the same time. Even in the United States, where divided government has been common, before 1956 only one of the congressional elections held in a presidential election year failed to produce a legislative majority for the incoming president's party. After 1956 the increasing tendency of voters to elect candidates of one party to Congress and candidates of another party to the presidency has made divided government more common; nonetheless, the share of seats won by the president's party has generally been lower in midterm elections—those elections that come halfway between presidential elections—than in presidential election years. Examples of presidential systems in which presidents and congresses are always elected at the same time are Costa Rica, the Dominican Republic, and Venezuela. In these cases, it has been rare for the president's party not to have a majority or at least a strong plurality (more than 40 percent) of the seats in the congress.

In some countries, elected officials may serve only a limited number of terms. Although some presidents—for example, those of the Dominican Republic, France, and Nicaragua—can serve an unlimited number of terms, others face restrictions. Some can serve only two terms, consecutive or not. This has been the rule in the United States since 1951 and also in Bulgaria, Namibia, Portugal, and Romania. Presidents in other countries are barred from being immediately reelected; they must wait for one term to pass before being eligible again, as in Argentina, or for two terms to pass, as in Venezuela. The presidents of Colombia, Costa Rica, and Mexico, among others, may serve no more than one term.

Rarely are there also limits on the terms that legislators may serve. Costa Rican, Ecuadoran, and Mexican legislators may not serve consecutive terms; few return to the legislature for second terms, as legislative service is a stepping stone in a political career that typically progresses to presidentially appointed bureaucratic posts for party loyalists. Several U.S. states have recently adopted limits on the number of terms that may be served by their state legislators and representatives to Congress. Legislative term limits were enacted in the Philippines in 1988. Supporters of term limits claim that limiting terms discourages members' abuse of their office by forcing turnover and thus assuring more competitive elections. Opponents say that limiting terms denies voters their primary means for influencing representatives—being able to defeat or reelect them.

See also *Accountability of public officials; Parliamentarism and presidentialism.*

Matthew Soberg Shugart

BIBLIOGRAPHY

Benjamin, Gerald, and Michael J. Malbin, eds. *Limiting Legislative Terms.* Washington, D.C.: CQ Press, 1992.

Carey, John M. "Term Limits and Legislative Representation." Ph.D. diss., University of California, San Diego, 1993.

Keech, William R. "Thinking about the Length and Renewability of Electoral Terms." In *Electoral Laws and Their Political Consequences,* edited by Bernard Grofman and Arend Lijphart. New York: Agathon Press, 1986.

Lijphart, Arend. *Democracies: Patterns of Majoritarian and Consensus Government in Twenty-one Countries.* New Haven and London: Yale University Press, 1984.

Shugart, Matthew S., and John M. Carey. *Presidents and Assemblies: Constitutional Design and Electoral Dynamics.* New York and Cambridge: Cambridge University Press, 1992.

Thailand

A constitutional monarchy of Southeast Asia and the only nation of that region never colonized by Western powers. The history of politics in Thailand (formerly known as Siam) is a history of authoritarian rule. From its earliest kingdom in Sukhothai (c. 1238–1350), Thailand was led by paternalistic kings whose duty it was to solve all the problems of their subjects. In the Ayuthaya period (1350–1767) these rulers were transformed into autocratic god-kings. Even today that perception remains an important element of the veneration shown to the king. The king was Lord of Life, with total power over every aspect of society.

The destruction of the city of Ayuthaya by invading Burmese in 1767 was a traumatic event in Thai history. The kingdom was nearly destroyed, but the Thais soon recovered and established life under a new centralized

government in Bangkok. Once again a dynasty was established. The ninth monarch of the Chakri dynasty, King Bhumibol Adulyadej, was Thailand's reigning monarch in the early 1990s.

The Chakri kings strengthened their position by creating a more "modern" and efficient governmental system led by Western-trained bureaucrats. Several of the Chakris were reformers who unintentionally brought about their own demise as they opened the kingdom to Western ideas of limited government. In 1932 the absolute monarchy was overthrown and replaced by a new oligarchy consisting of Western-trained bureaucrats and members of the military. These new forces promulgated constitutions, making the nation a constitutional monarchy. They continued to dominate Thai politics in the early 1990s. The kingdom was renamed Thailand in 1939.

Fashioning a Semidemocracy

The political culture of Thailand, with its emphasis on deference to authority and hierarchical social relations, is not conducive to democratic rule. Nevertheless, in the 1980s Thailand fashioned a semidemocracy that defied the expectations of most observers of Thai politics. *Semidemocracy* refers to the balance between Western-style democracy and the authoritarian values that favor and buttress military involvement in governmental affairs. The balance is uniquely Thai, a blend that has been legitimated in the minds of both the rulers and the ruled.

The success of Thailand's semidemocracy was partly a result of the economic boom of the 1980s, which allowed the government to meet the needs of the citizenry. This remarkable period of economic development brought high levels of education, literacy, access to the media, and travel—all of which heightened Thais' awareness of democratic values and expanded their horizons.

The Thai people approved of the semidemocracy because of the orderly society and economic growth that accompanied it. In the past, the democratic orientations of the Thais had been a matter of form rather than substance. Other values—security, development, deference, personalism, and economic stability—took precedence over those more directly related to citizen participation in governmental affairs. The economic achievements of the 1980s helped the Thais appreciate democratic values as much as other cherished values. The semidemocracy also provided the Thai people with an example of successful democratic government. Most viewed the earlier period of democracy, from 1973 to 1976, as a time of chaos, disorder, and economic travail.

In the 1980s and early 1990s the Thai political system seemed well able to cope with the changing needs and demands of the people. This ability was due in part to the strengthening of political institutions and in part to the rise of pressure groups representing the interests of an increasingly pluralistic society. These changes accompanied the process of democratization, which drew more citizens to become involved in the political sphere. Democratization also reduced the importance of personalism as it increased the observance of laws and the recognition of governmental institutions in public-policy decision making.

The clearest sign of change in contemporary Thai politics was the rise to power in 1988 of Chatchai Choonhavan, the first elected member of parliament to become prime minister since 1976. Chatchai became prime minister following the 1988 elections, when the political party he led received the largest plurality of votes. Chatchai's predecessor, Gen. Prem Tinsulanond, had led Thailand during a period of economic growth. His administration had been deemed acceptable to both civilians and the military, and he had been expected to continue in office. His refusal to be a candidate opened the way for civilian leadership under Chatchai.

The smooth transition reflected the new optimism about Thailand's evolution toward democracy. Chatchai was able to assume power without relying on the support of the army, and the constitutional provisions for elections worked well in the transfer of political power. Thus it was all the more shocking when a military coup d'état took place in February 1991. The coup was an assault on the notion that Thailand had successfully institutionalized democratic and civilian government.

The 1991 Coup and Its Aftermath

The last successful coup had taken place in 1977. The peaceful interval of more than a decade lulled the Chatchai administration into believing that the days of coups were over. Furthermore, the communist insurgency that had plagued Thailand in the 1960s and 1970s had been quelled, and there was no external threat to Thai security. There seemed to be no compelling motive for military intervention in governmental affairs. The stronger role of political parties and the parliament, as well as a general attitude favorable to democratic civilian rule, also seemed to have reduced the influence of the military. The determination of King Bhumibol Adulyadej to oppose a military coup was believed to lessen the chance that such a coup would succeed. Moreover, Thailand's remarkable economic growth of 11 percent per year (the highest in the world for three years) seemed to provide a bulwark against intervention by the military. Military leaders had a stake in the status quo because they benefited from the enormous profits generated by the booming Thai economy. Finally, the Thai military was thought to have accepted Chatchai, himself a former army general, because of the generous budget he allotted to the military.

But counter to this analysis, and against all expectations, Sunthorn Kongsompong, who was supreme commander, and Suchinda Kraprayoon, the army commander in chief, abrogated the constitution on February 23, 1991, and dismissed the elected government. In its place they set up a temporary National Peacekeeping Council, with powers of martial law, and established themselves as the ultimate arbiters of public policy. Initially the Thai people made no resistance to the coup, though they did not enthusiastically support it; there were no public protests or demonstrations.

The 1991 coup demonstrated that democratization had not ended the personalism and factionalism of traditional Thai politics. Even among the partners in the ruling coalition that was in power when the coup occurred, factional conflict remained the norm as party leaders vied for the most influential cabinet positions.

A problem related to personalism was corruption, which also continued to be an important part of the political scene. The phenomenal economic growth of the 1980s had brought large amounts of capital into the financial system, and these new resources were the target of public officials out for private gain. Thai citizens were skeptical about the Chatchai administration's professed concern for the majority, which did not benefit from the growth of the economy.

The National Peacekeeping Council claimed that corruption, factionalism, and the rise of a "parliamentary dictatorship" were the main reasons for the coup. In particular, the military complained of rampant vote buying, leading to the election of the rich rather than the most qualified. In fact, the number of wealthy capitalists elected to parliament and chosen for the cabinet had risen steadily in the past decades, but the increase was especially clear in the Chatchai administration.

The complaint of corruption was an important legitimizing rationale for the coup. The more direct cause, however, was a pattern of slights inflicted by Chatchai, which the military perceived as threats to its traditional prerogatives. Chatchai set forth the principle that the military must be subordinate to a civilian prime minister. This principle was intolerable to the military rulers, who had enjoyed greater influence in past military and civilian administrations.

The coup temporarily ended Thailand's steady progress toward democratization and embarrassed the nation in its expanding international affairs. The conventional wisdom was not completely wrong in holding that coups were a thing of the past, however. Realizing that times had indeed changed, the National Peacekeeping Council moved quickly to establish an interim constitution and name a prime minister. The council chose Anand Panyarachun, a distinguished civilian diplomat, administrator, and businessman, to serve as prime minister. His appointment was a sign that the military believed the people would not long tolerate direct military rule.

Anand scheduled a nationwide parliamentary election for March 1992. Corruption was widespread. Political parties sold their names and vote-mobilizing organizations to candidates. Candidates received up to several hundred thousand dollars each for campaign purposes. These funds were often given in cash, so they could not be accounted for. Candidates used the money they received from political parties to pay potential voters for their support. Corruption became the centerpiece of the Thai electoral system.

The elections on March 22 resulted in a narrow victory for parties aligned with the military. Eventually the coalition named General Suchinda as prime minister despite his unequivocal declaration that he would not accept the office. His nomination was approved by the king and the parliament with the concurrence of the speaker of the parliament, and Suchinda took office. In what Thais referred to as "the second coup" or "the silent coup," General Suchinda had engineered military control over the position of prime minister. In so doing he reversed the steps Thailand had taken toward democratic government. To express their dismay, some 50,000 protesters demonstrated against the new government following the announcement of Suchinda's appointment.

Suchinda's time in office was brief: he was driven from office after only forty-eight days. Massive anti-Suchinda demonstrations by hundreds of thousands of Thais took place in May, and hundreds died when the military tried to stop the protests. The conflict between Thailand's reverence for tradition and its headlong plunge into modernity was the major factor in these events. Suchinda mistakenly bet that the forces of tradition as exemplified by the military would prevail. He underestimated the power of the ideal of democracy among the country's increasingly educated and sophisticated citizens.

Suchinda misunderstood the reaction he would generate by approving a violent response to the antigovernment demonstrations. He declared a state of emergency, which effectively took away citizens' civil liberties. At the same time, censorship of the media and the sight of police officers and troops bludgeoning demonstrators wiped out any appearance of legitimacy Suchinda might have had. His claim that the demonstrators and their leaders were pawns of "communist" elements who desired the end of the monarchy was vintage rhetoric from the 1960s, irrelevant to the realities of the 1990s.

Return to Civilian Government

When the crisis of May 1992 turned into chaos and potential civil war, King Bhumibol Adulyadej stepped in to play a crucial role in determining political succession. His extraordinary intervention on May 20 forced the resignation of Suchinda and placed the immense prestige of the monarch on the side of democratic rule. Suchinda had no choice but to resign.

The establishment of a civilian administration was more difficult than the removal of Suchinda, who went into hiding, protected by troops loyal to him. In a second extraordinary intervention, the king approved the return of Anand Panyarachun as prime minister. The appointment was enthusiastically received by most Thais, who recalled that Anand had won international praise for running an honest and efficient government following the 1991 coup.

The election that took place September 13, 1992, was considered one of the fairest in Thai history because of the oversight of "watchdog" groups. A coalition of pro-democracy parties, plus one party that had supported the military in the previous administration, formed a government under the leadership of a civilian politician. Chuan Leekpai, the soft-spoken, fair-minded, moderate leader of the Democrat Party from Trang Province, became prime minister. He led a 207-seat coalition in the 360-member House of Representatives. Prime Minister Chuan's challenge was to find a balance between democratic rule and sensitivity to the traditional prerogatives of the Thai military.

The struggle between state officials led by the military, on the one hand, and politicians and business elites, on the other, continued to be at the center stage of Thai political activity. The 1991 military coup and the subsequent debate on how to fashion a new government exemplified both the attempt and the failure to resolve this struggle. The public explanations for the coup—corruption and parliamentary dictatorship—were rationalizations by military leaders who moved to secure prerogatives they thought were threatened by civilian leadership.

There are many reasons for optimism about continued stable, democratic rule and a continuing move away from military-dominated, authoritarian, self-serving centralized government. First, Thailand has successfully ended internal insurgency. Second, there are no serious outside threats to the kingdom's security. Third, with one of the highest economic growth rates in the world and a reputation for conservative fiscal management, Thailand has excellent prospects for continued development. Fourth, there has been increasing professionalization of the armed forces. Finally, the international movement toward democratization has penetrated most of the major groups in Thai society, including the military.

The rise of an educated, cosmopolitan middle class is often viewed as essential to stable government. In Thailand the middle class has increasingly become a focal point of economic and political decision making. Supporting the middle class are new interest groups that are demanding rights and resources formerly thought to be reserved for the elites. Along with political parties and parliament, these new organizations are taking on the functions once served by patron-client networks.

Prime Minister Chuan faced the challenge of finding the proper balance between the desire for stability and the desire for democracy, between the requirements of order and of civil liberties, between respect for authority and empathy for the demands of the people, and between the role of the military as the guarantor of security and the desire for civilian dominance. The kingdom's custom of treading the middle path augured well for the nation's democratic future.

See also *Asia, Southeast.*

Clark D. Neher

BIBLIOGRAPHY

Girling, John L. S. *Thailand: Society and Politics.* Ithaca, N.Y.: Cornell University Press, 1981.

Laothamatas, Anek. *From Bureaucratic Polity to Liberal Corporatism: Business Associations and the New Political Economy of Thailand.* Boulder, Colo.: Westview Press, 1991.

Likhit, Dhiravegin. *The Bureaucratic Elite of Thailand.* Bangkok: Thai Khadi Research Institute, Thammasat University, 1978.

Morell, David, and Chai-Anan Samudavanija. *Political Conflict in Thailand: Reform, Reaction, Revolution.* Cambridge, Mass.: Oelgesclager, Gunn, and Hain, 1981.

Neher, Clark D. *Modern Thai Politics, from Village to Nation.* 2d ed. Cambridge, Mass.: Schenkman, 1979.

———, and Mungkandi Wiwat, eds. *U.S.–Thailand Relations in a New International Era.* Berkeley: Institute of East Asian Studies, University of California, 1990.

Somsakdi, Xuto, ed. *Government and Politics of Thailand.* Oxford: Oxford University Press, 1987.

Wilson, David A. *Politics in Thailand.* Ithaca, N.Y.: Cornell University Press, 1962.

Thatcher, Margaret

Conservative prime minister of Britain from 1979 to 1990, the longest serving prime minister of the twentieth century and the first woman to hold that position. While Lady Thatcher (1925–   ) was in office, neoliberalism became the dominant strand within the Conservative Party, and the postwar political consensus concerning the role of the state in economic policy was broken. Thatcher gave her name to a constellation of values and policies known as *Thatcherism,* which Nigel Lawson, her Chancellor of the Exchequer for six years, defined as "a mixture of free markets, financial discipline, firm control over public expenditure, nationalism, 'Victorian values,' privatization, and a dash of populism."

The daughter of a successful shopkeeper and local politician, Thatcher was educated at the local girls' school and then at Oxford University. She was elected a Conservative member of Parliament in 1959 and was secretary of state for education in the government of Edward Heath (1970–1974). In 1975 she was elected leader of the Conservative Party.

Thatcher's economic philosophy combined the belief that good housekeeping equals good economics with the conviction, arising from her reading of Friedrich von Hayek's *The Road to Serfdom* (1944), that only markets free of state controls will produce an "enterprise culture." Acting on these beliefs, Thatcher's government reduced state intervention in financial and labor markets. State-owned utilities were "privatized" and shares sold to the public. Working-class families who had been tenants of public housing were encouraged to buy their dwellings. Individuals were encouraged through generous tax allowances to make their own provisions for old age and illness. Thatcher believed that such policies would enhance individual freedom and choice, which, in her view, depended on private property rights.

To reshape the welfare state, the autonomy and power of local government—as well as of central government bureaucracies, the professions, and the trade unions—had to be reduced. The attack on the welfare state did not begin in earnest until Thatcher's third term in 1988, by which time she had achieved these earlier objectives. As a consequence of the weakening of many institutions essential to a pluralist democratic society, Thatcher's policies have meant that the central state—comprising senior ministers and top officials—has to reckon with far fewer countervailing powers. Thatcher's critics charge that British civil society, once diverse and stable, was damaged and democracy weakened in the process.

The British central state in the 1990s is indeed far more powerful than before, and it is less accountable to its citizens. Market norms govern more areas of social life. The power, resources, and responsibilities of democratically elected local government have been reduced and replaced by numerous unelected, quasi-autonomous nongovernmental organizations (known as *quangos).* Their members are disproportionately male, white, and drawn from the business world. Many are active Conservative Party supporters. The provision of housing, pensions, education,

and health care have all become more market based. This is as Thatcher intended. After all, as she said (in a 1987 interview with *Woman's Own* magazine), "There is no such thing as society, only individuals and families."

Reshaping the welfare state by withdrawing state resources for benefits and services widened inequalities in Britain. Thatcher accepted this consequence of her policies but argued that "it means you drag up the poor people because there are more resources to do so." The income of poorer families in Britain fell by 17 percent in the 1980s, while that of the richest increased by 62 percent. In 1979, 10 percent of Britain's children were living in poverty; ten years later this number had increased to one-third.

Thatcher showed that gender need be no barrier to strong leadership. She had the conviction and courage to make radical changes. In doing so she challenged much that had been taken for granted in postwar British society. In the short run the effects were damaging to democracy, but in the long run they may be beneficial as the limits of applying market principles to all areas of life become clearer.

See also *Civil society; Market theory; United Kingdom.*

Hilary Land

BIBLIOGRAPHY

Gamble, Andrew. *The Free Economy and the Strong State: The Politics of Thatcherism.* London: Macmillan, 1988.

Hutton, Will. *The State We're In.* London: Jonathan Cape, 1994.

Kavanagh, Dennis. *Thatcherism and British Politics: The End of Consensus?* 2d ed. Oxford: Oxford University Press, 1990.

Lawson, Nigel. *The View From No. 11: Memoirs of a Tory Radical.* London: Corgi Books, 1992.

Thatcher, Margaret. *The Downing Street Years.* London: Macmillan, 1993.

Young, Hugo. *One of Us: A Biography of Margaret Thatcher.* Rev. ed. London: Pan Books, 1990.

Theory, African

African democratic theory is an aspect of African political thought that shows ambivalence toward the role of democracy in the management of African public affairs. The attention of theorists to democratic modes in Africa has sometimes been indirect, as it was in the political arrangements of precolonial Africa. In many other instances, democratic issues have been addressed more directly, as has been the case during the colonial and post-colonial periods.

Precolonial Indigenous Societies

The parentage of modern African studies can be traced to colonial social anthropology. Scholars in that field studied the principles of government in Africa's indigenous societies in order to facilitate the administration of European colonies established in the last quarter of the nineteenth century. The most famous formulation of these principles was provided by Meyer Fortes and E. E. Evans-Pritchard in their distinction between hierarchically organized societies, which were ruled by chiefly aristocratic orders, and egalitarian societies, which were governed by more democratic processes (*African Political Systems*, 1940).

The more egalitarian societies were based on kinship lineages that organized their fluid politics on the basis of situational alliances. The modern construction of democratic thought in Africa has grown largely from this egalitarian version of indigenous politics—a kind of precursor of democracy, or protodemocracy, which respected and protected the role of individuals in traditional politics—and has been opposed to the principle of aristocratic governance.

The most illustrious example of protodemocratic governance in indigenous Africa is the Igbo political system in southeastern Nigeria. Igbo public affairs were managed on the basis of open discussions involving all adult male members of the community in a democratic forum. Social anthropologists paid considerable attention to the politics of egalitarian and protodemocratic societies exemplified by the Igbo system. Such other indigenous groups as the Tiv in northern Nigeria, the Nuer in Sudan, and the Tallensi in Ghana provided the model of what social anthropologists labeled *segmentary lineage systems;* in these groups, politics was organized on the basis of varying kinship alliances. Although these stateless societies lacked the aristocratic hierarchies of kingdoms, they were able to govern themselves effectively. Their unit of political action was the kin group to which the individual was firmly tied—in place of a formal state.

Although the egalitarian systems had an apparent relationship to democratic means of governance, some traditional aristocratic societies also had features that could foster democratic behaviors. For instance, many traditional states in Africa excelled in creating the kinds of consti-

tutional formations on which liberal democracy thrives. Succession in most indigenous states was regulated by custom and constitutional usage. Furthermore, many traditional states practiced constitutional restraint. For example, the Fanti confederacy, a collection of traditional Akan states situated in modern Ghana, was formed in 1867 as a constitutional arrangement to stop warfare among neighboring states and to promote cohesion.

Unfortunately, in the wider sphere of precolonial African geopolitics, the simpler stateless societies fell victims to the ambitions of more powerful neighboring kingdoms. This was especially the case during the era of the slave trade in Africa, when aristocratic societies exploited weaker ones that were based on popular and democratic modes of governance.

The Slave Trade

The slave trade sharpened the distinction between aristocratic societies and stateless societies in Africa. The democratic principle was threatened by the Arab slave trade (c. 950–1850) and the European slave trade (1480–1850). These were enforced by state organizations, and most kin-based stateless societies in Africa suffered disproportionately. There is ample evidence that the internal protodemocratic organization of stateless societies deteriorated during the slave trade. For example, the Igbo institution of *osu* forbade the bestowal of citizenship status and privileges on kinless persons. That principle led to the utter degradation of kinless persons in a society suffused with kinship, and it palpably diminished the potential for the development of democratic processes in Igboland.

The problems of the slave trade brought to the fore of African politics the antagonism between democratic advocacy and practice and aristocratic privilege. The community of ex-slave "recaptives" of Sierra Leone advocated and practiced democratic self-governance for a short while in the latter half of the nineteenth century. The organization of this community was conceived by the leadership of the descendants of those whom British abolitionist expeditions had recaptured from slave-running ships in the Atlantic and resettled in Sierra Leone. The community's leader, James Africanus Horton, a direct descendant of an Igbo recaptive, designed a mode of self-government that was based on British democratic institutions but fully run by Africans. This system of self-government was practiced briefly in Horton's own political base on McCarthy Island in Sierra Leone. In contrast, native African aristocrats preferred to retain traditional African aristocratic institutions as a definition of African independence.

Democracy's Misfortunes in Africa

European contact with Africa from the end of the eighteenth century onward coincided with the growth and expansion of democratic institutions and traditions in Western Europe. Indeed, the four French communes of Saint-Louis in Senegal, including its African residents, were part of the original experimentation with democracy following the French Revolution (1789) and the revolution of 1848. By 1848 the residents of Saint-Louis were holding local elections, involving both the French and the Africans, to run their own affairs. At one point a Creole Senegalese was elected mayor of Saint-Louis. African leaders in this era—including especially the influential Edward Wilmot Blyden, a statesman based in Liberia who was of Caribbean origin and descended from former Igbo slaves—encouraged the expansion of European contact with Africa because they were convinced that Africa would benefit from the burgeoning democratic impulse in Europe.

Subsequent European expansion and imperialism in Africa actually had the opposite result. The colonizers nullified democratic self-rule among the Sierra Leonean recaptives; they severely limited, for Senegalese, the democratic benefits from the republicanism of the revolution of 1848; and they disenfranchised Africans in the Cape Colony of South Africa. Indeed, European imperialism not only limited the democratic potential inherent in indigenous African institutions but also denied Europe's African colonies any potential benefits from the growing democratic movement inside imperial European nations.

The three dominant models of European colonial rule in Africa were intrinsically antidemocratic. These were indirect rule, assimilation, and separatist doctrine. The British doctrine of indirect rule grew out of negotiations in the early part of the twentieth century between the Fulani aristocracy, the old conquerors of Hausaland in modern northern Nigeria, and the British, the region's new conquerors. Forerunners of the practice can be traced to English rule in Ireland and British rule in India.

From its outset indirect rule involved layers of hierarchy based on chiefs and discouraged democratic practices, even those inherent in traditional rulership. Indirect rule imposed new aristocratic orders on egalitarian societies. For example, British colonial rulers created a new rank of warrant chiefs among the egalitarian Igbo by issuing warrants or certificates of authority to men who previously exercised no special political powers. Indirect rule also curtailed the traditional checks and balances that had restrained rulers from arbitrary and despotic rule in traditional states.

In French colonies the doctrine and practice of assimilation set criteria for Africans to become French citizens, thus devaluing the political worth of ordinary individuals, the overwhelming majority, in the colonies. This practice was a major breach and reversal of the democratic principles of the French Revolution.

Various separatist doctrines and devices informed colonial rule in European settler colonies—ranging from Kenya, Rhodesia, and the Portuguese colonies to South Africa with its system of apartheid. These practices represented open denials of democratic self-rule for Africans.

Colonialism's attack on democratic prospects in Africa had two devastating results. First, colonialism devalued Africa's political cultures, placing them beneath Europe's and implying that they were not capable of organizing democratic self-government. Second, the colonial state treated the individual as a subject rather than as a citizen. Consequently, Africans were alienated from the colonial state and found their political forums in kinship enclaves, which thus became politicized. Kinship systems expanded enormously under colonialism, and the public realm became fragmented. Such fragmentation is hardly hospitable to democracy, which thrives best when citizens operate within a single public realm that they value and nourish.

Anticolonialism

Anticolonialism arose from the ranks and works of pan-Africanism, the movement begun by Africans residing in the United States and the Caribbean at the beginning of the twentieth century. Its primary purpose was to improve the political and social situation of Africa and Africans. Pan-African advocates of the nineteenth and early twentieth centuries were confident that European colonialism would be beneficial for Africans largely because they believed that the introduction of European political institutions would lead to liberal democratic rule in Africa. This was clearly their expectation at the time of the First Pan-African Congress, which was held in London in 1900 and was largely organized and directed by W. E. B. Du Bois, the African American intellectual. Du Bois and the congress wanted European colonialism to prepare Africans for democratic rule, primarily through education.

Pan-African nationalism quickly turned against colonialism when these expectations foundered, leading Du Bois, forty-five years after the First Pan-African Congress, to characterize colonialism as the antithesis of democracy and freedom. Anticolonialism turned European imperialism on its head, charging it with tyranny and subversion of democracy. A series of native African nationalists—beginning with Nnamdi Azikiwe from Nigeria and including Kwame Nkrumah (Ghana), Mbonu Ojike (Nigeria), and many others, who were educated in the United States and Europe—challenged European imperialism for its antidemocratic character.

Anticolonialism's conception of democracy was, however, remarkably different from contemporary European usage. Whereas European democracy emphasized the unique individual's rights, democracy-professing anticolonialism attacked imperialism for devaluing African cultures and for allowing aliens to rule indigenous African peoples. While democratic freedom meant the achievement of positive rights for the ordinary European, for the African nationalist democracy had a negative meaning of gaining the right not to be ruled by foreigners. Accordingly, individuals never much mattered in the anticolonialist concept of democracy. Whereas domestic tyranny was the enemy of democracy in European politics, Pan-African anticolonialists preached that democracy would be achieved if Africans rid themselves of foreign tyranny. This lack of attention to the needs of the individual, and the emphasis on collective rights of Africans, colored the meaning of democracy in colonial Africa. That limited concept now haunts African politics, for foreign tyrannies have departed and internal tyrants have replaced alien colonial rulers.

Evolution of Democratic Institutions

African independence movements had two parts whose distinction from each other will help to clarify the construction of democratic institutions in Africa. There was, first, a period of anticolonialism marked by unmitigated antagonism between the European imperialists and their main critics, African nationalists. This period was followed in some countries by decolonization, a period of negotiation and cooperation between the colonizers and their African challengers in arrangements for terminating colonial rule. The relationship between anticolonialism and decolonization is paramount in assessing the potential for democracy in any African nation.

Anticolonialism was widespread in twentieth-century Africa and can be identified in every region of Subsaharan Africa. In West Africa it took the form of elitist confrontation with colonialism, sometimes in fierce rhetoric, for which Azikiwe and Nkrumah were particularly famous. It also involved civil disobedience by trade unions and student organizations. In West Africa such actions were punished by the colonizers and resulted in court trials for many nationalists, earning jail terms for some, like Nkrumah in Ghana and Anthony Enahoro in Nigeria.

In East Africa in the 1950s the Mau Mau war was waged against white settlers in the Kenyan highlands. The British countered in heavy reprisals, court trials, and imprisonment of many nationalists, including Jomo Kenyatta, who eventually became Kenya's first prime minister. The Kenyan experience was to be repeated in other British settler territories in Rhodesia and South Africa. Anticolonialism was particularly bloody in the Portuguese colonies because of Portugal's absolutist definition of its colonies as Outer Portugal. Varying degrees of anticolonialism can be traced in other colonial experiences—in the Belgian Congo (Zaire) and in the French colonies in West and Central Africa.

Although all colonial regimes and regions experienced anticolonialism, not all of them had organized programs of decolonization. The need to grant independence to its African colonies was first recognized by Great Britain following World War II. The pattern of negotiations with British colonies had been established in India, which was granted independence in 1947.

In general, British colonies went through the routine of decolonization in two stages. First, there was an attempt in each case to reconcile the aspirations and claims of the nationalists with the objectives of the British government in granting self-rule. The nationalists who fostered anticolonialism had demonized the imperialists as enemies; conversely, the colonizers had portrayed nationalists as dangerous and irresponsible. Decolonization afforded each side the opportunity to reevaluate the opponent's positions.

Second, decolonization included various attempts to reconcile competing proposals for governmental arrangements by vested interests in the colonies. This reconciliation process was particularly important in dealing with the rift between anticolonial nationalists and the chieftains who collaborated with colonial rulers and who tended to reject the call by the anticolonial nationalists for full-blown democracy.

In Ghana, there were attempts to reconcile Nkrumah's

expansive political ambitions with the more conservative opposition to his call for wholesale democracy involving all regions of Ghana in one undifferentiated forum. In Nigeria, Azikiwe's notion of a common platform for all voters had to be reconciled with the views of Obafemi Awolowo and Ahmadu Bello. Awolowo was the leader of the powerful Yoruba, whose idea of a "people's republic" was a confederation of small ethnic states (the "people" in Awolowo's people's republic referred to cultural groupings, not to individuals). Bello represented the Fulani aristocracy, which was fighting for a restoration of its nineteenth-century empire in northern Nigeria. In Zimbabwe, compromises had to be forged not only between the African nationalists and the white settlers but also between two major factions among the nationalists.

Above all else, decolonization was a period of constitution making, embodying compromises between competing viewpoints. Under the British sphere, decolonization was partially a process of building governmental structures that were for the most part patterned on British parliamentary democracy.

Other European colonial powers did not fare as well as the British in negotiating decolonization for their African colonies. After a period of denying the need to do so, the French began a regime of decolonization following the general referendum in France's African colonies in 1958. Guinea, under Ahmed Sékou Touré's guidance, was allowed to opt for immediate independence, while all other French colonies chose gradual weaning toward independence in 1960. Decolonization in the French colonies included copying French ideals of democracy.

In contrast, there was little opportunity for decolonization in colonies ruled by Belgium and Portugal. Zaire, Rwanda, and Burundi were plunged into immediate independence from Belgium, without any period of measured decolonization. The Portuguese colonies of Angola, Mozambique, and Guinea-Bissau went through treacherous wars of liberation in order to gain their independence from Portugal, without the opportunity of negotiation under the aegis of decolonization.

In general, African nations that had marked transitions from periods of anticolonialism to regimes of decolonization have had fewer problems with the management of the institutions of parliamentary democracy than have those nations that never experienced a weaning transition from anticolonialism to decolonization. The political disasters in all the former Belgian and Portuguese colonies may well have multiple causes—but the inability of opponents in these nations to compromise may ultimately be traced to their lack of preparation under a regime of decolonization. Democracy thrives in a political culture of tolerance such as was cultivated by regimes of decolonization. On the other hand, democracy does poorly in circumstances of intolerance such as the absolutism that anticolonialism fomented. The weaning from anticolonialism to decolonization was an act of institutional political socialization that may have fostered the ability to run democratic regimes and to revive them when they are imperiled.

The Cold War Period

Whatever its inherent benefits, decolonization was of short duration and in most instances represented a hurried attempt to reverse the dictatorship of imperialism by replacing the institutions of colonial rule with new democratic structures. The democracies that followed colonialism faltered badly, in most instances yielding to military dictatorships, personal rule, or one-party state dictatorships. It is entirely possible that the failures of these democracies were the natural consequence of Africa's harsh history of tyranny under colonial rule and that the democratic pretensions of decolonization could not overtake an entrenched political culture of dictatorship.

Even so, the international environment of the 1960s through the mid-1980s was inhospitable for emerging democracies. During this cold war era the Western democracies were willing to support dictatorships in African countries in exchange for their promise to take sides with the West against the menace of Soviet communism. As a consequence, democratic stirrings in Africa did not receive wholesale support from established Western democracies, and, more remarkably, dictatorship gained specious respectability as an acceptable alternative to democracy.

Aristide Zolberg's *Creating Political Order* (1966) captures the views of postcolonial African leaders who monopolized power on the claim that their first responsibility was to create political order and improve the prestige and economic health of their nations. Touré of Guinea, Nkrumah of Ghana, Kenneth Kaunda of Zambia, and many other monopolizers of power in African nations were sophisticated men of letters, who read what Western social scientists wrote about them. They followed and encouraged "charismatic legitimation theory," which argued that the apparent dictatorship of charismatic rulers would eventually pay dividends for their nations. Various dictators embraced this version of the principle of developmental dictatorship, which contended that rapid escape from economic backwardness required a period of dictatorship.

The rationalization of dictatorship attained its intellectual peak in the theory of one-party state democracy in Tanzania under the benign guidance of Julius Nyerere, Tanzania's first president. The goal of one-party state democracy was the people's sovereignty and strong government. Missing from this ideology was any reference to the needs of the unique individual, the concern of liberal democracy. Clearly, the theory of one-party state democracy inherited the collectivistic strands of anticolonial nationalist thought.

One-party state democracy sought to enforce communal consensus and to avoid the dissension that seemed to be the nemesis of liberal democracy. In pursuing these goals, its protagonists have frequently misstated and exaggerated the degree of consensus in the traditional African societies they sometimes claimed as their model. In reality, one-party state democracy—as much in capitalist Kenya as in socialist Tanzania—was closer to the command politics in the Soviet Union than to traditional African politics. Not unexpectedly, the appeal and legitimacy of this form of government waned with the end of the cold war.

Prospects in the Multiethnic States

Despite the barriers to democracy in postcolonial Africa, especially during the cold war, the basis for democratic governance has not been eradicated. Richard Sklar, who has provided a major analysis of democracy in Africa, maintains that democracy's infrastructure is not absent from Africa's social and cultural institutions. Although three of Africa's smallest and relatively uncomplicated nations—Mauritania, Gambia, and Botswana—have usually provided examples of surviving democracies, the lasting elements of democracy are more apparent in less homogeneous countries. The cost of managing dictatorship in multiethnic nations is very high, and trends toward the compromises of democracies may be encouraged by these nations' own political momentum. That is why Nigeria's and South Africa's political experiences may contain seeds of democracy that will survive as lasting examples for other African nations.

From 1976 to 1979 Nigerians sought to overcome their political divisions through constitutional engineering.

The principal problems that faced Nigeria's constitution makers were two. First, Nigerians owed their loyalties primarily to their ethnic groups, starving the greater nation of badly needed support. Second, ethnic groups competed to obtain common public goods for their own exclusive benefit; stronger groups were able to monopolize power. The solution was to organize a constitution in which access to power required winning support from more than one's own ethnic or subethnic constituency and in which common benefits and public goods had to be distributed on the basis of the federal attributes of the nation or its subunits. This was what the constitution makers branded *federal character*. Its inept administration by a corrupt regime turned out to be unsatisfactory, but most Nigerians believe the principle of federal character was sound.

Although establishing democracy was not the announced purpose of Nigeria's 1979 constitution, the consequences of the constitution were clearly democratic. As a democratic document, however, it was marked by a characteristic endemic to African democratic thought. It made individuals, and their needs, the instrument of public policy rather than its goal. The aim of the constitution was to strengthen the state by redirecting individuals' loyalties and also to protect all ethnic groups. Western liberal democracy sees the individual as the end of politics, whereas African political thought since the era of the slave trade has consistently belittled the worth of the individual, subsuming the person's essence under some kinship grouping. Although individuals do have value within their own ethnic groups, they count for little in the wider national arena. The worth of the individual is a strand of liberal democratic thought that has not taken root in Africa.

Ironically, in light of the country's dismal record, South Africa's political experience may supply such liberal elements to African political thought. David Horowitz, in *A Democratic South Africa?* (1991), has suggested that the Nigerian constitutional experience could be helpful to South Africa by leading it to design a constitutional system that compels contestants for power to look beyond their ethnic base. But South Africa has a different political tradition from Nigeria's, one that is liable to enrich Africa's political thought further. The liberal tradition of respecting the individual's worth and dignity is strong in those fragments of South Africa (Afrikaners, the English, and the Jews) that have been included in the state—although the same regard has not been extended to the African masses who were until recently outside the South

African apartheid state. In neighboring Zimbabwe the settlers' political culture is being blended with that of the indigenous people. Similarly, one imagines that the South African state will accord the same respect to its indigenous African citizens as to those already privileged to be South African citizens; in so doing, it will increase the notional worth of the ideal citizen by focusing on the unique individual's needs and on individual human dignity as the goal of public policy.

Prospects for the Second Liberation

Democracy has fared poorly in Africa since colonial times. The hopes for a democratic order in postcolonial Africa have largely been unfulfilled. However, given favorable new international circumstances since the end of the cold war, and disgust with dictatorship in domestic affairs, prospects for renewed engagement with democracy in African nations appear good. Unfortunately, Samuel Huntington's conclusions in *The Third Wave* (1991), which accords economic prosperity a large share in the emergence of democracy, are not wholly encouraging with respect to Africa's chances. There is clamor among informed Africans, scholars, and politicians, as well as foreign scholars of African politics, for renewed commitment to democracy, a call labeled in the late 1980s and 1990s the *second liberation*. The diagnosis of democracy's ills—and hopes for cure through the second liberation—varies widely.

The first credible African voices calling for second liberation democracy tied it to popular struggles. In *Popular Struggles for Democracy in Africa* (1987), the Kenyan political scientist Peter Anyang' Nyong'o and his African coauthors saw popular struggles against dictatorship as the means to democracy. The control of the state is at issue here, and this view permits the establishment of participatory one-party state democracy. Indeed, much of the blame for Africa's undemocratic circumstances has been laid to states' inefficiency in the hands of corrupt and inept tyrants.

Other scholars, such as Michael Bratton, see the absence of the institutions of civil society as the cause of Africa's problems with democracy, sometimes implying that such institutions could be alternatives to the state. The ultimate quest of the second liberation movement is to "liberate" the African masses. Questions remain about what structures and processes the masses should be liberated from. The diversity of viewpoints on the second liberation is troubling to African democratic theory and suggests the need to specify the elements of that theory, since in this area familiarity with Western notions of democracy often imposes false categories on African political thought.

There are three constructs whose interrelationship provides the context for African democratic theory. These are the state, kinship, and the individual.

Derived from the colonial state, the modern African state is the civil arm of African nations. Although the African state may look like the Western state, on which it was originally modeled, its functions and its relationships with society and the individual are radically different from the familiar pattern of the Western state. The elements of the state have not been fully aligned with those of society because the African state's origins are outside indigenous African societies. Moreover, the individual has largely been alienated from the state—a relationship that persists from colonialism and one that postcolonial states have not corrected.

Kinship, broadly conceived to include ethnic groups and other categories of assumed blood relationships, is the most potent representation of society in Africa. From the slave trade era through colonialism and into our times, kinship has acquired an extraordinary significance in African public affairs. It provides an alternative public forum to the state's civic public. For their political actions, many Africans have come to rely on kinship's primordial publics, political forums limited to those bonded by the same moral ties of assumed blood relationships. Whereas the state has largely had difficult relationships with the individual, primordial publics have managed individuals' welfare. Many Africans live outside the purview of the state and rely on kinship groupings for their security. But the price that Africa pays for this arrangement is that the public realm is severely fragmented along the fault lines of kinship groupings.

For the individual, the second liberation can mean only two types of freedom. First, individuals need negative freedom from kinship groupings. But that freedom will become a possibility only if the state provides the essential personal security for which individuals now rely on their kinship networks. Second, the individual can enjoy positive freedom only by gaining legal, political, and social rights in the state's civic public realm. Only when individuals gain the freedom to exercise their rights in the civic public domain can Africans expect to participate fully in democratic freedoms. The romantic views of those advocating civil society as a replacement for the state to the contrary, the second liberation calls for the state's strengthening into a responsible organization, not its weakening.

See also *Africa, Horn of; Africa, Lusophone; Africa, Subsaharan; African independence movements; African transitions to democracy; Azikiwe, Nnamdi; Civil society; Colonialism; Kenyatta, Jomo; Multiethnic democracy; Nkrumah, Kwame; Nyerere, Julius; Theory, African American.*

Peter P. Ekeh

BIBLIOGRAPHY

Diamond, Larry, Juan J. Linz, and Seymour Lipset, eds. *Democracy in Developing Countries: Africa.* Boulder, Colo.: Lynne Rienner; London: Adamantine Press, 1988.

Du Bois, W. E. B. *Color and Democracy: Colonies and Peace.* Millwood, N.Y.: Kraus-Thomson, 1945.

Ekeh, Peter P. "Colonialism and the Two Publics in Africa: A Theoretical Statement." *Comparative Studies in Society and History* 17 (1975): 91–112.

———, and Eghosa E. Osaghae, eds. *Federal Character and Federalism in Nigeria.* Ibadan, Nigeria: Heinemann, 1989.

Eribor, Festus, Oyeleye Oyediran, Mulatu Wubneh, and Leo Zonn, eds. *Window on Africa: Democratization and Media Exposure.* Greenville, N.C.: Center for International Programs, East Carolina University, 1993.

Jennings, Ivor. *Democracy in Africa.* Cambridge: Cambridge University Press, 1963.

Nyong'o, Peter Anyang', ed. *Popular Struggles for Democracy in Africa.* Atlantic Highlands, N.J., and London: Zed Books, 1987.

Padmore, George, ed. *History of the Pan-African Congress.* London: Hammersmith Bookshop, 1963.

Sklar, Richard L. "Democracy in Africa." In *Political Domination in Africa,* edited by Patrick Chabal. Cambridge: Cambridge University Press, 1986.

Wiseman, John A. *Democracy in Black Africa: Survival and Revival.* New York: Paragon House, 1990.

Theory, African American

African American democratic theory encompasses the body of reflections by African Americans on whether or how a democratic government can govern well in the United States. These reflections are marked by the conviction that democracy—whatever its merits as a form of government in general—has been misused in the United States to the detriment of blacks. As Malcolm X (1925–1965), the preeminent African American radical, once observed, black people in America are victims of democracy.

Some African Americans, such as separatists Martin Delany (1812–1885), Marcus Garvey (1887–1940), and more recently Elijah Muhammad and Robert S. Browne, have always been pessimistic about black prospects in a democratic United States. They fear that whites are a permanent majority and will always use the democratic principle of majority rule to continue their tyranny over blacks. They recommend that the United States be reconstituted into black and white states, either through secession or through emigration. But most African American theorists of democracy believe that democracy can be a good form of government in the United States.

Since the Emancipation Proclamation (1863), African Americans have had to overcome many hurdles to gain full citizenship. Their first challenge was to secure voting rights for the black population after the Thirteenth Amendment to the Constitution abolished slavery in 1865. The opponents of black suffrage argued that each state should be allowed to decide—by majority rule—who should be allowed to vote, expecting that white majorities would decide that blacks should not be allowed to vote. Frederick Douglass (1817–1895), the black abolitionist, retorted to this ploy that if blacks knew enough to be hanged, they knew enough to vote. His point was that majority rule is fair only if the majority making the decisions is a majority of all those who are expected to know enough to conform to the decisions.

Another argument against black suffrage was that freed slaves were ignorant and would misuse their votes. Douglass's rebuttal, that blacks would learn how to use their votes only if they were allowed to vote, was forceful, but the argument persisted. By the turn of the century it was used to justify policies that circumvented the Fifteenth Amendment, which granted suffrage regardless of race or color or prior servitude, by placing educational requirements on the right to vote. These requirements disenfranchised the bulk of the black population. Booker T. Washington (1856–1915), the accommodationist principal of Tuskegee Institute in Alabama, endorsed these policies, insisting only that they be applied to blacks and whites impartially. Critics have charged that Washington was obeying his capitalist supporters, who wanted to block any alliance of poor whites and blacks. He claimed that blacks would get the vote, and would be in a position to use it responsibly, when they became educated and economically independent.

W. E. B. Du Bois

No matter how intelligently blacks voted, however, the white majority could always use the principle of majority rule to pass legislation contrary to black interests. Democracies have tried to deal with this problem of the tyranny of the majority by guaranteeing all citizens a set of rights—like those in the amendments to the U.S. Constitution known as the Bill of Rights. African Americans have energetically used the rights to freedom of speech and of the press granted by the First Amendment to try to persuade the majority of the irrationality and injustice of its racist practices and to shame it into mending its ways. To this end they have also used illegal forms of moral suasion such as civil disobedience, although Martin Luther King, Jr. (1929–1968), the foremost African American exponent of civil disobedience, argued that the laws he disobeyed were unjust or unconstitutional and so were not laws at all.

To increase their representation in lawmaking bodies, African Americans have proposed changes to existing procedures for choosing representatives. Because existing procedures generally involve voting districts from which only one representative is elected, legislatures often include no one representing African American viewpoints. Race-conscious districting deals with this problem by deliberately creating voting districts that contain a majority of black voters. This strategy, however, encourages residential segregation. And, as a 1976 Supreme Court case—*United Jewish Organizations v. Carey*—showed, it may split one minority's votes even as it consolidates another's. Moreover, the Court ruled in *Shaw v. Reno* (1993) that race-conscious districting may violate whites' rights to participate in a "color-blind electoral process."

In the early 1990s Lani Guinier, a law professor at the University of Pennsylvania, urged the adoption of proportional representation to improve representation for African Americans in lawmaking bodies. Proportional representation substitutes multiple-member voting districts for single-member voting districts. Without subverting the principle of majority rule, it enables every group to be represented in legislatures in proportion to its numbers. This feature has long commended the idea to theorists who believe that minorities should be heard in legislatures. The nineteenth-century political philosopher John Stuart Mill extolled its virtues; W. Arthur Lewis, the 1979 Nobel laureate in economics, recommended it for the culturally pluralist states of West Africa; and Du Bois argued that it was essential in the United States.

Democracy is the best form of government for cultur-

Washington's great opponent, the intellectual W. E. B. Du Bois (1868–1963), disagreed, pointing out that blacks were unlikely ever to become economically independent without the right to vote. But Du Bois's early defense of black suffrage was qualified. He was influenced by Alexander Crummell, an African American Episcopal priest. Crummell objected to Thomas Jefferson's view in the Declaration of Independence that the authority of government rested solely on the consent of the governed. He believed the authority of government also depended on the counsel of a religious, moral, and cultural elite. Du Bois followed Crummell in believing that society should be led by a moral and cultural elite, which he called the "talented tenth." He endorsed black suffrage, which came at the end of the Civil War, only because he thought the talented tenth was shirking its responsibility to lead society. Later Du Bois demanded black suffrage absolutely, though he always tried to leave place for the counsel of the talented tenth.

ally and racially homogeneous societies. Its gravest challenge is posed by culturally and racially pluralist societies, especially those in which an economically dominant cultural and racial group is a clear majority. The halting advance of African Americans in the United States intimates that they may one day force the nation to find a solution.

See also *King, Martin Luther, Jr; Majority rule, minority rights; Multiethnic democracy; Proportional representation; Racism; Slavery; Theory, African; United States Constitution.* In Documents section, see *Constitution of the United States (1787).*

Bernard R. Boxill

BIBLIOGRAPHY

Crummell, Alexander. "The Assassination of President Garfield." In *Destiny and Race,* edited by Wilson Jeremiah Moses. Amherst: University of Massachusetts Press, 1992.

Douglass, Frederick. *The Life and Times of Frederick Douglass.* New York: Collier, 1962.

Du Bois, W. E. B. "Of the Ruling of Men." In *Darkwater.* New York: Kraus-Thomson, 1975.

———. *The Souls of Black Folk.* New York: Everyman's Library, 1993.

Guinier, Lani. "The Representation of Minority Interests: The Question of Single-Member Districts." *Cardozo Law Review* 14 (April 1993): 1135–1174.

King, Martin Luther, Jr. "Letter from Birmingham City Jail." In *Civil Disobedience in Focus,* edited by Hugo Adam Bedau. London: Routledge, 1991.

Lewis, W. Arthur. *Politics in West Africa.* New York: Oxford University Press, 1965.

Little, Malcolm (Malcolm X). "The Ballot or the Bullet." In *Malcolm X Speaks.* Edited by George Breitman. New York: Grove Press, 1966.

Theory, Ancient

Ancient democratic theory is the study of democracy in Greek and Roman antiquity by such thinkers as Thucydides, Socrates, Plato, Xenophon, Aristotle, and Cicero. Ancient theory may seem to be of merely historical interest, with no more to teach us about modern democracy than ancient architecture has to teach us about skyscrapers. After all, what we mean by democracy was unknown to the ancients: a political system of representation governing a huge, often continental, and heterogeneous country under a written constitution that protects the equal natural rights of all citizens. As reflection on this description of modern democracy would show, not only has democracy changed fundamentally, so too has political

science. Natural rights, for example, were a discovery or invention of early modern political science.

Moreover, democratic theory as we know it did not exist in ancient times. Contemporary democratic theory is dedicated to the study and advocacy of various types of democracy. It classifies those types, articulates their principles, investigates how each works, and takes for granted that one type or another is the just and good political order. By contrast, the ancient study of democracy forms part of another study—the study of or inquiry into what the ancients called the *best regime.* The ancients did not take for granted that any type of democracy was the just and good political order. Indeed, they were deeply critical of democracy. Aristotle went so far as to classify democracy among the deviant political orders or regimes.

But perhaps it is just this feature of ancient democratic theory, or ancient political science, that has something of value to teach us. Ancient political science achieved a critical distance from democracy not likely to be encountered in modern democratic theory. Although the ancients understood something different by democracy from what modern readers of their thought understand, this difference is not so great a difficulty as it first appears. All democracies have something in common: the rule of the people. That rule may be direct or indirect, but in either case the ultimate authority in a democracy is the people. Ancient political science was concerned with understanding whether and in what sense the people ought to have that authority.

The Method of the Ancients

Greek and Roman thinkers approached the study and teaching of politics with much the same concerns as ordinary citizens, and they used much the same vocabulary to articulate those concerns. They began by taking political partisans and statesmen at their word. If, for instance, the partisans of democracy claimed that they deserved to rule because they were as free by birth as the wealthy, the ancients did not immediately look beyond this claim to some ulterior motive, such as economic self-interest, alleged to be more fundamental than the concern for justice. Rather, they investigated what it would mean to deserve to rule and whether free birth or any other quality could confer such an entitlement. Nor did the ancients return to an alleged state of nature to see how a political community might legitimately come into existence. The question of what makes a political community with its particular political order legitimate or just was answered instead by examining the various claims about legitimacy or justice together with due reflection on human needs and on the requirements of political community.

Ancient political science thus approached political life as it was lived. Thucydides helps us to examine the justice and goodness of democracy by presenting both the actions of the Athenians and the speeches by which they defended them during the Peloponnesian War between Athens and Sparta in the fifth century B.C. Because this account would give only part of the story, however, Thucydides invites us to compare the Athenians' actions and speeches with those of the Spartans, who lived under an oligarchy (which means "rule of the few"), and of the other participants in the war. Aristotle approaches the question of who should rule as a political dispute that arises typically after a democratic revolution. The democrats assert that democracy alone is just because it exists not through domination but for the common good. The oligarchs claim to deserve to rule because of their wealth, while the democrats claim to deserve an equal share in ruling because they are equal to the wealthy in freedom. This method of beginning from ordinary political opinions, from politics as it manifests itself in both ordinary and extraordinary times, compels thoughtful readers to think through and evaluate those opinions for themselves.

The most famous praise of Athenian democracy is found in Thucydides' *Peloponnesian War*. That praise comes not from Thucydides, however, but from Pericles, the Athenian statesman and general whose name is attached to a period of spectacular artistic, political, and imperialist achievement. In his funeral oration for the first Athenian soldiers killed in the Peloponnesian War, Pericles declares that Athens is worthy of the greatest admiration and love. According to Pericles, the Athenians combine extraordinary liberty with the stern discipline needed to fight wars. Moreover, the individual can devote himself to public affairs while developing himself to the fullest as a human being. Above all, Athens rules a marvelous empire that testifies to its power to do good and evil alike.

Thucydides does not endorse this praise; rather, he turns immediately to describe the plague that devastated Athens. He thus invites us to rethink Pericles' assessment of the Athenians in light of what was revealed about their nature by the selfishness and brutality that surfaced under the havoc of the plague. In addition, elsewhere in his work Thucydides praises Sparta for obtaining good laws earlier than any other city and for being moderate in prosperity. Athens, Thucydides makes clear, was never moderate but always restlessly bold. During the peace that marked the end of the war with Sparta (or, as it turned out, the end of the first half of that war), the Athenian people undertook and then, fearing for their own rule, rashly bungled the conquest of remote Sicily. Moreover, a careful reading of Pericles' funeral oration points to certain limits of the Athenians that Pericles praises. For example, a man who minds his own business, not meddling or joining in the affairs of the city, is counted a good-for-nothing. Judging from this, we might say that democratic Athens was remarkably successful at turning out citizens dedicated to democratic Athens. But the ancient political scientists doubted that a dedicated citizen was identical to a good human being.

It should be noted here that Socrates, the founder of political philosophy, was put to death by democratic Athens for impiety and corrupting the young, that is, for undermining the traditional authorities of the democracy—the people and the gods. It was Socrates who developed the method of proceeding from ordinary opinions about morality and politics, through contradictions in those opinions, to what he claimed were noncontradictory truths about morality and politics. In more than thirty dialogues Plato shows Socrates conversing with Athenian citizens and statesmen as well as foreigners. In most of the dialogues Socrates brings to light contradictions in his interlocutors' opinions, some of which are the authoritative opinions of democratic Athens. From the beginning, then, there was a tension between democracy, on the one hand, and the study of democracy, on the other. That tension reveals an important limit of democracy.

The Question of the Best Regime

The study of democracy was, as we have said, part of the inquiry into the best regime. To understand that inquiry, we must first consider what was meant by a regime. The ancients spoke of regimes where we speak of forms of government. Democracy was looked upon as much more than just a form of government; like every other kind of regime, democracy was looked upon as a political order—an order of the whole city or political community in which one particular group ruled. The word *politeia* (regime) denoted both the political order and the ruling group or class. (*Politeia* may also be translated as "constitution," but it never means a written document.) So important was the regime as a theme of ancient political science that the title of Plato's most famous political dialogue, the *Republic*, is in Greek the *Regime*, and every book of Aristotle's *Politics* after the first one is explicitly about the regime.

Ancient political science focused on the regime because the ancients considered the regime the most important fact of political life. According to the ancients, a city's regime decisively shapes the lives of its citizens. Every regime imparts to those who live under it a specific notion of justice—that is, of what human beings owe to one another—and each regime holds up one thing as most honorable and therefore most worthy of being pursued. In oligarchy, for instance, wealth is honored above all else, while in democracy, freedom or equality is most honored. The character of a city or country changes according to the kind of regime that governs it.

The influence of the regime on the lives of citizens is much more pervasive than is implied in the terms "form of government" and "the democratic process." Because of the pervasive influence of the regime, Aristotle speaks of the regime as the way of life of the city. In light of the ancient view, the principle of legitimacy articulated by early modern thinkers such as Thomas Hobbes and John Locke and most widely accepted today—the consent of the governed—necessarily leads to a regime that is fundamentally democratic; the actual form of government comes to be of secondary importance. The closest modern approximation to the ancient analysis of democracy as the way of life of a country was supplied by Alexis de Tocqueville's *Democracy in America* (1835–1840).

Because the ancient Greek cities did not have substantial middle classes, they were divided into two main factions: the wealthy and the poor. As a result, democracy and oligarchy were the two kinds of regime most frequently found. In democracy, the people ruled; in oligarchy, a much smaller number of citizens (typically the wealthy) ruled in their own right and were not answerable to the rest. Each kind of regime or ruling class could defend its rule by appealing to some notion of justice. According to oligarchic justice, the wealthy deserve to rule because of their special economic contribution to the city; according to democratic justice, the poor deserve to share in rule as much as the wealthy because they are equally free by birth.

In mediating between the claims of the wealthy and those of the poor, the ancients were compelled to ask whether the democratic or the oligarchic view of justice and of what is most honorable in life was true; they were compelled to ask what the best regime was. Even this question had a direct connection to politics. When political life breaks down—in times of revolution, for instance—political partisans are forced to make arguments for their political preferences. All such arguments implicitly invoke notions of the best regime. A defense of democracy for Athens must argue that democracy is superior to any alternative. It must argue that democracy is just and good or that democracy is a necessary step in the right direction. To make these arguments, it must have recourse to what is just and good simply or by nature.

The argument for democracy seems at first to be stronger than arguments against it. Whereas other regimes exclude some from full citizenship, democracy excludes no one. Democracy is the one regime that is inclusive; it alone serves the common good. To this view, the ancients responded as follows. Although no one is excluded from citizenship in a democracy, inclusion does not mean that the concerns of every citizen are given equal weight. Democracy (which means "people power") is the rule of the people (*demos*), of the majority. In a democracy the concerns of the common people predominate. For that reason the ancients viewed democracy as a partisan political order, a political order in which one part of the community rules over the rest. The claim that democracy is the just and good regime cannot rest on the unfounded assertion that democracy is the rule of all. Moreover, in the eyes of the ancients the fact that the largest class in a democracy rules does not automatically make democracy more just than other possibilities.

That democracy is not in and of itself a just and good political order was also recognized in recent times by thoughtful men sympathetic to democracy. James Madison and Tocqueville, for example, saw the potential for various forms of majority tyranny inherent in popular governments. What, after all, is to prevent a pure democracy from acting tyrannically? Do the people necessarily rule for the good of all or the common good? A complete answer to that question would require an investigation, such as Aristotle undertook in the *Politics*, into the character of "the common good" and its relation to the comprehensive good of individuals. If there were not a common good between rulers and ruled, all regimes or ruling classes would exercise rule with a view to their own good; all political orders, democracy included, would be essentially despotic. Plato presents the Sophist Thrasymachus challenging Socrates with precisely this position in the *Republic*. And in the *Memorabilia*, Xenophon, the other great student of Socrates, presents the young Alcibiades, companion of Socrates and future Athenian statesman, arguing this position against his guardian, Pericles. Leaving aside the difficult question of the content and character of the common good, however, it was at least the contention of the ancients that not every people could be trusted with political power. A given people might, for example, attempt to seize and redistribute the property of the wealthy out of resentment, plunging the city into civil war. And, of course, the wealthy as such were no more trustworthy than the common people.

Furthermore, the fact that the people met in assembly to conduct the business of the city meant that those individuals with the greatest rhetorical gifts became the de facto leaders of the people. Hence the danger always existed that the people would fall under the sway of mere demagogues (literally, "popular leaders") tapping into various forms of resentment. It was only by chance that Pericles, who would not stoop to flattering the people, was the most gifted Athenian speaker of his day. It was also by chance that Cleon, "the most violent of the citizens," was a few years later the most gifted Athenian speaker. Under the influence of Cleon, an indignant Athenian people came close to executing all the adult males and enslaving the women and children of Mytilene, an island city that Cleon had accused of grave injustice for revolting against imperial Athens. The Athenians were saved from error on this occasion by the all but miraculous intervention of an even more gifted speaker, Diodotus, from and about whom we never hear another word.

We find in the third book of Aristotle's *Politics* the most complete working out and assessment of the claims to deserve to rule advanced by the well-off and by the multitude. Those competing claims are based on different principles: according to the well-off, the political community exists above all to protect and to increase wealth; according to the multitude, its primary purpose is to protect freedom. Each group claims that its contribution to the city is the decisive one. This fact enabled Aristotle to assess these claims in part by investigating the purpose of the political community. Here Aristotle, like the ancients generally, disagrees with the characteristic modern answer—that the political community or country exists to protect life, liberty, and property. Although the country's purpose might include such protection, it cannot be limited to this goal. Aristotle pointed out that every country must claim that obedience to its laws is good for the citizens, but the laws necessarily place limits on liberty as well as on the acquisition of property. Then, too, every country has a regime, and every regime teaches the citi-

zens to hold a particular view of justice and to honor a particular way of life. Moreover, every country teaches the overwhelming importance of being just and may demand the sacrifice of some of its citizens in war, the "supreme sacrifice." In light of these observations the highest purpose of the country seems to be the nobility or virtue of its citizens. Those with virtue, or political virtue, should have a larger share in ruling because they contribute more to this purpose than do either the wealthy or the multitude.

But contribution to the country is not the only criterion for assessing the claims of political partisans to deserve to rule. Because the ruling class exercises enormous power, its members ought to possess extraordinary character and judgment. Furthermore, they ought to possess the knowledge relevant to making sound domestic and foreign policy. In view of these considerations the claim that wealth or freedom entitles a class of citizens to rule appears defective. If the people do not collectively possess the judgment and character required to rule well, placing the ultimate authority in their hands entails certain risks. Moreover, even if the people are well intentioned and not uneducated, a democratic regime reflects their concerns, not those of extraordinary individuals. Hence ancient thinkers feared that even a moderate democracy would not do enough to lead its citizens toward the best way of life and might even be a hindrance in this regard. In the language of Aristotle the virtue of the good man and that of the dedicated citizen can be the same only in the best regime.

For all these reasons the ancients thought the best regime would be one in which the best men ruled. By the best they meant something akin to what Thomas Jefferson meant when he wrote to John Adams of the "natural aristoi." The ancients were less certain, however, that the natural aristoi, described by Jefferson as possessing "virtue and wisdom" or "virtue and talents," could be discerned and elected by the people and that the natural aristoi would or should wish to rule chiefly with a view to the good of the common man. Be that as it may, according to the ancients, not only would those who are best rule most competently, but a regime in which those who are best occupy the place of honor would also be the most likely to lead capable citizens toward virtue and wisdom.

Moreover, this regime treats outstanding individuals with the appropriate respect for their capacities. Democracy, by contrast, constrains outstanding individuals by subjecting them to laws created by people whose judgment and character are inferior to their own. Those laws are shaped by the people, whether intentionally or inadvertently, with a view to their own good. For the people cannot help but view the common good in terms of what they believe to be good for themselves, any more than the merely wealthy can. The people, for instance, aim first and foremost at preserving their own rule, even at the expense of other goods they may desire; hence ancient democracies from time to time ostracized those of exceptional political talent.

Democracy does not treat excellent human beings appropriately or justly, according to the ancient thinkers, and it discourages their development in the first place. Democracy constrains excellence through the combination of its defining principles, freedom and equality. By honoring freedom above all, it downplays the importance of the uses to which freedom is put. By presupposing equality for political purposes, it tends to deny the existence of meaningful inequalities. For if all are presumed equal regarding so demanding and honorable a task as exercising authority for a whole country, any inequalities that persist must be of no more than secondary importance. Moreover, if any qualities are acknowledged as "virtue and talents," those qualities will be ones that dispose and enable an individual to satisfy the wishes of the people; hence individuals with potential for extraordinary accomplishments will tend to become ministers to the people's needs and desires.

Because what the ancient political scientists meant by genuine human virtue or excellence is exceedingly rare, they thought the best regime would be the rule of, at most, a few men. Indeed, it would be fortunate if even one such person were to be found in a given time and place. In part for that reason, the ancients investigated monarchy and the conditions that favored it. So we find Plato or Socrates experimenting in speech with the possibility of a philosopher-king; Xenophon holding up Cyrus the Great, the founder of the Persian empire more than a century earlier, as a model ruler of human beings; and Aristotle maintaining that the best regime is the absolute monarchy of the man of outstanding virtue. Only the rule of such individuals, unhampered even by law, which in circumstances that are always particular must be inferior to the judgment of the wise ruler, could be thought to satisfy all the requirements of a just and good regime. The certainty that such outstanding virtue does not even exist appeared to the ancients as no more than a prejudice instilled by democratic regimes.

Moderate Democracy and the Mixed Regime

Ancient political scientists were more than skeptical that genuine human virtue could ever be the principle of an actual political order. For one thing, genuine virtue arises only in very civilized times, the same times in which the majority—all those who do not possess that virtue—refuse to be ruled as children or worse. Because of the obstacles to such rule, including the opposition of the people, the best practicable political order would have to be based on something other than human virtue. Consequently, the argument for monarchy, or for aristocracy in the precise sense, has the character not of a practical political proposal but of an articulation of the nature of politics, as Cicero explained in his *Republic.* Only after one has answered the question of the best regime can one accurately assess the quality of actual regimes.

The ancient political scientists were not idealists. They did not advocate aristocratic revolutions, nor did they think that all regimes other than the best regime were unjust. The best possible regime might be a certain kind of aristocracy that falls short of rule by the truly best, an aristocracy in which gentlemen rule with a view above all to the noble or beautiful use of leisure—what today we loosely would call culture. Although the appreciation of culture differs considerably from what the ancients found to be the best life—that is, the life of the mind, or philosophy—it at least reminds us of that life and points to it as the culmination of culture.

The conjunction of conditions necessary for this aristocracy cannot be brought about by human effort, however, and is most unlikely to come about by chance. These conditions include human beings of just the right nature; a location easy to defend; land suitable for farming, mining, and pasturing; a population and territory small enough for every citizen to be familiar with the qualities of every other citizen; a carefully controlled plan for procreation; and, in a pretechnological age, a docile slave population fit to do the work of the city and also fit for eventual emancipation.

The ancients thought that an aristocratic republic devoted to culture, though not impossible, was beyond the reach of the vast majority of cities. Hence, to the question of the best regime, the ancients characteristically gave a second answer: the best regime is not aristocracy but a mixture of elements from two or more regimes—democracy, oligarchy, aristocracy, and kingship. The reason is not that the mixed regime promotes human excellence or treats outstanding individuals appropriately but that it achieves a stability that other regimes do not. To that extent it permits the cultivation of human excellence. A mixed regime might even make something like excellence one basis for election to ruling offices.

Most likely, a mixed regime will combine elements of democracy and oligarchy alone. By giving to this form of the mixed regime the name *polity*, the same word that means regime, Aristotle implies that the rule of the poor together with the well-off is most appropriately spoken of as a regime. If a regime is a stable arrangement of the city with respect to the ruling offices, that regime which incorporates both the rich and the poor and thus forestalls factional strife is perhaps especially deserving of the name. This regime is characterized by a combination of oligarchic and democratic arrangements or by arrangements that are midway between the two. For example, it is democratic to have ruling officials chosen by lot with no property qualification, while to have officials elected, and elected from among those with at least a certain amount of property, is oligarchic.

In polity, then, the officials might be elected rather than chosen by lot but elected from among all the citizens without regard to property. Another arrangement of a polity might be to ensure the attendance of both the well-off and the poor at courts and assemblies by paying the poor so that they can afford to attend while fining the well-off if they do not attend.

In the best case, the well-off will be of good birth, educated, and decent or fair. A mixed regime in which the well-off have these traits might for all practical purposes be called aristocracy. True aristocracy, as distinct from the aristocracy the ancients experimented with in thought, comes down to a mixture of oligarchy and democracy in which the well-off are men of some refinement who are concerned with administering the laws fairly.

Even the mixed regime, however, was thought to lie beyond the reach of most cities. The reasoning appears to have been as follows. In every city the real power is likely to lie either with the well-off or with the poor; neither will have a clear incentive to compromise with the other, a difficulty often exacerbated by the fact that each class views the regime as the prize for victory in factional struggle. Indeed, even the kind of democracy or oligarchy a city has is beyond the means of any human being to control. In a democracy, for instance, the farmers might make up the majority, or the majority might consist of the urban working class; the character of the democracy will vary accordingly. Moreover, the distribution of power between rich and poor in a given city has little to do with choice.

In Athens, for example, the strength of the poor grew after the naval victory over the Persians at Salamis in 480 B.C. Because of their importance to the navy in manning the ships, and because of the importance of the navy to the defense of Athens, concessions had to be made to the poor. Athens thus came to be more democratic at that time as a result of military necessity, not of legislation. Either a city's regime cannot be legislated, or the scope for such legislation is much narrower than one might wish. The laws do not establish the regime but reflect it; that is, they reflect the character of the class that holds power.

Because this version of the best regime could not be legislated but depended largely on the distribution of power, the ancients turned to a more modest version— the regime based on a large middle class. A middle class that outnumbered the well-off and the poor and had interests in common with each would stand as a sort of umpire between the two. Thus the stability of the middle-class regime would not depend on the justice or benevolence of any class. The middle class would have neither the arrogance and contempt characteristic of the wealthy nor the humility and envy characteristic of the needy; the middle-class regime would be characterized more than other regimes by civic friendship or fraternity. Aristotle goes so far as to call the regime based on the middle class the best regime and to imply that it is the standard by which actual regimes should be judged. The realization of such a regime became the undertaking of early modern political science.

In antiquity, however, the emergence of the middle-class regime was seen to depend more on fortune than on legislation. As mentioned earlier, ancient cities tended to have small middle classes. To the ancients it appeared that the best possible regime for a given city was likely to be some form of oligarchy or democracy. For that reason, the ancients were not averse to giving advice on making modest improvements to these inferior or "deviant" regimes and even on preserving them. In their view, revolutions were more likely to lead to something worse than to something better, and, in any case, the best regime they could conceive of had been shown to be impossible. But by gradually uncovering the virtues of the middle-class regime, beginning with the investigation into the best regime, the ancients supplied legislators and good citizens with the theoretical considerations needed for improving or preserving their own regimes.

Both oligarchies and democracies could be improved

by using legislation to add to the ranks of the middle class. This means, of course, that the middle-class regime, a second form of polity, is not so different from either oligarchy or democracy. In fact, it bears a close resemblance to the moderate forms of both. Aristotle initially characterizes polity as the correct, or good, form of the rule of the multitude, whereas he gives the name democracy to the bad, or deviant, form. One way to achieve a polity, understood now as the middle-class regime, would be to institute a property qualification for full participation in political life. The best amount for qualifying would be that which is required to purchase and maintain heavy arms needed for serving in the infantry or cavalry. In other words, the ability to serve in the armed forces of the city would be the prerequisite for full citizenship, for sharing in all the rights and duties of the citizen. This requirement would give the polity an oligarchic cast but would justify it on the ground of contribution to the city's defense. It would incidentally ensure that those participating in the regime would have more force at their disposal than those not participating, a necessary component of stability.

The best practicable regime differs little from a moderate democracy. The ancients thought the best form of democracy was that in which the people governed least; the best democracy existed in less civilized times, when the mass of the people were farmers. The reason for this opinion was not that the ancients discerned special virtues in an agrarian people but that an agrarian people living in the country had little access to the instruments of government. Such a people would be content to allow wealthy citizens, who had the leisure to engage in politics, to govern the city—according to the established laws—as long as the people retained the right to elect them and to review their performance. The power of the people to elect and review would help to keep the well-to-do officials decent. Aristotle calls this arrangement "most beneficial in regimes." As the artisans and laborers become more numerous, however, and as the urban population grows, the rule of law and the balance between the well-off and the poor erodes. The poverty of an urban populace eventually opens the way to extreme democracy, in which not the law but the assembly of the people reigns supreme, and the well-off are at the mercy of the multitude and the demagogues who lead them.

The Best Way of Life

Because in middle-class regimes the common people remain the ultimate authority, these regimes are exposed to the most serious objections raised earlier to the rule of the people; they cannot be simply just. But the fact that the ancients could speak of some form of democracy as the best regime reveals another side of their view of democracy. In Plato's *Republic,* in the middle of a sharp critique of democracy, Socrates tacitly compares democracy with the golden age of the heroes in the poet Hesiod's account of the world. Only when speaking of democracy does he mention even in passing the presence of philosophy. And Aristotle calls democracy the mildest and the least bad of the bad regimes—that is, of those regimes that are "bad" by the standard of genuine aristocracy—as well as the most stable and lasting.

It is worth recalling that Socrates, Plato, and Aristotle all lived and taught in Athens and that Thucydides begins his work by identifying himself as an Athenian. Because the freedom to live as one likes is one defining principle of the regime, democracy tends to ignore or implicitly denies the possibility that one way of life is best. At the same time, it accidentally makes room for those rare individuals who, not succumbing to the influence of democracy, use that freedom to investigate the truth about the city and about the whole within which the city exists.

As the death of Socrates shows, however, the freedom to live as one likes has strict limits. Democracy frowns upon those who question the goodness of making that freedom the principle of a regime, and who question the goodness of majority rule and hence the existence of gods who sanction that rule. The ancients thought that of the two ways of life that attracted serious individuals, the philosophic and the political, the philosophic way of life was superior. They thought that a truly good human being, though he might serve as a teacher of statesmen, would not wish to be a practicing statesman himself. Even the philosopher-king of Plato's *Republic* would have to be pushed into ruling in the best regime, which was still based on a lie, however noble.

The ancients thought that ignorance regarding human affairs, especially justice, and the divine was the most shameful condition for an individual to be in. The study of the justice and goodness of democracy, and the ancient political science of which that study was an important part, was strictly subordinate to the pursuit of knowledge of the whole, or philosophy in the original sense.

See also *Aristotle; Cicero; Class; Classical Greece and Rome; Communitarianism; Hobbes, Thomas; Leadership; Locke, John; Madison, James; Majority rule, minority rights; Montesquieu; Participatory democracy; Plato; Religion, Civ-*

il; *Rhetoric; Rousseau, Jean-Jacques; Tocqueville, Alexis de; Virtue, Civic.* In Documents section, see *Pericles' Funeral Oration (431 B.C.).*

Robert Goldberg

BIBLIOGRAPHY

Aristotle. *The Athenian Constitution.* Translated by H. Rackham. Cambridge: Harvard University Press, 1971.
———. *Nicomachean Ethics.* Translated by Martin Ostwald. New York: Macmillan, 1962.
———. *The Politics.* Translated by Carnes Lord. Chicago: University of Chicago Press, 1984.
Cicero. *The Republic.* Translated by Clinton Walker Keyes. Cambridge: Harvard University Press, 1977.
Plato. *The Apology of Socrates and Crito.* In *Four Texts on Socrates.* Translated by Thomas G. West and Grace Starry West. Ithaca, N.Y.: Cornell University Press, 1984.
———. *The Laws of Plato.* Translated by Thomas L. Pangle. New York: Basic Books, 1980.
———. *The Republic.* Translated by Allan Bloom. New York: Basic Books, 1968.
Strauss, Leo. *The City and Man.* Chicago: University of Chicago Press, 1977.
———, and Joseph Cropsey. *History of Political Philosophy.* 3d ed. Chicago: University of Chicago Press, 1987.
Thucydides. *The Peloponnesian War.* Translated by Thomas Hobbes. Chicago: University of Chicago Press, 1989.
Tocqueville, Alexis de. *Democracy in America.* Edited by J. P. Mayer. Translated by George Lawrence. Garden City, N.Y.: Anchor/Doubleday, 1969.
Xenophon. *Constitution of the Athenians.* In *Scripta Minora.* Translated by G. W. Bowersock. Cambridge: Harvard University Press, 1971.
———. *Cyropaedia.* Translated by Walter Miller. Cambridge: Harvard University Press, 1968.
———. *Memorabilia.* Translated by E. C. Marchant. Cambridge: Harvard University Press, 1968.

Theory, Postwar Anglo-American

Postwar Anglo-American democratic theory is the systematic inquiry into the conditions, institutions, purposes, and meaning of democratic political practices since World War II. The practice of this inquiry is distinctive in two respects. First, it has taken place within societies where democracy was nearly universally taken to be a good thing and wherein the way of life was widely understood to be democratic. Second, democratic theory in these societies has been, for better or worse, largely the preserve of professional academics rather than political actors or public intellectuals.

The development of democratic theory in the twentieth century is closely bound up with the rise of social science as a profession practiced on a massive scale in Anglo-American universities. Scholarly arguments concerning the criteria identifying democratic governments often became at the same time arguments concerning the criteria of theory itself, encompassing concepts of evidence, validity, and scientific objectivity. This commingling of issues of political theory with issues of the philosophy of science at times generated confusion and more than a little mutual miscomprehension among those involved in the debates. Still, incredible vitality and intellectual energy resulted from this development. Within the discipline of political science, no issue in the twentieth century attracted so many of the best minds and spurred them to such heights of intellectual endeavor and achievement.

Another factor contributing to the vibrancy of democratic theory has been its close and relatively evident connection with the turbulent political history of the twentieth century. The encounter with totalitarianism in the first half of the century and the continuing fragmentation of traditional sources of moral, political, and social authority in the latter half are reflected in many of the themes discussed by democratic theorists. These discussions have attracted greater attention in the culture at large than is usually the case with the works of academics. In turn, this practical relevance has served as a spur to innovation in the academy.

Finally, it is not surprising upon reflection that in long-standing and relatively successful democratic regimes, the topic of democracy should be a perennial and primary concern of intellectual, and indeed civic, life. A people who would rule themselves will have a great deal to talk about, including how to go about ruling themselves. There are as many democratic theories as there are possibilities in that regard.

It is impossible to state an agreed-on set of propositions or axioms that might be taken to define democratic theory. The term *democracy* itself admits of no canonical definition beyond the abstract "rule by the people." But what constitutes a "people"? How is "rule" to be known when it exists, and how is it to be distinguished from "coercion" and "force"? The questions multiply endlessly. There is not a single definition of democracy that has not been rejected by some student of the subject.

To proceed, then, we will do best to avoid any attempt to define once and for all the domain and concerns of democratic theory. Instead, let us examine what those conventionally referred to as "democratic theorists" have chosen to discuss. We shall first look at this from a historical point of view, describing the primary types of democratic theory that emerged in the course of the twentieth century. We shall conclude by adopting a more analytical point of view, examining briefly three problems that have been of interest to democratic theorists throughout the century.

Revisionist and Classical Theory

In the years between 1945 (at the end of World War II) and 1970 there developed a distinctive way of understanding democracy that came to be called the "revisionist" theory of democracy. Among the works best exemplifying this view were Joseph Schumpeter's *Capitalism, Socialism, and Democracy* (1942), Robert Dahl's *Preface to Democratic Theory* (1956), and Seymour Martin Lipset's *Political Man* (1960). The revisionists understood themselves to be revising a "classical" theory of democracy, which was seen to be deeply flawed in a number of respects. The classical theory comprised three major points, which the revisionists criticized.

First, the classical theory supposed a relatively high degree of rationality and political knowledge on the part of democratic citizens. In its popular version the classical theory is personified in the image of the New England town meeting as a participatory expression of the essential good sense and knowledge of the common person. The revisionists, however, pointed out that this image was largely a myth. As evidence, they cited the results of the first large-scale studies of public opinion carried out on the basis of systematic polling in accordance with the standards of scientific method. Study after study demonstrated that citizens were far less aware of, and knowledgeable about, political issues and affairs than the classical theory would have led one to expect.

Moreover, and even more unsettling, a series of empirical studies showed that at least at the level of opinion, ordinary citizens were decidedly less attached to the ideals of democratic tolerance and respect for different views than were political elites. These studies thus were taken to suggest that democracy was not so much threatened, as had traditionally been thought, by the usurpation of power by elites as it was by the incapacities of its citizens. The recent

memory of the mass basis of fascism in Germany and Italy only served to buttress this view.

Second, critics faulted the classical theory for failing to distinguish systematically between normative speculation and empirical scientific inquiry. Revisionist democratic theory was closely tied to the behavioralist movement in Anglo-American social science. This movement attempted to model the social sciences on the natural sciences, especially with regard to method. In this view, "theory" was understood to denote a systematic set of empirically testable propositions aimed at predicting the behavior of operationally defined variables, as opposed to a more traditional and less scientific understanding that theory in politics was to be concerned with issues of values and morality. The behaviorists tended to dismiss normative theory as hopelessly subjective and unscientific, an impediment to the progress of objective and value-free social scientific inquiry.

This behaviorist attitude is manifest in many of the works of revisionist democratic theory. The revisionists understood themselves to be scientific realists, testing and often debunking the more grandiose speculative claims of classical theorists, who were portrayed as unsophisticated amateurs. The classical theorists had been concerned with the normative question of how democracy ought to work; the revisionists were concerned with the scientific question of how it actually worked.

A third criticism often made by revisionists was the classical theory's alleged failure to account for the need for leadership in democratic politics. The classical theory saw democracy as primarily the collective work of citizens and valued widespread participation in politics. It tended, perhaps unwittingly, to downplay the significance of the role of leadership in the organizations of democracy because the greater that significance, the less democratic the practices would seem. The revisionists, especially and most sharply Schumpeter, criticized what they portrayed as squeamishness regarding the unavoidable fact of leadership, and hence inequalities of actual power, on the part of classical theorists.

Faced with overwhelming evidence that the citizens of the Anglo-American polities were far less interested in, knowledgeable about, and capable of effectively dealing with the highly complex issues of modern politics than had been supposed, students of democracy could make one of two moves. One response was to take the evidence as suggesting that the political systems of the Anglo-

American polities in the mid-twentieth century were in fact simply not very democratic. By making this move, they would maintain the classical theory's criteria of democracy but jettison the postulate that the regimes most proud of referring to themselves as "democratic" were in fact that. Christian Bay (in *Strategies of Political Emancipation,* 1981) expounded such a view, suggesting that democracy was such a fine idea it was a shame no nations were willing to try it out.

Proponents of the revisionist theory made the other move. They revised the criteria of "democracy" so as to render the idea consistent with the observed realities in the Anglo-American polities. The battle between adherents of these differing responses to the first wave of modern empirical social science was immediate, hostile, and longstanding. Indeed, it can fairly be said to continue, though in a somewhat muted fashion, to this day.

Main Elements of Revisionist Theory

The revisionist theory of democracy acknowledged the failings of citizens and found a compensation for each of them elsewhere in the system. Did citizens lack the skill and experience necessary to rule successfully? The revisionist theory expected less; citizens were not literally to rule themselves but were to choose their rulers through exercising the vote in competitive elections. Were citizens less intensely active in political affairs than the civics textbooks advocated, participating only sporadically in relatively undemanding activities? This very lack of involvement was said to provide the slack necessary within the system to allow political leaders to manage policy efficiently. Were citizens less attached to norms of civil tolerance than were elites, and hence more open to the destructive appeals of demagogues and charismatic, but undemocratic, leaders? All the more reason to recognize that apathy on the part of such citizens could be seen as a functional component of a healthy democratic system, rather than a detraction from it.

Were political organizations, especially parties, organized internally along hierarchical rather than democratic lines? Did the parties shape more than respond to the issue preferences of ordinary citizens? Perhaps. But again the revisionists pointed to the systemic functions served by such arrangements. A democratic system as a whole, it was argued, need not be democratic all the way down throughout every internal subsystem. Indeed, balance could be achieved only if this was not the case. Moreover,

given the degree to which individual political attitudes were discovered to be derived from emotional and symbolic sources rather than from cognitive bases of information, the role of parties and elites in providing guidance to civic energy seemed not only beneficial but absolutely necessary.

Aside from recognizing and affirming a much more significant role for political elites in a democracy, the revisionist theory also highlighted the importance of groups, rather than individuals, as a basic component of a viable democratic polity. David Truman and Robert Dahl were among the most eloquent and insightful analysts in this respect. Modifying Schumpeter's point that democracy was better understood as a method for choosing rulers than as a method of direct rule, Dahl emphasized the importance to democracy of a pluralism of groups within society. In Schumpeter's view the democratic method required only that there be more than one elite (party) competing for the votes of the electorate in order to ensure governmental accountability.

Dahl's view of democracy was not so minimalist. The range and diversity of interest groups at the level of civil society was seen to be as important a factor as elite competition. A system composed only of political elites controlling the state, on the one hand, and, on the other, a relatively unorganized and quiescent body of citizens was dangerously unbalanced. A diversity of interest groups seeking to advance their respective claims in the political arena would serve as a buffering level between the other two strata, functioning both to protect and to advance individual interests more efficiently than individuals could and also to provide a watch and check upon the responsiveness of governors. From a systemic point of view, the existence of a multiplicity of groups also compensated for the lack of competency on the part of individual citizens.

Reaction to Revisionism: Participatory Theory

Just as revisionist theory developed through a critique of classical democratic theory, so another theory, which we can label "participatory," developed out of the critical response to revisionism. The critics of revisionist theory did not, by and large, challenge the descriptive adequacy of the theory. It was agreed that the facts were pretty much as the revisionists related them. The challenge was over what exactly should be made of those facts and how they should be properly understood.

The critics of revisionism advanced four major claims.

First, they argued that the notion of a classical democratic theory was something of a straw man created by the revisionists, implying greater homogeneity among prerevisionist theorists than had actually existed. Although there is some basis for this complaint, it is largely misguided. Obviously, no two theorists agreed upon everything, but there was a recognizable thrust to prerevisionist theory that was, broadly speaking, quite optimistic about the potential and capacity of ordinary citizens if only they were provided with sufficient opportunity for exercising democratic rights of participation. The writings of John Dewey in America *(The Public and Its Problems,* 1927) and A. D. Lindsay in England *(The Essentials of Democracy,* 1935) are characteristic.

A second frequently made criticism was that the revisionist theory had abandoned the aspirational elements of democratic values, transforming the idea of democracy from a vision that looked forward to, in John Stuart Mill's famous words, "the improvement of mankind," to a "mere" procedural mechanism. Critics complained that the revisionist view of human nature and human capabilities was unduly static and pessimistic. C. B. Macpherson *(Democratic Theory,* 1973; *The Life and Times of Liberal Democracy,* 1977) argued that the observed political failings of citizens in the Anglo-American regimes were a consequence of too little institutional opportunity and incentive to develop the powers of citizenship, rather than any intrinsic or necessary limit rooted in human nature. The idea was that citizens would develop the powers of citizenship if more avenues of meaningful democratic participation were opened to them so that they might actually learn by doing. The revisionists were seen as being committed to blocking this development, insofar as their thought suggested that democracy was not something that needed to be built and achieved but rather was what citizens of "democratic" countries were already doing, apparently rather well.

This point led to a third criticism, in many ways the most biting (and contentious), for it directly challenged the scientific self-image of the revisionists. The critics' claim was that revisionist theory was not so much a scientific theory dispassionately derived from facts as it was an ideological defense of the political status quo. The implication was that the academics articulating the revisionist theory were not the objective and neutral observers of political reality they claimed or aspired to be but in effect were the intellectual servants of the dominant political powers.

Thus the debate over democracy between the revisionists and their critics became entangled not only with the debate in Anglo-American social science generally over the possibility of scientific objectivity and the relationship between truth and power but also with the political conflicts of the period between, roughly, 1955 and 1975. These conflicts were intense and divisive, especially the conflict at the level of public opinion in the United States over American military involvement in Southeast Asia. Academics were as much a part of that conflict as were the students they taught, and the debates between revisionists and their more radical critics during this period bear the traces of those political conflicts.

The fourth criticism was that the pluralism of groups and the consequent dispersal of power envisioned in the revisionist portrait of the Anglo-American regimes was more apparent than real. Although most critics granted that these regimes were not characterized by the concentration of power generally found in the communist world, they nevertheless denied that power was dispersed enough to constitute the degree of egalitarianism required by democracy. Critics charged that the needs and interests of large-scale corporations were systematically privileged over those of other interest groups and that hierarchy rather than pluralism characterized the political process.

The difference between the two positions was exemplified in two works that became classics: Robert Dahl's *Who Governs?* (1961) and C. Wright Mills's *The Power Elite* (1956). An entire generation of graduate students would cut their political science teeth on the analysis of these two works and the perspectives they embodied.

Dahl and other pluralists argued that, while groups were not equal in their power and resources, the inequalities were not cumulative. Different groups were seen to have advantages in different issue areas, the competition between them serving to prevent the development of a monopoly on political power by any single elite or group. The political system provided opportunities for participation sufficient to ensure that no significant interests were blocked from success in the political process. Mills saw something different when he looked at the American political system. He claimed that the political conflict highlighted by the pluralists described only the "middle levels" of power. Above this, he argued, was a cohesive and interlocking "power elite" comprising economic, political, and military leaders at the apex of their institutional hierarchies.

The criticisms of the revisionist theory went hand in

hand with the development of an alternative, participatory theory of democracy. Participatory theory aimed at criticizing and contributing to the transformation of Anglo-American political reality rather than scientifically describing it; in many ways the new theory harked back to the moral and developmental themes of classical theory. Prominent examples were Carole Pateman's *Participation and Democratic Theory* (1970) and Benjamin Barber's *Strong Democracy* (1984).

Drawing on the critical points just discussed, participatory theorists advocated the extension of democratic procedures of decision making to what had conventionally been understood as "nonpolitical" spheres of collective life. Employer-employee relations in the workplace were deemed especially significant in this respect. Theorists argued that it was unrealistic to expect citizens to develop the civic competencies necessary to rule themselves actively so long as most of their experience with decision making and authority occurred within the unequal and authoritarian context of the workplace structured on owner-employee lines. The democratization of industry and the workplace thus became the focal point of the practical reforms advocated by participatory theorists.

Of course, calls for increasing the power and control of workers over economic decision making directly challenge the traditional rights and prerogatives attaching to the ownership of property and capital in the capitalist market economies of the Anglo-American world. Such calls have been strenuously, and thus far successfully, resisted. Advocates of participatory theory often take this result to testify to the ability of corporate power to thwart mass demands for more democracy, but it is not at all evident that the demand for democratization attributed to "the people" by participation theorists is really there. Defenders of the status quo argue that the absence of widespread mass demand for the dismantling of capitalist property relations and for greater worker ownership and control of the economy is testimony not to corporate power but to the common sense of the worker, who appreciates the economic efficiency and productivity of capitalist economic relations.

Participatory democrats have tended to be critical of the elements of individualism and the consequent emphasis on the rights of individuals (rather than the good of the community) prevalent in Anglo-American political culture. They are more committed to a populist concept of democracy than to a liberal one—that is, they are more committed to a politics aimed at giving expression to a majority or "popular" will said to characterize the political community as a whole than to a politics aimed at the more mundane purpose of securing individual freedom, including the freedom to avoid the public realm.

On the whole, participatory theorists have taken a relatively optimistic view of human nature, seeing the cure for democracy to be more democracy. This view conforms with the idea that democratic participation is an educational process through which citizens will develop ever greater levels of interest and rationality.

More conservatively inclined theorists see the participatory idea of democracy as dangerous insofar as it aims at politicizing more and more areas of social life. The conservative sees this tendency as the unwarranted intrusion of the public realm into the private—a process the ultimate end of which is totalitarianism, the penetration of political concerns and categories into every aspect of human life. Critics of participatory theory have also tended to hold a somewhat more pessimistic (they would say "realistic") view of human nature, one that counsels citizens to be wary of political power and its inevitable abuses. This counsel is applied to democratic politics as well as to other forms, and it is argued that the participatory theorists fail to appreciate the dangers arising from politicization.

The Crisis of Democracy: Overload and Legitimation

From 1975 onward the rancor of the debate between the revisionists and the participatory democrats tended to decline. This is not to say that much agreement on the political issues dividing them was reached. Rather, the conflict over behavioralism and issues of the scientific status of the social sciences simply lessened to a great degree. A "live and let live" mentality with regard to these issues became more prevalent. Stripped of the entanglement with issues of science and method, however, the conflict between the two perspectives continues today; the basic differences are the same even though some of the labels, catchwords, and names have changed.

Beginning in the mid-1970s and throughout the 1980s a major concern of scholars was the so-called crisis of democracy. Adherents of one view maintained that an "overload of demand" severely threatened the stability of the Anglo-American governments. More and more demands were being placed on the system by increasingly aggressive and self-interested groups, especially those trying to increase their access to a greater range of entitlements provided by the welfare state—that is, the poor. These thinkers argued that too much democracy was dangerous. Because traditional cultural norms of deference and restraint that had checked the level of demand in the past had broken down, and because the world economy had changed in ways that severely restricted the capacity of the Anglo-American economies to grow at the rate they had maintained in the post–World War II era, the state, it was argued, could not effectively meet the demands being placed on it by the populace. The democratic electoral process only exacerbated this condition, because, in order to be elected, politicians had to promise more to a demanding electorate than they could possibly deliver. These promises then encouraged even greater levels of demand in turn.

The solution for this vicious circle resulting in "demand overload" was seen to lie in the direction of a more frankly authoritarian mode of firm and decisive leadership, especially in the executive branch of government. Such leadership would be willing to say "no" rather than capitulate to the various interests charged with creating the problem. Representative examples of this view are Samuel Brittain's "The Economic Contradictions of Democracy" (*British Journal of Political Science*, 1975), and *Democracy in Deficit: The Political Legacy of Lord Keynes* (1977), by Nobel Prize–winning economist James Buchanan and R. E. Wagner.

A very different view was taken by another group of thinkers who saw a "crisis of legitimacy" of the democratic state. They were greatly influenced by the work of the important German social thinker Jürgen Habermas, especially his *Legitimation Crisis* (1976). Leading Anglo-American exemplars of this view are James O'Connor's *The Fiscal Crisis of the State* (1973) and John Keane's *Public Life and Late Capitalism* (1984).

These thinkers attributed the inability of the contemporary state to manage economic policy in a way sufficient to achieve the levels of growth and productivity necessary to meet mass demands for goods to the state's inability to escape the controlling thumb of corporate capital. Thus, whereas the more conservative "overload" view blames the public and its demands for the crisis of democracy, the more radical "legitimation crisis" view places the blame on the system of capitalism, which requires that the interests of capital take priority over public interests. The leftist view claimed to detect a growing popular dissatisfaction with the state that was potentially the source of widespread dissatisfaction with the capitalist economy within which it was embedded. From this view arose the idea of a crisis in the degree to which the state could legitimate itself to its citizens as being genuinely democratic. Although it is certainly true that dissatisfaction with the state and alienation from public life are ever increasing in Anglo-American regimes of the late twentieth century, it is not the case that capitalist economic relations are widely and consciously seen as the cause of these phenomena.

The contrast between the overload and legitimation views of the alleged crisis of democracy is reminiscent of that between the revisionist and the participatory democratic theorists. Like the revisionists, the overload theorists fear greater mass participation in politics and see it as a destabilizing force threatening efficient policy making and administration. Like the participatory theory of democracy, the legitimation crisis view sees democracy as stunted and inhibited by the power of economic elites, and it looks forward to the dismantling of this power through the democratization of society and the politicization of citizens. Each side yearns for what the other fears.

The rhetoric of crisis applied to the Anglo-American regimes came to seem inappropriate, and fell out of use, with the fall of Eastern European communism in the late 1980s. In the last decade of the century a great new wave of interest in democratic theory and democracy arose throughout many parts of the world that had been under authoritarian rule and were attempting a transition to democracy—especially in South America and Eastern Europe.

This renewed vigor and interest in democracy in other parts of the world came at a time when the Anglo-American systems increasingly seemed to be exhausted with the demands of democracy. Civic alienation and cynicism continued to plague the health of the Anglo-American systems, and democratic theory continued to oscillate between what John Dunn calls the "dismally ideological" voice of the latest version of revisionist theory and the "blatantly utopian" voice of the latest version of participatory theory. If the democratic theory of the twenty-first century is to be helpful in alleviating these difficulties and reinvigorating Anglo-American democracy, the inspiration will likely come, ironically, from political energies, inventions, and discoveries in polities that, throughout much of the twentieth century, were considered by most Anglo-American thinkers to be incapable of practicing democracy.

Having completed the historical overview, we can conclude by examining three topics that perennially attract the attention of democratic theorists. These are the relation between political equality and social inequality, the nature of representation, and the justifiability of civil disobedience.

Political Equality and Social Inequality

At the least, political equality entails the equal legal status of all adult citizens within the democratic regime: all are equal as persons before the law, and each is possessed of the same set of political rights, permissions, and duties. There can be no second-class citizenship in a democracy. Yet to say these words is merely to specify the formal and legal requirements of political equality; the question of the degree to which political equality is compromised by the existence of inequalities in the social, economic, and familial spheres of collective life has been hotly debated throughout the twentieth century.

Democratic theorists have adopted a variety of positions in regard to the relationship between political status and the inequalities in wealth and power arising from economic class differences. At one (leftist) extreme are those Marxist socialists who maintain that democracy rightly understood is necessarily incompatible with a capitalist economy; true democracy requires a socialist economy comprising the public ownership of productive resources and a radically egalitarian (re)distribution of income shares. The underlying premise is that one's economic class identity is of such great significance that it tends to determine one's actual political status. Economic class division between those who own capital and those who do not is held to undermine and subvert the rhetoric of democratic political equality, revealing it to be a sham.

At the other (rightist) extreme are those libertarians who maintain a sharp conceptual division between the various spheres of collective life and who thus argue that formal or legal equality is itself a sufficient condition of political equality. Indeed, these thinkers argue that reformist state policies aimed at decreasing the amount of inequality in nonpolitical spheres of life so as to contribute to the realization of equal citizenship in the public sphere result in exactly the opposite. The libertarian claim is that such policies destroy political equality in the pursuit of social equality.

Of course, the great majority of democratic thinkers who address this issue take a position somewhere between these extremes. Defenders of the capitalist welfare state, ranging from American Republicans to European social democrats, disagree about the amount of redistribution of wealth to be undertaken by the state, but nevertheless they accept in principle some conceptual and practical connection between political status and economic class. Thus, for example, it is nearly universally accepted that children should have access to publicly funded education without regard to their parents' ability to pay. The premise here is that one cannot meaningfully be described as an equal citizen if one is illiterate and unable to understand the rudiments of political affairs.

Obviously, however, there is abundant room for debate and reasonable disagreement even among those who accept the general idea of a connection between political and economic status. This is not least because there is no singular or "correct" definition of political status. Whether an aspect of a person's identity or status is political or nonpolitical is dependent on the historically contingent definitions of "political" that the community has created over time. These definitions change and shift, expanding and contracting as a result of the practice of politics. An excellent account of this process of the development of "shared understandings" and its relationship to democracy is that of Michael Walzer in *Spheres of Justice* (1983).

Economic status is not the only form of social inequality that raises serious questions about the meaning of political equality. Race, especially in the United States, has since the beginning of the regime been the dimension of "social" status that has made a lie of the proudest boasts of the realization of political equality. With the development of feminist consciousness and theorizing, gender, once conceived as a quintessentially private and nonpolitical dimension of identity, has increasingly come to be seen as highly salient to the meaning of political equality. Indeed, much of the most interesting contemporary democratic theory is being formulated by young thinkers looking at race and gender, rather than economic class, as factors bearing on democracy and political equality. Examples would include Anne Phillips (*Engendering Democracy,* 1991) and Derrick Bell (*And We Are Not Saved: The Elusive Quest for Racial Justice,* 1987).

The Nature of Representation

What is the proper task of the legislator in representative democracy? The "passive" view of representation maintains that the legislator should, in principle and to the degree possible, aim at literally "re-presenting" the preferences of those for whom he or she stands. In this view the legislator is a channel for passing information, necessary only as a concession to the constraints of time and space that make it impossible for all citizens to "present" their own views.

In an "active" view of representation, the representative bears a much greater responsibility and consequently is charged with more tasks than is the passive legislator. The representative is to lead and educate the people he or she represents, not simply respond to their demands. Leadership requires that the representative exercise his or her own judgment about what is wise and prudent policy, even should this judgment diverge from the expressed preference of the majority of those represented. In that case the educative function of representation requires that the representative engage in the process of shaping constituents' opinion in the direction of the policy choices that the representative thinks are wise and prudent.

Participatory democrats tend to be hostile to representation generally, and especially hostile to the active view of representation, which is seen as paternalistic, manipulative, and elitist. Revisionist democrats tend to take the opposite view, seeing in active representation a counterweight to the inadequacies of the ordinary citizen.

Civil Disobedience

The question of the justifiability of civil disobedience arises in the context of any political regime, but it is especially acute in democracy. Democracy more than any other regime is built on the political competency of the ordinary citizen. The systematic development of this competency means that the regime has an investment in positively encouraging citizens to understand themselves as a source of valid political claims who need offer no apology for exercising their voices in the public realm. Consequently, the limits to such activity, which are essential from the point of view of the order and stability of the regime as a whole, are always controversial and subject to challenge by citizens.

The democratic regime's primary claim on the obedience of its citizens, even when some particular citizens disagree with the substance of the policy pursued by the regime, derives from an appeal to the fairness of the democratic procedure of majority rule among political equals. Insofar as the process can correctly be said to have been a fair one, citizens, including those whose preferred policy or candidate lost, nevertheless are expected to obey. To refuse to do so is to claim an individual veto power inconsistent with the recognition of oneself as a political equal

with one's civic peers. Hence civil disobedience would seem to be unjustifiable in terms of democracy.

Matters are not quite this simple, however. First, although it is true that fairness as modeled through a democratic procedure is considered a good thing, it is certainly not the only good thing, and it can and does conflict with other goods. Many claims to justifiable civil disobedience make appeal to some wider notion of justice or right, which is taken to limit and trump democratic procedure when the two conflict. While it would be foolish to say that such claims are valid simply as claims, it would be equally foolish to jump to the opposite conclusion and deny out of hand the justifiability of any such claim. Ultimately, such justification must depend upon the truth, whatever it is, in regard to ultimate right. Defenders of democratic procedure may be tempted at this point to claim that such procedures allow us to avoid having to inquire into and render judgment on such contentious and disputable matters. This claim is shortsighted, however, for democratic procedure is not itself self-justifying, and the chain of reasons by which a defense of democratic procedure is given will lead back to these very same perplexing matters.

Second, it is possible to argue plausibly in support of justifiable civil disobedience even within the confines set by the values of democracy itself. Indeed, it is ordinarily thought that one important factor distinguishing civil disobedience from mere crime or lawlessness on the one hand and revolutionary action on the other is that the aim of civil disobedience is to strengthen and improve, not destroy, the system of civil law disobeyed by bringing to public light and consciousness some defect within it in need of reform. The actor thus disobeys the law for the sake of the law itself, giving practical expression to this commitment by accepting the penalties that attach to the "crime."

Civil disobedience in a democracy could thus be understood as action in the service of democracy itself. Indeed, this is precisely the sort of public justification that has been given in many cases of civil disobedience in the Anglo-American regimes in the twentieth century. For example, one justification given of the various acts of civil disobedience carried out by civil rights activists in the American South in the 1960s was that these actions were necessary to goad and provoke Americans to change their blatantly undemocratic behaviors with regard to race so as to live up to their own professed democratic commitment to the political equality of all persons.

See also *Almond, Gabriel; Capitalism; Civil disobedi-*

ence; Class; Communitarianism; Dahl, Robert A.; Dewey, John; Elites, Political; Future of democracy; Lipset, Seymour Martin; Macpherson, C. B.; Representation; Schumpeter, Joseph.

Patrick Neal

BIBLIOGRAPHY

Arblaster, Anthony. *Democracy.* Minneapolis: University of Minnesota Press, 1987; Ballmoor: Open University Press, 1994.

Bay, Christian. *Strategies of Political Emancipation.* Notre Dame, Ind.: University of Notre Dame Press, 1981.

Dahl, Robert. *Democracy and Its Critics.* New Haven and London: Yale University Press, 1989.

———. *A Preface to Democratic Theory.* Chicago: University of Chicago Press, 1956.

Duncan, Graeme, ed. *Democratic Theory and Practice.* Cambridge: Cambridge University Press, 1983.

Green, Philip, ed. *Democracy: Key Concepts in Critical Theory.* Atlantic Highlands, N.J.: Humanities Press, 1993.

Held, David. *Models of Democracy.* Cambridge: Polity Press, 1986; Stanford, Calif.: Stanford University Press, 1987.

Levine, Andrew. *Liberal Democracy: A Critique of Its Theory.* New York: Columbia University Press, 1981.

Lipset, Seymour Martin. *Political Man.* New York: Doubleday, 1960.

Macpherson, C. B. *The Life and Times of Liberal Democracy.* Oxford and New York: Oxford University Press, 1977.

Pateman, Carole. *Participation and Democratic Theory.* Cambridge: Cambridge University Press, 1970.

Pennock, J. Roland. *Democratic Political Theory.* Princeton: Princeton University Press, 1979.

Plamenatz, John. *Democracy and Illusion.* New York: Longman, 1973.

Sartori, Giovanni. *The Theory of Democracy Revisited.* 2 vols. Chatham, N.J.: Chatham House, 1987.

Schumpeter, Joseph A. *Capitalism, Socialism, and Democracy.* New York: Harper and Row, 1942.

Stankiewicz, W. J. *Approaches to Democracy.* New York: St. Martin's, 1980.

Theory, Twentieth-Century European

Twentieth-century European democratic theory incorporates the diverse range of continental thinking on the possibility of democracy. The renaissance of democracy in Europe today is an event of immense practical as well as theoretical importance. Democratic or constitutional government originally found its home in modern Europe in England, Holland, Italy, and France, but in the twentieth century these achievements often have been eclipsed by misfortune. The Continent has endured two world wars, the Holocaust, and until the early 1990s the division between the West and the Soviet-dominated East.

Moreover, Europe was the home of the earliest expressions of democratic thought and sentiment in the writings of Benedict de Spinoza, the Baron de Montesquieu, Jean-Jacques Rousseau, and Alexis de Tocqueville. But, despite some rare exceptions, these considerable achievements have often been overlooked by equally powerful critics of democracy.

Critics of Democracy

The critics of democracy have stemmed primarily from two opposing camps. Karl Marx set forth the left-wing attack on democracy. In an essay titled "On the Jewish Question" (1843), he identified the achievements of democracy in France and North America with the emergence of capitalistic economies. Marx's attack on democracy stems from a radicalization of Rousseau's famous statement in his *Discourse on the Origins of Inequality* (1755), which attributed the foundation of civil society to the enclosure of private property. Rousseau was not a communist, but it would be difficult to find a more heartfelt denunciation of the evils attending the creation of property and the establishment of social classes. Representative or, as the Marxists later called it, bourgeois democracy, was taken to be no more than a mask for protecting the property interests of the newly enfranchised middle class.

The right-wing attack on democracy goes back to the assault by Joseph-Marie de Maistre (1753–1821) on the French Revolution, but its more powerful and plausible critics were Friedrich Nietzsche (1844–1900) and Martin Heidegger (1889–1976) in Germany and José Ortega y Gasset (1883–1955) in Spain. These critics saw democracy as part and parcel of the emergence of a new phenomenon: mass society. This term was understood not simply as a numerical or quantitative category but as a new egalitarian social order, which brought with it the destruction of the network of corporate ties, guilds, churches, and landed estates that had functioned as the bedrock of premodern, traditional society. Democracy was often linked to the brutalization and uglification of life that went hand in hand with the new industrial order.

In many respects, the attacks on democracy from the right and the left were not as far apart as they often appeared. For example, Max Horkheimer (1895–1973) and Theodor Adorno (1903–1969), founders of the Frankfurt school of Marxism, took great delight in reviling what they called "the culture industry" for cheapening European art and literature through television, the cinema, and other instruments of the mass media.

The left- and right-wing attacks on democracy have declined, even if they have not disappeared altogether. After World War II the rightist assault went into eclipse because of its political associations with the defeated fascist regimes in Italy and Germany. In the wake of the emergence of the Soviet Union as a world power in the 1950s, however, the Marxist critique continued to gain power and influence even in the noncommunist West. Even though so-called Western Marxists usually repudiated the despotic features of the Soviet model, they sought to keep Marxism alive as a "critical theory" of culture and society. This endeavor often involved considerable feats of intellectual gymnastics in which Marxist theory was combined with other doctrines culled from a variety of philosophic quarters. Thus at various times in the twentieth century Marxism sought to align itself with existentialism (Jean-Paul Sartre), phenomenology (Maurice Merleau-Ponty), Freudianism (Herbert Marcuse), and structuralism (Louis Althusser). These attempts at intellectual synthesis proved exceedingly thin, and with the collapse of the Soviet Union in 1991 there was no longer any reason to retain the pretense. The result has been the greatest resurgence of democratic theory in continental Europe since the French Revolution.

Procedural Theory of Democracy

Arguably, the most important work of democratic theory in the twentieth century was written by an Austrian economist. Joseph Schumpeter's *Capitalism, Socialism, and Democracy,* published in the United States in 1942, developed what became known as the procedural theory of democracy. This theory has had greater resonance in the United States and Great Britain than on the European continent, but the central European origins of the work are unmistakable. Schumpeter's defense of the method of democracy was developed in explicit opposition to the totalitarian experiment in "people's democracy" then under way in Soviet Russia, not to mention the rise of populist demagogues—Adolf Hitler and Benito Mussolini—in Germany and Italy.

Schumpeter's definition of democracy was based on a rejection of what he regarded as the two cardinal tenets of the classical theory of democracy. The first was the belief in "the common good," which could be determined by a rational electorate working in concert. The second was the belief in the "will of the people," which, like the common good, Schumpeter regarded as artificially manufactured or created by political leaders. In place of the classical theory,

Schumpeter offered his own account of democracy as a method for arriving at collective decisions by means of a competitive struggle for people's votes. This purely functional definition, intentionally stripped of all abstract notions such as human rights or the utilitarian goal of "the greatest happiness for the greatest number," was thought to have the advantage of reducing democracy to its bare essentials: electoral politics, pure and simple. Schumpeter's contribution was to see democracy along the lines of a market in which political parties, like firms, compete with one another for votes.

Schumpeter's definition of democracy has been vastly influential and has inspired the work of theorists such as Maurice Duverger in France and Robert Dahl, Anthony Downs, and Mancur Olson in the United States. Like any influential work, however, *Capitalism, Socialism, and Democracy* has also met with severe criticism. In the first place, Schumpeter's identification of democracy with electoral politics seemed overly austere and indifferent to the whole range of democratic values without which competitive elections would be meaningless. Competitive elections, while necessary, are not a sufficient criterion to establish democracy, which must equally be concerned with political participation, deliberation, and the formation of a democratic character among citizens.

Second, Schumpeter's concept of democracy has been widely criticized as economistic and reductionist. Not surprisingly, it has gained its widest adherence among students of "public choice" and the "logic" of collective action, who view politicians as entrepreneurs and voters as consumers in the marketplace of politics. His analogy between electoral politics and the marketplace was either blind or indifferent to the very real differences in political power and resources mobilized by different groups. Furthermore, without introducing philosophically contestable notions such as "fair" or "free" to describe elections, Schumpeter had no grounds for asserting that Hitler, who gained power through popular election, was not a democrat.

Return of the Political

Schumpeterian democracy has become virtually the norm in all Western European countries and the states of North America, but the matter has not rested there. In opposition to the procedural theory of democracy, a new group of theorists drawing on the tradition of classical republicanism extending from Niccolò Machiavelli to Alexis de Tocqueville to Hannah Arendt has attempted to revive such traditional concerns as freedom, rights, equality, and deliberation as central to democracy. Recent European democratic theorists have been concerned not only with securing procedural goods, such as fair elections and party competition, but substantive goods, such as citizen participation, social justice, and the affirmation of distinct cultural and collective identities. To be sure, these themes have been developed unevenly by different writers representing diverse political experiences and unique national contexts. But rather than examining these themes for their internal tensions and inconsistencies, we will treat them here as parts of a single family seeking to adapt democratic theory to the realities of a postcommunist world.

A first step in the direction of a renewal of democratic theory has been undertaken by Claude Lefort. An early associate of Merleau-Ponty's and coeditor of the journal *Socialisme ou Barbarie,* Lefort has written widely on bureaucracy, ideology, and totalitarianism and has published a defense of democratic theory entitled *Democracy and Political Theory* (1988). Under the guise of "rehabilitating" the political, Lefort has sought to establish political experience as something autonomous, distinct from sociological phenomena such as class or economic development.

Lefort plays on an ambiguity in the French language that distinguishes between the terms *le politique* (the political) and *la politique* (politics or policy). Politics or policy refers to a specific set of procedures or activities susceptible to observation and testing that can be studied alongside other empirical phenomena (for example, economics and society). The political, however, refers not to actual distributions of power or resources but to the principles that generate society or, more accurately, different forms of society. An investigation into the political, then, must take the form of a search for the "regime" and its "shaping" of human coexistence and relations of power. It is the specific historical shape or form of power that constitutes the regime and that provides the basic unit of political analysis.

Following Leo Strauss, Lefort maintains that the concept of the regime is worth maintaining only if it refers to more than the formal structure of power. It must also take into account those traditions and beliefs that testify to a set of implicit norms determining notions of just and unjust, good and evil, noble and ignoble. The concept of the regime refers to the existence of something like a political culture that defines the shared values of a people or its way of life.

Lefort's distinctive claim is that modern democracy represents a new kind of regime unprecedented in history. Every previous regime has been based on a particular identification of power with the representation of truth. In medieval Europe, for instance, all power was thought to emanate from the monarch who was both a political agent and the representative of God. In twentieth-century totalitarian societies, all power is said to emanate from the political party, which is both representative of "the people" and the ultimate guardian of the knowledge of the laws of history and society. The modern democratic polity is unique because it breaks from all these previous attempts to identify power with a localized political space and has instead constituted a new form of sovereignty as "an empty place."

Lefort's idea is that in modern democracies power belongs simultaneously to no one and to everyone. It is characterized precisely by the breaking up of the old standards of certainty that defined traditional politics. Democratic regimes have instituted a sense of uncertainty regarding the uses of power, law, and the representation of truth. Rather than regarding this new configuration of power as dangerous or destabilizing, however, Lefort sees in it exciting new possibilities for the future. At the least, modern democracy prevents any person or group of persons from monopolizing power and thus claiming a lock on the truth. More positively, democracies have instituted a new skepticism about the uses of power. Implicit in the social practices of democracy and the periodic contestations or redistributions of power is the belief that no one has the definitive answers to the problems of society and that all attempts to restore the previous landmarks of certainty can only result in totalitarian thought control. Lefort's paradoxical formulas for democracy are "power belongs to no one" and "those who exercise power do not possess it."

In Lefort's view, what makes democracy distinctive is that it not only welcomes but preserves indeterminacy at its core. It is not so much a new constitution of authority but a continuous, albeit controlled, challenge to all authority. What Lefort does not indicate, unfortunately, are the means by which the periodic challenges to power are controlled. What is it that prevents a democratic contest for power from degenerating into a Hobbesian struggle to the death? Lefort's pleasing picture of democracy thus presupposes what it needs to establish, namely, people who are already committed to democratic norms and procedures. Instead of considering the conditions that help to create and preserve democratic indeterminacy, Lefort invites us to consider the possibility that democracy is no longer a regime bounded by law but rather is founded on an ongoing debate about what the role of law should be, about the very boundaries of the legitimate and the illegitimate.

Rule of Law

The problems of democracy raised by Lefort have been addressed with equal seriousness by his Italian contemporary, Norberto Bobbio. Like Lefort a former Marxist, Bobbio has since come to stress the need for an independent legal framework capable of preserving the fundamental rights of individuals. His works, such as *Liberalism and Democracy* and *The Future of Democracy,* have shown great indebtedness to the works of Schumpeter, Dahl, and Giovanni Sartori. Unlike Lefort, who sees democracy as an empty place full of open-ended possibilities, Bobbio regards it first and foremost as a set of procedural rules for arriving at collective decisions.

The advantage of this procedural definition of democracy, Bobbio contends, is that it fits closely with the predominantly individualistic character of modernity. Rejecting organic models of society that have a discomfiting relation to fascism (which in the past have been used to subordinate individual rights and liberties to some theoretical "general will"), Bobbio maintains that democracy is best understood in Schumpeterian terms as a form of representative government in which competitive political parties are authorized to act as intermediaries between individual actors and the government.

Bobbio's model is, then, a defense of representative government as opposed to leftist appeals for direct or participatory democracy. In historical terms he takes the defense of "modern liberty" made by the French politician and writer Benjamin Constant de Rebecque (1767–1830) against Rousseau's and the French Revolution's appeal to the absolute power of the general will. Bobbio is not insensitive to the shortcomings of existing democratic norms and procedures. In the past the problem of democracy was confined to such issues as extending the franchise, removing obstacles to voting, and holding representatives publicly accountable. These tasks, he acknowledges, have been more or less accomplished, but the surface of the problem has only been scratched. The question for democrats is not the old one of who can vote, but what people may vote for. The process of democratization has not even begun to penetrate the twin pillars of contemporary autocracy: big business and the bureaucracy.

The task for future democratic leaders will be to extend democratic procedures outside the political arena, narrowly conceived, to wider areas of civil society.

To his credit, Bobbio is as aware as anyone of the pitfalls of extending democracy to the range of private and semiprivate institutions that populate modern society. He traces with considerable skill the sometimes uneasy historical alliance between liberalism and democracy. The democratic movement (which historically has enlisted the aid of socialism) has defined itself by the demand for greater equality and collective participation in all walks of life, chiefly including the workplace, while liberalism has demanded recognition of individual rights against the state, principally meaning economic liberties. Rejecting radical egalitarianism, Bobbio has defended the historical achievements of liberalism as an effective bulwark against the autocratic state. At the same time, he worries whether liberalism has the internal resources adequate to deal with the problems of inequality and social justice. Bobbio does not give a formula for how much democratization of society is either possible or desirable. Rather his procedural definition of the term leaves it open for people to decide for themselves how far to extend the democratic mandate.

The one norm on which Bobbio insists is strict adherence to the rule of law. As a former Marxist, he is all too aware of how easy it is to denounce law as an instrument of class interests and to oppose to it the rule of charismatic leaders claiming to speak for the interests of the people as a whole. But, he admits, law remains the best defense of democracy and liberty. Considering the classic question framed by Aristotle in the *Politics* whether the rule of law is to be preferred to the arbitrary rule of either the few or the many, Bobbio leaves no doubt as to the superiority of the former. Democracy is nothing other than the rule of law, and what is law but a set of rules for the peaceful resolution of conflict? The task of a democratic government today is to instill a rigorous respect for the rule of law. Without this it will become indistinguishable from the various autocracies that have haunted the chronicles of human history.

Recovery of Human Rights

The conflict between liberal and democratic values that Bobbio traces with great historical skill has been treated with even greater philosophical cogency by Luc Ferry and Alain Renaut. Because they belong to a younger generation of democratic theorists, their ideas were relatively untouched by the epic struggles between communism and fascism in which the thought of Lefort and Bobbio developed. Although deeply skeptical of Marxism, they have concentrated their attention on a critique of the French philosophy of the 1960s and the postmodern critique of Western metaphysics and its characteristic forms of rationality. In place of these postmodernist assaults, which were inspired by Heidegger and Michel Foucault (1926–1984), Ferry and Renaut have defended an interpretation of rights understood as powers and freedoms.

In an Anglo-American context, this last statement would come as no particular surprise, but in the overheated debates of contemporary French thought it stakes out a highly contested terrain. In their three-volume *Political Philosophy,* Ferry and Renaut have responded to the various "antihumanisms" that have come to populate the European scene. The most important of these derives from Heidegger's critique of democracy as inseparable from the technological urge to dominate and control the earth.

According to Heidegger, democracy is one vast, technological feeding frenzy erected upon a philosophy of the "subject" as the omnipotent and arrogant "lord of Being." In their various works, Ferry and Renaut have sought to rehabilitate the autonomy and dignity of the moral agent from the Heideggerian and Foucauldian assaults of the postmoderns. Drawing on the insights of the German philosophers Immanuel Kant (1724–1804) and Johann Gottlieb Fichte (1762–1814), they treat the individual as a moral agent open to an undetermined and in principle undefinable future. The meaning of their self-proclaimed juridical humanism is that human beings lack any determinate essence beyond a capacity for free agency. It is this capacity that surpasses in value all other historical, social, or national markers of identity.

Although Ferry and Renaut have defended the idea of the free individual as the most enduring legacy of modernity, they cannot help but note that the idea of democracy has suffered from the outset from a fundamental ambiguity in its understanding of rights. Drawing on the work of the American political theorist Hannah Arendt (1906–1975), they trace this ambiguity back to its origins in the American and French Revolutions, respectively. The American Revolution is identified with the liberal concept of rights as permissions that individuals exercise on their own behalf and that serve as a bulwark against the intrusive incursions of state power. The French Revolution by contrast developed a democratic concept of rights as entitlements, which are not to be entrusted to individuals as such but are the property of the state to implement for the improvement of the collective welfare.

This distinction between rights as permissions and rights as entitlements has helped to define the shape of democracy over the past two centuries. The balance has slowly shifted from fundamentals—such as life, liberty, and the pursuit of happiness—to encompass an enlarged package of social, cultural, and economic rights to such entitlements as universal health care, paid vacation and leave time, and the right to work.

Ferry and Renaut recognize that both the liberal and the democratic traditions of rights contain flaws. If the democratic (and later socialist) concept of rights as entitlements is allowed to go unchecked, it may expand indefinitely the power of the state over civil society. But the liberal concept of rights as permissions seems unable to address adequately the needs of social justice and ways to correct inequality. The solution they offer to this alleged contradiction is an idea that is neither strictly liberal nor strictly democratic. The "republican idea" centers on the rights of political participation exercised through the vote. Rights of participation are not just permissions to vote for representatives who will then be held publicly accountable; they also provide citizens with an opportunity to form political judgment, exercise responsibility, and establish new bonds of collective solidarity among themselves. Political participation is a means not only to satisfy private, nonpolitical goals but also to ensure a more fully developed, more fully human, life.

Democracy and Civil Association

Where the new European democratic theorists have often gone beyond the older Schumpeterian concept of democracy is in their concern with the problems of citizenship in multiethnic, increasingly pluralistic societies. With the collapse of communism, where these issues were systematically repressed or denied, Eastern European theorists like Václav Havel, Adam Michnik, and Georg Konrad have turned their attention to the phenomenon of "civil society" as an alternative to the state. Originally used by John Locke and the leading members of the Scottish Enlightenment, the term entered the European political lexicon through G. W. F. Hegel's *Philosophy of Right* (1821). For Hegel, civil society referred to a web of semiautonomous associations, independent of the state, that bound citizens together in matters of common concern. Today the term has been rehabilitated to indicate the domain of uncoerced cultural, religious, and economic associations that can fill the void left by the demise of the Leninist state.

The concept of civil society has been used by democratic theorists in at least two ways. The first grew out of dissident movements in countries such as Czechoslovakia, Hungary, and Poland. These movements saw civil society as an alternative to the coercive state apparatus. Their strategy was essentially antipolitical; they regarded politics and the state as irredeemably hostile to freedom and urged citizens to join with others in sharing a life organized around nonpolitical goals. Today, however, the term has been used less as an alternative to politics than as a means of widening and enhancing the sphere of citizen participation within the framework of parliamentary systems. For thinkers like Jürgen Habermas and Claus Offe, democratic institutions require an attitude of democracy that only the institutions of civil society can provide.

The most important aspects of the civil society argument stem from the effort to sustain and promote a democratic culture and new forms of democratic citizenship. Sometimes this argument is stated in terms of reestablishing an atmosphere of trust as a fundamental precondition for a stable democratic regime, in contrast to the overwhelming environment of fear and servility imposed by the Leninist state. Citizens must be able to trust one another as well as their representatives if democracy is to prove viable. At other times, civil society is charged with reestablishing the basic norm of civility, or the mutual recognition of the worth and dignity of every individual. Unless citizens recognize one another as worthy of basic esteem and respect, democracy will not flourish. Finally, it is alleged that civil society is the very means by which democratic society can be legitimized. Civil society crucially includes the institutions of public debate through which opinion is formed. In the absence of the older means of legitimizing power, public opinion takes on an enhanced role in shaping the character of democracy and the citizens who will inhabit it.

Civil society is related to the phenomenon of political education or culture mentioned earlier. Political theorists as different as Habermas and Hans-Georg Gadamer have interpreted civil society as tied not to the pursuit of power but to the open recognition of differences and the need for a nonmanipulative kind of communication. Habermas's version of a democratic society is one in which collective decisions are arrived at through a process of argument and debate, not distorted by disparities of power. Civil society is thus conceived, somewhat idealistically,

along the lines of the ancient Greek and modern German concepts of education, both of which convey a model of a liberally cultivated person.

For many of the theorists of civil society, democracy represents something like a condition of difference within a shared identity. Democracy is based upon certain common values, such as respect for the uniqueness and freedom of the individual, a market economy, and the rule of law. At the same time, the principles of a democratic culture must serve to foster an awareness of human diversity (cultural, linguistic, religious) and educate citizens toward a tolerance of and respect for these differences. Civil society today is, then, ultimately an educational institution whose goal is toleration of diversity. Democratic toleration is not simply a concession to the brute fact of difference and the frailty of human judgment. It grows out of an awareness of the deep-rooted pluralism of human association. This recognition of the multifold character of the human condition offers the best hope of promoting a democratic culture in Europe today.

Resurgence of Democratic Theory

The reemergence of democratic theory in Europe is one of the most hopeful signs on the political horizon today. Many of the debates and concerns touched upon here mirror or even reproduce arguments that have long been familiar to the Anglo-American world. But these concerns are often enriched by a language and vocabulary shaped by distinct political experiences and intellectual traditions. European democratic theorists are more likely to draw inspiration from Hegel than from Mill, from Fichte than from the writers of the *Federalist,* from Spinoza than from Locke. American political theorists who confront this renascent European democracy with an open mind and willingness to learn may well find their own understandings enlarged by the experience.

It would be foolishly optimistic to believe that the resurgence of democratic theory will be sufficient to guarantee the success of many of the new experiments in democratic rule and constitution making now abounding in Eastern Europe and the former Soviet Union. As the breakdown of Yugoslavia has demonstrated all too graphically, talk of equal rights and citizenship are fragile entities when confronted with ancient ethnic and religious hatreds. Furthermore, the survival of democratic institutions, especially in Germany, in the post–World War II years has been in large part sustained by the cold war and the artificial division of Europe by the iron curtain.

Whether the future of democracy will flourish in new, radically altered conditions remains a troubling question with which political theorists will have to grapple.

See also *Aron, Raymond; Civil society; Class; Dahl, Robert A.; Duverger, Maurice; Kant, Immanuel; Marxism; Mass society; Montesquieu; Nietzsche, Friedrich; Rousseau, Jean-Jacques; Schumpeter, Joseph; Tocqueville, Alexis de.*

Steven B. Smith

BIBLIOGRAPHY

Arendt, Hannah. *On Revolution.* New York: Viking, 1963.

Bobbio, Norberto. *The Future of Democracy: A Defence of the Rules of the Game.* Translated by Roger Griffin. Oxford: Polity Press, 1987.

———. *Liberalism and Democracy.* Translated by Martin Ryle and Kate Soper. London: Verso, 1990.

Ferry, Luc, and Alain Renaut. *The French Philosophy of the Sixties: An Essay on Anti-Humanism.* Translated by Mary Cattani. Amherst: University of Massachusetts Press, 1990.

———. *From the Rights of Man to the Republican Idea.* Vol. 3 of *Political Philosophy.* Translated by Franklin Philip. Chicago: University of Chicago Press, 1992.

Gadamer, Hans-Georg. "The Diversity of Europe: Inheritance and Future." In *Hans-Georg Gadamer on Education, Poetry, and History.* Edited by Lawrence Schmidt and Monica Reuss. Albany: State University of New York Press, 1992.

Habermas, Jürgen. "Justice and Solidarity: On the Discussion Concerning State 6." In *Hermeneutics and Critical Theory in Ethics and Politics.* Edited by Michael Kelly. Cambridge: MIT Press, 1990.

Havel, Václav. *The Power of the Powerless: Citizens against the State in Central-Eastern Europe.* Edited by John Keane. London: Hutchinson, 1985.

Lefort, Claude. *Democracy and Political Theory.* Translated by David Macey. Minneapolis: University of Minnesota Press, 1988.

———. *The Political Forms of Modern Society: Bureaucracy, Democracy, Totalitarianism.* Edited by John Thompson. Cambridge: Polity Press, 1986.

Schumpeter, Joseph. *Capitalism, Socialism, and Democracy.* New York: Harper and Row, 1942, 1962.

Seligman, Adam. *The Idea of Civil Society.* New York: Free Press, 1992.

Taylor, Charles. "Modes of Civil Society." *Public Culture* 3 (1990): 95–118.

Thiers, Louis-Adolphe

French politician, historian, and first president of the French Third Republic (1870–1940). In many ways Thiers (1797–1877) was the bridge between the monar-

Louis-Adolphe Thiers

chists who dominated the nineteenth century and the republicans who laid the foundations of democracy in the twentieth. In the terms of his times he was a political moderate who served as a minister during Louis-Philippe's reign (1830–1848) and became one of the most prominent republican politicians of his day. Despite his claims to being above politics—a claim often made by conservatives—Thiers's survival and eventual effectiveness depended on very substantial political skills.

Thiers was born to a family of modest means in Marseilles, where he attended *lycée* (academic high school) as a scholarship student. He went on to study law in Aix-en-Provence and moved to Paris in 1820. After establishing himself as a serious historian with the publication in 1827 of his *Histoire de la révolution française*, a passionate defense of constitutional monarchy, Thiers became a journalist. He founded the liberal newspaper *Le National* in 1829.

The very critical line of the paper toward the Legitimist

(that is, pro–Bourbon dynasty) government of Auguste-Jules-Armand-Marie de Polignac almost landed him in jail. Fortunately for Thiers, the arrival of the Orléans monarchy of Louis-Philippe in July 1830—which he had supported—saved him from incarceration. Eventually, Thiers would be named to various ministries in Louis-Philippe's July (or Bourgeois) Monarchy, including those of agriculture, interior, and foreign affairs.

Because Thiers's opinions were relatively liberal (for a monarchist), he was elected to the parliament in the next regime, the Second Republic (1848–1851), where he voted with the conservatives. The coup d'état of Napoleon III in 1851, with its early populist leanings, proved initially inhospitable to Thiers, who was incarcerated, then exiled for a year. On his return he was elected as a representative for Paris in the Second Empire's Legislative Assembly.

When the Government of National Defense was formed in the wake of the 1870 defeat of Napoleon III by the Prussians in Sedan, Thiers distanced himself from it. However, he was elected chief of the executive power by the National Assembly in 1871. His charge was to extract France from its war with Prussia, a war he had initially opposed because France was not prepared for it. Thiers ended the war by giving Otto von Bismarck, the Prussian chancellor, everything he wanted in the Treaty of Frankfurt (1871). Bismarck got the provinces of Alsace and Lorraine, which were rich in coal and iron ore, along with substantial reparations. When the reparations were paid, thanks to government loans negotiated by Thiers, the Prussians ended their occupation of France.

Thiers's political skills were put to the test when the first parliament of the Third Republic emerged from elections with a monarchist majority. His skill at playing off different factions of the monarchist camp, divided by their dynastic loyalties, allowed the republican institutions to survive.

Thiers was no modern democrat. He was responsible for the brutal repression of the Paris Commune in 1871. The Commune, which took its name from an earlier (1793) radical experiment during the French Revolution, was declared by local Parisian officials when the new government of the Third Republic, installed in the suburb of Versailles, ended the wartime moratorium on rent and debt payments. Parisians, who had borne the considerable hardship of the Prussian siege, were in no mood to compromise on this issue with the national government, dominated by the rich and propertied. Although little that the Commune advocated was very radical, Thiers sent in troops, themselves provincials who detested Parisians. The troops fired on the resisters, causing more deaths than had occurred during the Terror of the Revolution. This bloody repression had a precedent. Thiers had reacted the same way to the workers' risings in Lyons and Paris in 1834, when he was Louis-Philippe's minister of the interior.

Although Thiers's inclinations were conservative, most of his actions were pragmatic. In his famous rivalry with the fiery republican Léon Gambetta, Thiers had argued for a more conservative republic in order to attract a broader base of support, a strategy to which Gambetta was eventually won over. In a country that was deeply divided on many issues, where the overwhelming majority of people lived in the countryside, and where the representatives of the principal religion were hostile to the republic, conservative republicanism may have been the only kind of democratic system that could have endured.

See also *France; Gambetta, Léon-Michel.*

Harvey B. Feigenbaum

BIBLIOGRAPHY

Allison, John M. S. *Thiers and the French Monarchy.* Hamden, Conn.: Archon Books, 1968.

Bury, J. P. T., and Robert Tombs. *Thiers, 1797–1877: A Political Life.* Boston: Allen and Unwin, 1986.

Pomaret, Charles-Henri. *Monsieur Thiers et son siècle.* Paris: Gallimard, 1948.

Three People's Principles

The ideological principles developed by Sun Yat-sen (1866–1925) for the Chinese Nationalist Party (Kuomintang, or KMT). The Three People's Principles embody the ideas of Sun, frequently called the father of modern China, on revolution and governance in China. The first two principles, nationalism and democracy, formed part of Sun's thinking when he founded the Revive China Society in 1894. The third principle, the people's livelihood, derived from Sun's observations of English social problems during a stay in London in 1897. These three principles eventually became the guiding ideology of the Chinese United League, a precursor to China's Nationalist Party founded by Sun and others in 1905.

The Three People's Principles took their final form in 1924 with encouragement from Mikhail Borodin, a Comintern agent who persuaded Sun Yat-sen to deliver a series of lectures on his political philosophy. (The Comintern, or Communist International, was a group founded by Russian Bolsheviks to promote international revolution.) Sun's speeches were later edited into *The Three People's Principles,* the book that became the Kuomintang's ideological tract during the Nationalist Revolution of 1926–1928, which reunified China. It remains the guiding thought of the Nationalist Party. Sun's 1924 lectures included six each on the principles of nationalism and democracy. He gave only four lectures on the principle of the people's livelihood, however, before ill health and one last effort to maneuver in the world of warlord politics caused him to cease lecturing and travel to Beijing. He died there in March 1925.

Sun's lectures on the Three People's Principles are by no means a systematic treatise. Rambling, wordy, and frequently self-contradictory, they convey a sense of ideals more than a coherent program for revolutionary success and governance. Nevertheless, their embodiment of the Chinese people's aspirations to national independence, popular sovereignty, and common prosperity gave them wide appeal in their own day and explain their continuing impact on Chinese thought today.

Sun compared his principles of nationalism, democracy, and people's livelihood to Abraham Lincoln's concept of a government of the people, by the people, and for the people. Sun's principles, however, actually reflect traditional Chinese notions of equalization of wealth and popular welfare, leavened with Sun's readings of Western socialism and the anti-imperialist passions of his day, more than Lincolnian ideas of democracy. A close look at each principle reveals the very real gap between Sun's thought and Western notions of democracy.

Nationalism

Sun's concept of *nationalism* grew out of frustration with China's international weakness and internal division. The China of Sun's day was subject to economic and political exploitation by imperialist powers. Sun traced China's inability to stand up to imperialist pressures to the country's lack of nationalism. The loyalties of the Chinese, he argued, were directed toward families and clans rather than toward the nation as a whole. As a result, Sun compared China to a plate of loose sand. China did not, according to Sun, suffer from a lack of individual freedom but rather from an excess; nationalism would be the force that would unite the Chinese into an unyielding body—like a firm rock formed by adding cement to sand.

Unlike China's May Fourth intellectuals, who blamed the Chinese family for stifling individualism and regarded it as the root cause of autocracy in Chinese society, Sun looked to family loyalties as the foundation of national unity. He argued that it would be much easier to weld together the 400 or so clans of China (here he considerably understated the number of effective clans) than it would be to forge national unity among the 400 million individuals of China. Family loyalty could thus become the basis of national loyalty. Sun's conservative nationalism was also reflected in his rejection of the cosmopolitan ideals of the May Fourth intellectuals. Cosmopolitanism might be all right for developed nations, he said, but it was a luxury that developing nations like China could not afford.

Strong Government and Popular Sovereignty

Sun's notion of *democracy* (sometimes translated as "the people's rights") differed substantially from the Western use of that term. For Sun, the development of democracy in the West reflected a very different historical process and need from that which confronted China. Western democracy, Sun maintained, developed out of a struggle against autocracy, and therefore it placed a premium on liberty and the restraint of government. The Chinese people, on the other hand, did not suffer from autocracy according to Sun; the emperor collected taxes but otherwise left the people to live and die on their own.

Thus China's problem was not a struggle for liberty—of which China already had too much—but rather for strong government that would govern in the interests of the people. In Sun's view, it was necessary to distinguish between "sovereignty" and "ability." This distinction, which Sun never argued very coherently, would solve one of the key problems of Western democracy. The citizens of Western democracies, said Sun, feared that a strong government would get away from them. Sun argued that China could combine powerful government with popular sovereignty by delegating the running of government to people of ability.

However obscure the distinction between sovereignty and ability, there is no doubt that it fit well with Sun's elite view of democracy and his long-held belief in a natural hierarchy among humans. Sun divided the world into three types of people: those like himself who were thinker-inventors, their disciples, and the unconscious performers.

Sun liked to illustrate these types through the image of building a house. An architect draws up blueprints, a foreman reads them, and workers, without understanding architecture, nevertheless follow these instructions to build the house.

Vision of a Moral Society

Sun's final principle, the *people's livelihood,* can be thought of as a type of socialism that drew eclectically on a smattering of Western political views and traditional Chinese ideals of equalizing wealth. In Sun's view, China's fundamental problem was not inequality of wealth but rather the poverty of the country as a whole. Sun argued that China's conditions and the application of his principle of people's livelihood could prevent the sort of inequalities and class antagonisms that Karl Marx's theories were meant to address. Capital and labor, Sun said, could work together to create wealth that would benefit the whole nation.

Sharply refuting the Marxist belief in class struggle, Sun argued that class collaboration was the key both to social harmony and the prosperity of China. In the course of economic development, however, it was essential for the government to play an active role in restricting capital. For instance, Sun advocated the use of taxation and laws to ensure that capitalists used their money for the good of society. Sun also supported a policy that would equalize land ownership through a policy of government purchase and distribution rather than confiscation. Finally, great concentrations of wealth and power could be prevented by the development of state-owned enterprises that would command the heights of the Chinese economy. Industries that were central to the economy, such as railroads, mining, and shipping, should be owned by the state.

See also *China; May Fourth Movement; Sun Yat-sen; Taiwan.*

Joseph Fewsmith

BIBLIOGRAPHY

Linebarger, Paul. *Sun Yat-sen and the Chinese Republic.* New York: AMS Press, 1969.

Schiffrin, Harold Z. "The Enigma of Sun Yat-sen." In *China in Revolution: The First Phase, 1900–1913,* edited by Mary Clabaugh Wright. New Haven: Yale University Press, 1968.

———. *Sun Yat-sen and the Origins of the Chinese Revolution.* Berkeley and Los Angeles: University of California Press, 1968.

Sharmon, Lyon. *Sun Yat-sen: His Life and Its Meaning.* Stanford: Stanford University Press, 1968.

Sun Yat-sen. *Fundamentals of National Reconstruction.* Taipei: China Cultural Service, 1953.

———. *San Min Chu I: The Three Principles of the People.* Translated by Frank W. Price. Edited by L. T. Chen. Shanghai: Commercial Press, 1929.

Wilbur, C. Martin. *Sun Yat-sen: Frustrated Patriot.* New York: Columbia University Press, 1976.

Tobago

See *Caribbean, English*

Tocqueville, Alexis de

French statesman, political thinker, and historian. Tocqueville (1805–1859) was born in Paris to a distinguished aristocratic family. As a youth, he witnessed the fall of Napoleon Bonaparte and the recovery of his family's estates and at least a portion of the status they had before the French Revolution.

These events, however, did not cause Tocqueville to hope for anything like a restoration of the pre-revolutionary regime. Through study and thought, he had concluded that the fundamental idea of democracy, that of liberty as everyone's birthright, had revealed itself so clearly to humanity in general that it could no longer be resisted. He therefore took an oath of allegiance to the liberal monarchy of Louis-Philippe when it displaced the Bourbon monarchy in 1830. Taking the oath was in effect a declaration of independence from his aristocratic lineage. Henceforth Tocqueville would devote his life of writing and public service to the legitimization and improvement of democracy.

Public Career and Writings

Tocqueville's legacy consists almost entirely of two books: *Democracy in America* (1835–1840), which he wrote at the beginning of his public life, and *The Old Regime and the French Revolution* (1856), written in his final years. In the intervening years, Tocqueville devoted himself to a career in politics. He served his constituents of Volognes as a member of the Chamber of Deputies from 1839 until the end of the Second Republic in 1851. To his frustration, however, his influence as a statesman never matched his fame as an author. He labored valiantly to preserve the republic, participating in the drafting of a new constitution in 1848. Near the end of his career, he was appointed by the president, Louis Napoleon, to be minister of foreign affairs. He held this office for only five months, however, because his opposition to Louis Napoleon's ambitions of dictatorship became clear. When Tocqueville protested the coup d'état that ended the republic, he had to retire from public service.

During the last two years of his political career, Tocqueville wrote some *Recollections*—his memoirs of the events of 1848 and their aftermath. These observations, like much of his work, were not intended for publication. Had Tocqueville lived longer, some of the material in his *Souvenirs* might have found its way into his projected work on *The European Revolution*. He was able to complete only part of this ambitious project: *The Old Regime and the French Revolution*.

In *The Old Regime and the French Revolution*, Tocqueville presented his account of the causes of the French Revolution, an account still influential among historians of the period. He showed how the decadence and political ineptitude of the French aristocracy ultimately provoked the violence of 1789. Tocqueville also began to trace the gradual emergence of the idea—or perhaps it should be called the feeling—that is at the core of modern democracy and is responsible for its overwhelming power and grandeur—namely, the equal right of all human beings at birth to liberty.

By returning to this inspiring core of the French Revolution and of democracy, Tocqueville intended to overcome what he viewed as the sadly farcical politics of the mid-nineteenth century. His best hope for this book, as for all of his writings, was that it might begin to generate a level of statesmanship equal to the brightest prospects of democracy—but which there is no guarantee that democracy will produce. *The Old Regime* contains an implicit call for modern democratic statesmanship to provide social and political forms through which the democratic idea can be manifested in a healthy, active way. But there is little or nothing in *The Old Regime* that shows just what that might mean.

Tocqueville left no clearer or fuller prescriptions for democratic statesmanship than those in the book of his early years, *Democracy in America*. Despite the many reasons that American democracy could not, according to Tocqueville, stand as a model for Europe, *Democracy in America* came closest to providing some positive direction

Alexis de Tocqueville

for European legislators. The book remains Tocqueville's masterpiece.

The Question of Equality

The two volumes of *Democracy in America* complement one another in the presentation of what Tocqueville intended as a "new political science for a world quite new." By this he meant at least that the new world is a democratic one; a system of government that depends upon the authority of any natural elect—anyone superior by nature or labeled as chosen by God—is no longer possible. Political science will have to be guided by the fact that equality and the passion for equality are the dominant facts of political life. But what equality? An informing new political science is needed, Tocqueville maintained, because *equality* is an ambiguous term; the love of equality can take either a noble form or a debased form.

At its worst the love of equality is merely jealousy, hostile to any kind of individual distinction. In Volume One of *Democracy in America,* Tocqueville shows how this base passion gives to the democratic majority its own propensity to tyranny. It is as if the majority were a being with a soul that insisted on administering every aspect of human life, embarrassed by the success of anything not brought about by its own will. The most likely, and very noxious, consequence of this tyranny is an excess of political and especially administrative centralization that robs individuals of any necessity or even opportunity for self-reliance.

In Volume Two, Tocqueville further shows how the love of equality tends to break down all forms of human association subordinate to the democratic community as a whole. Because a person's belonging to a family or a voluntary association, or even a friendship, might provide the psychological support as well as the ground for resisting the democratic majority's authority, the democratic majority tends to suppress these things or tolerate them only in a truncated form. The result is an atomization of civil society. Individuals are denied almost any emotional connection with anything outside themselves, imprisoned, as it were, within their own personal opinions and their own immediate self-interest.

Tocqueville calls this phenomenon *individualism.* By this he does not mean the independence and strength of soul that the word has come to connote as a result of John Stuart Mill's usage in his later work *On Liberty* (1859). What Tocqueville means is almost the opposite of that. By individualism, he means the isolation, and hence the weakening, of the individual. Ultimately, Tocqueville fears that democratic individuals will offer no resistance to the absolute tyranny of a single person; they may even welcome tyranny so long as the tyrant promises to protect the condition of social equality. Short of that, however, Tocqueville is also concerned about the danger of a softer tyranny, of public opinion, among democratic citizens who are so weakened by individualism that they cannot really think or even feel for themselves.

The antidote to these horrors is the healthy or noble love of equality—a love of the political and moral equality among self-legislating human beings that Tocqueville almost certainly learned from the writings of the eighteenth-century philosopher Jean-Jacques Rousseau. Tocqueville's debt to Rousseau is indicated most clearly in the second chapter of Volume One of *Democracy in America,* which he says contains the "germ" of everything that follows. Here Tocqueville gives his description of the New England Puritan communities, where the real spirit of American democracy was implanted long before there was an American nation.

The outstanding, even startling, fact about the New England communities is that no aspect of life was held private, beyond the community's concern. The Puritans had come to America to establish a "city on a hill," to be governed directly by the laws of the Old Testament. In their zeal for their idea, they imposed upon themselves a code of civil legislation that often contained terrible penalties for what Tocqueville considers relatively light offenses.

The fact that Tocqueville declares the Puritans "free" shows how far he is from thinking of freedom as the limited license of, say, John Stuart Mill. Rather, the liberty to which we have equal right at birth means active involvement in our own self-government. Fundamentally, the definitive democratic passion is a sort of instinct for the general will. And Tocqueville's "new science of politics" has the aim of showing how this principle can act.

Local Autonomy and Voluntary Associations

Throughout the remainder of *Democracy in America,* Tocqueville seeks to explain how the Americans are able to keep alive anything of the spirit of those Puritan towns. It is intriguing because, obviously, the conditions that made the political experiment of the Puritans possible no longer existed. The active involvement in public life by all citizens of those New England towns was possible in part because of their small size and relative isolation. But the existence of such small entities is itself a violation of the forces tending toward democratic civilization, guided as those forces are by the growing perception of the commonality among human beings. The democratic world is a world of great nations, perhaps even empires. How, then, can a degree of local autonomy be maintained that allows people a direct active involvement in public life when the local jurisdictions are not politically independent?

Tocqueville's description of how Americans find an answer to this question is richly detailed, in a way that accounts for much of the early prestige of the book. Part of the answer lies in the American scheme of complex government and administrative decentralization. The surprising conclusion is that Americans do not really overcome the tyranny of the majority. Its effects, however, are mitigated so as to render it less despotic and less enervating than it might be. He explains that Americans connect democratic equality and local autonomy through a chain that has several links. For them, democratic equality entails the idea of popular sovereignty. Popular sovereignty, in turn, involves the notion that government is legitimized by the free consent of individuals, and, therefore, the individual is sovereign outside the sphere of authority to which the people have given their consent. This concession to the limited autonomy of the individual within government is then extended so as to sanction a similar concession to the autonomy of local administrations in relation to the central government.

The energy and vigor of American democracy also stem from American adeptness at forming voluntary associations for all sorts of tasks. These voluntary associations as well as the local governmental jurisdictions are the mechanisms through which Americans overcome the individual impotence that democracy may produce. They function indirectly as schools through which Americans develop the habits of free people. Moreover, in a way that parallels what Tocqueville said about complex governmental administration, American reasoning connects vigorous voluntary associations with democratic equality. The link, in their minds, is "self-interest rightly understood." Tocqueville shows somewhat wryly how the crude doctrine of self-interest can be accepted almost beyond question by a democratic people like the Americans and how it can lead them to at least small acts of sacrifice such as are necessary for cooperative endeavor.

The more Tocqueville leads us to understand the attitudes that underlie the health and vigor of local government and voluntary associations in America, the more clearly we see that these things are in fact the results of democratic freedom rather than its fundamental causes. Assumptions about an easy compatibility between individual interests and any common good are highly questionable. Tocqueville merely observes—but does not defend the thought—that Americans share those assumptions. Ultimately, Americans believe what they do because it suits them. They have learned from their own practical experience the advantages of their complicated institutions. What they say in their defense is only the verbalization of what they feel, and what they feel is a result of lucky accidents—of America's geographical circumstances and its almost purely democratic tradition at all levels.

Mores and Religion in American Democracy

What, then, is the inference to be drawn by the democratic legislator? It is clear that in a democratic country

unlike America, where the traditions of local freedom and voluntary association did not already exist, they would be difficult to implant. From the perspective of the nation, such localities and associations tend to appear as exceptions, even points of resistance, to the sovereign will of the nation. Put another way, if Tocqueville's argument is that local government and voluntary associations are preventive medicine against the grinding, atomizing effects of egalitarian jealousy, his argument seems to beg the question of why those institutions will not themselves be ground down by that very jealousy where it might already exist.

This much is certain: American political and social institutions would not have their beneficial effects for other democratic peoples. They can be of benefit to Americans because of peculiar American attitudes, or, in Tocqueville's broader word, *mores*. To understand completely why American democratic citizens are free, and what corollaries might be available in their own nations, democratic legislators need to consider the whole system of mores. Ultimately, as Tocqueville says explicitly, more than physical circumstances or even laws, it is mores that are responsible for maintaining republican freedom in America.

Tocqueville discusses mores in democracy, and in American democracy in particular, in both volumes of *Democracy in America*. This discussion is the richest and subtlest dimension of the work, with many features that are of interest to contemporary students of social psychology. The crown of the entire examination of mores, and thus the crown of Tocqueville's thought as a whole, is his discussion of religion. It turns out that the peculiar, marvelous combination of the spirit of religion with the spirit of freedom is just as fundamental to the health of American democracy as it was to that of the early Puritan New England towns—albeit not quite in the same way.

The religion of most of Tocqueville's Americans, that is, the preponderant religion, is Protestantism—of a sort that has made a full accommodation to this world. Protestantism includes the notion that humankind is on the road toward an indefinite perfection, and it interprets progress in material well-being as the sign of such perfectibility. This idea means that Americans are in fact animated to engage in industrial and commercial undertakings not simply from avarice or anxiety but from some satisfaction of grander emotions that they derive from their labors. They even seem to practice a kind of heroism in their commerce. They are sure that the wealth and power of their nation reflects the glory of God.

Not only is American religion worldly, but it is also in an intriguing way very conscious of itself as that. Americans are convinced that religion is indispensable to the maintenance of republican institutions. They take for granted that freedom depends upon a level of virtue among the citizens and, that to be relied on, such virtue needs the support of religion. In particular, virtue needs the support of the promise of reward and the threat of punishment in an afterlife. But Tocqueville confesses that it is very hard to tell whether Americans actually believe in such an afterlife. They say they do, but the secrets of the heart are hard to read. All that can be said for certain is that Americans believe that they ought to believe. Political freedom requires it. Tocqueville reports that this ironic attitude is held not only by the laity but even by ministers.

Tocqueville's analysis of religion in America continually leads to the question whether Americans are genuinely sincere in it. Is the faith they profess something devout, or rather is it politic? Ultimately, Tocqueville's teaching about American democracy revolves around his answer to this question: their faith is both. The best illustration of how this duality might be possible is what Tocqueville says about the separation of church and state in America. Tocqueville shares with Americans the conviction that separation of church and state is enormously valuable, not only to save the state from the ravages of sectarian conflict but also to preserve genuine religious feeling from unnecessary doctrinairism.

When liberated from politics, religion comes into its own, so to speak, as one lofty form of hope from which very few human beings are ever cut off. Sensing this, Americans are not professing the indifference of politics toward religion when they assert the advantages of separation of church and state. Rather, in a way, this separation is their religion. Their faith, at bottom, is something that might be called "natural." Their God is a humane one who loves an honest conscience (which they believe they have) more than doctrinal rectitude. Another way of putting it is to say that Americans make a sort of religion of tolerance; they blithely ignore the sources of such genuine diversity as would require much tolerance.

Tocqueville's showing that mores are the key to American democratic freedom—that they are the cause more than the effect of America's excellent political institutions—makes his reader aware of the artificiality that laces the American way of life. By this he does not intend an indictment. His broadest reflection is that all of human life is beset with artificiality, but that does not necessarily rob it of the prospects for genuine greatness.

What it does mean is that if democracy is to exhibit its own peculiar form of greatness, the artifices by which it lives must be guided by a legislator who sees through them and beyond them. Just who Tocqueville means by his legislator is hard to say. The word clearly does not refer to anyone who sits in Congress or in a state legislature. In the broad sense, Tocqueville's legislator may not even hold a political office but may exercise a natural authority by dint of a peculiar genius. Thus the equal birthright of all human beings to liberty does not cancel out the relevance of a fundamental inequality among human beings. It does, though, probably require more subtlety among the practitioners of the new science of politics.

See also *Mill, John Stuart; Popular sovereignty; Religion, Civil; Revolution, French; Rousseau, Jean-Jacques.*

John C. Koritansky

BIBLIOGRAPHY

Rousseau, Jean-Jacques. *The Social Contract.* Translated by Maurice Cranston. London: Penguin Books, 1968.

Tocqueville, Alexis de. *Democracy in America.* Translated by George Lawrence; edited by J. P. Mayer. New York: Harper and Row, 1966.

———. *Journey to America.* Translated by George Lawrence. Edited by J. P. Mayer. New Haven: Yale University Press, 1960.

———. *The Old Regime and the French Revolution.* Translated by Stuart Gilbert. Magnolia, Mass.: Peter Smith, 1978.

———. *Recollections.* Translated by George Lawrence. Edited by A. P. Kerr. Garden City, N.Y.: Doubleday, 1970.

Togo

See *Africa, Subsaharan*

Trinidad

See *Caribbean, English*

Tunisia

A presidential republic located between Algeria and Libya on the northern coast of Africa. Inhabited by descendants of its original Berber-speaking inhabitants, Tunisia has a distinctively Mediterranean culture and reflects the influences of successive waves of invaders, including the Phoenicians, Romans, Arabs, Turks, and French. Tunisia is the most arabized country of North Africa, although to continue its economic development, the country remains dependent on Western investment, capital, trade, and tourism.

The Arabic influence stems from a succession of Islamic monarchies dating back to the seventh century. The traditional ruler, the bey, strengthened the authority of the central state by creating a bureaucratic elite and initiating political reforms along European lines. Before the colonial era, Tunisia adopted—in response to growing Western encroachments—a constitution promoting Western values: fair taxation, property rights, religious freedom, and centralized administration. After France declared Tunisia a formal protectorate in 1883, the country continued to absorb Western ideas and practices in spite of their limited popularity. While the country remained under French control, the traditional leaders served as nominal rulers and exercised influence as the religious and political elite.

Early in the twentieth century a group called the Young Tunisians demanded an updated Islamic legal system, a renewal of Arabic culture, Western education, and democratic reforms. Nationalistic demands resurfaced in the 1920s and again in the 1930s when a new generation of leaders founded the Neo-Destour (New Constitution) Party. The French granted Tunisia full independence in 1956. Habib Bourguiba, the leader of the modern nationalist movement, became the country's first president. During his first years in office he used his image as father of the nation to consolidate power, maintain legitimacy, and gain popular support.

Habib Bourguiba, Father of the Nation

Bourguiba's New Constitution Party supporters won all the seats in the first Constitutional Assembly elections held in 1956 and quickly consolidated their power. In 1957 the new government abolished the monarchy, proclaimed Tunisia a republic, and elected Bourguiba to the new office of president. A 1959 constitution codified the exist-

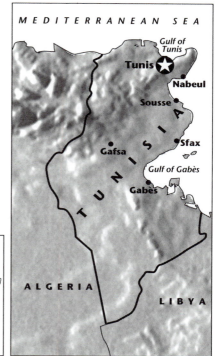

ing presidential system. The president was assigned broad discretionary powers, including the authority to legislate by decree and to appoint all civil and military officials, including the prime minister, the cabinet, and the governors of the country's twenty-three provinces. In fact, the president became head of state and government and supreme commander of the armed forces.

President Bourguiba dominated all aspects of political life in Tunisia during the postindependence era. He ran unopposed in presidential elections and was declared "president for life" by the National Assembly in 1975. His supporters in the New Constitution Party, renamed the Destourien Socialist Party in the 1960s and the Democratic Constitutional Assembly in 1988, continued to win all the seats in the National Assembly in spite of a declaration proclaiming Tunisia a multiparty system.

This fusion of state and party was reinforced over the years through the use of patronage and other privileges for the urban, Western-oriented elite. Bourguiba maintained a highly personalized system of patronage networks centered on himself. He prevented his ministers from forming coalitions and limited the participation of military leaders in politics. Leaders of organized centers of opposition were neutralized through co-optation and repression. The General Union of Tunisian Workers, which had been a powerful ally in the independence struggle, was quickly made a junior partner in the first government, and opposition political parties were banned until 1981. The party-government apparatus founded a host of affiliated organizations, allegedly to represent all segments of society.

Bourguiba's early popularity permitted his government to implement far-reaching political, social, and religious reforms, including universal suffrage and a uniform code of justice that abolished many common Islamic practices. Among Bourguiba's most enduring legacies are the substantial legal, political, and social rights enjoyed by women in modern Tunisia. Western aid assisted Bourguiba's implementation of reforms throughout the cold war era. After his government abandoned socialist reforms in 1969, Bourguiba cultivated an international image as a pro-Western, moderate leader pursuing a modernization strategy based on a pragmatic mixture of socialism and capitalism. Even as Bourguiba's popularity waned and he increasingly relied on authoritarian measures and repression to quiet opponents, Western governments continued to support him as an important cold war ally and a moderate leader who was opposed to Islamic fundamentalism. Western financial support became increasingly important by the mid-1980s, as the regime faced critical fiscal and debt crises.

These crises had their roots in the widespread discontent produced by governmental efforts to collectivize agriculture in the 1960s. Although abandoned in 1969, the program dislocated large numbers of peasants, alienated much of the Sahelian landed bourgeoisie, and was partially responsible for the governmental policy of holding the wages of organized labor constant for several years. Political alienation continued through the 1970s after the government switched to a Western-type economic liberalization program. A small Western-oriented elite was the main beneficiary of economic growth. During the 1970s the living standards of the workers, peasants, students, and youth deteriorated. But unauthorized strikes halted once the government arrested labor union leaders and, in 1978, declared a general state of emergency. Economic and social unrest resurfaced in the mid-1980s, when the government lifted price subsidies on food as part of an economic austerity program. Urban riots and street violence were stopped only after Bourguiba personally intervened to reverse food price increases, the government postponed implementation of several features of the structural ad-

justment program, and another state of emergency was imposed.

By the 1980s the government also faced increased challenges by Islamic fundamentalists. In 1980 a group calling itself the Tunisian Armed Resistance caught the government off guard by attacking the mining town of Gafsa. Although the army recaptured Gafsa, throughout the 1980s the government viewed Islamic opponents as a serious threat to political order.

In 1981, to cope with a growing crisis of legitimacy, the government engaged some of the weaker non-Islamic political parties in the legislative elections. In response to this political opening, a new organization, the Islamic Tendency Movement, was established. It claimed to offer a religious-political alternative to official Tunisian Islam at the ballot box. The movement's leader, Rachid Ghanouchi, denounced violence and urged religious opponents to participate in the electoral process. But Bourguiba undermined the credibility of this political opening by rigging the elections and eliminating the Islamic Tendency Movement as a political force. In fact, he imprisoned or forced into exile the group's entire leadership. As a result, popular support for political Islamicists increased markedly, and the movement splintered into factions, including several factions espousing violence.

When thirteen foreign tourists were injured by bomb explosions at resort hotels in 1987, Bourguiba used the pretext of foreign involvement to arrest at least 3,000 Islamic fundamentalists. In September 1987 the highly publicized trial of 90 Islamic fundamentalists accused of plotting against the government resulted in the acquittal of 14 defendants; 7, however, received the death penalty. Bourguiba was rumored to have been infuriated by the outcomes, but before he could order new trials, he was removed from power in a palace coup.

Ben Ali and a New Political Consensus

Bourguiba's prime minister, Zine el-Abidine Ben Ali, with the support of other cabinet ministers, forced Bourguiba to retire in November 1987, after Bourguiba exhibited increasingly erratic behavior. Once in power, Ben Ali, a former minister of the interior and army general, promised to initiate reforms designed to ensure greater political freedom and popular participation. And, indeed, in its first few years his regime implemented several actions that were widely supported and suggested that the government was sincere about its commitment to forge a new political consensus. Opposition newspapers were permitted to publish; the National Assembly approved legislation limiting the period a person could be held in police custody without charge; the State Security Court and prosecutor-general post were abolished; and thousands of political and nonpolitical detainees were freed. Tunisia also became the first Arab nation to ratify the United Nations convention against torture.

The government implemented a number of political reforms designed to widen participation in government. In 1988 the presidency-for-life was abolished, new guidelines for presidential succession were established, and legislation establishing a multiparty system was passed. Although this legislation legalized political parties, any groups organized along religious, racial, regional, or linguistic lines were prohibited from operating as political parties. In a national pact proposal in 1989, the government invited non-Islamic party leaders to stand for national election in a coalition with the Democratic Constitutional Assembly. Although this offer was rejected, all of the non-Islamic opposition parties, except the Communist Party, participated in the 1989 elections. Moreover, supporters of the Islamic Tendency Movement organized as a newly formed political party, the Renaissance Movement (known as Nahda), and ran as "independent" candidates in nineteen of the twenty-five voting districts. But none of the legally recognized opposition parties won any seats in this election, and the Democratic Constitutional Assembly retained all the National Assembly seats. Although Ben Ali was said to have received 99 percent of the vote in the presidential election, various Islamic "independents" received between 13 and 25 percent of the vote among Assembly constituencies. The aggregate vote indicated that the government's main opponents would continue to be political Islamicists.

After the election, in an effort to find an alternative to legalizing political Islamicists, the government instituted additional reforms designed to increase participation by the six legal non-Islamic political parties and other groups in government. In 1991 President Ben Ali permitted increased media coverage of the activities of the legal opposition parties, promised financial aid for the electoral campaigns and party activities of these parties, and invited opposition leaders to participate in discussions of the five-year development plan. In 1992 he announced that presidential and parliamentary elections would be held in March 1994. Throughout 1993 the government and opposition parties held talks designed to ensure some non-Democratic Constitutional Assembly representation in the National Assembly after the next general elections. The government also agreed in principle to allow some seats in the chamber to be elected through proportional representation, whereby representatives of a given party are elected according to the proportion of the popular vote that party receives.

In the early 1990s the government also took steps to eliminate the Islamic opposition. In 1991 the newly legalized arms of Nahda, the newspaper *Al Fajr* and the Tunisian General Union of Students, were crushed. Demonstrations by Islamic militants were violently suppressed, and Nahda was blamed for student protests and worker unrest. In May 1991 the government, claiming to have discovered a plot, detained thousands of Nahda activists.

Increased security crackdowns and the conviction of Nahda leaders and activists for subversive activities in a series of highly publicized trials during September 1992 effectively marginalized political opponents. Most of Nahda's leadership and a high proportion of its members were imprisoned or forced to live abroad. The government, however, had to counteract negative publicity at home and abroad, including allegations of torture of political detainees. While Ben Ali continued to stress the need for strong-arm tactics to prevent chaos in Algeria from spilling over into Tunisia, he also emphasized Tunisia's commitment to economic and political liberalization.

Most observers do not believe that the parliamentary reforms will lead to a representative opposition bloc in the National Assembly or will meet the expectations of an increasingly sophisticated and educated electorate for meaningful political reforms. It now appears that Ben Ali attempted to maintain his reputation abroad as a champion of human rights and political change, while using the party-state apparatus and the military to strengthen his power base, to stop political protests, and to crush Islamic opponents at home. After assuming the presidency, Ben Ali replaced Bourguiba's relatives and close associates in the cabinet with military officers, but he retained many of the practices introduced by Bourguiba to control the party. To manage internal security, Ben Ali formed a new National Security Council (consisting of himself, the prime minister, the minister of state for defense, the minister of foreign affairs, and the minister of the interior). Although a larger role for the military in government has prevented overt Islamic political activities, the political elite and growing numbers of the middle class remain concerned about future political stability as they witness a resurgence in support for Islamic fundamentalism. The battle between the government and Islamic militants is likely to continue. The outcome may depend on the success of economic and political reforms.

See also *Colonialism; Fundamentalism; Islam.*

Helen E. Purkitt

BIBLIOGRAPHY

Entelis, John P. *Comparative Politics of North Africa: Algeria, Morocco, and Tunisia.* Syracuse: Syracuse University Press, 1980.

Moore, Clement Henry. *Politics in North Africa.* Boston: Little, Brown, 1970.

Nelson, Harold D., ed. *Tunisia: A Country Study.* 3d ed. Washington, D.C.: Library of Congress, Government Printing Office, 1988.

Parker, Richard B. *North Africa: Regional Tensions and Strategic Concerns.* New York: Praeger, 1987.

"Tunisia." In *The Middle East and North Africa, 1993.* 39th ed. London: Europa Publications, 1993.

Vandewalle, Dirk. "From the New State to the New Era: Toward a Second Republic in Tunisia." *Middle East Journal* 42 (autumn 1988): 602–620.

Ware, L. B. "Ben Ali's Constitutional Coup in Tunisia." *Middle East Journal* 42 (autumn 1988): 587–601.

Zartman, I. William, and William Mark Habeeb, eds. *Polity and Society in Contemporary North Africa.* Boulder, Colo.: Westview Press, 1993.

Turkey

A predominantly Islamic nation in Asia and Europe that began its transition to democracy in the late 1940s. After the final defeat of the Ottoman Empire in World War I, Turkey emerged, under the leadership of Kemal Atatürk, as the only sovereign successor state.

Between the fourteenth and seventeenth centuries the realm of the Ottoman sultans had expanded into a large empire that extended from Hungary to Yemen and from Algeria to the Caucasus. Its military and administrative hierarchies and much of its agricultural population were Islamic. Yet Christians (in the Balkans, in Lebanon and Egypt, and in the capital of Istanbul) and Jews (in Istanbul, Salonika, and other major cities) lived by their own traditional laws and dominated much of the empire's

economy. From 1683 to 1913 the Ottoman Empire lost its Balkan and African territories in military defeats. As a result of the final defeat of 1918, most of the remaining empire (including its capital of Istanbul and its Arab-speaking territories of Syria, Lebanon, Palestine, and Iraq) was occupied by the victorious powers of Britain, France, and Italy, and its Anatolian heartland was invaded by Greek military forces.

National Identity and Political Institutions

From 1919 to 1923 a Turkish war of independence, organized under Atatürk's leadership, defeated the Greek invasion and other attempts at partition. After the Treaty of Lausanne in 1923 provided international recognition for the new state, the Republic of Turkey, with its capital in Ankara, was officially proclaimed. Whereas Ottoman leaders had felt ambivalent about their commitment to the Ottoman tradition, Islam, or Turkish nationhood, the defeat of 1918 and the victory of 1923 firmly established Turkey's national identity.

The country's commitment to Westernization, initiated by the Ottoman upper class in the nineteenth century, soon turned, under Atatürk's presidency (1923–1938), into a peaceful cultural revolution that included secular laws and education, religious freedom, adoption of the Roman alphabet, and equality of men and women. Yet, except for two brief experiments with legal opposition—in 1924–1925 and again in 1930—Turkey remained a single-party authoritarian system based on Atatürk's Republican People's Party.

Ismet İnönü, the military commander in the war of independence and prime minister under Atatürk (1923–1924, 1925–1937), succeeded Atatürk as president (1938–1950). In the early years of the cold war after 1945, İnönü launched what soon became a second peaceful revolution: the country's transition from single-party dictatorship to multiparty competition. Although the movement toward democracy suffered major setbacks in the military interventions of 1960–1961, 1971–1973, and 1980–1983, each time the military reproclaimed democracy. Since the mid-1980s public opinion has been firmly on the side of democracy, making future military interventions highly unlikely. The landmarks in this final transition were the 1983 parliamentary elections, in which an opposition party decisively defeated the artificial parties sponsored by the 1980 junta, and the 1987 national referendum, which by a close but clear majority amended the provisions of the 1982 consti-

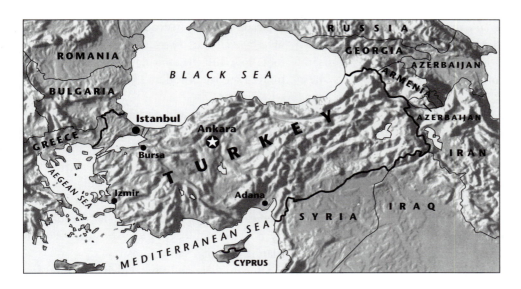

tution that had banned the party leaders of the 1970s from political participation.

Turkey's constitutional system has been strongly parliamentary, with a unicameral legislature in the First Republic (1923–1960) and Third Republic (1983–   ) and a bicameral legislature in the Second Republic (1961–1980). Throughout, presidents of the republic have been elected by the legislature (Grand National Assembly), although those of 1961–1980 and 1982–1989 were military figures selected in the wake of coups.

Some significant shifts in Turkey's pattern of political parties have stemmed from changes in its election laws. The voting system inherited from Atatürk's single-party days was a multiple-member plurality system (similar to that used by the U.S. electoral college), which guaranteed the concentration of voters within two parties and heavy majorities for the winning party. Because the government of Adnan Menderes (1950–1960) had relied on those heavy majorities (86 percent in 1950, 93 percent in 1954, and 70 percent in 1957) in setting its increasingly authoritarian course, the 1961 constitution shifted to the opposite extreme: a system of proportional representation that allocates seats among party lists in multiple-member districts, much as in Germany's Weimar Republic or in Israel.

Under this system the Justice Party won parliamentary majorities in 1965 and 1969, yet by the 1970s the result was a fragmentation of parties and recurrent deadlocks before coalition governments could be formed or a new president elected. This governmental paralysis encouraged the

mounting wave of terrorism of the late 1970s and the military intervention of 1980. Under the 1982 constitution Turkey has proceeded to a more balanced electoral system that guarantees some proportionality without encouraging party splintering or deadlocks in forming governments.

Meanwhile, the social base of Turkish politics has expanded substantially. The party leaders of the 1960s and 1970s had been drawn from the urban upper class, much like those of the single-party regime under Atatürk and Inönü. By contrast, the ban imposed from 1982 to 1987 on party leaders and members of parliament of the 1970s encouraged the emergence of new leaders, including many successful businesspeople attracted to the Motherland Party. Tansu Çiller's accession to the premiership in 1993 appeared to mark the coming of a new generation, which, amid the intense party realignments of the early 1990s, might overcome the splits and rivalries resulting from the military coup in 1980 and the ban on former politicians in 1982.

Democratic Transition and
Military Intervention

Turkey's transition toward democracy began in mid-1945 as President Inönü announced that, in view of the democracies' victory in World War II, Turkey must take seriously Atatürk's populist principles. Thus Inönü lifted restrictions on freedom of the press and on the formation of opposition parties. Turkey had remained neutral in World War II, except for making a last-minute declaration of war on the Axis powers in February 1945 in order to join the San Francisco conference that was to establish the United Nations. Nonetheless, years of maximum military mobilization and isolation from foreign trade had produced economic hardship and much political dissatisfaction.

Above all, Turkey was facing Soviet demands for the cession of three northeastern provinces and joint control of the Turkish straits (Bosphorus and Dardanelles): this was Moscow's opening move in what soon became the cold war. Thus Inönü was eager both to relieve domestic pressures and to secure the support of the United States, as later provided through the Truman Doctrine of aid to Greece and Turkey in 1947 and Turkey's entry into the North Atlantic Treaty Organization in 1952.

Inönü envisaged his own role in the new democratic system as that of a politically neutral president. Yet his withdrawal from day-to-day political leadership prompted the authoritarian elements in his governing Republican People's Party to prolong their grip on power by calling early elections in July 1946. The elections were fraught with dishonest counts. But, as public indignation mounted and was reported in the newly freed press, Inönü installed a more liberal party leadership and informed the citizenry that both the government and the opposition were legitimate contenders for power. When an honest election in 1950 gave a large majority to the opposition Democratic Party under Adnan Menderes, Inönü refused military advice that the problem could be solved by a coup, yielded his presidential office to the Democratic chair, Celal Bayar, and assumed the new role of opposition leader in parliament.

Nonetheless, the political role of the military was to remain ambiguous for several decades. By the late 1950s growing economic dissatisfaction led Menderes's government to drift toward authoritarianism by harassing newspapers; closing down the Nation Party, an opposition group with an Islamic base; and having the police disrupt other opposition meetings.

Amid mounting unrest the military refused to let themselves be used for Menderes's plans of restoring order by martial law. Instead, they formed a National Unity Committee of leading officers, who in their May 1960 coup proclaimed the need to restore democracy. Democratic Party leaders were tried for violating the constitution, and Menderes himself was sentenced to death by hanging. Yet the junta under Gen. Cemal Gürsel rejected plans of its own right-wing members to impose a perma-

nent authoritarian regime. Instead, a new constitution was formulated by a civilian assembly, and, after free elections in October 1961, full civilian rule was restored, except for the continuing service of military presidents from 1961 to 1989.

By 1971, as cabinet crises and parliamentary deadlocks paralyzed Turkey's Second Republic, the military intervened in what became known as the "coup by memorandum," forcing the parliament to accept a cabinet of bureaucrats endorsed by the military. Following the 1973 elections the initiative shifted back to the civilians. A cabinet was formed early in 1974 by the center-left Republican People's Party, now led by Inönü's successor Bülent Ecevit, and by the Islamic National Salvation Party.

In July 1974 this unlikely coalition, which agreed on few domestic issues, eagerly ordered the Turkish invasion of northern Cyprus in response to a Greek nationalist coup in Nicosia instigated by the right-wing military government in Athens. Soon Turkey faced more parliamentary crises and a surge of partisan gun battles in city streets, with the Marxist Turkish Labor Party acquiring its weapons from Syria and the Soviet bloc and the rightist Nationalist Action Party acquiring its weapons from the illegal drug trade and secret connections in the Turkish military.

In 1980, in response to the mounting terrorism on the streets and an endless deadlock in parliamentary elections for the next president, the military once again intervened, initially with much public approval. Later the junta convened a civilian constitutional assembly and imposed a ban on all the parties and leaders of the 1970s. It then organized a Nationalist Democracy Party under a retired officer and a Populist Party under a bureaucrat, which it expected to see elected as the government and the opposition. The junta's scheme of pseudo-democracy was foiled, however, by a clever maneuver of Turgut Özal, who had been the government's expert on foreign debt and who in 1980–1982 was the junta's chief economist. Registering his Motherland Party just before the deadline, Özal launched a folksy, populist campaign at public meetings and on television and secured a decisive Motherland Party victory in November 1983.

Liberalization and the Consolidation of Democracy

The following years brought a period of informal collaboration, with Gen. Kenan Evren in the presidency making major foreign policy decisions and Özal and his

Motherland Party majority developing their neoliberal economic policies. Within a few years the military-sponsored parties disappeared, and the political parties of the 1970s reappeared under new names. Turkey now enjoyed full freedom of expression, and the continuing ban on the politicians of the 1970s became highly controversial. In 1987 a referendum restored those former leaders to full participation.

The neoliberal economic policies of the Özal government had mixed effects: they stimulated private business, but they also contributed to mounting inflation and unemployment. When Evren's presidential term expired in 1989, Özal used his heavy parliamentary majority to have himself elected president, even though opinion polls showed his Motherland Party at an all-time low. Although he had previously criticized Evren for playing too political a role in the presidency, Özal himself made extensive and controversial use of his own presidential powers in the Persian Gulf war of 1991. For instance, he authorized the use of Turkey's Incirlik air base against Iraq without legislative approval or consultation, thereby prompting high-level military resignations.

In the October 1991 elections the Motherland Party lost its parliamentary majority, and the next government was formed by a coalition of Süleyman Demirel's leading True Path Party and Erdal İnönü's Social Democratic People's Party. Several months after Özal's death in April 1993, Demirel was elected president. He was succeeded as True Path Party leader and prime minister by Tansu Çiller, the first woman to head Turkey's government.

Political Parties and Policy Issues

The pattern of political parties in Turkey since the late 1940s has been remarkably consistent, despite reorganizations and name changes imposed by the coups of 1960 and 1980. (See Table 1.) Electoral competition has focused mostly on two major parties.

On the center-left, Ismet İnönü's Republican People's Party at first appealed mainly to the urban middle class, but by the 1970s, under Bülent Ecevit's leadership, it had moved in a democratic-socialist direction with strong support from labor unions. By the 1980s its successor was called the Social Democratic (or later Social Democratic People's) Party.

On the center-right, the Democratic Party under Bayar and Menderes built up a network of support in the country's agricultural districts and small towns and, with U.S. aid in the 1950s, initiated such major changes as rural road

networks and improved irrigation. The same line was continued by the Justice Party (so named in obvious protest against the hanging of Menderes by the 1960 junta) and the True Path Party, both led by Süleyman Demirel. In the vacuum produced by the military's ban on former parties, Turgut Özal's Motherland Party emerged in 1983 as another center-right party, with its main support from business circles.

On the far left the Turkish Labor Party emerged in the mid-1960s. Severe restrictions on organizations with (or suspected of) communist connections reduced its effectiveness, however.

Toward the right of the spectrum, there always has been a party advocating a return from secularism toward Islam, such as the (Republican) Nation Party of the 1950s and, since the 1970s, the National Salvation and Welfare Parties led by Necmeddin Erbakan. Their appeal has been limited, however, in part because government parties made some minor concessions from Atatürk's rigid secularism. For example, the Islamic prayer call in Arabic was restored in 1950—it had been pure Turkish since Atatürk's days—and theological faculties at universities and optional religious classes were reinstated in public schools.

Interestingly, secularism has given more freedom to Turkey's Alevi Muslims, a dissident group related to but not identical to the Shi'ites and variously estimated at 10–20 percent of Turkey's total population. Most of the Alevis are concentrated in central Anatolia, and they strongly endorse such secularist parties as the Republican People's or Democratic Left, which they consider to be the best guarantee against oppression by the Sunni Muslim majority.

All in all, Turkey has become a society in which citizens may be as religious or as nonobservant as they choose. And, although observance is predominant in villages and small towns (where shopkeepers do not dare to open their stores during the Muslim holy month of Ramadan), the steady stream of migration allows anyone to move to medium-sized and large cities, where secularism and religious choice set the tone. It also is symbolic of Turkey's full commitment to Western values that its 1987 application for membership in the European Community (now the European Union) was sponsored by Prime Minister Özal, a former pilgrim to Mecca who kept his religious beliefs strictly private.

On the far right, there has usually been an ultranationalist party, notably the Nationalist Action and Nationalist

TABLE 1. Major Turkish Political Parties and Their Popular Votes, 1950–1991 (in percent)

Party leaning	First constitution			Second constitution					Third constitution		
	1950	1954	1957	1961	1965	1969	1973	1977	1983	1987	1991
Left					3.0	2.7		0.1			
Center-left	39.5	35.4	41.1	36.7	28.7	27.4	33.3	41.4	30.5	33.3	30.8
Center			3.8	13.7	3.7	8.8	17.2	3.8	23.3	7.1	
Center-right	52.7	57.6	47.9	34.8	52.9	46.5	29.8	36.9	45.2	55.4	51.1
Right	3.1	4.9	7.0	14.0	8.5	9.0	16.9	15.4	10.1	16.8	
Other	4.8	2.2	0.1	0.8	3.2	5.6	2.8	2.5	1.1	1.2	1.3

SOURCES: Calculated by the author from data in Klaus Detlev Grothusen, *Tümurkei: Südosteuropa-Handbuch IV* (Göttingen: Vandenhoeck and Ruprecht, 1985), 738–741; and *Türkiye İstatistik Yilligi* (Ankara: Devlet Istatistik Enstitüsü), 1984–1992.

NOTE: Major parties (and their leaders):

Left: Turkish Labor, 1961–1971, 1975–1980

Center-left: Democratic Left, 1985– (Ecevit); Republican People's, 1923–1980 (Atatürk, I. Inönü, Ecevit); Social Democratic, 1983–1985 (E. Inönü); Social Democratic People's, 1985– (E. Inönü); Populist, 1983–1985 (sponsored by military)

Center: Nationalist Democracy, 1983–1986 (sponsored by military); various splinter parties, 1957–1980

Center-right: Democratic, 1946–1960 (Menderes); Justice, 1961–1980 (Demirel); True Path, 1984– (Demirel, Çiller); Motherland, 1983– (Özal, Akbulut, Yilmaz)

Right (Islamic, Nationalist): Nation, 1948–1953; (Republican) Nation, 1954–1958; Unity, 1966–1980; National Salvation, 1972–1980 (Erbakan); Welfare, 1984– (Erbakan); Republican Peasants' Nation, 1958–1969 (Türkeş); Nationalist Action, 1969–1980 (Türkeş); Nationalist Labor, 1985– (Türkeş)

Labor Parties, both founded by Col. Alpaslan Türkeş, who had been the leader of the authoritarian minority of the 1960 junta. The main tenet of these groups was Panturkism—that is, political unity between Turkey and the Turkic-speaking Central Asian republics. Its followers were closely involved in the terrorist battles of the 1970s between the left and the right. The Islamic and Panturkish right were briefly united in the early 1960s, and typically their joint or separate support since the 1970s has ranged from 9 to 17 percent of the popular vote. It also should be noted that, whereas Panturkism remained a utopian dream throughout the Soviet period, Ankara governments have cultivated close economic and cultural relations with the postcommunist countries from Romania to Kyrgyzstan (for example, by establishing the Black Sea Economic Cooperation Zone in 1992 and encouraging frequent visits between Turkish and Central Asian governments).

The Unresolved Kurdish Problem

One significant development of the early 1990s was the increasing acceptance of Turkey's substantial Kurdish minority as equal citizens. In 1925 a major rebellion broke out against the newly proclaimed Republic of Turkey, led by Islamic religious groups and centered on the Kurdish-speaking areas in the southeast. From that time on, it was illegal to speak Kurdish in public, and much of the Kurdish-populated southeast remained under martial law for many decades. As a result of this suppression (and also because many ethnic Kurds now speak Turkish as their mother tongue), no reliable figures on Turkey's Kurdish population are available, although their number has been variously estimated at 4 to 11 million (or 7 to 20 percent of the total population).

In February 1991 the ban on speaking Kurdish in public was lifted, and Kurdish-language publications began to appear. In the October 1991 elections a party allied with the Social Democratic People's Party openly appealed to Kurdish support in the southeast, and in the 1991–1993 Demirel cabinet both the foreign minister and the head of the newly established Human Rights Ministry were known to be of Kurdish background. Indeed, the Ankara government took care to establish friendly relations with the leadership of the Kurdish autonomous region in northern Iraq. Nonetheless, in the early 1990s the Kurdish terrorist activities intensified throughout Turkey's southeast, as the Kurdish Workers' Party moved its headquarters from Syrian-controlled Lebanon to semi-independent northern Iraq. The Turkish military escalated its repressive actions against those terrorist inroads.

Consolidation of Democracy

Clearly in the past half-century Turkish democracy has gone through serious crises and temporary setbacks. Yet the remarkable outcome is that democratic institutions and attitudes have been progressively consolidated and Turkey has become the only fully established democracy in the Muslim Middle East—and, indeed, one of the few throughout Asia or Africa. Three factors have contributed crucially to this result.

First, Turkey's secular national identity has been firmly established since the 1920s, in contrast to those of the Arab peoples, many of whom still are insecure in their national identities based on their present borders (Algeria, Egypt, Iraq, and Kuwait, among others), or on a common Arab language (from Morocco to Oman), or on Islam. Second, Turkey, unlike many developing countries, has an effective and impartial government because the new republic inherited most of the Ottoman Empire's bureaucratic and educational institutions. And, third, the organizational links between Ankara and the provinces developed in Atatürk's days of benevolent authoritarianism have been vastly expanded since the 1950s through party competition, internal migration, and the development of economic enterprises.

As in other Middle Eastern or developing countries, the major alternative to democracy has remained military-authoritarian rule, but here too Turkey differs significantly from its neighbors. Its military, from late Ottoman days and victory in Turkey's war of independence (1919–1923) to the cold war alliance with the United States, has been oriented toward the West and has maintained the highest professional standards. Thus military interventions have remained of short duration. Above all, the increasingly strong commitment of the population to democracy ultimately has given military leaders a choice only between accepting democracy or imposing a degree of military tyranny that they could not square with their own principles.

In summary, Turkey, aside from its unresolved Kurdish problem, has a well-structured political and social framework for democracy. Half a century after Ismet İnönü's first democratic moves in 1945, the country's commitment to an open political process seems beyond question, the crucial turning points being the outcomes of the 1983 election in favor of the nonmilitarily sponsored Motherland Party and of the 1987 referendum on the reentry of former politicians into the political arena.

See also *Atatürk, Kemal; Islam.*

Dankwart A. Rustow

BIBLIOGRAPHY

Ahmad, Feroz. *The Turkish Experiment in Democracy, 1950–1975.* Boulder, Colo.: Westview Press; London: C. Hurst, 1977.

Bianchi, Robert B. *Interest Groups and Political Development in Turkey.* Princeton: Princeton University Press, 1984.

Hale, William M. *The Political and Economic Development of Modern Turkey.* New York: St. Martin's, 1981.

Harris, George S. *Turkey: Coping with Crisis.* Boulder, Colo.: Westview Press, 1985.

Heper, Metin, and Jacob M. Landau, eds. *Political Parties and Democracy in Turkey.* London: I. B. Tauris, 1991.

Lewis, Bernard. *The Emergence of Modern Turkey.* 2d ed. London and New York: Oxford University Press, 1968.

Rustow, Dankwart A. "A Democratic Turkey Faces New Challenges." *Global Affairs* 8 (spring 1993): 58–70.

———. *Turkey: America's Forgotten Ally.* New York: Council on Foreign Relations, 1987.

Tachau, Frank. *Turkey: The Politics of Authority, Democracy, and Development.* New York: Praeger, 1984.

Weiker, Walter F. *The Modernization of Turkey: From Atatürk to the Present Day.* New York: Holmes and Meier, 1981.

Types of democracy

Various types of democracy other than the forms of liberal representative government that constitute the prevailing democratic systems in the contemporary world have been found in practice or have been advocated by various political thinkers. Some of these types of democracy have not been based on principles of representation. Others are based on methods of representation that differ markedly from those found in most liberal democracies. Nevertheless, many of these alternatives to conventional representative government have strong claims to be considered democratic.

Definitions of Democracy

The core definition of democracy is "the rule of the people." The word derives from the ancient Greek *demokratia,* which was composed from the word for the people *(demos)* and the word for power *(kratos)*. This apparently straightforward definition, however, conceals considerable problems of political theory and practice since the meaning of neither *the people* nor *rule* is self-evident.

The reference to the people implies that in a democracy all those within a country are equally entitled to participate in ruling. The composition of the people, however, has been a matter of dispute throughout the history of democracy. In ancient Athens, for example, slaves were a majority of the population but did not have the rights of citizens and were not part of the people. Nevertheless, the word *demos* also connoted the masses, and democracy was sometimes regarded as the rule of the poor. Other states have termed themselves democracies while denying political rights to persons of a particular color or race. Only in this century have women gained the vote. In most countries those below the age of eighteen cannot vote and, in some sense, are not part of the people who rule.

The people may also be considered either as a unified body with a single will or as composed of numerous individuals, a majority of whom rules on the basis of counting votes. Democracy has therefore sometimes been defined as government in which the will of the majority of qualified citizens prevails. This definition, however, raises the question how far the preferences of the minority may be ignored in a democracy. It is also necessary to consider what constitutes a majority (whether policy can be made according to the vote of the largest group—a plurality—or whether it is necessary to have the support of more than half the voters—the majority) and whether the consent of a majority can be obtained for every proposal.

The concept of *rule* is no less problematic. The original type of democracy entailed direct decisions by the people, meeting in an assembly. In modern democracies, decisions are made by representatives elected at intervals; hence, the rule of the people is indirect and is exercised through the accountability of the representatives to the electorate.

For these reasons, no single definition of democracy is entirely satisfactory. A broad definition might be as follows: democracy is a system of government in which all adult persons within the unit of rule are entitled to participate equally in making general laws and policy. Each of the elements within this and most other definitions will require further specification. In the course of such elaboration most theories go beyond description and definition to some statement of democratic ideals.

Direct Democracy

Direct democracy refers to political systems in which the citizens make the laws themselves rather than choose representatives to make the laws on their behalf. The ancient Greek democracies about which evidence survives were all direct democracies. In this sense, direct rather than liberal representative democracy is the original type of democratic government. The most celebrated example is ancient Athens, where direct democracy was the form of government with brief interruptions from 507 B.C. to 322 B.C.

In ancient Athens the entire citizen population was entitled to sit in the Assembly, which was the supreme governing body of the state. At the height of Athenian democracy, in the fifth century B.C., the Assembly was responsible for passing laws. It made decisions on matters of foreign policy, such as the signing of treaties with other states or the declaration of war. The Assembly elected some of the chief executive officers and magistrates. It could also make decisions about taxation.

The Assembly of the people could be described as sovereign. Although some of its powers were curtailed in the fourth century B.C., it remained the determining body within the state. The Assembly met about forty days a year. Within it every citizen had an equal right to speak and to initiate a proposal for debate. Decisions were made on the basis of majority rule.

In Athens the principles of direct democracy applied not merely to the legislative process but also to the executive aspect of government. Most administrative offices were performed by the ordinary citizens themselves. Thus the Council of Five Hundred, which handled the agenda of the Assembly, was filled by lot. In addition, many offices were rotated. A few offices, particularly those concerned with the military, were recognized as requiring more than average technical competence. These were elected annually by the Assembly, and the officeholders were permitted to stand for reelection repeatedly. Some, notably Pericles, gained positions of great influence.

Direct democracy in Athens also extended to the judicial process. There were no appointed judges or professional lawyers. The courts dealt with a wide range of matters, including criminal cases, civil disputes, the award of state contracts, and allegations of administrative incompetence or political corruption. The court was presided over by private citizens. For major political cases the verdicts were reached by mass juries of up to 2,501 citizens. The juries were chosen by lot from those who put themselves forward.

The combination of these direct democratic devices made for an intense level of citizen participation in politics. It has been calculated that a third of the citizens had served on one occasion as members of the council and a quarter had been its president (in a sense, the leader of Athens) for one day in their lives.

Nevertheless, by modern standards of democracy Athens fell far short. The citizens who held democratic rights were only a minority of the adult population. Only a man born of Athenian parents counted as a citizen. Women had no rights of citizenship. The large number of foreigners living in Athens (like resident aliens and "guest" workers in modern states) did not enjoy the full rights of citizens. Finally, Athens was a slave society. Slaves labored in mines, on farms, and as domestics. The numbers are not known, but estimates range up to five times the number of citizens—perhaps 150,000 in the fourth century, when the citizen population was probably 30,000. Accordingly, it has always been a controversial question whether the direct democracy of Athens was made possible by the existence of slavery, which enabled the male citizens to spend time in the Assembly, the council, the juries, and the administration and on active duty in the army and navy.

Scholars usually have argued that such direct democratic systems can exist only in small states. Among the city-states of ancient Greece, Athens was unusually large. Yet its territory was only 1,000 square miles. The total population in the fourth century, including male citizens, women and children, foreigners and slaves, might have been 400,000. Some other city-states had populations of about 10,000.

Athens was at the limits of the size of a "face to face" society, the type of society that many believe to be a precondition for direct democracy. In such a society, citizens could possess a personal knowledge of the characters and abilities of the leading political activists. They would be aware of the domestic and external social, economic, and political circumstances of the country. Their lives would be immediately affected by policy decisions. Advocates of direct, participatory democracy have argued that such conditions stimulate civic virtue. The system depends on participation and encourages political awareness and involvement. Civic activity is itself educational and creates a politically mature citizenry. By contrast, advocates of direct democracy allege that indirect, representative democracy discourages citizen involvement and favors professional political elites.

Criticisms of direct democracy have, however, persisted since ancient times. Some conservative writers of the time pointed out that not everyone lived up to the ideals of participation. Although all 30,000 citizens could in principle attend and vote in the Assembly, the quorum was 6,000, which is all the meeting place could hold. Even the daily payment for attendance might be interpreted as reliance on an economic incentive rather than civic virtue to obtain participation.

The most influential critic was the philosopher Plato. He argued that decisions, rather than being made by persons who were expert in political matters, were in the hands of an Assembly composed of people from all walks of life who had no special understanding of government. Consequently, direct democracy was in reality mob rule. The decisions were rash and inconsistent. The voters were swayed by rabble-rousing demagogues who appealed to emotion and prejudice rather than to reason. In his comedies the Greek dramatist Aristophanes indulged in satire at the expense of members of the Assembly who were barely literate, were politically ignorant, and could be persuaded to follow any political leader.

The importance of the Athenian instance of direct democracy is that it defined the meaning of the term *democracy* for more than 2,000 years. Until the advent of ideas of representative democracy about the time of the American Revolution, the term referred to direct democracy on the Athenian model. For most thinkers, democracy was not a viable form of government, carrying the connotations of mob rule and confined to small states. Most strikingly, there was no further example of a democracy in Western history after the fall of the Athenian system in 322 B.C.

Modern Direct Democracy

Direct democracy has never died out as an ideal in the modern era. Moreover, local examples of direct democracy have been put into practice. Political thinkers have regularly revived its central ideas within the theory of participatory democracy. A major attempt can be found in the work of Jean-Jacques Rousseau in the eighteenth century. Rousseau advocated a system of popular sovereignty in which, as in Athens, all male citizens would vote on the laws in an assembly. He did not, however, favor direct citizen participation in the executive process. He recognized that such a system of popular rule could occur only within a very small city-state.

An attempt to reconcile direct democracy with the complexities of large states can be found in the writings of

Karl Marx in the nineteenth century. While Marx's views on democracy have to be pieced together from several sources and are a matter of some controversy, it is clear that he believed that elements of direct popular rule were essential to the achievement of the goal of freedom as he understood it. Liberal, representative, constitutional democracy was merely a competition between bourgeois parties to sustain class repression. Instead, the people should determine their own affairs. At the smallest community level they would deliberate and vote directly on issues. Beyond this there would be a pyramid structure in which the community would elect delegates to a district assembly to deal with wider issues. The district would itself elect delegates to a national assembly. To keep these delegates under popular control, they were to be given strict instructions on how to vote and were subject to "recall"—that is, they would be required to go back to the electors for new instructions and possibly face the forfeit of their authority.

Marx also aimed to introduce direct democracy into the executive process. Administrators and judges would be subject to frequent election. The army would be replaced by a citizen militia. Ultimately, Marx believed, in a communist society in which the abolition of property had removed the prime source of conflict, even these aspects of direct democratic government would become superfluous. In place of the state there would be a system of self-regulation. The actual practices of regimes that have claimed to be inspired by Marxism have diverged markedly from Marx's democratic proposals.

Participatory Democracy

Participatory democracy is a term applied to theories of democracy that seek to involve the ordinary citizen more fully in the decision-making processes than is normal within representative democracy. Participatory democrats usually seek both to reform representative systems and to combine them with certain elements of direct democracy. Reforms to representative government might include holding more frequent elections or opening up a wider range of offices to election. In this sense, the United States is already more participatory than most European democracies, where fewer offices are open to election. In addition, participatory democracy would entail more active involvement by citizens in community affairs, social movements, and interest groups. Advocates of participation often support greater democracy in the workplace,

sometimes termed *industrial democracy*. Supporters of participatory democracy usually look to civic education to encourage a more politically interested and active citizenry.

Direct democratic devices that might be incorporated within participatory democracy include direct popular rule at the local neighborhood level, combined, somewhat in the manner of Marx, with delegation to higher bodies dealing with district issues. Participatory theorists also usually favor the more extensive employment of recall (used in some states of the United States), as well as referendum and initiative (familiar in many liberal democracies, such as Switzerland and the United States, but rarely used in others, such as the United Kingdom).

The most notable surviving examples of direct democracy in practice are the town meeting in the United States (especially in New England) and the commune assemblies (*Landsgemeinde*) in Switzerland. Both are examples of local democracy and therefore differ significantly from the politically autonomous city-states of ancient Greece.

In the purest form of New England town meeting the citizens assemble from one to several times a year to determine policy for the community. They can determine school budgets, zoning regulations, levels of road repair, approaches to local policing, and appropriate taxation. They also elect the town's executive officers. In some towns the procedure is to delegate powers of action to executives for a determinate period. The town meeting has been widely praised by commentators at earlier periods of American history, such as Thomas Jefferson and Alexis de Tocqueville, as an instrument of civic education. Although the powers of the town meeting remain quite extensive, however, even by the standards set for local self-government by some participatory democrats, it has much less autonomy today than in earlier periods. The town must exercise its control within the context of policies laid down by the state and the federal governments, not to mention the international economic and political environment. It would be harsh to say that the town meeting has great power but only over small issues, since many of these matters affect peoples' lives closely. Nevertheless, the degree of direct democratic self-government that a town can exercise in the modern world is restricted.

The Swiss *Landsgemeinde* is an assembly of citizens meeting as a direct democracy in a small local community. The first such assemblies met in the fourteenth century. At their height there were hundreds of these assemblies, which determined all matters affecting their villages. They survive in only five cantons and half-cantons, but the practice of direct democracy in Switzerland is sustained by the exceptionally extensive resort to the referendum and citizen initiative at local (cantonal) and national (federal) levels. Switzerland also retains the direct democratic concept of the citizen army.

Direct democracy has in the past been confined to small states or local governments, but in recent years it has been argued that modern communications technology has made it possible to arrange for direct mass participation in the affairs of the largest states. The term *teledemocracy* has been used to describe this new political phenomenon, of which there are many potential variants. In its most radical form the new direct democracy would involve equipping every citizen's home with a voting device so that every citizen could vote on legislative propositions for the whole nation, for the locality, or for a group such as a labor union. The votes would be registered by computer; so a popular vote could be taken instantaneously, as in ancient Athens. The ease and simplicity of home voting might increase levels of participation.

Objections to teledemocracy echo objections to earlier direct democracy. First, as in any form of referendum, it would be important to determine how questions to be voted on are phrased and who is to ask them. These procedures are notoriously susceptible to manipulation.

Second, critics since Plato have charged that voters would not possess the level of education and knowledge necessary to enable them to make informed choices on legislative propositions. This is a general objection to the referendum and similar devices. Accordingly, it is said that the electorate is equipped to choose who is to decide rather than to decide itself. Some advocates of teledemocracy respond by claiming that interactive communication technology enables citizens to call up large quantities of information and data on the television screen to facilitate their choice. Arguments for and against various propositions could be listed more fully than with current referendums. The charge of citizen incompetence, however, remains at the core of critiques of direct democracy and of all types of democracy.

Third, it is argued that teledemocracy does not permit the debate between the voters that is feasible in a direct democratic assembly. The technology is limited in this respect. Yet modern means of communications such as electronic mail can permit voters to exchange views or to put questions to those who have brought the propositions forward. Call-in shows and teleconferences can also, to a degree, help to re-create in the modern world certain features of the direct democratic assembly.

It is, however, more likely in the short run that interactive communications technology will be employed to supplement the established procedures of indirect, representative democracy than to replace them. The technology would facilitate greater use of the referendum and the initiative and is already being used extensively in polling public opinion. Although the size of modern states and the complexity of society have previously rendered direct democracy a largely outmoded system, it is possible that direct democracy is due for a partial revival as a result of technological advances.

Whether direct democracy—or, more generally, participatory democracy—is considered desirable depends on views about the political knowledge, judgment, and interest of the mass of citizens. It is wrong to suppose that direct democratic votes are clear and unambiguous expressions of the will of the people. The work of Kenneth Arrow and other social choice theorists has demonstrated that even in systems that seek fully to consult individual preferences, it is impossible to ensure that the outcome of votes is consistent and procedurally fair. Direct democracy lies at the origin of all democracy but is not a panacea.

Direct democracy is not the only alternative to liberal representative democracy. Many other forms of democracy based on representation have been proposed, and some have been used in government systems. Most suggest that interests rather than persons should be the basis of representation.

Statistical Representation

The idea of statistical representation derives from the notion that representatives should be a microcosm of the electorate and proposes that such representatives be selected by statistical sampling methods. A probability sample of the country could generate a government of representatives that would be a more accurate microcosm of the society than any electoral system yet devised. The process is analogous to the ancient Greek direct democratic procedure of selection by lot, and also to the selection of juries in American and British courts, so as to be a cross section of the public. A variant of this proposal is that issues that affect a particular segment of the population, for example, hearing-impaired people, would be decided by a commission composed of a probability sample from that segment who wished to stand for the office. Rather than having all citizens participate in choosing decision makers across the whole range of matters facing a nation, this system would have representatives of the affected interests determine special issues.

The democratic nature of the idea of statistical representation relies on its claim to be entirely representative. Although the method supposedly would give each person an equal chance to be selected, its basis is the representation of the interests or functions that comprise a society rather than of persons, in contrast to traditional forms of democratic representation. As a realistic proposal, statistical representation faces difficulties in coordinating policies favored by the various interests and in identifying those who are affected by a given policy issue, even if only indirectly as taxpayers.

Functional Representation

Proponents of functional theories of representation argue that the major functions or interests in modern society should be represented in the processes of decision making. According to these arguments, society is composed of a number of associations and organizations that have specific purposes. Each of these purposes can be represented by elective bodies. Such associations or organizations might range from industries to educational institutions.

Among the most elaborate versions of functional representation is that of the Guild Socialists, a group of British antistate socialists writing in the first two decades of the twentieth century. The most notable theorist was George Douglas Howard Cole (1889–1959). Cole argued that the representation of one person by another person was impossible because each individual has a variety of different purposes. Functions such as industry could be represented, however. Consequently, representative bodies for each industry and for industry as a whole should be established alongside the traditional political representative legislature; the legislature's tasks would be confined to matters of common concern to all persons and functions. Within each function there would be a hierarchy of representative bodies from the local to the national. Persons would have votes in every functional body in which they were involved. The objective was a participatory and pluralist democracy in which the sovereignty of the state would be restricted.

As a theory, functional representation faces difficulties in specifying which functions constitute the distinct interests to be incorporated into the representative process. There are also problems in balancing the autonomy of the functions with the need for coordination of functions and with more transcendent considerations of equality and justice. As a movement, Guild Socialism declined after the 1920s. Nevertheless, in practice functional representation is widespread in modern democracies where associations representing major industrial, commercial, labor, agricultural, and professional interests have established consultative positions in the policy-making process.

Corporatist Democracy

Corporatist democracy can be defined as a system in which associations, or "corporations," representing a restricted number of major interests in society are formally recognized by the state and are involved in the consultative stages of policy making and in their implementation. Corporatism is a form of functional representation. Conventionally, it is divided into state corporatism and liberal corporatism. These have different implications for democracy.

State corporatism theories developed in the second half of the nineteenth century in a number of European countries in opposition to both liberal and socialist thought. In contrast to liberal emphases on the individual and the market, and to socialist ideas of structural class conflict, corporatism advanced the idea that society constituted an organic whole to which the major interests of society, especially industry and labor, contributed. Hence the term *organic democracy* has also been applied to such theories. These ideas were influenced by Roman Catholic teaching, which perceived the various sectors of society as serving the greater divine order. This type of corporatism also appealed to nationalists, who regarded the state as the unit within which all elements in society found their common interests.

The democratic credentials of state corporatism were often seen as tenuous in both theory and practice. State corporatism explicitly rejected the ideas of individualism and equality associated with liberal democracy. Proponents of state corporatism also opposed conventional ideas of majority rule, based on one person, one vote, as divisive and atomized. The democratic aspect, to the extent that it was acknowledged, consisted of the state's recognition of the major corporations as representative of essential functions and as possessing formal consultative status. In turn, the theory proposed that the corporations had powers of self-regulation and responsibilities for implementing policies. These responsibilities included influence over prices, production levels, industrial relations, wages, and welfare. The overall objective was a solidarist, consensual community that would avoid the class conflict and the economic crises generally found in capitalist economies.

In practice, state corporatism was associated with authoritarianism rather than democracy. It came nearest to implementation in Italy in the fascist era (1922–1943) and in Portugal under the dictator António de Oliveira Salazar (premier, 1932–1968). Corporatist institutions were also to be found in certain Latin American countries. The European instances were marked by strong state control, and the corporations did not play the representative role intended by corporatist theory.

Liberal corporatism, also termed *neocorporatism,* developed after World War II within a number of liberal democracies in Europe. The "peak associations" representing major interests in a country, such as employers, professions, agricultural producers, and labor, are given a privileged position by the state in negotiations over policy making. In return, the associations deliver support from their members for the resultant policies. Liberal corporatist arrangements provide a form of functionalist representation alongside orthodox parliamentary institutions. Liberal corporatist democracy differs from pluralist democracy in that certain interest groups are privileged over others and in that the distinction between public and private authorities is less sharp.

The prime examples of liberal corporatist democracies are Austria and Sweden; corporatist processes also occur in the Netherlands and in Germany. The United States is usually regarded as the least corporatist of major nations in its politics. In many countries, however, there are middle-level corporatist arrangements. In these, interest groups within specific sectors of society and the economy are granted privileged positions in the consultative and regulatory processes. Frequent examples are found in agriculture. Defenders of liberal corporatism often claim that it promotes consensus and legitimacy for policies with beneficial effects for the economy and society. Critics are concerned about the privileged access to influence that powerful interests may gain at the expense of other groups in society.

Consociational Democracy

Consociational democracy is a type of representative government in which, in contrast to majoritarian systems, power sharing is institutionalized. Consociational practices typically have developed in countries that are deeply divided by clear-cut religious, ethnic, or linguistic differences. The aim of consociationalism is to ensure that all the major cleavages or segments in society are represented in the government in proportion to their size in the society. Power sharing implies that the government is a coalition of the representatives of the major segments, rather than composed of the single winning party, as in a majoritarian system such as the United Kingdom. Policy is produced as a result of negotiations between the leaders of the segments in a process known as "elite accommodation." The system of power sharing may also extend to the allocation of senior civil service posts or positions in significant public authorities.

The organizations representing each social segment are guaranteed considerable autonomy in determining which issues affect that particular grouping. Each segment may also possess rights of veto over matters that affect their vital interests, such as religious or linguistic schooling. Advocates of consociationalism argue that such power-sharing devices enable deeply divided societies to hold together. Countries that have had well-developed consociational democracies for considerable periods include Belgium, Switzerland, the Netherlands, Malaysia, and, in some views, Lebanon.

People's Democracy

People's democracy is a term used by those who wish to claim that the one-party states of the former Soviet Union, its former Eastern European satellites, and the People's Republic of China constitute a type of democracy. The claim rests on a number of arguments within Marxist-Leninist doctrine. Although *democracy* means the rule of the people, Marxist-Leninist theory argues that conventional liberal democracies do not provide genuine government by the people. The equal political rights and constitutional guarantees amount only to a "formal" democracy, since they are not reinforced by substantive economic and social equality. Liberal democracy is a shell that protects capitalism and the bourgeois ruling class.

The genuine rule of the people would imply control of government and the economy by the proletariat, or working class. The proletariat is identified with the people on the ground that within the Marxist scheme of history the proletariat constitutes variously the majority, the poor masses, and also the emancipatory, revolutionary class that represents the interests of humanity. The rule of the proletariat, and hence of the people, is not necessarily exercised directly. It may be exercised through the agency of the Communist Party, the vanguard of the proletariat. The party possesses a knowledge of the line of march to the realization of the proletariat's interests. The proletariat may fail to understand its true interests as a consequence of oppression and manipulation in the bourgeois era. Rule by the vanguard Communist Party is government for the people and, if only indirectly, by the people. Ultimately, in a true communist society in which the sources of class repression have been abolished, this rule will be superfluous and will wither away to a form of self-regulation.

One-party states in a number of African countries have justified their claims to being democracies by similar kinds of argument to those advanced in people's democracies. The dominant party in those instances claims to be leading the nation, formerly oppressed by colonialism, to a condition of economic development.

Plebiscitarian Democracy

Plebiscitarian democracy refers to political systems in which constitutional amendments are put to the people in a plebiscite or in which the head of state derives authority from being directly elected. A plebiscite (derived from the Latin term for a vote of the people, *plebs,* in ancient Rome) is a vote by the electorate on a proposed change in some aspect of the constitutional arrangements. As such it is a form of referendum, and the two terms are not always strictly differentiated. The French Fifth Republic (which began in 1958) is an example of a democracy that allows for plebiscites. A system in which the head of state is directly elected is also termed plebiscitarian, in that the person elected gains a legitimacy from the people distinct from that acquired by the representatives in the legislature. The powerful presidency of the French Fifth Republic is an instance. By extension, it is sometimes argued that modern representative democracies are becoming more plebiscitarian in that general elections increasingly are perceived as competitions between rival leaders who appeal directly to the people rather than as competitions between the political parties.

See also *Christian democracy; Classical Greece and Rome; Corporatism; Dominant party democracies in Asia; Federalism; Industrial democracy; Local government; Marx, Karl; Participatory democracy; Referendum and initiative; Rousseau, Jean-Jacques; Social democracy; Theory, African; Theory, Ancient.*

Geraint Parry

BIBLIOGRAPHY

Arterton, F. Christopher. *Teledemocracy: Can Technology Protect Democracy?* Newbury Park, Calif.: Sage Publications, 1987.

Barber, Benjamin. *Strong Democracy: Participatory Politics for a New Age.* Berkeley: University of California Press, 1984.

Burnheim, John. *Is Democracy Possible?* Cambridge: Polity Press, 1985.

Finley, Moses I. *Democracy Ancient and Modern.* London: Chatto and Windus, 1973.

Hansen, Mogens H. *The Athenian Democracy in the Age of Demosthenes: Structure, Principles, and Ideology.* Oxford and Cambridge, Mass.: Blackwell, 1991.

Held, David. *Models of Democracy.* Cambridge: Polity Press, 1987.

Hirst, Paul Q., ed. *The Pluralist Theory of the State: Selected Writings of G. D. H. Cole, J. N. Figgis, and H. J. Laski.* London and New York: Routledge, 1989.

Holden, Barry. *Understanding Liberal Democracy.* Oxford and Atlantic Highlands, N.J.: Philip Allan, 1988.

Lijphart, Arend. *Democracy in Plural Societies: A Comparative Exploration.* New Haven: Yale University Press, 1977.

Lively, Jack. *Democracy.* Oxford: Blackwell, 1975.

Mansbridge, Jane J. *Beyond Adversary Democracy.* New York: Basic Books, 1980.

Pennock, J. Roland. *Democratic Political Theory.* Princeton: Princeton University Press, 1979.

Sartori, Giovanni. *The Theory of Democracy Revisited.* Chatham, N.J.: Chatham House, 1987.

Stockton, David. *The Classical Athenian Democracy.* Oxford and New York: Oxford University Press, 1990.

Williamson, Peter J. *Varieties of Corporatism: A Conceptual Discussion.* Cambridge: Cambridge University Press, 1985.

U

Uganda

A landlocked country in East Central Africa where attempts at multiparty democracy have not precluded state-sponsored violence. Today Uganda is experimenting with novel forms of political participation.

Since gaining independence from Great Britain in 1962, Uganda has experienced many types of political structures, veering from civilian to military regimes to near anarchy. Not only were Uganda's episodes with formally democratic institutions under civilian rule highly unstable; they often provided a context for heavily repressive government policies.

Currently, Ugandans are bringing a maturity, and a cynicism hardened by years of political violence and economic decline, to discussions of democracy—in particular, the form democracy should take in their country and the way it should be expressed in a new constitution. The present government, the National Resistance Movement (NRM) led by President Yoweri Kaguta Museveni, is both facilitating and attempting to influence this debate. One arena of popular cynicism toward democracy in Uganda has been the performance of its political parties—especially the Uganda People's Congress (UPC) and the Democratic Party. All parties, but particularly the UPC, have practiced extraconstitutional and nondemocratic behavior.

From Independence to Idi Amin

In many ways Uganda's political parties have embodied the contradictions of a British colonial legacy, beginning in 1894. In constructing a protectorate in Uganda, the British both entered into treaties with collaborating precolonial polities and defeated recalcitrant groups in

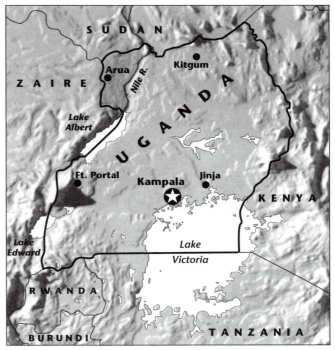

warfare. The final boundaries of the protectorate combined into a single administrative unit centralized kingdoms, the remnants of precolonial empires, and decentralized political groupings.

The British developed the south and left the north as a reserve for labor and military recruitment. They left the central government weak while strengthening the ethnic consciousness of subunits through policies of "indirect rule." The most significant result of these policies was the quasi-autonomous status of the southern kingdom of Buganda, led by its *kabaka* (king) and his chiefs. Buganda had the largest ethnic grouping in the protectorate (the Baganda tribal group represented 20 percent of the population), and it also was the most economically vibrant region. During this period, Buganda alternated between threats to become a separate state and efforts to secure dominance in an independent Uganda. Northern ethnic groups—particularly the Langi and Acholi—perceived their interests as circumscribed by Buganda's privileged position.

The UPC, led by Milton Obote, was the party of government for two periods of Uganda's postindependence history (1962–1971 and 1980–1985). It emerged before independence as a loose coalition of local elites with followings in various ethnic communities. What bound the UPC together was a desire to share in the spoils of political control, a vision of a strong central state that would supersede the federal tendencies fostered by colonial policies, and the Anglican faith of most of its leaders. By 1961 it controlled most district councils, with the key exception of Buganda, where its antifederal stance was deeply resented.

Ironically, the UPC entered into an alliance with the subnationalist party of Buganda—Kabaka Yekka, meaning "the king alone"—and defeated the Democratic Party in Uganda's independence elections in 1962. Obote became prime minister. This marriage of convenience proved to be short lived: members from other parties crossed the floor to join the UPC, giving it an absolute majority in the parliament. Freed from dependence on Buganda, Obote moved toward disassembling Uganda's federal structure by repressing opposition and abolishing all four of Uganda's kingdoms, including Buganda. (Several of these kingdoms were restored in 1993.) In addition, he imposed a new constitution that established a highly centralized state apparatus, giving direct control over local governments to the national executive. Obote declared himself president within this new structure. Ideologically, he labeled this shift a "move to the left," which was formalized in his Common Man's Charter. But more important in the long run was the domination of the UPC by the interests of political elites from the north of Uganda—the home region of both Obote and the bulk of the Ugandan army, upon which he was becoming increasingly dependent.

The origins of the Democratic Party lay in the mobilization of educated Catholics, at first in Buganda and later throughout the country. The party's most important leader, Benedicto Kiwanuka, served briefly as prime minister

after a Democratic Party victory in the pre-independence elections of 1961. Buganda's Anglican political elite greatly resented this outcome, leading to its ill-fated alliance with the UPC.

After the Democratic Party's defeat in the 1962 elections, it took on the role of parliamentary opposition. Within the next few years many parliamentarians in the party, who were enticed by promises of patronage and ministerial posts, joined the UPC rather than remain in opposition. The Democratic Party became virtually moribund in the late 1960s as the UPC moved toward one-party rule.

By 1969 Uganda had become a one-party state. Elections within a one-party framework were planned for 1971, the first since independence. But the coup led by Maj. Gen. Idi Amin in that year preempted the elections. Amin banned all political parties, and many UPC leaders went into exile. A notorious military dictatorship was established, with Amin declaring himself "life president." He quickly expelled Uganda's Asian population, the backbone of the commercial sector of the economy, and embarked on a reign of terror against intellectuals, members of the armed forces from supposedly disloyal ethnic groups, and all critics and opponents of the regime. Human rights violations occurred on a massive scale, with estimates of 100,000–250,000 deaths.

More Years of Turmoil

Obote returned to the political scene after the 1979 defeat of Amin's army by Tanzanian troops and a broad dissident force, the Uganda National Liberation Army (UNLA) and the Uganda National Liberation Front. The National Liberation Front, the political wing, appointed and then deposed several heads of state within a brief period before calling elections in 1980. These elections, organized by an electoral commission largely sympathetic to the UPC, resulted in a victory for the UPC and for Obote—a victory that many observers and most Ugandans regarded as rigged.

The Democratic Party had reconstituted itself for the 1980 elections under the leadership of Paul Ssemogerere, who, according to most accounts, would have become president if not for the rigged results. Once again it became a parliamentary opposition party and through its newspaper strongly denounced the army's human rights record. After the election it was evident that the social base of the party had been transformed. In addition to retaining some support among Catholics, the Democratic

Party swept Buganda, where it had made common cause with those who hated Obote and the UPC.

Among the prominent Ugandans rejecting the election results was Museveni, who formed the National Resistance Army (NRA) and began a guerrilla struggle. The north-south divide in Uganda was starkly revealed in the course of the guerrilla war, which was fought entirely in the south, particularly the region of Buganda known as the Luwero Triangle. The UNLA's counterinsurgency killed hundreds of thousands of civilians, even surpassing the excesses of Amin's regime. In addition, the UPC cadre and its youth wing ran roughshod over the population, persecuting Democratic Party and suspected NRA supporters. That such events could occur in a nominally democratic, multiparty regime was a lesson not lost on most Ugandans, and it is a source of their cynicism today.

In 1985, with the NRA capturing portions of western Uganda, a factional squabble within the military led to a successful coup, removing Obote once again. The Democratic Party declared its support for the leader of the coup, Tito Okello Lutwa, and his followers despite their involvement in the army's atrocities. This declaration of support was regarded as opportunistic by many Ugandans. Like the floor crossings of the mid-1960s, it compromised the Democratic Party's image as a party committed to democratic rule. When Museveni and the NRA captured Kampala, the capital, in January 1986, the Democratic Party reversed itself and entered into a fragile grand coalition with the new National Resistance Movement government.

Government Under the National Resistance Movement

By the time the NRM captured state power, the polarization between north and south in Uganda was at its peak. The NRM has its base of support in the south, and various rebel movements in the north have resisted its rule. In combating these groups, the NRA has tarnished its reputation for discipline and observance of human rights, upon which its legitimacy is largely based.

Although the NRM has roots in the Uganda Patriotic Movement, a small party once headed by Museveni, it is generally hostile to multiparty competition and blames the behavior of parties for much of Uganda's political troubles. At the same time the NRM has experimented with novel forms of popular participation that have been embraced with guarded optimism by Uganda's weary population.

The NRM has instituted a nationwide system of popular councils from the village to the district level. These "resistance councils" mandate direct elections to village committees and indirect elections to councils at each higher level of administration. While the indirect feature has come under criticism, the resistance council system allows Ugandans to participate more fully in politics than they had before. The councils are also used to elect members of the parliament indirectly, although some seats are reserved for the army (NRA) and presidential appointments. Thus far political parties, while not banned, are not allowed to campaign openly. The NRM considers itself an inclusive, populist movement, and it sees the resistance council system as the foundation for a "no-party" democracy.

In addition, the NRM appointed a commission to write a new constitution for Uganda. Commissioners have encouraged input from all sectors of Ugandan society and have traveled to remote rural areas to solicit opinions. The commission submitted a draft constitution in December 1992, and a Constituent Assembly was elected on March 28, 1994. The two most important issues facing the assembly were whether to return to a multiparty system and the restoration of the kingdoms. Candidates favoring the NRM's opposition to a return to multiparty electoral competition did well in these elections. The status of the kingdoms and the degree of federalism of the constitution were hotly debated, though the assembly was expected to ratify the constitution.

Overall, the NRM has demonstrated an ambiguous stance toward democratic politics. While occasionally showing authoritarian tendencies and limiting alternative political organization, it has encouraged popular participation in governance, especially at the local level. Most promising is the openness and engagement with which Ugandans are debating such issues given their skepticism toward political formulas of any kind. In the north, skepticism may still outweigh engagement, and the most difficult challenge for the NRM may be to ensure that whatever political arrangement is decided, it will reflect the genuine participation of all Ugandans.

See also *Africa, Subsaharan.*

Ronald Kassimir

BIBLIOGRAPHY

Apter, David E. *The Political Kingdom in Uganda: A Study of Bureaucratic Nationalism.* 2d ed. Princeton: Princeton University Press, 1967.

Hansen, Holger Bernt, and Michael Twaddle, eds. *Changing Uganda: The Dilemmas of Structural Adjustment and Revolutionary Change.* London: James Currey, 1991.

———. *Uganda Now: Between Decay and Development.* London: James Currey, 1988.

Kasfir, Nelson. *The Shrinking Political Arena: Participation and Ethnicity in African Politics, with a Case Study of Uganda.* Berkeley: University of California Press, 1976.

Kokole, Omari H., and Ali A. Mazrui. "Uganda: The Dual Polity and the Plural Society." In *Democracy in Developing Countries: Africa,* edited by Larry Diamond, Juan J. Linz, and Seymour Martin Lipset. Boulder, Colo.: Lynne Rienner; London: Adamantine Press, 1988.

Mamdani, Mahmood. "Contradictory Class Perspectives on the Question of Democracy: The Case of Uganda." In *Popular Struggles for Democracy in Africa,* edited by Peter Anyang' Nyong'o. London: United Nations University and Zed Books, 1987.

Mutibwa, Phares. *Uganda since Independence: A Story of Unfulfilled Hopes.* Trenton, N.J.: Africa World Press; London: Hurst, 1992.

Oloka-Onyango, Joe. "The National Resistance Movement, 'Grassroots Democracy,' and Dictatorship in Uganda." In *Democracy and Socialism in Africa,* edited by Robin Cohen and Harry Goulbourne. Boulder, Colo.: Westview Press, 1991.

Ukraine

An Eastern European country north of the Black Sea that declared independence from the Union of Soviet Socialist Republics in August 1991. Ukraine has a population of nearly 52 million people, almost 73 percent of whom are Ukrainian and 22 percent of whom are Russian. In addition, there are substantial minorities of Jews, Belarusians, Moldovans, Bulgarians, and Poles.

As a newly independent state emerging from the collapse of the Soviet Union, Ukraine began building its state institutions after a referendum on December 1, 1991, ratified the country's independence by a margin of more than four to one. In the first years of independence, Ukraine's newly established democratic institutions were weak. The absence of democratic traditions complicated Ukraine's transition to democracy. Civil society was at a formative stage, recovering from a legacy of seventy years of totalitarian and authoritarian rule under communism. In addition, the country lacked the durable political, public, and nongovernmental structures that evolve naturally in an independent state.

Although political parties were numerous, they were weak financially and administratively. Still, in elections in 1991 and 1994 the country consistently adhered to the orderly transfer of power through the will of the people. By the mid-1990s Ukraine had completed a series of major nationwide elections at all levels of governance.

Ukraine's first president, Leonid Kravchuk, once part of the Communist elite, remained in power from December 1991 until his defeat in July 1994. Despite some lapses, he adhered to democratic electoral procedures. In the autumn of 1994 Ukraine nominated its first civilian defense minister.

Historical Background

Since the thirteenth-century demise of the princely state of Kiev Rus', which was founded in the ninth century, Ukraine has had only brief periods of independence. The first period of independence lasted from the mid-seventeenth to the mid-eighteenth century, when large portions of Ukraine were controlled by Cossacks. During this time an independent proto-state emerged that was based on the Cossack *hetmanate,* in which leadership came from one top official—the hetman, who was elected by Cossack detachments. This official shared some legislative and executive powers with the *rada,* or council, the highest popular representative body. The Cossack period contained the seeds of democratic governance and democratic precedents, including the principle of the direct election of top leaders. The apogee of the Cossack bands was during the hundred years when Hetman Bohdan Khmelnytsky (1648–1657), Hetman Ivan Mazepa (1687–1709), and Hetman Pylyp Orlyk (1710–1742) ruled. Orlyk was an early Ukrainian voice for constitutionalism and limited power. His influence was felt primarily in the western part of Ukraine.

In the nineteenth century, eastern Ukraine's Cossacks were increasingly drawn into the centralized rule of the Russian czars, while western Ukrainian regions were under the dominion of the Austro-Hungarian Empire. Ukrainians actively participated in the Decembrist uprising of 1825 against Czar Nicholas I, which embodied revolutionary republican ideas. In the Russian empire, modern Ukrainian political thought emerged in the writings of the great nineteenth-century national poet Taras Shevchenko and his contemporary, the historian Mykola Kostomarov. Both were founders of the Brotherhood of Saints Cyril and Methodius, a group that preached national independence, freedom, and social justice. The brotherhood, created in 1845, was influenced by Polish, French, Czech, and

Slovak democratic nationalist and revolutionary thinkers. Kostomarov's writings—including the *Book of Genesis of the Ukrainian People*—are suffused with the ideas of Christian morality, democracy, and Slavic community. The brotherhood was dissolved by czarist decree in 1847; its activists were sentenced to prison or Siberian exile.

Russian imperial repression drove leading eastern Ukrainian political thinkers into exile in central Europe. There they joined in political dialogue with social democratic thinkers who had shaped their views in western Ukrainian regions. Social democratic ideas dominated Ukrainian political life as the nineteenth century drew to a close.

The most influential thinker of the period was the historian and political theorist Mykhaylo Drahomanov (1841–1895). Drahomanov was an influential voice within the Kiev Hromada, a clandestine political association that published a newspaper and supported archeological and cultural activities. Drahomanov developed a constitution that reflected democratic ideas and was aimed at establishing a federation of Slavic communities within the Russian empire. Other influential social democrats were the poet, novelist, and political theorist Ivan Franko and the historian Mykhaylo Hrushevsky, who later became president of the Central Rada (parliament), which proclaimed an independent state in 1917—commencing Ukraine's second period of independence.

Social democratic thinkers played a central role in the failed attempts at statehood in the years 1917 to 1921, which saw a succession of governments, including a democratically oriented Central Rada, a German-backed Hetmanate, and a Directory headed by Simon Petlyura, a military officer. The Rada authorities established a government that ensured broad protections for national minorities. The weakness of the Rada, however, and its inability to raise an effective army led to antidemocratic governments that sought to preserve sovereignty and state independence.

The defeat of the last of the governments (under Petlyura) ended efforts to preserve Ukraine's sovereignty. This government was followed by Bolshevik rule and the drift toward totalitarianism, the elimination of millions of people through state terror, and the eradication of independent civic life and civil society.

The Soviet Period

In 1922 Ukraine became one of the republics within the Soviet Union. Under Soviet rule, mounting repression culminated in the period of terror under the rule of Joseph Stalin. Imprisonment, execution, and exile claimed many of Ukraine's political and cultural elite from 1932 to 1934. The forced collectivization of the countryside claimed between 4.5 and 7 million lives, as grain, livestock, and seed were expropriated by the state. Much of it was sold for export to finance Stalin's program of rapid industrialization.

From the mid-1940s until 1951 the Ukrainian Insurgent Army fought a futile guerrilla war against Soviet authorities in the hope of establishing an independent Ukrainian state based on democratic principles. Progress toward democratization and the reemergence of civil society began with the cultural relaxations after Stalin's death in 1953, including the publication of previously banned writers and poets.

In the post-Stalin period, voices calling for the defense of human rights and civil liberties courageously upheld democratic values. Ukrainian dissent blossomed in the mid-1960s and focused on adherence to Soviet constitutional provisions guaranteeing freedom of speech and of religion. Subsequently, dissent also focused on adherence to Ukraine's and the USSR's ratification of international human rights documents, including the 1975 Helsinki Accords. Another theme of Ukrainian dissent was the defense of Ukraine's cultural and linguistic rights.

Most leading human rights activists were imprisoned—many for terms of seven to ten years, some for as long as twenty-five years—for anti-Soviet agitation, propaganda, and even treason. Many dissidents were imprisoned for long periods in psychiatric hospitals.

Independent organizations and mass democratic activism increased rapidly between 1987 and 1989, under Soviet leader Mikhail Gorbachev's encouragement of glasnost ("openness"). Demonstrations of 50,000 to 300,000 participants became common in Kiev, the Ukrainian capital, and other large cities. In July 1989 a strike in the eastern coal-mining region of the Donbas involved more than 250,000 workers and contributed to the birth of strike committees, free trade unions, political associations, and other independent organizations.

Peaceful pressure by independent civil society played a central role in the collapse of Soviet rule. The groups pressing for statehood were adherents of liberal democratic and free market ideas. The pressure to create a sovereign Ukrainian state came from organizations and associations united within Rukh, the Popular Movement of Ukraine. Rukh was created in September 1989 by liberally oriented writers, scholars, and former political prisoners. Because of its grassroots democratic structure, Rukh's membership quickly grew to more than 700,000, and it adopted more radical positions. As mass opinion radicalized, Rukh began to press for Ukraine's secession from the USSR.

In January 1990 a 300-mile-long "human chain" involving as many as 500,000 participants stretched from Kiev to Lviv as part of Rukh's efforts to promote state independence. Amid this ferment, democrats captured more than 25 percent of the seats in the Ukrainian Soviet Socialist Republic's parliament by March 1990.

Several important political parties emerged from the dissident movement. In addition to Rukh, which evolved into a party of national-democratic and liberal economic orientation, there were the Democratic Party of Ukraine, the Ukrainian Republican Party, and the Congress of Ukrainian Nationalists, which was linked to the émigré Organization of Ukrainian Nationalists. These parties had a broadly democratic orientation and supported a parliamentary or parliamentary-presidential system. Other parties originated from reform movements within the Communist Party and the Ukrainian Young Communist League (Komsomol). Among them were New Ukraine, the Party for Democratic Renewal of Ukraine, and the Ukrainian Social Democratic Party.

Obstacles to Reform in the Newly Independent State

The 1991 presidential elections and the referendum on independence produced a voter turnout of 85 percent. The first and second rounds of parliamentary elections in 1994 produced voter turnouts of 76 percent and 67 percent, respectively. The presidential elections of June 26, 1994, attracted a 68 percent turnout. In the runoff Leonid Kuchma was elected president. Polls conducted by the Democratic Initiatives organization in March-April 1994 showed that 63 percent of voters were certain that their vote mattered for the future of Ukraine.

On the eve of the 1994 electoral season, there were signs of growing political violence. Rukh leaders and other democratic activists were subjected to attempted kidnappings and beatings; acts of arson and occasional terrorist attacks were directed against their property. The party's executive director, Mykhaylo Boychyshyn, disappeared in October 1993 and was presumed to have been murdered. Political violence also was widespread in Crimea, where pro-Ukrainian Crimean Tatars and Russian secessionists were wounded or assassinated in a series of politically motivated attacks.

Despite widespread fears among democratic forces, and despite clear advantages enjoyed by local incumbents and by President Kravchuk in terms of access to television, foreign observers judged the electoral process to have been free and reasonably fair. In the aftermath of President Kuchma's victory, political violence abated and violent attacks on political leaders appeared to be linked primarily to organized criminal groups.

Because democratic movements struggling against the

communist system shaped and advanced the main arguments for Ukrainian statehood, and because democratic protest and use of the ballot box achieved statehood, Ukraine's citizens associate their statehood with the principles of democratic consent. Public opinion samplings conducted in 1993 and 1994 registered broad support for democracy based on the "Western" or "West European" model.

Although public support for the broad concepts of Western-style democracy was strong, Soviet rule in most of Ukraine (western Ukraine was annexed by the USSR in 1939) had left a deleterious legacy. Accustomed to centralized decision making and inundated by propaganda against private ownership and business—and at the same time innately mistrustful of political parties and organizations—much of Ukrainian society was disoriented by rapid social, economic, and political changes and newfound freedoms. While Ukrainians grappled with the particulars of representative democracy (such as the accountability of elected officials and individual civic responsibility) and the challenge of forging a modern market economy, some, particularly pensioners and older workers, were nostalgic for the certainty and order of the old system.

In addition, the collective farm directors had a stranglehold on the electorate in the countryside. These officials, and those whom they influenced, constituted a potent and cohesive bloc that resisted reform, although by the summer of 1995 some voices for reform had emerged in the agricultural sector.

A worrisome ethos was represented by Ukraine's Communist Party and its ally, the Agrarians. Wedded to the terminology of the past, they advocated the idea of Soviet democracy, the building of a centralized system in which power ostensibly derives from councils at the local, regional, and national levels. And they opposed efforts to privatize state property.

This clash of opposing sensibilities, both among the public and in the political leadership, hampered decisive action on the scope and pace of economic reform. Reformers were pitted against recalcitrant bureaucratic and agro-industrial elites. This dynamic has played an important role in Ukraine's post-Soviet elections and political life.

Reconciling Regional and Other Differences

Regional factors influence political differentiation in Ukraine. An emphasis on integration into the structures of Europe has appealed primarily to voters in central and—especially—western Ukraine. These areas, which were incorporated into the Soviet Union only in 1939, had experienced a market economy and a modicum of democratic self-rule under the Austro-Hungarian Empire and later under Poland. The heavily industrialized eastern and southern Ukraine, home to many of the country's 11 million ethnic Russians and "Russified Ukrainians," has been drawn to statist economic ideas and nostalgia for the Soviet period.

Although regional, ethnic, and demographic differences remain a key factor in Ukraine's cohesion, it should be remembered that a 1990 sovereignty declaration was overwhelmingly supported in all regions and by all ethnic groups. Moreover, an election law that minimized the importance of political parties prevented regional cleavages from coalescing around powerful central structures or regional leaders. Despite such flare-ups as sovereignty demands by the heavily Russian Crimean peninsula, Ukraine's central government has managed, with political and financial support from the West, to secure Ukraine's sovereignty and national unity in the face of protestations and veiled threats from an increasingly bellicose Russia.

More difficult to secure than independence have been political and market reforms, including privatization. At the end of 1994 reformist president Kuchma had made the necessary economic adjustments to secure Western and International Monetary Fund loans, but he continued to face a reluctant Rada. With the absence of strong national parties, the Rada had coalesced into distinct political blocs dominated by neocommunists and local agro-industrial bureaucrats, who had used their former influence and power to capture many of the 393 elected seats.

While parliamentary alliances continued to shift, the neocommunist left controlled approximately 146 seats and included a coalition of agrarians and socialists, many of whom favored a command economy and restoration of the Soviet Union. So-called centrists controlled about 115 seats; they represented a spectrum of forces, ranging from state administrative and industrial bureaucrats to economic reformers from central and eastern Ukraine who favored close cooperation with Russia. The national democrats and national liberals, with 103 seats, included Rukh members who supported liberal economic reform, moderates formerly aligned with former president Kravchuk, and radical free marketeers who supported lowering of tax rates, the creation of a stable currency based on strict budgetary discipline, and tight monetary policies. Independents were not a cohesive force; they ranged from a small faction of far-right nationalists contemptuous of democratic practice to Communist-era apparatchiks.

Civil Society and Constitutionality

In the mid-1990s a number of residual Soviet-era organizations continued to dominate Ukrainian society. The Federation of Trade Unions, which claimed 21 million members, was the successor to a Soviet-era state-controlled organization. It remained a major source of employment for Communist-era apparatchiks, but in such regions as western Ukraine, key leadership positions had been taken over by activists from Rukh and other democratic organizations.

Five independent unions, joined under the Consultative Council of Free Trade Unions, united some 200,000 workers from among miners, locomotive engineers, air traffic controllers, and aviation personnel. There were also newly created unions of maritime workers and journalists.

At the end of 1994 there were more than 150 business associations, ranging from groups representing local small businesses to a national League of Industrialists and Entrepreneurs, which represented some 2,000 member businesses and included many of Ukraine's industrial giants. The group had been headed by Leonid Kuchma.

Church life, too, underwent a considerable renewal with the end of repression of religious life associated with Communist rule. Religious leaders, for the most part, stayed out of political life.

With independence, Ukraine's media partly freed themselves from the shackles of state control and influence. Censorship was no longer practiced, but journalists could be tried on criminal charges for slandering state officials and ordinary citizens. The economic vulnerability of the media, including dependency on government subsidies and state control of newsprint as well as of major printing and distribution facilities, made them susceptible to outside influence. Although there were more than 2,000 newspapers, many were little more than mouthpieces of local government.

National—and much local—television remained in the hands of the state. Radio showed a higher degree of diversity than did television. Local television witnessed a proliferation of cable and regional broadcasters, most of them private, but little of their programming was oriented toward news and information. Much broadcast activity was conducted without registration or proper licensing.

Therefore, many broadcasters were vulnerable to state sanction. By the summer of 1995 state television was broadcasting material from independent producers.

The constitution adopted under Soviet rule in 1978, and significantly modified by the Rada between 1991 and 1994, was the basis for independent governance. Although there was no reliable constitutional basis for property rights, these rights were respected in many instances. Human rights and the rights of ethnic and religious minorities were well protected in practice and were codified in the Criminal Code and other legislation. Although these rights were occasionally abused, the abuses were not endemic or institutionalized. Most judges who held office at the end of 1994, especially at the local level, were holdovers from the Soviet period. There was no functioning Constitutional Court.

The adoption of a new constitution was a major unresolved item on the agenda facing the new Ukrainian state. In October 1994 Kuchma indicated that he intended to support a draft constitution creating a presidential-parliamentary system, subject to adoption by referendum. In May 1995 the parliament and the president agreed to abide by a temporary year-long agreement that strengthened presidential rule, before a new constitution was to be adopted.

Prospects for the Future

Many issues concerning Ukraine's transformation into a stable democracy are unresolved, but there are reasons for guarded optimism. Although cultural differences between Russian-speaking eastern Ukraine and Ukrainian-speaking western Ukraine remain, Russia's brutal invasion of Chechnya in December 1994, according to numerous polls, has dampened enthusiasm for any sort of political, economic, or military union with Russia, thus bolstering Ukrainian sovereignty and the government's control over Crimea. President Kuchma's determination to press through his economic reform program won strong support from the West, particularly the United States, improving his stature and wearing down parliamentary resistance. Civil society and democratic institutions continue to grow and solidify, and a young generation of post-Soviet Ukrainians has embraced the need for democratization, modernization, and change.

Another encouraging fact is that, despite several years of severe economic decline, Ukraine's citizens continue to have confidence in democratic values and in the electoral process. An increasingly outspoken press and a public with growing self-confidence and knowledge of its rights also are positive indicators.

Yet there are storm clouds on the horizon. Three successive years (1992–1994) of steep economic decline; a mounting trade deficit with Russia, Turkmenistan, and other principal energy providers; and a state budget vastly out of balance with revenues have created a brittle economy. The looming danger of widening poverty and the specter of mass unemployment might strengthen the appeal of antidemocratic movements. A further concern is evidence of widespread corruption among high-ranking government officials and signs of the growing influence of the criminal economy on political life.

See also *Union of Soviet Socialist Republics.*

Adrian Karatnycky

BIBLIOGRAPHY

Dzyuba, Ivan. *Internationalism or Russification? A Study in the Soviet Nationalities Problem.* London: Weidenfeld and Nicolson, 1968.

Kubijovyc, Volodymyr, ed. *Encyclopedia of Ukraine.* 4 vols. Toronto: University of Toronto Press, 1990–1994.

Motyl, Alexander J. *Dilemmas of Independence: Ukraine after Totalitarianism.* New York: Council on Foreign Relations Press, 1993.

Subtelny, Orest. *Ukraine: A History.* 2d ed. Toronto: University of Toronto Press, 1993.

Union of Soviet Socialist Republics

Heir of the Russian empire, which collapsed in 1917 under the impact of war and revolution. Under the rule of the czars, the empire had expanded over the centuries to become one of the great powers of Europe and Asia, extending from the Baltic to the Black Sea and Central Asia, and from the border of Poland to the Pacific Ocean. In the chaotic environment of World War I and its aftermath, a number of non-Russian territories declared their independence, but they were forcibly reannexed by the new Soviet state and incorporated into what became the Union of Soviet Socialist Republics (USSR).

The Revolution of 1917

The Russian empire on the eve of World War I was a largely agrarian society, lagging behind Europe in eco-

nomic development and ruled by a highly centralized, bureaucratic autocracy which, however reluctantly, was beginning to embrace significant political reforms. The Bolshevik revolution of 1917 cut short Russia's slow, gradual progress toward constitutional democracy, reversing the series of reforms that had begun to alter some of the autocratic features of the czarist system. Legal reforms in 1864 had created the foundation for judicial independence and due process, and the creation of local government assemblies *(zemstva)* in 1863 provided new, though limited, opportunities for broader participation in governance.

The first organized legal political parties made their appearance after the turn of the century. And the Revolution of 1905 brought about the establishment of the Duma, the first elected nationwide representative body, though its authority and suffrage were severely limited. Fitfully and against formidable obstacles, Russia seemed to be moving in the general direction earlier traversed by Western Europe toward representative government, broader participation, and accountability.

Whether these and other reforms would ultimately have produced a democratic system in Russia is a matter of dispute. In any event, World War I strained the czarist state and triggered its collapse. The Provisional Government that took its place in February 1917 was, in its majority, committed to political democracy, but it was unable to survive, let alone carry out any significant reform, under the crisis conditions of the time. The "October Revolution" of 1917 produced a Soviet state, with Vladimir Ilich Lenin as its leader.

Lenin and the Bolsheviks

The Bolsheviks represented one wing of the Russian Social Democratic Labor Party, which, under Lenin's leadership, had insisted on the need for tight organizational discipline. The initial organizational disagreements between the Bolsheviks and Mensheviks later broadened into doctrinal disagreements over the nature of the revolution itself.

Leninism was in many regards an amalgam of contradictory elements derived from Marxist origins and the impact of the Russian revolutionary scene. It joined a utopian vision of an egalitarian, classless society that would permit the full and free development of each individual, and in which participatory democracy would allow for the withering away of a coercive state, to an authoritarian and elitist revolutionary organization that re-

garded violence as a necessary and legitimate tool of social transformation.

As the seizure and exercise of power reinforced the centralizing and authoritarian tendencies of the Bolshevik elite, and as the utopian promise receded ever further into the future, the egalitarian and democratic strains in the Bolshevik tradition were deprived of operational significance and transformed into myths and rituals that provided a fig leaf of legitimacy to an antidemocratic and repressive political system. Yet their preservation in Bolshevik discourse left open the possibility that under propitious circumstances they could be invested with real meaning and invoked in behalf of systemic reform.

The Bolsheviks greeted the collapse of the czarist system and the creation of the Provisional Government in February 1917 with some ambivalence. On the one hand, the replacement of autocracy by what they labeled "bourgeois democracy" represented progress in their view of Russia's historical development. Indeed, in early 1917

Lenin described Russia as the "freest country in the world." On the other hand, the Bolsheviks viewed political democracy as a sham that merely disguised the economic exploitation of the masses of workers by the ruling class. Only a socialist revolution that destroyed the economic foundations of inequality could create the conditions for genuine proletarian democracy.

Lenin's singular contribution to the theory and practice of revolution was his longstanding insistence on the need for a tightly knit party of professional revolutionaries to serve as the vanguard of the proletariat. In the chaos of 1917, he saw an unexpected opportunity to seize power. Despite opposition from within the party's leadership, Lenin pressed for an insurrection that would replace the newly established parliamentary republic with a republic of soviets, the hastily improvised councils of workers', soldiers', and peasants' deputies that had emerged spontaneously alongside the Provisional Government. The seizure of power in the capital, Petrograd (later renamed Leningrad), proved surprisingly easy. Spurning pressure to form a broad coalition with the other socialist parties, the Bolsheviks installed a government under their leadership, which claimed to rest on the power of the soviets.

They went further in January 1918. Rejecting the outcome of the November 1917 elections to the Constituent Assembly—the first free nationwide elections in Russia's long history—in which they had received less than a quarter of the vote, the Bolsheviks forcibly dispersed the Constituent Assembly, cutting short Russia's embryonic movement toward parliamentary democracy.

Lenin would later justify the Bolsheviks' seizure of power in defiance of any electoral mandate by arguing that, although the proletariat (as represented by the Leninists) ultimately needed to win the support of a majority of the population, it would be impracticable and foolish, given the class-based antagonism of the bourgeoisie, to make such a mandate a condition of coming to power. Rather, it was the task of the new Soviet government to create forcibly the conditions that might ultimately generate mass support.

Civil War and Consolidation of Soviet Power

The Bolshevik seizure of power led to a civil war (1918–1920), which, intertwined as it was with the final stages of World War I and foreign intervention in Russia, further strengthened the authoritarian and ruthless proclivities of the Leninists, who emerged victorious. The following years saw the consolidation of Soviet—that is, Bolshevik—power and the progressive elimination of all political competition, beginning with the monarchists (including the execution of the czar and his family in 1918) and right-wing parties, then extending to centrist and socialist parties, and culminating in the destruction of organized opposition within the Bolshevik (Communist) Party itself. In March 1921, the Tenth Party Congress adopted a ban on "factions" that effectively destroyed the basis for open discussion and dissent within the party.

The closing down of the political arena was accompanied by a crackdown on freedom of the press, including the closure of opposition newspapers, the imposition of censorship, and the nationalization of printing presses and paper. Although many Bolsheviks were willing to tolerate violations of freedom of the press as a temporary emergency measure, the imposition of total control over the press—and the treatment of criticism of the party as tantamount to counterrevolution—went far beyond what had been envisioned in prerevolutionary programs.

Soviet rule was marked by a growing resort to repression, including the creation of a sizable political police network, administrative arrests, and, later, deportations to labor camps. As early as 1918 the repression was codified; the constitution promulgated that year denied to individuals and groups rights that they might use to the detriment of the socialist revolution. In the lawless atmosphere of the civil war, the leadership rejected the adoption of any legal restraints on state power and justified the use of terror in behalf of the revolution.

The effort to consolidate the power of the new Soviet state and to weaken or destroy alternative sources of social and political power was also reflected in the economic policies of the Bolshevik leadership. The underlying hostility to private ownership of the means of production, combined with the desire to use expropriation to win worker and peasant support, prompted a sweeping policy of nationalization. Among the earliest acts of the Soviet government was the seizure of the "commanding heights" of the economy, such as railroads, banks, mines, and large industrial enterprises, and the expropriation of their former owners. These assets remained in state hands even when, beginning in 1921, the Bolsheviks embarked on the "New Economic Policy," which restored small-scale private ownership and retail trade in an effort to overcome the crisis created by radical economic policies.

Even the trade unions, some of which had established a measure of "workers' control" at the beginning of the revolution, were now deprived of their autonomy and subordinated to state and party control.

Looking on the peasantry—the vast majority of Russia's population—as a long-term enemy but a temporary ally, Lenin had encouraged it to divide up the estates of the gentry and the church. Despite the forcible confiscation of grain during the civil war, private farming was tolerated in the 1920s. But most Soviet leaders were predisposed to see an independent peasantry as a bulwark of petty capitalism and ultimately a threat to the consolidation of Soviet power.

Throughout the 1920s there still remained some elements of autonomous social organization. Though subjected to harassment and pressures, a variety of institutions—among them the Orthodox Church, academic institutes, peasant communes, and literary journals—still preserved a degree of independence. But by the time of Lenin's death in 1924, the authoritarian, centralizing, and hierarchical thrust of Bolshevism had triumphed over populist, egalitarian, and syndicalist strands.

The consolidation of Soviet power in Russia was accompanied by the reabsorption of most non-Russian areas of the former czarist empire through essentially coercive means. The new federal structure, which was first created in Russia and then expanded to form the Union of Soviet Socialist Republics, or Soviet Union, was erected with ample use of pseudo-democratic and pseudo-libertarian phraseology. Just as the Soviet leaders eliminated rival political movements and leaders within Russia, they also destroyed rival national parties and leaders in non-Russian republics who challenged Soviet rule.

Stalin and Totalitarian Rule

The death of Lenin in January 1924 set off a protracted succession struggle within the party leadership from which Joseph Stalin emerged victorious. A harsh and ruthless party organizer of Georgian nationality who lacked the cosmopolitan education and experience abroad of other important Bolshevik leaders, Stalin utilized his considerable organizational skills as well as his control over key party institutions to outmaneuver his major competitors—most importantly Leon Trotsky and Nikolai Bukharin.

With Stalin's accession to supreme power by 1928, the monolithic concentration of power was further accelerated. A crash program of industrialization launched in 1928 and the brutal collectivization of agriculture (1929–1933) eliminated the remaining centers of independent economic activity and, with the creation of a centrally planned command economy, completed the fusion of economic and political power in the hands of the party-state.

The very notion of an autonomous intellectual or cultural realm was likewise challenged in the name of an increasingly dogmatic ideology that claimed to provide authoritative guidance on virtually every aspect of life, from child rearing to genetics. At the same time, Stalin himself was glorified as the unassailable authority on almost every subject and the infallible personification of the revolution itself.

The growing reliance on the secret police and terror as instruments of rule, and the atmosphere of ubiquitous insecurity that they generated, effectively eliminated the remaining constraints on the exercise of state power. It is this Stalinist era of Soviet history that most properly deserves the label "totalitarian." The massive purges of the mid- and late 1930s, ostensibly directed at enemies of Soviet power, engulfed the Bolshevik elite itself, including among their millions of victims a large part of the military high command as well as most of the "Old Bolsheviks" who had fought alongside Lenin in the 1917 revolution.

Ironically, it was in the midst of these developments, in 1936, that the Soviet regime promulgated what it called the most democratic constitution in the world. The constitution professed to guarantee a broad range of individual freedoms (including freedom of speech, conscience, press, and assembly; the inviolability of the person; and the right to privacy) as well as socioeconomic rights. It claimed to introduce universal suffrage, secret elections, the independence of the judiciary, and ostensibly representative legislative bodies. It also reaffirmed that the USSR was a federal state whose union republics retained the right of secession from the Soviet Union. In fact, however, the individual liberties were hedged with restrictions and obligations, and the republics' nominal autonomy was undercut by the centralization of economic and political decision making in Moscow.

What had emerged in fact was a unitary system with a hierarchical structure of power in which the Communist Party was the pervasive institution. It duplicated all agencies of government and penetrated all economic enterprises, the military, the secret police, and cultural institutions. Power was concentrated at the apex of the party pyramid—in the general secretary and the Politburo—with the self-perpetuating leadership vetting appointments throughout the land by means of the *nomenklatura* system. This system was a device for ensuring that key appointments in all areas of Soviet life were filled by suitable personnel ultimately controlled and allocated by the Party Secretariat and its cadre departments at all levels of the system. The legislative branch, with the Supreme Soviet at its top, functioned as little more than a rubber stamp, and elections to the parliament amounted to rituals of affirmation, without competitive candidacies.

The Soviet experience in World War II, as a consequence of the German invasion of June 22, 1941, saw vast stretches of territory overrun by invading armies, millions of soldiers captured by the enemy, destruction and devastation inflicted on an incredible scale, and well over 20 million casualties. Yet, ultimately, the Soviet army emerged victorious in an upsurge of patriotism that added significantly to the perceived legitimacy of the regime. The Soviet Union emerged after the war as a global power, with a sphere of control in Eastern Europe and East Asia. Within a few years of the end of the war, it also had the capability to produce atomic weapons of its own.

Khrushchev, Brezhnev, and Generational Change

Stalin's death in March 1953 and the succession struggle from which Nikita Sergeevich Khrushchev emerged as victor brought important changes in the nature of the Soviet system. Khrushchev, a particularly colorful Soviet leader of peasant background and populist inclinations, dissociated himself from his earlier role as one of Stalin's close associates to launch the contentious processes of de-Stalinization and "peaceful coexistence" with the capitalist West. The execution of Lavrenti Beria, the head of the secret police empire, and its subordination to the party ended the large-scale use of terror as an instrument of rule and altered the nature of political competition within the elite: political defeat was no longer tantamount to a death sentence. A cultural thaw accompanied political and economic reforms aimed at narrowing the chasm between regime and society.

Khrushchev's consolidation of power was accompanied by a dramatic, if selective, attack on Stalin in which Khrushchev sought simultaneously to distance himself from responsibility for some of the worst crimes of the Stalin era and to initiate important new developments in both domestic and foreign policy. Even this limited process of de-Stalinization, however, had far-reaching domestic and international repercussions, shattering faith in the infallibility of the party and the correctness of past decisions and pointing to the culpability of a whole generation for Stalin's crimes. De-Stalinization was particularly traumatic in Eastern Europe, where it undermined the legitimacy of dominant elites; it triggered major upheavals in Poland and Hungary.

The disruptive effects of Khrushchev's domestic and foreign policies, and especially of his efforts to challenge the status and prerogatives of the party elite, resulted in his forced resignation in October 1964. He was replaced as party first secretary by Leonid Brezhnev, who lost no time in assuring his party colleagues that they could henceforth enjoy both security and privilege.

Recruited into the party apparatus in the final years of the purges, Brezhnev served as a political officer in the armed forces during World War II and then in high party positions in Ukraine and Moldova before joining the central apparatus in Moscow in 1956. Brezhnev, a participant in the plot to oust Khrushchev in 1964, succeeded him as party leader and repudiated Khrushchev's bold and often impulsive initiatives, instituting instead a more cautious, conservative, and oligarchical style of leadership. The Brezhnev era saw improvement in the living standards of the Soviet population and a strengthening of Soviet military and political influence in international affairs. The achievement of superpower status and rough strategic parity with the United States, however, came at a high price: by the late 1970s declining rates of economic growth, a widening technological gap, and growing social malaise posed new challenges with which the aging Brezhnev leadership proved incapable of coping.

Whereas mass political terror in the Stalin years had deterred the expression of dissent, the cessation of terror under Khrushchev permitted the emergence of networks of dissenters who conducted clandestine discussions, circulated their own writings (samizdat), at times sent manuscripts abroad, and created rudimentary informal organizations. Their causes varied, ranging from political, religious, and cultural to nationalist dissent. Under Brezhnev, Soviet adherence to the Helsinki Accord of 1975 stimulated the monitoring of human rights violations by concerned volunteers, loosely grouped in Helsinki committees. When dissidents were arrested and put on trial, the defendants and their lawyers would often invoke the otherwise fictitious letter of the law in defense of their freedoms. Although the dissenters all advocated greater tolerance within the system, only a fraction among them could properly be labeled democrats in their beliefs and values.

Brezhnev's death in 1982 brought to the Soviet leadership the energetic and widely respected head of the KGB, Yury Vladimirovich Andropov. Despite his association with the repression of dissidence, Andropov's accession to power promised a rejuvenation of economic and political life, an emphasis on professional competence rather than on cronyism, and an effort to stem the erosion of civic morale through a reimposition of discipline. It also held out the prospect of new initiatives in Soviet foreign policy, including an effort to repair Sino-Soviet relations.

This promise was never fulfilled; Andropov's rapidly failing health was followed by his death in February 1984 and his replacement by Konstantin Chernenko, a close associate of Brezhnev's and a man of limited abilities and vision. Chernenko's brief tenure as party secretary prolonged the sense of stalemate and decline that had characterized Brezhnev's last years and further postponed decisions on the major domestic and foreign policy challenges of the day. His death in March 1985 brought to an end a long period of aging and indecisive leadership and brought to the fore a new generation of Soviet leaders committed to serious reform of the Soviet system.

The Gorbachev Reforms

Mikhail Sergeyevich Gorbachev represented the first generation of party leaders to come of age politically in the more liberal atmosphere that followed the death of Stalin. A graduate of the Law Faculty of Moscow University, with training and experience in agriculture as well, he quickly attracted the attention of several patrons in the party apparatus in Moscow. His rapid rise in the party hierarchy brought him to Moscow in 1978 and to full membership in the Politburo in 1980, where he became closely identified with Andropov. Lacking sufficient political support to succeed Andropov after his death, Gorbachev served as de facto second secretary under Chernenko and, despite opposition from the party's old guard, was elevated to the party leadership on Chernenko's death in March 1985.

The emergence of a reform-oriented coalition within the Soviet leadership reflected the growing recognition that deteriorating economic performance seriously jeopardized domestic stability and international power. But Gorbachev and his associates increasingly came to recognize that economic stagnation had its roots in deeper social and political problems and that far-reaching changes were necessary if these problems were to be addressed successfully. Gorbachev's concept of perestroika ("restructuring") thus evolved from its initial focus on economic acceleration to a broader and more radical agenda: the elaboration of a new model of socialism in which political democratization occupied a central place.

Gorbachev's struggle to revitalize the Soviet system became a struggle on two fronts: against conservatives in the party and state establishment who viewed his policies as a betrayal of socialism and as a threat to the unity and stability of the Soviet state, and against a variety of radicals (many of whom were also Communists) pressing for more drastic changes, including the introduction of a market economy, abolition of the party's monopoly

of power, and the creation of a genuine federal system.

How and why Gorbachev came to appropriate many of the ideas about political reform circulating among Soviet intellectuals is an interesting question in its own right. What is important here is that Gorbachev implicitly rejected the view that a viable economic system required the maintenance of political authoritarianism. The fusion of economic and political power in the USSR meant that the "command-administrative system" had to be attacked simultaneously on both fronts.

Though the political democratization Gorbachev envisioned was by no means a turn to a Western-style parliamentary democracy based on a multiparty system, it involved significant new departures in political principles as well as in institutions and practices. Just as his economic reforms were intended to enhance performance by introducing novel elements of competition, his political reforms were intended to revitalize political life by injecting the competition of political ideas and forces into Soviet practice.

In assessing the degree of democratization introduced in the course of Gorbachev's reforms, it is helpful to use as benchmarks five features of Western practice that, taken together, constitute the core of political democracy: (1) freedom of speech and press, which are prerequisites of political competition and accountability; (2) freedom to form and join parties and other organizations capable of representing interests and ideas, autonomous of the state; (3) mechanisms for making government responsive to the preferences of citizens; (4) checks and balances, including separation of powers between central and local authorities as well as between different branches of government; and (5) legal protection of individual and group rights against arbitrary state action. In one form or another, Gorbachev's reforms began to address all five.

The fundamental prerequisite of political reform was the delegitimation of the Stalinist system, indeed the very equation of Stalinism with socialism. Not only did this involve a highly controversial reassessment of Soviet history, it also challenged fundamental political values and institutions, which were now described in such unflattering terms as "partocracy," the "command-administrative system," and even "totalitarianism," and were charged with violating elementary and universal principles of democracy and human rights. One of the consequences of this process was not only to erode the authority of existing institutions, incumbents, and policies but also to elevate the status of former dissidents, from Andrei Sakharov to Aleksandr Solzhenitsyn. More broadly, it triggered a fierce debate over what features of the old system should be preserved and what should be replaced.

The endorsement of glasnost ("openness"), with its connotations of candor and public disclosure, was an essential step in the direction of increased freedom of public expression. By enshrining the principle of the public's right to know, glasnost also introduced an element of political accountability into a system where it had been absent. Glasnost, initially an effort to increase the new leadership's credibility with its own population and to win the intelligentsia's support in the struggle for reform, curtailed the information monopoly traditionally enjoyed by state authorities and paved the way for the emergence of the media as a major new political actor. It brought a progressive expansion of the range of subjects open to public discussion, a reduction of the scope of censorship, and greater frankness in addressing shortcomings and problems, from natural disasters to social pathologies to official incompetence.

Not only did Soviet newspapers, journals, and television programs become increasingly rich and bold, with differentiated political orientations, they also became a source of new political initiatives and a forum for communicating and debating the leading issues of the day and alternative political approaches. Although there was a steady breaching of taboos as topic after topic was opened to public discussion, the leadership maintained the ability to muzzle the media on select occasions, to dictate mandatory themes for the press to embroider, and to control the allocation of newsprint. Much-needed legislation on the freedom of the press was long bogged down in disputes. A Law on Press Freedom was finally adopted in 1990.

A second critical element in the process of political democratization was the endorsement of "socialist pluralism." Gorbachev acknowledged that the leadership lacked a ready-made recipe for solving major problems—a striking departure from past practice—and stated explicitly that open discussion of competing ideas and approaches was as essential to progress in social and political affairs as in scientific and technical domains. This shift from the notion of a "single truth" to a recognition of the legitimacy, and even necessity, of divergent opinions was a fundamental departure from the ideological premises of a Leninist vanguard party. Coupled with the recognition that Soviet society was itself composed of diverse and potentially conflicting social interests and that these required

some form of expression, it opened the way for the emergence of autonomous groups and organizations not sponsored by the state or the party.

The remarkable explosion of independent sociopolitical activity was one of the most striking consequences of the entire reform process. Thousands of informal groups and social movements emerged, with varying degrees of official tolerance in different regions of the country, ranging from small clusters of like-minded individuals to broad "popular fronts" embracing millions of members and supporters. Although many engaged in nonpolitical activities, such as sports and music, others represented single-issue lobbies, embryonic political parties, or movements covering the entire spectrum of interests and ideologies from Russian nationalists to environmentalists to Christian democrats. In the non-Russian republics, common national identity proved to be the most potent basis of political organization. Not only did national movements in these republics attract a considerable following, but they compelled the dominant Communist Party organizations there to bend to or even adopt many of their demands.

A third step toward political democratization involved the introduction of new political institutions and practices, notably competitive elections and new legislative bodies (the Congress of People's Deputies and a new Supreme Soviet), which not only promoted a new responsiveness to popular constituencies but altered the entire policy-making process. Combined with the role of television in bringing politics into the apartments of millions of Soviet citizens, the transformed institutions and practices contributed to a process of political education and mobilization, transforming a population long described as inert and passive into an aroused citizenry that used its new-found political clout to inflict massive defeats on unpopular party officials.

The spectacle of the Congress of Deputies reviewing the qualifications of ministerial appointees, challenging the heads of the KGB and the armed forces, establishing legislative oversight of foreign and military policies, and creating investigative commissions to examine explosive events such as the Molotov-Ribbentrop Pact of 1939 and the massacres in Tbilisi in April 1989 dramatized the fact that at the all-union level the legislative bodies were no longer a rubber stamp but rather actors in an authentic political process.

Despite its activism and freedom to act, the Congress of Deputies operated within severe constraints. Legislative drafting remained largely in the hands of the cognizant ministries. The deputies lacked the staff, the expertise, and the organizational capacity to challenge the domination of the party-state bureaucracy over the legislative process. Many of the (excessive) hopes invested in the new legislative bodies were disappointed. But they clearly became important new political arenas.

Despite the party's fierce resistance to giving up its formal monopoly of political power, its role was being significantly weakened by the political and economic reforms. Some of its previous functions were taken over by soviets, by market forces, or by enterprises. It was exposed to the political competition of new movements and contested elections; it lost members in unprecedented numbers, as did its youth affiliate, the Komsomol. There was a widespread crisis of morale among its members, no longer certain of its raison d'être; and the system of *nomenklatura* for making appointments to key positions around the country was undermined by grassroots nominations and elections of candidates who were not vetted by the center (and who occasionally were not even party members). Ideological conformity proved increasingly difficult to sustain in the absence of the once mandatory "general line"; organizational discipline was profoundly disrupted by the growing fragmentation of the party along national lines.

When in June 1988 the Armenian party leadership voted to support the incorporation of Nagorno-Karabakh, a disputed enclave populated largely by Armenians but administered by Azerbaijan, while the Azerbaijani party leadership voted against it, the Soviet party had reached a watershed. Greater responsiveness to local constituencies was bound to mean greater independence from Moscow. The decision of the Communist Party of Lithuania to separate from the all-union party and the Central Committee's quandary in responding to the challenge highlight the dilemmas Gorbachev faced in seeking to reconcile democratization with the traditional tenets of a "vanguard party."

Democratization also entailed an attack on the previous overcentralization of power. It involved a significant restructuring of the Soviet federal system to shift more responsibilities and resources to the republic and local levels as well as a marked reduction in the overall scope of governmental controls. In practice, however, the shrinking of the central Soviet bureaucracy turned out to be a daunting task, resisted by powerful bureaucratic interests.

Finally, political reform also included a commitment to the creation of a law-bound state. New (for the Soviet Union) principles proclaimed that individuals and groups were entitled to protection from arbitrary or illegal acts by state agencies and officials; that the uniform application of the law must take precedence over individual authority; that the quality and independence of judicial institutions must be strengthened; that the principle of the universality of human rights must be acknowledged in Soviet law and practice; and that Soviet laws must be reviewed for conformity to international norms. Although the observance of human rights improved dramatically during these years, the enactment and codification of these principles had scarcely begun.

The reform program of the Gorbachev coalition also set distinct limits to the scope of anticipated change, insisting that the goal was the renewal of socialism rather than its dismantling. Economic reform was not intended to introduce capitalism (and indeed marketization and private ownership remained highly contested within the elite); political democratization was to stop short of a multiparty system; and the right of national self-determination was not intended to include the right to secede from the USSR. Time and again, however, efforts to draw a line between permissible and impermissible change were overtaken by events, and the boundaries of toleration steadily widened.

Moreover, in pursuing an increasingly radical program and reaching out for allies among other reformers, Gorbachev gradually alienated the more conservative part of his original coalition and successively removed many of its key spokesmen from positions of power. At the same time, he generated expectations and pressures for change that went well beyond what he was prepared to do. His effort to hold together a centrist coalition was undermined by a growing polarization in which Boris Nikolayevich Yeltsin, expelled from the Politburo in October 1987, emerged as the advocate of more far reaching reform.

Yeltsin, a party functionary in the Sverdlovsk region who was appointed first secretary of the Moscow party committee in December 1985, attracted the attention and support of Muscovites by his outspoken criticism of corruption and privilege within the party elite. His populist style, dramatically demonstrated by his use of public transport in place of an official limousine, precipitated growing conflicts with Politburo colleagues. Removed from the Politburo and from the Moscow party leadership, Yeltsin emerged from a personal and political crisis to compete in the 1989 elections for a seat in the Congress of People's Deputies. His overwhelming victory in the Moscow constituency, despite fierce opposition from the party apparatus, propelled him back into the political limelight as an opposition leader and advocate of more radical reform. Elected president of Russia in June 1991, thereby winning a popular mandate that Gorbachev never sought, Yeltsin forged a coalition of radical reformers and advocates of decentralization and republic sovereignty.

Increasingly alarmed at the prospect of the disintegration of the Soviet system and at the imminent signing of a new federal treaty, a coalition of leading figures in the party, state, army, and police establishment attempted a coup on August 18, 1991. The successful resistance by Yeltsin and the reformers in the capital returned a chastised Gorbachev to power, but the attempted coup had further discredited and weakened the Soviet system. Escalating conflict between Yeltsin and Gorbachev and between the Russian republic and the Soviet "center" culminated in the disintegration of the Soviet Union and its breakup into fifteen states, twelve of which joined together in a new Commonwealth of Independent States. On December 25, 1991, Gorbachev resigned as president of the Soviet Union, and the red flag over the Kremlin was lowered for the last time.

The Soviet Legacy

How the Soviet experience and its memory affect the prospects for democracy in Russia and the other successor states of the Soviet Union remains a matter of controversy. Clearly, the revelations, particularly about the Stalin era, generated a distinct antitotalitarian mood and a massive rejection of terror and repression. Public opinion polls have revealed widespread and consistent, albeit superficial, support for a "democratic" system, though the meaning of the term remains uncertain.

The way in which the Soviet system collapsed was important in shaping its legacy. The speed, the lack of preparation, and the incompleteness of the collapse were all bound to leave their marks. All the newly independent states faced the enormous challenge of building democratic institutions while at the same time carrying out economic reform and engaging in state and nation building with personnel largely lacking in relevant experience.

Understandably, then, despite the collapse of the Communist Party and its various affiliates in virtually all the successor states (with the partial exception of the Baltic states), there has been a remarkable continuity of institutions, elites, attitudes, and patterns of behavior.

Antidemocratic forces, both communist and nationalist, have benefited from a general disappointment with the West and with the initial experience with "democracy," given exaggerated expectations, mounting corruption and crime, the harsh impact of market reforms, and spreading cynicism about politics. Moreover, as firsthand knowledge of the Soviet past recedes and living conditions deteriorate, popular nostalgia feeds on the myths of past Soviet achievements. While the processes of marketization and democratization are unlikely to be reversed, the Soviet legacy makes it likely that the effort to construct and consolidate genuinely democratic institutions will be protracted and problematic.

See also *Baltic states; Belarus; Europe, East Central; Gorbachev, Mikhail Sergeyevich; Leninism; Marxism; Russia, Post-Soviet; Russia, Pre-Soviet; Sakharov, Andrei Dmitrievich; Ukraine; Yeltsin, Boris Nikolayevich.*

Gail W. Lapidus

BIBLIOGRAPHY

Bahry, Donna. "Society Transformed?" *Slavic Review* 52 (fall 1993): 512–554.

Bialer, Seweryn. *Stalin's Successors.* New York and Cambridge: Cambridge University Press, 1980.

Brown, Archie. "Political Change in the Soviet Union." *World Policy Journal* (summer 1989): 469–501.

———, ed. *New Thinking in Soviet Politics.* London: Macmillan, 1992.

Dallin, Alexander, and Gail W. Lapidus, eds. *The Soviet System: From Crisis to Collapse.* Boulder, Colo.: Westview Press, 1995.

Fainsod, Merle. *How Russia Is Ruled.* Rev. ed. Cambridge: Harvard University Press, 1963.

Hahn, Jeffrey. *Soviet Grassroots.* Princeton: Princeton University Press; London: I. B. Tauris, 1988.

Hosking, Geoffrey A. *The First Socialist Society.* Rev. ed. Cambridge: Harvard University Press, 1993.

———, Jonathan Aves, and Peter J. S. Duncan. *The Road to Post-Communism.* New York: St. Martin's; London: Pinter, 1992.

Lapidus, Gail W., and Andrei Melville, eds. *The Glasnost Papers.* Boulder, Colo.: Westview Press, 1990.

Lapidus, Gail W., and Victor Zaslavsky, eds. *From Union to Commonwealth.* New York and Cambridge: Cambridge University Press, 1992.

Moore, Barrington. *Soviet Politics: The Dilemma of Power.* New York: Harper and Row, 1965.

Schapiro, Leonard. *The Origin of the Communist Autocracy.* London: Bell, 1955.

Toker, Rudolf L., ed. *Dissent in the USSR.* Baltimore: Johns Hopkins University Press, 1975.

Tucker, Robert, ed. *Stalinism.* New York: Norton, 1977.

Unions, Labor

See *Class relations, Industrial; Industrial democracy*

Unitary state

A term generally applied to a state in which executive and legislative powers are centrally concentrated and not shared to any substantial extent with institutions below the national level. The term is often contrasted with *federalism,* a term applicable to states in which there is a constitutionally entrenched division of powers, shared between central and state or provincial governments.

Frequently the broad definition of unitary state turns out to be unhelpfully elastic. The numerous states throughout the world that might commonly be described as unitary, including many European, African, and South American countries, differ widely in terms of the constitutional and institutional relationships between their central, regional, and local governments.

The Federal-Unitary Distinction

The distinction between unitary systems and federal systems, which also are characterized by numerous variations, is far from clear-cut. For some purposes the states of a federation may be considered unitary substates, with their own systems of local government.

The distinction is highly elusive, not least because the conditions that characterize a given state as unitary or federal may change over time. There may be a tendency for powers to gravitate upward from the state or provincial governments to the federal government at the center. And, whatever a constitution may say about the relationships between the states and the federal government, there is always in practice a high degree of interdependence between the two levels of government. As Brian Smith observes in *Decentralization* (1985), the main characteristic of a federal state is that it is more difficult than in a unitary state for the central government to encroach upon the powers and status of regional governments.

The picture is further complicated in many countries by recent policies of privatization and contracting out. Thus the upward gravitation of the functions of the local government to the central government may be accompanied by a redistribution of some central and local functions to the private sector and to quasi-government agencies. A state may become more unitary in constitutional form at the same time that it is shrinking and disengaging.

The ambiguities are exacerbated by the political rhetoric that colors the labels that states choose to adopt. Unitary labels signify national strength and unity of purpose, particularly in the international and military arenas. Federalist labels stress a commitment to pluralist democratic values and a willingness to accommodate the diverse needs of a heterogeneous population, particularly in domestic policy.

Types of Unitary States

Unitary states vary greatly in the status they give to local government. Thus the constitution of Japan, ostensibly unitary, defines substantial areas of local government autonomy. In Denmark most domestic public spending is in the hands of elected local authorities. A very different unitary example is to be found in France, which has traditionally operated through a network of centrally appointed prefects, who supervise local affairs in association—or sometimes in conflict—with the elected local authorities of the provincial governments, which are known as departments. The early 1980s saw a decentralization of power from the prefects to the local authorities but not to an extent that significantly altered the unitary character of the French state.

The United Kingdom provides an interesting variation that is almost unique because it has no codified constitution. From 1920 to 1973 the special circumstances of Northern Ireland were accommodated by a quasi-federal arrangement, whereby the province had its own semidetached executive and legislature, with substantial powers. Scotland and Wales are nations within a nation, subject to the authority of the government of the United Kingdom and its Parliament, but with distinct administrative arrangements through territorial ministries. In the late 1970s, when James Callaghan was prime minister, the government got into great difficulty through its unsuccessful attempts to devise coherent legislation that would grant more autonomy to Scotland and Wales while at the same time preserving the unity of the United Kingdom.

Similar policies have reemerged on the political agenda of the United Kingdom in the 1990s. The significant erosion of the already limited autonomy of elected local government has further reinforced the centralist, unitary character of the state in a period when the reverse tendency has been observed in a number of other European countries. Contrasts between the unitary government of the United Kingdom and some federal countries like the United States are sharpened by the fact that the British constitution is based on a fusion rather than a separation of executive and legislative powers. In Britain the prime minister and other members of the government are also members of Parliament. In the United States the executive operates independently of Congress, though with checks and balances between the two. This is not a definitive feature of the federal-unitary distinction, however. Some countries of the British Commonwealth, for instance, are federations with a fusion of powers similar to the Westminster, or British parliamentary, style.

Decentralization and Democracy

The central concentration of power that characterizes unitary states gives rise to many concerns on democratic grounds, particularly in countries with politically significant subunits—such as Scotland in the United Kingdom. These concerns are accentuated as states become more ethnically and culturally diverse. The pluralist position is more or less defined by an antipathy toward such concentration of power and by a preference for decentralization and for federal constitutions. As Patrick Dunleavy and Brendan O'Leary comment in *Theories of the State* (1987), pluralists see unitary states as being constantly vulnerable to capture by political parties or interest groups, a condition that will reduce or even eliminate meaningful political competition. Many totalitarian regimes have adopted arrangements whereby local administration is entrusted to puppets of the central leadership.

Decentralization is seen as a way of improving access for pressure groups and of facilitating and encouraging citizen participation. Decentralization in the form of strong elected local government is a particularly important feature of pluralist thinking. Elected local authorities bring public services closer to the populations they serve. Strong local government provides a counterweight to strong central government; it encourages local awareness of political issues, and it transmits local perspectives and concerns to the central government. It can also be an antidote to overload in the central government. But the success of decentralization depends very much on the nature and the effectiveness of local government systems, and on citizens' perceptions of them.

In summary, the concept of a unitary state provides a useful baseline for discussion of the democratic implications of federalism and decentralization. But the usefulness of the study of unitary states is limited by imprecise definitions and by the tendency of such states not to fit neatly into categories.

See also *Decentralization; Federalism; Local government; Separation of powers.*

Gavin Drewry

BIBLIOGRAPHY

Bogdanor, Vernon. *Devolution.* Oxford: Oxford University Press, 1979.

Dunleavy, Patrick, and Brendan O'Leary. *Theories of the State: The Politics of Liberal Democracy.* Franklin, N.Y.: New Amsterdam Books, 1987.

Lijphart, Arend. *Democracies: Patterns of Majoritarian and Consensus Government in Twenty-One Countries.* New Haven and London: Yale University Press, 1984.

Page, Edward C. *Localism and Centralism in Europe: The Political and Legal Bases of Local Self-Government.* Oxford and New York: Oxford University Press, 1992.

Smith, B. C. *Decentralization: The Territorial Dimensions of the State.* New York: Routledge, 1985.

United Kingdom

An island nation of 58 million people, located between the Atlantic Ocean and the North Sea, that comprises Great Britain (England, Scotland, and Wales) and Northern Ireland. The United Kingdom is a constitutional monarchy and was the birthplace of parliamentary democracy. The country has 94,216 square miles of territory. England, with 50,335 square miles, is the home of more than four-fifths of the entire population. Most live in the southeastern portion of the country, and about 7 million of these live in the capital city of London.

Small size and geographic insularity have strongly influenced the historical development of Britain's democratic polity. Territorial compactness has allowed for remarkably easy communication and centralized government. As an island, Britain has been protected from invasion for nearly a thousand years by the moat that is the English Channel.

The British people thus have been able to develop their political system free from the invasions that ravaged neighboring European states. Change has been accomplished at almost every period of political stress without external intrusion. No unbreachable divisions have opened within the society, as occurred in France after 1789. Rather, the process of negotiated change has progressively legitimized the political system to a remarkable degree. This wide and strong support for its political system explains the reluctance of some in Britain to cede political authority and attendant decision making about public policy to the European Union.

Britain's Political History

Political authority over the centuries has flowed in broad terms from royal absolutism to power sharing between the monarch and the nobility and clergy to, in recent centuries, a widening and deepening of mass participation. As early as the eleventh century, monarchs in Britain had centralized their rule. More than European rulers, they were able to create a direct relationship with landholders, forging a fairly strong network of loyalties. The king thus became an institution of authority, and it was against him that the nobility struggled to preserve its freedom of action. King John's assent to the Magna Carta in 1215 did not create popular democracy in Britain but rather acknowledged that the nobility had the right to resist the monarch's power. The struggle between the strong monarch and the contentious aristocracy in the succeeding centuries established the rule of law and, thereby, limits on the authority of both sides.

Over time, Parliaments and the courts became the institutions in which the struggle between the monarch, the nobility, and the clergy was played out. In its earliest days, Parliament was little more than an informal gathering of representative knights. Meetings were brief and debate was limited to requests the monarch wished to have considered. Only as the king relied more heavily on Parliament's support did the institution take on real importance. The monarchy's need for revenues gave Parliament its leverage. And it was from the arguments about whether and how revenues should be raised that Parliament began to scrutinize what the king intended to do with the money and, subsequently, to insist that the monarch hear and consider its opinions on a widening number of issues.

The seventeenth century was a particularly important time in British political development. Parliament, increasingly aware of its own power, clashed heatedly with a succession of monarchs who either refused to acknowledge power sharing or wished to recapture lost monarchical prerogatives. Bit by bit the monarchy lost its battles and by the terms of each new formal or informal settlement recognized more parliamentary power. During the sixteenth century, Queen Elizabeth I had been a firm ruler who had held the loyalty of Parliament, but her successor, James I, irritated Parliament by his intolerance and arbitrariness.

James's successor, Charles I, worsened relations even more, ruling for eleven years without Parliament, taxing without parliamentary authority, and imprisoning without trial. By the 1640s Britain was in full-scale civil war between those who supported the rights of the Parliament, including Puritans (Calvinistic Protestants), who vocally criticized monarchical power and the nobility, and Anglicans, adherents of the Church of England who supported Charles. In 1649 Charles was beheaded, and Oliver Cromwell became Lord Protector, leading Britain's first and only period of republican government with its only written constitution.

Cromwell was not very successful in the decade of his rule. When he died in 1658, there was little opposition to the restoration of the monarchy. Charles II assumed the throne but with sharply weakened authority. Although he would have preferred a stronger hand, Charles was very careful throughout his more than twenty years on the throne not to provoke open clashes with Parliament. His brother, James II, was not so careful, however, and his open support of Roman Catholicism after he became king in 1685 sparked renewed conflict that ended three years later with his overthrow.

James's daughter Mary and her husband, William of Orange, accepted the throne in 1688 after they had formally agreed to a Bill of Rights in which they recognized the right of Parliament to meet regularly and pass on all revenue matters. Thirteen years later, at the beginning of the eighteenth century, the longstanding religious conflict ended with the Act of Settlement, by which it was agreed that no Catholic could be king of England. The Protestant House of Hanover, it was agreed, would succeed to the throne following the rule of Queen Anne, and Britain formally became a Protestant nation with a Protestant monarch.

Britain could not be considered a modern democracy at the beginning of the eighteenth century (nor even a century later at the beginning of the nineteenth). But the experiences of the seventeenth century established a pattern of power sharing and change within the context of continuing political institutions. The notion of a limited monarch who deferred to the rights of Parliament was established, thus creating the underpinnings for further modernization and democratization of the polity.

The modern era of British politics—characterized by the advent of democratic and representative government—opened with the passage in 1832 of the first Reform Act, which gave more than a half-million men from the upper-middle class the right to vote. The Reform Act was not a gesture of goodwill or generosity by the privileged but a very pragmatic action by those who feared that Britain would suffer violent rebellion unless the door was opened to wider political participation. Many in the British elite were frightened by the example of the French Revolution and were willing, in self-defense, to allow the rising commercial and industrial elite a share of political power. They also were willing to allow significant reform of the membership of the House of Commons. Many critics had vigorously attacked the system of "rotten boroughs" by which influential men controlled seats in the House of Commons based on electoral districts that might contain only a few dozen voters. The reforms of the middle portion of the nineteenth century replaced rotten boroughs with a much more rational and representative system of electoral districts.

It was this reform of the House of Commons, coupled with two additional enfranchisements during the balance of the nineteenth century, that propelled British politics into its more contemporary democratic pattern. Politicians, faced with an electorate that now included nearly all adult men, needed to take notice of and appeal to a very much larger audience. To do this, they began to recognize the necessity of offering voters coherent policy programs and to organize their activities and appeals through permanent party organizations both inside and outside Parliament.

British politics thus arrived in the twentieth century in a form very different from that in which it had begun the nineteenth. Although the supremacy of Parliament and, overwhelmingly, of the House of Commons was well established by 1800, politics was still an elite activity in which a small percentage of British men were enfranchised. By the end of the nineteenth century, politics included most of the adult male population, and competitive and disciplined political parties debated in detail and at length the great issues of the day.

Peaceful Change and Compromise

Although the formal structure of the British political system looks almost as it did in the time of Queen Eliza-

beth I, with the monarch as the head of state, the distribution of power is quite different. Today, the prime minister heads the British government, and the monarch is little more than a ceremonial ruler. Successive prime ministers have held the position because they led the political party that won the most seats in the House of Commons in the previous election—not because they were favored by the king or queen.

The contribution of British history to its political development is therefore the durability of its institutions, the long tradition of generally peaceful change based on compromise (to which the civil war of the seventeenth century and the Chartist riots of the nineteenth were the exception), and the resulting high level of consensus about basic political norms and values. There is a wealth of contemporary evidence that demonstrates the high level of legitimacy the system enjoys, although consensus has been increasingly harder to reach in recent times.

Surveys in Britain over the past several decades have confirmed this dedication to peaceful change through compromise and to the political system, despite the contemporary disgust with incumbent governments and leaders. Few respondents can imagine any situation in which they feel it would be right to violate the law. In practice, as well, the British confirm their support for the rule of law. Many scholars have pointed to the United Kingdom's low rate of crime, especially compared with that of the United States. Even in political life, where the British elite have a penchant for personal misadventures, nearly all of their notoriety stems from sexual adventures of one kind or another, rather than from the financial and political corruption found in other systems.

Functioning of Democracy in Contemporary Britain

The preceding historical review of the emergence and development of British political democracy explains how Britain came to enjoy its constitutional monarchy with a parliamentary form of government headed by a prime minister and cabinet elected directly in free elections. What still needs to be explained, however, is how that parliamentary system actually performs democratically. This question, at first glance, would hardly seem to need any discussion. If citizens freely elect their Parliament, and if the leader of the largest party almost always leads the government, is this not quite naturally a functioning democracy? The answer is, not necessarily.

The British government is dominated by the prime minister and the prime minister's cabinet, with the usually unwavering support of the majority party's members in the House of Commons. (The House of Commons is Britain's only elected parliamentary body; the members of the House of Lords either inherit their seats or are appointed by the monarch.) With nearly certain formal support, the prime minister and the cabinet can almost always expect that they will exert very strong power over the crafting of public policy. Their legislation will be approved by Parliament and implemented by the civil service. Cabinet ministers operate their departments without significant oversight by Parliament.

Given such concentration of political power, therefore, where is Britain's democracy to be found? After all, how effective can an opposition be between elections when it almost never has any chance to defeat legislation proposed by the government? The incumbent government only rarely can be ousted on a vote of confidence. It is also very difficult to conduct serious parliamentary scrutiny of executive actions or policies, as is done through the committee system used by the U.S. Congress to monitor the executive branch. How does the system operate democratically when the formal distribution of political power suggests that a much more dictatorial polity exists?

There is embedded in Britain's politics a subtle but pervasive set of restraints on the government that force it to pay keen attention to the views of the ruling party, the opposition, and the public at large. A few examples of restraining or countervailing processes should illustrate this point.

"Question Time" in the House of Commons

Several devices built into the process of work of the House of Commons preserve the ability of the opposition at least to embarrass the government of the day. One of the most important restraining devices is "question time." On each weekday, except Friday, members of the House of Commons spend a half-hour at the beginning of the session questioning members of the cabinet about their work as leaders of the various ministries. Each minister takes a turn at answering questions; the prime minister appears twice a week.

Members of the government party and the opposition alternate in asking questions, and the event is televised throughout Britain—as is the whole of the House's session each day. Because cabinet ministers and the prime minister do not know what questions will be asked, they must come well prepared.

Little in British politics compares with the excitement of question time. The prime minister in particular is besieged at every appearance, as the opposition seeks to pose embarrassing questions that the prime minister may not be able to answer fully. At the same time, the leader of the opposition tries to defeat the prime minister in the cut and thrust of argument.

To be a successful political leader in Britain, and certainly to become prime minister, means being able to overcome this daily onslaught. For the most part, members of the government do quite well. When the government or the prime minister is in real trouble, however, question time can become a powerful political instrument for the opposition.

In October 1957 Prime Minister Anthony Eden ordered British forces to collaborate with the French in taking possession of the Suez Canal. Their purpose was to prevent the Egyptian government from nationalizing the canal and restricting its use. Almost immediately, the American government objected to the Anglo-French action, and public opinion polls showed a high degree of disapproval by the British electorate. Seizing the opportunity, the opposition Labour Party skillfully used question time to embarrass the Eden government by drawing on, and fueling, the public's growing disapproval. Although the government was never in any danger of losing its majority in the Commons, the embarrassment of question time gradually wore down its resolve. In the end, Eden ordered a British withdrawal. Within a few months he had resigned, his career in ruins.

Restraints on Legislating

The ruling majority is restrained as well by the manner in which British governments develop legislation. The legislative process often begins with political party manifestos at election time. Comparatively speaking, British political parties—unlike their counterparts in the United States—largely follow the policies and plans they describe in these election platforms. With a majority in the House of Commons, however, the government should, in theory, be free to legislate whatever policies it wishes once in the office.

The actual course of policy implementation by legislation turns out to be somewhat different. Although the government drafts its legislative proposals within the ministries, ministers are expected, as a matter of democratic practice, to consult widely with individuals or groups that will be affected by the legislation. Usually, these consultations lead to a discussion document called a *green paper* and eventually to a finished draft of the proposed legislation, called a *white paper*. The idea in both cases is that there should be wide and deep consideration of the proposals.

The discussions that grow out of this process tend to be thorough. The notion is that if the government can use its majority to do whatever it wants, it needs to be especially careful at the prelegislative stage to listen to every possible argument about its plans. In general, the government usually proceeds to accomplish its purpose. However, the details of legislation are often changed in the process of consultation, frequently to a considerable extent. Some legislative proposals do not survive the process; if consultations with relevant interest groups show the ideas to be unworkable, or if they provoke such resistance among the affected groups that they will not be implemented to a useful extent, they may be dropped. Either way, the practice of consultations is a strong example of countervailing power against a majority that could have its way if it was not concerned with being accountable and representative.

During the 1980s the government of Prime Minister Margaret Thatcher was often less flexible than its predecessors in negotiations over proposed legislation. In many cases, however, the government's concessions were often greater than its rhetoric implied. The persistence of social welfare programs after nearly twelve years of Thatcher's Conservative stewardship (1979–1990) is evidence of the prime minister's sensitivity to the fact that the electorate, at bottom, continued to support the basic structure of the welfare state.

The Fall of Margaret Thatcher

The most interesting example of countervailing power in British politics was Margaret Thatcher's fall from power in November 1990. Thatcher was brought down not by the British electorate but by her own Conservative colleagues in the House of Commons. The episode showed convincingly that despite the power of the government, a potential countervailing power is held by the prime minister's usually pliant supporters in the House of Commons.

More than any other British politician in this century, Thatcher dominated her cabinet, her party, the opposition, and British politics in general. She pressed to the maximum the advantages that the British political system offers to the prime minister. For the most part, Thatcher's admirers reveled in her strength, believing that she was the first leader with clear and sensible ideas that Britain had had in generations. They applauded her triumph over interest groups and over dissenters in her own cabinet who wished to take "soft" policy approaches on social welfare programs, defense, foreign affairs, or economic and financial affairs.

By contrast, Thatcher's critics opposed what they saw as her attack on the very fiber of British democracy, arguing that the prime minister stifled dissent from every quarter, even from her most senior colleagues. They complained that over time she eliminated every dissenting voice from her cabinet. Moreover, the House of Commons seemed to them to allow less time for opposition-sponsored debate than previously. Certainly, they felt that Thatcher stifled serious examination of government policies. Specifically, they pointed to questionable actions during the 1982 Falkland Islands war with Argentina, to her interference in freedom of speech and the press, and to her cabinet struggle over policies about the European Community with her chancellor of the exchequer and foreign secretary, Sir Geoffrey Howe. Many argued that Thatcher's eleven-year "rule" had demonstrated the urgent need for legislating a new British "bill of rights" to formally guarantee freedoms and rights that had always been understood before coming under her relentless attack.

During her first eight years in office, Thatcher's enemies, whether in the Conservative Party or in the opposition, enjoyed precious few victories. The Falkland Islands victory, her 1983 and 1987 election victories, the defeat of Britain's coal union in 1985, repeated legislative successes, and comparative economic prosperity were all, as Thatcher would say, part of her pride. By 1988 she stood at the pinnacle of her power, widely admired and respected as Britain's "Iron Lady."

Even her detractors were coming to believe in the truth of Thatcher's promise to "go on and on." It seemed almost certain that she would lead the Conservatives in the next election, which had to be called by 1992. Without a credible threat from the Labour Party, which was still reeling from three straight election defeats, there seemed little reason to expect that Britain would have any other prime minister for the foreseeable future.

Between 1988 and 1990, however, the once buoyant economy sank into its longest and deepest recession since the end of World War II. Politicians in any society lose popularity in times of economic difficulties, but Thatcher had staked much of her reputation on her stewardship of the economy.

Thatcher had come to power out of the ashes of a failed Labour government headed by James Callaghan. That government had suffered a barrage of union strikes during the winter of 1979 that proved to be the final straw in a decades-long struggle by governments of both parties to develop economic policies through consultation and negotiation with myriad pressure groups, especially the unions. The idea had been that British government would provide full employment and social welfare support for British workers in exchange for union cooperation in developing and maintaining economic prosperity by restraining wage and price inflation. The goal was to keep British exports competitive in world trading markets so that Britain could buy what it wanted and needed abroad.

The problem was that government-union deals eventually failed in every instance and the British economy

floundered. Union militancy grew ever more destructive over the years as the economy deteriorated into serious crisis during the late 1960s and 1970s. The voters' rejection of the Callaghan government in 1979 was a rejection of the pattern of politics practiced by both Conservative and Labour governments after 1945. The election of Thatcher's Conservatives brought to power a government with a very different purpose from that of those preceding it.

Thatcher's incumbency was a watershed. Her purpose was the adoption of a new approach to economic, monetary, and fiscal policies that deemphasized government management and enhanced market forces. It also included the abandonment of postwar collectivism in favor of greater central political authority. In this sense, Thatcher was a radical leading the Conservative Party. The uniqueness of her views was to prove quite potent over time in enhancing her power.

The bite of the British recession therefore kicked the pins from underneath Margaret Thatcher's most important strength and greatest self-proclaimed triumph. By 1990 the Conservative Party no longer had confidence that their leader was a political asset for the next election. Public opinion polls, which showed the Conservatives trailing Labour by substantial margins for more than a year, confirmed this pessimism. Eventually, Thatcher's most loyal and long-serving colleagues used the rules of the Conservative Party to oust her as party leader and therefore to remove her from her position as prime minister.

The events leading to Thatcher's resignation occurred with almost lightning speed and surprised almost everyone. The trigger was the resignation of Sir Geoffrey Howe, leader of the House of Commons, deputy prime minister, and the only member of the 1979 government still in the cabinet. Howe had been Thatcher's most loyal and continuous source of support, serving as both chancellor of the exchequer and foreign secretary. Beginning in the mid-1980s, however, he and his replacement as chancellor, Nigel Lawson, had quarreled repeatedly with the prime minister over economic policy and Britain's role in the European Community. Britain's participation in the European exchange rate mechanism, which tied the British currency to the rates of other European currencies led by the German mark, was a particularly sensitive issue. Thatcher had always been less favorable to the European Community than her colleagues were, and she was especially hostile to the idea of British membership in the exchange rate mechanism. Over time these rows had become quite bitter, leading to Lawson's resignation (1988) and Howe's demotion (1989) and eventual resignation (1990). Howe used the occasion of his resignation speech to the House of Commons to attack Thatcher's leadership and policies. He concluded by suggesting that perhaps the time had come for others to take up leadership.

With this opening, provided by Thatcher's most loyal colleague, the onslaught against the prime minister quickly moved into full swing. Using Conservative Party rules that provided for possible annual leadership elections, Thatcher's archrival and former minister Michael Heseltine stood against her. Although Thatcher won a majority of the votes on the ballot, her totals were not enough to ensure victory under party rules. A second ballot was called. Initially, Thatcher declared her resolve to fight on, but she soon realized that the fight was hopeless. Facing the prospect of ultimate defeat, she withdrew and threw her support to two new participants in the contest, Chancellor John Major and Foreign Secretary Douglas Hurd. In the end, Major won when Heseltine, realizing that his own support was fading, withdrew.

The foregoing examples offer just a sample of the arsenal of power that can be brought to bear against the British government and its political leaders. The art of pressing the government is well developed and much used. The example of Thatcher's political demise is an extreme case, however; question time occurs every day and usually does no more than embarrass the government. All the tools described above offset but do not trample on the considerable strength the majority enjoys to govern Britain effectively.

See also *Churchill, Winston; Commonwealth, British; Disraeli, Benjamin; Gladstone, William E.; Ireland; Thatcher, Margaret.* In Documents section, see *Magna Carta (1215).*

Gerald A. Dorfman

BIBLIOGRAPHY

Almond, Gabriel, and Sidney Verba, eds. *The Civic Culture Revisited.* Boston: Little, Brown, 1980; London: Sage Publications, 1989.

Bagehot, Walter. *The English Constitution.* 2d ed. Garden City, N.Y.: Doubleday, 1961; London: Fontana Press, 1988.

Beer, Samuel H. *Modern British Politics.* London: Faber and Faber, 1969.

Butler, David, and Donald Stokes. *Political Change in Britain.* New York: Macmillan, 1975.

Dorfman, Gerald A. *British Trade Unionism against the Trades Union Congress.* London and Stanford, Calif.: Macmillan and Hoover Institution Press, 1983.

Dunleavy, Patrick, et al., eds. *Developments in British Politics.* Vol. 3. New York: St. Martin's, 1993.

Finer, Samuel. *Adversary Politics and Electoral Reform.* London: Anthony Wigram, 1975.

Jones, Bill, et al., eds. *Politics UK.* New York: Philip Allan, 1991; 2d rev. ed. London: Harvester Wheatsheaf, 1994.

McKenzie, R. T. *British Political Parties.* New York: Praeger, 1966.

Norton, Philip. *The British Polity.* New York: Longman, 1991.

United Nations

An international organization, created in 1945 at the close of World War II, intended to prevent war. The United Nations (UN) succeeded the League of Nations. Today it includes as a member every sizable independent state except Switzerland. It is based in New York City but houses some important functions in Geneva, Switzerland, and Vienna, Austria.

When the UN was created, it was assumed that it would have to avoid and remedy the defects of the League of Nations. The League, established in 1919 after World War I, had been unable to prevent another world war. Any attempt merely to renew the League probably would have been unsuccessful.

Founding Principles

The interconnection of the United Nations with political democracy was somewhat more complicated than what had been envisaged for its predecessor. An important premise on which the League of Nations had been founded was that a collective security system maintaining peace would function well if the principal nations in the system were democracies. Thus in 1919 the Soviet Union under the control of V. I. Lenin and imperial Germany were excluded from designing or joining the League of Nations. In 1945, however, given the importance of the Soviet Union after the defeat of Germany and Japan, advocates of the United Nations felt that a more "realistic" assessment of international linkages would have to be brought to bear.

It was crucial to the viability of the United Nations that the United States be a member. Americans had been involved in planning the League of Nations but then had declined to join. If a concern about surrendering certain attributes of sovereignty had played a role in the U.S. Senate's refusal to join the League, some rethinking of the UN Charter would be in order.

Perhaps the greatest difference between the United Nations and the League of Nations (albeit a difference that might be easy to exaggerate) is the veto given permanent members of the UN Security Council. Members of the Security Council's forerunner, the League of Nations Council, had lacked formal veto power. This change addressed two concerns: it ensured that the United States would be a member of the organization, and it took into account the powerful position and expressed wishes of Joseph Stalin's Soviet Union, a nation that, despite some wartime propaganda, could hardly be interpreted to be a political democracy.

The League of Nations had been founded on the premise that democratic self-government might incline every nation toward international peace—including Germany once the kaiser had been deposed and a constitution implemented. The United Nations, in contrast, was founded on the premise that the Axis powers—Germany, Japan, and Italy, the initiators of World War II—were in fact likely to disturb the peace. Although the UN Charter generally renounced war, two provisions (Articles 53 and 107) explicitly exempted interventions against the former Axis powers from this ban.

Thus the United Nations is a hybrid—partly a continuation of the wartime alliance against Germany and its allies (which the French had wanted the League of Nations to be in 1919) and partly a renewal of the League's commitment to collective security and self-government. On a theoretical level the League's commitment to self-determination had been clear. In practice, however, the League made glaring and seemingly hypocritical departures from this mandate. For example, it drew questionable political boundaries in Europe and gave India a seat while that country was still under British rule. The UN's commitment to self-determination and democracy had to be more vigorous, if only because of the Soviet Union's military prominence in 1945.

Some of the specialized agencies and activities of the League of Nations were carried forward into the United Nations, including the World Health Organization and the World Meteorological Organization. (A few changed their names.) The UN's foremost challenge was understood to be keeping the peace.

Membership and Self-Government

Charter membership in the United Nations was to be extended to any nation that had declared war against the Axis powers during World War II. Even Argentina under Juan Perón's dictatorship slipped in because it had made a last-minute declaration of war against Germany. Stalin demanded sixteen memberships in the organization, one for each of the sixteen republics in the Soviet Union. He was placated with three, one membership for the entire country and one each for the Ukrainian and Byelorussian Soviet Socialist Republics.

A few other states were admitted in the first years of the United Nations' existence, but as the cold war settled into place, a period of logjam set in. The Soviet Union proposed membership for the former German-occupied countries in Eastern Europe, states that were saddled with communist dictatorships subservient to Moscow. Western members of the Security Council regularly voted down these memberships, and the Soviets in turn vetoed the admission of states proposed by the West.

In a mild thawing of the cold war, which said more for a perceived need to extend the reach of the United Nations than for a need to promote free elections and democracy, this logjam was broken. In 1955 sixteen nations were voted in as a package deal, with members on each side of the cold war withholding their vetoes. The United Nations might be useful in maintaining peace, regardless of whether democracy was present in the countries involved.

In other ways, however, the United Nations could be seen as vitally committed to democratic self-government. The colonies of France, Great Britain, and other imperial powers were to be admitted to membership in the United Nations only after they had achieved self-government—that is, only after they no longer were ruled from Paris or London or Brussels. The former colonies of Italy and Japan were to be administered as UN trusteeships. Germany had already lost its colonies when it lost the First World War; the former German colonies, which had been administered as League of Nations mandates, became UN trusteeships. UN trusteeships had the same philosophical basis as that articulated by U.S. president Woodrow Wilson for the League of Nations mandates: for a time people might need to be prepared for self-government, but self-government in the near future was the goal. Some international oversight would be required to make certain that territories were not simply shifted from one imperial overlord to another.

Many colonies achieved independence, whether or not they passed through the status of mandates and trusteeships, and UN membership increased dramatically, from 51 members at the inception of the organization to more than 180 in the mid-1990s. To the dismay of believers in democracy, most of these former colonies, now collectively labeled "the third world," did not stick by the basics of democracy very long. Multiparty elections and freedom of the press often gave way to ideological and authoritarian versions of single-party rule. "One man, one vote," a popular slogan for African nationalists, erased any special status for the white minority that had governed their territories. Cynics remarked that this typically meant "one man, one vote, one election."

Democracy and Self-Determination Within the Member States

These new nations, however, even if they arbitrarily overruled contested elections, could in some sense claim to be democratic and representative of the wishes or needs of their people. Consistent with the UN's commitment to democracy, virtually every one of the countries entering the United Nations would describe itself as democratic. (Saudi Arabia and Ethiopia under Haile Selassie were probably exceptions.) Some of these countries, like Sukarno's Indonesia, would speak of "guided democracy." Even the communist countries would claim that their regimes were the will of the people. They never explicitly denounced democracy but described their systems as more democratic than those of noncommunist countries because wealth was shared more equally. (The communist regime in East Germany called itself the German Democratic Republic.) Western ideas about the importance of a free press or competitive elections were ridiculed as "bourgeois democracy."

These countries' claims to be democratic highlight the distinction between political democracy and economic democracy. Political democracy is the principle of government by the consent of the governed. Each person has an equal vote. In addition, political democracies permit freedom of the press and freedom from arbitrary arrest; otherwise, elections would be meaningless because opposition to an incumbent could be stifled. Economic democracy, on the other hand, stresses an equal distribution of wealth. Forthright advocates of communism will admit that they consider economic equality to be so important that competitive elections and a free press should be eliminated wherever they stand in the way of economic equality.

In the 1970s and 1980s it might have seemed to Western liberals and other advocates of political democracy that a majority of nations in the United Nations, in particular the seventy-seven or more self-styled third-world countries, considered economic leveling to be more important than free elections. The votes of the UN General Assembly and of subagencies such as the United Nations Educational, Scientific, and Cultural Organization tended to downplay Western standards of freedom of the press, freedom of speech, and multiparty elections. The suggestion was that justice, economic progress, and economic democracy were more important than the principles of liberal democracy.

The general state of international affairs has somewhat mirrored the trends in domestic politics. The collapse of communist rule in Eastern Europe and in the former Soviet Union has been matched by a disenchantment with one-party rule and Marxist economic approaches throughout much of the undeveloped world. The overall tone of the United Nations in the 1990s is noticeably more consistent with basic concepts of political democracy than it was in the 1970s.

The connection between democratic self-government and international peace has always been entangled with issues of ethnicity and religion. In Asia the boundaries of former colonies that have become independent countries have roughly corresponded with ethnic divisions. The opposite has been the case across Africa, however, where imperialist European states had capriciously carved up the continent. As a result, virtually every country in Africa has had major problems with becoming fully democratic and committed to self-determination. Coordinated through the Organization of African Unity, the newly independent African states (with the important exception of Somalia) basically have forsworn any irredentist claims to "redeem" their ethnic kin across existing boundaries. (These were the kinds of claims that plagued European politics before and after World War I, for example, with Germany seeking to claim ethnic Germans in Eastern and Central Europe and Italy looking at neighboring territory inhabited by Italians.)

The policy of the Organization of African Unity in effect parallels that of the nineteenth-century Austrian statesman Klemens von Metternich in the decades after the defeat of Napoleon Bonaparte: suppressing one important aspect of self-rule and self-determination because it might lead to chaos and war. The inheritance of imperial rule, however, has often enough caused one tribal group to seek to ignore or dominate another (with Rwanda offering a frightening example in 1994), an attitude hardly conducive to fostering political democracy.

Voting

Questions of democracy can be raised in regard to the UN's voting procedures. Some of the new countries admitted to the United Nations were very large in population, while others (like Grenada with only 60,000 people) were very small. If the democratic goal is "one person, one vote," the question can be asked, Will the deliberations of the General Assembly not be skewed by the equal vote given to each sovereign nation, no matter its size?

Moreover, the UN Security Council gives particular voting strength to its permanent members—China, France, Great Britain, Russia, and the United States. The permanent members were chosen not on the basis of demographic size but because they had been major powers in the victorious alliance against the Axis in World War II. These five nations, like the permanent members of the League of Nations Council, always have a vote, while other nations have to take their turn. The permanent members, under the UN Charter, also have the veto.

Some UN components, for example, the International Monetary Fund, have based voting arrangements on financial contribution rather than on size of population or military power. Donors of funds would be unwilling to donate if they did not have a proportionate voice on how the funds were used. But this practice, while realistic, cannot be described as illustrating a commitment to the principle of global political democracy.

Despite these problems, the countries of the world seem basically committed to the principle by which tiny Grenada has the same vote as India in the General Assembly. This commitment shows the importance attached in the UN, as in the League of Nations, to the principle of sovereignty. U.S. senators who opposed the League of Nations regarded the prerogatives of sovereignty as crucial to safeguarding democracy within the United States. Similarly, other democracies have doubted whether a world government could ever be liberal and democratic enough to protect freedoms already established at home. Thus the Swiss have refused to join the United Nations, even though Switzerland hosts many UN activities in Geneva. The traditional Swiss plebiscite, that most democratic of institutions, has voted down UN entry even when the Swiss government recommended it.

But what about the large number of nondemocratic regimes, which have caused so much disappointment and distrust for believers in democracy? Why are these nondemocratic regimes so committed to an equal vote for each state? For most of them, membership in the United Nations, and the accompanying equal prerogatives of sovereignty, are elementary demands of a nationalism that has imitated the older nationalisms of Europe. The insistence on equal votes for all states probably reflects not so much the fear that the United Nations will become a world government as the view that the United Nations serves as an international forum in which governments can assert and express themselves.

If every nation were to become as democratic as Denmark, India, Switzerland, or the United States, would there be less objection to allowing the United Nations to assume governmental functions? Would some countries demand that the votes of the United Nations reflect the relative populations of the member states, rather than assigning nations equal votes or assigning votes on the basis of military or economic power?

Only some of the resistance to a fuller governmental role for the United Nations can be attributed to a desire to protect democracy. A skeptic might note the enormous economic inequalities of the world, with, for example, Denmark, Switzerland, and the United States much richer on a per capita basis than India. Even though India is a democratic state, it might be seen as a tremendous sacrifice for Americans to be taxed by a democratic parliament that assigned votes on the basis of population and thus gave Indians three or four times as many votes as it did Americans. In addition to nationalistic cravings for sovereignty and practical considerations of military power, the elementary selfishness of those who hold a large share of the world's wealth (and desire to keep it) is a prime concern.

Sovereignty Versus Human Rights

In part to ensure U.S. entry into the United Nations, the UN Charter included provisions specifically forbidding intrusions into the domestic affairs of member states. As noted, these provisions are consistent with a concern for preserving democracy and self-determination in any country that already has achieved these goals. Similarly, for states governed by other political systems, these provisions can be seen as protecting the attributes of sovereignty and the prerogatives of existing rulers. The trend nonetheless has been to erode this prohibition. For example, concerns for human rights in the 1980s and 1990s have come to be formulated more broadly than in the past.

The concept of human rights is somewhat unevenly linked to notions of political democracy. Freedom from arbitrary arrest, for example, must be seen as a vital attribute of representative government: an opposition to an incumbent regime cannot make its case to the voters if candidacy leads to arrest and torture or assassination. But opposing torture might be more basic than merely reinforcing representative government. Even if we cannot find an example of democratic governments going to war against each other, we surely can find numerous accusations, even in full-fledged democracies, that police authorities are mistreating prisoners and subjecting people to "cruel and unusual punishment." Human rights thus may seem more basic than democracy, as something to be supported even if democracy is not imminently threatened. Some other kinds of human rights—for example, entitlements to health care and adequate nutrition—seem even less essential than freedom from torture and thus move more in the direction of economic democracy.

If we turn to specific cases of intervention within what once might have been regarded as the preserve of sovereignty, concerns for political democracy play a role as well, though never an exclusive or predominant role. The willingness of the United Nations to intervene in the internal affairs of South Africa, through resolutions condemning apartheid, restrictions on the regime's full participation in UN activities, and finally votes endorsing economic sanctions, reflected a widespread perception that the white government in Pretoria did not represent the great majority of the people living in South Africa.

Perhaps the black African states were being inconsistent, in questioning the self-government of South Africa while never questioning that of Poland under communist rule. The feelings of developing nations—typically states admitted to the United Nations after being released from white colonial rule—surely were understandable on this issue. South Africa, though already a member of the United Nations, was simply being subjected to the same tests that Kenya or Ghana or other developing states had to pass before becoming members of the United Nations. The South African governance of Southwest Africa (Namibia), which Pretoria had ruled as a mandate under the League of Nations but had declined to regard as a trusteeship of the United Nations, was an object of UN concern on the same ground—that the great majority of

the population was being governed without its consent.

UN ventures into deploying military forces have mostly been exercises in stopping wars ("peacekeeping") rather than commitments to establishing democracy. Again, however, an interesting pattern is developing. Foreign interventions in Cambodia after the Communist takeover by the Khmer Rouge in 1975 ultimately led to the deployment of UN peacekeeping forces. These forces, which were charged with conducting a democratic election to establish the next Cambodian government, probably never would have emerged out of concern for self-determination. Rather, they were deployed because of the enormity of the massacres inflicted by Pol Pot's regime.

Here, as in the cases of South Africa and Namibia, one sees a standard of human rights that transcends democracy. The absence of democracy pales when compared with more basic transgressions against the human condition. Perhaps democracy is an antidote to war or to massacres and holocausts; perhaps it is not. Most UN intervention has been aimed at ending wars and holocausts. But—as shown by its reentry into the business of monitoring elections, as it did at the beginning of the 1990s in Cambodia and El Salvador—the UN has not completely renounced the idea that democracy is appropriate as a means of preventing wars and massacres.

The immediate problem in Somalia in 1992 was the prospect of large numbers of people starving rather than the absence of free elections. If Somalia had simply remained one of the many member states of the United Nations that permitted no free press or multiparty elections, no Security Council or General Assembly votes would have been taken on its future, and no UN-sponsored military intervention would have taken place. In view of the breakdown of political and social structures in Somalia, there could hardly have been designs to set up a democratic structure for its future governance. Yet the bias of the United Nations—like that of Woodrow Wilson and his colleagues who drew up the League of Nations—is still largely that, in the long run, self-government is the only appropriate arrangement for this territory, as for any other.

When the United Nations intervenes in the internal affairs of territories, it still tends to justify the intervention by declaring that there is a threat to peace in that particular situation. The definition of *peace* is very broad. A "realist" might note that Somalia posed a greater threat to peace when it had some government and military structure than when its foundations were in a shambles. As long as Somalia had some structure, it had threatened Ethiopia and other neighbors (using the classic arguments that ethnic Somalis were being governed against their wills and natural inclinations in Ethiopia, Djibouti, and Kenya). Thus starvation in Somalia may have supported rather than undermined international peace. Starvation is horrible, intolerable to an outside world watching it on television, but it rendered Somalia incapable of pursuing any new wars with Ethiopia.

Similarly, the UN intervention in the former Yugoslavia in the early 1990s was broadly defined as seeking to preserve international peace. The United Nations and the major Western powers had been quick to recognize the independence of Slovenia, Croatia, and Bosnia-Herzegovina so that any "crossing of boundaries" would be an act of war. Yet the boundaries had been created so recently that political and military conflict was bound to occur, causing frustration for the UN in its peacekeeping efforts. The major motivation for this UN intervention was not strictly the keeping of international peace but rather a response to the democratic preferences of the peoples involved—of the non-Serbs who did not want to be governed by Belgrade. But preserving self-government and preventing "ethnic cleansing" proved much more difficult than simply preserving peace.

An Uncertain Future

The United Nations promises to be a vehicle, more often indirectly than directly, for democracy. Entry into the United Nations has, to some extent, been predicated all along on self-government, even though no such explicit requirement exists. Its original structure was somewhat bent to take into account the character of the Soviet Union and its satellites, but these states have been replaced by governments that are pursuing political democracy. Concerns about peace, and about preventing starvation or discord or massacres, are usually tied, indirectly, to support for free elections. With the people of many nations now seeing post–cold war events as favorable to political democracy around the globe, it will not be surprising if the United Nations becomes more closely engaged in democratic pursuits.

Much of what happens in the United Nations depends on whether democracy truly takes hold in Latin America, Eastern Europe, the former Soviet Union, and the parts of Asia that are trying to abandon Marxist economic systems while retaining one-party political systems. If democracy

solves many domestic problems, as it has in North America and Western Europe, the international workings of the United Nations may become intertwined with a commitment to government by the consent of the governed, thus pushing this organization in the direction envisaged by Wilson for the League of Nations. But if democracy fails in Russia or India or Brazil, or if it does not develop in China, the United Nations may revert to its 1960s and 1970s role of moderating and reflecting international power competition and serving as a battleground for various ideologies.

See also *Human rights; International organizations; League of Nations*. In Documents section, see *Universal Declaration of Human Rights (1948)*.

George H. Quester

BIBLIOGRAPHY

Barros, James. *The United Nations: Past, Present, and Future.* New York: Free Press, 1972.

Claude, Inis L. *Swords into Plowshares.* New York: Random House, 1971.

Falk, Richard, ed. *The Strategy of World Order.* New York: World Law Fund, 1966.

Finkelstein, Lawrence, ed. *Politics in the United Nations System.* Durham, N.C.: Duke University Press, 1988.

Gati, Toby Trister, ed. *The U.S., the U.N., and the Management of Global Change.* New York: New York University Press, 1983.

Haas, Ernst B. *Collective Security and the Future International System.* Denver, Colo.: University of Denver Press, 1968.

Humphrey, John P. *Human Rights and the United Nations.* Dobbs Ferry, N.Y.: Transnational Publications, 1983.

McWhinney, Edward. *United Nations Law Making.* New York: Holmes and Meier, 1984.

Meron, Theodor. *Human Rights Law-making in the United Nations: A Critique of Instruments and Processes.* Oxford and New York: Oxford University Press, 1986.

Peterson, M. J. *The General Assembly in World Politics.* Boston: Allen and Unwin, 1986; London: Routledge, 1990.

Schiffer, Walter. *The Legal Community of Mankind.* New York: Columbia University Press, 1954.

Taylor, Paul Graham. *International Institutions at Work.* New York: St. Martin's; London: Pinter, 1988.

United States Constitution

The fundamental law that establishes the U.S. government's structure, defines its jurisdiction, and declares the rights of persons in that nation. The Constitution was drafted at a constitutional convention in Philadelphia in 1787 and ratified in 1788. The original Constitution establishes a federal republic; the amended Constitution provides the legal framework of American democracy.

The unamended Constitution is a remarkably brief document composed of seven articles. The first and longest article concerns the composition and powers of Congress. Because Congress was to have only the powers delegated to it, a broad range of topics was covered: the powers to tax, to regulate commerce, and so on. The second article establishes the offices of president and vice president and defines their powers. The third article establishes the Supreme Court, authorizes subordinate tribunals, and explains their jurisdictions. The fourth article controls interstate relations. The fifth article establishes the procedures for amending the Constitution. The sixth article declares that the Constitution is the supreme law of the land and all public officials are sworn to uphold it. The last article declares that the Constitution shall take effect when it is ratified by nine of the then thirteen states.

Twenty-seven amendments have been added to the original Constitution, the first ten of which, added in 1791, are called the Bill of Rights. The American Revolution was fought to protect the claimed rights of the colonists; the Constitution with the Bill of Rights sought to protect the rights of Americans. The concept of constitutionally protected rights was part of the English heritage.

Colonial Background

The colonists in America believed that English rights and liberties came with them when they crossed the ocean. Indeed, several of the colonies' charters stated that those born in the colonies would be entitled to all the liberties of the English born. Many of the colonial charters specified that orders and statutes must not be contrary to the laws of England.

When the colonists declared their separation from Great Britain in 1776, to become independent states, they parted with the constitutional rights of the English. Without membership in the British Empire, they could no longer claim the protection of the English constitution. Consequently, the revolutionary foundation for rights and liberties reflected a radical shift in position.

In place of the rights of the English, the Declaration of Independence proclaimed the natural and inherent rights of man. There was no need for the protection of the En-

glish constitution when an appeal could be made to a higher authority, the laws of nature and of nature's God. The historic claim in Great Britain that citizens might not be taxed without the consent of representatives of their own choosing was expanded in the Declaration to the broader claim of citizens not to be governed without their consent.

The unwritten British constitution was a composite of statutes, principles, and judicial orders, which could be changed at any time by a simple act of Parliament. The constitutions of the newly independent states were written documents intended to be beyond the reach of simple legislative majorities. Only the body politic acting through representatives chosen for the task, or exceptional majorities of the legislature, could draft a constitution. The law contained in a written constitution was the higher law of republican government.

Eleven states drafted written constitutions, in response to the Continental Congress's call to the states to establish their own frames of government; Connecticut and Rhode Island continued government under their self-governing charters. Virginia, in 1776, was the first to draft a state constitution; this constitution included a section ensuring certain rights. Several other states used the Virginia rights language as a model. In style similar to the Declaration of Independence, the section on rights stated that all men by nature were equally free and possessed inherent rights of which they could not be deprived when they entered society; these rights were life, liberty, with the means of acquiring and possessing property, and pursuing and obtaining happiness and safety. The underlying theory was that even governments based upon the consent of the governed needed to be restrained by constitutional checks when they approached the sensitive area of personal liberty.

Creating the System

A basic claim to liberty found in many revolutionary documents asserted that people ought to be protected from abusive and arbitrary government. The difficulty faced by the Framers of the Constitution in 1787 was how to achieve a political system strong enough to govern yet so contrived as not to be arbitrary or abusive. Monarchy and arbitrary power existed almost everywhere in the Old World. Was it possible to establish a durable republic in the New World containing checks within the system that would protect the liberties of the people?

The system developed by the Framers was remarkably innovative. The government would be republican, rather than monarchical, aristocratic, or directly democratic. Offices would be held in accordance with representative principles, but much of the representation would be indirect: electors would choose the president and vice president; state legislators would select the senators (changed by the Seventeenth Amendment in 1913 to popular election); delegates to the House of Representatives would be elected by the people; judges would be appointed by the president, subject to confirmation by the Senate. The terms of office holding were so arranged that there would not be a complete turnover of power in one election. Delegates to the House of Representatives would be elected for two years; senators would be elected for six years, with the terms staggered so that only one-third of the senators would be selected every two years; the president would be selected every four years; judges would hold office for life (assuming good behavior).

The Constitution established a federal system in which power was divided; some was held by the states and some by the new federal government. The power placed in the central government was delegated; that remaining in the states consisted of all those powers not delegated to the federal government and not prohibited to the states. The central government guaranteed to the states a republican form of government.

Within the Constitution, prohibitions were placed on Congress as well as the president. There was a functional division of power among the branches of the federal government. The French philosopher Montesquieu, John Adams (who became the second president of the United States), and others believed that a separation of power among the legislative, executive, and judicial branches was essential to protect the liberty of the citizens. Tyranny consisted of consolidating these separate powers in one office. The Constitution set up the proper procedures for the exercise of power so there were checkpoints throughout the system. For example, the passage of laws required the concurrence of both houses of Congress as well as presidential approval.

Another feature of the Constitution, which was implied though not stated, was that the judicial branch of the government had the power of judicial review. That is, the courts in cases actually before them could determine whether legislative or executive actions had violated the Constitution. If these actions were found to be in viola-tion of the Constitution, they could be declared void. The Constitution was declared to be the supreme law of the land. This interpretation of judicial power was clearly explained in *The Federalist* by Alexander Hamilton, who later became the country's first secretary of the Treasury. In *Marbury v. Madison* (1803), Chief Justice John Marshall established a precedent for judicial review by declaring an act of Congress unconstitutional.

Ratification

This constitutional system, the Framers hoped, would protect the citizenry from arbitrary and abusive power. Interestingly, the Constitutional Convention did not provide for a bill of rights. The issue of a bill of rights in the new Constitution did not come up until late in the convention, when George Mason—who had been one of the drafters of the Virginia Constitution—suggested that one could be written in just a few hours and that it would give great quiet to the people. He proposed that a committee be appointed for that purpose. The convention, voting by states, rejected the proposal.

When the Constitution was put out to the states for ratification by conventions held in each state (the assent of nine states was required), it was evident that the issue would be very close in Massachusetts, New York, and Virginia. The support of these large and important states was critical.

In the debate over ratification, those who favored the new constitution as written were called Federalists; those opposed were called Antifederalists. A series of newspaper articles were written in 1787 and 1788, to persuade the voters in New York to ratify the Constitution. The authors were Hamilton, James Madison (who became fourth president of the United States), and John Jay (later chief justice). The articles were also published in book form as *The Federalist*. Thoughtful, erudite, and lucid in exposition, these articles have endured as the clearest statement of what the Founders of the U.S. political system intended by their labors.

Those who opposed ratification, the Antifederalists, included Mason, Richard Henry Lee, and Elbridge Gerry. They argued that among other deficiencies the document lacked a bill of rights. The Antifederalists believed that a new convention should be held to revise the whole plan before the states should be called upon to ratify it.

Hamilton responded to these criticisms in *Federalist* Nos. 84 and 85. He argued that no power had been delegated to the federal government to do the things that a bill of rights would prohibit. Furthermore, there were already basic rights in the Constitution: bills of attainder (which declare a person or group guilty of a crime and impose punishment without a trial) and ex post facto laws (which are applied to acts committed prior to passage of the laws) were prohibited; the writ of habeas corpus could not normally be suspended; crimes had to be tried before juries in the state where the crime had been committed. Indeed, Hamilton argued, to specify particular rights in a bill of rights might be harmful, as it would suggest that the only rights citizens had were those specified in the Constitution.

Several of the Federalists, however, seeing their plan in trouble, agreed to a compromise schedule. They wanted to proceed with ratification, and they promised that a bill of rights would be added in the form of amendments at the first opportunity. Several states, including Massachusetts, New York, and Virginia, had attached proposed bills of rights to their ratifications. Fortunately, the Framers of the Constitution had designed a workable system of amendment. Amendments might be proposed by two-thirds of both houses of Congress or by a convention called for by two-thirds of the state legislatures. Such amendments would take effect when ratified either by the legislatures in three-fourths of the states or by conventions in three-fourths of the states. Congress would decide which mode of ratification would be used. This strategy was successful. The Constitution was ratified in 1788, and the national government was organized under it in 1789.

Madison and the Bill of Rights

In Madison's view, the Constitution was incomplete without a bill of rights. Elected as a representative from Virginia, he brought up before the first Congress the issue of the promised bill of rights. Some of the Federalists stressed again that because the federal government had only those powers delegated to it, it could not act where power was not delegated; therefore a federal bill of rights was unnecessary. Delegated federal power was not like the reserved powers held in the states, it was argued; states required bills of rights to curb potential abuses of their reserved power. Antifederalists argued that wherever federal power bore directly on individuals there was the possibility of abuse. Federal power could not be checked by state bills of rights which applied only to state governments. The Antifederalists also pointed out that two of the states,

North Carolina and Rhode Island, which had not ratified the Constitution, were holding back until there was a bill of rights.

Madison made a strong plea for a list of rights to be enacted as amendments to the Constitution. He argued that even if the proposed rights were unnecessary, they could do no harm as extra precautions against an abuse of power. The passage of such amendments would bring reassurance to those who had doubts about the Constitution, of whom he thought there were still a great many. Thus a bill of rights would increase support for the new government, and there was, after all, nothing to lose. Furthermore, Madison argued, even if a list of rights constituted only a paper barrier and was ineffective in checking abuses of power, it would help to focus attention on these rights and arouse public opinion to support them; moreover, the courts would consider themselves the guardians of those rights.

Madison proposed a set of rights which he thought would be agreeable to all of the states. He proposed a preamble to the Constitution that would state the purpose of government in terms similar to those used in the Declaration of Independence and in the Virginia Constitution of 1776. He recommended that the additional specific rights be fitted into the existing framework of the Constitution, rather than added on to it. Congress, however, rejected that arrangement in favor of listing amendments at the end of the original Constitution.

This first Congress proposed twelve amendments; conventions in the states ratified ten of them by 1791. Neither of the defeated proposals was directly concerned with rights. One applied to the size of Congress in relation to population, and it soon became obsolete with the rapid growth of the population. The other prohibited Congress from voting itself pay raises that would become effective before the next election. Curiously, this amendment received the requisite number of state ratifications about 200 years later, in 1992.

Constitutional Rights

The passage of the Bill of Rights would not have been possible had there not been broad agreement among the people as to what liberties were of such basic importance that without their protection one's life, liberty, property, and pursuit of happiness would be in jeopardy. Among the more than two dozen rights listed in the first ten amendments are those that prohibit Congress from establishing a religion or impeding the free exercise of religion and those that prohibit Congress from abridging free speech, freedom of the press, the right of assembly, or the right to petition government. People have the right to bear arms and to be secure against unreasonable searches and seizures. Troops may not be quartered in citizens' private homes.

Several of the amendments deal specifically with judicial procedures and processes. These include the right of the accused to be indicted by a grand jury, to call witnesses, to confront the accuser, to have counsel, to be entitled to reasonable bail, and to have a speedy public trial before a jury drawn from the district where the crime was committed. No punishment may be cruel or unusual. Following the enumeration of specific rights are two general amendments. The Ninth Amendment declares that the enumeration of rights is not meant to deny or disparage others retained by the people. The Tenth Amendment declares that those powers not delegated to the federal government, nor prohibited to the states, remain with the states and the people.

One of Madison's proposed amendments, which passed the House of Representatives but failed in the Senate, would have prohibited any state from violating the equal rights of conscience, freedom of the press, or trial by jury. Madison believed that these rights would be more endangered by the state governments than by the federal government. Had this amendment become part of the Constitution, states would have been subject to the same restrictions as the federal government regarding conscience, the press, and jury trials.

It was not until the enactment of the Fourteenth Amendment in 1868 that the states were prohibited from denying any person the equal protection of the laws or from depriving any person of life, liberty, or property without due process of law. Even then, these prohibitions were narrowly interpreted for a time. For nearly 150 years the courts found the restrictions in the Bill of Rights applicable only to the federal government. Then, commencing in the 1920s, and in an increasing number of cases over the next forty years, the Supreme Court ruled that the prohibitions in the Fourteenth Amendment meant that no state could violate the fundamental rights listed in the Bill of Rights. Today substantially all of the rights in the Bill of Rights apply in the states as well as at the federal level.

Since the Constitution has been in effect, it has been changed more often by decisions of the Supreme Court than by the formal amendment process. For example, the Court held in 1896 that racial segregation was acceptable under the Constitution, but it overruled this decision in 1954. Among the twenty-seven amendments enacted by the formal amending process, only one has radically altered the constitutional edifice erected by the Founders. That amendment (the Seventeenth, ratified in 1913) made senators popularly elected rather than selected by the state legislatures. In this case, as well as in the cases of most of the other amendments, the political thrust of the changes has been to democratize the Constitution. In essence, the constitutional amendments have democratized the political bases of office holding while they have extended the rights of the citizenry. The republic established in the late eighteenth century has become more nearly a democracy in the late twentieth.

See also *Adams, John; Antifederalists; Checks and balances; Constitutionalism; Contractarianism; Declaration of Independence; Federalism; Federalists; Freedom of speech; Hamilton, Alexander; Locke, John; Madison, James; Marshall, John; Natural law; Property rights, Protection of; Separation of powers; States' rights in the United States.* In Documents section, see *Constitution of the United States (1787).*

Alan P. Grimes

BIBLIOGRAPHY

Anderson, Thornton. *Creating the Constitution: The Convention of 1787 and the First Congress.* University Park: Pennsylvania State University Press, 1993.

Bernstein, Richard B., and Rice, Kym. *Are We to Be a Nation? The Making of the Constitution.* Cambridge, Mass., and London: Harvard University Press, 1987.

Farrand, Max, ed. *The Records of the Federal Convention of 1787.* Rev. ed. 4 vols. New Haven and London: Yale University Press, 1966.

Grimes, Alan P. *Democracy and the Amendments to the Constitution.* Lanham, Md.: University Press of America, 1987.

Kammen, Michael. *A Machine That Would Go of Itself: The Constitution in American Culture.* New York: Knopf, 1986.

Lutz, Donald S. *A Preface to American Political Theory.* Lawrence: University Press of Kansas, 1992.

Miller, William Lee. *The Business of May Next: James Madison and the Founding.* Charlottesville: University Press of Virginia, 1992.

Morgan, Robert J. *James Madison on the Constitution and the Bill of Rights.* Westport, Conn., and London: Greenwood, 1988.

Storing, Herbert, ed. (with Murray Dry). *The Complete Anti-Federalist.* 7 vols. Chicago: University of Chicago Press, 1981.

Wood, Gordon S. *The Creation of the American Republic, 1776–1787.* Chapel Hill: University of North Carolina Press, 1969.

United States of America

The largest and one of the oldest of the world's democracies. The United States was not born as a democratic nation. The original European settlers of North America brought with them deeply embedded ideas about the normality of economic and social distinctions—rigid hierarchies of power, privilege rooted in status, and deference to one's betters. Their system of beliefs undergirded the reality of the social and political inequality in which they all lived. These traditional notions and practices were deeply planted in the soil of the New World. Social distinctions and great inequalities of status and wealth were a reality from New Hampshire to Georgia, along with the most undemocratic of social and economic institutions: slavery and indentured servitude.

Yet dynamic forces pushing toward democratic changes were also present from the beginning of colonial America. Rooted in seventeenth-century movements in England that were directed against the unchecked power of the monarchy, and reinforced by religious ideas that challenged rule from the top, these forces included notions of more widespread access to power, the right of free debate, and liberty of individual conscience. The two revolutions against English kings in the seventeenth century, and the rise of parliamentary power—that is, rule by popularly elected representatives—affected the attitudes of Americans as well as those of the English. Radical democratic ideas promoting greater political power for the masses, first heard in the English Civil War of the 1640s, were heard in America as well. Although such ideas never became dominant, they did help seed the ground from the beginning with a sense of human relationships that stressed political equality and the will of the people.

It is easy to treat a democratic triumph in the New World as inevitable, evolving inexorably from the seventeenth through the twentieth centuries. But democracy never grew smoothly in American soil and always contained contradictions and anomalies. It was, at first, fiercely contested by opponents who doubted the fitness for political democracy of the poorly educated, the non-English immigrants, and the lower classes. Over time, that resistance weakened significantly, but it never disappeared entirely. As a result, democratic achievement occurred in fits and starts; had setbacks, limitations, and inconsistencies; and emerged largely as a result of events in three transformative eras.

When Americans celebrated democracy it was, for much of the nation's history, as a national ideal to be achieved largely in terms of specific political practices. But there always was a tension between two kinds of political democracy: individual and representative democracy. The solution was to extend political rights to each citizen who, in turn, exercised that right by casting a vote for someone to represent him in the government. Yet claims were also made from the first that political democracy could not be achieved outside a local community context in which free individuals came together directly, not through elected representatives, to deal with problems of governance themselves, acting as both legislators and constituents, and subordinating their individual desires and needs to the larger common good.

From the seventeenth century on, individual democratic rights rooted in suffrage and majority rule gained the upper hand in America over the communitarian notions that were also present. The people delegated authority to representatives who acted as their agents in a larger government framework. These representatives had to obey the people's mandate or risk losing their seats in a subsequent election. Communitarian democratic ideas never completely disappeared, however; they reemerged as a significant force from time to time, particularly in moments of crisis when some people found representative power rooted in suffrage more restrictive and less democratic than they thought it should be.

Colonial Setting

As they emerged, colonial political practices reflected the conditions of the settlers' background. As in England, political offices were dominated by social and economic elites. Elections to colonial legislative assemblies occurred quite early, but only a small portion of the population could take part: men who had the property and status that presumably ensured their commitment to the common welfare. Under such terms, most settlers were unable to participate in elections or hold office. Voters were expected to, and did, defer to those who held high status in the society, even when casting a free vote in an election. Finally, responding to the "will of the people" was, at best, a minor aspect of traditional political practice. Although those in power might consider public opinion at times, they were unlikely to be heavily influenced by it. As a result, democratic popular expression was limited in the formal institutions of colonial government, although there were individual acts of discontent, occasional mass

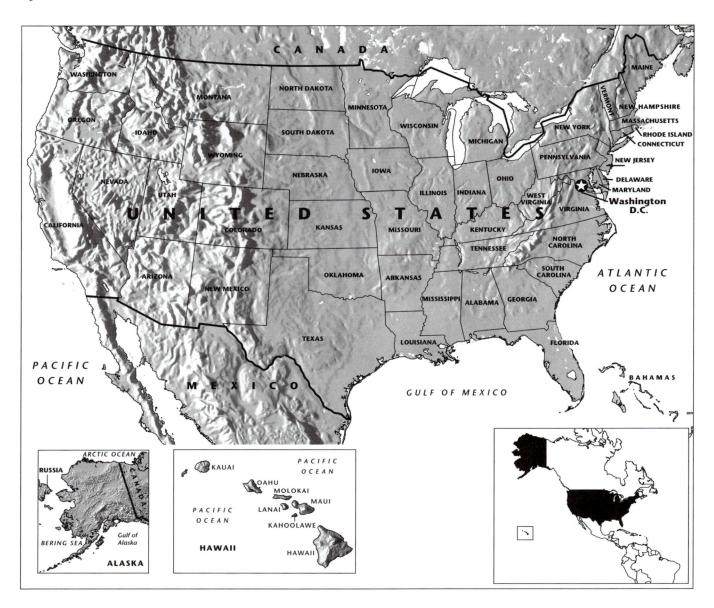

demonstrations, or outbreaks of rioting over specific grievances.

A cluster of economic, ideological, and circumstantial factors helped modify these long-established, undemocratic practices. Conditions in the New World made the usual social hierarchies and inequalities less stable than they were in the home country. From the first, some white men, at least, found themselves freer than anyone had anticipated from the kinds of restrictions on movement, economic aspirations, speech, and behavior that characterized their original homeland. In the colonies there was more freeholding (independent ownership of property),

the basis of access to power, than in England. In addition, the lack of aristocratic structure and the fierce competitiveness of local political warfare promoted a relatively broader distribution of economic and social power and of political opportunity than had been the case in anyone's previous experience.

At the time, hierarchical church structures and exclusionary religious creeds were still dominant, if no longer unchallenged, in England. In contrast, colonial America had a much larger number of sects that were less authoritarian in organization and creed and thus more democratic in their political implications. Among Puritans, power resided not in appointed archbishops and bishops but in small congregations in which direct participation and face-to-face exchange among relative equals characterized relationships. Such churches did not directly challenge authority, but their tenets argued against automatic submission to earthly hierarchies, questioned traditional notions of power and authority, and reframed the issue of how inclusion in decision making was determined.

The democratic implications of these different elements quickly became clear. Individual changes occurred, from styles of address between former unequals to the assertiveness of colonists claiming their rights. As politics evolved, unworkable or obsolete restrictions on political expression and participation were ignored, and community decision-making gatherings such as New England town meetings became a democratic reality (even when they were dominated by elite community leaders). Community elites found themselves appealing to masses of people for support during difficult battles over economic policies or against the distant authority of the English government. Colonial life was filled with examples of democratizing impulses, ideas, and practices, all taking root in a society that was still theoretically nondemocratic.

These antiauthoritarian and democratic tendencies appeared at different times and developed at different rates. At first, only partially egalitarian results were possible. Conflicting ideas about the extent of the people's right to rule, as well as a profusion of both democratic and undemocratic forms, institutions, and practices, brought with the settlers from their European homelands, continued to exist side by side. Many of the groups who had always been excluded from the right to political participation were still excluded.

Property holding remained the main indicator of having a stake in the society and consequently the determinant of the right to vote. Although landholding in the colonies was greatly liberalized in comparison with that in Europe, it did not extend to the majority. Thus many more settlers remained excluded from the political process than were incorporated into it. Office holding remained the province of those with high social status. In nearly every colony, voting restrictions based on religious affiliation and residency prevented some groups from participating in politics. Into the 1760s democracy, while clearly a growing factor in colonial life, was far from a fully realized condition.

From the Revolution to the Jacksonian Era

Between the 1760s and the 1830s American society and politics took a significant democratic leap forward in the first of the three transformative episodes in which traditional undemocratic elements were diluted and the nation largely democratized. The American Revolution began as a war for independence from England and a revolt against the unchecked power of the king. It became much more: an internal upheaval that significantly advanced colonial democratic tendencies. Over time the institutions of political competition, originally established among elites, incorporated an ever widening range of citizens. The right to vote spread, and the institutions of democratic expression and competition became institutionalized, accepted, and largely routinized. From the Revolution onward a persistent democratic discourse and egalitarian everyday behavior permeated American life.

The nation's revolutionary Founders were not democrats: they challenged the king's power in the name of a representative republican government, in which elites ruled, although not arbitrarily. They also recognized the right of citizens to participate in political decision making. Local notables, however, quickly found their traditional control of the levers of power challenged—and overturned in many parts of the emerging nation—by an upsurge of communitarian democracy. Crowds took control of the revolutionary situation in different localities, bypassed formal political authorities, and sought to rule on behalf of all, as the Declaration of Independence's commitment to universal equality and rights was taken seriously in the first flush of the social upheavals of the 1770s.

The communitarian democratic impulse dominated matters only briefly. Formal institutions of government made a strong comeback during and after the Revolution, albeit with more extensive democratic qualities. The pluralism of interests competing for power on the scene played an important role in these developments. As elite groups jostled for advantage at the levels of state and nation, new political practices and structures emerged as combatants found them useful. During the Revolution competing gentry courted the people in election campaigns, often incorporating populist rhetoric into their appeals. They even conceded some reforms; in particular, they agreed to expand popular suffrage. Their courting and concessions helped, slowly, to open the formal government system to democratic impulses and popular involvement in state and national decision making.

The newly drafted state constitutions of the 1770s began to fix the democratic impulse firmly into place. Property qualifications and religious tests for voting were weakened or eliminated as citizenship and an individual's stake in society were redefined. In some states the franchise was extended to those who paid taxes or had served in the military. In the most democratic expansion yet, residency, rather than social status or economic condition, became more prominent as a defining norm of political participation. More frequent elections were mandated, along with secret ballots. Single-house legislatures became more common, independent of review by an undemocratic second institution (a house of lords or a governor's council), as had been the norm. Clearly, a consensus was forming, derived from the Declaration of Independence, that government drew its authority from the consent of the governed.

This commitment to democracy did not go unchallenged. Democratic practices and participation were often sporadic, irregular, and uneven in effect. Some states were slower than others to respond, and not all democratic measures spread everywhere. Many pockets of undemocratic restrictions and practices remained. The notion that democratic politics must include restraints on the popular will was never lost. Requirements for political participation changed, but restrictions were still present. Leadership remained largely in the hands of community elites. Critically, the years after the Revolution were a time of popular disturbances in America on behalf of broader reforms, which gave force to those who argued against further political equality. Democracy, they contended, would too often descend into dangerous anarchic behavior, as it had in Shays's Rebellion in Massachusetts in 1787, when riotous crowds had challenged the regularly elected government of the state. Such outbursts made it clear that the people could not be trusted to behave responsibly without political checks on them.

The U.S. Constitution codified most of the practices that were already in place, especially the authority of elected representative institutions, and elaborated protections for individuals against arbitrary acts of the government. At the same time, safeguards against popular impulsiveness were also included: a second legislative house, with membership based on territory, not population, and elected indirectly; a president who was also chosen indirectly; and an unelected Supreme Court. The Supreme Court and the president were equal in power to the representa-

tive institutions included in the new framework. Insistence on the need for such constraints was to echo repeatedly in American political thought until well into the twentieth century as one of the persistent anomalies of American culture and practice.

Despite these setbacks American democratizing impulses continued to exert pressure on the scene after 1787, often as the unplanned byproduct of ongoing political battles. Those who joined with Thomas Jefferson and James Madison in the Democratic-Republican Party in the 1790s used egalitarian rhetoric to counter the threat of a strong national government. In their efforts to resist the powerful centralizing tenets of Alexander Hamilton's policies at the national level, Jefferson and Madison strongly championed the ideal of local authority and supported popular resistance to a central government power that threatened to crush the will of individuals and majorities. Their political movement called on voters to serve as the bulwark against the continuing threat from the antipopular government elements in the United States.

Although the Democratic-Republican Party never pushed democratic impulses to their fullest extent, its successors came much closer to doing so, especially in the areas of suffrage, representation, and leadership. In the Jacksonian era and its aftermath, between the 1820s and 1850s, the expansion of political democracy touched all but a very few American white men. President Andrew Jackson, and the movement that he led, did not create these currents. Some of the Jacksonians' behavior ran counter to democratic ideals, and their rhetoric went beyond what they actually accomplished. But their challenge, in the name of the people, to the dominant political establishment of the day transformed the democratic impulse into a full-blown conception of democratic nationalism limited primarily by race and sex. As a result, persistent democratic tendencies in the United States became ever more firmly rooted, and significant challenges to democratic purpose and practice all but disappeared.

What impelled the surge forward at that time? Certainly, the origins lay in the loosening of old restraints on individual expression, rights, and majority power that had occurred in the colonial and revolutionary periods; an array of more recent changes in American society had vigorously pushed these democratizing impulses beyond their original limits. Although in the first third of the nineteenth century, economic and social disparities remained prominent in the United States, a democratic temper—in speech, outlook, behavior, and, ultimately, in the realities of political power—grew stronger and stronger. Democratization was once again furthered by religion, as revivals sweeping the nation in the 1830s invigorated the notion that individuals stood equally before their God, not needing clergymen to mediate their relationship.

The remains of the old social hierarchies, rooted in the English past, had weakened significantly, and the new hierarchies that emerged were different in important ways. Property still defined position in America. But access to land and rapidly expanding commercial opportunities in cities opened new possibilities so that more people were able to move into an increasingly permeable, extended, and politically empowered middle class. The expansion of suffrage rights continued to define the widening political democracy of the nation. Individual states ended almost all the remaining property qualifications for voting and substituted minimal residence requirements. As a result of these changes, by the 1840s, most adult white male citizens in the United States could vote, and a large number of them did.

The Jacksonians organized these social and economic elements into a national movement dedicated to the further democratization of all the institutions of society. Their rhetoric emphasized common virtues, individual rights, and majority rule, more fervently than had ever been the case before. They were adept at borrowing and expanding populist techniques and commitments, originally developed by various mass political movements at the state level, to further their own purposes. They took every opportunity to set a democratic tone beyond anything that previously had been the norm, including such dramatic individual demonstrations as the unprecedented opening of what had been called the Presidential Palace (today's White House) to the people on Jackson's inauguration day in 1829. This invitation was joyously taken up with much damage to the president's home but also with a powerful sense of popular participation and belonging.

Political parties took on new meaning in this environment. Organized competition and distinctive policy proposals became a regular feature of democratic politics. Both Democrats and Whigs sought to mobilize the largest possible electorate behind their competing policy views. Political competition between these two mass-based political parties repeatedly stressed populist themes as the bases of their appeals, reducing complex policies to easily understood scenarios of the people versus their enemies.

Party organizations provided both symbolic and real opportunities for leaders and citizens to interact with each other. Candidates and officeholders frequently met with the voters in regular local meetings and in the course of widespread campaign activities. Through these interactions leaders learned the boundaries of what they could do.

During the Jacksonian era opportunities to hold office, though never fully egalitarian, expanded beyond the long-established social hierarchical pattern of leadership. Social elites still held most offices. But the basis of political leadership broadened to include small-town lawyers, newspaper editors, farmers, businessmen, and professional, full-time politicians. Historians remain skeptical that many Americans rose to the higher reaches of political power from the lower portions of society; however, many people attained higher positions in the political world than had earlier been possible.

All this profoundly affected the meaning of elections, which remained the central forum of popular expression and control in the Republic. Their number was extraordinary. Every year, somewhere in the nation, elections for local officials, party officers, and national positions took place, all with the trappings and realities of a democratic political culture. As parties organized themselves for these frequent elections, they advanced—partly by accident, partly by design—the democratic revolution in style and structure that was already under way. Candidates for office had to stress their roots in the people, and ostentatious behavior was a political liability. Like Jackson, all candidates had to become the people's champion.

Jackson's enemies, the leaders of the Whig Party, stung by charges that they were the heirs of earlier Federalist opponents of America's democratic destiny, were quick to align themselves with populist currents. They appealed to the masses with much the same populist vigor that the Jacksonians brought to election contests. Although some saw deception in Whig behavior, one could see this behavior as a result of the degree to which democratic notions and behavior had permeated American politics.

To be sure, many of these democratic practices glossed over the continuing realities of elite power, undemocratic conditions, and less popular control of politics than was claimed. Amid the exuberant celebration of individual freedom, some Americans continued to search for community-centered democratic norms. As long as people who were voted into office could decide matters for everyone, elites would remain in control. As an alternative, many would have preferred that people in a community come together to work things out.

Nevertheless, despite limitations and criticism, the electoral activities promoted and managed by the political parties provided arenas for the most widespread participation in political activities yet known in American life. Hundreds, even thousands, turned out to rally for their party in campaign meetings, including people who were not eligible to vote. Large numbers actively participated in the excitement of a form of popular access to the political world that was otherwise unknown. Voters responded in extraordinary numbers to all these democratic activities, claims, and demands. Popular turnout to vote increased significantly from 1828 onward, soaring to unprecedented heights in the 1840s, as the people flocked to the polls to make their will known.

Unfinished Business

By the end of the Jacksonian revolution, although many social and political inequities remained in America, the democracy that had evolved went well beyond anything known to that point, anywhere. But American democracy had not reached all Americans, the complacency of the people and the claims of publicists and politicians notwithstanding. Democracy remained more circumscribed than popular rhetoric and belief had it. Protest meetings and mass demonstrations were held at times, as some continued to feel that their democratic rights were denied. One such mass protest, led by Thomas Dorr in Rhode Island in the 1840s, on behalf of the democratization of the state's ballot laws and of its government, actually took on the status of a revolt. Dorr's Rebellion was brief and intense, but it remained a significant indicator of the meaning of democracy and a reminder that all levels of government must not hesitate in reaching the full implications of national democratic purpose.

Gaps in the democratic matrix remained, and efforts to expand democracy continued to be hindered by those who saw in unbridled democracy serious threats to American well-being. Jackson's triumph had not convinced everyone of the virtues of full democracy, even as most went along with the changes that had occurred.

Efforts to prevent further expansion of democratic practices persisted. Nativists made a brief but potent effort to question the right of the massive wave of immigrants that came to the United States in the 1840s and 1850s to participate freely in American elections. Many of the immigrants were illiterate peasants from Ireland and Germany, unable, it was claimed, to vote in a reasoned way. Furthermore, many of these immigrants were Catholic, and nativists alleged that they were not capable of free thought and behavior, since they were under the control of priests and the pope. Presumably, such immigrants could not be good citizens; their participation would debase American democracy. Nativists organized to try to impose rigorous restrictions on the newcomers, demanding that naturalization laws include a twenty-one-year residency requirement for voting. Yet, significantly, even the nativists did not try to do more than impose delays on voting, acknowledging the right of immigrants to vote at some point.

The most critical gaps in the democratic reality of the middle of the nineteenth century were in the areas of gender and race. Women did not enjoy equal status with men economically, socially, or politically. They could not vote, and their other civil rights—to own property, to enter into contracts, and to have individual standing in court—were severely circumscribed. Women were largely confined by custom and law to the domestic sphere of family and home, and they were all but totally dependent on their husbands or fathers.

Similarly, the nation still contained the greatest anomaly of all in a democratic system: slavery. In the United States this institution began with the colonists' taking advantage of an opportunity to obtain cheap labor by buying Africans who had been kidnapped and enslaved. Slavery took hold throughout the colonies but was abolished in the industrialized North by the early nineteenth century. It grew stronger in the South, however, as the labor-intensive cotton economy expanded. By the 1830s more than three million African slaves lived below Mason and Dixon's line; none of them had any democratic civil, social, or political rights at all. Northerners and southerners alike accepted, and even defended, that status quo. Here was a massive contradiction between theory and practice. But in the United States democratic rights were assigned to whites only; many Americans accepted this racial distinction and strongly resisted both ending slavery and extending rights to free blacks. (Immigrant Asians, as nonwhites, were denied citizenship as well, under the provisions of a naturalization law passed in 1790.)

Thus, while white suffrage expanded during the Jacksonian era, many northern states, in keeping with the racial notions that characterized American democratic practice, denied or severely restricted voting rights for the African Americans living among them. At the beginning of the nineteenth century some northern states allowed free blacks to vote. By the 1850s most of them no longer did, as a result of state laws passed during the previous generation. Many northern states also forbade African Americans to reside within their borders. Neither the Whigs nor the Democrats challenged the assumptions underlying these measures. In *Dred Scott v. Sandford* (1857), Chief Justice Roger B. Taney (a Jackson appointee) led the Supreme Court to elaborate a theory of racially limited citizenship and democratic rights. (Taney also maintained that in such racial matters the Supreme Court was not obligated to follow the views of electoral majorities in the nation.)

Expansion and Contraction

As a consequence of the Civil War and Reconstruction, from 1861 to 1877, a second major expansion of political democracy occurred in the United States. Organized efforts on behalf of granting basic civil rights, including suffrage, to women and African Americans had been undertaken from the 1840s onward. Both the abolitionist and the women's suffrage movements kept up a persistent campaign into the 1860s, despite powerful opposition to their position. They were frequently disappointed. Most northern states refused to extend the right to vote to African Americans even with the abolition of slavery at the end of the Civil War. But sympathetic Republican leaders in Congress proved strong enough to overcome such hesitancy and pass, then secure the ratification of, the Fourteenth and Fifteenth Amendments to the Constitution by 1870. (Similar attempts to extend economic democracy to former slaves through the distribution of land to them failed.) For the first time there was a national definition of citizenship and a universal (if negative) standard for democratic eligibility: no state could deny someone the right to vote on the basis of race. Consequently, those relatively few African Americans who lived in the North were able to vote and, for a brief period, so could thousands of former slaves and their descendants in the southern states.

Women's rights leaders had yoked themselves to the movement for African American rights in the expectation that they too would win the vote. But their specific demand for women's suffrage was not enacted into national law at the same time as the Fourteenth and Fifteenth Amendments. There was powerful resistance to women's suffrage as well as threats to African American gains. Moreover, in the case of *Minor v. Happersett* (1875), the Supreme Court ruled that the Fourteenth Amendment's "equal protection of the laws" clause did not justify claims that women could also vote.

That major setback was partially offset when some states subsequently enacted limited women's suffrage for some types of elections, usually local elections or those concerned with family and education matters (traditionally women's concerns). Disappointment in this limited outcome was profound. The suffragist movement continued to press its case vigorously in the last decades of the nineteenth century. But this pressure had little effect. In a male-dominated society, democratic political rights still eluded most women.

The late nineteenth century was a troubled time for American democracy in both the political and the economic spheres. From the 1870s to World War I, the process of democratic political expansion in America was reversed in several areas. One was the disenfranchisement of African Americans in the South. Aroused by the civil rights gains of the Reconstruction era, white-dominated southern state legislatures in the 1890s enacted a wide array of restrictions and barriers to voting participation. The Mississippi Plan of 1890, which was widely copied and extended by other southern states, included extraordinarily complicated procedures for voter registration, literacy and character requirements for eligibility, and overwhelmingly confusing ballot procedures to greet those who made it to the polls on election day. These provisions successfully thwarted the purpose of the Fifteenth Amendment and eliminated the franchise of almost all blacks (and many poor whites) who lived in the former slave states. The Supreme Court and Congress went along, agreeing that states retained the authority to set voting qualifications as they always had and taking a narrow view of the national rights standards supposedly embodied in the Fifteenth Amendment. Obviously, the power of racial distinctions still held sway in a society otherwise dedicated to democratic ideals.

At the same time even many of those who usually championed American democracy were increasingly beset by fears that it was in growing danger and had to be protected. They saw compelling evidence toward the end of the nineteenth century that democracy was being corrupted by an onslaught of new forces led by avaricious party bosses, masses of voters indifferent to American traditions and values, and selfish economic royalists determined, and able, to hold sway over popularly elected governments. The flood of immigration from eastern and southern Europe from the 1880s on created a particularly dangerous crisis, in some minds, for America's democratic tradition and the future of the nation. Nativist polemics once more became a feature of American political discourse.

These fears for the nation's future came at a crucial moment in American life. A major economic transformation, the Industrial Revolution, had reshaped the American landscape and social order by the late nineteenth century. Concentration of economic power in the hands of a new class of financial and industrial leaders, such as J. P. Morgan and John D. Rockefeller, threatened the nation's democratic institutions as such men used their unprecedented economic power to dominate the political sphere. Through their financial clout they corrupted politicians and controlled the political parties, Congress, state legislatures, and the courts to an unprecedented extent. Government, including the courts, appeared to be hostage to them. Individuals seemed defenseless in the face of such economic power. The outrage expressed against this state of affairs was widespread, loud, and repetitive.

In the 1890s the Populists argued that fundamental economic and social changes could still save American democracy. The socioeconomic underpinnings that had nurtured American democracy had been dislodged by the new urban industrialism, with its overwhelming concentration of economic power. Political democracy, the Populists argued, could not be effective without a return to economic equality and the vesting of real authority in local communities. They worked to reclaim democracy by attacking concentrated economic power and its allies, the corrupt, undemocratic urban political machines, which had as their base of support many of the recent immigrants. They challenged the commitment of most Americans to the two major political parties as well, because both Democrats and Republicans were captives of the industrial monoliths. Despite their energy and commitment, the Populists largely failed in their efforts, since they confronted a world that had grown very different from what they had hoped for and a society in which communitarian democratic arguments no longer took hold in any large-scale way.

In the next decade another group of reformers, the Progressives, focused their efforts on the machinery of political decision making. Like the Populists, they sought to rein in concentrated economic power and the authority of party leaders. In particular, they pushed a number of proposals that, they argued, would expand democratic capabilities. These included the direct election of U.S. senators as well as changes in ballot procedures to guarantee the nonpartisan administration of elections and fair counts of the results. The Progressives also advocated new forms of direct democracy so that concerned citizens, rather than corrupt party representatives, could set public policies. The direct primary (in which citizens, not party bosses, nominated candidates for office), the initiative (which permitted people to petition to place policy proposals on the ballot in the absence of legislative actions), the referendum (to permit people to vote directly on policy proposals even if the legislature had already passed them), and recall (of elected officials by a new popular vote) all promoted democratic participation unmediated by, and often directed against, state and national representative institutions.

The Progressives used democratic rhetoric incessantly, even when they put forward antipartisan proposals that reduced the democratic control of government decisions. In an effort to weaken the control of party bosses (and of the immigrants who backed them), they worked to make many administrative positions appointive rather than elected. They advocated government by experts—in which policies would, they claimed, be formulated scientifically and carried out by trained technicians secure from the power of removal by the electorate and changes in party power. They also pushed forward, as others had in the 1850s, restrictions on voting by recent immigrants. In addition, the Progressives mounted a widespread campaign to save democracy by promoting it at home through mass education and patriotic reminders of the nature of the American heritage.

The result of the Progressives' efforts was a redefinition of democratic participation that restricted suffrage through more stringent voter registration laws and expanded the use of literacy tests for potential voters. Both proposals successfully limited the political rights of recent immigrants who did not speak English. Still, as in the past, the right of white male immigrants to achieve democratic participation in elections was not fully denied by these restrictions, as it continued to be for women, African Americans, and Asian Americans.

Completion of Political Democracy

America's democratic possibilities seemed to reach their apogee during and immediately after the two world wars of the twentieth century, the third period of democratic expansion. Persisting constraints on the democratic ideal gave way to the logic of the nation's commitments, powerfully stimulated by the totalitarian threats of the kaiser's and Hitler's Germanies. Progressives had vigorously pressed for the expansion of American democratic values overseas into less friendly, unenlightened areas. President Woodrow Wilson's assertion that the United States entered World War I in 1917 to make the world safe for democracy epitomized the notion that, having successfully secured the most democratic state in the world at home, the United States had an obligation to defend its values against outside enemies and to take democratic lessons everywhere. As a result of these battles to make the world safe for democracy in 1917–1918 and in 1941–1945, there was much pressure to complete democratic commitment in the United States by extending the right to vote, and guaranteeing the exercise of that right, to all adult citizens.

As before, this reform wave did not immediately sweep all before it. Patterns of undemocratic behavior and values persisted through both wars. In World War I, aliens and dissenters were victims of arbitrary actions by the government as well as of popular repression through mob action, often in the name of saving democracy. In World War II, Japanese Americans were interned in the name of defending the nation, an action upheld by the Supreme Court.

Many Americans resisted extending democratic political rights to women or guaranteeing them to African Americans and other people of color. It was nearly impossible to change these Americans' convictions, which supported a divided society, regardless of the changes that had taken place.

Women's suffrage was achieved with the ratification of the Nineteenth Amendment to the Constitution in 1920. The long years of agitation by reform groups finally bore fruit, aided by the enlarged role women had played in public life during the Progressive Era, and especially during World War I. As women went to work in war plants, and joined or worked with the armed forces to defend American democracy, opposition to political participation by women weakened significantly and then gave way. Women became enthusiastic participants in elections from the mid-1920s onward, although few went the next step up the democratic ladder to hold elective office.

In the 1920s and 1930s little changed politically for most African Americans. The New Deal under Franklin D. Roosevelt, which began in 1933, saw an expansion of government regulation of economic matters, and elite power was further limited. Given the power of southerners in the Democratic Party and in Congress, however, Roosevelt and his colleagues, for fear of endangering the rest of their policy agenda, hesitated to try to extend the rights of African Americans. Yet, as women's role in World War I had helped advance their rights, the forces unleashed by World War II advanced the cause of African American political rights. The process was slow and painful, but the issues raised by the war itself and the battle against a uniquely violent antidemocratic Nazi state awakened Americans to the destructiveness of limiting democratic rights on the basis of racial prejudices. (The same forces worked to persuade Congress, at last, to remove the 150-year-old ban on citizenship for immigrant Asians.)

As Asian Americans and African Americans fought in the armed forces, and as thousands of African Americans migrated north during and after the war in search of economic opportunities in shipyards and defense plants, their potential political power was not ignored by politicians. Because they were able to vote in the northern states, and were mobilized to do so by party leaders, African Americans began to emerge as a powerful bloc in the Democratic Party in the years after 1945. Civil rights organizations effectively mobilized a reform coalition on behalf of rights long denied. As a result, civil rights for African Americans became prominent on that party's, and the nation's, political agenda from 1948 on. The Democrats split that year over putting a civil rights plank in their national platform. This was only the first episode in a long series of battles in the 1950s and 1960s, including demonstrations by civil rights organizations and violence against demonstrators, which culminated in the passage by Congress of a number of civil rights laws. The most important of the civil rights laws was the Voting Rights Act of 1965.

Fired by the unrealized implications of the American democratic tradition, civil rights and voting rights organizations maintained constant political pressure on Congress, the president, and the courts. In a meaningful shift in tactics, these groups began to focus almost exclusively on the national government as the key to democratic fulfillment. Government was no longer seen as democracy's enemy. Rather, it had become democracy's promoter and guardian. Since the 1920s, for example, the Supreme Court had moved toward taking the Fourteenth Amendment's equal protection clause more seriously by weakening the most egregious restrictions on African Americans' right to vote in southern state party primaries. But it took the 1965 Voting Rights Act to fully mobilize the national government to ensure that African Americans could register to vote and go to the polls unhindered.

The civil rights revolution of the 1960s also successfully promoted federal laws and constitutional amendments that ended the poll tax—an expense that had prevented poor blacks (and whites) from voting—and extended the right to vote in national elections to eighteen-year-olds. (The states soon lowered their age requirements as well.) From the 1950s to the 1980s the Supreme Court also pushed the state and national governments to widen electoral opportunities. The federal courts, in fact, became unique promoters of democratic expansion from the 1950s on. They moved far from their earlier role as a bastion of unelected, lifetime-tenured defenders of limits on democracy.

By the 1970s all adult citizens in the United States could vote if they registered to do so. Literacy and state residence requirements had loosened a great deal. African Americans began to turn out in large numbers, and consequently to transform southern politics, from the 1970s onward. Ultimately, they appeared in southern sheriffs' offices, city councils, mayors' offices, state legislatures, governors' offices, and Congress for the first time since their brief experience of freedom during Reconstruction a century earlier.

Democracy and Its Discontents

Many Americans believed that the nation had reached a prosperous, egalitarian, democratic pinnacle by the 1960s. There were frequent celebrations in the popular media and in election campaigns of the uniqueness and pervasiveness of American democracy. Every aspect of American life seemed to be democratic. American cultural expression and activities became more populist and leveling than ever before, as elitism in American culture from education to art came under repeated attack. In the face of such assaults the remaining barriers to most forms of popular expression, control, and direction fell.

Yet, as always, anomalies in the democratic condition complicated the celebration. If the first definition of political democracy was citizens' participation at the polls, the nation was in serious trouble. As more Americans had won the franchise, fewer had turned out to vote; the decline was precipitous from the 1940s onward. Toward the century's end only about half the eligible citizens regularly turned out to vote in presidential elections, and only about one-third of those eligible voted in the off-year congressional elections. A surprising number of Americans do not register to vote; their lack of participation in the political process indicates that too many procedural barriers remain in place.

The decline of political parties, once the most important mobilizers and organizers of voters, has meant the loss of effective mechanisms to bring people into the voting universe, stimulate them, and keep them there election after election. Some analysts have argued that turnout has declined as citizens have become cynical and indifferent because political leaders have consistently failed to live up to their promises, have repeatedly deceived the people, and have not been accountable to their constituents. These analysts are concerned that the people's indifference and cynicism is weakening American democracy.

As democracy expanded in America, its meaning seemed to change. In the eighteenth and nineteenth centuries, and for much of the twentieth as well, democracy had clearly meant that the most individuals possible would have access to political expression and that leaders could be expected to take their cues from the voters. By the late twentieth century, however, critics of American democracy believed the ballot box was no longer the forum for democratic expression; so voting was not the epitome of political democracy. Echoing many earlier critics, they argued that voting rights and competitive elections were not enough, especially in the changed and much more complicated conditions of late industrial America.

More and more government decision making seemed resistant to electoral decisions or democratic control. Virtually all political institutions—parties, legislatures, bureaucracies—reached their decisions in ways that cut them off from their own alleged source of legitimacy, the will of the people. In the media age Americans now inhabited, critics suggested, elites had learned how to engineer consent from the public. Public support, or at least acquiescence, could be obtained through the effective building and manipulating of images in the press—especially on television—in ways that brought elites the results they wanted. The public, meanwhile, believed the fiction that they were making unfettered choices.

Critics charged that, once elected, representatives became separated from the will of those who had elected them, bowed to the power and authority of large campaign contributors, not their constituents, or were powerless to accomplish anything in the face of undemocratic power centers. Democratic majorities no longer had more, or even as much, power as did specific organized interests, which could blithely ignore the will of the people. Government now largely consisted of appointed, permanent bureaucracies, free of direct electoral control. Most of their decisions were beyond the review of the electoral arena and often were made with indifference to voters' wishes. The result was ill-advised and contentious policies, such as U.S. engagement in the war in Vietnam in the 1960s and 1970s, which were quickly seen as illegitimate. Representative democracy had become meaningless. What good were voting, political parties, or duly elected representatives of the people?

Some reformers responded to the democratic distemper of the 1960s by demanding the further democratization of political institutions and more direct access by more people to the levers of power. They called for and helped pass laws to open up party nominations and conventions and to expose government activities to the widest possible publicity and public scrutiny. Others sought change through technology, calling for the mobilization of public opinion on specific issues through the use of modern media such as television rallies, call-in shows, and interactive presentations that allowed the people to be heard.

Other critics suggested such tinkering or technological activities were not good enough. Instead, they sought alternative means of democratic expression, often outside the electoral arena and representative assemblies. To Tom Hayden, a leader of Students for a Democratic Society, America was a "false democracy" ripe for reform, if not revolution. He and other critics suggested that democracy would be reinvigorated only through the widespread adoption of participatory democracy. This was to be undertaken first through the building of small communities at the workplace, in schools, and in politics, unfettered by large-scale institutions and free of the power of important groups, which only got in the way of democratic expres-

sion. Such communitarian ideals—a vision of equal people living together harmoniously, making decisions together democratically, in the interests of all—which had always been present in American democratic thought, took on new vigor in the 1960s.

Confrontation became common as groups turned to street demonstrations and other direct challenges to specific government policies. The new left, civil rights activists, and anti–Vietnam War groups persisted in massive challenges to most existing institutions of authority, making constant attempts to reform, or even to destroy, them in the name of a more democratic United States.

Changes in Democracy

Although the methods and aims of these critics varied, they were united by their refusal to accept traditional notions of political democracy rooted solely in the vote. To most Americans, however, popular elections still mattered; yet something had to change. The exercise of electoral democracy had not produced social and economic equality. Democratic reality, many realized, was not achieved through electoral access alone. It would be necessary to move beyond the individual to recognize the undemocratic reality of group deprivation because of longstanding, unyielding prejudice and majority indifference to minority needs. The emphasis, reformers argued, should be on group-based, not individual-based, democracy. If groups could not realize their aims because they were outvoted or dispersed, they could not enjoy the fruits of democratic rights. In a democracy, the majority could not deny minorities their rights or voting would be a tool of oppression, not a democratic liberation.

Race-blind approaches to voting and office holding, and simple faith in majority rule, then, were inadequate to remedy a situation that had systematically put racial minorities at a disadvantage. The issue of representation came to the fore. Assuming that minority voters would be represented most faithfully by members of their own racial community, it would be necessary to create legislative districts that could favor the election of someone from that community.

The Supreme Court under Chief Justice Earl Warren and the lesser federal courts, taking their cues from the top, issued an unprecedented series of decisions in voting rights cases from the 1960s on. These decisions confirmed both the symbolism and the substance of democratic rights. In perhaps the farthest reaching decisions, the

Court mandated a mathematical standard of representation in the apportionment of congressional seats by state legislatures. Organized protest groups, this time particularly in the African American community, had brought the issues into the judicial system. Once again such groups had proven instrumental in an expansion of democratic political rights.

Not everyone favored wholesale changes in American democracy in the 1960s and later. Observers from varied political camps instead focused on the nation's democratic achievements, not its failures. The cold war had provided a number of opportunities to push democratic ideas abroad through private and government propaganda agencies such as the Voice of America and the National Endowment for Democracy, as well as through a variety of American education and aid programs. Such efforts helped American democracy grow even stronger. The end of the cold war in the late 1980s proved how strong and important the American democratic tradition was, as people breaking free from totalitarian domination in Europe and elsewhere turned to the United States for guidance in bringing democracy to their lands.

Such triumphs and appeals, some people argued, underscored that whatever problems existed American democracy remained the best there was anywhere. Many who felt that way were outraged by the criticisms and demands of the dissatisfied in the United States. They saw a tendency toward anarchy and the breakdown of American national unity in the anti-institutional, group-rights outlook of the post–Vietnam War, post–civil rights movement generation. Multicultural democracy was pulling apart the sinews of a common history and ideology. The government was oversympathetic, in their view, to these destructive notions. All sorts of license were now permitted, endangering national cohesion, prosperity, and democracy itself.

Echoes of earlier ideological differences and political battles were clear in this debate. Critics continued to reveal anomalies in the democratic experience, and democratic ideas were still vigorously in play at the end of the twentieth century. Thus conflicts over the nature and adequacy of American achievements were certain to persist in a society that many times in its history had believed that it had finally achieved full democratic reality, certainly more than any other place on earth, only to discover that much was left to accomplish.

See also *Adams, John; Americans, Ethnic; Civil rights; Communitarianism; Declaration of Independence; Jackson, Andrew; Kennedy, John F.; Lincoln, Abraham; Madison, James; Marshall, John; Revolution, American; Roosevelt, Franklin D.; Roosevelt, Theodore; Slavery; States' rights in the United States; United States Constitution; Washington, George; Watergate; Wilson, Woodrow; Women's suffrage in the United States.* In Documents section, see *American Declaration of Independence (1776); Constitution of the United States (1787).*

Joel H. Silbey

BIBLIOGRAPHY

Barber, Benjamin. *Strong Democracy: Participatory Politics for a New Age.* Berkeley: University of California Press, 1984.

Countryman, Edward. *The American Revolution.* New York: Hill and Wang, 1985; Harmondsworth, England: Penguin Books, 1991.

Dahl, Robert A. *Democracy and Its Critics.* New Haven and London: Yale University Press, 1989.

Dubois, Ellen. *Feminism and Suffrage: The Emergence of an Independent Women's Movement in America, 1848–1869.* Ithaca, N.Y.: Cornell University Press, 1978.

Ginsberg, Benjamin. *The Consequences of Consent: Elections, Citizen Control, and Popular Acquiescence.* Reading, Mass.: Addison-Wesley, 1981.

Goodwyn, Lawrence. *Democratic Promise: The Populist Moment in America.* New York and Oxford: Oxford University Press, 1976.

Graham, Hugh Davis. *The Civil Rights Era: Origins and Development of National Policy, 1960–1972.* New York and Oxford: Oxford University Press, 1990.

Hanson, Russell L. *The Democratic Imagination in America: Conversations with Our Past.* Princeton: Princeton University Press, 1985.

Kousser, J. Morgan. *In Pursuit of Power: Southern Blacks and Electoral Politics.* New York: Columbia University Press, 1985.

———. *The Shaping of Southern Politics: Suffrage Restriction and the Establishment of the One-Party South, 1880–1910.* New Haven: Yale University Press, 1974.

Morgan, Edmund Sears. *Inventing the People: The Rise of Popular Sovereignty in England and America.* New York and London: Norton, 1989.

Morone, James. *The Democratic Wish: Popular Participation and the Limits of American Government.* New York: Basic Books, 1990.

Nieman, Donald G. *Promises to Keep: African-Americans and the Constitutional Order, 1776 to the Present.* New York: Oxford University Press, 1991.

Rogers, Donald W. *Voting and the Spirit of American Democracy: Essays on the History of Voting and Voting Rights in America.* Urbana: University of Illinois Press, 1992.

Tate, Katherine. *From Protest to Politics: The New Black Voters in American Elections.* Cambridge, Mass., and London: Harvard University Press, 1993.

Uruguay

A small country in South America located between two powerful neighbors, Argentina and Brazil, which has one of the oldest party systems in the world. In the early twentieth century, Uruguay was well known for advanced political and social experiments, which caused it to be dubbed a "model country."

Uruguay is also known for its unusual electoral system—double simultaneous vote—which permits factions of the same party to accumulate votes toward winning the presidency. Under this system, electoral officials count the ballots to determine which party won the election. The candidate of the majority faction of the winning party is then elected president.

In spite of its long democratic record, Uruguay in the 1960s and early 1970s experienced revolutionary warfare, which led to the breakdown of democracy in 1973. Twelve years of military rule followed. During this period, political activity was forbidden for the parties and social movements of the left and was frozen for the traditional parties.

An initiative to modify the national constitution was promoted by the armed forces then in power, but it was rejected in a 1980 plebiscite. The military then negotiated a transition to democracy with the political parties. A democratic government was installed in 1985, after a competitive election from which one of the main actors was excluded.

Roots of Uruguayan Democracy

After a brief colonial history as a frontier territory coveted and disputed by the Spanish and Portuguese empires, Uruguay became an object of contention among factions of revolutionaries seeking independence from the Spanish crown. The region comprised a fortified port city, Montevideo, and an open interior, where cattle and *gauchos* (cowboys) roamed free. The unruly and combative gauchos posed a perennial threat to the authority of Montevideo. They were responsible for the egalitarianism that became a distinctive trait of Uruguayan society.

The rebellion of 1811 began the process of independence from colonial rule. It was an uprising of *criollo*, or landowners of Spanish descent, against the merchants of Montevideo. The landowners were led by a radical rural chief, or *caudillo*, José Artigas. Influenced by the ideas of

the American Revolution, Artigas advocated federalism and provincial autonomy and upheld the right of the people to bear arms and resist oppression. From the philosophers of the French revolution, he adopted the ideas of egalitarianism and the defense of the "rights of man and the citizen," including religious freedom.

Artigas's ideas and the myth surrounding him left their imprint on Uruguayan political culture. A decade of pacification followed the rebellion, first under Portuguese rule and then under the control of Argentina. Uruguay became independent in 1828, thanks to the mediation of Great Britain. The newly founded republic had an important geopolitical role in the Rio de la Plata region, as a buffer state between two powerful antagonists, Argentina and Brazil.

The New Nation

The new Uruguayan state was a republic with a restricted, tax-based franchise. The government, based in Montevideo, favored the interests of the port over those of the interior. The character of the republic created by the cultivated elite of Montevideo was at odds with that of the rest of the country, which was dominated by *caudillos* and their armed bands. The first form of solidarity among Uruguayans was based on those patrimonial groups, bound by strong bonds of loyalty and dependent on a caudillo. They identified themselves through *divisas,* or badges.

The two traditional parties—the Blanco, later officially known as the National Party, and the Colorado—were established in the nineteenth century out of the unstable association between groups of urban leaders and rural *caudillos.* In that period civil wars became the common way of solving conflicts between different interests: Montevideo versus Buenos Aires, Argentina versus Brazil, the city versus the countryside. Conflicts within the traditional parties and struggles between parties tore apart the republic, but neither party was ever able to destroy the other. In the process, enduring myths and identities were constructed.

In the last quarter of the nineteenth century, Uruguay underwent social and economic modernization. Changes in land exploitation and waves of foreign immigration transformed the social structure. The population grew and diversified. These social changes were accompanied by profound changes in the political system. The government extended its area of territorial control and increased its efficiency.

Schools helped transform newly arrived immigrants into full members of Uruguayan society. Gradually the traditional parties evolved into organizations prepared to appeal to an increasing mass of citizens. In 1904 Aparicio Saravia, the last of the traditional *caudillos* of the National Party, was defeated by a professional army led by President José Batlle y Ordóñez. This event was a turning point in Uruguayan history.

The Model Country

Under the two administrations of Batlle y Ordóñez (1903–1907 and 1911–1915), the processes of state formation and of the democratization of society and politics converged. Batlle y Ordóñez and his followers developed an anticipatory, or proactive, style of government in dealing with social demands. They also made state intervention an instrument for perfecting society. In this way they created the modern Uruguayan state. Progressive social reforms coupled with economic prosperity caused Uruguay to be considered a "laboratory country."

The Batllista model of politics continued to dominate in Uruguay long after Batlle y Ordóñez's death in 1929. A strong belief in the power of lawmaking and political engineering to improve political practices and society led to experiments at both the constitutional and the electoral levels. The constitution of 1919 established a mixed, presidential-collegial executive. A president had charge of a minimal liberal state, while a collegial body directed the new social and economic functions of the state.

The new constitution also consecrated the principle of proportional representation. In 1925 the first electoral laws gave guarantees to voters by creating the electoral court and permanent register of voters. Since then, Uruguayan politics has been marked by a trend toward power sharing between the two major parties. Under the principle of coparticipation, the minority party has representation in all areas of political and institutional life, from the boards of directors of public enterprises to the state bureaucracy.

Coparticipation gave a share in the system to the opposition, but it also colonized the state apparatus and hindered the formation of a neutral civil service. To maintain this equilibrium born of consensus, pacts between parties were accompanied by formulas of political engineering intended to deal with intraparty conflicts and factionalism. Thus Uruguay's electoral laws banned the possibility of ticket splitting, forcing voters to choose all candidates for local government and for the executive and legislative branches of the national government from the same party. At the same time, the electoral practice of double simultaneous vote effectively prevented the multiplication of parties by making it more convenient for political actors to form alliances within the two traditional parties.

In 1933 the dynamics of democratic politics in Uruguay reached a deadlock that was resolved by a presidential coup d'état at the hands of Dr. Gabriel Terra. This coup resulted in a *dictablanda*—a dictatorial regime without notorious violation of human rights—which intensified the process of social reform in a newly restrictive political context. The constitution of 1934 reflected the new situation of exclusion of the opposition. The *ley de lemas,* or party laws, of 1934—reformulated in 1938—gave control of each party to its majority faction. This measure punished any attempt at intraparty dissent by letting the members of the majority faction decide who belonged to the party and who could present a list of candidates under that party's label.

The "good coup" of elected president Alfredo Baldomir in 1942 restored democracy. The constitution of 1942 maintained the basic tenets of the constitution of 1934 but eliminated the barriers that kept minority sectors from political participation.

During the 1940s and 1950s an imperfect welfare state largely succeeded in buffering tensions and social conflicts. Despite its problems, this period became known as the "happy Uruguay." The politics of consensus, however, was hostile to innovation, and a political elite adhering to the motto "slow but sure" firmly held the reins of power.

Decline and Fall of Uruguayan Democracy

In 1952, as a result of a pact between conservative sectors of the two traditional parties, Uruguay adopted another new constitution. This constitution modified the form of the executive, making it fully collegial, a kind of government by committee. But instead of helping parties adapt to changed social circumstances, this step led the entire Uruguayan political system to stagnation.

The 1950s marked the end of "happy Uruguay" and the beginning of disenchantment. Uruguay's political myths began to crumble, while its citizens began to see that there were limits to equitable social well-being in a developing economy.

The crisis of Uruguayan democracy deepened during the 1960s. In 1967 a new constitutional reform took place that reinstated a strong presidential executive. Uruguay entered an era of radicalism and ideological polarization. A coalition of parties of the left, the Broad Front, was formed for the 1971 election. There was economic instability, accompanied by labor strikes. Organized political violence erupted with the Movement of National Liberation–Tupamaros and other lesser groups.

In 1973, after a "long coup" that lasted from February to June, the armed forces took control of the country. President Juan María Bordaberry, who had decreed the dissolution of the National Assembly on June 27, 1973, was in turn ousted by the military when he tried to institutionalize an authoritarian regime in 1976. After 1976 Uruguay was ruled by a combination of military leaders and technocrats. Traditional parties survived in a state of suspended animation; leftist parties and movements were ostracized. A culture of fear prevailed.

Recovering Democracy

The military tried to institutionalize the dictatorship through a new constitution in 1980. The document was submitted to a plebiscite, which meant that the government had to restore a limited degree of party activity and allow for controlled public opposition. The proposed reforms were defeated, and the process of liberalization began. Rounds of talks with the opposition were held, and the internal life of the parties revived.

General elections were held in 1984, although Wilson Ferreira Aldunate, the leader of the National Party, was still proscribed. Julio María Sanguinetti was elected president. A major problem facing Sanguinetti's administration was how to handle the divisive issue of human rights violations. This problem was solved through a plebiscite in April 1989. In November 1989 a new general election was held. Alternation of parties occurred at both the national and local levels. Dr. Luis Alberto Lacalle of the National Party was elected president, and Dr. Tabaré Vázquez of the Broad Front became mayor of the capital city of Montevideo.

Also in the 1989 election, a plebiscite to improve retirement pensions was passed with 81 percent of the votes. The measure succeeded even though it was expected to worsen economic inflation. President Lacalle faced many problems of governance in his attempts to make a severe economic adjustment. He tried to privatize the many existing state enterprises through the Law of Privatization of Public Enterprises, passed by the congress after long negotiations. But his efforts were checked in 1992 by a plebiscite against the law.

In the general election of November 1994 the Colorado Party won the election over the National Party led by Alberto Volonté. Sanguinetti, the former president, ran again as the principal candidate of the Colorado Party and won a close race.

See also *Batlle y Ordóñez, José; Proportional representation; Sanguinetti, Julio María.*

Juan Rial

BIBLIOGRAPHY

Fitzgibbon, Russell H. *Uruguay: Portrait of a Democracy.* New Brunswick, N.J.: Rutgers University Press, 1954; London: Allen and Unwin, 1956.

Gillespie, Charles Guy. *Negotiating Democracy: Politicians and Generals in Uruguay.* New York: Cambridge University Press, 1991.

González, Luis E. *Political Structure and Democracy in Uruguay.* Notre Dame, Ind.: University of Notre Dame Press, 1991.

Perelli, Carina. "The Legacies of Transitions to Democracy in Argentina and Uruguay." In *The Military and Democracy: The Future of Civil-Military Relations in Latin America,* edited by Louis Goodman, Johanna Mendelson, and Juan Rial. Lexington, Mass.: Lexington Books, 1990.

———. "Putting Conservatism to Good Use: Women and Unorthodox Politics in Uruguay, from Breakdown to Transition." In *Women's Movement in Latin America: Feminism and the Transition to Democracy,* edited by Jane S. Jaquette. Boston: Unwin Hyman, 1989.

Real de Azúa, Carlos. *¿Uruguay: una sociedad amortiguadora?* Montevideo: Ediciones de la Banda Oriental, 1985.

Rial, Juan. "The Social Imaginary: Utopian Political Myths in Uruguay (Change and Permanence during the Dictatorship)." In *Repression, Exile and Democracy: Uruguayan Culture,* edited by Saúl Sosnowsky and Louise B. Popkin. Durham, N.C.: Duke University Press, 1993.

———. "The Uruguayan Elections of 1984: A Triumph of the Center." In *Elections and Democratization in Latin America, 1980–85,* edited by Paul Drake and Eduardo Silva. San Diego: University of California Press, 1986.

USSR

See *Union of Soviet Socialist Republics*

Utilitarianism

The ethical theory holding that actions and policies should be approved of if they maximize happiness. The historical association of utilitarianism with democracy originated with Jeremy Bentham (1748–1832), one of the creators and most important proponents of utilitarian theory and a strong advocate of democracy. Bentham's slogan about the doctrine of utility promoting "the greatest happiness of the greatest number" has a democratic ring. Although he and most of his disciples promoted democracy, there is no necessary or logical connection between utilitarianism and democracy. Some notable utilitarians, for example, John Austin and James Fitzjames Stephen, were opposed to democracy.

Bentham approved of democracy because it counteracted the tendency of all governments to be corrupt. According to his analysis, those who exercised power would,

if they had an opportunity, use it for personal gain. Their interest was separate from that of the people and was therefore sinister. Because one could not rely on the honesty or sense of justice of those who held public office, the only way to prevent them from exploiting their opportunity to serve themselves instead of the people was to establish democracy. Democracy would give a political voice to the people, whose interest, by virtue of encompassing the entire populace, was whole and universal.

To promote the universal interest, the electoral institutions of democracy were required. Universal suffrage would allow the voice of the people to be reflected in the legislature; frequent elections would subject the conduct of representatives to popular scrutiny; and the secret ballot would make it likely that the votes cast were a true reflection of the people's interest. Bentham called the institution of these procedures "democratic ascendancy." In his analysis he distinguished between interests that were separate, corrupt, and sinister and the interest of the people, which was universal and democratic. This utilitarian rationale for democracy rested on the claim that democracy is an effective obstacle to corrupt government and not on any claim of justice or natural right. As a utilitarian, Bentham was concerned with happiness more than with justice.

Bentham's understanding of democracy was adopted and disseminated by many of his disciples, most notably by James Mill and a prominent group of intellectuals and politicians known as the philosophic radicals. Among them was John Stuart Mill, who subsequently made important revisions in Bentham's theory, becoming one of the most important nineteenth-century theorists of democracy.

The character of democracy, as Bentham understood it, was determined by other features of the utilitarian theory of government, all of which made his concept of democracy majoritarian but left it without checks or obstacles to the unrestrained exercise of power. One feature of utilitarian theory was opposition to the very idea of constitutional limitations; such a notion was incompatible with the utilitarian view that sovereignty was indivisible and incapable of legal limitation. Thus for utilitarians it was illegitimate to claim that limits on sovereign power could be derived from extralegal notions of morality or tradition. Bentham thought it absurd and an abuse of language to talk about government exceeding its authority or going beyond its right. He believed that utilitarianism could be linked to a science of legislation that would become the source of laws maximizing happiness, therefore making it unnecessary to place constitutional limitations on legislators.

In light of the utilitarians' opposition to constitutional limitations, it is not surprising that Bentham and most of his disciples, while admiring American democracy, criticized the American institutions that were established as constitutional limitations. These included federalism, separation of powers, judicial review, and the establishment of the Senate as a second chamber.

Another feature of the utilitarian theory of government that promoted unchecked democracy was its denial that there were human rights other than those created by a sovereign power. Utilitarians rejected the language of natural, inalienable, and universal rights. The belief that such rights were the basis of valid claims was rejected by Bentham as fictional and as originating in false views about laws of nature. He called natural rights "nonsense on stilts," saying they were invented by poets and dealers in moral and intellectual poisons. He criticized both American and French references to the rights of man during their respective revolutions.

The language of rights was objectionable for another reason. Rights, Bentham said, were proclaimed in "terrorist language"; they led to anarchy and chaos. When he encountered the passage in the Declaration of Independence asserting that all men are created equal and are endowed with certain unalienable rights, Bentham decided that the Americans had reached an extreme of fanaticism. These features of the utilitarian theory of government allowed the exercise of power without limitations, thus raising the specter of democratic despotism.

During the twentieth century the utilitarian rationale for democracy has been regarded as incomplete and defective, for it has been maintained that popular sovereignty should be combined with protections for individual liberty and constitutional limitations on political power. One challenge to the utilitarian argument has been posed by rights-based theorists, such as John Rawls, who have criticized utilitarianism generally and the utilitarian rejection of individual rights in particular. The strong interest in the concept of democracy developed by James Madison and Alexis de Tocqueville, both of whom sought to protect individuals against the threat of democratic despotism, also points up the current dissatisfaction with utilitarianism.

See also *Enlightenment, Scottish; Human rights; Mill, John Stuart.*

Joseph Hamburger

BIBLIOGRAPHY

Bentham, Jeremy. *An Introduction to the Principles of Morals and Legislation.* Edited by J. H. Burns and H. L. A. Hart. London: Athlone Press, 1970.

———. *Plan of Parliamentary Reform.* Vol. 3 of *The Works of Jeremy Bentham.* Edited by John Bowring. Edinburgh: William Tait, 1843.

Hamburger, Joseph. "Utilitarianism and the Constitution." In *Confronting the Constitution,* edited by Allan Bloom. Washington, D.C.: AEI Press, 1990.

Long, Douglas G. *Bentham on Liberty: Jeremy Bentham's Idea of Liberty in Relation to His Utilitarianism.* Toronto: University of Toronto Press, 1977.

Mill, John Stuart. *Utilitarianism.* Edited by George Sher. Indianapolis: Hackett, 1979.

Stephen, Leslie. *The English Utilitarians.* 3 vols. New York: A. M. Kelley, 1968; Bristol: Thoemmes Press, 1991.

V

Venezuela

A republic that lies on the north coast of South America along the Caribbean Sea. Venezuela poses a paradox for theorists of democracy. Until 1958 the country saw decades of virtually uninterrupted authoritarian rule, yet it is home to Latin America's second oldest democracy—one that has survived strong challenges from both revolutionary and military authoritarian alternatives. That some form of democracy still persists is due to a combination of factors not found elsewhere in Latin America: petroleum revenues and political pact making. But the former became scarcer and the latter less practiced in the 1980s. Venezuelan democracy therefore must find a new equilibrium based on lower oil revenues and different political rules.

Historical Background

Considered a backwater by Spanish colonialists who unsuccessfully sought the golden city of El Dorado within its borders, Venezuela was ruled by military *caudillos* (leaders) and shaped by warfare after its most famous citizen, Simón Bolívar, led the move for South American independence from Spain in the early 1880s. Venezuela gained international significance with the discovery of "black gold" at the beginning of the twentieth century. The development of oil production coincided with the birth of the modern Venezuelan state during the twenty-seven year rule (1908–1935) of the caudillo Juan Vicente Gómez.

As a result of this historic accident of timing, both U.S. multinationals and the U.S. government became essential props sustaining the country's authoritarian arrangements. Colliding with a weak and fragmented civil society,

foreign oil companies had an overwhelming effect: petrodollars became the bulwark of a ruling alliance that included military caudillos, the coffee and cacao producers of the Andes, and the commercial and financial elite in Caracas. Foreign influence was directly felt: Gómez seized power through a U.S.-backed coup in 1908, and revenues paid by foreign oil companies to his government provided stable financing for authoritarian rule for almost three decades.

But the exploitation of petroleum also set in motion long-term structural changes in the economy that provided the social basis for democracy. The petroleum economy hastened the decline of an already stagnating agricultural sector, thereby weakening the landlord class that had proved to be a strong barrier to political democracy in Latin America. It also provoked rapid industrialization, the fastest urbanization rate in Latin America, and the rise of a middle class whose aspirations for better jobs and education were blocked by authoritarian rule. Pushed by militant oil workers organized primarily by the Communist Party and led by dissidents from the student "Generation of 1928" who had protested Gómez's dictatorial rule, new political forces appeared and began to clamor for a more open polity. Prominent among these were two parties that later would be the primary shapers of Venezuelan democracy: Democratic Action and the Social Christian Party.

Democratic Action was given an unexpected chance to govern in 1946—a mere two years after the party's founding. After Gómez's death from natural causes, the military rule of Generals Eleazar López Contreras and Isaías Medina Angarita alternated between liberalization and repression, reflecting the slowly approaching collision between new urban social forces and a dying but unyielding authoritarian alliance. Unable to govern on their own in the heady atmosphere of democratic sentiment that swept Latin America in the wake of World War II, military leaders asked Democratic Action to share power—an invitation that lasted only three crisis-filled years.

Nevertheless, these brief years in power gave party founder Rómulo Betancourt the opportunity to develop a platform based on exploitation of the country's petroleum resources. Betancourt established Democratic Action headquarters in every region of the country and built an organized popular constituency through the Confederation of Venezuelan Workers and the Federation of Venezuelan Peasants. Although both organizations became illegal after the government of 1946–1948 was ousted by the military, they provided the organizational basis for the party's political advantages over other parties in the future.

The government of 1946–1948 was a product of elite military responses to the changing international and domestic context after World War II rather than the actual political capacity of an emerging mass party. Brought down in part by Democratic Action's failure to make alliances with potential allies, the sectarianism of all political parties, and the opposition of the Roman Catholic hierarchy, it was also strongly opposed by economic elites and foreign oil companies, which feared the nationalization of petroleum. Although military rule was promptly restored, the structural transformation of the economy and society accelerated rapidly during the 1946–1948 period, and it was just a matter of time until the disjuncture between an outmoded polity and an increasingly complex country provoked a crisis once again.

Breakdown of Military Rule and Beginning of Reform

The new authoritarian rule of Gen. Marcos Pérez Jiménez lasted less than a decade. Confronted with growing demands for participation, Pérez Jiménez alienated many of the key economic interests underlying Venezuela's traditional authoritarian alliance and stimulated a process of breakdown from within. At the same time, political party members united in an umbrella organization, the Patriotic Junta, to coordinate the clandestine activities of the opposition. Protesting both Pérez Jiménez's decision to succeed himself after a fraudulent plebiscite and a deep fiscal crisis provoked by the government's extraordinary overspending in the wake of the 1950s oil boom, the Junta organized a general strike and massive civilian demonstrations in downtown Caracas, which ultimately led to Pérez Jiménez's ouster in 1958.

The nature of Venezuela's new democracy was profoundly affected by the manner in which military authoritarian rule broke down. Although long-term structural changes provoked by the oil-led economy had strengthened emerging middle-class forces at the expense of traditional elites, the ability of these new actors to define a different order through a political party system was always constrained by the persistent effort of elites from the past alliance to limit reform.

In the midst of the acute political and economic crisis that followed the overthrow of Pérez Jiménez, right-wing military officers attempted several coups to block the implementation of a political party system. Panicked businessmen sought to circumscribe the power of newly legalized unions, and foreign oil companies, fearful of social unrest that might lead to nationalization, threatened to move their operations to the Middle East. The U.S. government sent marines into the Caribbean in the event their assistance would be required. Other political parties and the Catholic Church, remembering policies unfavorable to them that Democratic Action had implemented when it shared power in 1946–1948, and worried about that party's possible hegemonic aspirations, added their weight to those who wanted to limit Democratic Action's reformist policies. With such strong potential opposition, the threat of reversion to authoritarian rule loomed over Venezuela's democratic transition.

In order to accommodate the demands and desires of new political actors without significantly threatening the interests of those strong enough to reverse the process of change, democratization in Venezuela was based on an explicit definition of the rules of the game, both formal and informal. These institutional arrangements were established through several interlocking elite-negotiated arrangements formulated in 1958 and refined during the presidency of Rómulo Betancourt. The Pact of Punto Fijo and the Minimal Program of Government, documents signed by all presidential candidates prior to the country's first elections, spelled out these arrangements. Essentially, they bound all signatories to the same political and economic program, regardless of the electoral outcome. Only the Communist Party was excluded from the two agreements.

The first important compromises represented by these pacts were political. All parties agreed to respect the electoral process and institute a process of power sharing commensurate with the voting results. The parties promised to form coalitions and distribute the benefits of oil revenues in such a way that each party was guaranteed some share of the economic and political pie through access to state jobs, a partitioning of ministries, and a complicated spoils system. A clear agreement also was reached between the military and civilians: in exchange for leaving power and accepting an apolitical role, the armed forces received the promise of civilian leaders to modernize equipment, improve the economic situation of officers, and guarantee an amnesty for human rights abusers. Even the Catholic Church, worried about the spread of secular education, received assurances that it would have greater independence from the state.

Reform was further circumscribed by an economic accord specifying the broad outlines of a new development program that would distribute oil revenues. All parties agreed to accept a development model based on foreign and local private capital accumulation, and they also promised huge state subsidies to the private sector. Although the new government program proposed agrarian reform, it ruled out the nationalization of foreign-owned oil and steel companies and confirmed a strong presence for the multinationals in the country's extractive industries—a significant retreat from Democratic Action's original nationalistic stance. In return for these concessions, the private sector accepted the state's leading role; new benefits for organized labor, peasants, and the middle class; trade union rights; and substantial privileges for party members.

The Crisis of "Pacted Democracy"

Taken together, the agreements that permitted Venezuela's "pacted democracy" to be sustained rested on the country's petroleum wealth even more than on the statecraft of the regime's founders. Petrodollars served as the chief lubricant, smoothing social conflict during the transition and consolidation of democracy. Oil provided the revenues to make feasible a development model based on simultaneously subsidizing the private sector, the middle classes, and some sectors of the working classes. Specifically, pact making rested on the capacity to grant extensive state favors, contracts, and infrastructure to entrepreneurs, while charging the lowest taxes on the continent, permitting some of the highest profits, and supporting a mode of collective bargaining that resulted in the highest wages, price controls, and food subsidies in South America.

For many years, oil revenues meant that democracy could be built with very few losers. The advantages of this arrangement were clear: the country had regular elections and numerous transfers of power between opposition parties until 1993. Not surprisingly, the first three presidents—Democratic Action's Rómulo Betancourt (1959–1963) and Raúl Leoni (1964–1968) and the Social Christian Party's Rafael Caldera (1969–1973) were among the principal designers of Venezuela's pacted arrangements.

But pacted democracy also incurred significant costs. Because Venezuelan democracy was based on agreements that carved up the state through a complicated spoils system, norms of efficiency and productivity were corroded, and corruption was rampant. These problems became especially apparent during the first administration of President Carlos Andrés Pérez, which coincided with the oil boom of 1973. The combination of the influx of petrodollars and barriers to access within the party system itself created strong incentives to freeze existing political arrangements. Political parties, the guardians of access to the public sector, were transformed into mere machines for extracting revenues and protecting existing privileges. This arrangement seemed to work—at least as long as huge oil revenues continued to flow. Oil revenues mitigated the problems of extreme partisanship, economic inequalities, and insufficient growth that threatened democracies elsewhere in South America.

Problems arose, however, in the early 1980s as state spending soared out of control, international oil prices declined, and the combination of oil revenues and massive foreign borrowing failed to cover a growing fiscal deficit. Faced with a financial crisis whose roots were visible as early as 1976, democratic governments continued to pursue the politics of appeasement through public spending—even when there were no more petrodollars to spend. Most striking in the period covering the administrations of Democratic Action's Carlos Andrés Pérez (1974–1978), the Social Christian Party's Luís Herrera Campíns (1979–1983), and Democratic Action's Jaime Lusinchi (1984–1988) was the persistent effort, regardless of party affiliation, to postpone the profound political and economic policy changes that had to be made if Venezuelan democracy was to survive.

Although it became increasingly evident that distortions of all kinds were accumulating at an alarming rate, the reaction was, at best, partial reforms, half-measures, and perpetual debt renegotiations. At worst, it was increasing corruption and revenue-seeking behavior from both politicians and entrepreneurs. In this context, the pact-making habits of the past were severely undermined.

Venezuela's ability to live beyond its means came to an abrupt end in 1989, just as Carlos Andrés Pérez became the first politician to become president for a second term. With inflation and budget deficits soaring and wages and foreign reserves plunging, Pérez implemented a stabilization program imposed by the International Monetary Fund that involved a complete rejection of the economic policy making of the past. The harsh austerity measures he imposed triggered the worst riots in the country's democratic history on February 27, 1989. Following two attempted military coups that narrowly missed ending the democratic regime altogether, Pérez was indicted for embezzlement. Charges of corruption were also leveled at former president Jaime Lusinchi and other politicians.

By the mid-1990s Venezuelan democracy had reached a critical juncture. After the Pérez government finally abdicated in the face of tremendous popular protest, an interim regime presided over by a respected independent, Ramón José Velásquez (1993–1994), provided continuity until elections were held in December 1993. These resulted in the victory of Rafael Caldera who, though he was one of the progenitors of the pacted system and the founder of the Social Christian Party, ran as an independent in order to communicate to the electorate that he could be trusted to confront the sclerotic party system.

The challenges Caldera's administration faces are twofold. First, both governability and faith in the capacity of democratic institutions must be restored. Paradoxically, this accomplishment requires some type of democratic renewal under the leadership of many of the same actors who benefited from the old rules of the game. Second, democratic renewal must occur in the context of a transition from an economy based on petroleum revenues to a more diversified, productive, and austere economy. If Venezuela's democracy is to survive into the twenty-first century, it will have to design new rules that can accommodate losers as well as winners.

See also *Betancourt, Rómulo; Central America.*

Terry Lynn Karl

BIBLIOGRAPHY

Karl, Terry Lynn. *The Paradox of Plenty: Oil Booms, Venezuela, and Other Petro-States.* Berkeley: University of California Press, 1995.

———. "Petroleum and Political Pacts: The Transition to Democracy in Venezuela." *Latin American Research Review* 22 (1987).

Levine, Daniel. *Conflict and Political Change in Venezuela.* Princeton: Princeton University Press, 1973.

McCoy, Jennifer, William C. Smith, Andres Serbin, and Andres Stambouli, eds. *Venezuelan Democracy under Pressure.* New Brunswick, N.J.: North-South Center/Transaction, 1995.

Naim, Moises. *Paper Tigers and Minotaurs: The Politics of Venezuela's Economic Reforms.* Washington, D.C.: Carnegie Endowment, 1993.

Veto, Liberum

The liberum veto, in the kingdom of Poland from the fourteenth century to the late eighteenth century, was the legal right of each deputy to parliamentary gatherings of the nobility to strike down any measure under consideration or to dissolve the parliament and nullify all acts passed during its session. It was rooted in medieval tradition and codified during the period known as the Noble Republic (1569–1795), in which the Polish nobility held supreme power and the monarchy was transformed into an elective office.

This right was derived from the assumed political equality of all members of the Polish nobility and the principle of unanimity in deciding the affairs of the state. Neither the national parliament (Sejm) nor the regional parliaments (sejmiki) could pass a resolution unless it gained unanimous consent. The requirement of unanimity in political decisions was not an unusual feature in the constitutional practice of European monarchies. However, it assumed an extreme form in Polish politics during this time.

The right to veto legislation and dissolve parliamentary gatherings evolved gradually in the Polish constitutional tradition. It was intended originally to ensure consensus and a sense of responsibility among delegates for the resolutions they passed. In practice, it protected the rights and privileges of the nobility from the crown and allowed individuals and groups to pursue their own advantages. Initially, the right applied to groups of deputies representing provinces, not to individual deputies. After deliberations, the provinces in the minority would join those in the majority for the sake of the common good; then a measure would be passed by a unanimous decision of the national parliament. The liberum veto of a single deputy was effective only if it was supported by a faction of the deputies attending the meeting. Thus the veto was usually a device by which the parliamentary minority could intimidate and defeat the majority.

In 1536 the first session of the Sejm was dissolved because representatives of regions failed to reconcile their differences. After the constitution of the Noble Republic in 1569, the liberum veto became a common practice. During Stefan Batory's reign (1576–1586) it was used frequently, and under Sigismund III (1587–1632) only one session of the Sejm succeeded in passing any legislation. During this period the protests of individual deputies were customarily ignored. In 1652, however, the Sejm was dissolved as the result of a protest by a single deputy. Although such individual irresponsibility shocked the members of the parliament, the delegate's action was upheld by the speaker of the parliament, creating a dangerous precedent.

Gradually, the number of sessions of both regional and national parliaments that were terminated either by an individual or by a group of deputies increased. Between 1576 and 1763, 53 of some 150 parliamentary gatherings failed to enact any legislation. The liberum veto was used not only to obstruct reforms introduced by the king but also to support factional struggles between groups within the Polish nobility. Abuse of the liberum veto paralyzed the government. It made state reforms and any centralization of power impossible and left Poland vulnerable to the influence of foreign powers that bribed deputies to prevent the passage of legislation contrary to their interests.

The principle of the liberum veto preserved the feudal features of Poland's political system, weakened the role of the monarchy, led to anarchy in political life, and contributed to the economic and political decline of the Polish state. Such a situation made the country vulnerable to foreign invasions and ultimately led to its collapse. Stanislaw II August Poniatowski, who was king from 1764 to 1795, introduced constitutional reforms that limited the use of the liberum veto, making economic and legal affairs subject to simple majority vote.

The liberum veto was abolished in the constitution of May 3, 1791, in the final hours of Poland's monarchy. In the Polish political tradition it has become a synonym for political anarchy and the willfulness of politicians as well as the weaknesses of democracy.

See also *Poland*.

Grzegorz Ekiert

BIBLIOGRAPHY

Davies, Norman. *God's Playground. A History of Poland*. Vol. 2. New York: Columbia University Press, 1982.
———. *Heart of Europe. A Short History of Poland*. Oxford and New York: Oxford University Press, 1986.
Michalski, Jerzy, ed. *Historia Sejmu Polskiego*. Vol. 1. Warsaw: Panstwowe Wydawnictwo Naukowe, 1984.

Vietnam

See *Asia, Southeast*

Virtue, Civic

Civic virtue is the public spirit required of citizens if a republic is to survive and flourish. It requires a readiness to set the public good above one's private interests. In the classical republican tradition, virtue is the opposite of corruption. In recent republican thought public spirit is contrasted with the self-interested individualism taken to be characteristic of liberal societies.

The Classical Concept of Virtue

Reflections on civic virtue are at the heart of traditional republican thinking. In the ancient world, republics in which power was shared among the citizens were vulnerable to conquest from without and to civil war and tyranny from within. Their autonomy, insofar as they managed to remain independent and stable, was attributed largely to the solidarity and courage of the citizens, and particularly to the citizens' willingness to sacrifice their lives and private interests for the city. Sparta's warrior-citizens, often regarded as models of civic virtue, were formed by means of a harsh and intensive discipline designed to make them hardy, brave, and totally identified with their comrades. The long stability and military success of Sparta were widely attributed to this ethos.

Virtue in the classical context was the characteristic of a male citizen (Latin, *vir*), and its connotations are overwhelmingly military. It denotes the qualities that make good soldiers and good armies: courage, toughness, loyalty, and solidarity. It was strongly associated in the classical mind with simplicity of life (epitomized by the notoriously unsavory black broth eaten at Sparta's communal meals), and it was contrasted with the "corruption" induced by wealth. From Aristotle onward it was agreed that citizens needed some property (preferably in the form of land) if they were to have the leisure and independence to be virtuous citizens.

The point of economic activity, however, was to serve politics, rather than vice versa, and the ideal citizen possessed property without seeking or enjoying wealth. Where a modern observer might see a rise in the standard of living, ancient moralists saw luxury, which threatened civic virtue in a number of ways. For one thing, softer living made citizens less able to face the physical rigors of military campaigns. For another, it sowed dissension among citizens by increasing divisions between rich and poor and undermining justice. Above all, if citizens were attending to their private wealth and material possessions, their energies were diverted from the public good. An ideal example of the priorities befitting a virtuous citizen was provided by the Roman hero Cincinnatus, summoned from the plow in 458 B.C. to take charge as dictator in a military crisis. After leading the Romans to victory, he rode in triumph with the army but did not seek personal profit and went straight back to his frugal agricultural life.

Aristotle's claim that life as a citizen is necessary for human fulfillment may seem to imply that the welfare of the individual and that of the city are ultimately compatible. Republican moralists in the ancient world, however, more often assumed that the public good requires the sacrifice of private interests and attachments. Rome's early histori-

ans underlined this point with their stories of citizens whose heroic dedication to the republic had made Roman freedom and greatness possible, such as Lucius Junius Brutus, the founder of the republic, who executed his own sons for conspiring to restore the monarchy. Another example held up before the eyes of budding citizens was that of the Roman general Regulus, who was captured by the Carthaginians in 255 B.C. and sent to Rome bearing peace terms, under oath to return to execution in Carthage if the terms were rejected. Concentrating selflessly on the public interest, he persuaded the Senate to reject peace and returned to certain death in fulfillment of his oath.

Certainly no republican supposed that civic virtue came naturally. Virtuous citizens had to be molded by education and by the general ethos of the city. It followed that attitudes, habits, and the conduct of what a liberal might regard as private life were matters of political importance because laxity here might undermine the city's defenses. Classical republicanism had a strong puritanical streak that gave rise to laws controlling consumption and display. In their anxiety to preserve civic virtue, the censors of the Roman Republic prohibited women from wearing colored robes, limited the number of guests at banquets, and even controlled the details of menus. In the second century B.C. Cato the Elder acquired a reputation for virtue in part because of his rigor as a censor in taxing such items as jewels.

The conundrum faced by moralists of the later Roman Republic was (as the historian Livy explained) that the virtues that had made Rome great thereby undermined themselves. As a united band of tough, frugal, hardy soldiers the Romans had conquered much wealthier societies than theirs. Once left to enjoy their conquests in peace, however, they succumbed to the temptations of luxury and avarice and began to lose their military virtues and public spirit. When Rome yielded to imperial rule, the first-century writers Juvenal and Sallust attributed this submission to the effeminacy and self-centered avarice into which former citizens had sunk.

The classical concept of civic virtue was profoundly conservative, with a deeply pessimistic attitude toward time. Change tended to be equated with decay, and virtue was located in the past, in the days of the heroic founders of the republic. The efforts of those concerned with virtue were therefore directed toward preservation rather than toward improvement. One of the main reasons for Sparta's exalted reputation was that it had stayed the same and resisted corruption for an exceptionally long time.

The Renaissance and Enlightenment

From late antiquity until the Renaissance these classical views became overshadowed by a different concept of virtue. Although the Roman moralists continued to exert an influence, moral thinking was dominated by the Christian Church. Puritanism and ideals of self-sacrifice were common to both traditions, but Christianity redirected attention away from secular glory to individual salvation in the next world. When efforts were made during the Italian Renaissance to recover ancient civilization, including classical republicanism, Niccolò Machiavelli openly complained that Christianity was incompatible with civic virtue. His concept of *virtù* was from a Christian point of view an amoral resolution to confront fortune and to strive by all necessary means for glory in this world, instead of submitting humbly to the decrees of Providence. In his republican *Discourses on Livy,* Machiavelli contrasted Christianity with ancient Roman religion, which had been a civic religion wholly supportive of the state and its interests. Christianity, Machiavelli complained, glorified "humble and contemplative men," thereby offering no resistance to the wicked. The ancient Roman religion, by contrast, glorified victorious generals and engaged in bloody sacrifices that reinforced the ferocity of the soldiers.

As this example makes clear, the classical concept of civic virtue reaffirmed by Machiavelli in the early sixteenth century was incompatible not only with Christianity but also with the liberal values that began to emerge in Western Europe a little later. By the end of the seventeenth century educated Europeans had available to them not only the classical concept of freedom as the collective achievement of an armed band of virtuous citizens but also a new concept of freedom as the private possession of peaceful individuals living their own lives within the order established by a modern state. The challenge to militarist values included a new stress on happiness that legitimized material comfort and a new humanism that condemned violence and cruelty instead of regarding them as reassuring signs of military prowess.

As the commercial wealth of Western Europe grew rapidly in the eighteenth century, opinion was divided between those who hailed a new age of improvement and progress and the more classically minded who saw ominous similarities with the luxury and corruption that had destroyed republican Rome. These debates were particularly common in Britain and its American colonies be-

cause the parliamentary monarchy that had emerged from the constitutional struggles of the seventeenth century was widely interpreted (in language derived from classical sources through Machiavelli and James Harrington) as a kind of classical republic. If this interpretation was accurate, Britain's freedom must lie in the virtue of her citizen-soldiers, the freeholders of the shires, who were (in the guise of a civil militia) the proper defenders of the realm. From the republican point of view, threats to liberty could be seen just as clearly in the country's ever increasing commercial wealth as in the king's standing army and the systematic corruption of Parliament by the king's ministers. Britain's impending ruin was presaged by luxurious practices such as tea drinking and material comforts such as warm, draft-free houses. From a liberal point of view, by contrast, material wealth could be seen as evidence of progress.

Although it is possible in retrospect to discern a conflict between radically different systems of political values, most eighteenth-century political thinkers and actors oscillated uneasily between republican and liberal attitudes. For example, in his enormously influential *Spirit of the Laws* (1748), Montesquieu reiterated the importance of classical virtue in republics, but he also proclaimed that political liberty was to be found under the shelter of the balanced constitution of England, in spite of that country's commercial society and lack of ancient virtue. Among the thinkers of the Scottish Enlightenment, including Adam Smith, notions of the benefits of economic growth and of a natural development of human society from barbarism to civilization were worked out in an intellectual context still deeply suspicious of the moral and political implications of commercial activity. Bernard Mandeville's satirical poem, *The Fable of the Bees: or Private Vices, Public Benefits* (1714), which foreshadowed Smith's account of how the "invisible hand" of the free market transforms material self-interest into general welfare, depended for its effect on the lingering conviction that concern for wealth and material consumption were vices.

Rousseau and the Age of Revolution

In America the debates surrounding the Revolution and the adoption of the Constitution were complicated by the difficulty of adapting a discourse derived from the militaristic republics of antiquity to fit a modern commercial society. Classical echoes can be found in the Jeffersonian assumption that armed citizen-farmers leading frugal lives are the bastions of republican liberty as well as in more unexpected quarters. For example, Thomas Paine, in most respects a thoroughly modernist liberal, observed that commerce threatens patriotism and military valor, while John Adams remarked as a matter of course that in a republic "Virtue and Simplicity of Manners" are indispensable. The extent to which Antifederalist opposition to the Constitution can be understood in terms of classical republican values is a matter much disputed among historians.

The most influential exponent of the idea of civic virtue among eighteenth century political thinkers was Jean-Jacques Rousseau, in whose ambiguous writings classical themes underwent some interesting transformations. Rousseau was one of the chief progenitors of the modern concept of "positive liberty," according to which true freedom is enjoyed not by the freestanding individuals of liberal theory but by participants in civic life. Characteristically, Rousseau's thought contains two incompatible versions of this notion—one democratic, the other romantic and potentially fascist.

One of the strands in Rousseau's *Social Contract* (1762) is an ideal of participatory democracy, that is, popular sovereignty in the most literal and direct form, with law-making carried out in a face-to-face assembly of all the citizens of a small city-state. Civic virtue in this context consists in putting the general will one shares with one's fellow citizens above the private will for the satisfaction of one's selfish interests. Rousseau implies that such conduct is not only virtuous but also rational and satisfying. Modern sympathizers with classical republican thinking usually follow this democratic strand in Rousseau's thought. A different and more disquieting theme, however, takes up the classical emphasis on the importance of a republic's ethos. Building on Machiavelli's criticisms of Christianity, Rousseau argues that a republic needs a civil religion; he also maintains that it needs a lawgiver who will lick the citizens into shape as the legendary Lycurgus had formed the Spartans in the ninth century B.C.

Classical republican theory had always recognized the importance of socialization in molding citizens and inspiring them to virtue. Most thinkers had assumed that civic virtue does not come naturally but demands the suppression of natural human inclinations, from fear and love of pleasure to family loyalties. In a famous passage in *Emile,* his book on education (1762), Rousseau sharpened this point, contrasting education for humanity with edu-

cation for citizenship and arguing that the latter demands complete loss of self and immersion in the life of the community. In stating this, Rousseau was doing more than reiterating classical clichés. For ancient republicans the point of self-abnegation on the battlefield was simply that without that kind of commitment a republic could not remain free. With Rousseau, however, loss of self in identification with an intense community became part of the romantic quest for wholeness in opposition to the fragmentation of modern life. In the subsequent thinking about civic virtue and the nature of citizenship, hard-headed analysis of the ethos necessary for the survival of free states has often been overlaid by romantic rejections of modern individualism and yearnings for community and wholeness.

Tocqueville and the Modern Age

Alexis de Tocqueville, pondering the nature and prospects of American democracy (in *Democracy in America,* 1835–1840), did not indulge in romantic nostalgia for ancient community. It seemed to him, however, that although freedom appeared to be firmly established in the United States, it could not be taken for granted in modern societies. Republican thinking, up to and including that of Rousseau, had always assumed that although a particular republic might be "democratic" in the sense that its citizens had equal political rights, citizenship itself was a privilege restricted to a small part of the population. The United States, by contrast, was not only an exceptionally large republic but also an unprecedentedly inclusive one in which citizenship was diluted by extension. Tocqueville feared that the advance of democracy (by which he meant a society without hereditary ranks) would tend to give rise to "individualism," an atomization of society into a mass of separate and impotent individuals, each immersed in private concerns. By undermining public spirit, this fragmentation could make possible a new kind of despotism.

Tocqueville considered that in America this tendency was counterbalanced by the high rate of participation in political and voluntary organizations, which drew people out of their narrow private concerns and involved them in efforts to advance the welfare of the republic. He also observed that the strength of religion in America restrained its citizens from the worst excesses of selfish materialism. A century and a half later, with political participation down, religion weakened, consumption vastly increased, and the atomization of society proceeding apace, recent commentators have been less sanguine than Tocqueville and have drawn upon the republican tradition of thinking about civic virtue in criticizing the excesses of liberal individualism. Communitarian critics of liberalism tend to maintain that liberalism is incompatible with civic virtue.

If civic virtue is understood in the classical sense, with all its overtones of aggressive militarism, puritanical censorship of private life, and rigid hostility to change, any form of liberalism must be opposed to it. No modern republican, however, wishes to resurrect the tradition of civic virtue in its original inhumane, exclusively male, deeply illiberal form. Those who have recently borrowed from the tradition have tended to play down its puritanism and to emphasize the Aristotelian idea of fulfillment through participation in ruling and being ruled rather than the Spartan ideal of patriotic self-sacrifice. In response, defenders of liberalism have pointed out that many notable liberal thinkers, such as John Stuart Mill, enthusiastically supported political participation and public spirit while at the same time celebrating individual diversity.

One battleground for struggle between liberals and classically minded communitarians concerns education for citizenship. The republican tradition is antimaterialistic in two senses: it condemns material consumption, and it stresses the importance in politics of nonmaterial elements such as the ethos of the republic. If republics depend on the virtue of their citizens to maintain their freedom, common attitudes must be matters of public interest, and the moral formation of future citizens becomes particularly important. This concern conflicts with the recent liberal tendency, most famously expressed in John Rawls's *Theory of Justice* (1971), to negotiate the problems of modern pluralistic societies by claiming that citizens can be united in accepting principles of justice without sharing any substantive moral commitments at all.

One of the points at issue here is a question of historical sociology. Does the process of economic development naturally lead to free and democratic societies, or are free republics always rare and fragile exceptions in a world where tyranny is the norm? If the former is the case, more citizen participation and public spirit may be desirable, but neither is crucial; if the latter, civic virtue may be a matter of life and death for the republic. One of the first neorepublican thinkers, Hannah Arendt, was driven back to classical thinking by the experience of Nazi and Soviet totalitarianism, which she analyzed as subordination of human interests to material forces, made possible by a lack of public-spirited citizens prepared to take responsibility for defending freedom. Although she argued, like her successors, that political action is intrinsically satisfying, the ultimate point of active citizenship, for her as for Machiavelli and the ancients, was that without it freedom cannot last.

Since World War II attempts have been made in a great many states to establish republican and democratic institutions, in most cases without success. Although many complex reasons may be given for such failures, political scientists agree that one important problem is corruption in the sense of diversion of public funds to private purposes and that some level of public spirit is indeed a necessary condition for the flourishing and perhaps the survival of free states.

See also *Antifederalists; Aristotle; Classical Greece and Rome; Communitarianism; Enlightenment, Scottish; Federalists; Liberalism; Machiavelli, Niccolò; Mill, John Stuart; Montesquieu; Participatory democracy; Popular sovereignty; Republicanism; Rhetoric; Rousseau, Jean-Jacques; Theory, Ancient; Tocqueville, Alexis de.*

Margaret Canovan

BIBLIOGRAPHY

Arendt, Hannah. *The Human Condition.* Chicago: University of Chicago Press, 1958.
Aristotle. *The Politics.* Edited by Stephen Everson. Cambridge: Cambridge University Press, 1988.
Machiavelli, Niccolò. *The Discourses.* Edited by Bernard Crick. Harmondsworth: Penguin Books, 1970.
Montesquieu, Charles-Louis de Secondat, Baron de. *The Spirit of the Laws.* Edited by A. M. Cohler, B. C. Miller, and H. S. Stone. Cambridge: Cambridge University Press, 1989.
Oldfield, Adrian. *Citizenship and Community: Civic Republicanism and the Modern World.* London and New York: Routledge, 1990.
Pocock, J. G. A. *The Machiavellian Moment: Florentine Political Thought and the Atlantic Republican Tradition.* Princeton: Princeton University Press, 1975.
Rahe, Paul A. *Republics Ancient and Modern: Classical Republicanism and the American Revolution.* Chapel Hill and London: University of North Carolina Press, 1992.
Rousseau, Jean-Jacques. *The Social Contract, with Geneva Manuscript and Political Economy.* Edited by R. D. Masters. New York: St. Martin's, 1978.
Sinopoli, Richard C. *The Foundations of American Citizenship: Liberalism, the Constitution, and Civic Virtue.* Oxford: Oxford University Press, 1992.
Tocqueville, Alexis de. *Democracy in America.* Translated by G. Lawrence. Edited by J. P. Mayer and M. Lerner. New York: Harper, 1966; London: Fontana, 1968.

Voting

See *Participation, Political*

Voting behavior

Voting behavior is determined by the political attitudes, assumptions, policy preferences, and partisan loyalties of individuals and the political and institutional context within which they cast their votes in an election. It is studied in order to discover why people choose to support particular parties or candidates in elections. Elections are primarily occasions when governments defend their policies and voters hold them accountable by confirming them in office or "kicking the rascals out." In the process, elections legitimate the government by giving it a mandate for future action.

These functions of legitimation and control are central to democracy. For this and other reasons, the question why people choose to support a particular party or candidate when voting at elections has long been of interest. If voters did not take account of government performance or the promises of candidates, there would seem to be little chance that elections would perform the functions of accountability and control. When voters do behave as required, questions may remain about whether their votes are properly translated into government actions, but accountability is more likely to be achieved.

Until the advent of scientific public opinion polling, the assumption was generally made that voters choose between candidates or parties on the basis of careful evaluation of past performance and campaign promises, bearing in mind their own preferences and concerns. With scientific polling came the realization that most people at most elections vote not on the basis of careful evaluation of competing options but on the basis of what has been called a *standing decision* to support a particular political party. So explaining this "partisan voting" (and assessing its rationality) means that we need to explain how these standing decisions are reached.

Socialization, Immunization, and Partisan Voting

Although children presumably must reach a certain age before they acquire political opinions, there is an impor-

tant sense in which party preference is inherited at birth. It is the political complexion of the family, neighborhood, and school that most strongly influences initial partisanship and hence the choice between parties and candidates that is made when an individual first votes. If these influences reinforce each other, with neighbors echoing the political preferences of family and school, then the likelihood is strong that the initial vote will be in conformity with these influences.

If the influences are contradictory, they will dilute each other, and it may be hard to predict which of the influences (if any) will be reflected in a person's vote. In such situations the influence of the family tends to be paramount, but in no case can we say that individuals are more than strongly inclined to vote in accordance with family tradition. The more this tradition is diluted by other influences, the more people are liable to be affected by additional factors (the nature of the times, the influence of advertising, the attractiveness of a candidate, and so on).

Socialization does not stop with adulthood. Entering the labor market or going to college exposes people to new experiences that may reinforce childhood influences or (further) dilute them. Moving out of the parental home brings the possibility of a new neighborhood with new political influences. Even late in life a change in social situation accompanying a new job or retraining may give rise to influences that can trigger a change in political outlook.

The extent to which individuals are open to new influences and considerations is not only a function of the extent to which previous influences have reinforced each other. At least as important as reinforcement is another concept that appears to be similar: the concept of immunization. Immunization occurs once people actually start to cast votes in elections. The act of voting can turn a tendency into a commitment that, with the passage of time and with repetition, can become ingrained. Effectively, by repeatedly voting for the same party a person can become immunized against influences that might otherwise have led him or her to vote differently in the future. On the other hand, if at successive elections a voter does not reassert his or her commitment to a specific party but instead makes different choices, such a voter may remain unimmunized and open to new experiences and influences.

It used to be thought that as people grew older they became more set in their ways. In the context of voting choice this would mean that older voters would prove less open to influence from events and tides of opinion particular to a specific election. They would see these events in the light of their preexisting commitment to a particular political party. In fact, it has been found that this openness to new ideas and choices is a function not of age but of immunization. Older voters are indeed more likely to be set in their ways, but only because they have had more time in which to become immunized against change. Older voters who have repeatedly changed their party allegiance throughout their lives are in fact no more set in their ways than are young voters who have not yet had a chance to become immunized against change. By contrast, a voter may be as young as thirty and already be immunized as a consequence of having voted the same way at every opportunity since reaching voting age. The passage of time merely increases the number of opportunities for a voter to be caught by the immunization process.

The fact that so many people vote on the basis of a standing decision means that in the course of an election campaign very few people will change their minds. This lack of change would not be surprising in parliamentary democracies, where election campaigns typically last a month or less, but it is true even in the United States, where campaigns for presidential elections last the best part of a year. In both types of system (but especially in the United States) vast sums are expended in trying to influence a very small number of voters: those who are not (yet) immunized against change—the young and the nonpartisan older voters. Unfortunately, of all voters these older nonpartisans are the least interested in politics, the most poorly educated, and the most likely to be influenced by ephemeral considerations such as the candidate's personality and physical appearance or the hint of scandal.

Because politicians know that well-informed and thoughtful voters are likely to have made up their minds long before the campaign started, they are often tempted to focus on the ignorant and thoughtless, who are more likely to engage in what has sometimes been called *personality voting*. These voters, who can most easily be influenced, are the most likely to be targeted. If "sound bites" and headlines appear to treat voters like fools, this is largely because the fools among the voters are the easiest to influence. Of course, voters who are uninterested in politics are quite likely not to vote, but their large numbers among the undecided make them appealing targets for the pandering of politicians. What politicians forget is

that the people being targeted are not the only ones who read newspapers or watch the news on television. Well-informed and thoughtful voters see the messages too, and their reactions of distaste help to put politics and politicians into disrepute.

Persistence and Change in Party Systems

In the days before television, when political ideas were transmitted mainly by word of mouth and when communities were stronger and more localized, the mechanisms of socialization and immunization tended to produce voters who were strongly committed to particular political parties. These mechanisms, by building strong party loyalties which were then transmitted to successive generations, ensured the persistence of party systems over long periods of time. Indeed, early students of party competition characterized these systems as "frozen."

In the United States the salient divisions underlying party identification reflected the different sides taken in the American Civil War (1861–1865) and the patterns of migration and immigration that occurred since then. The Republicans had been the party of Abraham Lincoln and so were strong in the North. The Democrats had been the party of the South. The development of cities and the influx into them of immigrants who knew nothing of the Civil War gave Democrats in the North and Republicans in the South the opportunity to make gains. Westward migration then projected these allegiances to newly settled states in sometimes complex patterns as the wagon trails (and later the railroads) crisscrossed their way across the continent. Until the 1950s American politics were fundamentally explicable in terms of these historic loyalties.

In Europe voters also remained loyal to sides taken in past conflicts. But the past went back much further, to conflicts that had preceded other conflicts (for example urban versus rural, church versus state, middle class versus working class). The result was a mosaic of loyalties often more complex than those seen in the United States. With the coming of democratic institutions, party choice in European countries tended to follow the lines of social demarcation that had resulted from these historic conflicts. Because the distinction between supporters of one party and another became, in such countries, coterminous with the boundaries or cleavages between social groups, these types of political linkages are often referred to as *cleavage politics*.

Within the confines of the political alternatives defined

by historic conflicts, the balance of political forces could change from election to election, but generally this balance changed only marginally and temporarily, with previous loyalties reasserting themselves quite soon. In some countries (notably the United States and Great Britain) realignments during the course of the twentieth century altered the balance of political forces significantly, bringing Franklin D. Roosevelt's New Deal to the United States in the 1930s and a Labour government to Great Britain in 1945. But in most longstanding democracies the original pattern of cleavage politics endured (sometimes bridging interruptions in the continuity of democratic institutions) until the 1960s or later.

Changes in the balance of political forces, such as those that occurred in the United States in the 1930s and in Great Britain in the 1940s, are not hard to explain in a fashion consistent with the presence of socializing and immunizing mechanisms. Even though people may seldom change their political allegiances, the specific individuals who comprise the electorate are constantly changing. Old people become infirm and die, to be replaced by young people who may not have exactly the same political ideas and preferences. In any given election about one in ten voters will be voting for the first time, replacing about the same number who are no longer participating.

Although the inheritance of political ideas by a new generation can result in the transmission of strong allegiances once the new generation becomes immunized against change, there is a weak spot in the process that can last for a decade or more. During this time the younger generation can be deflected from its inherited partisanship by the arrival of new ideas and concerns. If the younger generation is unusually large (a baby boom generation, for example) this deflection can have major political consequences.

Moreover, political systems are not necessarily closed. Immigration can provide a pool of unimmunized individuals, and the extension of the franchise can bring into the electorate people with concerns that were not previously represented (or not represented in such great numbers). In the contemporary era the extension of the franchise in most countries to include individuals in their late teenage years had implications for the balance of political forces that were not trivial and that go some way toward explaining the support for new political parties in many countries. It is also possible that normal mechanisms of socialization and immunization go into abeyance during periods of political turmoil, when political passions are roused and people are less likely to follow unthinkingly a standing decision made in more normal times.

It is hard to be definitive about these matters because our methods for studying voters and party choice were in their infancy during the great realignments of this century, and the explanations that we have developed for understanding continuity and change are of recent vintage. It seems likely, however, that realignments involve both the coming of age of a new generation of voters with ideas that are radically different from those of their elders and a greater than usual amount of conversion among established voters.

Dealignment and Voting Choice

In recent years the number of unimmunized individuals available to be energized by new political ideas seems to have increased greatly in many countries. Since the early 1970s we have seen a growing number of new social movements concerned with defending ecological diversity, the needs of women, and minority interests of every kind; and the adherence of individuals to these movements is no longer mediated by face-to-face contact. Some new social movements have given birth to new political parties whose advent seems to have coincided with a decline in the predictability of electoral choice based on partisan voting—a development sometimes referred to as *dealignment* because it involves a breakdown in the close ties between particular parties and particular social groups. Furthermore, although the number of supporters of new political parties is small, the number of people who are voting for a traditional party for nontraditional reasons seems to be large and growing. Voters are increasingly making their choice not on the basis of inherited partisan loyalties and identifications but on other grounds, some of them very specific and particular to the individual concerned.

The decline of cleavage politics seems to have gone further in some countries than in others, apparently because the decline started at different times. In Great Britain, France, Australia, and New Zealand, the importance of cleavage politics was apparently already on the wane by the time of the earliest nationwide election studies, which were conducted in the 1960s. In Sweden, Denmark, Belgium, and the Netherlands, by contrast, cleavage politics was apparently still strong in the 1960s and started to decline only thereafter. In Norway and Italy, finally, cleavage politics remained strong even in the 1980s, though the characteristics of the youngest voters made it seem likely that such a decline would soon be evident.

Other countries fit the pattern less clearly, either because of the absence of comparable opinion poll data or for other idiosyncratic reasons. This blurring of the situation, together with the different timing of the decline of cleavage politics in different countries, makes it difficult to see all these developments as part of a single pattern. Nevertheless, the argument has been made that all countries with functional democratic systems eventually see a decline in cleavage politics. Such a decline quite likely occurred in the United States and Canada before the advent of polling data and will almost certainly happen soon in Norway; the 1994 election in Italy indicates that cleavage voting there has declined.

How do we account for the apparent universality in democracies of these developments in voting behavior? Many suggested explanations were designed specifically to suit the situation in particular countries (the ending of military conscription in Great Britain, for example), and they fail as soon as we recognize that the developments to be explained occur more widely. Others (such as the widely touted suggestion that increasing affluence has led to the rise of a new generation to which questions of quality of life and self-actualization were more salient than material concerns) do not square with the large differences in timing of the decline of cleavage politics in different countries.

A suggestion designed to fit the facts is that the decline of cleavage politics is evidence of the successful resolution of past conflicts. After all, the representation of social groups was also the representation of conflicting interests, and the accommodation of conflicting interests is precisely what democratic procedures are supposed to achieve.

Confirmation of this hypothesis cannot be found among the countries for which we have adequate opinion poll data, since all such countries are examples of successful democratic systems; but suggestive evidence is provided when we contrast the successful democracies with countries such as Northern Ireland and Lebanon in which democratic processes were not successful—and with countries of Eastern Europe and the former Soviet Union in which democratic processes were deliberately suppressed. In Northern Ireland and Lebanon social conflicts have never been resolved, and social groups remain the defining basis of political life. In countries in which the suppression of democratic procedures also suppressed the means for conflict resolution, the demise of tyrannical regimes has lifted the lid to reveal ancient conflicts still smoldering. The contrast with countries where democratic processes have been operating for a hundred years or more strongly suggests that those processes have had consequences for the nature of political conflict—resolving or defusing the most deep-seated differences.

The Particularization of Voting Choice

The decline of cleavage politics in European countries, like the decline of party identification in the United States, reduces the extent to which we can explain the voting choice of individuals on the basis of inherited characteristics. The question arises, then, of what has replaced partisan voting in the calculus of voting choice. At first sight it might appear that what was previously a somewhat unflattering picture of voters choosing between parties on the basis of unconsidered loyalties inherited, so to speak, at birth will have given way to the even less flattering picture of voters dancing to the tune of random and idiosyncratic forces.

Research in the United States, Great Britain, the Netherlands, and elsewhere, however, has suggested that the declining power of party identification to structure party choice has been matched by a rise in the importance of issues. Voters who are concerned about the environment or women's issues are responding to concerns particular to them, but these concerns are aroused by news items that publicize the issues involved. Few people based their votes on environmental concerns before Greenpeace brought those concerns before the public; few voted for consumer protection before Ralph Nader exposed the safety record of American automobiles. The fact that publicity for policy concerns can yield votes in favor of those concerns is a new phenomenon that speaks of voter rationality and bodes well for the future of democratic politics.

The particularization of voting choice that comes with these developments was predicted by Alvin Toffler in *The Third Wave* (1981). Contemporary innovations in social organization and communications technology have removed the need for peer groups to meet in person. Satellite and cable television, the lower costs of long-distance telephone calls, and the explosion of special-interest publications that cater to people on the basis of their concerns rather than of their affiliations have led to the development of societies that are fragmented along many lines of competing interest rather than along a few lines of social cleavage.

Because interests are less durable than group loyalties, particularized voting can be quite volatile. New concerns can lead to large variations in the strength of parties from one election to the next, and there is no longer the same likelihood that previous loyalties will reassert themselves. With greater volatility in electoral choices, immunization is less likely to occur. Consequently, political life can now yield quite unexpected electoral outcomes, as we saw with the virtual elimination of the Canadian Conservative Party in the election of 1993. The decline of partisan voting also makes possible increasingly sophisticated voting decisions that are not purely designed to register support for the party each individual prefers.

Tactical Voting

So far we have focused on voters' choice between parties as though each choice contributed equally to an electoral outcome so that no vote was wasted. Such a translation of votes into outcomes is indeed a feature of countries in which the electoral system is designed to yield proportional representation. But elections in many countries are held in the context of "winner takes all" (plurality) electoral systems.

In plurality systems each person's vote varies considerably in its effect on the final outcome of the election. In Great Britain, France, the United States, and other countries with plurality voting in single-member districts (or constituencies) there are many "safe" districts where historical experience or local opinion polls have made it clear that one candidate is far ahead and that the outcome of the contest is a foregone conclusion. In such districts those who do not support the leading candidate may well conclude that their votes for others would be wasted. Votes can also be wasted on third parties or candidates with no chance of winning. Such votes do not help to determine the outcome of the election; thus many supporters of small parties are effectively disenfranchised in plurality electoral systems.

Tactical voting occurs when individuals choose to support a party other than the one they really prefer so that their vote will not be wasted. Recent research has indicated that the balance of political forces in particular districts can have a considerable bearing on how people vote. In a closely contested seat, voters who prefer a minor party with no realistic chance of winning may choose to vote for one of the two main contenders if their vote might prove decisive in determining the outcome in the district. By contrast, votes for minor parties will be more numerous when the outcome in the district is not in doubt or the voter has no preference between the two main contenders.

Tactical voting can be instrumental (when the vote is

intended to affect the outcome) or expressive (when the vote is for a party that cannot win). The former type of tactical voting has received considerable attention, especially in recent British elections. There it has been found to occur very widely in suitable situations (where the first two parties in the district are running neck and neck, where the voter cares about the outcome, and where his or her own party is a long way behind). In such districts and among such individuals, almost one-fifth of the votes can be tactical, rising to one-half among voters who are highly educated and aware of the tactical situation in the district.

The other form of tactical voting has been less widely studied, but it may ultimately turn out to be more important. For, although instrumental tactical votes will be frequent only in districts where voters might have supported a third party but are induced to vote otherwise in order that their vote not be wasted, expressive tactical votes can be cast any time the outcome in a district appears to be a foregone conclusion—a much more frequent phenomenon. Expressive tactical votes are not intended to affect the outcome of an election. Rather they are designed to send a message: generally a message of discontent about the options offered by the major contestants.

Thus it seems likely that many of those who voted for Ross Perot in the U.S. presidential elections of 1992 did so not because they seriously expected their vote to help him become president but because they hoped that by voting for him they would send a message of discontent to the party they would otherwise have supported. Considerations of this kind will almost certainly prove an increasingly common feature of voting behavior in elections that are conducted without the straitjackets of party identification or cleavage politics.

Individual Voting and Election Outcomes

However individual voting choice is explained, it must be recognized that the importance of an election lies not in individual votes but in aggregate outcomes. It matters whether parties gain votes or lose votes. At the margin a government may lose its majority and be replaced; and, even if the government is not replaced, the experience of losing votes may lead to changes in government policy. Evidently, many individuals can change their votes without changing the relative standing of different parties, if the changes in favor of one party cancel out the changes in favor of another. But if such shifts do not cancel each other out, even a relatively small change in the strength of parties (perhaps the result of new voters with distinctive concerns) can result in a change of government or at least of government policy.

The link between individual voting choice and election outcomes is not simple or straightforward, yet the outcome of the election—the overall standing of parties and candidates and whether they gain or lose votes compared with the previous election—determines how countries are governed. To see how elections can lead to changes in government, or at least to changes in government policy, we must shift our attention from individual voters to the electorate in general and consider whether the aggregate process is a rational one.

Strong signs of rationality are detected by those who see the electorate in recent elections as responding primarily to concerns about the economy. "The economy, stupid!" was not just a staff reminder during Bill Clinton's campaign in 1992 for the U.S. presidency; it is a slogan that might as well be chalked up on the board in every introductory college class on voting behavior. Contemporary electorates do seem frequently to punish incumbent governments for bad economic times by removing them from office while rewarding them for good economic times by renewing their mandates.

Though rational in a sense, such behavior would not be much more flattering than votes cast purely on the basis of group loyalties or inherited party identification. The state of the economy may or may not be the fault of the government in office. Sophisticated voters should be able to differentiate between bad times that are the fault of the incumbent government and bad times that are the result of world recession or other external forces.

There is some evidence that indeed voters are more sophisticated than the simple theory of retrospective economic evaluations would indicate. The electorate of Great Britain did not eject the Conservative Party in 1992, despite the stubborn persistence of bad economic times. Moreover, although Clinton made much of George Bush's poor economic management in the U.S. election of 1992, objectively the economy was well on its way to recovery. Bush's failure to be believed when he pointed this out was arguably more fundamental to his electoral defeat than was the objective economic situation.

If we look beyond elections to the continuous polling of public opinion that takes place today in all Western countries, it seems clear that public policy is shaped by shifts in public mood that occur over long periods. Such responsiveness by government to changing electoral demands raises the question of whether the electorate pays attention to policy changes. If it did not, there would be no incentive for governments to take account of public demands; but the latest research shows that, at least in the United States, changes in public policy are indeed registered by the electorate and are reflected in changes in mood. This feedback between public demands and policy changes happens just as though the public were acting as a thermostat that sends signals when policy changes are wanted and stops sending them once policies have altered enough to match demands.

Of course, the extent to which the public pays attention to policy outputs varies among different components of public policy. Defense expenditure is better publicized than expenditure on education, and there is evidence that the public pays closer attention to the former than to the latter. In areas such as foreign aid that people know very little about, they can hardly respond to policy changes. In general it seems clear that the public is more aware of domestic than of foreign policies (except when foreign policy failures lead to large numbers of deaths in battle or otherwise), and in most countries governments have traditionally been granted a freer rein in foreign policy matters than in domestic matters.

The Electoral Verdict

Because there are areas in which the public is relatively uninformed, one must be careful about interpreting election outcomes as verdicts upon government policies. Just because politicians campaign for votes on a particular issue or issues does not mean that the voters choose between parties on the basis of those issues. In particular, an election that is ostensibly about foreign policy issues may actually be found to hinge on the domestic situation. This problem of voter attention (or, more properly, inattention) becomes particularly important when voters are consulted about some policy proposal in a referendum. It may be that the outcome of the referendum reflects not public sentiments about the ostensible subject but simply the standing of the parties that are arguing on either side.

In France and Denmark in 1992, when voters were asked their opinion about the Treaty on European Union, they appear to have voted primarily to show their displeasure with the domestic performance of the government of the day. A similar tendency on the part of voters should be taken into account when interpreting results of elections for the European Parliament. The elections ostensibly are about European affairs, but since voters know little about such matters they cast their vote largely according to their domestic party preferences, turning European elections into "beauty contests" of little more importance than an opinion poll.

The most famous occasion on which voters were asked to judge a politician on one basis and actually judged him on another was probably the British election of 1945. Winston Churchill asked British voters to reward him as a war leader by giving him a chance to "win the peace." In fact, Churchill was repudiated by a landslide, not because the British were not grateful to him as a war leader (his personal popularity stood at more than 80 percent) but because they did not see the need for a war leader after the defeat of Germany.

This election was merely a particularly dramatic example of the fact that politicians cannot always determine the criteria upon which they will be judged by voters; so the electoral verdict can easily hinge on things that are not the ostensible subject of the election. Some see this result as a manifestation of irrational voting, but it is not. Voters surely have the right not only to judge the relative merits of different candidates (or parties) but also to determine the issues on which the judgment will be made. What is important is for politicians not to make the mistake of supposing that voters are necessarily voting on the grounds proposed by them (or even that all the members of the electorate voted on the same grounds). Election outcomes are the product of a multitude of judgments, many of which cancel out, and the basis of which in individual preferences is often hard to determine.

The Consequences of Elections

If elections are held to legitimate and control the government, it matters whether outcomes correspond with voters' intentions. An election outcome can be considered rational if the election leads to government or policy changes in line with changes in voter preferences as registered at the election. If the consequence of an election is otherwise, the outcome might be considered irrational.

In multiparty systems, where coalition governments are the norm, the electoral verdict and the complexion of the governing coalition that is formed afterward need not correspond. The bargaining process that takes place after an election can completely vitiate the desires of individual voters, as in Israel in 1988, when a government took office that represented a minority point of view on virtually every major issue. Even in so-called two-party systems, where single-party governments are the norm, voter preferences are not necessarily translated into changes in gov-

ernment (or government policy) if there are in fact more than two parties competing.

Between 1979 and 1994 the Conservative Party won four successive elections in Great Britain, remaining in government throughout that period despite not once having won a majority of the popular vote. Because the opposition to the Conservatives was split between Labour and other parties, the working of the electoral system ensured that the Conservatives remained in office. An even more perverse outcome occurred in 1951, when the Conservative Party won more seats in Parliament than did Labour, despite winning almost 1 percent fewer popular votes.

These problems in translating electoral outcomes into government outcomes constitute a major deficiency in democratic politics from which no country is immune; but perverse outcomes happen seldom enough or are benign enough that the rules that translate individual voting acts into government formations receive widespread acceptance. In Great Britain and in Israel, perverse outcomes are accepted as long as the rules have been followed. The same would probably be true elsewhere. Elections in a democracy are not even close to being perfect mechanisms for controlling governments and holding them accountable. They are merely the best mechanisms we have.

See also *Churchill, Winston; Class; Coalition building; Election campaigns; Electoral systems; Multiethnic democracy; Participation, Political; Parties, Political; Party systems; Polling, Public opinion; Rational choice theory; Social movements; Socialization, Political.*

Mark N. Franklin

BIBLIOGRAPHY

Eijk, Cees van der, Mark N. Franklin, et al. *Choosing Europe? The European Electorate and National Politics in the Face of Union.* Ann Arbor: University of Michigan Press, forthcoming.

Eijk, Cees van der, and Kees Neimoller. *Electoral Change in the Netherlands.* Amsterdam: CT Press, 1983.

Franklin, Mark, Thomas Mackie, Henry Valen, et al., eds. *Electoral Change: Responses to Evolving Social and Attitudinal Structures in Western Countries.* Cambridge and New York: Cambridge University Press, 1992.

Franklin, Mark, Michael Marsh, and Christopher Wlezien. "Attitudes to Europe and Referendum Votes." *Electoral Studies* 13 (1994): 117–121.

Franklin, Mark, Richard Niemi, and Guy Whitton. "Two Faces of Tactical Voting." *British Journal of Political Science* 24 (1994): 549–557.

Inglehart, Ronald. *The Silent Revolution: Changing Values and Political Styles among Western Publics.* Princeton: Princeton University Press, 1977.

Key, V. O., Jr. *Public Opinion and American Democracy.* New York: Knopf, 1961.

Lewis-Beck, Michael S. *Economics and Elections: The Major Western Democracies.* Ann Arbor: University of Michigan Press, 1988.

Lipset, Seymour Martin, and Stein Rokkan, eds. *Party Systems and Voter Alignments.* New York: Free Press, 1967.

Nie, Norman, Sydney Verba, and John Petrocik. *The Changing American Voter.* 2d ed. Cambridge: Harvard University Press, 1979.

Stimson, James. *Public Opinion in America: Moods, Cycles, and Swings.* Boulder, Colo.: Westview Press, 1991.

Toffler, Alvin. *The Third Wave.* New York: Bantam Books; London: Pan Books, 1981.

Wlezien, Christopher, and Malcolm Goggin. "The Courts, Interest Groups, and Public Opinion about Abortion." *Political Behavior* 15 (1993): 381–405.

Voting rights

The right to vote, along with freedom of expression, assembly, association, and press, is one of the fundamental requirements of modern constitutional democracy. The political right of electoral participation, indisputable in the theory of democracy since the French Revolution, was achieved at different times in different countries and only after a long historic process. Elections are among the most important forms of institutionalized participation and, because of voting rights, are a form of participation in which social, economic, ethnic, and other factors matter little.

Principles of Suffrage

Today, there exist four principles of democratic suffrage: suffrage must be universal, equal, secret, and direct. These principles must be viewed from a juridical-historical as well as from a conceptual point of view. That is, one must consider not only if and when suffrage became universal, equal, secret, and direct but also how those terms were defined by different societies in different eras. For example, in the nineteenth century, *universal* meant only the right of men to vote.

First, the norm of universality requires that all citizens of the state—regardless of their sex, race, language, income, land holdings, profession, class, education, religion, or political beliefs—have the right to vote and to be elect-

Haitians, holding their registration cards, wait outside a polling place in Port-au-Prince. The November 29, 1987, presidential and congressional election was called off after only a few hours because of violence and intimidation.

ed. The fact that certain prerequisites are demanded, such as age, nationality, residence, sound mind, citizenship, or absence of a criminal record, does not negate this principle. In pre-democratic systems, suffrage was limited in essentially three ways: through the direct exclusion of a certain sector of the population, such as ethnic or religious minorities, dependents, or women; through the imposition of a poll tax, which discriminated against the poorer elements of society; and through educational or professional requirements, which disenfranchised illiterates.

Second, the principle of equality demands that the value of each vote be the same, that votes not be weighted according to property, income, education, religion, race, social class, sex, or political belief. In pre-democratic political systems this principle was routinely violated in a number of ways. One way was through class suffrage, in which the electorate was divided into groups of very different size, each of which elected a fixed number of legislators. Another was through weighted voting, in which the number of votes each qualified elector could cast was different, and additional votes were granted to predetermined groups of persons (landowners or heads of households, for example).

The principle of equality is also important for the technical organization of elections, above all, for deciding constituency boundaries. To guarantee numerical equality, the constituency boundary must be designed so as to maintain a proportion of qualified voters to representatives that is approximately equal across constituencies. The principle of equal suffrage is today the most important of all the principles of suffrage, in practical terms.

Third, the principle of secrecy requires that the voting act cannot be known by a third party. This differs from all forms of open vote casting (signed voting) or public vote casting (nominal voting). Secrecy in voting is achieved under the guidance of an electoral organization that provides secret booths or rooms and secret ballot boxes.

Finally, under the principle of direct elections the voters select their leaders for themselves; with indirect elections intermediate bodies (such as an electoral college) stand between the voters and the elected officials. One must distinguish, however, between pro forma intermediary bodies (whose members are bound by the vote of the citizens) and substantive intermediary bodies (whose members are free to ignore the popular vote and to elect the leaders according to their own criteria).

The Process of Achieving Democratic Suffrage

Historically, universal and equal suffrage ("one person, one vote, one value") developed quite differently in various parts of the world. Let us first look at some early industrializing countries.

The democratization of suffrage—which together with the parliamentarization of political systems is a key line of constitutional transformation since the French Revolution—took approximately one hundred years in Europe. Before 1848 universal male suffrage did not exist in any country. After World War II all four principles of democratic suffrage had been realized in every European country, with only a few exceptions: Switzerland, where women were denied the vote until 1971, and Spain and Portugal, where open, competitive elections were not held until the mid-1970s.

Some countries introduced universal male suffrage at an early date; France, Germany, Switzerland, and New Zealand had all instituted universal male suffrage by 1889. Other countries, including Australia, Finland, and Austria,

established it shortly before World War I. And still others established it either during or after World War I. By 1920 universal male suffrage was in force in all Western industrialized countries.

For women, suffrage came later. Before 1900 women were allowed to vote only in New Zealand; shortly after the turn of the century they were also enfranchised in Finland and Norway. After World War I a majority of countries introduced female suffrage (some at the same time as universal male suffrage). In France, Italy, Belgium, Portugal, Spain, and the special case of Switzerland (all countries heavily influenced by Roman Catholicism), women had to wait until after World War II to obtain the right to vote.

In the United States universal suffrage was introduced for white males at an early stage, in many states during the so-called Jacksonian Revolution of the 1830s. Black males were enfranchised by a constitutional amendment adopted after the American Civil War. Whites, however, through various kinds of manipulation, contrived to hinder black males' right to vote. This discrimination did not end until the 1960s. The experience of the United States highlights the important difference between the formal, legal right to vote and the practical application of that right.

Within any given country the dissolution of limitations on suffrage was generally a gradual process in which the four principles of suffrage were introduced one after the other, until finally the modern standards of full democratic suffrage were achieved. The process differed from state to state, however. In Prussia during the empire (1871–1918), for example, the right to vote evolved in three distinct steps: unequal suffrage, indirect suffrage, and open suffrage similar to universal suffrage. In Belgium, the extension of suffrage went hand in hand with an increased inequality in the value of the votes. Germany established direct and secret suffrage after World War I.

The evolution of democratic suffrage in every society followed one of two basic patterns: the slower, more deliberate English model or the French model. The English pattern is characterized by the gradual extension of the right to vote, by a lack of relapses, and by long periods of formal recognition of inequalities. The French model is characterized by the early and sudden introduction of rights that tend to correlate with the principles of universality and equality, but it is also characterized by frequent relapses and plebiscites to gain the support of the masses. Great Britain, in 1948, was the last country to abolish unequal suffrage and to abandon special voting rights for university graduates.

The development of suffrage in most countries fell between the extremes of the British and French cases. Normally, the working-class parties demanded and fought for universal suffrage. In exceptional cases, such as that of Belgium, the socialists voted for a long time against female suffrage, fearing the more conservative preferences of women. In Switzerland attempts to introduce female suffrage were repeatedly defeated. In Denmark the electorate rebelled against the lowering of the voting age to eighteen years in 1969 but approved the measure in a second referendum ten years later.

The extension of suffrage in developing countries tended to begin later, to consist of more stages, and to take longer. Also, in these countries the process of extending suffrage did not coincide with the establishment of stable and durable democracy. It is an open question whether the differences in the extension of suffrage between the developing and the Western industrialized countries are more pronounced than those between countries within the developing world. In any case, generalizations for such a heterogeneous group are difficult to make. There are some countries—Argentina and Uruguay among them—that adopted universal male suffrage at the same time as did the Western industrialized countries. But we also find other countries—such as the Islamic monarchies—that still do not have universal suffrage.

There are important differences in the developing world between those countries that were decolonized in the first half of the nineteenth century and those that gained their independence in the second half of the twentieth century. In countries that were decolonized early in the nineteenth century, distinct stages are observable in the extension of suffrage: first, universal male suffrage; then, female suffrage; next, enrollment of all formally qualified voters in electoral registers; and, finally, suffrage for illiterates. For example, in Chile, which gained its independence from Spain in 1818, women received the right to vote only in 1952 (and illiterates only in 1970). In Uruguay, the other South American country with democratic traditions, universal suffrage was introduced in 1916 and included illiterates. Moreover, the formal condition necessary for voting—enrollment in electoral registers—was a great obstacle to the extension of suffrage to the lower segments of the population, especially the peasants. In Chile, for example, the difference between the legally qualified voters and the entire electorate amounted to 1.3

million persons at the beginning of the 1960s, or one-third of the presumed electorate.

In the countries that decolonized later, by contrast, democratic suffrage was introduced in a single stage, generally before political independence. In most of the countries of the British West Indies, universal, equal, secret, and direct suffrage was guaranteed at the beginning of the 1950s, which in the case of Antigua and Barbuda was thirty years before the country became independent.

In the African countries, universal direct suffrage was introduced with the help of the colonial powers—primarily Great Britain and France—immediately before political independence. Exceptions were Rhodesia, where unequal suffrage based on census and skin color was maintained until 1971, and South Africa, where a racially restricted suffrage excluded more than two-thirds of the population. Suffrage was not extended to blacks in South Africa until 1994.

Political regression in some countries has also limited universal suffrage, as in the case of Sri Lanka, where the Tamils lost the right to vote after the country gained political independence from Great Britain. Such cases are rare, although the realization of equal suffrage remains a problem in almost all ethnically heterogeneous countries. Often, attempts are made to maintain existing precarious power relations without regard to the changing demographic proportions of ethnic groups (Lebanon, for example). Sometimes, the population census becomes a political question of utmost importance, preventing equal suffrage from being achieved.

In some countries of the developing world the achievement of full suffrage did not signify any real progress because of limited or nonexistent competition in the political system. In such political systems the function of elections was distorted. Also, the political-administrative structures of these countries were often not sufficient to ensure honest elections, thus diminishing the legitimacy of the election results. Such manipulations have often been the cause of violent attempts to overthrow the power holders. In recent years, international election assistance and observation have made an essential improvement in these situations. Furthermore, since voting rights are now considered to be human rights, the international community is exercising increasing pressure on national political actors to guarantee political rights in each country. In some cases, ensuring voting rights is an important condition for a country's receiving economic assistance from abroad.

Expansion of Suffrage

Many variables must be considered in analyzing the expansion of suffrage. For the Western industrialized countries, the most relevant factors are the level of industrialization and its timing; transformations in the social structure; migration flows; differences in sociocultural relations (especially ethnic and religious); constitutional changes (parliamentarization); the capacity for moderation and cooperation on the part of elites; and the processes of secession and war.

The relationship between industrialization and the extension of suffrage varied considerably from country to country. Given that a direct relationship between industrialization and the strength of the socialist party or the workers movement cannot be established, it is not possible to develop a general model, even for this limited field of causal factors relevant to the expansion of suffrage. For example, the strength of the Finnish Socialists, who entered the government in 1916, did not result from the level of industrialization, from its timing, or from the relatively early introduction of universal suffrage but from the expression of political conflicts lingering since the nineteenth century.

Nor was the relationship between the democratization of suffrage and the parliamentarization of the political system linear. In Great Britain, under limited suffrage, Parliament had relatively homogeneous representation with respect to social interests. Contrary to the British line of development, the parliamentarization of the political system in Sweden and Germany was achieved only after the democratization of suffrage.

The temporal relationship between parliamentarization, industrialization, and universal suffrage had lasting consequences in several respects: (1) for the integrative capacity of the political system and the legitimacy of the decisions taken by it; (2) for the structure of party competition; and (3) for the extent of ideological differences between the parties that were articulating social conflicts.

Where universal suffrage resulted from a difficult struggle by an already existing workers movement, radical workers parties were formed based on the idea of class conflict. In countries where access to rights of electoral participation was achieved more easily, the workers parties had a more reform-oriented character and were more willing to collaborate with bourgeois parties. The Scandinavian countries—Denmark, Norway, and Sweden—are examples of the latter course of development. A similar process of integration can be seen in Great Britain where,

under gradually expanding suffrage and a "first past the post" electoral system, the Liberals were willing to make electoral pacts with the workers movement even though a consistent segment of the working class voted for the Conservative Party. On the contrary, in the German empire the Socialists were strictly repressed, and suffrage was granted by the government in such a way as to benefit conservative-agrarian interests. The government took measures to enfranchise the dependent voters in rural areas in order to overcome the political opposition of bourgeois progressives in largely urban areas.

The major long-run consequence of the expansion of suffrage was the growth of workers parties. Although they did not fundamentally call into question the rule of capital, they articulated fundamental social conflicts within the political system—and in so doing became less radical. Once the workers movement opted for representation by a labor party, it fought for an electoral system based on the principles of proportional representation in order to achieve political representation mirroring the social structure of the electorate. Because the integration of the workers movement in the Anglo-American countries occurred early on, there were at first no demands for change in the electoral system. Universal suffrage and the stability of the principle of representation (that is, election by majority or proportional representation) "froze" the party systems by World War I along the lines of social conflict.

In the developing world, only in a few cases—notably Argentina and Uruguay—did the extension of suffrage begin concurrently with the process of industrialization and with the related process of social modernization. In most other developing countries, democratic norms were implemented without the requisite social and political structures having been realized. In many cases the extension of suffrage could not be maintained for long.

In view of the great social disparities and the lack of social participation of the broad masses of the population, universal suffrage in most developing countries did not have the same significance as in the industrialized states. The social and political forces that supported the extension of suffrage were not sufficiently strong to force the traditionally dominant segments of society to accept the participation of new strata. In some cases, the dominant forces were strong enough to suspend democracy altogether.

Contrary to the course of development of the Western democracies, political participation and political competition—the two dimensions of modern democratic development—were not mutually reinforcing but rather were conflictual. Political participation excluded competition. In many Central American countries, for example, authoritarian structures in the political system were not substantially altered when the masses were allowed to participate in elections. In addition, recognition of the principles of democratic suffrage was often pro forma, just as the election process was frequently corrupt.

See also *Citizenship; Elections, Monitoring; Electoral college; Voting behavior.*

Dieter Nohlen
Translated from the German by Cindy Skach

BIBLIOGRAPHY

Lipset, Seymour Martin. "Radicalism or Reformism: The Sources of Working Class Politics." *American Political Science Review* 77 (January 1983): 1–18.

Mackie, Thomas T., and Richard Rose, eds. *The International Almanac of Electoral History.* 3d rev. ed. London and New York: Macmillan, 1991.

Nohlen, Dieter, ed. *Encyclopedia electoral latinoamericana y del Caribe.* San José, Costa Rica: Inter-American Institute of Human Rights, 1993.

Nuscheler, Franz, and Klaus Ziemer. *Politische Organisation und Repraesentation in Afrika.* Berlin and New York: De Gruyter, 1978.

Rokkan, Stein. *Citizens, Elections, Parties: Approaches to the Comparative Study of the Processes of Development.* Oslo: Universitetsforlaget, 1970.

Rueschemeyer, Dietrich, Evelyne Huber Stephens, and John D. Stephens. *Capitalist Development and Democracy.* Oxford: Polity Press, 1991; Chicago: University of Chicago Press, 1992.

Wales

See *United Kingdom*

Walesa, Lech

President of Poland and a founder of Solidarity, the first independent trade union in communist Eastern Europe. Walesa (1943–) became a symbol of Poland's struggle against communist rule and was a principal actor in the country's nonviolent transition to democracy in 1989. He was elected president of Poland in 1990. Walesa's charismatic personality, courage, and keen sense of politics propelled him from humble beginnings to a spectacular political career. Since 1989 he has played a pivotal and often controversial role in Poland's politics.

Born to a peasant family, Walesa received a primary and vocational education, which was followed by two years of military service. In 1967 he moved to Gdansk to work as an electrician at the Lenin Shipyard, one of the largest and most important enterprises in the Polish economy. In December 1970 workers along the Baltic coast rebelled against food price increases introduced by the government. Their protests were brutally suppressed by the Communist regime. During the rebellion, Walesa became a member of the shipyard's strike committee. He was arrested but was released a few days later. In 1976 he was dismissed from the shipyard for criticizing the regime's policies at a trade union meeting, and he remained unemployed for a few months.

Lech Walesa

Later that year another food price increase caused unrest and riots. Again protests were brutally suppressed. Prosecution of workers who participated in the riots led to the formation of the Committee for Workers Defense and the rise of oppositional activities across the country. Walesa became deeply involved in oppositional activities in Gdansk. He collaborated with an underground paper and coordinated illegal activities of the Free Trade Unions of the Baltic Coast. He was detained by the police many times and was fined and dismissed from jobs in 1979 and again in February 1980.

In the summer of 1980 Poland was engulfed by a serious economic and political crisis, and strikes erupted in many enterprises. In August, Walesa, who headed the strike committee in the Lenin Shipyard, gained national attention as the strikes expanded throughout the region. He became the leader of the Interfactory Strike Committee, representing some 500 enterprises. The committee negotiated ground-breaking agreements with the Polish authorities that allowed the formation of independent trade unions. With the strikes concluded, Walesa became chairman of Solidarity, which rapidly grew to a nationwide trade union of 10 million members. He was elected president of the union during its first national congress, in September 1981. During subsequent months, Walesa negotiated with Polish authorities, represented the union abroad, mediated conflicts and strikes, and curbed radical and militant groups within the union. During this time he represented moderate political views and was committed to negotiating a compromise with Poland's Communist rulers.

On December 13, 1981, the Polish government declared martial law and banned Solidarity, which continued to operate underground. Walesa was interned and kept in isolation until November 1982. After his release, he worked to establish himself as a viable political figure, collaborating with leaders of the underground movement, meeting foreign journalists and politicians, organizing consultative committees, and urging Polish authorities to negotiate with the opposition. In the fall of 1983 Walesa received the Nobel Peace Prize, which reaffirmed his worldwide reputation and international support for the Solidarity movement.

The postmartial law regime failed to solve Poland's political and economic problems, and its repressive policies became ineffective. In 1988, facing resurgent workers' strikes and demands for the restoration of Solidarity, the Communist leaders began formal talks with Walesa, the undisputed leader of the Polish opposition, and the team of opposition activists selected by Walesa. These negotiations became Walesa's personal triumph and put him at the center of Poland's politics. The agreement reached on April 5, 1989, relegalized Solidarity and established a power-sharing arrangement between Solidarity and the Communist authorities based on semifree elections. Walesa played a critical role in mobilizing support for the coming parliamentary elections. Representatives of a broad Solidarity coalition known as the "Walesa team" achieved a stunning victory, taking all but one of the seats that were freely contested. The political and moral success of the opposition resulted in the formation of a non-Communist government led by Tadeusz Mazowiecki and paved the way for fundamental political and economic reforms.

During the initial phase of the transition to democracy, Walesa declined to accept any political post. Early in 1990, however, he turned against the power-sharing arrangement he had negotiated, challenged the Solidarity-led government he had helped to create, and urged new parliamentary and presidential elections. He declared "a war at the top," which ultimately destroyed the original Solidarity-sponsored coalition and caused growing political conflicts and the fragmentation of Polish politics. The presidential campaign of fall 1990 pitted Walesa against Prime Minister Mazowiecki. In the first round of elections, Walesa received only 40 percent of the vote, necessitating a runoff election, which he won overwhelmingly. On December 22, 1990, Walesa was sworn in as Poland's first democratically elected president since World War II.

Walesa's term as president was marred by controversies. He sought to expand the powers of the presidency and in the process alienated many of his former friends and advisers. He was criticized for blocking constitutional reforms and for destabilizing Poland's new democracy. Although his approval rating dropped significantly, he remains one of Poland's most important politicians.

See also *Poland; Solidarity.*

Grzegorz Ekiert

BIBLIOGRAPHY

Ascherson, Neal, ed. *The Book of Lech Walesa.* New York: Simon and Schuster, 1982.

Craig, Mary. *The Crystal Spirit: Lech Walesa and His Poland.* London: Hodder and Stoughton, 1986.

Kurski, Jaroslaw. *Lech Walesa: Democrat or Dictator?* Translated by Peter Obst. Boulder, Colo.: Westview Press, 1993.

Walesa, Lech. *The Struggle and the Triumph: An Autobiography.* New York: Arcade, 1992.

———. *A Way of Hope. An Autobiography.* New York: Holt, 1987.

War and civil conflict

War and civil conflict have figured prominently in the history of democracy. Violent conflicts between states and between domestic groups have been causes of, reasons for, and consequences of democracy. However, war and civil conflict are qualitatively different phenomena. Their significance in the history of democracy has not been the same. Moreover, in the long, discontinuous history of democracy, from ancient Greece to the present day, the relationship between war and civil conflict on the one hand and democracy on the other has shifted.

Historically, states have been above all military organizations, organizations designed for war. Democracy refers to the distribution of power within a state. Inevitably, the form of war and its organization have influenced and have been affected by the pattern of internal political power and political rights.

Arms and Classical Democracy

In premodern times the control of territories and populations was the source of power and wealth. The competition for power and wealth was largely an armed zero-sum game, in which one state's victory was another's defeat. In this context the power of the people—that is, the extent of democracy—depended heavily on the distribution of arms and the mode of waging war.

The relatively broad political participation in classical Greece was based in large part on the infantry, pioneered by Sparta and sustained by relatively affluent propertied farmers. The wider Athenian democracy rested militarily on a navy in addition to the infantry. The Athenian navy, which was the main force of the empire, was staffed by the poorer elements of the citizenry.

The democracy of the Nordic Viking age—most typically in its kingless Icelandic form with a national annual *Althing* (parliament) of adult, male freehold farmers, but common to all Viking-ruled territories—was based on an egalitarian distribution of the means of violence: the sword and the spear. The participants in Nordic assemblies were usually armed, and the clashing of weapons was a frequent means of expressing opinion.

Ancient Greek and, in particular, Athenian warfare depended on the collective contribution of the citizenry. The ancient Nordic organization of violence, on the other hand, was built on individual freeborn men and their personal arms. The Nordic system was prone to armed civil conflict and feuding, and eventually led to the breakdown of Icelandic democracy in the thirteenth century. In Athens, civil strife and conflict generally took nonarmed forms.

Because European armies—in contrast to military organizations in China and other Asian empires—generally tended to be self-equipped, the soldiers, whether farmers or knights, and their commanders had a certain autonomy with regard to the central ruler. Cities usually developed as combinations of fortresses and marketplaces. The unique feature of the European city was its legal and political autonomy from the local ruler. This trait derived largely from the military organization of the West, together with the relative weakness of kinship ties, which also favored territorially based self-organization. This classical tradition, which links a widespread distribution of property, arms, and political participation, has been carried into modernity in some of the former British colonies, notably the United States and Australia.

Gradually, the people in arms of the ancient democracies were replaced by imperial armies, imported mercenaries, and, for a time in medieval Europe, wealthy, mounted knights. Patriarchal democracies across Europe gave way to monarchical empires, to feudalism, and to absolutist rule. Among the old European democracies, Switzerland has been the only enduring exception to the pattern, keeping both its militia and its autonomous assemblies while exporting formidable soldiers of fortune to France, Italy, and other places.

External War and Modern Democracy

The modern concept of the nation provides a crucial link between external war and modern democracy. Broadly defined, a nation is a population of a territory, actual or desired, defining itself as a political community. Democracy is a political system in which political power within the territory is vested in the whole adult population of the territory. External wars in a system of nations become wars of nations and of whole populations. The modern era has, therefore, returned to the classical notion of democratic peoples in arms, a tendency recently reversed with the substitution of professionals for conscripts.

In premodern times a nation's only means of increasing its power was through expansion—the acquisition of additional territory and populations. That fact has given way in modern times to the improvement of a nation's existing territory, including its resources and infrastructure, and of its existing population, through education and motivation. Conquest is no longer the major road to power and wealth, but in the event of war the quality of the population matters significantly.

The first major steps toward a genuinely national army were taken during the French Revolution (1789–1791), when France promulgated a constitution guaranteeing universal male suffrage and an army based on national mass mobilization. Neither succeeded very well by later standards. Ninety percent of eligible voters abstained from the elections of 1792. Because of the war, the civil terror, and the subsequent coup d'état against Maximilien Robespierre, the virtual dictator, in July 1794, the June 1793 constitution was never applied. The revolution's call to arms got a massive response, and revolutionary-nationalist reforms brought about a formidable war machine, but the principle of voluntary participation was not upheld in practice, nor was universal military service instituted. (Universal military service was established in France only in 1872.)

For all its limitations the French Revolution witnessed the first connection between popular rights and modern warfare. Far more than the original revolutionary message of freedom, equality, and fraternity, it was the military success of a politically motivated mass army, the consciousness of the nation, and the realization of the dependence of that nation on armed power that forged the new link between war and democracy. Nations emerged in the wake of the French Revolution; wars were perceived as deciding the fate of nations, not only of kings; and victory in war seemed to be decided by the strength of nations. The health and the living standards of the national population came to be perceived as important resources for war.

National warfare did not supplant or override civil class conflict over the issue of democracy. The dissolution of feudalism—which in Europe was also largely an effect, direct or indirect, of the French Revolution—and the ascendancy of capitalism gave rise to large numbers of independent farmers and of free workers, with increased capacities for organizing themselves and for demanding political rights. War—preparation for it, waging it, and the outcome of it—intervened, often decisively, between the forces for and against democracy.

War has brought many democracies into being. The two world wars of the twentieth century (1914–1918 and 1939–1945) were critical to the democratization of the world's most socioeconomically developed nations. The actual conduct of war, however, is usually detrimental to democracy and to popular political rights. War calls for the discipline of command and the conformity of unquestioned loyalty. It fosters suspicion, surveillance, incarceration, and deportation. But war has been conducive to democracy or to an extension of popular political rights in two major ways.

First, the promise of democracy or of widened citizens' rights can be a means to mobilize for war and to smooth over civil conflict during wartime mobilization. This course could be called "democratization by national mobilization." Second, democracy can emerge as a consequence of the military defeat of an authoritarian regime. This might be called "democratization by defeat."

Means and Effects of War Mobilization

Among the most clear-cut Western examples of democratization by national mobilization were the Italian franchise reform of 1912, which was instituted to legitimate Italy's colonial war in Libya, and the Canadian War Times Election Act of 1917, which was intended to pave the way for that country's entry into World War I. Granting the right to vote was intended to bring the people closer to the state and its war policy. In the Canadian case, it was also intended to weaken the resistance to conscription.

Democratization can also be used as a stratagem during war. In 1866 the German nationalist chancellor Otto von Bismarck of Prussia proposed equal and universal male suffrage for a new constitution of the German Confederation in a calculated move to undercut support for Austria. The ploy contributed to Prussian victory in the Austro-Prussian War in the battle of Königgrätz. After another successful Prussian war, this one against France in 1870–1871, the German Reich was proclaimed under a Prussian emperor. The Reich had universal male suffrage and a legislature with severely limited powers.

In a number of non-Western states that were threatened but never colonized by European and North American powers, political rights were granted to the populations by local rulers as means of national mobilization in preparation for defensive war. The menace and superior strength of the Western powers was acknowledged, and their institutions of popular participation were associated with this strength. Such institutions were therefore imported as a means to mobilize for resistance.

The first example of such democratization under threat

of colonization was the Tanzimat ("reorganization") reforms of the Ottoman Empire in 1840. The 1881 Imperial Rescript of Meiji Japan, issued under similar circumstances, promised (and delivered in 1889) a constitution with significant popular rights, although it fell short of establishing democracy. In 1908 the Chinese imperial court announced a similar, gradual introduction of parliamentary government, which was begun in 1909 but was cut short by the republican revolution in 1911 and the subsequent civil conflict.

Examples of the democratic effects of consensual wartime mobilization include the Danish conservatives' acceptance of democracy in 1915, the institution of universal male suffrage in the Netherlands and Belgium in 1917–1918, the enlarged suffrage of the British Reform Act of 1918, the institution of female suffrage in the United States in 1920, and its acceptance in Belgium, France, and Italy in 1944–1946.

Democratization by Defeat

The first modern democracy to arise from a nondemocratic regime's defeat in an external war was France after 1871. Defeat in the Franco-Prussian War finished off the French Second Empire, although the issue of universal male suffrage was left until the late 1870s.

The end of World War I led to a number of new democratic states, which broke off from the defeated empires, and to the temporary democratization of the defeated states themselves—Austria and Germany. The most renowned manifestation of this democratization by defeat was the Weimar constitution of Germany, written by the distinguished scholar-politician Hugo Preuss, who before the war was a constitutional monarchist and not a democrat.

Defeat can affect democratization indirectly as well. The Swedish right wing, for example, was adamantly opposed to parliamentary democracy in the early part of the twentieth century, and its resistance had been strengthened by the rising might of the German Reich. After the Reich's defeat and fall in 1918, however, a constitutional transition to democracy became possible in Sweden.

The democratic outcomes of World War I were contested by antidemocratic forces, often successfully for a while. A number of new dictatorships arose in southern and central Europe. Yet another wave of democratization by defeat took place after World War II, when democracy returned to Austria, Finland, and Germany and, for the first time, prevailed in Italy and Japan. In Germany and,

particularly, in Japan, the victorious Allied army was the crucial midwife of democratization.

Defeat in external war has been important in later processes of democratization as well. Examples include Pakistan in 1971, after the loss of East Pakistan, which became Bangladesh; Greece in 1974, after its disastrous attempt to capture Cyprus in the face of an acute Turkish threat; Portugal in the same year, after protracted losses in colonial wars; and Argentina in 1982, after its catastrophic attempt to wrest the Falklands/Malvinas Islands from the British.

The Legacy of Civil Wars

Whereas external wars have had an overall positive effect on modern democratization, the legacy of civil wars has generally been negative. It is true that ancient Athenian democracy was established in 508 B.C. after a brief civil war and lasted for a century, until it was overthrown by a short-lived oligarchy in 411 B.C. It would seem that the outcome of modern civil wars, however, has been restrictive in terms of citizens' rights, regardless of which side has won. A civil war implies an enemy within, with which a reconciliation is very difficult.

The enemy in a civil war is typically regarded as a traitor and is likely to be treated as such after its defeat. The outcome of the American Civil War (1861–1865) is a good example. In spite of President Abraham Lincoln's efforts at national reconciliation, the effective postwar alternatives were either reconciliation with the Southern whites at the expense of the blacks or emancipation of the blacks at the expense of the white racists. In any case, full democracy did not ensue from the American Civil War.

In the postrevolutionary civil war in Russia (1917–1921), neither side stood for democracy—neither the Bolsheviks nor their counterrevolutionary enemies, the so-called Whites. The effect of the civil war was a general devastation of the country and a brutalization of all the forces involved. Similarly, in the 1940s the protracted civil war in China between the Communists and the Nationalists (Kuomintang) strengthened authoritarian tendencies on both sides and led to nondemocratic regimes in Nationalist-ruled Taiwan and in Communist-ruled mainland China.

In the Finnish civil war of 1918, both communists and noncommunists were originally open to democratic ideas. But the German-aided victory of the noncommunists ushered in severe repression. Moreover, there is no indication that the effect on elementary human rights would have been different with another outcome.

The Spanish civil war (1936–1939) was won by the anti-democratic forces of Gen. Francisco Franco, and almost three decades of dictatorship ensued. A victory by the republican forces would most probably have led to democracy in Spain much earlier, but hardly without an initial wave of repression.

Civil Conflict: Property and Poverty

The socioeconomic issues involved in democracy were very clear to the ancient Greeks 2,500 years ago. Democracy was from the very beginning an assertion of the rights of the common people against the rich and against the aristocracy. Class conflict is a thread running throughout the history of democracy: ancient, medieval, and modern. Demands for democracy have been raised by the middle classes, especially by those strong and self-confident enough to demand their rights—that is, small farmers, artisans, skilled workers, and industrial workers.

In modern times the labor movement has been the most consistent pro-democratic force across nations. The modern labor movement began in the 1830s with the British Chartists, supporters of the "People's Charter," which demanded universal male suffrage, use of the secret ballot, elimination of property qualifications for members of Parliament, and other reforms. The movement was carried on by the international organization of Social Democratic labor parties and trade unions, which comprised the Second International of 1889–1914.

Fear of democracy, or more precisely fear of the non-propertied mass of the population, is a recurrent theme in political theory, which until the end of the nineteenth century was written by people from or associated with the privileged classes. Classical Athenian democracy had in fact not involved any redistribution of land or other property, but Greek philosophers remained hostile to democracy nonetheless. The Founders of the United States were also fearful of democracy, but they retained a republican commitment to accountability to a broad citizenry.

The most principled battles for and against democracy were fought in Europe. The battles were developed in the aftermath of the English civil war in the mid-seventeenth century but gathered momentum only with the French Revolution. The issue of popular political rights took on a new character after Napoleon III showed, in the 1850s, that it was possible to run a propertied empire with universal male suffrage. Until the 1888 presidential election in the United States, the largest electorate in world history was that of the French Second Empire. Prime Minister Benjamin Disraeli in England and Bismarck in Prussia soon learned as well that universal suffrage did not mean an abdication of the prerogatives of the executive and of the aristocracy. The dynamics and outcomes of war, therefore, had great importance for the achievement of democracy.

The Legitimacy of Debate and Channeling Conflict

The legitimacy of conflict and debate within democracy was questioned for a long time. In classical Greece, *stasis* (meaning "faction," "discord," "dissent," or "sedition") was held to be the great evil to which democracies were prone. Faction was also singled out for severe criticism in the *Federalist,* written by James Madison, Alexander Hamilton, and John Jay in support of ratification of the U.S. Constitution. One of the first principled defenders of parties was the English Whig Edmund Burke, in 1770, but party conflict and party government became legitimate only in the nineteenth century, and then only in some countries. The replacement of partisan conflict—whether based on ideology, class differences, or ethnic cleavages—by national unity has been a recurrent theme of modern dictatorial regimes.

The extent to which democracy presupposes or promotes certain forms of social conflict is still open to debate. Elitist theories of modern democracy see democracy as primarily an institution for selecting political leaders by competition. In this view a certain insulation of the polity from the population and from society's strife is necessary if elites are not to become "overloaded" by popular demands. In pluralist conceptions of democracy the polity is the arena of conflict between a large number of dispersed and competing interests of various sorts. Democracy is in danger, the purveyors of pluralist theory argue, when interests coalesce and cumulate into polarized social blocs.

Other theories of democracy and civil conflict have started from a perception that modern democracies often contain socioeconomic and sociocultural interests that coalesce in stable, even polarized, constellations. To account for the compatibility of democracy and such patterns of social conflict, two theories have evolved: consociationalism, which is based on cooperation between the elites representing the major segments of a divided population, and corporatism, which is based on an institutionalized regulation of socioeconomic conflict by interest associations. The importance of negotiations and transactions between different interests and forces has also been stressed in studies of democratization and democratic consolidation.

Democracy can affect the forms of civil conflict. Modern democracy provides outlets for civil conflict in the form of elections for political office. Thereby, conflicts may be channeled into institutionalized patterns. Recurrent elections with uncertain outcomes tend to reduce the pain of defeat and to restrain the enjoyment of the fruits of victory in conflict.

Competitive elections have also proved to be compatible with persistent violence and social oppression. In such situations, certain parts of society are sealed off from the democratic process. This oppression is most likely to be directed against impoverished ethnic-minority groups and those in outlying parts of the state who contest central authority. The worst example of this kind of persistent and violent mass repression coexisting with formally democratic central institutions is probably Guatemala, since the military coup of 1954. The combination of repression with formal democracy has been widespread in the developing world generally as well as in such places as Sicily and the Kurdish areas of southeastern Turkey.

War and Peace

The modern developmental paths to power and wealth, which by and large coincided with democratization, have tended to diminish the frequency of wars. There is little evidence, however, that democracy must be peaceful. Many wars, notably World War I, have been popular, at least at the outset.

Democratic great powers seem to be no less inclined to armed intervention in other countries than nondemocratic ones, though the reasons may differ. After World War II the Soviet Union intervened militarily four times in other countries: in East Germany in 1953, in Hungary in 1956, in Czechoslovakia in 1968, and in Afghanistan in 1979. The United States intervened directly five times in the same period: in Korea, Vietnam, Grenada, Panama, and Iraq. After the collapse of the Soviet Union in 1991, the United States intervened militarily in a sixth country—Somalia—not to mention conducting covert war operations elsewhere. France fought wars in Vietnam, Madagascar, Algeria, Egypt, and Chad.

It appears that there is no straightforward relationship between peace and democracy but that universal socioeconomic developments promote both peace and democracy. Military dictatorships and military coups are related more to domestic situations and to weaknesses of internal civil society than to external war. The long series of military putsches and regimes characterizing some Latin American countries, such as Bolivia and Haiti, are being repeated in many African countries. They are manifestations of unbuilt nations, of populations never fully nationally mobilized for war or for any other purpose.

The two world wars demonstrated that democracies can wage war very well, even protracted wars in which they suffer initial defeats. But the French war in Algeria and the American war in Vietnam also showed the possible strength of domestic antiwar opposition and the sensitivity of conscripted armies to that opposition. The current tendency toward professional armies, protected and backed by immense technological power, renders the leaders and commanders of democratic states less dependent on national mobilization, and even on popular legitimacy, than they have been in the past. On the other hand, television has made the violence of war more visible. A new relationship between war and democracy is just beginning.

See also *Burke, Edmund; Classical Greece and Rome; Disraeli, Benjamin; Revolution, French; Revolutions.*

Göran Therborn

BIBLIOGRAPHY

Eckstein, Harry, ed. *Internal War: Problems and Approaches.* Glencoe, Ill.: Free Press, 1963.

Finer, S. E. *The Man on Horseback: The Role of the Military in Politics.* Harmondsworth, England: Penguin Books, 1976.

Finley, M. I. *Democracy Ancient and Modern.* Rev. ed. New Brunswick, N.J.: Rutgers University Press, 1985.

Hintze, Otto. "Military Organization and State Organization." In *The Historical Essays of Otto Hintze,* edited by Felix Gilbert. New York: Oxford University Press, 1975.

Huntington, Samuel P. *The Third Wave.* Norman, Okla., and London: University of Oklahoma Press, 1991.

Líndal, S. "Early Democratic Traditions in the Nordic Countries." In *Nordic Democracy,* edited by Erik Allardt et al. Copenhagen: Det Danske Selskab, 1981.

Therborn, Göran. "The Right to Vote and the Four Routes to/through Modernity." In *State Theory and State History,* edited by Rolf Torstendahl. London and Newbury Park, Calif.: Sage Publications, 1992.

———. "The Rule of Capital and the Rise of Democracy." *New Left Review* 103 (May–June 1977): 3–41.

Tilly, Charles. *Coercion, Capital, and European States.* Rev. ed. Cambridge, Mass., and Oxford: Blackwell, 1992.

Washington, George

Commander in chief of the Continental army during the American Revolution and first president of the United States. Washington (1732–1799), the younger son of a minor landowner, was deprived by his father's death of education abroad. In his early twenties, he became known throughout the colonies and in England as leader of Virginia's regiment in the French and Indian War. Frustrated in his efforts to join the British regulars at a suitable rank, he resigned from military life in 1759 and devoted the next sixteen years to cultivating and improving his estate, Mount Vernon, which he possessed as a consequence of his eldest brother's death and expanded thanks to wealth acquired in a felicitous marriage.

Persuaded by 1774 that the colonies and Britain must eventually separate, Washington, the following year, accepted from the Second Continental Congress appointment as commander in chief of American forces in the rebellion already under way in Massachusetts. His success on the battlefield ultimately depended upon his extraordinary ability to recruit and train a Continental army and officer corps and to persuade the Congress to support them. Immensely popular with his soldiers and with the people of the new United States, Washington was staunch in his devotion to republican principles. He refused compensation for his services during the war and squelched a movement after independence was won to offer him a crown. In 1783 he resigned his commission after the Treaty of Paris recognized the independence for which he had fought.

Washington encouraged those who sought to strengthen the federal government, agreeing to attend the Federal Convention of 1787 once he was convinced that it would radically confront the vices of the Articles of Confederation (the first written instrument of federal union) and establish a strong federal government. Elected unanimously to the presidency established by the new Constitution and conscious that his every deed would set precedent, he gave form and life to an office that, by all accounts, had been designed with him in mind.

Leaving initiative on most matters to Congress and his brilliant cabinet, which included Alexander Hamilton and Thomas Jefferson, Washington supported the addition of a Bill of Rights to the Constitution. He oversaw the establishment of the executive departments, the development of a stable system of government finance, the proclamation of neutrality in the wars of the French Revolution, the ratification of treaties with Britain and Spain, and the suppression of a rebellion against a federal excise tax. Generally successful in staying above the bitter partisanship that emerged from within his cabinet, he determined to retire from the presidency after his second term, setting a precedent unbroken until 1940 and now codified in the Twenty-second Amendment to the Constitution. He urged in his Farewell Address continued attachment to the principles of union and independence.

Amiable and energetic, dignified and self-restrained,

tolerant and generous, Washington bequeathed a model of republican greatness to the nation that he, first among equals, helped to found.

See also *Revolution, American; United States Constitution; United States of America.*

James R. Stoner, Jr.

Watergate

The American political crisis that began in June 1972, with a burglary at the Democratic campaign headquarters in Washington, D.C. The break-in was organized and funded by Republican president Richard M. Nixon's campaign organization, the Committee to Reelect the President. This political burglary sparked the most critical American constitutional conflict since the Civil War. The crisis ended in August 1974, when President Nixon resigned his office, the first president to do so in the history of the United States. The two-year period tested the fundamental democratic tenet that the legal demands of office must take priority over personal and purely political interests. In the eyes of most observers, American democracy withstood the test.

Watergate must be understood in the context of the 1960s, which in the United States were marked by intense social movements struggling for and against change. The civil rights movement challenged the institutional and cultural foundations of the American South. The youth movement crystallized startlingly different forms of sexual, moral, and community life. These left-wing movements enjoyed great political and cultural success in the mid-1960s. By 1967, however, they had provoked overwhelming resistance, not only because of vested social and cultural interests but because of the polarization generated by the increasingly unpopular Vietnam War. Some officials in the executive branch of the U.S. government tried to restore order through extrademocratic means. Lyndon B. Johnson (president from 1963 to 1969) had secretly authorized extensive spying on left-wing activist groups, and the FBI engaged in disruptive undercover activities and blackmail against leftists.

Backlash movements developed among those whom Richard Nixon later would call "the silent majority," while movements on the left splintered into moderate and revolutionary groups. In 1968 Nixon rode the backlash movement into office as president. Elements in his administration, and often the president himself, felt themselves under siege by leftist movements who would, they believed, resort to any means necessary to achieve their goals against a legitimately elected conservative regime.

When majority opinion backed by the Constitution refused to allow the administration to wield power in an unconstrained way, some administration officials took the law into their own hands. In the midst of massive public demonstrations disrupting Washington, D.C., Attorney General John Mitchell ordered summary arrests of tens of thousands of activists, an act of repression that was attacked by the nation's leading newspapers and dismissed by its courts. Defying Supreme Court rulings and decades of moral and legal precedent, Mitchell authorized covert wiretapping on the private telephones of opposition leaders and groups.

In the years between 1970 and 1972 the challenges of radical groups declined dramatically. Civil rights demonstrations dwindled, the antiwar movement largely faded away, and the youth culture virtually disappeared in its most visible and socially radical forms. Yet the American public's perception was exactly the opposite: opinion leaders and ordinary citizens alike believed that political and cultural polarization was increasing. George McGovern's selection as the Democratic party candidate in the 1972 presidential election seemed to confirm this perception. An early and outspoken opponent of the Vietnam War, McGovern championed many of the causes of the sixties and brought activists into his campaign. To many members of the Nixon administration, and to a significant number of Americans, the threat to civil society seemed more palpable than ever before.

In June 1971 President Nixon and John D. Ehrlichman, head of the President's Domestic Council, created a small spying operation—the so-called Plumbers—headed by E. Howard Hunt, a former CIA agent, and G. Gordon Liddy, a former FBI agent. In the early months of 1972, at Nixon's suggestion and under the orders of Mitchell, who later became director of Nixon's reelection campaign, this group became the core of a larger clandestine operation whose "dirty tricks" were designed to disrupt and manipulate the Democrats' presidential primary and general election campaigns. On June 17, 1972, five agents of this group were arrested during a burglary at Democratic campaign headquarters in Washington's Watergate Hotel complex.

By early 1973, after McGovern—the "leftist threat"—had been roundly defeated in the November 1972 election, centrist members of the Senate voted to organize a public investigation of "the Watergate crimes." Some administration officials who had been involved in the coverup of the break-in acknowledged their wrongdoing and cooperated with the investigation. The most important of these was John Dean, counsel to the president, who prepared damning testimony about Nixon's direct involvement, not only in the Plumbers' operations, dirty tricks, and the Watergate break-in, but also in the bribery, intimidation, and blackmailing that followed.

The Senate hearings, which lasted from May to August 1973, were nationally televised. Suspenseful and dramatic, they garnered a viewing audience of record-breaking size. Senators and witnesses alike evoked the simple yet sacred discourse of American civil society. Alongside accounts of the hidden exercise of public and private power and details of secret money trails, a grand and imposing narrative emerged that drew upon legends about the American nation's earlier times of trial. Once again, foolish, corrupt, and evil men had threatened to destroy the democratic foundations of the nation. The nation's Founders were evoked time and again, and to many viewers Sen. Sam Ervin, the fierce but courtly chair of the committee conducting the hearings, seemed a representation of the Founders in contemporary form. The universal obligations of law and office were enthusiastically confirmed.

Shortly after the conclusion of the hearings, on Saturday, October 20, 1973, President Nixon announced that he had fired Special Prosecutor Archibald Cox and abolished the office that Cox directed. The Office of the Special Prosecutor had been created only months earlier in response to increasing public demands for impartiality and for legal rather than political control. Cox had been pressing Nixon for full disclosure of relevant, possibly incriminating, material from the executive branch. Demonstrating support for Cox's inquiry, Attorney General Eliot Richardson resigned rather than carry out the president's order to fire Cox. Deputy Attorney General William Ruckelshaus was fired when he too refused to carry out the president's demand.

In response to what was widely perceived as a constitutional confrontation between democratic obligations and personal power—a confrontation promptly labeled the "Saturday night massacre"—there emerged over that Oc-

tober weekend what reporters called a "firestorm of protest." Three million angry Americans wrote, called, or telegraphed protests to Washington. Confronted by such an apparently unified public, Nixon rescinded his decision to shut down the special prosecutor's office and appointed Leon Jaworski as Cox's successor.

Facing subpoenas for tape-recorded meetings, injunctions from the special prosecutor's office, and eventually the congressional impeachment procedure itself, President Nixon and his supporters tried to justify their secret and illegal activities by their historical context. They made reference to the polarization of the 1960s and the threats to democracy it had engendered. However, the great civic ritual of Watergate—from the confrontational Senate hearings and the melodramatic Saturday night massacre to the somber, almost funeral impeachment hearings in the House of Representatives—seemed only to confirm that the United States was then, and had always been, a cohesive and civil community.

The crisis actually brought Americans together in an unprecedented way. The specifics of the polarization of the 1960s were forgotten, and the generalized ties so essential to maintaining democracy in complex modern societies were reestablished. Watergate drew a curtain on the period of intense and turbulent social change, creating a kind of public amnesia about how widespread anticivil sentiments had been and how strongly some had felt they required illegal means and intolerant ends in reply.

Scholars disagree about whether Watergate had significant long-term institutional effects. Without doubt, its most important effect was the creation of the Office of the Special Prosecutor, a potentially important vehicle for enforcing the moral obligations of public officials. Yet, though it was utilized on several significant occasions after 1974, the office was never able to regain the image of impartiality or the moral prestige of that earlier time. Proposals to reform campaign financing have been enacted, most conspicuously for presidential campaigns, but they have hardly succeeded in curbing the influence of "big money" on American politics. The War Powers Resolution of 1973 promised to curb presidential power in foreign policy, yet presidentially initiated military interventions have continued unabated. To decry the relative dearth of institutional reforms, however, misses what Watergate was really about. Watergate reached well beyond politics. It was a moral event, a gigantic civics lesson that had no precedent in the history of American political life.

Despite the agonies, duplicities, and political confrontations that marked the 1972–1974 period of crisis, polls and interviews at its conclusion confirmed that the process had affirmed, for some four out of five Americans, that theirs was a society built upon justice rather than retribution, that universal moral codes take precedence over personal or material power, that America is less a state, an economy, or a bureaucracy than a community whose members are united by trust, honesty, mutual respect, and the love of truth.

These symbolic, moral lessons of Watergate had profound and relatively long-term effects on American life. Most important, they reinforced trust in democracy, in the constitutional system upon which American government and society rests. At the same time this systemic legitimation had the surprising effect of ensuring that the conservative backlash against movements for liberal social reform would continue in an even more effective way. Separated by the interregnum of Watergate from the polarizing passions of the sixties, conservatism proceeded in a less radical, more moderate and civil way, and in more politically strategic terms, than it had before. Watergate also heightened citizens' distrust of powerful individuals and institutions.

This paradox has led many scholars to conclude that the Watergate crisis had largely negative effects on American democracy, increasing cynicism and undermining the kind of idealistic faith upon which democratic politics depends. The opposite argument can be made, however. Despite the lack of fundamental institutional reform, "post-Watergate morality" continues to exercise a salutary effect on political power in the United States. For Watergate was more than a political and social crisis: it challenged the moral foundations of American democracy itself. The crisis refurbished the mythical dimension of American democracy, the "memory of justice" upon which, Plato believed, the vitality of every experiment in self-government depends.

See also *Impeachment; United States of America.*

Jeffrey C. Alexander

BIBLIOGRAPHY

Alexander, Jeffrey C. "Culture and Political Crisis: 'Watergate' and Durkheimian Sociology." In *Durkheimian Sociology: Cultural Studies,* edited by Jeffrey C. Alexander. Cambridge and New York: Cambridge University Press, 1988.

———. "Three Models of Culture and Society Relations: Toward an Analysis of Watergate." In *Sociological Theory,* edited by Randall Collins. San Francisco: Jossey-Bass, 1984.

Kutler, Stanley I. *The Wars of Watergate: The Last Crisis of Richard Nixon.* New York: Norton, 1990.

Lipset, Seymour Martin, and Earl Raab. "An Appointment with Watergate." *Commentary* 56 (September 1973): 35ff.

Lipset, Seymour Martin, and William Schneider. *The Confidence Gap: Business, Labor, and Government in the Public Mind.* New York: Free Press; London: Collier Macmillan, 1983.

Schudson, Michael. *Watergate in American Memory: How We Remember, Forget, and Reconstruct the Past.* New York: Basic Books, 1992.

Weber, Max

A founding thinker of sociology and an important German theorist of the connections between capitalism, bureaucracy, and democracy. Karl Emil Maximilian Weber (1864–1920), as he was christened, suffered from a nervous disorder that forced him to resign his professorship early in a budding academic career. He nevertheless became Germany's most important sociologist and contributed enormously to the rise of modern social science.

Weber is best remembered for his study of how early Protestantism helped generate the cultural basis for modern capitalism. His scholarship also encompassed pathbreaking work on the philosophy and methodology of social science, multifaceted conceptual and empirical studies, and sweeping comparative historical research on Eastern and Western societies from antiquity to modern times. He stressed in particular the role of the distinctively rational aspects of Western culture in the rise of modern capitalism, bureaucracy, and democracy. Weber influenced not only conservative and libertarian views of democracy but also the views of progressives and the radical left. His ambivalent vision of "mass democracy" continues to be debated and appropriated in divergent ways today.

Early in his career Weber argued that Germany should follow Britain's path of "liberal imperialism," but he later abandoned this stance. After supporting Germany's entry into World War I, he attacked its territorial annexations and aggressive submarine warfare. Against the prevalent garrison state mentality, he called for a strengthened parliament and a popularly elected chancellor.

Weber held that authoritarian rule had stunted the development of parliamentary institutions and democratic leadership in Germany. Following the war, he helped prepare the German reply to charges of war guilt made at Versailles during the Paris Peace Conference, helped

Max Weber

general citizenship, occupations open to talent, and representative politics.

The nation-state ended city autonomy in early modern Europe by the sixteenth or seventeenth century, but monarchs, competing with relatively equal neighbors and depending on urban resources, tolerated the independence of the bourgeoisie. Weber held that, although new central governments consolidated disparate European fiefdoms and cities, competition among the nation-states and bourgeois interests within them prevented the type of total power manifested in ancient empires and permitted the continued development of capitalism and liberal democracy.

Contradictory aspects of Western democratization are visible in Weber's treatment of the Reformation. Puritan values of tolerance, ethical community, and principled dissent, combined with the sovereignty of a congregation composed exclusively of individuals who had demonstrated their qualification for full membership, prepared the way for democratic civil society and voluntary association. Moreover, the Puritan ethic of "duty in a calling" gave rise to secular values of commitment and responsibility in professional vocations.

But Weber also linked Puritanism to ruthless capitalistic acquisition, pessimistic individualism, and pure utilitarianism. In his view, Puritan culture contributed indirectly to the class polarization, cultural homogenization, and authoritarian statism characteristic of mass democracy, while also providing the resources to resist these same forces.

The Power of Bureaucracy

Modern bureaucracy, according to Weber, is the unparalleled means for coordinating large numbers of functionally specialized workers. Its rational discipline, technical knowledge, precision, and "objective discharge of business" are all essential to capitalism and continue to shape contemporary culture. Like all modern bureaucracies, governments require small numbers and secrecy for fast, decisive, and efficient action. Thus heads of state and appointed officials make many important decisions away from public view.

Professional staffs in political parties do the same. Citizens are targets of every cheap demagogic means of persuasion at election time and are otherwise treated as inert objects of administration. Weber implied that political legitimacy depends mainly on suffrage and legal equality and on a minimum of material support and security, but

found the German Democratic Party, and contributed to the drafting of the Weimar constitution. Prophetically, he warned that "a polar night of icy darkness and hardness" would emerge from Germany's national humiliation and social disintegration and from the despotic tendencies of romantic extremism of both the right and the left.

Weber's ideas about democracy are scattered throughout his scholarly works. In antiquity, he argued, all-encompassing state power throttled capitalism and democracy. Landowning elites amassed wealth through military expropriation and widespread slavery and dependency. They dominated the cities, from which they administered the hinterlands and extracted surpluses from rural producers. In medieval Europe, by contrast, craftsmen and merchants made revolutionary breaks from the landed aristocracy, turning towns into centers of production and commerce. The ascendant bourgeois class liberated slaves and serfs and created liberal institutions, such as equality before the law, rational trial procedures, individual rights, he recognized that these offer the masses neither participation nor social justice. Rather, mass democracy produces relative powerlessness below the bureaucratically based elites.

Genuine revolutionary transformation, in Weber's view, becomes increasingly improbable with the growth of bureaucracy. Victors and vanquished alike depend upon quick restoration of administrative machinery. Weber's point that bureaucracies function smoothly even under enemy occupation showed a chilling prescience about France a few decades later.

While thinkers of both the right and the left promised harmonious futures, Weber saw conflict among values, interests, and groups as modernity's most precious resource. Peaceful struggles, alliances, and compromises produce cultural dynamism and create space for minority opinions and individuality. Weber feared, however, that competing organizations would someday be fashioned into a singular bureaucracy, destroying the countervailing forces upon which pluralism depends. In the name of nationalism or social justice, a new total state would forge an inescapable, top-to-bottom system of mass surveillance and control, with no independent unions, no professional associations, no parties, and no news. Weber predicted that communist regimes like the Soviet Union's would be thoroughly bureaucratic and repressive and that similar authoritarian systems could arise from the right.

Yet Weber believed that efforts to increase social justice and democracy do not inevitably expand the state. They also produce tensions, struggles, and changes that enhance diversity and prevent inflexible orthodoxy.

Even bureaucracy has some democratizing tendencies. Unclear jurisdictions, lack of consistently applied rules, and broad official prerogative made premodern states opaque, rigid, and immune to reconstruction. By contrast, modern bureaucracy's small number of ultimate decision makers, clear hierarchy, and rational legalism fix responsibility with specific individuals and open organizations to critique, challenge, and reform. Functional specialization, moreover, raises the costs of authoritarian rule. Arbitrary, rigid micromanagement unduly restricts specialized knowledge and skill and generates technical failures, malingering, and even outright resistance.

Overall, Weber implied that multicentered bureaucratic societies, although resistant to revolution, are open to substantial democratic change. Reforms, however, will not free the working class from authoritarian work settings or from compulsion "by the whip of hunger." Thus Weber saw German constitutionalism as legitimating capitalist inequality, and he considered participatory democracy to be a pipe dream.

The Power of Politics

A vibrant political sphere is the countervailing force against bureaucracy, Weber believed, with politics and administration being fundamentally different domains. In contrast to the hierarchical rule in state and party officialdom, politics is a struggle between different values and voices, originating in divergent sociocultural interests and different locations in socioeconomic hierarchies. Whereas officials are expected to be obedient, loyal, and technically competent, politicians must be able to articulate convictions, calculate consequences, make autonomous decisions, and, above all, lead. Such skills are honed in electoral and parliamentary battles, not in administrative offices.

Although he viewed the politics of plebiscites as inherently demagogic, Weber saw value in subjecting potential leaders to public scrutiny and choice. Even the Caesarist tendencies of such politics break the ruts of administrative and economic control. Critics fault Weber on this point for exaggerating the threats of bureaucracy and understating the dangers of charismatic demagogues.

Weber held that the long authoritarian rule of Otto von Bismarck (1815–1898) as chancellor left Germany with a tyranny of officials, a toothless parliament, deformed politics, and an obsequious intelligentsia. Although cultural pessimism and an aversion to political prophecy discouraged Weber from theorizing about an alternative, more strongly democratic regime, he argued that two core ethics of Puritan culture—conviction and cool reserve—had the power to revitalize democratic politics. He called for a new breed of politicians, who would combine passionate vision with an ethic of responsibility about the consequences of their normative and electoral postures. They would be able to face bitter realities without illusions, to tame demagogic aspects of mass culture, and to control the vanity inherent in creative leadership.

In the wreckage of the Treaty of Versailles after World War I, however, Weber thought that Germany's lethal mixture of political demagoguery, leaderless bureaucracy, and dispirited masses pointed directly toward the total state. His premature death in 1920 spared him from seeing his nightmare realized in Nazi Germany.

See also *Bureaucracy; Germany.*

Robert J. Antonio

BIBLIOGRAPHY

Beetham, David. *Max Weber and the Theory of Modern Politics.* 2d ed. Cambridge: Polity Press; New York: Blackwell, 1985.

Eden, Robert. *Political Leadership and Nihilism: A Study of Weber and Nietzsche.* Tampa: University Presses of Florida, 1983.

Käsler, Dirk. *Max Weber: An Introduction to His Life and Work.* Translated by Philippa Hurd. Cambridge: Polity Press; Chicago: University of Chicago Press, 1988.

Mommsen, Wolfgang J. *Max Weber and German Politics 1890–1920.* 2d ed. Translated by Michael S. Steinberg. Chicago: University of Chicago Press, 1984.

Scaff, Lawrence A. *Fleeing the Iron Cage: Culture, Politics, and Modernity in the Thought of Max Weber.* Berkeley and Los Angeles: University of California Press, 1989.

Weber, Marianne. *Max Weber: A Biography.* Translated and edited by Harry Zohn. New York: Wiley, 1975.

Weber, Max. *Economy and Society: An Outline of Interpretive Sociology.* 2 vols. Edited by Guenther Roth and Claus Wittich. Translated by Ephraim Fischoff et al. Berkeley and Los Angeles: University of California Press, 1978.

———. *From Max Weber: Essays in Sociology.* Translated and edited by Hans H. Gerth and C. Wright Mills. New York: Oxford University Press, 1958; London: Routledge, 1991.

Welfare, Promotion of

Promotion of welfare is a feature of modern nations that has ambivalent connections to democracy. Welfare and social security are the main functions of modern governments, which for this reason are often called welfare states.

The welfare state can be both broadly and narrowly defined. In the narrowest sense it consists of a set of social insurance laws (encompassing pensions, disability, health, work accidents, and unemployment). This legislation is designed to bridge gaps in income for individuals caused by various misfortunes, both natural and man-made, as well as by the inevitable consequences of aging. In a broader sense the welfare state includes, in addition to these programs of organized and often compulsory self-help, all other measures for redistributing money to various groups according to criteria other than those dictated by the market. Such programs naturally include measures that help poor people by providing them with resources that would not otherwise be available to them, such as subsidized housing, food for free or below market cost, and health services without fees or insurance premiums.

Programs aimed at and restricted to the poor, and delivered in contradiction of market principles of distribution, are what most Americans understand by the term *welfare.* By *social security,* most Americans understand the sorts of social programs that are at least partially paid for by the recipients. But the state's welfare function is by no means limited to the poor. To the contrary, in most countries programs aimed exclusively at the poor make up a rather small fraction of all the public monies redistributed. Many welfare programs are aimed at groups of citizens who generally are far from poor. These include subsidies to farmers, subventions for industrial producers (whether motivated by export ambitions, hopes for national sufficiency, or other, only partially economic, impulses), tax breaks to encourage home ownership and donations to charity, and public education, which all citizens, even those who make no use of it, regard as their right.

Social programs as usually understood are only one of the activities of the welfare state in the broadest definition. Some government interventions seek to promote increased production, while others—the "welfare" functions in the common sense of the word—redistribute a portion of the resources thus created. The latter types of programs are intended to ensure a minimum of fairness in the allotment of resources, both between social groups and across the lifespan of the individual.

In the broadest sense, the welfare state is a form of government that exists mainly to provide for the well-being of its citizens. This function is also its primary claim to citizens' allegiance and support. No longer is the greater glory of God or the aggrandizement of the nation or even, for that matter, the defense of the homeland the main objective of government. Instead, the goal is economic growth and a reasonably fair distribution of this ever growing pie. In this sense, every government, at least among developed nations, is a welfare state. All governments seek to encourage economic growth, and all promise to guarantee certain basic living conditions, a minimum standard of living below which no citizen is, in theory, allowed to fall.

Variations on the Welfare State

Variations among nations are found not at this fundamental level but rather in such issues as the extent of the state's role and the style of intervention expected from its authorities. In some nations, the state plays a dominant part, while in others it has a lesser role, with greater efforts expected from private initiative and charity. In the Scandinavian countries, for example, the state plays a very active role, providing its citizens from the cradle to the grave with a broad and generous set of benefits to cover most risks. The United States has a much more limited welfare state. For certain groups of citizens (such as veterans and the elderly), it provides coverage and benefits comparable to the social policy systems of Europe, while other kinds of coverage, which in other developed nations are taken for granted (such as health insurance), exist only in private and voluntary form.

Although nations clearly vary in the amount and scope of welfare benefits they provide, to some extent matters simply are arranged differently in different countries. For example, in England health insurance is provided in a government-organized national system. In Germany health insurance is furnished through various insurance schemes, many of which are nominally private but have compulsory membership. In the United States most people obtain health insurance through a wide variety of voluntary private and occupational schemes, while the government provides coverage for the very poor and the very old. For the average person who has coverage in one of these three systems, differences in the exact arrangement of benefits are probably not that important. But for those Americans who are not insured at all, the differences between welfare states are dramatic. In some nations, such as the United States, charity and private initiative play a major role and in effect supply what elsewhere falls to the responsibility of the state.

Nations also make different choices among the kinds of measures into which they can pour their resources. The United States has no national health insurance system, and its unemployment insurance is comparatively miserly and restricted. At the same time, the United States has traditionally spent considerably more on education, especially higher education, than the otherwise more extensive and generous European welfare states. This choice among possibilities was dictated by the American belief in equality of opportunities rather than equality of outcomes. It served to make education a means of social mobility and advancement for the academically talented. By allowing many people the chance to improve their position, the educational system to some extent served as a substitute for other sorts of welfare measures.

The Welfare State and Democracy

The welfare state, in the broadest definition, is clearly connected to democracy. The entrance of the populace onto the political stage, beginning in the mid-nineteenth century, evidenced in mass suffrage (and eventually universal suffrage), forced all governments to reorient their claims to legitimacy. Legitimacy now had to be based on the ability to satisfy the material interests of this enormously expanded pool of citizens. In the broadest sense, democracy created the welfare state.

But if we look more closely at the welfare state, examining the various ways governments have sought to satisfy the material ambitions of the populace, especially in the realm of redistributing resources, we see that matters become more complicated. In some nations democracy and the welfare state have gone hand in hand. In the Scandinavian countries welfare services expanded, beginning in the 1930s and continuing into the postwar era. This expansion was the outcome of the increasing power of the social democratic parties and their ability to represent effectively a broad coalition of workers, peasants, and the urban lower-middle classes. In these countries power shifted away from traditional social elites, allowing the construction of a wide-ranging, generous, and egalitarian form of social policy. Scandinavian welfare systems were characterized by the broad scope of state initiative, lifetime coverage, generous benefits, and the inclusion of all citizens, whether rich or poor, in social programs so that the poor were not stigmatized or marginalized.

The United Kingdom offers another example of the connection between democracy and the welfare state. In 1942 the social reformer William Beveridge published a report advocating extensive change in the British welfare state. After World War II, with the Labour Party in power, many of his proposals were implemented. In 1949 sociologist T. H. Marshall sketched out a vision of the development of the welfare state, based in large measure on the Beveridge/Labour reforms. In Marshall's view the connection between democracy and the welfare state seemed almost a matter of historical inevitability.

Marshall argued that three major stages characterized the development of Western democracies. In the first stage, during the eighteenth century, civil rights had been won (equality before the law, the right to own property, the right to settle at will, and so forth). In the second stage, a century later, political rights (above all the vote) became taken for granted. But, in spite of such advances, however notable, citizenship in a democratic polity remained an abstract and formal quality. All citizens were in theory equal members of the community, but in reality civil and political rights were often hollowed out by the vast disparities in material circumstances that still separated rich and poor. All citizens were treated equally in the eyes of the law: all, whether baron or bag lady, whether director or down and out, were forbidden to beg on the streets, steal bread, and sleep under bridges, as writer Anatole France put it in a famous sarcasm.

This situation was now corrected, according to Marshall, by the third and last stage in the development of democracy: the invention of social rights and their realization in the modern welfare state. Although political rights had limited the encroachment of the state on others, establishing the boundaries of personal autonomy, social rights made freedom into something positive. Social rights staked claims to a certain basic standard of living, a fundamental right not to be cut off from membership in the wider community by abject poverty. Social rights meant the ability to participate fully in civil life: freedom *to,* in other words, not just freedom *from.*

Of course, there had been social benefits in earlier societies. Charity, alms, and poor relief had given institutional voice to the unwillingness of past societies to leave the neediest to their fates. But such aid had been granted only on demeaning and stigmatizing terms, which marked recipients as incapable of maintaining themselves and thus as less than full members of the community. Social rights, in contrast, were now to be considered part of citizenship, a rightful claim that in no way diminished recipients' standing.

Social rights expanded the notions of citizenship, freedom, and rights and thus of democracy. Citizens in a democratic regime were no longer equal only in a formal sense; they now also had claims to a certain degree of material well-being. In Marshall's vision, the welfare state was the culmination of a long historical development of democracy, its fulfillment as social democracy.

The extent to which citizenship claims to social rights are today considered politically inviolable shows that Marshall was basically right. The continued growth of expenditures by the welfare state has prompted taxpayer revolts in several nations, with taxpayers seeking to limit entitlements and thus cut costs. Ironically, most such movements have tried to slash benefits aimed at the poor and unorganized and have not dared to threaten the vast bulk of middle-class entitlements. For this reason, even politicians like former U.S. president Ronald Reagan and former British prime minister Margaret Thatcher, who sought to roll back the welfare state, could only slow, and not actually reduce, the growth of social spending.

The Welfare State Against Democracy

Although the connection between democracy and the welfare state is taken almost for granted in modern societies, the two also stand in contradiction. The welfare state provides material benefits that may, as in Marshall's vision, expand and fulfill the civil and political rights that preceded them. But benefits may also serve as substitutes for such rights, as a way of buying off and deflecting claims to the basic and formal elements of democratic systems. The German statesman Otto von Bismarck founded the modern welfare state in the 1880s by passing some of the first social insurance legislation. In so doing he was not seeking to expand the civil and political rights of German workers—quite the contrary. As Prussian ambassador in Paris, he had learned from the French emperor Napoleon III that citizens' loyalty could be won for even an autocratic regime like the Second Empire through the wide distribution of small state pensions. At home, he sought to achieve a similar effect. By granting social insurance to workers, Bismarck hoped to demonstrate the state's concern for their well-being. He intended to woo them away from the social democrats and toward a system that was distinctly undemocratic or at least unparliamentary. He was offering pensions instead of, not in addition to, political empowerment.

Bismarck's aims, his hopes of substituting social for political reform, were no mystery to the organized working class. Working-class representatives generally opposed not the idea that the state should assume responsibility for helping its most hard-pressed citizens, but rather the specifically undemocratic manner in which their chancellor pursued the goal. German social democrats of that time would have preferred intervention more in line with the labor reform then taking place in Britain: laws regulating working conditions and hours. Such legislation promised to improve matters immediately for the working class on the job and struck directly at the ability of manufacturers to conduct business in the most profitable and least responsible fashion. Bismarck's approach, in contrast, was curative rather than preventive. It mopped up the consequences of long and dangerous work through increased access to medical care and payments to ease the loss of wages, eventually culminating in a small pension should the individual live that long.

This recognition that social policy could be used to limit the growth of democracy gave rise to the view, popular on the left, that the welfare state was at best a partial remedy, a reformist measure that did not fundamentally improve matters for society's disinherited. At worst, it appeared a conscious attempt by the ruling class to preserve its power, a sop thrown to workers in hopes of quieting discontent and preventing more serious challenges to the status quo. The idea also developed that there were different kinds of welfare states. Some, like the Scandinavian versions, expressed the hopes of the poor for a larger share of goods and a greater sense of security. Others, like the German and French systems, were more concerned with stabilizing the status quo than with improving conditions for the worst off. And some, like the American system with its limitations and residual nature, gave expression to deep-seated liberalism and antistatism.

This tension between social rights on the one hand and political and civil rights on the other, between individuals' claims to material benefits and their standing as full citizens in the community, continued, adding an ambiguous note to the otherwise positive connection between welfare and democracy. Means-tested benefits, targeted at the poor, tend to demean and stigmatize people in societies where market principles of allocation otherwise hold sway. Benefits that are given in kind rather than in cash, such as food stamps or subsidized housing, imply distrust of the recipient. The unexpressed fear is that, if people received cash benefits, they might squander the money on goods and services other than those intended.

Economic Tensions

There is a general problem here for Western capitalist democracies. Political and civil rights are unconditional. With a few exceptions, citizens possess the right to personal autonomy or the vote regardless of their income, intelligence, or morals. Despite Marshall's claims, social rights still are not universally viewed in the same light (though there are some exceptions, such as education and the British National Health Service). There remains a deeply ingrained sense that market principles ought to play a large role in allocation, that social benefits should be earned to be deserved, and that if not earned, they remain charity.

This tension between distribution according to market or social principles, between allocation of benefits according to merit or according to need, gave rise to the view that the welfare state is largely concerned with redistributing resources downward, from the middle to the lower classes. This contradiction affects even those with only few merit-based claims to resources, such as workers, who are often regarded as the main beneficiaries of the welfare state's efforts at redistribution. The organized working class has opposed employers' attempts to turn the redistributive logic of social benefits to their own advantage by using welfare programs as an alternative to better pay. In France, for example, employers supported family allowances because they targeted resources on workers with many dependents, which was cheaper than across-the-board pay increases—in other words, remuneration according to need, not achievement. In England, however, the labor movement successfully resisted the introduction of family allowances for precisely this reason, insisting instead on the working-class claim to wages high enough to support dependents without supplement.

Democracy and the welfare state are, at one level, inseparable. A concern with the political rights of all citizens cannot be wholly divorced from concern for their economic circumstances. Too wide a range of material circumstances undercuts the possibility of a stable, functioning democratic regime. To feel themselves members of the same political community, citizens must also be functioning members of the same economic marketplace. But within this most general level of association between democracy and the welfare state, there is room for considerable variation. The market principles of allocation still attached to many social benefits make them different from the formal and absolute political and civil rights that people possess in modern democracies. This is why some nations have been welfare states without being democracies and why even democracies vary greatly in their characteristics as welfare states.

See also *Income, Equality of; Roosevelt, Franklin D.*

Peter Baldwin

BIBLIOGRAPHY

Baldwin, Peter. *The Politics of Social Solidarity: Class Bases of the European Welfare State.* Cambridge: Cambridge University Press, 1990.

De Swaan, Abram. *In Care of the State: Health Care, Education and Welfare in Europe and the USA in the Modern Era.* Cambridge: Polity Press, 1988.

Esping-Andersen, Gøsta. *Three Worlds of Welfare Capitalism.* Princeton: Princeton University Press, 1990.

Flora, Peter, and Arnold J. Heidenheimer, eds. *The Development of Welfare States in Europe and America.* New Brunswick, N.J.: Transaction, 1981.

Goodin, Robert E., and Julian Le Grand, eds. *Not Only the Poor: The Middle Classes and the Welfare State.* London: Routledge, 1987.

Guttmann, Amy, ed. *Democracy and the Welfare State.* Princeton: Princeton University Press, 1988.

Harris, José. *William Beveridge: A Biography.* Oxford: Oxford University Press, 1977.

Marsh, David C. *The Welfare State: Concept and Development.* 2d ed. New York and London: Longman, 1980.

Marshall, T. H. "Citizenship and Social Class." In *Class, Citizenship, and Social Development.* Chicago: University of Chicago Press, 1963.

Rimlinger, Gaston V. *Welfare Policy and Industrialization in Europe, America, and Russia.* New York: Wiley, 1971.

Williams, Eric

Major Caribbean historian who became a leading political figure in Trinidad and Tobago and the country's first prime minister. Williams (1911–1981) was born in Trinidad. He won a scholarship to Oxford University in 1931, where he earned a doctor of philosophy degree in 1938. He began teaching political science at Howard University in Washington, D.C., in 1939. He returned to Trinidad in 1948 and became the first prime minister of the newly independent nation of Trinidad and Tobago in 1962. He held that position until his death in 1981.

As a historian, Williams helped shape the study of the causes and consequences of British West Indian slavery, of the ending of the British slave trade in 1808, and of the ending of the institution of slavery. As a political figure, he played a major role in Trinidad's transition to independence and in its development in the following two decades. He also encouraged a Caribbean sense of independence; in the 1950s he participated in the debates concerning a West Indian federation.

Capitalism and Slavery, Williams's most influential historical work, was published in 1944. Based on his Oxford dissertation, it presented several major arguments (including one on the expansion of racism), two of which became important to later scholarship. He contended that the slave trade and slavery played a central role in the Industrial Revolution in Great Britain. He further claimed that the emerging industrialists then moved to limit the West Indian "monopoly" of sugar in the British market so as to end the by now unprofitable slave trade and slavery and to foster economic gain for "the new industrial order." Williams later published other books dealing with West Indian history and historians, as well as an autobiography, *Inward Hunger.*

Williams had returned to Trinidad as deputy chairman of the Caribbean Research Council. After various conflicts with his superiors at the Caribbean Commission, he began an active political life in 1956. He launched the successful People's National Movement, which attained a majority in the next election. Williams then became chief minister of Trinidad and Tobago. Political controversies over West Indian federation and the presence of U.S. military bases in Trinidad and elsewhere in the Caribbean marked the years before independence.

At independence, Williams became prime minister, a position to which he was reelected several times. Problems with trade unions, East Indians, a black power movement (including an attempted coup in 1970), and the Tobagoan independence movement made his years of rule eventful. In addition, he did not always follow the U.S. policy line in international matters. He was helped by his political skills, the economic development of the country, and the revenue generated by the local oil industry (which helped give Trinidad and Tobago one of the highest per capita incomes of the Caribbean nations).

Although he became more reclusive over the years, Williams remained in office until his death. He was succeeded by a member of his party, without political strife.

Stanley L. Engerman

BIBLIOGRAPHY

Oxaal, Ivar. *Black Intellectuals and the Dilemmas of Race and Class in Trinidad.* Cambridge, Mass.: Schenkman, 1982.

Williams, Eric. *Capitalism and Slavery.* Chapel Hill: University of North Carolina Press, 1944.

———. *Forged from the Love of Liberty: Selected Speeches of Dr. Eric Williams.* Compiled by Paul K. Sutton. Trinidad: Longman Caribbean, 1981.

———. *From Columbus to Castro: The History of the Caribbean, 1492–1969.* London: Andre Deutsch, 1970.

———. *Inward Hunger: The Education of a Prime Minister.* London: Andre Deutsch, 1969.

Wilson, Woodrow

Twenty-eighth president of the United States (1913–1921), revered for his commitments to democracy and the League of Nations. A political scientist by profession, Thomas Woodrow Wilson (1856–1924) was president of Princeton University and governor of New Jersey before being elected president of the United States in 1912. He had grown up in the South, the son of a Presbyterian minister. Before entering politics, he wrote *Congressional Government* (1885) and was president of the American Political Science Association.

Ideologically, Wilson represented the Progressive movement within the Democratic Party. Progressives favored an increased governmental role in economic and other matters and a more equal sharing of wealth. One can easily find flaws in his record; in particular, his attitudes on racial segregation and the role of African Americans reflected his southern origins and were derived from widespread American biases at the time. But Wilson remains esteemed, by his own party and by the country at large, for attempting to round out democracy in the governance of the United States.

President Wilson has been both praised and criticized for wanting to export democracy to other countries. He displayed this desire early in his administration by withholding U.S. recognition of regimes in Mexico and elsewhere in Latin America, questioning whether these regimes were genuinely democratic.

Woodrow Wilson

World War I and the League of Nations

A similar attitude was instrumental in Wilson's decision in 1917 to bring the United States into World War I as an "associated power" with the Allied forces (originally France, Great Britain, and Russia) against Germany rather than as one of the Allies. When the war was over, in 1918, Wilson was committed to moving international politics away from the old balance-of-power mechanisms, which had been attuned to nonrepresentative governments, and to establishing a League of Nations based on self-determination and political democracy throughout the world.

Republican opponents of Wilson, including former president Theodore Roosevelt (himself a leader of the Republican wing of the Progressive movement), favored a more power-oriented approach to the American entry into World War I and in the peace negotiations afterward. Rather than caring about self-determination or democracy in Europe or Latin America, they urged the United States to be as self-interested as any other nation, watching for opportunities to acquire power and resources.

However, in the aftermath of the bitter experience of the 1914–1918 trench war, Wilson's vision captured the imagination of the European masses as well as of American voters. Wilson wanted to see governments shake off the selfish rivalries of the old diplomacy and seek to establish a diplomacy resembling the internal workings of a domestic democracy, with "open covenants, openly arrived at." This diplomacy would be based on the self-determination and political democracy of the countries being represented.

Many analysts at the time shared Wilson's view that the war had been caused by the ethnic grievances of people governed against their will: French speakers in Alsace-Lorraine, for example, and Czechs, Poles, Croats, and Serbs in the former German, Russian, and Austro-Hungarian empires. Wilson thus was not alone in believing that self-determination was the antidote to international tensions and wars. But his personal commitment to this vision, ahead of considerations of power, left him substantially at odds with the French government under Georges Clemenceau, who believed in strengthening the power of one's own nation regardless of others' desires for self-determination, and with most other European leaders.

During the negotiations of the Treaty of Versailles, in 1919, which ended World War I, Wilson reluctantly went along with some of the secret treaties negotiated among the Allies. These treaties divided up territories regardless of the ethnic composition or preferences of the people living in them. But Wilson assumed that violations of the principle of democratic self-determination could be remedied by the new League of Nations, once the Versailles treaty was in force and the League was in operation.

Wilson's greatest failure and biggest disappointment generally is considered to be the U.S. Senate's refusal to ratify the Treaty of Versailles and U.S. membership in the League of Nations. Had Wilson lived to see the developments of the 1920s and 1930s, however, he surely would have been disappointed with the fate of democracy in the central European republics created on the principle of self-determination. Of these, only Czechoslovakia survived through the interwar years as a political democracy.

Wilson has been viewed as the quintessential liberal American in the broadest and best sense of the term—someone who sees good things in politics as going together, who favors democracy within states as much as peace among states, and who sees no need to choose between these two human goals. Those among political scientists who are called realists (the most prominent are perhaps Hans Morgenthau and Kenneth Waltz) consider such views to be typical of what most Americans naïvely assume to be the way international relations work. These advocates of *realpolitik,* or power politics, consider Clemenceau's attitude at Versailles more sensible than Wilson's.

Wilson's Policies and Legacy

In the early years of the twentieth century the United States was just beginning to participate actively in international relations. The relationships Americans saw between their political experience and the outside world thus had to be articulated. Theodore Roosevelt had enunciated a set of theories by which the United States would behave "like other countries": seeking power, acquiring naval bases, and engaging in imperialism. Wilson, through his policies and speeches, presented a very different view. He encouraged the United States to behave in an exceptional way (in large part because it was a democracy): it would intervene to change the normal international practice of the world rather than joining in such practice, and it would help to spread democracy around the world.

Although formal public opinion polls did not yet exist (coming on the scene only at the end of the 1930s), the indirect evidence we have is that most Americans preferred Wilson's vision to the power-politics vision. It is an irony of the precautions built into the U.S. Constitution to protect American freedoms (in particular the provision requiring two-thirds of the members of the Senate to ratify a treaty) that Americans, in retrospect, remember themselves as having turned against the League of Nations and Wilson's hope of international order. In fact, more Americans favored the League than opposed it. Even in the 1920 election, Republican candidate Warren Harding, who succeeded Wilson as president, equivocated on whether he favored or opposed the League of Nations. Harding knew that outright opposition to Wilson's vision of a collective security system would lose him votes.

To attribute the vision of the League of Nations and the idea of making the world "safe for democracy" solely to Wilson would be an oversimplification. Others had endorsed the same idea, even before the disaster of World War I. (The idea can be traced back to the eighteenth-century philosopher Immanuel Kant.) Yet Wilson popularized the idea and was instrumental in bringing the conjunction of peace and democracy to the forefront of people's imaginations.

Like many image makers and their ideas in a democratic environment, Wilson and his ideas rode a roller coaster of popularity and rejection—by the U.S. Senate and by the French, Italians, and other Europeans who put their ambitions as the victors in World War I ahead of any abstract plans for a new diplomatic order of democratic self-determination. The rise of fascism in the 1930s and the experiences of World War II often are seen as proof that the concept of the League of Nations was somehow flawed. The United Nations, created at the end of World War II, was designed to be more attuned to the power relationships emerging in 1945 than the League had been in 1918. The United Nations, for example, was more capable of handling the fact that the Soviet Union was not a democracy in any political sense of the term.

Yet the spread of political democracy in the 1990s, with the end of the cold war and the breakup of the Soviet Union, and the example of the world's collective resistance in 1991 to Iraq's invasion of Kuwait, have led some analysts to see the call for a "new world order" made by George Bush, then U.S. president, as the belated realization of Woodrow Wilson's vision for the way in which the League of Nations was meant to function.

Critics of Wilson described him as stubborn and personally autocratic, unwilling to compromise and negotiate. He feuded with opponents at all stages of his career, perhaps thereby losing the opportunity to win a compromise acceptance of the Treaty of Versailles by the Senate and U.S. membership in the League of Nations. Yet effective democracy often requires strong leadership, and it is questionable whether the idea of the League of Nations or the United States's commitment to democracy abroad would ever have emerged as clearly if Wilson had not been president.

See also *Europe, East Central; League of Nations; Progressivism; United States of America; World War I.*

George H. Quester

BIBLIOGRAPHY

Bailey, Thomas Andrew. *Woodrow Wilson and the Lost Peace.* New York: Macmillan, 1944.

Baker, Ray Stannard. *Woodrow Wilson and the World Settlement.* Garden City, N.Y.: Doubleday, 1922.

Bell, Sidney. *Righteous Conquest: Woodrow Wilson and the Evolution of the New Diplomacy.* Port Washington, N.Y.: Kennikat, 1972.

Doyle, Michael J. "Liberalism and World Politics." *American Political Science Review* 80 (September 1986): 1151–1170.

Gardner, Lloyd C. *Safe for Democracy.* New York: Oxford University Press, 1984.

George, Alexander, and Juliette George. *Woodrow Wilson and Colonel House: A Personality Study.* New York: John Day, 1956.

Link, Arthur Stanley. *The Higher Realism of Woodrow Wilson.* Nashville, Tenn.: Vanderbilt University Press, 1971.

Stone, Ralph A., ed. *Wilson and the League of Nations: Why America's Rejection?* New York: Holt, Rinehart and Winston, 1967.

Wollstonecraft, Mary

Pioneering English writer and political theorist who challenged the virtual exclusion of women from contemporary thinking about freedom and equality. Determined to be economically independent, Wollstonecraft (1759–1797) supported herself first by teaching and then by writing. She married William Godwin after the father of her first child abandoned her. She died shortly after giving birth to a second child, Mary, who was to become the wife of the poet Percy Bysshe Shelley and the author of *Frankenstein.*

Wollstonecraft lived through a turbulent and politically unstable period. She was influenced by the experience of the French Revolution and by the writings of its political theorists, in particular Jean-Jacques Rousseau, as well as by William Blake, Thomas Paine, William Godwin, and Henry Fuseli in England. All these writers believed in the rights of man, but they generally understood those rights to apply differently, if at all, to women. Wollstonecraft accepted the view, developed by Enlightenment thinkers in the eighteenth century and later applied to nineteenth-century theories of sexual difference, that men and women have different duties within the "separate spheres" of the public world of civil society and the private world of the family. However, she did not interpret that idea to mean that women could not become full citizens.

According to liberal theory, citizens were to be governed by reason. Because women were thought to be governed by feeling—not least because they were closer to nature than men—citizenship was restricted to men. Wollstonecraft challenged the view that only men were capable of reason. Provided women were treated with the same dignity and shared the same privileges as men, they too could become rational beings and, at the same time, would honor their duties as wives and mothers more fully. As she wrote in *A Vindication of the Rights of Woman* (1792), "Why do they expect virtue from a slave, from a being whom the constitution of civil society has rendered weak, if not vicious?"

If women were not treated equally in the private sphere, Wollstonecraft believed, morality in the public sphere would be undermined, because "the virtue of men will be worm eaten by the insect whom he keeps under his feet." Her writings point to the limitations of liberalism, which posits a separation and an opposition between the public and private spheres of life and naturalizes women's subordinate place within the family.

See also *Feminism; Women and democracy.*

Hilary Land

Women and democracy

Women and democracy concerns the roles, especially the political roles, of women in democratic societies. Through the nineteenth century, even as democracy began to flourish in the world, most women were excluded from meaningful participation in the political processes of the nations in which they lived. Legal restraints, as well as societal norms and customs, kept women from exercising the rights that were accorded to men. Only in the twentieth century were women granted the right (and society's permission) to vote and run for office in democracies.

In most nations of the world at the end of the twentieth century, women have the same rights of citizenship as men. Like men, their participation in the democratic process is typically characterized by voting, serving in parliamentary bodies, and acquiring political leadership roles. In many nations, despite the removal of legal constraints on women's involvement in the democratic process, limitations on their ability to participate as full political beings remain. In fact, in all nations of the world, women are vastly underrepresented at the elite levels of power.

During most of the history of the world, political activism was viewed as an inappropriate role for women. Support for women's participation in the democratic institutions of government is a very recent phenomenon, and in many countries the commitment remains largely rhetorical. Article 21 of the Universal Declaration of Human Rights, ratified by members of the United Nations in 1948, proclaims everyone's right of participation in government. The struggle for women to achieve that goal has taken many forms, including the existence of active women's (and in many cases, feminist) movements, which also address other legal and social interests of women.

Women's Rights in the Industrial Democracies

Concern with women's rights can be traced back to the Enlightenment in eighteenth-century France. By the onset of the French Revolution in 1789, the lists of grievances submitted to the king contained demands for legal equality between men and women, including the reform of marriage laws. Olympe de Gouges's *Declaration of the Rights of Women,* which argued for economic and political equality between the sexes, was published in 1791 in the midst of revolution. Yet in 1793 the revolutionary leader Maximilien Robespierre reversed the progress that seemed possible when he banned all women's organizations and barred gatherings of more than five women.

After the revolution, with the enactment of the Napoleonic Code in 1804, women's rights were set back. The code firmly established women's subordination to their husbands in the home and denied women's equality outside the home. As part of this framework, women were considered legally incompetent in France until 1938, when the restrictions on women were removed.

Despite the setback in France, concern with women's equality grew with the spread of liberal democracy and the Enlightenment to other nations of the world. Soon after the onset of the French Revolution came advocacy of the rights of women in England, when Mary Wollstonecraft's *Vindication of the Rights of Woman* (1792) was published.

In the nineteenth century the women's movements in Great Britain and the United States increasingly worked toward extending the vote to women. In Great Britain, prostitution laws and the working conditions of women were early targets of the women's movement, and the Liberal Party was an ally of the women's groups for a time. John Stuart Mill, the philosopher and member of Parliament, published an essay called *The Subjection of Women* (1869). In Mill the suffrage movement had an influential advocate.

The movement became increasingly radicalized when one of its leaders, Emmeline Pankhurst, affiliated the movement with the Independent Labour Party and then formed the Women's Social and Political Union in 1903. The Women's Social and Political Union undertook a campaign of "direct action" that was characterized by attacks on property, followed by mass arrests of the women. In prison, Pankhurst's followers went on hunger strikes and were force fed by prison authorities. Women's suffrage in Great Britain was won in two stages: in 1918 women aged thirty and over were allowed to vote, and in 1928 women were enfranchised on the same terms as men (at the age of twenty-one).

Women's suffrage activity in the United States arose from the antislavery movement of the 1830s. Elizabeth Cady Stanton and Lucretia Mott, barred—like all women—from attendance at the 1840 World Antislavery Convention in London, convened the Seneca Falls Convention in 1848 to demand women's rights. At this convention, delegates adopted the first formal statement of the women's rights movement. Women remained committed to the abolition of slavery, but they were also beginning to express concern for the political, economic, and social status of women in society.

After the Civil War ended in 1865, women joined in support of a constitutional amendment to enfranchise the former slaves, hoping that it would include a provision granting women the right to vote as well. When the Fourteenth Amendment, ratified in 1868, extended suffrage only to male former slaves, women, including newly freed slaves such as Sojourner Truth, were divided over whether to support it.

Two rival suffrage organizations arose at this time, based in part on the split over support of the Fourteenth Amendment; they eventually combined in 1890 to form the National American Woman Suffrage Association. After a long struggle, the women's suffrage movement, led by Susan B. Anthony, Elizabeth Cady Stanton, Lucy Stone, Carrie Chapman Catt, and, later, Alice Paul, succeeded in securing the vote for women in national elections when the Nineteenth Amendment to the Constitution was ratified in 1920.

On the European continent, as in Great Britain and the United States, women in the nineteenth century organized on their own behalf. In several countries women's groups formed, but their progress was slow; few gains were made anywhere until the twentieth century. Aside from those of Great Britain, the most successful European women's movements emerged in the Scandinavian countries. Women won the right to vote in Norway and Finland before World War I.

Eventually, when women were well established as participants in the political system, they ventured into more and more arenas. By the 1960s a second wave of women's movement activity had emerged in North America, Great Britain, France, Germany, Italy, Denmark, the Netherlands, and even in Spain (after the death of Spanish dictator Francisco Franco in 1975). The most active of the women's organizations were, to varying degrees, influenced by radical philosophies, drawing heavily on Marxist and socialist thought. Many "women's liberation" and feminist groups were committed to reform of abortion laws so as to make abortion more accessible as well as reform of marriage and divorce laws. They also sought to expand women's social and economic opportunities.

Women's Rights in Other Parts of the World

The Soviet Union and its successor states present a different picture. With the success of the Russian Revolution in 1917, the constitution of the newly formed Soviet Union declared men and women equal. A byproduct of the formal declaration of equality was the subordination of women's issues to the problem of the class struggle. For ideological reasons, no independent concern for women was allowed to surface in the new revolutionary society. Despite obvious inequities in society—for example, women were expected to assume responsibility for all housework and child care as well as to participate in the labor force—it was not until the 1980s and Soviet leader Mikhail Gorbachev's perestroika that a women's movement was born.

Women carry their children as they wait to vote in South Africa's historic elections in April 1994. For the first time in the country's history all races were able to vote.

Amidst the tremendous changes taking place in the nations formed through the breakup of the Soviet Union in 1991, women are struggling to bring the question of the status of women to the political agenda. As before, it is possible that matters of special concern to women, such as economic discrimination, domestic violence, and reform of marriage and divorce laws, will become lost in the larger political debate.

In the less industrial countries, women became involved in many of the national liberation movements. Political unrest in colonial possessions provided opportunities for women to challenge men's domination in the political realm while contributing to the overthrow of the colonial regime. Women in Algeria, Cuba, and Vietnam succeeded to some extent in altering the status of women in the new regimes that sprang up with the victory of the revolutionary forces. With the victory of the Communist Party and the establishment of the People's Republic of China in 1949, women made major strides in improving their economic and social status. Even under the authoritarian regime, women's conditions with respect to marriage, education, and work improved. Nonetheless, women have generally been unable to overcome the patriarchal structure that dominates Chinese cultural and economic life.

In many of the nations of Latin America and Asia, women are hindered by authoritarian regimes and social and religious norms that militate against their participation in the democratic process. Women's movements have been unable to bring about effective political changes and have concentrated instead on revising sexual norms related to prostitution, abortion laws, and male violence against women. Women in India, Mexico, Pakistan, and Thailand have had some success, although quite limited for the most part, in these areas.

In most of precolonial Africa, women were legally subordinate to men. In traditional African societies, women had some autonomy because of their role in agricultural production. During the colonial period, African women's autonomy was diminished as men, aided by the colonial powers, increasingly began to control agricultural development. Reinforcing traditional views of the proper distribution of power within the family, the colonial powers helped strengthen male authority. The emerging colonial state created a distinction between public and private sectors in which women were relegated to a subordinate private role, and men became the dominant public actors. The modernization process thus undermined African women's economic base and forced them into subservient positions within the household and within the polity. By the time most Subsaharan African nations achieved independence, in the 1950s and 1960s, women had little economic or political power.

Although women played important roles in the liberation movements of the post–World War II era in Africa, for the most part they were unable to organize effectively when independence was won. Women are often considered outside the political process because many of their concerns are only marginally related to the larger picture of economic development and modernization.

The diversity among African nations makes generalization difficult, but many problems are common across the continent. Although African men are subject to many of these hardships, women suffer disproportionately from problems of illiteracy, unemployment, malnutrition, low life expectancy, and physical abuse. Women have achieved some success in protecting property rights in Zambia, instituting divorce law reform in Zimbabwe, and creating limited equality in marriage in Senegal, but social and political change to advance women's rights has often been sacrificed to competing economic and cultural interests.

Patterns of Enfranchisement

In the early twentieth century, after long decades of struggle, women were finally granted the vote in more and more of the democracies. Women in New Zealand could vote by 1893, and Australian women of European descent had won the vote by 1901. (Aborigines of both sexes in Australia were not allowed to vote until 1967.) Women had been allowed to vote for school committees in Nor-

way as early as 1889. By 1910 women had secured the right to vote in local elections, and in 1913 Norwegian women were enfranchised in parliamentary elections. Finnish women got the vote in 1906. In Canada, non-Indian women won the right to vote in federal elections in 1918, the same year as many women in Great Britain—although women's enfranchisement at the local and provincial levels in Canada came later. With limitations, Canadian Indians were permitted to vote in 1950; all Canadian adults were eligible to vote by 1960.

Most of the remaining countries of Western Europe granted women the right to vote between 1915 and 1919: Denmark and Iceland in 1915; Austria, Germany, Ireland, and Sweden in 1918; Luxembourg and the Netherlands in 1919. In Belgium, women connected to the military through their husbands or sons were granted the vote in 1919; all others, in 1948. Unable to overcome restrictive laws, French women were not permitted to vote until 1944. Swiss women were not able to vote in national elections until 1971. Women in Liechtenstein were finally allowed to vote in 1984.

Although the right to vote does not always signify the existence of real democratic institutions, many Eastern European women were eligible to vote in the post–World War I period: in Poland and the Soviet Union (1918) and in Czechoslovakia (1920). Not until the end of World War II were women permitted to vote in Albania and Hungary (1945) and in Yugoslavia (1949).

Women in some countries of Asia and the Middle East had been able to vote relatively early for those parts of the world: Lebanon (1926, far earlier than women in the colonial power, France, that administered the country), Sri Lanka (1931), Thailand (1932), and the Philippines (1937). Most other women in Asia and the Middle East were unable to vote until World War II had ended. In some cases, enfranchisement was simultaneous with the expiration of colonial rule. Indonesian women were thus able to vote in 1945, Vietnamese women in 1946, women in the Republic of Korea in 1948, Syrian women in 1949, Indian women in 1950, Egyptian women in 1956, and Algerian women in 1962. The People's Republic of China was engaged in civil war after World War II; women were granted the right to vote in 1949 with the final success of the Communist revolution.

Women's political emancipation in Japan was begun during the 1870s, when women were becoming a more visible part of the work force and began to agitate for better working conditions. Women's political activity was sharply curtailed by the Meiji constitution of 1889, which prohibited women from voting, joining political parties, or even attending political meetings. Although that constitution was later revoked, women were still banned from party activity until 1930, when they were allowed to join parties and vote in local elections. Japanese women attained suffrage in 1945 with the end of World War II.

The vote had come earlier to women in Latin America, where many had been enfranchised in the 1930s: in Chile (for local elections in 1931), Uruguay (1932), and Brazil (1934). In other Latin American countries, women were not allowed to vote until the 1940s and 1950s. These countries include Argentina and Mexico (1947), Chile (national elections, 1949), Peru (1950), and Colombia (1957).

In most African nations, women won the right to vote only after World War II. Enfranchisement often accompanied a nation's independence. The earliest votes for women came in Gabon in 1944 and Djibouti and Senegal in 1946. Postcolonial suffrage was granted to women in Tanzania in 1959, in Uganda in 1962, in Kenya in 1963, in Angola in 1975, and in the Central African Republic in 1986. Because voting rights in South Africa were based on race, nonwhite women were not permitted to vote until the nation's first democratic elections in 1994. As in many other nations of the world, having the right to vote, for either sex, does not guarantee access to other democratic rights. Few African countries are democracies.

Women today in most of the world have the same formal voting rights as men; indeed, according to a 1991 survey by the Inter-Parliamentary Union, the only exceptions to the worldwide enfranchisement of women are Kuwait and Bahrain. (As an absolute monarchy, Bahrain has no representative institutions—that is, no one can vote.) Having the right to vote, however, does not necessarily mean that women are deeply engaged in democratic governmental processes.

Women in Legislatures

One important indicator of women's participation in democratic society is the degree to which they seek and gain public office. In most nations the right to vote and the right to hold office were granted to women at the same time. In a significant number of countries, however—namely Mexico, New Zealand, Peru, Syria, Rwanda, Zaire, Zimbabwe, Belgium, Canada, Djibouti, the Netherlands, and the United States—the right to vote was not granted with the right to be elected to office. In the Netherlands and the United States, women were able to hold office before they were permitted to vote.

In many countries, women were elected to the national parliament soon after being allowed to run for office. In other nations, it took years for the first women to be elected after they became eligible to seek office. The gap was significant in Senegal (ten years), Uruguay (ten years), and New Zealand (fourteen years). In Singapore women had the right to run for office thirty-six years before the first women were elected; in Australia women of European descent were first elected forty-two years after becoming eligible. In 1992 there were still some countries, including Lebanon, Morocco, Tonga, the United Arab Emirates, and Djibouti, where no woman had ever been elected to national office.

The removal of legal constraints against women officeholders does not change the fact that they continue to hold only a small proportion of legislative seats. Although women make up more than half the population in most nations of the world, according to an Inter-Parliamentary Union survey, as of June 30, 1993, they constituted a little over 10 percent of the membership of the 170 national parliaments. This figure is slightly lower than the 13 percent tallied in June 1989.

The 1993 survey indicates that the parliament with the most parity between men and women representatives, the People's Assembly of Seychelles, had twenty-four members, eleven of whom were women (45.8 percent). The Scandinavian countries had the next highest percentage of women parliamentarians—39 percent in Finland, 35.8 percent in Norway, 33.5 percent in Sweden, and 33 percent in Denmark—followed by the Netherlands with 29.3 percent. Women made up 18 percent of the Canadian House of Commons. Most legislatures, though, from the British House of Commons to the French National Assembly to the Indian Lok Sabha to the Zambian National Assembly and the Greek Chamber of Deputies, had between 5 and 10 percent women members. After the general election of 1992, women made up 9 percent of the House of Commons in the United Kingdom. In the United States the proportion of women in the 103d Congress (1993–1995) was 10 percent, up from 6 percent in the previous Congress.

In some nondemocratic nations, where parliamentary power was not commensurate with political power, such as the People's Republic of China, Cuba, or the Democratic People's Republic of Korea, women representatives held more than 20 percent of the parliamentary seats. In the Soviet Union women had almost 15 percent of the seats in the Council of the Union. Seats had been reserved for women in some of the parliaments of East Central Europe; the demise of these communist states led to the eradication of this system. Consequently, the number of women parliamentarians in this part of the world has dropped since the advent of greater political competition in national parliamentary elections.

In the 1980s women on average held only 6 percent of national legislative seats in Subsaharan Africa, although they reached the 10 percent mark in Rwanda, Cameroon, Malawi, and Senegal. According to statistics compiled by the United Nations in 1986, women have never made up more than 25 percent of the membership in any African legislative body.

Women as Political Leaders

Despite some gains in legislative office holding, women are underrepresented in positions of political leadership in the nations of the world. A few women have held the highest posts (prime minister or president) in their countries: in Europe, Margaret Thatcher of Great Britain, Vigdís Finnbogadóttir of Iceland, Gro Harlem Brundtland of Norway, and Milka Planinc of Yugoslavia; in the Americas, Eva Perón of Argentina, Kim Campbell of Canada, and Violeta Chamorro of Nicaragua; and across the Middle East and Asia, Indira Gandhi of India, Golda Meir of Israel, Benazir Bhutto of Pakistan, Corazon Aquino of the Philippines, Sirimavo Bandaranaike of Sri Lanka, and Tansu Çiller of Turkey. The small number of women in top leadership posts is testimony to the difficulty women face in gaining power as government leaders or heads of state in the nations of the world.

Women have been infrequent occupants of lower ministerial positions as well. The United States has typically had only one or two women cabinet members since the 1930s. President Bill Clinton in the 1990s appointed four women to cabinet-level posts and others to high positions in the executive branch. Women have never held the key posts of secretary of defense, secretary of state, or secretary of the treasury. Despite their own positions as leaders, neither Indira Gandhi nor Margaret Thatcher appointed women to their cabinets. Women have most often served in the national cabinets of the Scandinavian countries and the Netherlands, and, when François Mitterrand was president in the 1980s and 1990s, in France. The record for the highest number of women in office goes to Norway, where almost half (40 percent) of Brundtland's Labour government from 1986 to 1989 were women.

Overall, women have fared less well in achieving cabinet-level positions in Eastern European and less industrialized nations. Although women may have held high-sounding titles, they fulfilled largely ceremonial roles. The number of women with positions of real power was very small. In 1982 Planinc of Yugoslavia became the first woman to be appointed prime minister in an Eastern European nation. And Alexandra Biryukova was appointed to a Central Committee post (as secretary) in the Soviet Union in 1986. (In the Soviet Union, most women who held government positions were restricted to local or regional offices.)

Women have been absent from cabinet positions in most of the Latin American nations. Costa Rica has been an exception. In 1979, 25 percent of the government positions there were held by women. In Asia, with the exception of a few women in national ministerial posts in Sri Lanka and India during the 1980s, the governments were almost entirely male. In Africa women held only 2 percent of the national ministerial posts, and half the states had no women cabinet officials.

The statistics on women in high positions do not by themselves reveal the type of positions women hold. For the most part, women are appointed as ministers of education, the family, or social development, not the "important" policy-making positions in which men still predominate. Despite their success in attaining positions of national office in the Scandinavian countries, most women even in these countries occupy positions that conform to stereotypical gender roles in society.

Promoting Women's Participation

Within the last century, virtually all of the formal limitations on women's political participation have been revoked. Yet women remain underrepresented in positions of political power. In recent decades the participation of women in the political life of their nations has attracted a good deal of national and international attention. The activities associated with the United Nations Decade for Women (1975–1985) have raised awareness of the issues. In addition, national and international feminist organizations, political parties, and other nongovernmental actors have pressured governments to integrate women more fully into political life.

Political parties and nongovernmental actors can often play a significant role in empowering women. For example, the Canadian Committee for '94 was created in 1984 with the goal of attaining gender equity in the Canadian House of Commons by 1994. Although this and other groups have lobbied for equal representation of women in Parliament, they have not achieved their goal for the Canadian House. The National Council of Women in Denmark, founded in 1899, has almost one million members; this organization plays an active role in encouraging women's political participation in Danish politics. The National Council on Women in the Philippines works to bring women's problems to the forefront of the national agenda. In the United States organizations such as the League of Women Voters and the American Association of University Women also promote civic awareness and participation among women.

Aside from their roles in the established political parties of their nations, women have also been instrumental in creating political parties, some devoted to women members and women's issues. Examples of such parties are the Feminist Party of Canada, the Chilean Women's Party, and the Nationalist Party of Korean Women in the Republic of Korea. Similarly, most national parties have women's branches that are designed to promote the participation of women in the political system as well as to foster adherence to the aims of the party among women.

Government action has often taken the form of establishing a ministry or cabinet office, or legislative committee, dedicated to improving the status of women. The 1991 Inter-Parliamentary Union survey indicates that twenty-four countries have created ministry-level governmental bodies. Fifty-seven nations have lower-level governmental agencies devoted to the status of women, such as the Department for Emancipation of Women in the Ministry of Social Affairs and Employment in the Netherlands and the General Directorate on the Status of Women in the Ministry of Labour and Social Security in Turkey. Of course, the numerical results of the survey do not indicate the effectiveness of nations' efforts and the commitment to change within each nation. Undoubtedly, many governments attempt to give the impression of concern about the roles and status of women without any hope or intention of accomplishing their stated goals.

Most national constitutions and laws prohibit discrimination against women in political participation. The United Nations has highlighted the problem of discrimination against women's political participation in a number of conventions and resolutions. The Convention on the Elimination of All Forms of Discrimination against Women was adopted by the UN General Assembly in 1979. Earlier, in 1967, the General Assembly had approved the Declaration on the Elimination of Discrimination against Women.

Women in most of the world remain underrepresented in the political arena, although legal barriers are few. Some states employ special measures designed to improve women's political status. Various mechanisms have been devised to increase the number of women in office: for example, a certain number of candidates for office must be women; the political party structure designates a certain number of women members; seats are reserved for women; or women are appointed by the head of the government. Quota systems for elective and appointive office are not common; affirmative action for women, like other forms of affirmative action in politics and business, is controversial.

In the twentieth century, women of the world have made significant progress in the political arena. In democratic societies, voting is now an established right for almost all women; most women have also won the right to seek election, or be appointed, to public office. In many democratic nations, however, women's political activity is constrained by cultural and economic restrictions. Until these obstacles are overcome, women's ability to participate fully in the democratic processes of their nations will continue to lag behind men's.

See also *Anthony, Susan B.; Feminism; Mill, John Stuart; Pankhurst, Emmeline; Stanton, Elizabeth Cady; Wollstonecraft, Mary; Women's suffrage in the United States.*

Susan Gluck Mezey

BIBLIOGRAPHY

Bystydzienski, Jill, ed. *Women Transforming Politics: Worldwide Strategies for Empowerment.* Bloomington: Indiana University Press, 1992.

Duverger, Maurice. *The Political Role of Women.* Paris: UNESCO, 1955.

Epstein, Cynthia Fuchs, and Rose Laub Coser, eds. *Access to Power: Cross-National Studies of Women and Elites.* London: Allen and Unwin, 1981.

Iglitzin, Lynne B., and Ruth Ross, eds. *Women in the World: A Comparative Study.* Santa Barbara, Calif.: Clio Books, 1976.

Kohn, Walter S. G. *Women in National Legislatures: A Comparative Study of Six Countries.* New York: Praeger, 1980.

Lovenduski, Joni. *Women and European Politics: Contemporary Feminism and Public Policy.* Amherst: University of Massachusetts Press, 1986.

———, and Jill Hills, eds. *The Politics of the Second Electorate: Women and Public Participation.* London: Routledge and Kegan Paul, 1981.

Norris, Pippa. "Women's Legislative Participation in Western Europe." *West European Politics* 8 (October 1985): 90–101.

Parpart, Jane L., and Kathleen A. Staudt, eds. *Women and the State in Africa.* Boulder, Colo.: Lynne Rienner, 1989.

Penna, David, et al. "Africa Rights Monitor: A Woman's Right to Political Participation in Africa." *Africa Today* 37 (1990): 49–64.

Rai, Shirin, Hilary Pilkington, and Annie Phizacklea, eds. *Women in the Face of Change: The Soviet Union, Eastern Europe, and China.* London and New York: Routledge, 1992.

Randall, Vicky. *Women and Politics: An International Perspective.* 2d ed. Chicago: University of Chicago Press, 1987.

Rowbotham, Sheila. *Women in Movement: Feminism and Social Action.* New York and London: Routledge, 1992.

Staudt, Kathleen. "Women's Politics, the State, and Capitalist Transformation in Africa." In *Studies in Power and Class in Africa,* edited by I. L. Markovitz. New York: Oxford University Press, 1987.

Wolchik, Sharon L., and Alfred G. Meyer, eds. *Women, State, and Party in Eastern Europe.* Durham, N.C.: Duke University Press, 1985.

Women's suffrage in the United States

Women's suffrage refers to women's right to vote, a right earned long after the principle of democratic participation for men had been established in the United States. As early as the American Revolution, Abigail Adams's letters to her husband, John Adams, who became the country's second president, reminded him of the importance of sharing power with women, of giving them a voice in the new government. Adams did not take her concerns seriously. He and his fellows made no attempt to include women in the nation's political activities.

By the 1840s women had become far more visible in public affairs, and they were especially intent on gaining influence in the broadening social arena. In the 1840s and 1850s women activists were committed to three causes of social reform: the temperance movement, the antislavery movement, and the women's rights movement. Most abolitionists, such as Elizabeth Cady Stanton, Lucretia Mott, and Henry Ward Beecher, advocated the enfranchisement of women as well as the abolition of slavery.

In some respects the women's movement grew directly from activists' experiences in the antislavery movement.

Not all abolitionists favored women's participation in political matters, even on behalf of the antislavery cause. Women who traveled to the World Antislavery Convention in London in 1840 were not seated as delegates, although the American delegation supported their attendance. Mott, the Quaker minister and social reformer, and Stanton, the early feminist and abolitionist, were banished with the other women from the convention floor. By the time the convention ended, the two women were determined to organize a women's rights convention in the United States.

Eight years later, in July 1848, the first Women's Rights Convention to discuss the social, civil, and religious rights of women was held in Seneca Falls, New York. The convention unanimously adopted the Declaration of Sentiments, which extended the egalitarian principles of the Declaration of Independence to women: "all men and women are created equal." Only after intense and prolonged debate, however, did delegates adopt Stanton's resolution proposing women's suffrage.

As the Civil War drew closer, the women put aside their own struggle to focus on the abolition of slavery. In 1863 Stanton and Susan B. Anthony formed the Women's Loyal League to gather signatures for petitions to be presented to Congress to demand the total abolition of slavery. The League was disbanded when slavery was abolished by the ratification of the Thirteenth Amendment to the Constitution (1865).

Post–Civil War Struggles

After the war, women renewed their efforts to win the vote, but—as the post–Civil War amendments demonstrated—the nation was not ready to accept women voters. The Fourteenth Amendment, ratified in 1868, was a major setback for women's rights. For the first time the word *male* was added to the Constitution, when the amendment specified penalties that would follow a state's refusal to permit male citizens over the age of twenty-one to vote. Stanton, Anthony, and Sojourner Truth were horrified at the omission of women, while Lucy Stone, Henry Blackwell, and Frederick Douglass insisted that the rights of black citizens were the immediate concern and that women's suffrage must wait. Two years later, women were again overlooked when the Fifteenth Amendment, which forbade voting discrimination based on race, color, or previous condition of slavery, did not secure their right to vote.

This difference of opinion over the urgency of the need

In 1869 Susan B. Anthony and Elizabeth Cady Stanton organized the National Woman Suffrage Association. The leaders are shown here with Anthony in the center.

for women's suffrage led to a division in the women's rights movement that lasted more than two decades. The split was precipitated by a struggle in Kansas over two state referendums on the enfranchisement of blacks and women. Although Stanton, Anthony, Stone, and Blackwell campaigned for both groups, they were attacked by Republicans who derided their efforts to enfranchise women. Stanton and Anthony were unwilling to continue to ally themselves with a Republican Party that opposed women's suffrage. Stone and Blackwell were disinclined to risk the loss of the franchise for black men by linking it to women's suffrage. The latter were also horrified that Stanton and Anthony accepted aid from white Democrats who, they believed, supported women's suffrage in an attempt to cloud the issue and forfeit the vote for black men.

Amid conflict over support for the Fourteenth and Fifteenth Amendments, two rival women's suffrage organizations were formed in 1869. Stanton and Anthony created the National Woman Suffrage Association (NWSA), and Stone and Beecher formed the American Woman Suffrage Association (AWSA). Ultimately, the differences between the two groups diminished, and in 1890 they merged to become the National American Woman Suffrage Association (NAWSA). Stanton was president until 1892, followed by Anthony, who served until 1900.

The issue of suffrage was brought to the Supreme Court in 1875 in the case of *Minor v. Happersett.* Three years earlier, Virginia Minor had sued a voting registrar, Reese Happersett, in St. Louis, Missouri, for refusing to allow her to register to vote. After losing in the Missouri Supreme Court, she appealed to the U.S. Supreme Court, claiming that the right to vote was a privilege of national citizenship protected from state infringement by the Fourteenth Amendment. In an opinion reminiscent of *Dred Scott v. Sandford,* in which the Court had repudiated black citizenship, the Court rejected Minor's appeal. The Court denied that the Fourteenth Amendment granted new privileges of citizenship, stating that it simply guaranteed the protection of existing rights.

Speaking for the Court, Chief Justice Morrison Waite explained that because the Fourteenth Amendment did not confer suffrage Minor could prevail only if women had been entitled to vote at the time the Constitution was adopted. This decision made it clear that women's suffrage was not going to be won through the courts.

Women's Demands for Suffrage

The two women's suffrage organizations differed over the best strategy to follow in order to achieve the vote. The National Woman Suffrage Association, which favored a national approach and passage of a federal constitutional amendment, succeeded in having the "Anthony amendment" introduced in Congress. The amendment was reintroduced year after year until it was finally approved by Congress.

The American Woman Suffrage Association advocated a state-by-state approach for suffrage and, although there were some successes, progress was uneven and very slow. Women won the right to vote in school board elections in a number of states, beginning in Kentucky in 1838. The territory of Wyoming adopted full voting rights for women in 1869; it became the first state in which women were freely allowed to vote when it was admitted to the Union in 1890. Three years later Colorado followed suit, and in 1896 Utah and Idaho democratized the ballot in their states by adopting women's suffrage. There were no further victories for women's suffrage, however, despite hundreds of campaigns in numerous states, until 1910.

Beginning in 1900, when Anthony resigned as president, a revitalized National American Woman Suffrage Association under the leadership of Carrie Chapman Catt renewed its efforts in national politics. When Catt retired as president of the NAWSA in 1902, she was succeeded by Anna Howard Shaw, a Methodist minister and physician who was also a leader of the Women's Christian Temperance Union. Catt resumed the presidency of the NAWSA again in 1915 and was ultimately responsible for coordinating the activities of the state affiliates on behalf of the Anthony amendment.

About the turn of the century, women's demands for suffrage took on a new tone. Previously suffragists had asserted that their claim to the ballot stemmed from an inalienable right of political equality as citizens. They had stressed their common interests with men and argued that democracy required equality of treatment. Now some suffragists began to argue that women differed from men and deserved the vote because they were more virtuous than men. They asserted that including women in the electorate would lead to reform of the political system as well as to other needed social reforms. They also proclaimed that the higher level of citizenship signified by the vote would allow women to produce more responsible citizenship in their children and would make them more interesting as wives. At the same time, many suffragists argued that they were entitled to the vote by virtue of their class and race, in contrast to foreign-born and nonwhite male working-class voters. They sought to convince the political leadership that women were more deserving of the franchise than such men.

In 1910 the National American Woman Suffrage Association began to redirect its energy toward grassroots activities, mounting referendum campaigns in Washington and California (in 1911), followed by Kansas, Oregon, and Arizona (in 1912). In these states, through their victories in referendums, women succeeded in securing state constitutional amendments granting them the right to vote. In Illinois, women won the right to vote for presidential electors by successfully lobbying the Illinois legislature. The failure of referendums in other midwestern states as well as eastern states led to renewed interest in the federal constitutional amendment that had long been the hope of Anthony and Stanton.

Winning the Vote

In 1913 a new suffrage organization, the Congressional Union for Woman Suffrage, was founded by Alice Paul, a Quaker social worker. The Congressional Union planned a massive demonstration on President Woodrow Wilson's inauguration day. Adopting a more radical approach than the NAWSA, the Congressional Union, which later became the National Woman's Party, held the Democratic Party accountable for its failure to enfranchise women. Increasingly influenced by the militant tactics of the English suffragists under Emmeline Pankhurst, the Congressional Union worked to defeat Democratic Party candidates who were not committed to suffrage. Beginning in January 1917, the National Woman's Party picketed in front of the

White House with signs and banners demanding immediate passage of the amendment for women's suffrage.

Women suffragists organized by the National American Woman Suffrage Association demonstrated at both the Republican and Democratic conventions in 1916 and demanded support of the Anthony amendment. At the same time, the NAWSA organized campaigns for state referendums, for legislative efforts in states where women could vote, and for the involvement of women in party politics. Despite the pacifist views of some of its leaders, the suffragists also supported the U.S. war effort in World War I.

The suffragists eventually secured the right to vote when the thirty-sixth state, Tennessee, ratified the Nineteenth Amendment on August 26, 1920. The amendment states: "The right of citizens of the United States to vote shall not be denied or abridged by the United States or by any State on account of sex."

See also *Anthony, Susan B.; Pankhurst, Emmeline; Stanton, Elizabeth Cady; United States Constitution; United States of America; Women and democracy.* In Documents section, see *Constitution of the United States (1787); Declaration of Sentiments (1848).*

Susan Gluck Mezey

BIBLIOGRAPHY

Barry, Kathleen. *Susan B. Anthony: A Biography of a Singular Feminist.* New York: New York University Press, 1988.

Evans, Sara. *Born for Liberty.* San Francisco: Free Press, 1989.

Flexner, Eleanor. *Century of Struggle: The Women's Rights Movement in the United States.* Rev. ed. Cambridge, Mass., and London: Harvard University Press, 1975.

Kraditor, Aileen S. *The Ideas of the Woman Suffrage Movement, 1890–1920.* New York: Columbia University Press, 1965; London: Norton, 1982.

Lutz, Alma. *Created Equal.* New York: John Day, 1940.

McGlen, Nancy, and Karen O'Connor. *Women's Rights.* New York: Praeger, 1983.

Mezey, Susan Gluck. *In Pursuit of Equality.* New York: St. Martin's, 1992.

Sochen, June. *Herstory.* New York: Alfred Publishing, 1974.

World War I

The First World War was waged from 1914 to 1918 between the Central Powers (principally Germany and Austria-Hungary) and the Allied forces (principally Great Britain, France, Russia, and, after April 1917, the United States). For American president Woodrow Wilson, the purpose of the war was "to make the world safe for democracy," but its effects nowhere favored democracy. In some cases, prewar democratic experiments gave way to authoritarianism, either during the war (as in Russia) or shortly thereafter (in Germany and Italy).

World War I changed the world forever. The emperors and generals who sent their men to war in August 1914 had thought the war would last weeks, not months, let alone years. Few foresaw the world catastrophe that would snuff out the lives of an entire generation and consign the next to disillusion and despair.

Background

The crucial events on the threshold of the war were the German pledge of support to Austria in Austria's policy toward independent Serbia, a source of Slavic separatist militancy that threatened the tottering Austro-Hungarian Empire; Austria's ultimatum to Serbia and the rejection of the Serbian response; and Germany's efforts to mediate and to restrain Austria. General war broke out on August 1, precipitated by Germany's declaration of war on Russia and the German invasion of Luxembourg and Belgium.

In the weeks leading up to the war the news of the assassination of the Austrian crown prince on June 28 by a Serbian nationalist at Sarajevo reached Germany's Kaiser Wilhelm II on his yacht near Kiel. His fury and indignation toward the Serbians were thoroughly aroused. He believed that the assassination represented a profound threat to the monarchical system that still prevailed throughout much of Europe. With characteristic impetuosity, but convinced that the entire civilized world, including Russia, would be sympathetic, the kaiser urged Austria to punish Serbia as quickly as possible. On July 5 he took the fateful step of assuring Austria that she could count on Germany's "faithful support" even if punitive action brought her into conflict with Russia, Serbia's ally.

Wilhelm II had not the slightest idea what the Austrians would do. Impelled by a generous loyalty to his assassinated friend, he offered what he thought would be no more than moral support to the aggrieved party. That this guarantee would entail military support never seriously occurred either to him or to the German military and governmental apparatus, which fully supported his move. Even more important, the kaiser believed that a common loyalty to monarchy would prevail over the bonds of ethnic kinship and that the Russian czar would support the kaiser against his fellow Slavs in Serbia. On both counts Wilhelm II proved to be terribly mistaken.

At the time of the Sarajevo assassination, the Austrian emperor, Franz Josef, was an exhausted and embittered old man. The wars he had waged in the past had ended in defeat or loss of territory. It is likely that the aged sovereign no longer fully grasped the consequences of the policies that his foreign minister, Count Leopold von Berchtold, was now pursuing. The count drafted an ultimatum to Serbia which, he was certain, that nation would reject. Protected by Germany, Berchtold thought, Austria could deal a mortal blow to Serbia without fear of intervention.

The Serbian prince regent, Peter, and his ministers were deeply shaken by the harshness of the ultimatum, suspecting that it was a pretext to eliminate Serbia as a sovereign state. In desperation, the prince regent cabled a plea for help to the Russian czar. The Serbian ministers then began to work on their reply, arguing bitterly over the intent of the ultimatum. The arguments were in vain, because the Austrians intended to go to war with Serbia, no matter what response they received. Even though the Serbs dispatched a conciliatory reply to the ultimatum, Austrian bombs fell on Belgrade a few hours later.

The war that broke out on July 28 was a localized conflict between Serbia and Austria-Hungary. The Austrians gambled that it would remain so. Count Berchtold was convinced that there was nothing to fear from Russia; after all, the czar, who also faced opposition from separatists and antimonarchists and lived in fear of assassination, was sure to sympathize with a determined Austrian move against Serbia. Even if this assumption was incorrect, a swift and decisive military victory over Serbia would confront the czar with a fait accompli. But most important, Berchtold was sure that the kaiser's guarantee to Austria would prevent Russian intervention.

Czar Nicholas and his ministers decided to side with Serbia and placed Russia's army in a state of partial mobilization against Germany and Austria-Hungary. This move, in turn, drove Kaiser Wilhelm to a decision to strike first. On July 31 the Kaiser proclaimed a "state of threatening danger of war" and issued a twelve-hour ultimatum to Russia demanding demobilization. When the Russian leadership refused to comply, Wilhelm promptly ordered full mobilization.

German Military Strategies and Pressures

As emperors and statesmen on all sides gradually lost control over the deepening crisis, generals and military staffs began to dominate the scene. During the final period before the outbreak of general war, one appalling fact became terrifyingly clear: the rigidity of military schedules and timetables on all sides made it difficult to reverse the slide toward war. Mobilization plans had been worked out in minute detail years before, in case war should come. Now that it was imminent, each general was terrified lest his adversary move first and thus capture the initiative. Everywhere, then, military staffs exerted mounting pressure on their chiefs of state to move schedules ahead so as to allow them to strike the first blow. What each plan lacked to an astonishing degree was even a small measure of flexibility.

For several years, the German generals had been committed to the Schlieffen Plan—the product of Count Alfred von Schlieffen, an illustrious disciple of the nineteenth-century Prussian strategic thinker, Karl von Clausewitz. The Schlieffen Plan envisaged a German attack on France through Belgium as the most promising first strike in the event of the outbreak of a general European war. Caught between his personal desire to begin a military campaign with a devastating blow against Russia and the plan of his general staff to invade Belgium and France, the kaiser began to dread the specter of a two-front war. He now believed that the German army should not launch an attack against France in the west but against Russia in the east. In the meantime, however, mobilization had been ordered, and the gigantic German war machine had begun to roll toward France.

Helmuth von Moltke, Schlieffen's successor, had planned for this day for a decade. In 1914, at the age of sixty-six, he was still living in the shadow of his illustrious uncle, the victor over France in the Franco-Prussian War of 1870. This burden had taken its toll: military decisions were agonizing for him, and he reached them only after searing self-doubt. The emotional cost of making them was so great that he found it next to impossible to alter them once made.

When the kaiser told Moltke of his plan, the chief of staff was aghast. The vision of 11,000 trains wrenched into reverse was simply too much for Moltke to bear, and he refused the Kaiser point-blank. In fact, it could have been done. Gen. Ludwig von Staab, the chief of the German railway division, was so shocked by Moltke's assertion that it could not be done that after the war he detailed how, given notice on August 1, he could have turned most of the armed forces around and deployed them against Russia by mid-August.

Be that as it may, Moltke convinced the kaiser on that fateful August 1 that the German machine that had begun to roll toward the west could no longer be stopped. The kaiser made one final effort: he dashed off a telegram to King George of England informing him that for "technical reasons" mobilization could no longer be countermanded; he also stated that if both France and England would remain neutral, he would deploy his troops elsewhere. Simultaneously, Wilhelm ordered his aide-decamp to telephone German headquarters at Trier, a point near the Luxembourg border where German troops were scheduled to cross the frontier at any moment. Moltke, according to his memoirs, refused to sign the order countermanding the invasion of Luxembourg. As it turned out, the kaiser's final effort had come too late. His phone order to Trier had not arrived in time. German soldiers had already crossed the border into Luxembourg. Almost simultaneously, the British informed the Germans that they would not remain neutral if Russia were attacked.

We cannot know with certainty what would have happened if Moltke had obeyed the kaiser's order to turn the army around and march toward the east. At the very least, however, valuable time would have been gained; quite possibly, the outbreak of general war might have been postponed or even averted. But the unrelenting logic of a military schedule, and the rigid mind of a military leader, foreclosed that possibility.

French and British Responses

In France a similar confrontation between a statesman and a general occurred. Premier René Viviani, haunted by the fear that war might erupt by accident, on July 30 took the extraordinary step of ordering a ten-kilometer withdrawal along the French-German border, from Switzerland to Luxembourg. In Viviani's words, France took a chance "never before taken in history." The French commander in chief, Gen. Joseph Joffre, trained to seize the offensive, regarded the withdrawal as suicidal and pleaded with the premier to mobilize. By the morning of August 1, he had declared that because each twenty-four-hour delay before general mobilization would mean a loss of up to twenty kilometers of territory, he would refuse to take responsibility for the consequences of the withdrawal. Sev-

eral hours later, he had his way, and the premier authorized full mobilization.

England was the only major European power that had no military conscription. The cabinet hoped to keep the nation out of war, but it also realized that England's national interest was tied to the preservation of democratic France. As the tension mounted, the cabinet became increasingly divided. The man who most clearly saw the imminent outbreak of war on the continent was First Lord of the Admiralty Winston Churchill. On July 28 Churchill ordered the fleet to sail to its war base at Scapa Flow, a remote northern outpost of the British Isles, thus preparing it for possible action and probably saving it from a surprise torpedo attack. When Germany declared war on Russia on August 1, Churchill, after consulting the cabinet, issued the order to activate the fleet.

The chiefs of state of every European nation involved in a military alliance were pressed by their general staffs to mobilize. The generals, under the relentless pressure of their self-imposed timetables, stridently demanded action lest even one crucial hour be lost to the enemy. The pressure on the brink was such that the outbreak of war, when it finally came, was greeted by many with relief rather than fear.

Trench Warfare, Blockades, and Russian and U.S. Involvement

The German general staff hoped for a quick victory over France by launching seventy-eight infantry divisions on its western front. For a few weeks the Schlieffen Plan seemed to work, but then things began to go wrong. The Russians, honoring their alliance with France, pushed two armies into Germany, and the Germans found themselves fighting a two-front war. In addition, the British ordered a fierce counterattack. Germany's hope of defeating France with a single blow was thus ended.

From that point forward, World War I assumed a new and devastating character: inconclusive trench warfare. The battle of the Somme, for example, lasted from July to October, 1916. It cost the Germans about 500,000 men, the British 400,000, and the French 200,000. Yet nothing was gained. Men died by the tens of thousands to gain a few feet of ground in endless battles that raged for months at a time. In the spring of 1915 the Germans used poison gas for the first time. Huge armies wearing gas masks and brandishing bayonets and hand grenades ventured out nearly every day during major campaigns.

Other new forms of warfare appeared as well. The British introduced the tank toward the end of the war, and aerial dogfights by fighter aces on both sides were watched from the ground almost like a sport. But mostly the life of the soldier at the front was lonely and miserable, and mortally dangerous.

Fearful of losing their new navy in direct engagements with the larger British fleet, the Germans used the submarine as their major naval weapon. They attempted a submarine blockade of England and sank enormous numbers of Allied ships. The May 1915 sinking of the British ship *Lusitania,* on which 118 American citizens died, brought the United States close to war with Germany. When Germany resumed unrestricted submarine warfare in 1917, the United States entered the fray (in April), with President Woodrow Wilson's promise of making the world "safe for democracy."

In February 1917 Czar Nicholas of Russia abdicated, and Russia was ruled for six months by a provisional government, led by democratic socialist Alexander Kerensky, which continued to wage war against Germany. President Wilson welcomed Kerensky as a "fit partner in a league of honor." The German high command, eager to knock Russia out of the war and thus escape from its two-front dilemma, made a deal with Kerensky's rival, Bolshevik revolutionary V. I. Lenin. The Germans would support the Bolshevik revolution in exchange for Lenin's promise to take Russia out of the war if he came to power. In October 1917, when Lenin led the Bolsheviks to power and created the Soviet Union, he kept his promise and made a separate peace with Germany in the Treaty of Brest-Litovsk.

Russia's defection enabled the Germans to mount a final offensive against Britain and France in the west, but the might of the United States swung the balance in the Allies' favor and an armistice was signed in November 1918. The final tally was horrible: each of the European combatants lost between one and two million men.

Peace

The victors assembled in Paris in the winter of 1919 to impose peace terms on Germany and Austria. The terms of the Treaty of Versailles, which applied to Germany, and the Treaty of St. Germain, which applied to Austria-Hungary, were very harsh indeed, imposing enormous reparation payments on the defeated Central Powers. The victorious Big Three—Woodrow Wilson of the United States, David Lloyd George of England, and Georges Clemenceau of France—had widely divergent views of a future world.

France demanded large parts of German territory, Britain insisted on a long-term Allied occupation of the Rhineland, and President Wilson of the United States fought passionately for his ideal of a League of Nations, a permanent international body in which all nations should settle their disputes without going to war. In return for concessions to Clemenceau and Lloyd George, Wilson was able to sell his allies on the League of Nations, but in one of history's great ironies, he was unable to sell it at home in the United States. It was defeated by the U.S. Senate, and thus the League of Nations came into existence without American participation.

The end of World War I signaled a temporary upsurge in democracy throughout Europe. The Austrian emperor abdicated in November 1918, and Austria and Hungary quickly proclaimed themselves republics, without waiting for the Paris peace conference. Czechoslovakia, Yugoslavia, and an enlarged Romania were among the other new states formed out of the war. The German empire crumbled in the weeks before the armistice, as the military elite conspired to put in place a civilian regime that would suffer the ignominy of seeking peace. The empire was replaced by a short-lived republic, known as the Weimar Republic.

By 1920, in keeping with the new principle of national self-determination, seven new independent states existed in Europe: Finland, Estonia, Latvia, Lithuania, Poland, Czechoslovakia, and Yugoslavia. In addition, Romania received adjoining areas from Hungary, Greece gained territory at the expense of Turkey, and Austria and Hungary were now small states shorn of their imperial status.

The triumph of national self-determination, unfortunately, did not signify a lasting victory for democracy. The Weimar Republic in Germany, for example, was soon superseded by Adolf Hitler's Nazi regime, which quickly conquered the fledgling democracies of Austria and Czechoslovakia. Democracy's great hope, the League of Nations, soon proved powerless against the onslaught of new dictatorships in Germany, Russia, and Italy. Thus, less than a generation after the signing of the Treaty of Versailles, the new democracies had fallen victim to new dictators: Hitler had swallowed Austria and Czechoslovakia; Joseph Stalin had annexed Estonia, Latvia, and Lithuania; and Benito Mussolini of Italy had conquered Ethiopia in Africa. Far from "making the world safe for democracy," the end of World War I had only set the stage for the holocaust of World War II.

See also *Churchill, Winston; Kerensky, Alexander Fedorovich; League of Nations; Wilson, Woodrow; World War II.*

John G. Stoessinger

BIBLIOGRAPHY

Clausewitz, Karl von. *On War.* New York: Modern Library, 1943.

Fay, Sidney B. *The Origins of the World War.* 2 vols. New York: Free Press, 1966.

Freud, Sigmund. *Civilization, War and Death.* London: Hogarth Press, 1953.

Kennedy, Paul. *The Rise and Fall of the Great Powers.* New York: Random House, 1987; London: Fontana Press, 1989.

Kurenberg, Joachim von. *The Kaiser.* New York: Simon and Schuster, 1955.

Stoessinger, John G. *Why Nations Go to War.* 6th ed. New York: St. Martin's; London: Macmillan, 1993.

Tuchman, Barbara T. *The Guns of August.* New York: Macmillan, 1962.

World War II

The Second World War was waged from 1939 to 1945 between the Axis powers (principally Germany, Italy, and Japan) and the Allied powers (principally Great Britain, France, the United States, the Soviet Union, and China). The leaders of the Axis powers—Adolf Hitler, Benito Mussolini, and Hideki Tojo—shared a bottomless contempt for the democracies, which they tried to destroy using blitzkrieg tactics. In the end, all three dictators led their countries to defeat and unconditional surrender.

Background

The seeds of the Second World War were sown in the soil of the First. Germany, tormented by hyperinflation during the 1920s, saw its middle class virtually wiped out. Caught between growing extremist movements and union demands it could not meet, the Weimar Republic, as the German government had come to be known, became more and more enfeebled. In 1923 Hitler, who had been a corporal in the German army during the war, founded the National Socialist (Nazi) Party, which promised jobs, an end to inflation, and the abrogation of the hated Versailles

treaty. Under Nazi leadership, Hitler promised, Germany would become a great power once again and avenge itself against the French and British democracies, which had imposed the onerous war reparations that burdened the German economy. Above all, Germany would rid itself of the Jews, whom Hitler viewed as an inferior race that nevertheless had managed to bring Germany to its present plight.

Mussolini, in a comparable assault on democracy, had proclaimed a fascist state in Italy in 1922. In the Soviet Union, V. I. Lenin's death in 1924 sparked a bitter struggle for succession that finally produced yet another ruthless dictator: Joseph Stalin emerged in the late 1920s as the undisputed head of the new communist state. In the Far East, imperial Japan pursued its expansionist visions by invading Manchuria (in northern China) in 1931.

In the early years of the worldwide depression that began in 1929 the Nazis consolidated their presence in the German legislature, and in January 1933 Hitler was appointed führer of the German Reich by the aging World War I leader, Paul von Hindenburg.

Nazi Germany began its assault on civilization when, in March 1938, it annexed neighboring Austria without firing a shot. An emboldened Hitler now demanded the German-speaking areas of Czechoslovakia, the Sudetenland. Britain and France, in a fateful conference with Hitler in Munich, sold out Czechoslovakia, seduced by Hitler's pledge that the Sudetenland would be his "last territorial demand."

Hitler invaded Czechoslovakia in March 1939; abandoned by their allies, the Czechs quickly surrendered. Britain and France now pledged to go to war if Germany attacked Poland. In preparation for doing just that, and to the consternation of the democracies, Hitler concluded a nonaggression pact with Stalin in August. The Nazi dictator hoped to avoid the trap of a two-front war, which had contributed to Germany's defeat in World War I. Stalin, in turn, calculated that Hitler and the Western allies would be locked in a long and bloody struggle from which only the Soviet Union would benefit. Reassured by his pact with Stalin, Hitler invaded Poland on September 1, 1939. Two days later, Britain and France declared war on Germany. Appeasement was over. The Second World War had begun.

The Blitzkrieg and the Bombardment of England

German military tactics in World War II differed sharply from those in the earlier war. Endless trench war-

World War II 1395

fare was replaced by blitzkrieg (lightning) war. The Germans quickly overran the western half of Poland, and Stalin annexed the eastern half. Stalin benefited further from his pact with Hitler by reincorporating the three Baltic states—Estonia, Latvia, and Lithuania—into the Soviet Union. In 1940 Hitler turned his fury against all of Western Europe. Once again, as in the First World War, Belgian neutrality was violated as Hitler attacked France through Belgium. This time, however, the German army reached Paris, and France surrendered. The conquests of the Netherlands, Denmark, and Norway followed in short order. Sweden and Switzerland managed to remain neutral.

Hitler now focused on England. For many months London was subjected to merciless aerial bombardments designed to soften up the island nation for a German invasion. Prime Minister Winston Churchill pledged that his nation would never surrender, and, despite relentless round-the-clock bombardments, England stood fast. It was, in Churchill's words, "her finest hour." For the first time, Hitler hesitated. U.S. president Franklin D. Roosevelt, while officially preserving America's neutrality, had earlier vowed to make the United States the great arsenal of democracy. To fulfill that promise, he lent the British some badly needed destroyers in exchange for the right to use British naval bases.

During the winter of 1940, Hitler, then at the zenith of his power, contemplated his next move. Should he persist in his attack on England and make his victory in Western Europe complete? Or should he turn east against his ally, Stalin, break the nonaggression pact, and invade the Soviet Union? Hitler's January 1941 decision to invade Russia bore within it the seeds of his destruction. It was the turning point of the Second World War.

Preparations for a Russian Campaign

To understand Hitler's hatred for Russia, one must appreciate the fact that he paved his road to power with communist blood. As the German population grew polarized between right and left because of the deepening economic crisis and a wave of unemployment, Hitler began to perceive the communists as his only serious obstacle and, next to the Jews, his worst enemies. His storm troopers confronted them in innumerable street battles, beer hall skirmishes, and fist fights in crowded meeting halls. Because Russia was the citadel of the communist movement, Hitler's military ambition to conquer the country grew into an obsession over the years.

As Hitler watched Stalin's attitude toward territorial conquest come to resemble his own, his rage against Bolshevik Russia assumed frenetic proportions. After Stalin's attack on Finland in late 1939, Hitler ordered his generals to prepare an attack on Russia by the autumn of 1940. Protestations by the general staff that such a short schedule would pose insuperable logistical problems made Hitler postpone the projected assault until the spring of 1941. As the German armies conquered Denmark and Norway in the spring of 1940, Stalin imposed Red Army bases in Estonia, Latvia, and Lithuania, in preparation for annexing those states. In June, Stalin took the provinces of Bessarabia and Bukovina from Romania, and on July 21 he annexed the three Baltic states. That same day, in a raging speech to his generals, Hitler ordered immediate feasibility studies for the conquest of Russia.

Hitler's obsession with the Soviet Union now began to color his view of Britain. So desperate was he to destroy Russia that he told his generals in July 1940 that Britain's stubborn determination to continue the war could only be explained by her hope that Russia would enter the war. Hence, Hitler argued, Russia had to be destroyed first. Hitler's hatred of Russia blinded him completely to the strategic realities that prevailed in the summer of 1940. Stalin had absolutely no intention of helping Britain in her plight. It is quite conceivable that Hitler could have dealt Britain a fatal blow had he not been mesmerized by his desire to annihilate the Soviet Union.

In the autumn of 1940 Hitler secretly transferred large segments of the German war machine, the Wehrmacht, to the east. May 15 was set as the date for the invasion of Russia. Throughout the winter Hitler planned "Operation Barbarossa," in which the Germans would penetrate the Soviet Union with two gigantic armies, one aimed at Leningrad in the north and the other at Kiev in the south. Moscow, in Hitler's view, would fall once the rest of western Russia had been conquered. There is no evidence that any of the generals who were taken into Hitler's confidence objected to Operation Barbarossa.

During this crucial period two events took place that prompted Hitler to postpone the invasion of Russia. In October 1940 Mussolini, eager for martial glory of his own, had invaded Greece in a surprise attack. Shortly thereafter, the Italian campaign turned into a rout, and by January 1941 Mussolini had to ask Hitler for military assistance. Hitler complied, and in April 1941 Nazi tanks rattled into Athens and the swastika flew from the Acropolis. The price of this diversionary maneuver, however, amounted to twelve German divisions mired down in Greece.

The second and more pivotal event was a coup d'état in Yugoslavia on March 26. That night the government of the regent, Prince Paul, a virtual puppet of Hitler, was overthrown. Peter, the young heir to the throne, was declared king, and the Serbs made it quite clear on the following day that Yugoslavia's subservience to Germany had ended. The Belgrade coup threw Hitler into one of the wildest rages of his life. Calling his generals into immediate session, Hitler declared that Yugoslavia would be crushed with unmerciful harshness and ordered an immediate invasion. The beginning of the Barbarossa operation would have to be postponed for up to five weeks.

Once again, none of the generals present objected. But six months later, when German troops were hit by deep snows and arctic temperatures three or four weeks short of what the generals thought they needed for final victory, the German chief of staff was to recall with deep bitterness that the postponement of Barbarossa was probably the most catastrophic military decision of the entire war. In order to vent his personal revenge on a small Slavic nation, the Nazi leader had thrown away the opportunity to annihilate the Soviet Union. Hitler came to the same conclusion shortly before his death. Just as Augustus had shouted to a pitiless sky, "Varus, give me back my legions!" Hitler, in the underground bunker of the Reich chancellery with the Russians only several blocks away, was said to have screamed in anguish at a portrait of Frederick the Great: "Give me back my five weeks!"

Invasion of Russia

The invasion of the Soviet Union was rescheduled to begin on June 22. Hitler described the coming campaign as a war to the death between two opposing ideologies. No quarter would be given. Breaches of international law would be excused since Russia had not participated in the Hague conferences and thus could not claim protection under their terms. Soviet commissars who surrendered were to be executed. Five years later at the Nuremberg war-crime trials, when the question of the notorious commissar order was brought up, several generals confessed that they had been horrified but had lacked the courage to object.

During the final weeks before the invasion, Hitler alternated between detailed military planning and fantasies of what he would do to the hated Russians. On the morning after the summer solstice, the German army would smash into Russia. Long before the winter solstice, Russia would disappear from the map.

When the German invasion began, Hitler was the absolute master of the most formidable fighting machine the world had ever seen: 154 German divisions, with additional Finnish and Romanian detachments, were massed on the Russian border; 3,000 tanks and 2,000 airplanes were ready for battle; generals fresh from a succession of victories were in command of the Wehrmacht.

The attack was a complete surprise, due not so much to Hitler's discretion as to Stalin's stubborn refusal to believe that a surprise attack was imminent. During the night of the invasion, Moscow slept peacefully. As dawn broke, the commander of a small Soviet frontier post was awakened by artillery fire. When he called the general in command to report the shelling, the reply was, "You must be insane." By this time the Germans had overrun the post and advanced deep into Russia.

Examining these events, one is struck by Hitler's private and personal involvement in the war against Russia. The need to destroy the hated Slavic nation blinded him completely to the strategic realities in Russia, both before and after the invasion. Thus German soldiers, sure of a summer victory, entered Russia wearing their light uniforms. No provisions had been made to cope with the Russian winter. Men and machines were tooled to perfection, but only for another blitzkrieg. The lessons of Charles XII of Sweden and of Napoleon Bonaparte, who had met their doom in the snows of Russia, were ignored. Yet Hitler chose for his greatest military venture two symbols of a strange and murky significance. Barbarossa had been a crusader of the Holy Roman Empire who had failed in his mission to the East and drowned. His corpse and the site of his burial were lost. Even more peculiar was the choice of June 22 as the day of reckoning. Hitler never mentioned the fate of Napoleon's Grande Armée in its retreat from Moscow in 1812, and it has not been established whether he knew that June 22 was the anniversary of Napoleon's invasion of Russia almost a century and a half before.

War in the East, U.S. Involvement, and Hitler's "Final Solution"

With the European colonial powers embroiled once again in war, Japan, allied with Germany and Italy since 1940, consolidated its hold over China and began to occupy French Indochina. On December 7, 1941, Japanese planes carried out a devastating preemptive strike against the American fleet at Pearl Harbor in Hawaii, bringing the United States immediately into the war. Japan, under its prime minister, General Tojo, intended to destroy the American fleet completely, push the United States out of the Pacific, and turn Asia into a "Greater East Asia Co-Prosperity Sphere," a euphemism for ruthless economic exploitation. Eager to obtain raw materials for its war machine, Japan overran Southeast Asia, the Philippines, French Indochina, the Dutch East Indies, and British Malaya.

Things looked very bleak for the Allies in 1942: Hitler was laying siege to Stalingrad deep in the Soviet Union; his North African corps had conquered much of North Africa under the direction of Field Marshal Erwin Rommel, Germany's "Desert Fox"; and Japan had made the Pacific Ocean a Japanese lake. But then the tide began to turn.

In the winter of 1942 Hitler abandoned the battle of Stalingrad, the first massive Nazi defeat of the war. Rommel suffered his first defeats at El-Alamein and other pivotal battles in North Africa. On the other side of the world, the Americans won a major naval battle against the Japanese at Midway. From that point forward, it was downhill for Germany and Japan. Over the next two years, Soviet and Nazi armies continued to clash in bloody and terrible battles as the Red Army pressed westward. Hitler attempted to consolidate his power on the European continent but never implemented his original plan of invading England. Instead, he turned his greatest ferocity against the Jews.

In 1942 at a special conference convened at Wannsee, the top Nazi leaders designed a program for the systematic extermination of European Jewry, the "Final Solution." Toward that end, huge extermination camps were set up in Germany (Dachau) and Poland (Treblinka, Sobibor, and, most terrible of all, Auschwitz). All in all, the Nazis murdered more than six million Jews in death camps before they were liberated by Allied soldiers in 1945. Even when the Nazis began to lose the war in 1944, the death trains to Auschwitz continued to run on time.

The Jews were not the only victims of Hitler's pathology of hate. The Nazi murder machine also annihilated five million members of other minority groups, including gypsies and homosexuals, whom Hitler regarded as subhuman.

Allied Victory and Aftermath

The weary people under Nazi occupation gained hope with the Allied landing on the beaches of Normandy, in northern France, on "D day," June 6, 1944. American, British, Canadian, and Free French forces under the overall command of General Dwight D. Eisenhower pushed forward toward the Rhine—only briefly interrupted by Hitler's last stand, the Battle of the Bulge in Belgium in the winter of 1944—and then entered Germany. In early 1945 Americans and Russians met at the river Elbe and cut Germany in half. On April 30, realizing that the war was lost, Hitler committed suicide in his bunker in Berlin. In his political testament he blamed Germany's defeat on world Jewry.

In the Pacific the war went on for another three months. In early August 1945, under orders from President Harry S. Truman, the United States dropped two atomic bombs on Japan, the first one on Hiroshima and the second on Nagasaki. Shortly thereafter, General Douglas MacArthur accepted Japan's surrender aboard the battleship *Missouri*. World War II had come to an end. The three Axis powers, Germany, Japan, and Italy, were forced to accept unconditional surrender terms from the victors—the United States, Britain, France, the Soviet Union, and China.

World War II was one of the most destructive conflicts in history. Almost 50 million soldiers and civilians perished between September 1939 and August 1945. Once again, as twenty years earlier, democracy experienced a partial victory over dictatorship. Germany was occupied by the United States, Britain, France, and the Soviet Union. While Stalin quickly turned East Germany into a Soviet satellite, the three Western allies prepared the ground for a democratic German state with its capital at Bonn; the Federal Republic of Germany was destined to be far more durable than its feeble predecessor, the Weimar Republic.

In the Pacific the United States became the sole occupying power in Japan. General MacArthur's new constitution for Japan forbade that nation ever to go to war again and laid the groundwork for a successful Japanese democracy. In both Germany and Japan, war criminals were brought to justice. The lesson of Versailles had been learned: no reparations were exacted from the defeated countries. Instead, both West Germany and Japan were encouraged to embark on a road to recovery, through the Marshall Plan, an American economic-assistance plan named for U.S. secretary of state and former general George C. Marshall, and other acts of reconstruction.

In Eastern Europe, however, democracy was not allowed to triumph. Stalin was still bent on expanding the Soviet empire. After the end of the war in the wake of the retreating Nazi armies, Stalin set up puppet governments in Hungary, Poland, Romania, Bulgaria, and Albania. In 1948 even Czechoslovakia, a comparatively robust democracy between the two world wars, became a communist state. The Second World War had not made the world safe for democracy, to use the phrase of Woodrow Wilson, America's president during World War I. War gave way to the long twilight struggle known as the cold war, which was to become a new sword of Damocles, suspended over humanity for forty years.

Democracy in the United States suffered a severe setback when the government placed Japanese Americans into relocation centers for the duration of the war, in violation of their rights as U.S. citizens. Conversely, democracy received a boost when the U.S. Army decided to desegregate the military during the war, in a policy shift that became permanent.

Perhaps the most lasting positive consequence of the war was the creation of the United Nations in 1945. Its plenary body, the General Assembly, now includes almost every nation on earth and has become a kind of global parliament, quite possibly an expression of democracy's slow but steady advance throughout the world.

See also *Churchill, Winston; de Gaulle, Charles; Fascism; Roosevelt, Franklin D.; United Nations; World War I*. In Documents section, see *Constitution of Japan (1947)*.

John G. Stoessinger

BIBLIOGRAPHY

Bullock, Alan. *Hitler and Stalin: Parallel Lives.* New York: Knopf, 1992; London: Fontana Press, 1993.

Claude, Inis L., Jr. *Swords into Plowshares.* 4th ed. New York: Random House, 1971.

Gilbert, Martin. *The Second World War.* New York: Holt; London: Weidenfeld and Nicolson, 1989.

Keneally, Thomas. *Schindler's List.* New York: Simon and Schuster, 1982; London: Hodder and Stoughton, 1994.

Prange, Gordon W. *At Dawn We Slept.* New York: Penguin Books, 1981.

Shirer, William L. *The Rise and Fall of the Third Reich.* New York: Simon and Schuster, 1960.

Stoessinger, John G. *Why Nations Go to War.* 6th ed. New York: St. Martin's; London: Macmillan, 1993.

Y

Yeltsin, Boris Nikolayevich

Former Communist Party official who became president of the Russian Federation in 1991, the first head of state in Russian history to have been directly elected by the citizens of his country. Yeltsin (1931–) had been, in effect, leader of the opposition during the last few years of the existence of the Soviet Union.

Born into a poor peasant home in the Sverdlovsk re-

gion of Russia, Yeltsin graduated as a civil engineer and worked in the construction industry. He joined the Communist Party in 1961, became a full-time official in 1968, and by 1977 was first secretary of the Sverdlovsk regional committee. A member of the party's Central Committee from 1981 until 1990, he was brought to Moscow as a department head (and soon a secretary) of the Central Committee in 1985 by the new leadership of Mikhail Gorbachev.

It was, however, as first secretary of the Moscow party organization from December 1985 until late 1987 that Yeltsin first made an impact on the political consciousness of his fellow Russians. He clashed with one of the most powerful members of the party leadership, Yegor Ligachev, and became popular with Muscovites as he opened pedestrian zones, relaxed controls over street traders, attacked privilege, and made well-publicized appearances on Moscow buses.

Yeltsin attacked party conservatives in an unscheduled speech to the Central Committee in October 1987. The episode led to his removal from the Moscow party leadership and from the candidate membership of the Politburo he had held since 1986. Although still officially a member of the Central Committee, Yeltsin was largely in the political wilderness for eighteen months—until Gorbachev introduced competitive elections for a new legislature, the Congress of People's Deputies of the USSR, in the spring of 1989.

Yeltsin made excellent use of the political space opened up by Gorbachev's electoral reform and overwhelmingly defeated, in a Moscow-wide district, the candidate favored by the party hierarchy. The following year, this time from his native Sverdlovsk (now Yekaterinburg), Yeltsin equally convincingly won a seat in the Congress of People's Deputies of the Russian republic. In May 1990 the

Congress elected him chairman of its inner body, the Supreme Soviet, from which post he became a thorn in the flesh not only of conservative Communists but also of Gorbachev.

Yeltsin had adopted an increasingly radical position on market reforms and on the devolution of powers from the federal authorities to the republics, including his own giant Russian republic. He also spoke up courageously in defense of the right to independence of the Baltic states and against the threatened crackdown on these states in early 1991. He was elected to the new post of president of Russia in June 1991, with an overall majority over five other candidates on the first ballot. By this time his power in Russia was at least equal to that of the Soviet president, Gorbachev. Yeltsin's domestic and international standing was greatly enhanced when, along with members of the Russian parliament with whom he was later at odds, he led the defense of Russian democracy in August 1991 against those who had launched a coup to restore the old order.

Following the failure of the putsch, during which Gorbachev had been under house arrest, Yeltsin pressed home his advantage and played a notable part in breaking up the Soviet Union rather than sign a union treaty that would grant a role to an "all-union" government and to Gorbachev in a loose federation or confederation. In December 1991 Gorbachev resigned, and Yeltsin moved into his offices in the Kremlin and in the former party Central Committee building.

With fewer constraints on his actions in post-Soviet Russia, Yeltsin from early 1992 supported the liberalization of prices and a privatization program as Russia moved, falteringly, toward a market economy. His relations with the Russian legislature, however, deteriorated. In September 1993 Yeltsin forcibly dissolved the Congress of People's Deputies and the Supreme Soviet and announced elections for a new bicameral Federal Assembly. Those elections, as well as a plebiscite on a new constitution which increased presidential power at the expense of the legislature, were held in December 1993. In an election characterized by low turnout, Yeltsin's constitution was approved, but radical reformers and committed Yeltsin supporters were in a minority within the State Duma (the more representative and influential of the two chambers of the new parliament). Yeltsin's popularity had also declined sharply from its 1991 high point. By 1995 it was still lower.

Confronted with a growing problem of organized crime, Yeltsin demonstrated his own tenuous grasp of the principle of the rule of law. He thought nothing of contradicting his own presidential decrees or even of contravening his tailor-made 1993 constitution. Despite his loss of enthusiasm for U.S.-style checks and balances, Yeltsin contributed greatly to the democratization of Russia during the reformist phase of his career.

See also *Russia, Post-Soviet; Union of Soviet Socialist Republics.*

Archie Brown

BIBLIOGRAPHY

Brown, Archie, Michael Kaser, and Gerald S. Smith, eds. *The Cambridge Encyclopedia of Russia and the Former Soviet Union.* Cambridge and New York: Cambridge University Press, 1994.
Morrison, John. *Boris Yeltsin: From Bolshevik to Democrat.* London and New York: Penguin Books, 1991.
Yeltsin, Boris. *Against the Grain: An Autobiography.* London: Jonathan Cape, 1990.
———. *The Struggle for Russia.* New York: Times Books, 1994.

Yoshida, Shigeru

Prime minister of Japan during most of the U.S. occupation (August 1945–April 1952), when many democratic changes were instituted. Reared in a wealthy family with aristocratic connections, Yoshida (1878–1969) served as a career diplomat in China and in Europe before World War II. A conservative and stubborn individual, he opposed Japan's militarists. He was briefly imprisoned because of his antiwar efforts, shortly before Japan's surrender on August 15, 1945.

Yoshida's clean record led to his appointment as foreign minister in September 1945. He became prime minister in May 1946, when the leading candidate was ruled ineligible by the occupying forces because of his prewar nationalist record. Yoshida's two main tasks were to get along with the supreme Allied commander, Gen. Douglas MacArthur, and to gain popular and parliamentary acceptance of the occupation's extensive reform program. He succeeded on both counts.

Yoshida vigorously defended the liberal constitution that MacArthur's staff had drafted. He won an overwhelming vote of approval for the constitution from the Diet (parliament), despite Japan's limited experience with popular sovereignty, representative government, and civil

Shigeru Yoshida

For most of the occupation, Yoshida was the dominant political figure in Japan, partly because he seemed to get along well with MacArthur. His government pushed through the occupation program that included freeing the labor movement, opening up education at all levels, giving tenant farmers ownership of the land they tilled, and creating a "national police reserve" (a 75,000-man paramilitary force ordered by MacArthur) when the Korean War began in June 1950.

Although he considered some reforms "excessive," Yoshida implemented them. Examples include the occupation's "lenient attitude" toward Japanese communists and left-wing labor leaders, the wide scope of the "purge" of wartime political figures, the prohibition of the teaching of "morals" in the schools, and the decentralization of the national police. Yoshida was suspicious of left-of-center parties and politicians, but he steadfastly abided by the principles of parliamentary government. Japan successfully conducted four general elections while Yoshida was prime minister.

Yoshida left office in December 1954. The Japanese hold him in high esteem because they believe he stood up for his country at a time of crisis and started it on the way to democracy, peace, and prosperity.

See also *Constitution of Japan (1947)* in Documents section.

Richard B. Finn

BIBLIOGRAPHY

Finn, Richard B. *Winners in Peace: MacArthur, Yoshida and Postwar Japan.* Berkeley: University of California Press, 1992.

Yoshida, Shigeru. *The Yoshida Memoirs.* Translated by Kenichi Yoshida. Boston: Houghton Mifflin, 1962.

liberties. With support from Emperor Hirohito, whom MacArthur kept on the throne as a symbolic figurehead, the constitution was adopted in 1947 and remains unaltered half a century later. Not all of its provisions have been fully implemented, however, and the spirit of democracy is sometimes wanting in Japanese political and social practice. Still, outside observers give Japan high marks for its protection of political and civil rights. Public opinion strongly supports the constitution, especially its no-war clause.

Yugoslavia

See *Europe, East Central*

Z

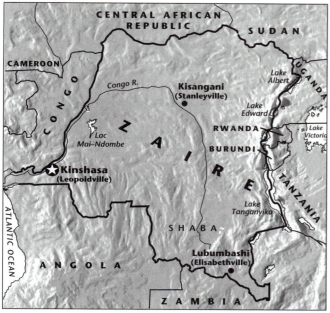

Zaire

A large central African state that has not known democracy since achieving independence from Belgium on June 30, 1960. The factors contributing to Zaire's absence of democracy include the country's  colonial legacy, the crisis-ridden first five years of independence (1960–1965), the tyrannical presidency since 1965 of Mobutu Sese Seko, and, until 1993, the firm political and economic support of Mobutu's external patrons and protectors—Belgium, France, and the United States. Because of the combination of these factors, democracy has never had a chance to succeed in this politically turbulent nation.

Historical Legacy and the Initial Crisis

Before the advent of formal colonial rule at the Berlin Conference in 1884–1885, the territory today known as Zaire was occupied by many different political forms. They ranged from highly centralized states such as the Kongo kingdom to decentralized village governments. These forms interacted with each other over the years in a long-term ebb and flow as people struggled to increase their autonomy. These struggles for political autonomy, however, were localized and were waged without the vocabulary of nineteenth-century European liberalism. While most villages and many precolonial kingdoms did have systems of checks and balances designed to prevent certain abuses of power, the democratic notions of competition among groups, inclusive political participation, and civil and political liberties were generally absent.

From 1885 to 1908 Zaire, then the Congo, was the personal fiefdom of King Leopold II of Belgium. Vicious plunder prevailed until international outrage and pressure forced the elected Belgian government to take legal control of the colony in 1908. Belgium moderated some harsher aspects of Leopold's order, but forced labor, crop restrictions, and frequent imprisonment for violations of agricultural regulations remained. The state continued to extract wealth from those who produced it.

The population had no say in determining colonial policies. Political parties were not permitted until the end of the colonial period; educational policy emphasized primary education rather than secondary schooling or higher education; indigenous, Christian groups such as the Kimbanguist Church and the Kitawalists were repressed because the colonial government saw them as subversive; and censorship ensured that no free interchange of political ideas could occur. The Belgian Congo was one of the most intensively administered states in

Subsaharan Africa. It was, in many ways, the antithesis of democracy.

The colonial period also reshaped the way Zairians thought about themselves. Precolonial nationalities such as Kongo suddenly became "tribes" or ethnic groups. The Belgians permitted cultural organizations based on a single ethnic identity, but they banned political parties transcending ethnic lines. Zairians used ethnic identities, even if artificial, as a means of political mobilization in the colonial state. Consequently, when independence arrived, Zairians found it all too easy to perceive the new world of competitive politics in predominantly ethnic terms.

Civil and political order disintegrated from 1960 to 1965 for three main reasons. First, although the Belgians bequeathed their colony a constitutional and ostensibly democratic order when they left in 1960, Zairians were unprepared to run their newly independent country. There were few college graduates, and there had been no period of planned decolonization with training in the practices of democratic self-rule. The entire transition was hasty and ill conceived. The new institutions, simple copies taken from the Belgian system, quickly proved unworkable. The second reason was politicized ethnicity. It made trust and political legitimacy impossible to achieve, fostered the secession of the copper-rich Katanga/Shaba Province, and fueled an ethnic civil war in Kasai Province. The final reason was the cold war, which contributed to the interventions of the Belgians, Soviets, Americans, and the United Nations. Under such difficult circumstances, Mobutu and his soldiers staged a military coup in 1965 and seized power from the civilians who had shown themselves incapable of governing the country.

Mobutu's Tyranny

Wearied by the ceaseless strife, many Zairians welcomed the new regime because the civilian order had completely lost legitimacy. Mobutu quickly tried to end instability by rebuilding the state. He created a rubber-stamp legislature and curbed pervasive ethnic conflict by decreasing the number of provinces, removing their political autonomy, and nationalizing their police. Provincial governors were named by the president. Single-party rule soon followed when Mobutu founded the Popular Movement of the Revolution in 1967. Although the constitution briefly permitted a second party, Mobutu would tolerate no other political organization, and he soon controlled all institutional arms of both state and party. A syndicate sponsored by the state absorbed trade unions; women's

and youth groups found a home in the Popular Movement of the Revolution. Mobutu was president-founder of the party, president of the republic, and commander in chief of the armed forces. A cult of personality emerged as sycophants massaged Mobutu's ego in the state-controlled media.

Ill-advised economic policies, grandiose and unsuitable development schemes, and a generally mismanaged economic sector created pervasive scarcity. Moreover, Mobutu's policies to rebuild the state added to the insecurity of government officials whose tenure depended on Mobutu's whim. Since few had ventured into the private sector, they used public office to create private wealth. Corruption became endemic. The powerful felt impelled to use their state offices as a means of extracting wealth from their fellow citizens. Insecurity and scarcity thus fed on each other. When generals stole their salaries, soldiers raided villages. When teachers went unpaid, they charged students. When state-employed physicians could no longer survive, they charged patients. This vicious chain of extraction prompted a national search for survival in the economy's burgeoning informal sector.

As the regime's legitimacy dwindled, Mobutu ruled increasingly through coercion. The Zairian army's primary purpose was to crush unarmed civilians. The civil guard, party youth wing, and political police also terrorized the citizenry. In 1982 some parliamentarians formed an opposition party, the Union for Democracy and Social Progress, but this movement was repressed at every turn. Until 1990 when Mobutu, under intense international pressure, opted to liberalize the system by legalizing political opposition, including the Union for Democracy and Social Progress, most Zairians remained silent for fear that they would be reported, jailed, or worse. In recent years Amnesty International has publicized the state's consistent abuse of fundamental human rights. It is no exaggeration to say that Mobutu's regime has sustained a reign of terror: extortion, arbitrary arrest, detention without trial, and extrajudicial executions have been all too common. Unsurprisingly, democracy has not flourished in this environment.

External Support

The final reason that democracy has not taken root in Zaire pertains to Mobutu's external support. From the republic's earliest days the cold war fostered external intervention in Zaire's internal affairs while impeding the emergence of a democratic political order. The initial international interventions of the early 1960s accomplished the removal from power of Patrice Lumumba, Zaire's first prime minister and the only politician who then had anything approaching a national following, because the West perceived him as a Soviet sympathizer. The rise to power of Mobutu, a strong anticommunist, was facilitated at certain key junctures by the U.S. government, and especially by the Central Intelligence Agency.

Throughout the cold war the United States and its European allies, France and Belgium, were quick to shore up the central government's political control whenever that became necessary. When, in 1964, a series of popular rebellions swept through two-thirds of the country, both Belgium and the United States provided military and logistical support so that the central government could defeat the insurgents. In 1977 and 1978 Zairian insurgents operating from Angolan and Zambian bases twice invaded Shaba Province in an attempt to topple Mobutu. Quickly, French and Belgian troops intervened to support the regime. Once again the United States provided logistical support.

By shrewdly playing his anticommunist card and pointing to "Kremlin-inspired" plots against him, Mobutu could shroud the deficiencies of his regime and get the attention of policymakers in Washington, D.C. Although these officials certainly knew that Mobutu's rule was substantially less than democratic, they rationalized their support for him because of his strong anticommunism and because—regardless of party affiliation—they did not wish to "lose" this country on their watch. External support enabled Mobutu to continue his ruthless regime even though it had lost all legitimacy at home.

When the cold war ended in the early 1990s, Mobutu's position became increasingly precarious. Long-suppressed internal dissent combined with global pressures toward democratization had weakened his hold on power and pushed Zaire toward a complete breakdown of civil and political order. In 1993 Mobutu lost his last vestiges of Western support. But by then the destruction of Zairian society had been so complete that it will take years to rebuild. Decades of Mobutu's misrule and repression took an enormous toll—politically, economically, and psychologically. As long as Zairians must worry about their survival, it seems unlikely that democracy will be uppermost in their minds.

See also *Africa, Subsaharan.*

Michael G. Schatzberg

BIBLIOGRAPHY

Callaghy, Thomas M. *The State-Society Struggle: Zaire in Comparative Perspective.* New York: Columbia University Press, 1984.

Kalb, Madeleine G. *The Congo Cables: The Cold War in Africa from Eisenhower to Kennedy.* New York: Macmillan, 1982.

MacGaffey, Janet. *Entrepreneurs and Parasites: The Struggle for Indigenous Capitalism in Zaire.* Cambridge: Cambridge University Press, 1987.

Schatzberg, Michael G. *The Dialectics of Oppression in Zaire.* Bloomington: Indiana University Press, 1988.

———. *Politics and Class in Zaire: Bureaucracy, Business, and Beer in Lisala.* New York: Africana, 1980.

Willame, Jean-Claude. *Patrimonialism and Political Change in the Congo.* Stanford, Calif.: Stanford University Press, 1972.

Young, Crawford. *Politics in the Congo: Decolonization and Independence.* Princeton: Princeton University Press, 1965.

———, and Thomas Turner. *The Rise and Decline of the Zairian State.* Madison: University of Wisconsin Press, 1985.

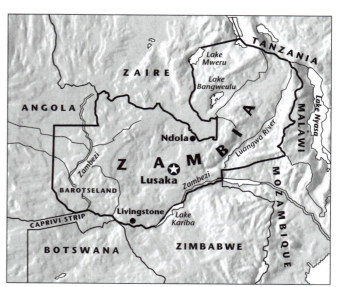

Zambia

A land-locked, low-income country in Africa bordered by Zaire on the north and Zimbabwe on the south. Zambia was the first English-speaking state in Africa to make an electoral leadership transition in the post–cold war period. In October 1991 voters rejected a seventeen-year experiment with single-party rule by the United National Independence Party (UNIP) in favor of a broad-based opposition movement that promised a return to pluralistic and competitive politics. By electing trade unionist Frederick Chiluba as their new president, Zambians disavowed Kenneth Kaunda, a founder of the Zambian independence movement and a prominent African nationalist.

The case of Zambia illustrates three truths about poor countries that attempt to reject authoritarianism. First, mass demands for democratization often originate in popular resentment of declining economic opportunities and living standards. Second, an economic crisis alone is insufficient to propel a successful transition to democracy: other political-institutional conditions must be in place, including a unified opposition and a relatively neutral bureaucracy and judiciary. Third, the resultant political regimes are extremely fragile, and democratic institutions prove difficult to consolidate.

From Traditional to One-Party Rule

The colony of Northern Rhodesia was created in the late nineteenth century to protect mineral concessions extracted from indigenous chiefs by the British South Africa Company, founded by Cecil Rhodes. The British Colonial Office, which ruled from 1924 to 1953, amalgamated many indigenous polities—each with its own language, culture, and institutions—into a hybrid political system in which central colonial authority was exercised and, to a degree, shared with local leaders. Although some traditional polities, such as the Lozi chiefdom, were highly centralized, others, such as the Tonga village, dispersed authority to headmen. Neither traditional nor colonial rule encouraged a democratic political culture since these regimes vested authority in appointed male elders and allowed few opportunities for political participation or competition.

Africans resisted colonial rule, initially by joining messianic religious sects and later through industrial strikes in the mining region, known as the Copper Belt. In response to the incorporation of Northern Rhodesia into the white settler–dominated Central African Federation in 1953, a new class of Western-educated leaders, including schoolteachers such as Kaunda, were able to build an anticolonial nationalist movement. Combining protest action with demands to broaden the electoral rolls, they pressured Great Britain into permitting the first African government in 1962 and granting full political independence within the British Commonwealth in 1964. In that year Kaunda became the first president of Zambia under a republican constitution that affirmed freedom of political expression and association.

The First Republic (1964–1973) was marked by lively multiparty competition in which the United National Independence Party's electoral dominance was gradually eroded by regional opposition parties. To promote national unity, Kaunda skillfully balanced competing ethnic interests by distributing political appointments among the country's main ethnic groups. He avowed a preference for single-party rule but promised that UNIP could win its desired monopoly through the ballot box. As it happened, however, Kaunda ultimately resorted to coercion. Faced with possible defeat for UNIP in the 1973 parliamentary elections, he detained or co-opted opposition leaders and declared a single-party state on December 13, 1973.

The revised constitution for Zambia's Second Republic (1973–1991) enshrined the principle of party supremacy and empowered the president to appoint all senior party and government officials. The National Assembly was reduced to a "rubber stamp" that endorsed decisions taken in the UNIP Central Committee. Inspired by the ideas of Tanzania's president, Julius Nyerere, Zambian "one-party participatory democracy" at first permitted a measure of political competition within the ruling party. Over time, however, Kaunda manipulated electoral rules to consolidate UNIP control over the recruitment of parliamentary candidates and to eliminate challenges to his presidency. Under the banner of a socialistic ideology of "humanism," he also appointed party loyalists to patronage posts in the network of public corporations that dominated the Zambian economy. Voters showed their dissatisfaction with these policies by staying away from the polls and casting growing numbers of "no" votes in presidential elections.

Democratic Transition

Popular disenchantment deepened in the 1980s as Zambia's economy entered a prolonged downturn because of falling international copper prices and economic mismanagement at home. Lacking opportunities for political participation within the ruling party or outside it, the people shifted the locus of their opposition to civil society. Church, student, and business associations became havens for liberal political views and vehicles for the expression of dissent. At the core of Zambian civil society was the labor movement organized under the umbrella of the Zambia Congress of Trade Unions. Its membership comprised more than 80 percent of formal employees, and by the mid-1980s it was twice the size of UNIP. Under the leadership of Chairman Frederick Chiluba, who was imprisoned briefly by Kaunda in 1981, it resisted UNIP's efforts to incorporate workers into the ruling party.

Frustrated by the reluctance of the government, Zambia's main employer, to engage in collective bargaining or take adequate steps to reverse the country's economic decline, the Congress demanded greater governmental accountability. By late 1989 Chiluba began to call openly for the restoration of multiparty politics. In defense of this view, he pointed to the collapse of communist regimes in Eastern Europe. Africans, he argued, also should forsake the one-party system.

Such demands for political pluralism were backed by massive street demonstrations in Zambia's populous urban areas. The political crisis was exacerbated by food riots, the worst political violence since independence, and an attempted military coup in June 1990. In response, Kaunda made a series of historic political concessions. First, he permitted a referendum on a multiparty system. Second, he called for competitive elections monitored by international observers. Finally, he allowed constitutional revisions to reduce the executive powers of the presidency. To take advantage of these political openings, labor and business leaders convened a loose opposition alliance, which was hastily converted into a political party. Chiluba was elected to lead this Movement for Multiparty Democracy (MMD) and to be the party's candidate for the nation's presidency in the October 1991 elections.

The 1991 election campaign pitted MMD's critique of economic mismanagement and political repression against UNIP warnings that competitive politics would foster ethnic violence. In the end Zambia's first democratic election in more than two decades hinged on personalities, with voters expressing a clear determination to rid themselves of Kaunda. Chiluba won 76 percent of the presidential vote, and MMD candidates captured 125 out of 150 National Assembly seats. Zambia's Third Republic was born on November 1, 1991, as Chiluba took office with a strong electoral mandate to restore both political rights and economic well-being.

Features of the Transition

Why was Zambia able to exit from authoritarian rule through a peaceful election, a landmark event on a continent where such transfers of power are rare? Several factors help explain the Zambian exception.

First is the quality of leadership. Kaunda's instinct for political compromise led him to concede to demands other African rulers had stubbornly resisted. Kaunda was generous even in defeat, stepping aside promptly once it became apparent that the opposition had won. Second,

compared with other African countries, Zambia has an unusually urbanized and well-educated population. This social structure laid the foundation for independent associational life, particularly among organized labor, and for energetic protest against elite corruption and declining living standards.

Third, the opposition in Zambia coalesced into a coherent political force. Although never a well-organized political party, the MMD did bring labor, business, professional, and religious interests together into a united social movement, unlike the fragmented opposition that characterized other regimes in Africa attempting transitions in the early 1990s. Finally, governmental institutions played vital independent roles. The courts, for example, ruled against UNIP in key court cases concerning the use of public resources for partisan political purposes. And the electoral commission displayed commendable impartiality in adjusting and enforcing electoral rules to ensure free and fair elections. Uncommonly for contemporary Africa, even the police and the military performed their roles neutrally.

All its institutional assets—reflective leaders, modern social classes, active voluntary associations, a professional bureaucracy—will be needed to consolidate democracy in Zambia. There is no going back from certain aspects of pluralism: the press, civic groups, and political parties have vigorously defended newly won freedoms of expression and association, and judges and civil servants have resisted politicians who sought to reassert supremacy over decision making. Nevertheless, certain generic problems of consolidating democracy in a poor country have become evident.

Problems of Democratic Consolidation

The political transition occurred rapidly in two short years between late 1989 and late 1991, allowing little time for the emergence of firm democratic institutions. Most notably, Zambia lacked a complement of effective political parties that could instill practices of popular participation and open competition: the MMD party organization began to fragment with the disappearance of the unifying goal of ousting Kaunda, and UNIP was reduced by its poor showing at the polls to a regional party with a base only in the Eastern Province. Indeed, MMD's lopsided electoral victory raised anew the prospect of one-party dominance of elections and the legislature.

Moreover, economic conditions in Zambia in the early 1990s hampered the consolidation of democratic gains. The MMD inherited a monumental national debt, a deteriorated physical infrastructure, a reputation for high risk among investors, and an accelerating rate of inflation. The government thus embarked on a radical economic reform program to reduce state employment, restore private ownership, and introduce free markets. In the short run this program deepened hardship for urban dwellers and increased opportunities for conspicuous consumption by economic elites. As strikes proliferated, especially in the public sector, former supporters turned against the MMD. The Zambian case supports the notion that democratic consolidation is not purely a political process but also demands social and economic change.

Most fundamentally, the consolidation of democracy requires a political culture in which elites and masses alike value democratic practices as part of the natural order of things. Such values are not widespread in Zambia. At the mass level, voter turnout remains low, registering just 45 percent in the historic transition elections of 1991 and below 14 percent in the local government elections of the following year. The mass celebrations in response to the erroneous news of Kaunda's ouster during the aborted coup attempt of June 1990 indicate that many Zambians were willing to accept any form of political change—democratic or not—as long as it removed an unpopular leader. Moreover, the habits of one-party rule have proved to be resilient among political elites. A hard-line faction of MMD cabinet ministers has displayed a predilection for arbitrariness (for example, by convincing Chiluba temporarily to declare a state of emergency in 1993). Elements within UNIP, for their part, have tended to resort to plots and intrigue and have failed to develop an ethic of loyal opposition. For all these reasons, the young democracy in Zambia remains fragile and unconsolidated.

See also *African transitions to democracy; Nyerere, Julius.*

Michael Bratton

BIBLIOGRAPHY

Bratton, Michael. "Zambia Starts Over." *Journal of Democracy* 3 (April 1992): 81–94.

Chanda, Donald. *Democracy in Zambia: Key Speeches of President Chiluba, 1991–92.* Lusaka: Africa Press Trust, 1993.

Gann, L. H. *A History of Northern Rhodesia: Early Days to 1953.* London: Chatto and Windus, 1964.

Gertzel, Cherry, Carolyn Baylies, and Morris Szeftel. *The Dynamics of the One-Party State in Zambia.* Manchester: Manchester University Press, 1984.

Kaunda, Kenneth. *Zambia Shall Be Free: An Autobiography.* London: Heinemann, 1962.

Tordoff, William, ed. *Politics in Zambia.* Manchester: Manchester University Press, 1974.

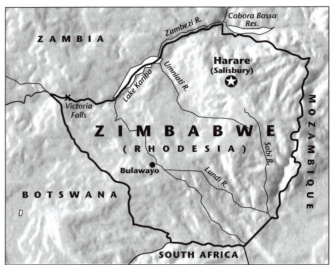

Zimbabwe

A landlocked country in southeastern Africa, which has had the constitutional form of democracy since 1980 but lacks electoral competition and free expression of ideas. The boundaries of Zimbabwe, originally called Southern Rhodesia, were drawn by the British South Africa Company in the 1890s. Before then the African population in the region consisted primarily of small-scale political organizations centered on villages, although the Ndebele in the Southwest had a hierarchical political structure centered on a king.

Historical Background

Led by Cecil Rhodes, the British South Africa Company searched the area for mineral wealth comparable to the rich deposits found in South Africa. The expected mineral bonanza never materialized, however. Faced with the company's virtual bankruptcy, the white settlers voted to become a self-governing colony of the United Kingdom in a 1922 referendum that excluded the participation of blacks. Although whites made up only a minuscule portion of the population, they took control of the region's internal affairs.

The whites were few in number, but there were still too many whites with a vested interest in controlling government to allow for the kind of easy decolonization that occurred in much of Africa. Rhodesian whites possessed a political voice and an ability to organize that made the colony fundamentally different from other African territories. On the other hand, there were not enough whites to institute a full-fledged program of apartheid as was being done in South Africa. Indeed, whites in what became Zimbabwe never represented more than 2 percent of the population, compared with a peak population share of almost 20 percent for whites in South Africa. Only after a long and bloody war of national liberation did Zimbabwe achieve independence through formal decolonization.

In the decades after the 1922 referendum, whites slowly consolidated their power. Africans were forced off their land and herded into Tribal Trust Territories. The Rhodesian state expanded and created a large number of state-owned corporations (parastatals) to foster infrastructure, agriculture, and an iron and steel industry. Especially after World War II, with a significant influx of whites fleeing the gloom of postwar England, the economy boomed. Oppressive laws ensured white supremacy and prevented protest by the black majority.

Yet, alongside this complex system of economic and legal controls to repress Africans, a tradition of democratic politics developed among white Rhodesians. Elections occurred routinely, and occasionally the incumbents lost. But there was never a tradition of competition among parties representing different political ideals. Always aware that they were a tiny minority, the whites were never as divided by issues as they were united by fear of the Africans coming to power.

End of Colonial Rule

In 1964, faced with demands from Great Britain that Southern Rhodesia follow the continental trend and grant political power to the African majority, Ian Smith, the prime minister, promulgated a Unilateral Declaration of Independence. The declaration was declared illegal by the United Nations, which then imposed mandatory comprehensive sanctions against the renegade regime. These sanctions, however, had little effect. By enacting even more repressive legislation and exploiting the many loopholes in the global embargo, white Rhodesians managed to prosper.

Soon after the declaration a war of national liberation began, but the military threat against the settler regime was very limited because of the disorganization of the guerrilla armies, the effectiveness of the Rhodesian counterinsurgency effort, and support from the South African military. The Zimbabwe African People's Union (ZAPU), led by Joshua Nkomo and supported by the minority

Ndebele, continued to fight from its bases in Zambia, but it was never a very effective organization. The party of the majority Shona was the Zimbabwe African National Union (ZANU), led by Robert Mugabe. Only in 1975, when Mugabe was able to open bases in newly independent Mozambique, did hostilities against the regime, based in Salisbury (now Harare), increase dramatically.

In 1979 Bishop Abel Muzorewa created a transitional regime. It was never acknowledged as legitimate by other countries, however, and it was clear to all inside the country that Smith was the power behind the throne. Demonstrating the oddity of that regime, the country was briefly known as Zimbabwe-Rhodesia. Its economy gradually deteriorated as a result of years of warfare, political uncertainty, sanctions, and white emigration.

Finally, the government regime was forced to negotiate with the Africans. The site of these negotiations, mediated by Lord Carrington, was Lancaster House in London. The elections held the following year were widely considered to be free and fair. Mugabe's Zimbabwe African National Union won a significant electoral victory: 63 percent of the vote and 57 of the 100 seats in Parliament. Most of Mugabe's support came from the Shona-dominated areas; he garnered less than 10 percent of the vote in the Ndebele-dominated areas of Matabeleland North and Matabeleland South. Muzorewa's party received almost no popular support.

The constitution drawn up at Lancaster House made numerous concessions to the whites. Most dramatically, a separate voting roll allowed whites to have a disproportionate number of seats in Parliament (20). To placate the politically important white farmers, seizure of land by the state was forbidden unless compensation was paid in foreign currency. These provisions could not be amended for seven years unless the white members of Parliament agreed.

The Government Since 1980

Zimbabwe's democratic experience since 1980 has been mixed. On a continent where many constitutions are irrelevant almost as soon as they are printed, the Mugabe regime has strictly adhered to the constitution, at least on a procedural level. Although the guaranteed white veto in Parliament was widely viewed as insulting, the constitution stood unchanged for the agreed seven years. Mugabe's government did not seize any land or nationalize any enterprises (unless market compensation was set). Only in 1987, at the end of the seven-year period specified in the Lancaster House constitution, did the government eliminate white seats in Parliament and enact legislation that permitted it to seize some land from white farmers. Within the parameters of the constitution, the courts in particular have been independent and energetic in defending individual rights, sometimes to the dismay of the government. There has been no retribution against the whites. Indeed, Ian Smith was allowed to participate fully in politics even though many in the country believe that he is a war criminal.

Beyond strict procedural adherence, Zimbabwe's democratic performance has been poor. Most dramatically, the regime probably killed between 1,000 and 2,000 people in Matabeleland in the mid-1980s, when Mugabe accused elements of the Zimbabwe African People's Union of collaborating with South Africa. Partially for ethnic reasons, the army of Zimbabwe went amok in this region, inflicting countless injuries and causing numerous people to flee their lands. Nearly a decade later the country still had not come to grips with this massacre. Ethnic conflict did lessen, however, in 1987 with the merger of ZANU and ZAPU to form the Zimbabwe African National Union–Patriotic Front (ZANU–PF).

Majority rule in Zimbabwe has been characterized by repression of ideas as well as violence. Because the government directly controls the electronic media, open debate and discussion are stymied. Especially during the 1980s, information on what was happening in the country was difficult to obtain. The state of emergency imposed by the minority white regime as well as other repressive laws were retained by the Mugabe regime during the 1980s, further inhibiting free political discussion.

The country did not experience a full-fledged national debate about its political system until 1989, when ZANU–PF was about to create a de jure one-party state (as opposed to the de facto one-party state that had existed since 1980). A series of events, including the collapse of communism in central Europe, the release of Nelson Mandela in South Africa, and the end of the state of emergency in South Africa (particularly important given the stridency of Zimbabwe's criticism of apartheid), as well as the global trend toward democracy, demonstrated just how anachronistic the Mugabe government's political project had become. Indeed, Western donors warned that Zimbabwe would appear badly out of step with the rest of the world if it outlawed political competition just when so many other countries were overthrowing dictatorships. At the same time domestic opposition to the creation of a political monopoly for ZANU–PF increased. This opposition was sparked not only by the wave of democratic transitions in the late 1980s but also by the genuine desire of many Zimbabweans for a pluralistic order and an end to the corruption and authoritarianism of Mugabe's regime.

The elections in 1990 were open to other parties, although only one, the Zimbabwe Unity Movement, emerged as significant. While ZANU–PF won the vote count handily, only 54 percent of the eligible population voted. This low turnout indicated that many people were displeased with the political and economic performance of the regime, although they did not find the opposition compelling.

Although the one-party state clearly lacks support in Zimbabwe, many questions remain about the country's political future. Political competition based on ideology has yet to emerge, and ZANU–PF continues to reserve for itself special access to the media. Like most African countries, Zimbabwe must develop innovative democratic institutions and procedures if its rural majority is to have political power commensurate with its interests. So far no democratic vision that would ensure full political participation has become generally accepted. The great democratic task ahead is for Zimbabweans to develop an indigenous democratic theory appropriate to their circumstances.

Jeffrey Herbst

BIBLIOGRAPHY

Baynham, Simon, ed. *Zimbabwe in Transition.* Stockholm: Almqvist and Wiksell, 1992.

Herbst, Jeffrey. *State Politics in Zimbabwe.* Berkeley: University of California Press, 1990.

Mandaza, Ibbo, ed. *Zimbabwe: The Political Economy of Transition, 1980–1986.* Dakar: Council for the Development of Economic and Social Research in Africa, 1986.

———, and Lloyd Sachikonye, eds. *The One-Party State and Democracy.* Harare: Southern Africa Political Economy Series Trust, 1991.

Moyo, Jonathan N. *Voting for Democracy: Electoral Politics in Zimbabwe.* Harare: University of Zimbabwe Publications Office, 1992.

Sithole, Masipula. "Zimbabwe: In Search of Democracy." In *Democracy in Developing Countries: Africa,* edited by Larry Diamond, Juan J. Linz, and Seymour Martin Lipset. Boulder, Colo.: Lynne Rienner; London: Adamantine Press, 1988.

Zionism

A democratic national liberation movement that arose in the late nineteenth century. The primary purpose of Zionism was to normalize the status of the Jewish people through the attainment of political sovereignty. In seeking to establish a homeland for the Jewish people in Palestine, Zionists asserted the historic link of the Jewish people to a land from which they had been exiled in the Diaspora ("Dispersion") nearly two thousand years earlier, when the temple in Jerusalem was destroyed in A.D. 70.

A major nondemocratic consequence of the success of Zionism in creating the modern State of Israel was that it led to the displacement of hundreds of thousands of Palestinians. Israel, as a nation, began as a British mandate under the League of Nations in 1917. When it declared its independence in 1948, it was attacked by neighboring Arab states, who opposed its creation. Those who remained as an Arab minority in the Jewish state were estranged from the Zionist political culture, which in becoming dominant muted their voices. The unresolved debate over the Jewish character of the state remains an issue that divides Israeli Jews deeply, as well as dividing Arabs from Jews, and has significant implications for the democratic nature of Zionism and the State of Israel.

Background

Zionism as a modern ideological and political movement arose as a response to the problem of the Jews (their persecution and insecurity as a consequence of anti-Semitism) and to the problem of Judaism (the threat that assimilation would undermine authentic Jewish culture). It rejected both the cultural assimilation characteristic of Jews of the West and the passivity of waiting for the Messiah characteristic of the more traditional Jews of Eastern Europe. According to tradition the Messiah will be a descendant of King David sent by the Lord to lead the children of Israel back to the Promised Land. Zionism defined the Jewish problem as a national problem and therefore called for national liberation.

Despite its modern and essentially secular nature, Zionism derived its power and legitimacy from its reinterpretation and adaptation of the traditional religious myth of the exile of the Jewish people from the Holy Land and the biblical promise of their return, which would result in collective (national) redemption. This myth gave Zionism both its conceptual orientation and a strategy for action. The most radical (and modern) innovation introduced was the call for human collective action to realize national redemption by returning to the Land of Israel rather than waiting for fulfillment of the divine promise of Messianic redemption.

From its inception the Zionist movement was merely one of many ideologies that competed for the hearts and minds of Jews around the world. Also from the beginning, the Zionist movement was torn by internal political and ideological divisions. For example, the political Zionists—led by Theodor Herzl (1860–1904), founder of the World Zionist Organization, who favored diplomatic efforts to gain an international charter for the creation of a Jewish homeland—were opposed by the practical Zionists, led by Chaim Weizmann (1874–1952) and David Ben-Gurion (1886–1973), who favored settlement of Jews in Palestine as the primary focus of Zionist activities.

In institutionalizing the new state, Zionists faced a monumental challenge: they had to create the impression of constituting a natural community. Perhaps the primary goal of Israeli political culture has been to persuade the world to accept, and even take for granted, the continuity of the contemporary nation-state with the ancient past. The Jews' right to statehood based on this historic link has been challenged by many both inside and outside Israel's borders. The challenge to inventing the secular Zionist tradition has therefore been daunting.

Democratic Dilemmas

By basing the legitimacy of a modern state on the claim to continuity with the biblical past, Zionism became established as the dominant motif of the political culture of the prestate Jewish community in Palestine in the late nineteenth and early twentieth centuries. This dominance was accomplished primarily through the use of symbols, myths, and rituals that were interpreted in various ways according to the ideological perspectives of competing political movements and parties.

Competition between groups not only determined which ideological interpretation was ascendant at different periods but also decided which views were marginalized or silenced. The debate within Zionism traditionally set the bounds of legitimacy within Israeli politics. Those who did not accept or who rejected its major tenets, for example, Arabs and non-Zionist Orthodox Jews, were on the political periphery. Although both have gained much greater political influence in the 1990s, the enduring cultural themes within Zionism continue to shape the rhetoric and discourse of Israeli political debate even for those who reject them.

Zionist symbols, myths, and rituals are less acceptable to the Arab/Palestinian citizens of Israel than to the non-Zionist Jews. Ironically, one of the consequences of the attempt to socialize Israeli Arab children with the symbols of Zionism has been their tendency to use the rhetoric of Zionism to identify the notion of a persecuted people without a homeland with the plight of their fellow Palestinians. Zionism has thereby become a means of expressing Palestinian nationalism.

The Zionists' secularization of the concept of Messianic redemption was perceived to be blasphemous by many of the ultra-Orthodox (fundamentalist) Jews, some of whose descendants still reject political Zionism and the State of Israel. The contradiction between the claims of Zionists and those of the anti-Zionist Orthodox Jews has not been reconciled. In the 1950s an alliance of two groups of Zionists formed the National Religious Party, in an attempt to bridge the gap between Orthodox Jewish tradition and modern political Zionism. (The National Religious Party has been a coalition partner in every Israeli government except the one formed after the 1992 election.) An ethnically based ultra-Orthodox religious party, Shas (Sephardic Torah Guardians), formed in 1984, challenges the conventional distinction between Zionist and non-Zionist.

Conflicting perspectives on the questions of what the Jewish character of Israel should be, and even whether there should be a Jewish state, continue to cause the most serious division among Jews and between Jews and Arabs in contemporary Israel. The absence of even minimal consensus on such basic principles has been the primary obstacle to agreement over a written constitution and has been one of the primary causes for coalition crises since the establishment of the state.

For a number of reasons this division is likely to increase in political importance in the future. Given the relative balance of power between the two major political blocs, Labor (the latest incarnation of the party that dominated Israeli politics from the founding of the state until 1977) and the Likud (the amalgamation of nationalist parties that led the governing coalition cabinets from 1977 to 1984 and shared power with Labor from 1984 until 1990), the power of the religious parties as key coalition partners increased tremendously during the 1980s and 1990s. As

greater concessions are made to the religious parties, the resentment of the non-Orthodox majority has grown, and signs of a backlash are apparent. In the future, however, a further influx of secular Jews from the former Soviet Union could reduce the electoral influence of the Orthodox parties.

Segregation between ultra-Orthodox, nationalist religious, and secular Jews—and between Jews and Arabs—is almost absolute in terms of residence, education, military service, and marriage. Almost all Arabs and thousands of ultra-Orthodox Jews are exempted (the former collectively and the latter individually) from compulsory military service. Because service in the Israel Defense Forces is one of the most important rites of passage for gaining individual and collective social acceptance, mobility, and legitimacy, those who do not serve tend to be marginalized.

The two most important democratic dilemmas facing Israel are how to reconcile the claims of the Palestinian national movement with those of Zionism and how to reconcile the democratic requirements of inclusion of, and responsiveness to, its Arab citizens while maintaining the Jewish character of the state and its special links to the Jews of the Diaspora. Arab citizens of Israel have increasingly identified with their brethren in the occupied territories—the Arab territories occupied by Israel during the Six-Day War with Egypt, Jordan, and Syria in 1967—thereby raising the stakes and making the resolution of this problem even more imperative.

Israel After the Six-Day War

Israel's record of preserving a dynamic democracy within its pre-1967 borders has been impressive, particularly given the persistent political challenges to its legitimacy and military challenges to its very existence. The country remains unique in the Middle East, and among new nations in general, for its competitive party system, free press, independent judiciary, and many other manifestations of a democratic system. The nondemocratic military occupation of territories conquered in the Six-Day War resulted in an anomalous situation, however.

In a sense Israel was reborn in 1967 as a Siamese twin. Within the borders created by the 1949 armistice (its independence was not recognized by any Arab state until 1979), democratic Israel has lived symbiotically linked with a Palestinian twin whom it dominates. The two radically different forms of regime and political cultures have inevitably affected each other. The Palestinians, subjects of

Israeli military rule until the process of withdrawal began in Gaza and Jericho in 1994, have seen the benefits of democracy enjoyed by the citizens of Israel (including those Palestinians who are Israeli citizens); this awareness intensifies their sense of the injustice of their conditions. Israeli democracy has been compromised by the prolonged maintenance of a military occupation, which is by its very nature antithetical to democracy. (The notion of a democratic military occupation is an oxymoron.)

The polarization of politics and the political stalemate partially created by and expressed in the election results from 1981 through 1992 have strengthened the bargaining positions of the religious parties and reduced the Zionist parties' paternalism toward the Arab voters. As a result of the 1992 election, the Labor Party, led by Yitzhak Rabin, returned to power heading a coalition with Shas and the liberal, dovish Meretz alignment of Mapam, the Citizens' Rights Movement, and Shinui (Change). Whereas the government received the parliamentary support of the Arab parties through their votes on crucial issues, Rabin preferred the partnership of a Jewish religious party with dubious Zionist credentials to that of the Arab parties, which lack even such tenuous links to the dominant political culture (particularly given the delicate diplomatic negotiations with the Palestine Liberation Organization, Jordan, and Syria, which began in secret after Labor came back to lead the government).

Part of the price for dependence on parties like Shas has been the weakening of some Zionist principles (for example, mass exemptions of students in higher-level religious schools from the military draft) and of efforts to strengthen democratic processes (for example, compromises on legislation codifying civil rights). If these electoral trends continue, future governments might be more dependent on non-Zionist religious parties or on Arab parties as full partners in the government than they have been in the past. Either scenario would lead to revisions of the Zionist vision as well as important changes in policy.

Negotiations for the Future

The mainstream Palestinian organizations have moved toward a grudging recognition of the existence of the State of Israel, while the majority of Israelis have moved toward a grudging recognition of the existence of the Palestinian national movement. In mid-September 1993, in a dramatic ceremony on the lawn of the White House in Washington, D.C., Prime Minister Rabin and Yasir Arafat, chairman of the Palestine Liberation Organization, shook hands and began a process of reconciliation and political negotiations. The militants in both camps continue to reject this trend and claim their exclusive rights to all of the same land as their birthrights.

The militant position sets forth a zero-sum situation in which only one side can win and the other will lose. The moderates claim that the militants' position implies that everybody loses, whereas compromise provides the basis for gains on both sides. For both Zionism and Palestinian nationalism to realize their democratic potentials and to resolve their century-old rivalry, they must compromise on their contradictory political objectives. Recognition of the legitimacy of the other through dialogue and negotiations is an essential first step. A hopeful sign is the peace treaty that was signed between Israel and Jordan in the latter part of 1993.

Zionism's unique blend of the particular with the universal provided a bridge through which the Jewish people collectively crossed from the premodern *kehilla* (the traditional Jewish social and religious community in the Diaspora) to modern national independence. Its present challenge is to undertake significant ideological transformation in order to accommodate the conflicting demands of democratic inclusion and ethnic exclusion. Zionism was one of the world's earliest and most effective national liberation movements. It has also pioneered in linking bonds of sympathy and loyalties that transcend the nation-state, a phenomenon associated with postmodernity.

Zionism has been invoked to frustrate the demands for greater democratic inclusion of Israel's Arab citizens. It has contributed to undermining aspects of the democratic character of Israel to the extent that it has been used to give legitimacy to the prolonged occupation of the territories of Palestinians who are not its citizens.

Ideological innovation in Zionism since the mid-1970s took place primarily on the right end of the political continuum—that is, on the more nationalistic end. The return of the Labor Party to the leadership of a government based on an alignment of even more liberal parties might provide a conducive environment for the emergence of more liberal ideological innovations in Zionism with greater sensitivity to democratic concerns. Such an outcome would be particularly likely if progress in the peace talks between Israeli and Palestinian leaders and between Israel and Syria are successful.

See also *Israel; Judaism.*

Myron J. Aronoff

BIBLIOGRAPHY

Aronoff, Myron J. *Israeli Visions and Divisions: Cultural Change and Political Conflict.* New Brunswick, N.J.: Transaction, 1989.

———. *Power and Ritual in the Israel Labor Party.* Revised and expanded ed. Armonk, N.Y.: M. E. Sharpe, 1993.

Avineri, Shlomo. *The Making of Modern Zionism: The Intellectual Origins of the Jewish State.* New York: Basic Books, 1981.

Halpern, Ben. *The Idea of the Jewish State.* Cambridge: Harvard University Press, 1961.

Hertzberg, Arthur. *The Zionist Idea.* New York: Basic Books, 1966.

Liebman, Charles S., and Eliezer Don-Yehiya. *Civil Religion in Israel.* Berkeley: University of California Press, 1983.

Lucas, Noah. *The Modern History of Israel.* London: Weidenfeld and Nicolson, 1974; New York: Praeger, 1975.

Medding, Peter. *The Founding of Israeli Democracy, 1948–1967.* Oxford and New York: Oxford University Press, 1990.

Vital, David. *The Origins of Zionism.* Oxford: Oxford University Press, 1975.

DOCUMENTS RELATING
TO THE DEVELOPMENT OF DEMOCRACY

INTRODUCTION TO THE DOCUMENTS

Following are twenty seminal documents relating to the development of democracy. The documents span the globe and two millennia, from Athens 431 B.C. to the 1994 Summit of the Americas. And they address the several fundamental beliefs that underlie democracy as the term is understood today: rule of law, as enshrined in constitutions; self-determination (the right of a people to govern themselves), as represented by declarations of national independence; and the rights of the individual, as stated in international declarations of human rights.

The documents reproduced here are illustrative of democracy as it emerged and has been practiced at different times and in different societies. No such selection could be considered comprehensive. And, while all of the following documents represent important milestones in democratization, no claim could be made to them being the twenty "most important" documents.

A brief headnote introduces each document, highlighting the features that make it unique or remarkable. The headnotes also provide historical context to help the reader understand the circumstances that gave rise to the document, and they draw comparisons among the documents.

The Use of Documents in Historical Research

Documents are important sources of information for historians and political scientists in explaining the development of a concept such as democracy and the factors that underlie the concept. A document—whether it is a constitution, a declaration, a legal code, a piece of legislation, or the transcription of a speech or other official pronouncement—provides insight into the society and historical epoch that gave rise to it. When documents from different societies and different eras are compared, clues emerge as to the intellectual heritage passed from society to society and generation to generation. Insight can also be gleaned from documents into the pattern of economic, social, political, constitutional, legal, and cultural development across time and space.

The interpretation of such "primary-source" informa-

tion as documents, however, is fraught with potential methodological and intellectual pitfalls. In juxtaposing these twenty documents relating to the development of democracy, it is all too tempting to draw a linear progression from document to document, to say, for example, that the Dutch Declaration of Independence begat the U.S. Declaration of Independence, which begat the Israeli Declaration of Independence. There is little doubt that the drafters of the American document were familiar with its Dutch predecessor, and that the founders of the Israeli state had some knowledge of the American document. But it would be too simplistic to suggest that the later documents were no more than updated versions of the earlier ones, or to suggest that there has been a teleological progression over time and space toward world democratization. Although historical narratives often draw a clear line between events, or individuals, or documents, the true nature of the legacy from one to another is much more subtle and difficult to discern.

The alternative interpretation of history as a series of unrelated people, events, and theories is equally inadequate. Clearly, the political theorists and practitioners of the eighteenth century owed a debt, consciously or unconsciously, to their predecessors. And those of the nineteenth to those of the eighteenth. And so on. The development of democracy from ancient Athens to the modern-day states was neither inexorable, toward a final "perfect" form, nor was it a series of disjointed events. The true nature of the developmental process is somewhere in between the two extremes.

The difficulties inherent in comparing documents of different eras is brought out most directly in the headnote to Magna Carta. Often touted as the forerunner of such modern concepts as trial by jury and the "community of the realm," Magna Carta was in fact a product of the feudal age. Although those concepts can be identified in embryonic form in the document, one must take care not to read twentieth-century values and political philosophies into a thirteenth-century document.

Analyzing a document within the context of the society

that gave rise to it is often as challenging as comparing documents across societies. Context is critically important to understanding the nature of a document. This aspect of historical inquiry is addressed most clearly in the headnote to the constitution of Argentina. The drafters of the Argentine constitution had borrowed liberally from the U.S. Constitution. Election procedures, political institutions and processes, and other aspects of American theory and practice were adopted with only minimal changes. Yet the character of Argentine democracy was very different from that of the American because the underlying intellectual, social, religious, and economic bases of Argentine society differed so greatly from the American.

A related methodological concern that should be kept in mind when studying the following documents is the issue of "normative" versus "nominal" democracy. The former refers to the prescriptive attributes of a political system; to the written guarantees of liberty, to the formally established government procedures and processes. Nominal democracy refers to the political establishment as it really exists and operates, as opposed to how it is normatively supposed to operate. Here again, the U.S. and Argentine constitutions are good examples; they are more alike in letter than in practice.

The distinction between normative and nominal democracy, between constitutional theory and practice, is sometimes for the better. For example, the U.S. Constitution makes no provision for judicial review of acts of Congress and the president. That practice emerged gradually, beginning with Chief Justice John Marshall's decision in *Marbury v. Madison*. Although the practice is well developed and universally accepted as "constitutional" in the United States, it was never added to the Constitution. The practice was so highly regarded by democratic theorists that it was formally written into a number of subsequent constitutions, including those of Argentina, Japan, and the Federal Republic of Germany. When reading the following documents, one must therefore keep in mind the difference between the written text and the actual practice of democracy.

The Roots of Democracy

Why did democracy emerge in particular societies at particular times? What is the relationship between the underlying factors—economic, social, and cultural—and the development of democratic ideals and forms of government? There are no universally accepted answers to those questions. But that renders the questions no less important.

Democracy is fundamentally an intellectual construct. It is the product of deeply held beliefs about the sanctity of individual rights and organization of political society in such a way as to guarantee those rights. But the correlation between certain economic and social factors and the development of a democratic political culture has to be acknowledged.

In a number of the headnotes, economic factors figure prominently in explaining the context of the document. Expanding commerce or a change in patterns of commerce is attributed with enhancing national identity in the Dutch provinces (Dutch Declaration of Independence) and the American colonies (American Declaration of Independence) and with contributing to the political unification of Argentina (Constitution of Argentina). The rise of a middle class, which is a natural consequence of industrialization and urbanization, is credited in several headnotes with buttressing democracy.

While there is a correlation between democracy and an economically advanced middle class, that does not prove causation. Clearly, certain economic and social characteristics reinforce democratic ideals, but the political system of any nation is more than a superstructure determined by its economic and social systems.

PERICLES' FUNERAL ORATION (431 B.C.)

Under Pericles (c. 495–429 B.C.), an intellectually gifted politician, military leader, and orator, the Greek city-state of Athens reached its zenith. Though Athens was a slave society in which citizenship was circumscribed, and though it was the ruler of a colonial empire, Athenian politics and society had many democratic features that were advanced for the time.

Fifth-century Athens was a prosperous society, with annually elected magistrates, called "generals," and broad citizen participation in such institutions as the Assembly and the Boule. The Assembly was the sovereign body, in which every citizen had an equal vote; the Boule, a 500-person body whose members were selected annually by lot from all citizens over the age of thirty, set the agenda for the Assembly, reviewed all state business, and controlled the magistrates.

Pericles was among the ten Athenians elected "general," a position that entailed political as well as military responsibilities, in 454 B.C. Although wealthy and of aristocratic

background, he supported the extension of democracy. Among his innovations was state payment for jury duty and other services to the state, a practice that allowed the poorer citizens of Athens to participate in running the government.

Pericles, whose extensive power as magistrate rested on his intellect and powers of persuasion, was selected in 431 B.C. to pay homage to Athenian soldiers killed in the first campaigns of the Peloponnesian War (431–404 B.C.). His address to the citizenry of Athens, saved for posterity by his contemporary, the historian Thucydides, provides insight into the Athenians' perception of their own political system. Unfortunately, the political character of Athens began to deteriorate soon after Pericles' death in 429 B.C. There were no statesmen of comparable standing and ability to replace his leadership, and the Athenian political system gradually grew unstable and eroded from broad-based democracy to oligarchy. In 404 B.C. Athens was defeated by Sparta and its Peloponnesian allies.

Many of those who have spoken here in the past have praised the institution of this speech at the close of our ceremony. It seemed to them a mark of honor to our soldiers who have fallen in war that a speech should be made over them. I do not agree. These men have shown themselves valiant in action, and it would be enough, I think, for their glories to be proclaimed in action, as you have just seen it done at this funeral organized by the state. Our belief in the courage and manliness of so many should not be hazarded on the goodness or badness of one man's speech. Then it is not easy to speak with a proper sense of balance, when a man's listeners find it difficult to believe in the truth of what one is saying. The man who knows the facts and loves the dead may well think that an oration tells less than what he knows and what he would like to hear: others who do not know so much may feel envy for the dead, and think the orator over-praises them, when he speaks of exploits that are beyond their own capacities. Praise of other people is tolerable only up to a certain point, the point where one still believes that one could do oneself some

of the things one is hearing about. Once you get beyond this point, you will find people becoming jealous and incredulous. However, the fact is that this institution was set up and approved by our forefathers, and it is my duty to follow the tradition and do my best to meet the wishes and the expectations of every one of you.

I shall begin by speaking about our ancestors, since it is only right and proper on such an occasion to pay them the honor of recalling what they did. In this land of ours there have always been the same people living from generation to generation up till now, and they, by their courage and their virtues, have handed it on to us, a free country. They certainly deserve our praise. Even more so do our fathers deserve it. For to the inheritance they had received they added all the empire we have now, and it was not without blood and toil that they handed it down to us of the present generation. And then we ourselves, assembled here today, who are mostly in the prime of life, have, in most directions, added to the power of our empire and have organized our State in such a way that it is perfectly well able to look after itself both in peace and in war.

I have no wish to make a long speech on subjects familiar to you all: so I shall say nothing about the warlike deeds by which we acquired our power or the battles in which we or our fathers gallantly resisted our enemies, Greek or foreign. What I want to do is, in the first place, to discuss the spirit in which we faced our trials and also our constitution and the way of life which has made us great. After that I shall speak in praise of the dead, believing that this kind of speech is not inappropriate to the present occasion, and that this whole assembly, of citizens and foreigners, may listen to it with advantage.

Let me say that our system of government does not copy the institutions of our neighbors. It is more the case of our being a model to others, than of our imitating anyone else. Our constitution is called a democracy because power is in the hands not of a minority but of the whole people. When it is a question of settling private disputes, everyone is equal before the law; when it is a question of putting one person before another in positions of public responsibility, what counts is not membership of a particular class, but the actual ability which the man possesses. No one, so long as he has it in him to be of service to the state, is kept in political obscurity because of poverty. And, just as our political life is free and open, so is our day-to-day life in our relations with each other. We do not get into a state with our next-door neighbor if he enjoys himself in his own way, nor do we give him the kind of black looks which, though they do no real harm, still do hurt people's feelings. We are free and tolerant in our private lives; but in public affairs we keep to the law. This is because it commands our deep respect.

We give our obedience to those whom we put in positions of authority, and we obey the laws themselves, especially those which are for the protection of the oppressed, and those unwritten laws which it is an acknowledged shame to break.

And here is another point. When our work is over, we are in a position to enjoy all kinds of recreation for our spirits. There are various kinds of contests and sacrifices regularly throughout the year; in our own homes we find a beauty and a good taste which delight us every day and which drive away our cares. Then the greatness of our city brings it about that all the good things from all over the world flow in to us, so that to us it seems just as natural to enjoy foreign goods as our own local products.

Then there is a great difference between us and our opponents, in our attitude towards military security. Here are some examples: Our city is open to the world, and we have no periodical deportations in order to prevent people observing or finding out secrets which might be of military advantage to the enemy. This is because we rely, not on secret weapons, but on our own real courage and loyalty. There is a difference, too, in our educational systems. The Spartans, from their earliest boyhood, are submitted to the most laborious training in courage; we pass our lives without all these restrictions, and yet are just as ready to face the same dangers as they are. Here is a proof of this: When the Spartans invade our land, they do not come by themselves, but bring all their allies with them; whereas we, when we launch an attack abroad, do the job by ourselves, and, though fighting on foreign soil, do not often fail to defeat opponents who are fighting for their own hearths and homes. As a matter of fact none of our enemies has ever yet been confronted with our total strength, because we have to divide our attention between our navy and the many missions on which our troops are sent on land. Yet, if our enemies engage a detachment of our forces and defeat it, they give themselves credit for having thrown back our entire army; or, if they lose, they claim that they were beaten by us in full strength. There are certain advantages, I think, in our way of meeting danger voluntarily, with an easy mind, instead of with a laborious training, with natural rather than with state-induced courage. We do not have to spend our time practicing to meet sufferings which are still in the future; and when they are actually upon us we show ourselves just as brave as these others who are always in strict training. This is one point in which, I think, our city deserves to be admired. There are also others:

Our love of what is beautiful does not lead to extravagance; our love of the things of the mind does not make us soft. We regard wealth as something to be properly used, rather than as something to boast about. As for poverty, no one need be ashamed to admit it: the real shame is in not taking practical measures to escape from it. Here each individual is interested not only in his own affairs but in the affairs of the state as well: even those who are mostly occupied with their own business are extremely well informed on general politics—this is a peculiarity of ours: we do not say that a man who takes no interest in politics is a man who minds his own business; we say that he has no business here at all. We Athenians, in our own persons, take our decisions on policy or submit them to proper discussions: for we do not think that there is an incompatibility between words and deeds; the worst thing is to rush into action before the consequences have been properly debated. And this is another point where we differ from other people. We are capable at the same time of taking risks and of estimating them beforehand. Others are brave out of ignorance; and, when they stop to think, they begin to fear. But the man who can most truly be accounted brave is he who best knows the meaning of what is sweet in life and of what is terrible, and then goes out undeterred to meet what is to come.

Again, in questions of general good feeling there is a great contrast between us and most other people. We make friends by doing good to others, not by receiving good from them.

This makes our friendship all the more reliable, since we want to keep alive the gratitude of those who are in our debt by showing continued goodwill to them: whereas the feelings of one who owes us something lack the same enthusiasm, since he knows that, when he repays our kindness, it will be more like paying back a debt than giving something spontaneously. We are unique in this. When we do kindnesses to others, we do not do them out of any calculations of profit or loss: we do them without afterthought, relying on our free liberality. Taking everything together then, I declare that our city is an education to Greece, and I declare that in my opinion each single one of our citizens, in all the manifold aspects of life, is able to show himself the rightful lord and owner of his own person, and do this, moreover, with exceptional grace and exceptional versatility. And to show that this is no empty boasting for the present occasion, but real tangible fact, you have only to consider the power which our city possesses and which has been won by those very qualities which I have mentioned. Athens, alone of the states we know, comes to her testing time in a greatness that surpasses what was imagined of her. In her case, and in her case alone, no invading enemy is ashamed at being defeated, and no subject can complain of being governed by people unfit for their responsibilities. Mighty indeed are the marks and monuments of our empire which we have left. Future ages will wonder at us, as the present age wonders at us now. We do not need the praises of a Homer, or of anyone else whose words may delight us for the moment, but whose estimation of facts will fall short of what is really true. For our adventurous spirit has forced an entry into every sea and into every land; and everywhere we have left behind us everlasting memorials of good done to our friends or suffering inflicted on our enemies.

This, then, is the kind of city for which these men, who could not bear the thought of losing her, nobly fought and nobly died. It is only natural that every one of us who survive them should be willing to undergo hardships in her service. And it was for this reason that I have spoken at such length about our city, because I wanted to make it clear that for us there is more at stake than there is for others who lack our advantages; also I wanted my words of praise for the dead to be set in the bright light of evidence. And now the most important of these words has been spoken. I have sung the praises of our city; but it was the courage and gallantry of these men, and of people like them, which made her splendid. Nor would you find it true in the case of many of the Greeks, as it is true of them, that no words can do more than justice to their deeds.

To me it seems that the consummation which has overtaken these men shows us the meaning of manliness in its first revelation and in its final proof. Some of them, no doubt, had their faults; but what we ought to remember first is their gallant conduct against the enemy in defense of their native land. They have blotted out evil with good, and done more service to the commonwealth than they ever did harm in their private lives. No one of these men weakened because he wanted to go on enjoying his wealth: no one put off the awful day in the hope that he might live to escape his poverty and grow rich. More to be desired than such things, they chose to check the enemy's pride. This, to them, was a risk most glorious, and they accepted it, willing to strike down the enemy and relinquish everything else. As for success or failure, they left that in the doubtful hands of Hope, and when the reality of battle was before their faces, they put their trust in their own selves. In the fighting, they thought it more honorable to stand their ground and suffer death than to give in and save their lives. So they fled from the reproaches of men, abiding with life and limb the brunt of battle; and, in a small moment of time, the climax of their lives, a culmination of glory, not of fear, were swept away from us.

So and such they were, these men—worthy of their city. We who remain behind may hope to be spared their fate, but must resolve to keep the same daring spirit against the foe. It is not simply a question of estimating the advantages in theory. I could tell you a long story (and you know it as well as I do) about what is to be gained by beating the enemy back. What I would prefer is that you should fix your eyes every day on the greatness of Athens as she really is, and should fall in love with her. When you realize her greatness, then reflect that what made her great was men with a spirit of adventure, men who knew their duty, men who were ashamed to fall below a certain standard. If they ever failed in an enterprise, they made up their minds that at any rate the city should not find their courage lacking to her, and they gave to her the best contribution that they could. They gave her their lives, to her and to all of us, and for their own selves they won praises that never grow old, the most splendid of sepulchers—not the sepulcher in which their bodies are laid, but where their glory remains eternal in men's minds, always there on the right occasion to stir others to speech or to action. For famous men have the whole earth as their memorial: it is not only the inscriptions on their graves in their own country that mark them out; no, in foreign lands also, not in any visible form but in people's hearts, their memory abides and grows. It is for you to try to be like them. Make up your minds that happiness depends on being free, and freedom depends on being courageous. Let there be no relaxation in face of the perils of the war. The people who have most excuse for despising death are not the wretched and unfortunate, who have no hope of doing well for themselves, but those who run the risk of a complete reversal in their lives, and who would feel the difference most intensely, if things went wrong for them. Any intelligent man would find a humiliation caused by his own slackness more painful to bear than death, when death comes to him unperceived, in battle, and in the confidence of his patriotism.

For these reasons I shall not commiserate with those parents of the dead, who are present here. Instead I shall try to comfort them. They are well aware that they have grown up in a world where there are many changes and chances. But this is good fortune—for men to end their lives with honor, as these have done, and for you honorably to lament them: their life was set to a measure where death and happiness went hand in hand. I know that it is difficult to convince you of this. When you see other people happy you will often be reminded of what used to make you happy too. One does not feel sad at not having some good thing which is outside one's experience: real grief is felt at the loss of something which one is used to. All the same, those of you who are of the right age must bear up and take comfort in the thought of having more children. In your own homes these new children will prevent you from brooding over those who are no more, and they will be a help to the city, too, both in filling the empty places, and in assuring her security. For it is impossible for a man to put forward fair and honest views about our affairs if he has not, like everyone else, children whose lives may be at stake. As for those of you who are now too old to have children, I would ask you to count as gain the greater part of your life, in which you have been happy, and remember that what remains is not long, and let your hearts be lifted up at the thought of the fair fame of the dead. One's sense of honor is the only thing that does not grow old, and the last pleasure, when one is worn out with age, is not, as the poet said, making money, but having the respect of one's fellow men.

As for those of you here who are sons or brothers of the dead, I can see a hard struggle in front of you. Everyone always speaks well of the dead, and, even if you rise to the greatest heights of heroism, it will be a hard thing for you to get the reputation of having come near, let alone equaled, their standard. When one is alive, one is always liable to the jealousy of one's competitors, but when one is out of the way, the honor one receives is sincere and unchallenged.

Perhaps I should say a word or two on the duties of women to those among you who are now widowed. I can say all I have to say in a short word of advice. Your great glory is not to be inferior to what God has made you, and the greatest glory of a woman is to be least talked about by men, whether they are praising you or criticizing you. I have now, as the law demanded, said what I had to say. For the time being our offerings to the dead have been made, and for the future their children will be supported at the public expense by the city, until they come of age. This is the crown and prize which she offers, both to the dead and to their children, for the ordeals which they have faced. Where the rewards of valor are the greatest, there you will find also the best and bravest spirits among the people. And now, when you have mourned for your dear ones, you must depart.

MAGNA CARTA (1215)

The English Magna Carta, or "Great Charter," contains none of the sweeping statements of principle on constitutional government or the rights of man to be found in such later documents as the American Declaration of Independence or the French Declaration of the Rights of Man and of the Citizen. To the contrary, it is a detailed prescription of remedies exacted from a king in the narrow self-interest of a feudal baronial class. Its value as a statement on the relationship between the government and the governed was realized only gradually, as reformers and philosophers hundreds of years later found support and justification in a document that had been drafted in a very different social and political context.

The Magna Carta was a redress of grievances forced upon King John (reigned 1199–1216) by a group of barons whose resentment of the crown had been rising for several decades. John's predecessors, Henry II (reigned 1154–1189) and Richard I (reigned 1189–1199), had encroached on the barons' customary rights and had increased the burdens of military service and taxation to support the Third Crusade and wars in France. John exacerbated the barons' resentment with his costly—and failed—attempt to regain the En-glish Crown's control over the Duchy of Normandy. John returned to England after his defeat at Bouvines in July 1214 to face the wrath of the barons.

On June 15, 1215, the barons met King John at Run-nymede, on the River Thames between Windsor and Staines, and forced upon him the Articles of the Barons, from which the Magna Carta was formally drafted several days later. The Magna Carta was repudiated by John shortly thereafter, leading to a brief civil war that ended when John died in October 1216. The document was reissued by John's successors with minor changes thirty-eight times over the following one hundred years.

Over the centuries, the Magna Carta lost its original character as a statement of current law, to be read instead as a statement of principles applying not only to the baronial class but to all people. The notions of individual freedom and trial by jury found in the U.S. Constitution (1787) and in England's Petition of Right (1628) and Habeas Corpus Act (1679) trace their lineage to Article 39 of the Magna Carta. Similarly, the notion of a "community of the realm," which is the bedrock of representative government, can be identified in embryonic form in Article 61.

John, by the grace of God, king of England, lord of Ireland, duke of Normandy and Aquitaine, and count of Anjou, to the archbishops, bishops, abbots, earls, barons, justiciars, foresters, sheriffs, stewards, servants, and to all his bailiffs and faithful subjects, greeting. Know that we, out of reverence for God and for the salvation of our soul and those of all our ancestors and heirs, for the honour of God and the exaltation of holy church, and for the reform of our realm, on the advice of our venerable fathers, Stephen, archbishop of Canterbury, primate of all England and cardinal of the holy Roman church, Henry archbishop of Dublin, William of London, Peter of Winchester, Jocelyn of Bath and Glastonbury, Hugh of Lincoln, Walter of Worcester, William of Coventry and Benedict of Rochester, bishops, of master Pandulf, subdeacon and member of the household of the lord pope, of brother Aymeric, master of the order of Knights Templar in England, and of the noble men William Marshal earl of Pembroke, William earl of Salisbury, William earl of Warenne, William earl of Arundel, Alan of Galloway constable of Scotland, Warin fitz Gerold, Peter fitz Herbert, Hubert de Burgh seneschal of Poitou, Hugh de Neville, Matthew fitz Herbert, Thomas Basset, Alan Basset, Philip de Aubeney, Robert of Ropsley, John Marshal, John fitz Hugh, and others, our faithful subjects:

[1] In the first place have granted to God, and by this our present charter confirmed for us and our heirs for ever that the English church shall be free, and shall have its rights undiminished and its liberties unimpaired; and it is our will that it be thus observed; which is evident from the fact that, before the quarrel between us and our barons began, we willingly and spontaneously granted and by our charter confirmed the freedom of elections which is reckoned most important and very

essential to the English church, and obtained confirmation of it from the lord pope Innocent III; the which we will observe and we wish our heirs to observe it in good faith for ever. We have also granted to all free men of our kingdom, for ourselves and our heirs for ever, all the liberties written below, to be had and held by them and their heirs of us and our heirs.

[2] If any of our earls or barons or others holding of us in chief by knight service dies, and at his death his heir be of full age and owe relief he shall have his inheritance on payment of the old relief, namely the heir or heirs of an earl £100 for a whole earl's barony, the heir or heirs of a baron £100 for a whole barony, the heir or heirs of a knight 100s, at most, for a whole knight's fee; and he who owes less shall give less according to the ancient usage of fiefs.

[3] If, however, the heir of any such be under age and a ward, he shall have his inheritance when he comes of age without paying relief and without making fine.

[4] The guardian of the land of such an heir who is under age shall take from the land of the heir no more than reasonable revenues, reasonable customary dues and reasonable services and that without destruction and waste of men or goods; and if we commit the wardship of the land of any such to a sheriff, or to any other who is answerable to us for its revenues, and he destroys or wastes what he has wardship of, we will take compensation from him and the land shall be committed to two lawful and discreet men of that fief, who shall be answerable for the revenues to us or to him to whom we have assigned them; and if we give or sell to anyone the wardship of any such land and he causes destruction or waste therein, he shall lose that wardship, and it shall be transferred to two lawful and discreet men of that fief, who shall similarly be answerable to us as is aforesaid.

[5] Moreover, so long as he has the wardship of the land, the guardian shall keep in repair the houses, parks, preserves, ponds, mills and other things pertaining to the land out of the revenues from it; and he shall restore to the heir when he comes of age his land fully stocked with ploughs and the means of husbandry according to what the season of husbandry requires and the revenues of the land can reasonably bear.

[6] Heirs shall be married without disparagement, yet so that before the marriage is contracted those nearest in blood to the heir shall have notice.

[7] A widow shall have her marriage portion and inheritance forthwith and without difficulty after the death of her husband; nor shall she pay anything to have her dower or her marriage portion or the inheritance which she and her husband held on the day of her husband's death; and she may remain in her husband's house for forty days after his death, within which time her dower shall be assigned to her.

[8] No widow shall be forced to marry so long as she wishes to live without a husband, provided that she gives security not to marry without our consent if she holds of us, or without the consent of her lord of whom she holds, if she holds of another.

[9] Neither we nor our bailiffs will seize for any debt any land or rent, so long as the chattels of the debtor are sufficient to repay the debt; nor will those who have gone surety for the debtor be distrained so long as the principal debtor is himself able to pay the debt; and if the principal debtor fails to pay the debt, having nothing wherewith to pay it, then shall the sureties answer for the debt; and they shall, if they wish, have the lands and rents of the debtor until they are reimbursed for the debt which they have paid for him, unless the principal debtor can show that he has discharged his obligation in the matter to the said sureties.

[10] If anyone who has borrowed from the Jews any sum, great or small, dies before it is repaid, the debt shall not bear interest as long as the heir is under age, of whomsoever he holds; and if the debt falls into our hands, we will not take anything except the principal mentioned in the bond.

[11] And if anyone dies indebted to the Jews, his wife shall have her dower and pay nothing of that debt; and if the dead man leaves children who are under age, they shall be provided with necessaries befitting the holding of the deceased; and the debt shall be paid out of the residue, reserving, however, service due to lords of the land; debts owing to others than Jews shall be dealt with in like manner.

[12] No scutage or aid shall be imposed in our kingdom unless by common counsel of our kingdom, except for ransoming our person, for making our eldest son a knight, and for once marrying our eldest daughter; and for these only a reasonable aid shall be levied. Be it done in like manner concerning aids from the city of London.

[13] And the city of London shall have all its ancient liberties and free customs as well by land as by water. Furthermore, we will and grant that all other cities, boroughs, towns, and ports shall have all their liberties and free customs.

[14] And to obtain the common counsel of the kingdom about the assessing of an aid (except in the three cases aforesaid) or of a scutage, we will cause to be summoned the archbishops, bishops, abbots, earls and greater barons, individually by our letters—and, in addition, we will cause to be summoned generally through our sheriffs and bailiffs all those holding of us in chief—for a fixed date, namely, after the expiry of at least forty days, and to a fixed place; and in all letters of such summons we will specify the reason for the summons. And when the summons has thus been made, the business shall proceed on the day appointed, according to the counsel of those present, though not all have come who were summoned.

[15] We will not in future grant any one the right to take an aid from his free men, except for ransoming his person, for making his eldest son a knight and for once marrying his eldest daughter, and for these only a reasonable aid shall be levied.

[16] No one shall be compelled to do greater service for a knight's fee or for any other free holding than is due from it.

[17] Common pleas shall not follow our court, but shall be held in some fixed place.

[18] Recognitions of *novel disseisin,* of *mort d'ancester,* and of *darrein presentment,* shall not be held elsewhere than in the counties to which they relate, and in this manner—we, or, if we should be out of the realm, our chief justiciar, will send two justices through each county four times a year, who, with four knights of each county chosen by the county, shall hold the said assizes in the county and on the day and in the place of meeting of the county court.

[19] And if the said assizes cannot all be held on the day of the county court, there shall stay behind as many of the knights and freeholders who were present at the county court on that day as are necessary for the sufficient making of judgments, according to the amount of business to be done.

[20] A free man shall not be amerced for a trivial offence except in accordance with the degree of the offence, and for a grave offence he shall be amerced in accordance with its gravity, yet saving his way of living; and a merchant in the same way, saving his stock-in-trade; and a villein shall be amerced in the same way, saving his means of livelihood—if they have fallen into our mercy: and none of the aforesaid amercements shall be imposed except by the oath of good men of the neighbourhood.

[21] Earls and barons shall not be amerced except by their peers, and only in accordance with the degree of the offence.

[22] No clerk shall be amerced in respect of his lay holding except after the manner of the others aforesaid and not according to the amount of his ecclesiastical benefice.

[23] No vill or individual shall be compelled to make bridges at river banks, except those who from of old are legally bound to do so.

[24] No sheriff, constable, coroners, or others of our bailiffs, shall hold pleas of our crown.

[25] All counties, hundreds, wapentakes and trithings shall be at the old rents without any additional payment, except our demesne manors.

[26] If anyone holding a lay fief of us dies and our sheriff or bailiff shows our letters patent of summons for a debt that the deceased owed us, it shall be lawful for our sheriff or bailiff to attach and make a list of chattels of the deceased found upon the lay fief to the value of that debt under the supervision of law-worthy men, provided that none of the chattels shall be removed until the debt which is manifest has been paid to us in full; and the residue shall be left to the executors for carrying out the will of the deceased. And if nothing is owing to us from him, all the chattels shall accrue to the deceased, saving to his wife and children their reasonable shares.

[27] If any free man dies without leaving a will, his chattels shall be distributed by his nearest kinsfolk and friends under the supervision of the church, saving to every one the debts which the deceased owed him.

[28] No constable or other bailiff of ours shall take anyone's corn or other chattels unless he pays on the spot in cash for them or can delay payment by arrangement with the seller.

[29] No constable shall compel any knight to give money instead of castle-guard if he is willing to do the guard himself or through another good man, if for some good reason he cannot do it himself; and if we lead or send him on military service, he shall be excused guard in proportion to the time that because of us he has been on service.

[30] No sheriff, or bailiff of ours, or anyone else shall take the horses or carts of any free man for transport work save with the agreement of that freeman.

[31] Neither we nor our bailiffs will take, for castles or other works of ours, timber which is not ours, except with the agreement of him whose timber it is.

[32] We will not hold for more than a year and a day the lands of those convicted of felony, and then the lands shall be handed over to the lords of the fiefs.

[33] Henceforth all fish-weirs shall be cleared completely from the Thames and the Medway and throughout all England, except along the sea coast.

[34] The writ called *Praecipe* shall not in future be issued to anyone in respect of any holding whereby a free man may lose his court.

[35] Let there be one measure for wine throughout our kingdom, and one measure for ale, and one measure for corn, namely "the London quarter"; and one width for cloths whether dyed, russet or halberget, namely two ells within the selvedges. Let it be the same with weights as with measures.

[36] Nothing shall be given or taken in future for the writ of inquisition of life or limbs: instead it shall be granted free of charge and not refused.

[37] If anyone holds of us by fee-farm, by socage, or by burgage, and holds land of another by knight service, we will not, by reason of that fee-farm, socage, or burgage, have the wardship of his heir or of land of his that is of the fief of the other; nor will we have custody of the fee-farm, socage, or burgage, unless such fee-farm owes knight service. We will not have custody of anyone's heir or land which he holds of another by knight service by reason of any petty serjeanty which he holds

of us by the service of rendering to us knives or arrows or the like.

[38] No bailiff shall in future put anyone to trial upon his own bare word, without reliable witnesses produced for this purpose.

[39] No free man shall be arrested or imprisoned or disseised or outlawed or exiled or in any way victimised, neither will we attack him or send anyone to attack him, except by the lawful judgment of his peers or by the law of the land.

[40] To no one will we sell, to no one will we refuse or delay right or justice.

[41] All merchants shall be able to go out of and come into England safely and securely and stay and travel throughout England, as well by land as by water, for buying and selling by the ancient and right customs free from all evil tolls, except in time of war and if they are of the land that is at war with us. And if such are found in our land at the beginning of a war, they shall be attached, without injury to their persons or goods, until we, or our chief justiciar, know how merchants of our land are treated who were found in the land at war with us when war broke out, and if ours are safe there, the others shall be safe in our land.

[42] It shall be lawful in future for anyone, without prejudicing the allegiance due to us, to leave our kingdom and return safely and securely by land and water, save, in the public interest, for a short period in time of war—except for those imprisoned or outlawed in accordance with the law of the kingdom and natives of a land that is at war with us and merchants (who shall be treated as aforesaid).

[43] If anyone who holds of some escheat such as the honour of Wallingford, Nottingham, Boulogne, Lancaster, or of other escheats which are in our hands and are baronies dies, his heir shall give no other relief and do no other service to us than he would have done to the baron if that barony had been in the baron's hands; and we will hold it in the same manner in which the baron held it.

[44] Men who live outside the forest need not henceforth come before our justices of the forest upon a general summons, unless they are impleaded or are sureties for any person or persons who are attached for forest offences.

[45] We will not make justices, constables, sheriffs or bailiffs save of such as know the law of the kingdom and mean to observe it well.

[46] All barons who have founded abbeys for which they have charters of the kings of England or ancient tenure shall have the custody of them during vacancies, as they ought to have.

[47] All forests that have been made forest in our time shall be immediately disafforested; and so be it done with riverbanks that have been made preserves by us in our time.

[48] All evil customs connected with forests and warrens, foresters and warreners, sheriffs and their officials, riverbanks and their wardens shall immediately be inquired into in each county by twelve sworn knights of the same county who are to be chosen by good men of the same county, and within forty days of the completion of the inquiry shall be utterly abolished by them so as never to be restored, provided that we, or our justiciar if we are not in England, know of it first.

[49] We will immediately return all hostages and charters given to us by Englishmen, as security for peace or faithful service.

[50] We will remove completely from office the relations of Gerard de Athée so that in future they shall have no office in England, namely Engelard de Cigogné, Peter and Guy and Andrew de Chanceaux, Guy de Cigogné, Geoffrey de Martigny and his brothers, Philip Marc and his brothers and his nephew Geoffrey, and all their following.

[51] As soon as peace is restored, we will remove from the kingdom all foreign knights, cross-bowmen, serjeants, and mercenaries, who have come with horses and arms to the detriment of the kingdom.

[52] If anyone has been disseised of or kept out of his lands, castles, franchises or his right by us without the legal judgment of his peers, we will immediately restore them to him: and if a dispute arises over this, then let it be decided by the judgment of the twenty-five barons who are mentioned below in the clause for securing the peace: for all the things, however, which anyone has been disseised or kept out of without the lawful judgment of his peers by king Henry, our father, or by king Richard, our brother, which we have in our hand or are held by others, to whom we are bound to warrant them, we will have the usual period of respite of crusaders, excepting those things about which a plea was started or an inquest made by our command before we took the cross; when however we return from our pilgrimage, or if by any chance we do not go on it, we will at once do full justice therein.

[53] We will have the same respite, and in the same manner, in the doing of justice in the matter of the disafforesting or retaining of the forests which Henry our father or Richard our brother afforested, and in the matter of the wardship of lands which are of the fief of another, wardships of which sort we have hitherto had by reason of a fief which anyone held of us by knight service, and in the matter of abbeys founded on the fief of another, not on a fief of our own, in which the lord of the fief claims he has a right; and when we have returned, or if we do not set out on our pilgrimage, we will at once do full justice to those who complain of these things.

[54] No one shall be arrested or imprisoned upon the appeal of a woman for the death of anyone except her husband.

[55] All fines made with us unjustly and against the law of the land, and all amercements imposed unjustly and against the law of the land, shall be entirely remitted, or else let them be settled by the judgment of the twenty-five barons who are mentioned below in the clause for securing the peace, or by the judgment of the majority of the same, along with the aforesaid Stephen, archbishop of Canterbury, if he can be present, and such others as he may wish to associate with himself for this purpose, and if he cannot be present the business shall nevertheless proceed without him, provided that if any one or more of the aforesaid twenty-five barons are in a like suit, they shall be removed from the judgment of the case in question, and others chosen, sworn and put in their place by the rest of the same twenty-five for this case only.

[56] If we have disseised or kept out Welshmen from lands or liberties or other things without the legal judgment of their peers in England or in Wales, they shall be immediately restored to them; and if a dispute arises over this, then let it be decided in the March by the judgment of their peers—for holdings in England according to the law of England, for holdings in Wales according to the law of Wales, and for holdings in the March according to the law of the March. Welshmen shall do the same to us and ours.

[57] For all the things, however, which any Welshman was disseised of or kept out of without the lawful judgment of his peers by king Henry, our father, or king Richard, our brother, which we have in our hand or which are held by others, to whom we are bound to warrant them, we will have the usual period of respite of crusaders, excepting those things about which a plea was started or an inquest made by our command before we took the cross; when however we return, or if by any chance we do not set out on our pilgrimage, we will at once do full justice to them in accordance with the laws of the Welsh and the foresaid regions.

[58] We will give back at once the son of Llywelyn and all the hostages from Wales and the charters that were handed over to us as security for peace.

[59] We will act toward Alexander, king of the Scots, concerning the return of his sisters and hostages and concerning his franchises and his right in the same manner in which we act towards our other barons of England, unless it ought to be otherwise by the charters which we have from William his father, formerly king of the Scots, and this shall be determined by the judgment of his peers in our court.

[60] All these aforesaid customs and liberties which we have granted to be observed in our kingdom as far as it pertains to us towards our men, all of our kingdom, clerks as well as laymen, shall observe as far as it pertains to them towards their men.

[61] Since, moreover, for God and the betterment of our kingdom and for the better allaying of the discord that has arisen between us and our barons we have granted all these things aforesaid, wishing them to enjoy the use of them unimpaired and unshaken for ever, we give and grant them the under-written security, namely, that the barons shall choose any twenty-five barons of the kingdom they wish, who must with all their might observe, hold and cause to be observed, the peace and liberties which we have granted and confirmed to them by this present charter of ours, so that if we, or our justiciar, or our bailiffs or any one of our servants offend in any way against anyone or transgress any of the articles of the peace or the security and the offence be notified to four of the aforesaid twenty-five barons, those four barons shall come to us, or to our justiciar if we are out of the kingdom, and, laying the transgression before us, shall petition us to have that transgression corrected without delay. And if we do not correct the transgression, or if we are out of the kingdom, if our justiciar does not correct it, within forty days, reckoning from the time it was brought to our notice or to that of our justiciar if we were out of the kingdom, the aforesaid four barons shall refer that case to the rest of the twenty-five barons and those twenty-five barons together with the community of the whole land shall distrain and distress us in every way they can, namely, by seizing castles, lands, possessions, and in such other ways as they can, saving our person and the persons of our queen and our children, until, in their opinion, amends have been made; and when amends have been made, they shall obey us as they did before. And let anyone in the land who wishes take an oath to obey the orders of the said twenty-five barons for the execution of all the aforesaid matters, and with them to distress us as much as he can, and we publicly and freely give anyone leave to take the oath who wishes to take it and we will never prohibit anyone from taking it. Indeed, all those in the land who are unwilling of themselves and of their own accord to take an oath to the twenty-five barons to help them to distrain and distress us, we will make them take the oath as aforesaid at our command. And if any of the twenty-five barons dies or leaves the country or is in any other way prevented from carrying out the things aforesaid, the rest of the aforesaid twenty-five barons shall choose as they think fit another one in his place, and he shall take the oath like the rest. In all matters the execution of which is committed to these twenty-five barons, if it should happen that these twenty-five are present yet disagree among themselves about anything, or if some of those summoned will not or cannot be present, that shall be held as fixed and established which the majority of those present ordained or commanded, exactly as if all the twenty-five had consented to it; and the said twenty-five shall swear that they will faithfully observe all the things aforesaid and will do all they can to

get them observed. And we will procure nothing from anyone, either personally or through anyone else, whereby any of these concessions and liberties might be revoked or diminished; and if any such thing is procured, let it be void and null, and we will never use it either personally or through another.

[62] And we have fully remitted and pardoned to everyone all the ill-will, indignation and rancour that have arisen between us and our men, clergy and laity, from the time of the quarrel. Furthermore, we have fully remitted to all, clergy and laity, and as far as pertains to us have completely forgiven, all trespasses occasioned by the same quarrel between Easter in the sixteenth year of our reign and the restoration of peace. And, besides, we have caused to be made for them letters testimonial patent of the lord Stephen archbishop of Canterbury, of the lord Henry archbishop of Dublin and of the aforementioned bishops and of master Pandulf about this security and the aforementioned concessions.

[63] Wherefore we wish and firmly enjoin that the English church shall be free, and that the men in our kingdom shall have and hold all the aforesaid liberties, rights and concessions well and peacefully, freely and quietly, fully and completely, for themselves and their heirs from us and our heirs, in all matters and in all places for ever, as is aforesaid. An oath, moreover, has been taken, as well on our part as on the part of the barons, that all these things aforesaid shall be observed in good faith and without evil disposition. Witness the abovementioned and many others. Given by our hand in the meadow which is called Runnymede between Windsor and Staines on the fifteenth day of June, in the seventeenth year of our reign.

DUTCH DECLARATION OF INDEPENDENCE (1581)

The Dutch Declaration of Independence, like its American counterpart nearly 200 years later, implies the existence of an unwritten contract between the government and the governed and proclaims the right of the people to rebel when the contract is broken. When a king becomes a tyrant, the document proclaims, the people have a natural right to "disallow his authority." In formulation, as well, the Dutch declaration is similar to the American document: it states in the first paragraphs the principles that justify the rebellion; it then states specific transgressions on the part of the king; it follows with examples of repeated attempts to rectify the problems short of rebellion; and it concludes that, all other courses of action having been attempted and failed, all political ties are henceforth broken. Furthermore, many of the specific indictments are similar in character: burdensome taxation, forced quartering of mercenary troops, suppression of individual liberty, confiscation of property, and summary justice.

After several centuries of territorial consolidation, dynastic changes, and royal intermarriages, the region now known as the Netherlands came under the rule of King Philip II of Spain in 1555. Relations between the Roman Catholic, feudal, and absolutist Spanish crown and the Protestant Dutch were strained from the outset over social, economic, and, most important, religious issues. The growing towns and expanding commerce of the Dutch contributed to a sense of local power and community, and the Dutch chafed at the centralized authority of the far-off king.

In 1568 King Philip's emissary, the Duke of Alva, began a bloody reign of terror in the northern Dutch provinces in an attempt to stamp out the Protestant religions and to consolidate Spanish control of the region. The Dutch resisted, and by 1571 the principalities of Holland and Zeelund were in open rebellion against the king. Several more provinces joined Holland and Zeelund in rebellion on January 23, 1579, when all united in the Union of Utrecht. The provinces in the union issued their declaration of independence from Spain in The Hague on July 26, 1581.

The struggle for independence was led by the House of Orange, first by William the Silent (1533–1584) and then by his son, Maurice of Nassau (1567–1625). Dutch victories over the Spanish on land and at sea, compounded by British and French wars against Spain, forced Spain to seek a truce in 1609. Dutch independence was formally recognized by Spain in the 1648 Treaty of Westphalia.

Despite the role played by the House of Orange, Dutch independence was fought for and won in the name of the States General of the United Netherlands. All sovereignty resided in the States General, which granted to the princes of Orange the title of stadholder (governor, or magistrate). Upon achieving independence, each of the provinces in the States General considered itself sovereign and independent, until the Netherlands became a unitary state in 1795.

The States General of the United Provinces of the Low Countries, to all whom it may concern, do by these presents send greeting:

As it is apparent to all that a prince is constituted by God to be ruler of a people, to defend them from oppression and violence as the shepherd his sheep; and whereas God did not create the people slaves to their prince, to obey his commands, whether right or wrong, but rather the prince for the sake of the subjects (without which he could be no prince), to govern them according to equity, to love and support them as a father his children or a shepherd his flock, and even at the hazard of life to defend and preserve them. And when he does not behave thus, but, on the contrary, oppresses them, seeking opportunities to infringe their ancient customs and privileges, exacting from them slavish compliance, then he is no longer a prince, but a tyrant, and the subjects are to consider him in no other view. And particularly when this is done deliberately, unauthorized by the states, they may not only disallow his authority, but legally proceed to the choice of another prince for their defense. This is the only method left for subjects whose humble petitions and remonstrances could never soften their prince or dissuade him from his tyrannical proceedings; and this is what the law of nature dictates for the defense of liberty, which we ought to transmit to posterity, even at the hazard of our lives. And this we have seen done frequently in several countries upon the like occasion, whereof there are notorious instances, and more justifiable in our land, which has been always governed according to their ancient privileges, which are expressed in the oath taken by the prince at his admission to the government; for most of the Provinces receive their prince upon certain conditions, which he swears to maintain, which, if the prince violates, he is no longer sovereign.

Now thus it was that the King of Spain after the demise of the emperor, his father, Charles the Fifth, of the glorious memory (of whom he received all these provinces), forgetting the services done by the subjects of these countries, both to his father and himself . . . did rather hearken to the counsel of those Spaniards about him, who had conceived a secret hatred to this land and to its liberty, because they could not enjoy posts of honor and high employments here under the states as they did in Naples, Sicily, Milan and the Indies, and other countries under the king's dominion. Thus allured by the riches of the said provinces, wherewith many of them were well acquainted, the said counselors, I say, or the principal of them, frequently remonstrated to the king that it was more for his majesty's reputation and grandeur to subdue the Low Countries a second time, and to make himself absolute (by which they mean to tyrannize at pleasure), than to govern according to the restrictions he had accepted, and at his admission sworn to observe. From that time forward the King of Spain, following these evil counselors, sought by all means possible to reduce this country (stripping them of their ancient privileges) to slavery, under the government of Spaniards, having first, under the mask of religion, endeavored to settle new bishops in the largest and principal cities, endowing and incorporating them with the richest abbeys, assigning to each bishop nine canons to assist him as counselors, three whereof should superintend the Inquisition. By this incorporation the said bishops (who might be strangers as well as natives) would have had the first place and vote in the assembly of the states, and always the prince's creatures at devotion; and by the addition of the said canons he would have introduced the Spanish Inquisition, which has been always as dreadful and detested in these provinces as the worst of slavery. . . . But, notwithstanding the many remonstrances made to the king both by the provinces and particular towns, in writing as well as by some principal lords by word of mouth. . . . And, although the king had by fair words given them grounds to hope that their request should be complied with, yet by his letters he ordered the contrary, soon after expressly commanding, upon pain of his displeasure, to admit the new bishops immediately, and put them in possession of their bishoprics and incorporated abbeys, to hold the court of the Inquisition in the places where it had been before, to obey and follow the decrees and ordinances of the Council of Trent, which in many articles are destructive of the privilege of the country. This being come to the knowledge of the people gave just occasion to great uneasiness and clamor among them, and lessened that good affection they had always borne toward the king and his predecessors. And, especially, seeing that he did not only seek to tyrannize over their persons and estates, but also over their consciences, for which they believed themselves accountable to God only. Upon this occasion the chief of the nobility in compassion to the poor people, in the year 1566, exhibited a certain remonstrance in form of a petition, humbly praying, in order to appease them and prevent public disturbances, that it would please his majesty (by showing clemency due from a good prince to his people) to soften the said points, and especially with regard to the rigorous Inquisition, and capital punishments for matters of religion. And to inform the king of this affair in a more solemn manner, and to represent to him how necessary it was for the peace and prosperity of the public to remove the aforesaid innovations, and moderate the severity of his declarations published concerning divine worship, the Marquis de Berghen, and the aforesaid Baron of Montigny had been sent, at the request of the said lady regent, the council of state, and of the States General, as ambassadors to Spain, where the king, instead of giving them audience, and redressing the grievances they had complained of . . . did, by the advice of Spanish council, declare all those who were concerned in preparing the said remonstrance to be rebels, and guilty of high treason, and to be punished with death, and confiscation of their estates; and, what is more (thinking himself well assured of reducing these countries under absolute tyranny of the army of the Duke of Alva), did soon after imprison and put to death the said lords the ambassadors, and confiscated their estates, contrary to the law of nations, which has been always religiously observed even among the most tyrannical and barbarous princes.

And, although the said disturbances, which in the year 1566 happened on the aforementioned occasion, were now appeased by the governess and her ministers, and many friends to liberty were either banished or subdued, in so much that the king had not any show of reason to use arms and violences, and further oppress this country, yet for these causes and reasons, long time before sought by the council of Spain (as appears by intercepted letters from the Spanish ambassador, Alana, then in France, writ to the Duchess of Parma), to annul all the privileges of this country, and govern it tyrannically at pleasure as in the Indies; and in their new conquests he has, at the instigation of the council of Spain, showing the little regard he had for his people (so contrary to the duty which a good prince owes to his subjects), sent the Duke of Alva with a powerful army to oppress this land, who for his inhuman cruelties is looked upon as one of its greatest enemies, accompanied with counselors too like himself. . . . The said duke, immediately after his arrival (though a stranger, and no way related to the royal family), declared that he had a captain-general's commission, and soon after that of governor of these provinces, contrary to all its ancient customs and privileges; and . . . he immediately garrisoned the principal towns and castles, and caused fortresses and citadels to be built in the great cities to awe them into subjection, and very courteously sent for the chief of nobility in the king's name, under pretense of taking their advice, and to employ them in the service of their country. And those who believed his letters were seized and carried out of Brabant, contrary to law, where they were imprisoned and prosecuted as criminals before him who had no right, nor could be a competent judge; and at last he, without hearing their defense at large, sentenced them to death, which was publicly and ignominiously executed. The others, better acquainted with Spanish hypocrisy, residing in foreign countries, were declared outlaws, and had their estates confiscated . . . besides a great number of other gentlemen and substantial citizens, some of whom were executed, and others banished so that their estates might be confiscated, plaguing the other honest inhabitants, not only by the injuries done to their wives, children and estates by the Spanish soldiers lodged in their houses, as also by diverse contributions, which they were forced to pay toward building citadels and new fortifications of towns even to their own ruin, besides the taxes of the hundredth, twentieth, and tenth penny, to pay for both the foreign armies and those raised in the country, to be employed against their fellow citizens and against those who at the hazard of their lives defended their liberties.

In order to impoverish the subjects, and to incapacitate them to hinder his design, and that he might with more ease execute the instructions received in Spain, to treat these countries as new conquests, he began to alter the course of justice after the Spanish mode, directly contrary to our privileges; and, imagining at last he had nothing more to fear, he endeavored by main force to settle a tax called the tenth penny on merchandise and manufacturing, to the total ruin of these countries, the prosperity of which depends upon a flourishing trade, notwithstanding frequent remonstrances, not by a single Province only, but by all of them united. . . . All these considerations give us more than sufficient reason to renounce the King of Spain, and seek some other powerful and more gracious prince to take us under his protection. . . .

So, having no hope of reconciliation, and finding no other remedy, we have, agreeable to the law of nature in our own defense, and for maintaining the rights, privileges, and liberties of our countrymen, wives, and children, and latest posterity from being enslaved by the Spaniards, been constrained to renounce allegiance to the King of Spain, and pursue such methods as appear to us most likely to secure our ancient liberties and privileges.

Know all men by these presents that, being reduced to the last extremity, as above mentioned, we have unanimously and deliberately declared, and do by these presents declare, that the King of Spain has forfeited, *ipso jure,* all hereditary right to the sovereignty of those countries, and are determined from henceforward not to acknowledge his sovereignty or jurisdiction, nor any act of his relating to the domains of the Low Countries, nor make use of his name as prince, nor suffer others to do it. In consequence whereof we also declare all officers, judges, lords, gentlemen, vassals, and all other inhabitants of this country of what condition or quality soever, to be henceforth discharged from all oaths and obligations whatsoever made to the King of Spain as sovereign of those countries. . . .

Moreover, we order and command that from henceforth no money coined shall be stamped with the name, title, or arms of the King of Spain in any of these United Provinces, but that all new gold and silver pieces, with their halfs and quarters, shall only bear such impressions as the states shall direct. We order likewise and command the president and other lords of the privy council, and all other chancellors, presidents, accountants-general, and to others in all the chambers of accounts respectively in these said countries, and likewise to all other judges and officers, as we hold them discharged from henceforth of their oath made to the King of Spain, pursuant to the tenor of their commission, that they shall take a new oath to the states of that country on whose jurisdiction they depend. . . .

We further command the president and members of the privy council, chancellor of the Duchy of Brabant . . . of Guelders . . . of Zutphen . . . of Holland . . . of Zeeland . . . of Friese . . . of Mechelen . . . of Utrecht, and to all other justiciaries and officers whom it may concern . . . to cause this our ordinance to be published and proclaimed throughout their respective jurisdictions . . . . And to cause our said ordinance to be observed inviolably. . . . And, for better maintaining all and every article hereof, we give to all and every one of you, by express command, full power and authority. In witness whereof we have hereunto set our hands and seals, dated in our assembly at The Hague, the six and twentieth day of July, 1581, endorsed by the orders of the States General, and signed, J. De Asseliers.

AMERICAN DECLARATION OF INDEPENDENCE (1776)

The American Declaration of Independence is the most eloquent and succinct statement of Enlightenment principles of self-government ever drafted. The declaration follows logically from a statement of the prevailing political theory of natural rights, to a list of transgressions attributed to King George III, to an enumeration of the failed attempts to seek redress short of revolution, to a proclamation of independence.

By the summer of 1776 tensions between the colonies and the English government over issues of taxation, commerce, and colonial administration had been on the rise for more than a decade. The battles of Concord and Lexington had occurred more than a year before, and the Continental Army under Gen. George Washington was in the field against the British army. On June 7, Richard Henry Lee introduced in the Second Continental Congress a resolution of the Virginia House of Burgesses declaring that "these United Colonies are, and of right ought to be, free and independent States."

Many delegates to Congress—and many Americans—opposed independence and still sought reconciliation with Eng-land. The delegates agreed on June 10, however, to a three-week postponement of debate, during which time a committee of five—Thomas Jefferson, John Adams, Benjamin Franklin, Robert Livingston, and Roger Sherman—were appointed to "prepare a Declaration to the effect of the said . . . resolution."

Thomas Jefferson drafted the declaration and, after minor changes by the other members of the committee, submitted it to Congress on June 28. After heated debate, Virginia's resolution proclaiming independence passed on July 2. Jefferson's declaration was then subjected to two days of extensive revision. Passages deemed to be personal attacks on King George III were deleted, as were passages censuring the English people, whom Jefferson had referred to as "unfeeling brethren." Most important, passages critical of the institution of slavery were excised when delegates from certain of the Southern colonies refused to support the declaration otherwise. In all, the declaration was cut by one-quarter, but its essential points and character remained unchanged. Congress approved the final draft on July 4.

In Congress, July 4, 1776

The Unanimous Declaration of the Thirteen United States of America

When in the Course of human events, it becomes necessary for one people to dissolve the political bands which have connected them with another, and to assume among the Powers of the earth, the separate and equal station to which the Laws of Nature and of Nature's God entitle them, a decent respect to the opinions of mankind requires that they should declare the causes which impel them to the separation.

We hold these truths to be self-evident, that all men are created equal, that they are endowed by their Creator with certain unalienable Rights, that among these are Life, Liberty and the pursuit of Happiness. That to secure these rights, Governments are instituted among Men, deriving their just powers from the consent of the governed. That whenever any form of Government becomes destructive of these ends, it is the Right of the People to alter or to abolish it, and to institute new Government, laying its foundation on such principles and organizing its powers in such form, as to them shall seem most likely to effect their Safety and Happiness. Prudence, indeed, will dictate that Government long established should not be changed for light and transient causes; and accordingly all experience hath shown, that mankind are more disposed to suffer, while evils are sufferable, than to right themselves by abolishing the forms to which they are accustomed. But when a long train of abuses and usurpations, pursuing invariably the same Object evinces a design to reduce them under absolute Despotism, it is their right, it is their duty, to throw off such Government, and to provide new Guards for their future security.—Such has been the patient sufferance of these Colonies; and such is now the necessity which constrains them to alter their former Systems of Government. The history of the present King of Great Britain is a history of repeated injuries and usurpations, all having in direct object the establishment of an absolute Tyranny over these States. To prove this, let Facts be submitted to a candid world.

He has refused his Assent to Laws, the most wholesome and necessary for the public good.

He has forbidden his Governors to pass Laws of immediate and pressing importance, unless suspended in their operation till his Assent should be obtained; and when so suspended, he has utterly neglected to attend to them.

He has refused to pass other Laws for the accommodation of large districts of people, unless those people would relinquish the right of Representation in the Legislature, a right inestimable to them and formidable to tyrants only.

He has called together legislative bodies at places unusual, uncomfortable, and distant from the depository of their Public Records, for the sole purpose of fatiguing them into compliance with his measures.

He has dissolved Representative Houses repeatedly, for opposing with manly firmness his invasions on the rights of the people.

He has refused for a long time, after such dissolutions, to cause others to be elected; whereby the Legislative Powers, incapable of Annihilation, have returned to the People at large for their exercise; the State remaining in the mean time exposed to all the dangers of invasion from without, and convulsions within.

He has endeavored to prevent the population of these States; for that purpose obstructing the Laws of Naturalization of Foreigners; refusing to pass others to encourage their migration hither, and raising the conditions of new Appropriations of Lands.

He has obstructed the Administration of Justice, by refusing his Assent to Laws for establishing Judiciary Powers.

He has made Judges dependent on his Will alone, for the tenure of their offices, and the amount and payment of their salaries.

He has erected a multitude of New Offices, and sent hither swarms of Officers to harass our People, and eat out their substance.

He has kept among us, in times of peace, Standing Armies without the Consent of our legislature.

He has affected to render the Military independent of and superior to the Civil Power.

He has combined with others to subject us to a jurisdiction foreign to our constitution, and unacknowledged by our laws; giving his Assent to their acts of pretended legislation:

For quartering large bodies of armed troops among us:

For protecting them, by a mock Trial, from Punishment for any Murders which they should commit on the Inhabitants of these States:

For cutting off our Trade with all parts of the world:

For imposing taxes on us without our Consent:

For depriving us in many cases, of the benefits of Trial by Jury:

For transporting us beyond Seas to be tried for pretended offences:

For abolishing the free System of English Laws in a neighbouring Province, establishing therein an Arbitrary government, and enlarging its Boundaries so as to render it at once an example and fit instrument for introducing the same absolute rule into these Colonies:

For taking away our Charters, abolishing our most valuable Laws, and altering fundamentally the Forms of our Governments:

For suspending our own Legislature, and declaring themselves invested with Power to legislate for us in all cases whatsoever.

He has abdicated Government here, by declaring us out of his Protection and waging War against us.

He has plundered our seas, ravaged our Coasts, burnt our towns, and destroyed the lives of our people.

He is at this time transporting large armies of foreign mercenaries to compleat the works of death, desolation and tyranny, already begun with circumstances of Cruelty & perfidy scarcely paralleled in the most barbarous ages, and totally unworthy the Head of a civilized nation.

He has constrained our fellow Citizens taken Captive on the high Seas to bear Arms against their Country, to become the executioners of their friends and Brethren, or to fall themselves by their Hands.

He has excited domestic insurrections amongst us, and has endeavoured to bring on the inhabitants of our frontiers, the merciless Indian Savages, whose known rule of warfare, is an undistinguished destruction of all ages, sexes and conditions.

In every stage of these Oppressions We have Petitioned for Redress in the most humble terms: Our repeated Petitions have been answered only by repeated injury. A Prince, whose character is thus marked by every act which may define a Tyrant, is unfit to be the ruler of a free People.

Nor have We been wanting in attention to our British brethren. We have warned them from time to time of attempts by their legislature to extend an unwarrantable jurisdiction over us. We have reminded them of the circumstances of our emigration and settlement here. We have appealed to their native justice and magnanimity, and we have conjured them by the ties of our common kindred to disavow these usurpations, which would inevitably interrupt our connections and correspondence. They too have been deaf to the voice of justice and of consanguinity. We must, therefore, acquiesce in the necessity, which denounces our Separation, and hold them, as we hold the rest of mankind, Enemies in War, in Peace Friends.

We, therefore, the Representatives of the United States of America, in General Congress, Assembled, appealing to the Supreme Judge of the world for the rectitude of our intentions, do, in the Name, and by Authority of the good People of these Colonies, solemnly publish and declare, That these United Colonies are, and of Right ought to be Free and Independent States; that they are Absolved from all Allegiance to the British Crown, and that all political connection between them and the State of Great Britain, is and ought to be totally dissolved; and that as Free and Independent States, they have full Power to levy War, conclude Peace, contract Alliances, establish Commerce, and to do all other Acts and Things which Independent States may of right do. And for the support of this Declaration, with a firm reliance on the Protection of Divine Providence, we mutually pledge to each other our Lives, our Fortunes and our sacred Honor.

JOHN HANCOCK

New Hampshire: Josiah Bartlett, William Whipple, Matthew Thornton.

Massachusetts-Bay: Samuel Adams, John Adams, Robert Treat Paine, Elbridge Gerry.

Rhode Island: Stephen Hopkins, William Ellery.

Connecticut: Roger Sherman, Samuel Huntington, William Williams, Oliver Wolcott.

New York: William Floyd, Philip Livingston, Francis Lewis, Lewis Morris.

Pennsylvania: Robert Morris, Benjamin Harris, Benjamin Franklin, John Morton, George Clymer, James Smith, George Taylor, James Wilson, George Ross.

Delaware: Caesar Rodney, George Read, Thomas McKean.

Georgia: Button Gwinnett, Lyman Hall, George Walton.

Maryland: Samuel Chase, William Paca, Thomas Stone, Charles Carroll of Carrollton.

Virginia: George Wythe, Richard Henry Lee, Thomas Jefferson, Benjamin Harrison, Thomas Nelson Jr., Francis Lightfoot Lee, Carter Braxton.

North Carolina: William Hooper, Joseph Hewes, John Penn.

South Carolina: Edward Rutledge, Thomas Heyward Jr., Thomas Lynch Jr., Arthur Middleton.

New Jersey: Richard Stockton, John Witherspoon, Francis Hopkinson, John Hart, Abraham Clark.

CONSTITUTION OF THE UNITED STATES (1787)

The Constitutional Convention that opened in Philadelphia on May 25, 1787, convened in a crisis atmosphere. In the six years since winning independence from Great Britain, the weak central government created under the Articles of Confederation had proven woefully incapable of handling the difficulties confronting the nation. The combined public debt of the states and Congress, much of it accrued during the war for independence, had reached $60 million, and the high taxes imposed to pay off the debt had led to civil disturbances in many states and to armed insurrection—Shays's Rebellion—in Massachusetts. Compounding these domestic difficulties, Great Britain, Spain, and France were interfering with increasing frequency with American commerce and navigation.

Domestic politics under the Articles of Confederation had been dominated by "republicans," who for reasons of philosophy and self-interest opposed the creation of a strong central government and strong executive authority. Their opponents, called "nationalists," gained strength as the crisis of the 1780s intensified. A large majority of the fifty-five delegates to the convention were ardent nationalists and arrived in Philadelphia determined to create a strong central government.

"Strong," however, was a relative term. The delegates dis-

agreed over just how much power the national government should have regarding the states and citizens as well as how that power should be apportioned between the executive and legislative functions. The debate over those broad issues overlapped with other disputes: between representatives of large states and small states, the latter favoring a strong central government; and between "democrats" and "aristocrats," over questions of suffrage, individual rights, ease of amendment, and susceptibility of the government to popular pressure.

The final draft of the U.S. Constitution was a masterful product of debate and compromise over the practical issues. In spirit it remained true to the Enlightenment objectives of justice, liberty, and equality and to the Enlightenment commitments to civil liberties and limited government that had given rise to the American Revolution a decade earlier.

Delegates to the convention approved a final draft on September 17, 1787, and the Constitution was submitted to the states for ratification. In a few states, ratification was swift and uncontroversial; in others, the Constitution's supporters had to persuade. The Constitution was declared in effect by the Continental Congress on September 13, 1788, after nine states had ratified the document.

We the People of the United States, in Order to form a more perfect Union, establish Justice, insure domestic Tranquility, provide for the common defence, promote the general Welfare, and secure the Blessings of Liberty to ourselves and our Posterity, do ordain and establish this Constitution for the United States of America.

ARTICLE I

Section 1. All legislative Powers herein granted shall be vested in a Congress of the United States, which shall consist of a Senate and House of Representatives.

Section 2. The House of Representatives shall be composed of Members chosen every second Year by the People of the several States, and the Electors in each State shall have the Qualifi-

cations requisite for Electors of the most numerous Branch of the State Legislature.

No Person shall be a Representative who shall not have attained to the age of twenty five Years, and been seven Years a Citizen of the United States, and who shall not, when elected, be an Inhabitant of that State in which he shall be chosen.

Representatives and direct Taxes shall be apportioned among the several States which may be included within this Union, according to their respective Numbers, which shall be determined by adding to the whole Number of free Persons, including those bound to Service for a Term of Years, and excluding Indians not taxed, three fifths of all other Persons. The actual Enumeration shall be made within three Years after the first Meeting of the Congress of the United States, and within every subsequent Term of ten Years, in such Manner as they shall by Law direct. The Number of Representatives shall not exceed one for every thirty Thousand, but each State shall have at Least one Representative; and until such enumeration shall be made, the State of New Hampshire shall be entitled to chuse three, Massachusetts eight, Rhode-Island and Providence Plantations one, Connecticut five, New-York six, New Jersey four, Pennsylvania eight, Delaware one, Maryland six, Virginia ten, North Carolina five, South Carolina five, and Georgia three.

When vacancies happen in the Representation from any State, the Executive Authority thereof shall issue Writs of Election to fill such Vacancies.

The House of Representatives shall chuse their Speaker and other Officers; and shall have the sole Power of Impeachment.

Section 3. The Senate of the United States shall be composed of two Senators from each State, chosen by the Legislature thereof, for six Years; and each Senator shall have one Vote.

Immediately after they shall be assembled in Consequence of the first Election, they shall be divided as equally as may be into three Classes. The Seats of the Senators of the first Class shall be vacated at the Expiration of the second Year, of the second Class at the Expiration of the fourth Year, and of the third Class at the Expiration of the sixth Year, so that one third may be chosen every second Year; and if Vacancies happen by Resignation, or otherwise, during the Recess of the Legislature of any State, the Executive thereof may make temporary Appointments until the next Meeting of the Legislature, which shall then fill such Vacancies.

No Person shall be a Senator who shall not have attained to the Age of thirty Years, and been nine Years a Citizen of the United States, and who shall not, when elected, be an Inhabitant of that State for which he shall be chosen.

The Vice President of the United States shall be President of the Senate, but shall have no Vote, unless they be equally divided.

The Senate shall chuse their other Officers, and also a President pro tempore, in the Absence of the Vice President, or when he shall exercise the Office of President of the United States.

The Senate shall have the sole Power to try all Impeachments. When sitting for that Purpose, they shall be on Oath or Affirmation. When the President of the United States is tried the Chief Justice shall preside: And no Person shall be convicted without the Concurrence of two thirds of the Members present.

Judgment in Cases of Impeachment shall not extend further than to removal from Office, and disqualification to hold and enjoy any Office of honor, Trust or Profit under the United States: but the Party convicted shall nevertheless be liable and subject to Indictment, Trial, Judgment and Punishment, according to Law.

Section 4. The Times, Places and Manner of holding Elections for Senators and Representatives, shall be prescribed in each State by the Legislature thereof; but the Congress may at any time by Law make or alter such Regulations, except as to the Places of chusing Senators.

The Congress shall assemble at least once in every Year, and such Meeting shall be on the first Monday in December, unless they shall by Law appoint a different Day.

Section 5. Each House shall be the Judge of the Elections, Returns and Qualifications of its own Members, and a Majority of each shall constitute a Quorum to do Business; but a smaller Number may adjourn from day to day, and may be authorized to compel the Attendance of absent Members, in such Manner, and under such Penalties as each House may provide.

Each House may determine the Rules of its Proceedings, punish its Members for disorderly Behaviour, and, with the Concurrence of two thirds, expel a Member.

Each House shall keep a Journal of its Proceedings, and from time to time publish the same, excepting such Parts as may in their Judgment require Secrecy; and the Yeas and Nays of the Members of either House on any question shall, at the Desire of one fifth of those Present, be entered on the Journal.

Neither House, during the Session of Congress, shall, without the Consent of the other, adjourn for more than three days, nor to any other Place than that in which the two Houses shall be sitting.

Section 6. The Senators and Representatives shall receive a Compensation for their Services, to be ascertained by Law, and paid out of the Treasury of the United States. They shall in all Cases, except Treason, Felony and Breach of the Peace, be privileged from Arrest during their Attendance at the Session of their respective Houses, and in going to and returning from the same; and for any Speech or Debate in either House, they shall not be questioned in any other Place.

No Senator or Representative shall, during the Time for which he was elected, be appointed to any civil Office under the Authority of the United States, which shall have been created, or the Emoluments whereof shall have been increased during such time; and no Person holding any Office under the United States, shall be a Member of either House during his Continuance in Office.

Section 7. All Bills for raising Revenue shall originate in the House of Representatives; but the Senate may propose or concur with Amendments as on other Bills.

Every Bill which shall have passed the House of Representatives and the Senate, shall, before it become a Law, be presented to the President of the United States; If he approve he shall sign it, but if not he shall return it, with his Objections to that House in which it shall have originated, who shall enter the

Objections at large on their Journal, and proceed to reconsider it. If after such Reconsideration two thirds of that House shall agree to pass the Bill, it shall be sent, together with the Objections, to the other House, by which it shall likewise be reconsidered, and if approved by two thirds of that House, it shall become a Law. But in all such Cases the Votes of both Houses shall be determined by yeas and Nays, and the Names of the Persons voting for and against the Bill shall be entered on the Journal of each House respectively. If any Bill shall not be returned by the President within ten Days (Sundays excepted) after it shall have been presented to him, the Same shall be a Law, in like Manner as if he had signed it, unless the Congress by their Adjournment prevent its Return, in which Case it shall not be a Law.

Every Order, Resolution, or Vote to which the Concurrence of the Senate and House of Representatives may be necessary (except on a question of Adjournment) shall be presented to the President of the United States; and before the Same shall take Effect, shall be approved by him, or being disapproved by him, shall be repassed by two thirds of the Senate and House of Representatives, according to the Rules and Limitations prescribed in the Case of a Bill.

Section 8. The Congress shall have Power To lay and collect Taxes, Duties, Imposts and Excises, to pay the Debts and provide for the common Defence and general Welfare of the United States; but all Duties, Imposts and Excises shall be uniform throughout the United States;

To borrow Money on the credit of the United States;

To regulate Commerce with foreign Nations, and among the several States, and with the Indian Tribes;

To establish an uniform Rule of Naturalization, and uniform Laws on the subject of Bankruptcies throughout the United States;

To coin Money, regulate the Value thereof, and of foreign Coin, and fix the Standard of Weights and Measures;

To provide for the Punishment of counterfeiting the Securities and current Coin of the United States;

To establish Post Offices and post Roads;

To promote the Progress of Science and useful Arts, by securing for limited Times to Authors and Inventors the exclusive Right to their respective Writings and Discoveries;

To constitute Tribunals inferior to the supreme Court;

To define and punish Piracies and Felonies committed on the high Seas, and Offences against the Law of Nations;

To declare War, grant Letters of Marque and Reprisal, and make Rules concerning Captures on Land and Water;

To raise and support Armies, but no Appropriation of Money to that Use shall be for a longer Term than two Years;

To provide and maintain a Navy;

To make Rules for the Government and Regulation of the land and naval Forces;

To provide for calling forth the Militia to execute the Laws of the Union, suppress Insurrections and repel Invasions;

To provide for organizing, arming, and disciplining, the Militia, and for governing such Part of them as may be employed in the Service of the United States, reserving to the States respectively, the Appointment of the Officers, and the Authority of training the Militia according to the discipline prescribed by Congress;

To exercise exclusive Legislation in all Cases whatsoever, over such District (not exceeding ten Miles square) as may, by Cession of particular States, and the Acceptance of Congress, become the Seat of the Government of the United States, and to exercise like Authority over all Places purchased by the Consent of the Legislature of the State in which the Same shall be, for the Erection of Forts, Magazines, Arsenals, dock-Yards, and other needful Buildings; —And

To make all Laws which shall be necessary and proper for carrying into Execution the foregoing Powers, and all other Powers vested by this Constitution in the Government of the United States, or in any Department or Officer thereof.

Section 9. The Migration or Importation of such Persons as any of the States now existing shall think proper to admit, shall not be prohibited by the Congress prior to the Year one thousand eight hundred and eight, but a Tax or duty may be imposed on such Importation, not exceeding ten dollars for each Person.

The Privilege of the Writ of Habeas Corpus shall not be suspended, unless when in Cases of Rebellion or Invasion the public Safety may require it.

No Bill of Attainder or ex post facto Law shall be passed.

No Capitation, or other direct, Tax shall be laid, unless in Proportion to the Census or Enumeration herein before directed to be taken.

No Tax or Duty shall be laid on Articles exported from any State.

No Preference shall be given by any Regulation of Commerce or Revenue to the Ports of one State over those of another; nor shall Vessels bound to, or from, one State, be obliged to enter, clear, or pay Duties in another.

No Money shall be drawn from the Treasury, but in Consequence of Appropriations made by Law; and a regular Statement and Account of the Receipts and Expenditures of all public Money shall be published from time to time.

No Title of Nobility shall be granted by the United States: And no Person holding any Office of Profit or Trust under them, shall, without the Consent of the Congress, accept of any present, Emolument, Office, or Title, of any kind whatever, from any King, Prince, or foreign State.

Section 10. No State shall enter into any Treaty, Alliance, or Confederation; grant Letters of Marque and Reprisal; coin Money; emit Bills of Credit; make any Thing but gold and silver Coin a Tender in Payment of Debts; pass any Bill of Attainder, ex post facto Law, or Law impairing the Obligation of Contracts, or grant any Title of Nobility.

No State shall, without the Consent of the Congress, lay any Imposts or Duties on Imports or Exports, except what may be absolutely necessary for executing it's inspection Laws: and the net Produce of all Duties and Imposts, laid by any State on Imports or Exports, shall be for the Use of the Treasury of the United States; and all such Laws shall be subject to the Revision and Controul of the Congress.

No State shall, without the Consent of Congress, lay any Duty of Tonnage, keep Troops, or Ships of War in time of Peace, enter into any Agreement or Compact with another State, or with a foreign Power, or engage in War, unless actually invaded, or in such imminent Danger as will not admit of delay.

ARTICLE II

Section 1. The executive Power shall be vested in a President of the United States of America. He shall hold his Office during the Term of four Years, and, together with the Vice President, chosen for the same Term, be elected, as follows:

Each State shall appoint, in such Manner as the Legislature thereof may direct, a Number of Electors, equal to the whole Number of Senators and Representatives to which the State may be entitled in the Congress: but no Senator or Representative, or Person holding an Office of Trust or Profit under the United States, shall be appointed an Elector.

The Electors shall meet in their respective States, and vote by Ballot for two Persons, of whom one at least shall not be an Inhabitant of the same State with themselves. And they shall make a List of all the Persons voted for, and of the Number of Votes for each; which List they shall sign and certify, and transmit sealed to the Seat of the Government of the United States, directed to the President of the Senate. The President of the Senate shall, in the Presence of the Senate and House of Representatives, open all the Certificates, and the Votes shall then be counted. The Person having the greatest Number of Votes shall be the President, if such Number be a Majority of the whole Number of Electors appointed; and if there be more than one who have such Majority, and have an equal Number of Votes, then the House of Representatives shall immediately chuse by Ballot one of them for President; and if no Person have a Majority, then from the five highest on the list the said House shall in like Manner chuse the President. But in chusing the President, the Votes shall be taken by States, the Representation from each State having one Vote; a quorum for this Purpose shall consist of a Member or Members from two thirds of the States, and a Majority of all the States shall be necessary to a Choice. In every Case, after the Choice of the President, the Person having the greatest Number of Votes of the Electors

shall be the Vice President. But if there should remain two or more who have equal Votes, the Senate shall chuse from them by Ballot the Vice President.

The Congress may determine the Time of chusing the Electors, and the Day on which they shall give their Votes; which Day shall be the same throughout the United States.

No Person except a natural born Citizen, or a Citizen of the United States, at the time of the Adoption of this Constitution, shall be eligible to the Office of President; neither shall any Person be eligible to that Office who shall not have attained to the Age of thirty five Years, and been fourteen Years a Resident within the United States.

In Case of the Removal of the President from Office, or of his Death, Resignation, or Inability to discharge the Powers and Duties of the said Office, the Same shall devolve on the Vice President, and the Congress may by Law provide for the Case of Removal, Death, Resignation or Inability, both of the President and Vice President, declaring what Officer shall then act as President, and such Officer shall act accordingly, until the Disability be removed, or a President shall be elected.

The President shall, at stated Times, receive for his Services, a Compensation, which shall neither be encreased nor diminished during the Period for which he shall have been elected, and he shall not receive within that Period any other Emolument from the United States, or any of them.

Before he enter on the Execution of his Office, he shall take the following Oath or Affirmation:—"I do solemnly swear (or affirm) that I will faithfully execute the Office of President of the United States, and will to the best of my Ability, preserve, protect and defend the Constitution of the United States."

Section 2. The President shall be Commander in Chief of the Army and Navy of the United States, and of the Militia of the several States, when called into the actual Service of the United States; he may require the Opinion, in writing, of the principal Officer in each of the executive Departments, upon any Subject relating to the Duties of their respective Offices, and he shall have Power to grant Reprieves and Pardons for Offences against the United States, except in Cases of Impeachment.

He shall have Power, by and with the Advice and Consent of the Senate, to make Treaties, provided two thirds of the Senators present concur; and he shall nominate, and by and with the Advice and Consent of the Senate, shall appoint Ambassadors, other public Ministers and Consuls, Judges of the supreme Court, and all other Officers of the United States, whose Appointments are not herein otherwise provided for, and which shall be established by Law: but the Congress may by Law vest the Appointment of such inferior Officers, as they think proper, in the President alone, in the Courts of Law, or in the Heads of Departments.

The President shall have Power to fill up all Vacancies that may happen during the Recess of the Senate, by granting Commissions which shall expire at the End of their next Session.

Section 3. He shall from time to time give to the Congress Information of the State of the Union, and recommend to their Consideration such Measures as he shall judge necessary and expedient; he may, on extraordinary Occasions, convene both Houses, or either of them, and in Case of Disagreement between them, with Respect to the Time of Adjournment, he may adjourn them to such Time as he shall think proper; he shall receive Ambassadors and other public Ministers; he shall take Care that the Laws be faithfully executed, and shall Commission all the Officers of the United States.

Section 4. The President, Vice President and all civil Officers of the United States, shall be removed from Office on Impeachment for, and Conviction of, Treason, Bribery, or other high Crimes and Misdemeanors.

ARTICLE III

Section 1. The judicial Power of the United States, shall be vested in one supreme Court, and in such inferior Courts as the Congress may from time to time ordain and establish. The Judges, both of the supreme and inferior Courts, shall hold their Offices during good Behaviour, and shall, at stated Times, receive for their Services, a Compensation, which shall not be diminished during their Continuance in Office.

Section 2. The judicial Power shall extend to all Cases, in Law and Equity, arising under this Constitution, the Laws of the United States, and Treaties made, or which shall be made, under their Authority; —to all Cases affecting Ambassadors, other public Ministers and Consuls; —to all Cases of admiralty and maritime Jurisdiction; —to Controversies to which the United States shall be a Party; —to Controversies between two or more States; —between a State and Citizens of another State; —between Citizens of different States; —between Citizens of the same State claiming Lands under Grants of different States, and between a State, or the Citizens thereof, and foreign States, Citizens or Subjects.

In all Cases affecting Ambassadors, other public Ministers and Consuls, and those in which a State shall be Party, the supreme Court shall have original Jurisdiction. In all the other Cases before mentioned, the supreme Court shall have appellate Jurisdiction, both as to Law and Fact, with such Exceptions, and under such Regulations as the Congress shall make.

The Trial of all Crimes, except in Cases of Impeachment, shall be by Jury; and such Trial shall be held in the State where the said Crimes shall have been committed; but when not committed within any State, the Trial shall be at such Place or Places as the Congress may by Law have directed.

Section 3. Treason against the United States, shall consist only in levying War against them, or in adhering to their Enemies, giving them Aid and Comfort. No Person shall be convicted of Treason unless on the Testimony of two Witnesses to the same overt Act, or on Confession in open Court.

The Congress shall have Power to declare the Punishment of Treason, but no Attainder of Treason shall work Corruption of Blood, or Forfeiture except during the Life of the Person attainted.

ARTICLE IV

Section 1. Full Faith and Credit shall be given in each State to the public Acts, Records, and judicial Proceedings of every other State. And the Congress may by general Laws prescribe the Manner in which such Acts, Records and Proceedings shall be proved, and the Effect thereof.

Section 2. The Citizens of each State shall be entitled to all Privileges and Immunities of Citizens in the several States.

A Person charged in any State with Treason, Felony, or other Crime, who shall flee from Justice, and be found in another State, shall on Demand of the executive Authority of the State from which he fled, be delivered up, to be removed to the State having Jurisdiction of the Crime.

No Person held to Service or Labour in one State, under the Laws thereof, escaping into another, shall, in Consequence of any Law or Regulation therein, be discharged from such Service or Labour, but shall be delivered up on Claim of the Party to whom such Service or Labour may be due.

Section 3. New States may be admitted by the Congress into this Union; but no new State shall be formed or erected within the Jurisdiction of any other State; nor any State be formed by the Junction of two or more States, or Parts of States, without the Consent of the Legislatures of the States concerned as well as of the Congress.

The Congress shall have Power to dispose of and make all needful Rules and Regulations respecting the Territory or other Property belonging to the United States; and nothing in this Constitution shall be so construed as to Prejudice any Claims of the United States, or of any particular State.

Section 4. The United States shall guarantee to every State in this Union a Republican Form of Government, and shall protect each of them against Invasion; and on Application of the Legislature, or of the Executive (when the Legislature cannot be convened) against domestic Violence.

ARTICLE V

The Congress, whenever two thirds of both Houses shall deem it necessary, shall propose Amendments to this Constitution, or, on the Application of the Legislatures of two thirds of the several States, shall call a Convention for proposing Amendments, which, in either Case, shall be valid to all Intents and Purposes, as Part of this Constitution, when ratified by the Legislatures of three fourths of the several States, or by Conventions in three fourths thereof, as the one or the other Mode of Ratification may be proposed by the Congress; Provided that no Amendment which may be made prior to the Year One thousand eight hundred and eight shall in any Manner affect the first and fourth Clauses in the Ninth Section of the first Article; and that no State, without its Consent, shall be deprived of its equal Suffrage in the Senate.

ARTICLE VI

All Debts contracted and Engagements entered into, before the Adoption of this Constitution, shall be as valid against the United States under this Constitution, as under the Confederation.

This Constitution, and the Laws of the United States which shall be made in Pursuance thereof; and all Treaties made, or which shall be made, under the Authority of the United States, shall be the supreme Law of the Land; and the Judges in every State shall be bound thereby, any Thing in the Constitution or Laws of any State to the Contrary notwithstanding.

The Senators and Representatives before mentioned, and the Members of the several State Legislatures, and all executive and judicial Officers, both of the United States and of the several States, shall be bound by Oath or Affirmation, to support this Constitution; but no religious Test shall ever be required as a Qualification to any Office or public Trust under the United States.

ARTICLE VII

The Ratification of the Conventions of nine States, shall be sufficient for the Establishment of this Constitution between the States so ratifying the Same. Done in Convention by the Unanimous Consent of the States present the Seventeenth Day of September in the Year of our Lord one thousand seven hundred and Eighty seven and of the Independence of the United States of America the Twelfth. In Witness whereof We have hereunto subscribed our Names,

George Washington, *President and deputy from Virginia.*

New Hampshire: John Langdon, Nicholas Gilman.

Massachusetts: Nathaniel Gorham, Rufus King.

Connecticut: William Samuel Johnson, Roger Sherman.

New York: Alexander Hamilton.

New Jersey: William Livingston, David Brearley, William Paterson, Jonathan Dayton.

Pennsylvania: Benjamin Franklin, Thomas Mifflin, Robert Morris, George Clymer, Thomas FitzSimons, Jared Ingersoll, James Wilson, Gouverneur Morris.

Delaware: George Read, Gunning Bedford Jr., John Dickinson, Richard Bassett, Jacob Broom.

Maryland: James McHenry, Daniel of St. Thomas Jenifer, Daniel Carroll.

Virginia: John Blair, James Madison Jr.

North Carolina: William Blount, Richard Dobbs Spaight, Hugh Williamson.

South Carolina: John Rutledge, Charles Cotesworth Pinckney, Charles Pinckney, Pierce Butler.

Georgia: William Few, Abraham Baldwin.

AMENDMENTS

AMENDMENT I

(First ten amendments ratified December 15, 1791)

Congress shall make no law respecting an establishment of religion, or prohibiting the free exercise thereof; or abridging the freedom of speech, or of the press; or the right of the people peaceably to assemble, and to petition the Government for a redress of grievances.

AMENDMENT II

A well regulated Militia, being necessary to the security of a free State, the right of the people to keep and bear Arms, shall not be infringed.

AMENDMENT III

No Soldier shall, in time of peace be quartered in any house, without the consent of the Owner, nor in time of war, but in a manner to be prescribed by law.

AMENDMENT IV

The right of the people to be secure in their persons, houses, papers, and effects, against unreasonable searches and seizures, shall not be violated, and no Warrants shall issue, but upon probable cause, supported by Oath or affirmation, and particularly describing the place to be searched, and the persons or things to be seized.

AMENDMENT V

No person shall be held to answer for a capital, or otherwise infamous crime, unless on a presentment or indictment of a Grand Jury, except in cases arising in the land or naval forces, or in the Militia, when in actual service in time of War or public danger; nor shall any person be subject for the same offence to be twice put in jeopardy of life or limb; nor shall be compelled in any criminal case to be a witness against himself, nor be deprived of life, liberty, or property, without due process of law; nor shall private property be taken for public use, without just compensation.

AMENDMENT VI

In all criminal prosecutions, the accused shall enjoy the right to a speedy and public trial, by an impartial jury of the State and district wherein the crime shall have been committed, which district shall have been previously ascertained by law, and to be informed of the nature and cause of the accusation; to be confronted with the witnesses against him; to have compulsory process for obtaining witnesses in his favor, and to have the Assistance of Counsel for his defence.

AMENDMENT VII

In Suits at common law, where the value in controversy shall exceed twenty dollars, the right of trial by jury shall be preserved, and no fact tried by a jury, shall be otherwise re-examined in any Court of the United States, than according to the rules of the common law.

AMENDMENT VIII

Excessive bail shall not be required, nor excessive fines imposed, nor cruel and unusual punishments inflicted.

AMENDMENT IX

The enumeration in the Constitution, of certain rights, shall not be construed to deny or disparage others retained by the people.

AMENDMENT X

The powers not delegated to the United States by the Constitution, nor prohibited by it to the States, are reserved to the States respectively, or to the people.

AMENDMENT XI *(Ratified February 7, 1795)*

The Judicial power of the United States shall not be construed to extend to any suit in law or equity, commenced or prosecuted against one of the United States by Citizens of another State, or by Citizens or Subjects of any Foreign State.

AMENDMENT XII *(Ratified June 15, 1804)*

The Electors shall meet in their respective states and vote by ballot for President and Vice-President, one of whom, at least, shall not be an inhabitant of the same state with themselves; they shall name in their ballots the person voted for as President, and in distinct ballots the person voted for as Vice-President, and they shall make distinct lists of all persons voted for as President, and of all persons voted for as Vice-President, and of the number of votes for each, which lists they shall sign and certify, and transmit sealed to the seat of the government of the United States, directed to the President of the Senate; —The President of the Senate shall, in the presence of the Senate and House of Representatives, open all the certificates and the votes shall then be counted; —The person

having the greatest number of votes for President, shall be the President, if such number be a majority of the whole number of Electors appointed; and if no person have such majority, then from the persons having the highest numbers not exceeding three on the list of those voted for as President, the House of Representatives shall choose immediately, by ballot, the President. But in choosing the President, the votes shall be taken by states, the representation from each state having one vote; a quorum for this purpose shall consist of a member or members from two-thirds of the states, and a majority of all the states shall be necessary to a choice. And if the House of Representatives shall not choose a President whenever the right of choice shall devolve upon them, before the fourth day of March next following, then the Vice-President shall act as President, as in the case of the death or other constitutional disability of the President. The person having the greatest number of votes as Vice-President, shall be the Vice-President, if such number be a majority of the whole number of Electors appointed, and if no person have a majority, then from the two highest numbers on the list, the Senate shall choose the Vice-President; a quorum for the purpose shall consist of two-thirds of the whole number of Senators, and a majority of the whole number shall be necessary to a choice. But no person constitutionally ineligible to the office of President shall be eligible to that of Vice-President of the United States.

AMENDMENT XIII *(Ratified December 6, 1865)*

Section 1. Neither slavery nor involuntary servitude, except as a punishment for crime whereof the party shall have been duly convicted, shall exist within the United States, or any place subject to their jurisdiction.

Section 2. Congress shall have power to enforce this article by appropriate legislation.

AMENDMENT XIV *(Ratified July 9, 1868)*

Section 1. All persons born or naturalized in the United States, and subject to the jurisdiction thereof, are citizens of the United States and of the State wherein they reside. No State shall make or enforce any law which shall abridge the privileges or immunities of citizens of the United States; nor shall any State deprive any person of life, liberty, or property, without due process of law; nor deny to any person within its jurisdiction the equal protection of the laws.

Section 2. Representatives shall be apportioned among the several States according to their respective numbers, counting the whole number of persons in each State, excluding Indians not taxed. But when the right to vote at any election for the choice of electors for President and Vice President of the United States, Representatives in Congress, the Executive and Judicial officers of a State, or the members of the Legislature thereof, is denied to any of the male inhabitants of such State, being twenty-one years of age, and citizens of the United States, or in any way abridged, except for participation in rebellion, or other crime, the basis of representation therein shall be reduced in the proportion which the number of such male citizens shall bear to the whole number of male citizens twenty-one years of age in such State.

Section 3. No person shall be a Senator or Representative in Congress, or elector of President and Vice President, or hold any office, civil or military, under the United States, or under any State, who, having previously taken an oath, as a member of Congress, or as an officer of the United States, or as a member of any State legislature, or as an executive or judicial officer of any State, to support the Constitution of the United States, shall have engaged in insurrection or rebellion against the same, or given aid or comfort to the enemies thereof. But Congress may by a vote of two-thirds of each House, remove such disability.

Section 4. The validity of the public debt of the United States, authorized by law, including debts incurred for payment of pensions and bounties for services in suppressing insurrection or rebellion, shall not be questioned. But neither the United States nor any State shall assume or pay any debt or obligation incurred in aid of insurrection or rebellion against the United States, or any claim for the loss or emancipation of any slave; but all such debts, obligations and claims shall be held illegal and void.

Section 5. The Congress shall have power to enforce, by appropriate legislation, the provisions of this article.

AMENDMENT XV *(Ratified February 3, 1870)*

Section 1. The right of citizens of the United States to vote shall not be denied or abridged by the United States or by any State on account of race, color, or previous condition of servitude.

Section 2. The Congress shall have power to enforce this article by appropriate legislation.

AMENDMENT XVI *(Ratified February 3, 1913)*

The Congress shall have power to lay and collect taxes on incomes, from whatever source derived, without apportionment among the several States, and without regard to any census or enumeration.

AMENDMENT XVII *(Ratified April 8, 1913)*

The Senate of the United States shall be composed of two Senators from each State, elected by the people thereof, for six years; and each Senator shall have one vote. The electors in each State shall have the qualifications requisite for electors of the most numerous branch of the State legislatures.

When vacancies happen in the representation of any State in the Senate, the executive authority of such State shall issue writs of election to fill such vacancies: Provided, That the legislature of any State may empower the executive thereof to make temporary appointments until the people fill the vacancies by election as the legislature may direct.

This amendment shall not be so construed as to affect the election or term of any Senator chosen before it becomes valid as part of the Constitution.

AMENDMENT XVIII *(Ratified January 16, 1919)*

Section 1. After one year from the ratification of this article the manufacture, sale, or transportation of intoxicating liquors within, the importation thereof into, or the exportation thereof from the United States and all territory subject to the jurisdiction thereof for beverage purposes is hereby prohibited.

Section 2. The Congress and the several States shall have concurrent power to enforce this article by appropriate legislation.

Section 3. This article shall be inoperative unless it shall have been ratified as an amendment to the Constitution by the legislatures of the several States, as provided in the Constitution, within seven years from the date of the submission hereof to the States by the Congress.

AMENDMENT XIX *(Ratified August 18, 1920)*

The right of citizens of the United States to vote shall not be denied or abridged by the United States or by any State on account of sex.

Congress shall have power to enforce this article by appropriate legislation.

AMENDMENT XX *(Ratified January 23, 1933)*

Section 1. The terms of the President and Vice President shall end at noon on the 20th day of January, and the terms of Senators and Representatives at noon on the 3d day of January, of the years in which such terms would have ended if this article had not been ratified; and the terms of their successors shall then begin.

Section 2. The Congress shall assemble at least once in every year, and such meeting shall begin at noon on the 3d day of January, unless they shall by law appoint a different day.

Section 3. If, at the time fixed for the beginning of the term of the President, the President elect shall have died, the Vice President elect shall become President. If a President shall not have been chosen before the time fixed for the beginning of his term, or if the President elect shall have failed to qualify, then the Vice President elect shall act as President until a President shall have qualified; and the Congress may by law provide for the case wherein neither a President elect nor a Vice President elect shall have qualified, declaring who shall then act as President, or the manner in which one who is to act shall be selected, and such person shall act accordingly until a President or Vice President shall have qualified.

Section 4. The Congress may by law provide for the case of the death of any of the persons from whom the House of Representatives may choose a President whenever the right of choice shall have devolved upon them, and for the case of the death of any of the persons from whom the Senate may choose a Vice President whenever the right of choice shall have devolved upon them.

Section 5. Sections 1 and 2 shall take effect on the 15th day of October following the ratification of this article.

Section 6. This article shall be inoperative unless it shall have been ratified as an amendment to the Constitution by the legislatures of three-fourths of the several States within seven years from the date of its submission.

AMENDMENT XXI *(Ratified December 5, 1933)*

Section 1. The eighteenth article of amendment to the Constitution of the United States is hereby repealed.

Section 2. The transportation or importation into any State, Territory, or possession of the United States for delivery or use therein of intoxicating liquors, in violation of the laws thereof, is hereby prohibited.

Section 3. This article shall be inoperative unless it shall have been ratified as an amendment to the Constitution by conventions in the several States, as provided in the Constitution, within seven years from the date of the submission hereof to the States by the Congress.

AMENDMENT XXII *(Ratified February 27, 1951)*

Section 1. No person shall be elected to the office of the President more than twice, and no person who has held the office of President, or acted as President, for more than two years of a term to which some other person was elected President shall be elected to the office of the President more than once. But this Article shall not apply to any person holding the office of President when this Article was proposed by the Congress, and shall not prevent any person who may be holding the office of President, or acting as President, during the term within which this Article becomes operative from holding the office of President or acting as President during the remainder of such term.

Section 2. This article shall be inoperative unless it shall have been ratified as an amendment to the Constitution by the legislatures of three-fourths of the several States within seven years from the date of its submission to the States by the Congress.

AMENDMENT XXIII *(Ratified March 29, 1961)*

Section 1. The District constituting the seat of Government of the United States shall appoint in such manner as the Congress may direct:

A number of electors of President and Vice President equal to the whole number of Senators and Representatives in Congress to which the District would be entitled if it were a State, but in no event more than the least populous State; they shall be in addition to those appointed by the States, but they shall be considered, for the purposes of the election of President and Vice President, to be electors appointed by a State; and they shall meet in the District and perform such duties as provided by the twelfth article of amendment.

Section 2. The Congress shall have power to enforce this article by appropriate legislation.

AMENDMENT XXIV *(Ratified January 23, 1964)*

Section 1. The right of citizens of the United States to vote in any primary or other election for President or Vice President, for electors for President or Vice President, or for Senator or Representative in Congress, shall not be denied or abridged by the United States or any State by reason of failure to pay any poll tax or other tax.

Section 2. The Congress shall have power to enforce this article by appropriate legislation.

AMENDMENT XXV *(Ratified February 10, 1967)*

Section 1. In case of the removal of the President from office or of his death or resignation, the Vice President shall become President.

Section 2. Whenever there is a vacancy in the office of the Vice President, the President shall nominate a Vice President who shall take office upon confirmation by a majority vote of both Houses of Congress.

Section 3. Whenever the President transmits to the President pro tempore of the Senate and the Speaker of the House of Representatives his written declaration that he is unable to discharge the powers and duties of his office, and until he transmits to them a written declaration to the contrary, such powers and duties shall be discharged by the Vice President as Acting President.

Section 4. Whenever the Vice President and a majority of either the principal officers of the executive departments or of such other body as Congress may by law provide, transmit to the President pro tempore of the Senate and the Speaker of the House of Representatives their written declaration that the President is unable to discharge the powers and duties of his office, the Vice President shall immediately assume the powers and duties of the office as Acting President.

Thereafter, when the President transmits to the President

pro tempore of the Senate and the Speaker of the House of Representatives his written declaration that no inability exists, he shall resume the powers and duties of his office unless the Vice President and a majority of either the principal officers of the executive department or of such other body as Congress may by law provide, transmit within four days to the President pro tempore of the Senate and the Speaker of the House of Representatives their written declaration that the President is unable to discharge the powers and duties of his office. Thereupon Congress shall decide the issue, assembling within forty-eight hours for that purpose if not in session. If the Congress, within twenty-one days after receipt of the latter written declaration, or, if Congress is not in session, within twenty-one days after Congress is required to assemble, determines by two-thirds vote of both Houses that the President is unable to discharge the powers and duties of his office, the Vice President shall continue to discharge the same as Acting President; otherwise, the President shall resume the powers and duties of his office.

AMENDMENT XXVI *(Ratified July 1, 1971)*

Section 1. The right of citizens of the United States, who are eighteen years of age or older, to vote shall not be denied or abridged by the United States or by any State on account of age.

Section 2. The Congress shall have power to enforce this article by appropriate legislation.

AMENDMENT XXVII *(Ratified May 7, 1992)*

No law varying the compensation for the services of the Senators and Representatives shall take effect, until an election of Representatives shall have intervened.

DECLARATION OF THE RIGHTS OF MAN AND OF THE CITIZEN (1789)

The French Declaration of the Rights of Man and of the Citizen followed in the tradition of the Dutch and American declarations of independence in asserting that the fundamental rights of liberty and equality derive from nature and that a government violating those rights is illegitimate and should be overthrown. Decreed by the revolutionary National Assembly on August 27, 1789, the declaration sanctioned the destruction of the old regime that was already under way.

Despite shared philosophical underpinnings, the French and American declarations differed in important ways, largely because of the contexts in which they arose. Whereas the American revolution against the British king had been almost exclusively political and ideological in nature, the French revolution against its own monarch included social and economic aspects; it was as much a class-based revolution against aristocracy and privilege as a political revolution. Consequently, many of the principles embodied in the French declaration were antithetical to the status quo: the right to legal equality in matters of taxation and employment were a reaction to aristocratic privilege; the right to representative government was a reaction to royal absolutism; and the right to rule of law was a reaction to the monarchy's arbitrary practices.

Another important difference between the documents stems from their respective intellectual forebears. Whereas the American declaration had been grounded in John Locke's theory that individuals have natural rights, the French declaration was influenced more by Jean-Jacques Rousseau. Rousseau held that individuals can realize their natural rights only in political society, whence derives the French declaration's emphasis on the rights of the citizen.

Preamble

The representatives of the French People, formed into a National Assembly, considering ignorance, forgetfulness or contempt of the rights of man to be the only causes of public misfortunes and the corruption of Governments, have resolved to set forth, in a solemn Declaration, the natural, unalienable and sacred rights of man, to the end that this Declaration, constantly present to all members of the body politic, may remind them unceasingly of their rights and their duties; to the end that the acts of the legislative power and those of the executive power, since they may be continually compared with the aim of every political institution, may thereby be the more respected; to the end that the demands of the citizens, founded henceforth on simple and uncontestable principles, may always be directed toward the maintenance of the Constitution and the happiness of all.

In consequence whereof, the National Assembly recognizes and declares, in the presence and under the auspices of the Supreme Being, the following Rights of Man and of the Citizen.

ARTICLE FIRST—Men are born and remain free and equal in rights. Social distinctions may be based only on considerations of the common good.

ARTICLE 2—The aim of every political association is the preservation of the natural and imprescriptible rights of man. These rights are Liberty, Property, Safety and Resistance to Oppression.

ARTICLE 3—The source of all sovereignty lies essentially in the Nation. No corporate body, no individual may exercise any authority that does not expressly emanate from it.

ARTICLE 4—Liberty consists in being able to do anything that does not harm others: thus, the exercise of the natural rights of every man has no bounds other than those that ensure to the other members of society the enjoyment of these same rights. These bounds may be determined only by Law.

ARTICLE 5—The Law has the right to forbid only those actions that are injurious to society. Nothing that is not forbidden by Law may be hindered, and no one may be compelled to do what the Law does not ordain.

ARTICLE 6—The Law is the expression of the general will. All citizens have the right to take part, personally or through their representatives, in its making. It must be the same for all, whether it protects or punishes. All citizens, being equal in its eyes, shall be equally eligible to all high offices, public positions and employments, according to their ability, and without other distinction than that of their virtues and talents.

ARTICLE 7—No man may be accused, arrested or detained except in the cases determined by the Law, and following the procedure that it has prescribed. Those who solicit, expedite, carry out, or cause to be carried out arbitrary orders must be punished; but any citizen summoned or apprehended by virtue of the Law, must give instant obedience; resistance makes him guilty.

ARTICLE 8—The Law must prescribe only the punishments that are strictly and evidently necessary; and no one may be punished except by virtue of a Law drawn up and promulgated before the offense is committed, and legally applied.

ARTICLE 9—As every man is presumed innocent until he has been declared guilty, if it should be considered necessary to arrest him, any undue harshness that is not required to secure his person must be severely curbed by Law.

ARTICLE 10—No one may be disturbed on account of his opinions, even religious ones, as long as the manifestation of such opinions does not interfere with the established Law and Order.

ARTICLE 11—The free communication of ideas and of opinions is one of the most precious rights of man. Any citizen may therefore speak, write and publish freely, except what is tantamount to the abuse of this liberty in the cases determined by Law.

ARTICLE 12—To guarantee the Rights of Man and of the Citizen a public force is necessary; this force is therefore established for the benefit of all, and not for the particular use of those to whom it is entrusted.

ARTICLE 13—For the maintenance of the public force, and for administrative expenses, a general tax is indispensable; it must be equally distributed among all citizens, in proportion to their ability to pay.

ARTICLE 14—All citizens have the right to ascertain, by themselves, or through their representatives, the need for a public tax, to consent to it freely, to watch over its use, and to determine its proportion, basis, collection and duration.

ARTICLE 15—Society has the right to ask a public official for an accounting of his administration.

ARTICLE 16—Any society in which no provision is made for guaranteeing rights or for the separation of powers, has no Constitution.

ARTICLE 17—Since the right to Property is inviolable and sacred, no one may be deprived thereof, unless public necessity, legally ascertained, obviously requires it, and just and prior indemnity has been paid.

CONSTITUTION OF NORWAY (1814)

Norwegian national consciousness began to rise, and the Norwegian monarchy began to consolidate, in the twelfth to fourteenth centuries. The development was interrupted, however, when the bubonic plague wiped out roughly half the population and decimated the economy in 1349–1350. The weakened nation joined in union with Denmark in 1387 and remained in union for more than five hundred years.

By the end of the eighteenth century Norwegians began to chafe under Danish rule. A growing economy contributed significantly to a sense of power and an awakening of national consciousness, as it had in America and the Dutch provinces.

In 1807 the Danish king, Frederik, allied with Napoleon against Great Britain and dragged Norway involuntarily into a war that was disastrous for the Norwegians. When Napoleon was defeated at the battle of Leipzig six years later, the Norwegians saw an opportunity to declare their independence from Denmark. Independence was short-lived, however, because Britain's ally, Sweden, coveted Norway. In an attempt to rally Norwegians in opposition to Sweden, Danish crown prince Christian Frederik summoned a constituent assembly, which drafted the constitution and elected Christian Frederik king of an independent Norway. The constitution was signed May 17, 1814. Two months later, Swedish troops chased Christian out of Norway.

For the next ninety-one years, Norway would remain in union with Sweden. However, the Swedes accepted the Norwegian constitution as essentially valid, and only insisted on minor constitutional amendments to recognize the Swedish king and Swedish control over foreign affairs. Norway had almost complete autonomy in matters of internal self-government, and the Storting (parliament) was permitted to operate. Nonetheless, by the late nineteenth century even Sweden's limited authority came to be resented in Norway. On June 7, 1905, the Storting declared the union void, and Sweden was powerless to do anything about it.

There was some sentiment in Norway for a republic, but the monarchists prevailed in a nationwide plebiscite. Prince Carl of Denmark was invited to accept the throne of Norway; he arrived November 25, 1905, and became Haakon VII. The constitution was again slightly revised. (The constitution is reproduced here as amended.)

The Norwegian constitution melded French revolutionary ideas, elements of U.S. constitutional doctrine and British parliamentary tradition, and some uniquely Norwegian features. The prominence of religion is particularly striking, as is the absolute executive power originally vested in the king (Sec. 3). The king was specifically granted the right to appoint cabinet members, civil servants, and military officials; to pass provisional ordinances; and to pardon criminals. However, modern constitutional practice differs substantially from the formal terms of the document, and the king's prerogatives have been substantially reduced. In fact, the modern-day king is largely a figurehead, as in other constitutional monarchies. The Council of State, which functions as a cabinet, is responsible to the Storting, which in turn is responsible to the people.

A. Form of government and religion.

Sec. 1. The Kingdom of Norway is a free, independent, indivisible, and inalienable realm. Its form of government is a limited and hereditary monarchy.

Sec. 2. All inhabitants of the Kingdom shall have the right to free exercise of their religion.

The Evangelical-Lutheran religion shall remain the official religion of the State. The inhabitants professing it shall be bound to bring up their children in the same.

B. The executive power, the King, and the Royal Family.

Sec. 3. The executive power is vested in the King.

Sec. 4. The King shall at all times profess the Evangelical-Lutheran religion, and uphold and protect the same.

Sec. 5. The King's person shall be sacred. He cannot be censured or accused. The responsibility shall rest with his Council.

Sec. 6. The order of succession shall be lineal and agnatic, so that only males, born in lawful wedlock, may succeed males, and the nearer line shall take precedence over the more remote and the elder in the line over the younger.

An unborn child shall also be included among those entitled to the succession and shall immediately take his proper place in the line of succession as soon as he is born into the world after the death of his father.

When a Prince entitled to succeed to the Crown of Norway is born, his name and the time of his birth shall be notified to the first subsequent Storting and be entered in the record of its proceedings.

Sec. 7. If there is no Prince entitled to the succession, the King may propose his successor to the Storting, which has the right to make the choice if the King's nominee is not acceptable.

Sec. 8. The age of majority of the King shall be stipulated by law.

As soon as the King has attained the age of majority fixed by law, he shall make a public declaration that he is of age.

Sec. 9. As soon as the King, being of full age, accedes to the government, he shall take the following oath before the Storting: "I promise and swear that I will govern the Kingdom of Norway in accordance with its Constitution and Laws, so help me God, the Almighty and Omniscient!"

If the Storting is not in session at the time, the oath shall be made in writing in the Council of State and be repeated solemnly by the King at the first subsequent Storting.

Sec. 10. (Repealed)

Sec. 11. The King shall reside in the Kingdom and may not, without the consent of the Storting, remain outside the Kingdom for more than six months at a time, otherwise he shall have forfeited, for his person, the right to the Crown.

The King may not accept any other crown or government without the consent of the Storting, for which two thirds of the votes are required.

Sec. 12. The King shall himself choose a Council from among Norwegian citizens who are entitled to vote. This Council shall consist of a Prime Minister and at least seven other Members.

More than half the number of Members of the Council of State shall profess the official religion of the State.

The King shall apportion the business among the Members of the Council of State, as he deems appropriate. Under extraordinary circumstances, the King may summon, apart from the ordinary Members of the Council of State, other Norwegian citizens, but no members of the Storting, to take a seat in the Council of State.

Husband and wife, parent and child, or two siblings may not, at the same time, have a seat in the Council of State.

Sec. 13. During his travels within the Kingdom, the King may delegate the government to the Council of State. The Council of State shall conduct the government in the King's name and on his behalf. It shall scrupulously observe the provisions of this Constitution as well as such particular directives in pursuance thereof as the King may instruct.

The matters of business shall be decided by voting, wherein in the event of the votes being equal, the Prime Minister, or in his absence, the highest-ranking Member of the Council of State who is present, shall have two votes.

The Council of State shall make a report to the King of the matters of business which it thus decides.

Sec. 14. The King may appoint State Secretaries to assist Members of the Council of State with their duties outside the Council of State. Each State Secretary shall act on behalf of the Member of the Council of State to whom he is attached to the extent determined by that Member.

Sec. 15. (Repealed)

Sec. 16. The King shall give directions for all public church services and public worship, all meetings and assemblies dealing with religious matters, and shall ensure that the public teachers of religion follow the rules prescribed for them.

Sec. 17. The King may issue and repeal ordinances relating to commerce, tariffs, trade and industry, and the police; they must not, however, be at variance with the Constitution or the laws passed (as hereinafter prescribed in Secs. 77, 78 and 79) by the Storting. They shall be in force provisionally until the next Storting.

Sec. 18. The King shall, as a general rule, cause the taxes and duties imposed by the Storting to be collected.

Sec. 19. The King shall ensure that the property belonging to the State, as well as its privileges and monopolies, are utilized and administered in the manner determined by the Storting and in the best interest of the general public.

Sec. 20. The King shall have the right in the Council of State to pardon criminals after sentence has been passed. The criminal shall have the choice of accepting the King's Grace or submitting to the penalty imposed.

In proceedings which the Odelsting causes to be brought before the Constitutional Court of the Realm, no pardon other than exemption from the death penalty may be granted.

Sec. 21. The King shall choose and appoint, after consultation with his Council of State, all senior civil, ecclesiastical, and military officials. Such officials shall swear or, if by law exempted from taking the oath, solemnly declare obedience and allegiance to the Constitution and the King. The Royal Princes must not hold senior civil posts.

Sec. 22. The Prime Minister and the other Members of the Council of State, together with the State Secretaries may be dismissed by the King without any prior court judgment, after he has heard the opinion of the Council of State on the subject. The same applies to senior officials employed in government offices or in the diplomatic or the consular service, to highest-ranking civil and ecclesiastical officials, commanders of regiments and other military formations, commandants of forts and officers commanding warships. Whether pensions should be granted to senior officials thus dismissed shall be determined by the next Storting. In the interval they shall receive two thirds of their previous pay.

Other senior officials may only be suspended by the King, whereupon legal proceedings should be instituted against them, but, unless judgment has been pronounced against them, they may neither be dismissed nor transferred against their will.

All senior officials may, without any prior court judgment, be discharged from office upon attaining the statutory age-limit.

Sec. 23. The King may award honors, upon whomever he pleases, as a reward for distinguished services, and this shall be announced publicly; but not any rank or title other than such as each office carries with it. The honor exempts no one from the common duties and burdens of citizens, nor does it carry with it any preferential admission to senior official posts in the State. Senior officials honorably discharged from office may retain the title and rank of their office. This does not apply, however, to Members of the Council of State or the State Secretaries.

No personal, or mixed, hereditary privileges may henceforth be granted to anyone.

Sec. 24. The King shall choose and dismiss, at his own discretion, his Royal Household and Court Officials.

Sec. 25. The King shall be Commander-in-Chief of the Army and the Navy of the Kingdom. These forces may not be increased or reduced without the consent of the Storting. They may not be transferred to the service of foreign powers, nor may the military forces of any foreign powers, except auxiliary forces against hostile attack, be brought into the Kingdom without the consent of the Storting.

The territorial contingent (landevern) and the other troops which cannot be classed as troops of the line may never, without the consent of the Storting, be employed outside the borders of the Kingdom.

Sec. 26. The King shall have the right to assemble troops, to enter into war in the defense of the Kingdom and to make peace, to conclude and denounce conventions, to send and to receive diplomatic envoys.

Treaties on matters of special importance, and, in all cases, treaties whose implementation, according to the Constitution, necessitates a new law or a decision by the Storting, shall not be binding until the Storting has given its consent thereto.

Sec. 27. All Members of the Council of State shall, unless lawfully absent, attend the Council of State and no decision may be taken there unless more than half the number of Members are present.

Members of the Council of State who do not profess the official religion of the State shall not take part in proceedings on matters which concern the State Church.

Sec. 28. Proposals regarding appointments to senior official posts and other matters of importance shall be presented in the Council of State by the Member under whose department they come, and such matters shall be dealt with by him in accordance with the decision adopted in the Council of State. Matters strictly relating to military command may, however, to the extent determined by the King, be excepted from proceedings in the Council of State.

Sec. 29. If a Member of the Council of State is lawfully prevented from attending the meeting and from presenting the matters coming under his department, these may be presented by another Member temporarily appointed by the King for the purpose.

If so many Members are lawfully prevented from attending that not more than half of the stipulated number are present, the requisite number of other men or women shall be temporarily appointed to take a seat in the Council of State.

Sec. 30. All the proceedings of the Council of State shall be entered in its records. Diplomatic matters which the Council of State has decided to keep secret shall be entered in a special record. The same applies to matters relating to military command which the Council of State has decided to keep secret.

Everyone who has a seat in the Council of State has the duty frankly to express his opinion, to which the King is bound to listen. But it rests with the King to make a decision according to his own judgment.

If any Member of the Council of State is of the opinion that the King's decision conflicts with the form of government or the laws of the Kingdom, or is clearly prejudicial to the Kingdom, it is his duty to make strong remonstrances against it, and also to have his opinion entered in the record. A Member who has not thus protested shall be deemed to have been in agreement with the King, and shall be answerable in such manner as may be subsequently decided, and may be impeached by the Odelsting before the Constitutional Court of the Realm.

Sec. 31. All decisions drawn up by the King shall, in order to become valid, be countersigned. Decisions relating to military command shall be countersigned by the person who has presented the matter, while other decisions shall be countersigned by the Prime Minister or, if he has not been present, by the highest-ranking Member of the Council of State who is present.

Sec. 32. The decisions adopted by the Government during the absence of the King shall be drawn up in the King's name and be signed by the Council of State.

Sec. 33. (Repealed)

Sec. 34. The nearest heir to the Throne, if he is the son of the reigning King, shall bear the title of Crown Prince. The other persons entitled to succeed to the Throne shall be called Princes, and the daughters of the Royal House, Princesses.

Sec. 35. As soon as the heir to the Throne has completed his eighteenth year, he is entitled to take a seat in the Council of State, but without vote or responsibility.

Sec. 36. A Prince of the Royal House may not marry without the consent of the King. Nor may he accept any other crown or government without the consent of the King and the Storting; to obtain the consent of the Storting, two thirds of the votes are required.

If he acts contrary to this rule, he and his descendants forfeit their right to the Throne of Norway.

Sec. 37. The Royal Princes and Princesses shall not be answerable personally to any other than the King, or to such person as he may appoint to sit in judgment on them.

Sec. 38. (Repealed)

Sec. 39. If the King dies and the heir to the Throne is still under age, the Council of State shall immediately summon the Storting.

Sec. 40. Until the Storting has assembled and made provisions for the Government during the minority of the King, the Council of State shall be responsible for the administration of the Kingdom in accordance with the Constitution.

Sec. 41. If the King is absent from the Kingdom, and not in the field, or if he is so ill that he cannot attend to the Government, the Prince next entitled to succeed to the Throne shall conduct the Government as being temporarily invested with the Royal powers, provided that he has attained the age stipulated for the King's majority. If this is not the case, the Council of State shall be responsible for the administration of the Kingdom.

Sec. 42. (Repealed)

Sec. 43. The choice of trustees to conduct the Government on behalf of the King during his minority shall be undertaken by the Storting.

Sec. 44. The Prince who, in the cases mentioned in Sec. 41, conducts the Government shall make the following oath in writing before the Storting: "I promise and swear that I will conduct the Government in accordance with the Constitution and the Laws, so help me God, the Almighty and Omniscient!"

If the Storting is not in session at the time, the oath shall be made in the Council of State and later be presented to the next Storting.

The Prince who has once made the oath shall not repeat it later.

Sec. 45. As soon as their conduct of the Government has ceased, the trustees shall submit to the King and the Storting an account of the same.

Sec. 46. If the persons concerned fail to summon the Storting immediately in accordance with Sec. 39, it becomes the unconditional duty of the Supreme Court, as soon as four weeks have elapsed, to arrange for the Storting to be summoned.

Sec. 47. The supervision of the education of the King during his minority shall, if his father has left no written directions, be determined by the Storting.

Sec. 48. If the male line of the Royal Family has died out, and no successor to the Throne has been designated, then a new King shall be chosen by the Storting. Meanwhile, the executive power shall be exercised in accordance with Sec. 40.

C. Rights of citizens and the legislative power.

Sec. 49. The people shall exercise the legislative power through the Storting, which shall consist of two divisions, the Lagting and the Odelsting.

Sec. 50. Those entitled to vote are Norwegian citizens, men and women, who have completed their 18th year at the latest during the year when the election is held.

The extent, however, to which Norwegian subjects who on election day are resident outside the Kingdom but who satisfy the abovementioned conditions, are entitled to vote shall be determined by law.

Sec. 51. The rules concerning the electoral registers and the registration of persons entitled to vote shall be determined by law.

Sec. 52. (Repealed)

Sec. 53. The right to vote shall be lost in the case of any person who:

a) is sentenced for criminal offenses, subject to such provisions as may be laid down by law;

b) enters the service of a foreign power without the consent of the Government;

c) ———

d) is found guilty of having bought votes, of having sold his own vote, or of having voted at more than one poll;

e) is declared incapable of managing his own affairs.

Sec. 54. Elections shall be held every four years. They shall be completed by the end of September.

Sec. 55. Elections shall be conducted in such a manner as shall be determined by law. Disputes as to the right to vote shall be settled by the returning officials, whose decision may be appealed to the Storting.

Sec. 56. (Repealed)

Sec. 57. The number of representatives to be elected to the Storting shall be one hundred and fifty-five.

Sec. 58. Each county shall be a constituency.

The distribution of representatives to the Storting from the Kingdom's constituencies shall be as follows: 8 shall be elected from the county of Østfold, 15 from the city of Oslo, 10 from the county of Akershus, 8 from the county of Hedmark, 7 from the county of Opland, 7 from the county of Buskerud, 7 from the county of Vestfold, 6 from the county of Telemark, 4 from the county of Aust-Agder, 5 from the county of Vest-Agder, 10 from the county of Rogaland, 15 from the county of Hordaland, 5 from the county of Sogn og Fjordane, 10 from the county of Møre og Romsdal, 10 from the county of Sør-Trøndelag, 6 from the county of Nord-Trøndelag, 12 from the county of Nordland, 6 from the county of Troms and 4 from the county of Finnmark.

Sec. 59. Each municipality shall constitute a separate polling district.

The elections shall be held separately for each polling district. At the elections the votes shall be cast directly for the representatives to the Storting, together with their proxies, for the entire constituency.

The system of election is by proportional representation. The rules to be applied hereto, and to the procedures in respect of the elections otherwise, shall be determined by law, subject to the relevant provisions laid down in the Constitution.

Sec. 60. Whether and in what manner those entitled to vote may deliver their ballot papers, without personal attendance at the polls, shall be determined by law.

Sec. 61. No one shall be eligible for election as a representative to the Storting unless he has resided for 10 years in the Kingdom, as well as being entitled to vote.

Sec. 62. The officials who are employed in government departments, although with the exception of the State Secretaries, as well as officials and pensioners of the Court, may not be elected as representatives to the Storting. The same applies to officials employed in the diplomatic or consular services.

Members of the Council of State may not attend meetings of the Storting as representatives while holding a seat in the Council of State. Nor may the State Secretaries attend as representatives while holding such office.

Sec. 63. It shall be the duty of anyone who is elected as a representative to accept the election, unless elected outside the constituency in which he is entitled to vote or prevented from attending for reasons which the Storting deems valid. If anyone has been present as a representative at all the ordinary sessions of the Storting following one election, he shall not be obliged to accept election at the next election for the Storting.

If anyone is elected as a representative without being bound to accept such election, he must, within the time and in the manner prescribed by law, make a declaration stating whether or not he accepts election.

The time within which, as well as the manner in which, a person elected as representative for two or more constituencies shall state which election he will accept, shall likewise be determined by law.

Sec. 64. The representatives elected shall be furnished with credentials, the validity of which shall be adjudged by the Storting.

Sec. 65. Every representative and proxy called to the Storting shall be entitled to receive from the Treasury such reimbursement as is prescribed by law for travelling expenses to and from the Storting, and from the Storting to his home and back again during vacations lasting at least fourteen days, as well as for expenses for medical treatment in the case of illness.

He shall further be entitled to remuneration, likewise prescribed by law, for attending the Storting.

Sec. 66. Representatives on their way to and from the Storting, as well as during their attendance there, shall be exempt from personal arrest unless they are apprehended in public crimes, nor may they be called to account outside the meetings of the Storting for opinions expressed there. Every representative shall be bound to conform to the rules of procedure therein adopted.

Sec. 67. The representatives elected in the aforesaid manner shall constitute the Storting of the Kingdom of Norway.

Sec. 68. The Storting shall as a rule assemble on the first weekday in October every year in the capital of the Kingdom, unless the King, by reason of extraordinary circumstances, such as a hostile invasion or infectious disease, designates another town in the Kingdom. If so, such a decision must by publicly announced in good time.

Sec. 69. Under extraordinary circumstances the King shall have the right to summon the Storting at a time other than the ordinary.

Sec. 70. An extraordinary session of the Storting of this nature may be prorogued by the King at his discretion.

Sec. 71. The members of the Storting shall act as such for four successive years, both in extraordinary and in ordinary sessions of the Storting held during that period.

Sec. 72. If an extraordinary session of the Storting is being held at the time when an ordinary session of the Storting is due to open, the former shall be prorogued before the latter assembles.

Sec. 73. The Storting shall nominate from among its members one fourth to constitute the Lagting; the remaining three fourths shall constitute the Odelsting. This nomination shall take place at the first ordinary session of the Storting that assembles after a new general election, whereafter the Lagting shall remain unchanged at all assembled sessions of the Storting after the same election, except in so far as any vacancy which may occur among its members has to be filled by special nomination.

Each Ting shall hold its meetings separately and nominate its own President and Secretary. Neither Ting may hold a meeting unless at least one half of its members are present. However, Bills concerning amendments to the Constitution may not be dealt with unless at least two thirds of the members of the Storting are present.

Sec. 74. As soon as the Storting is constituted, the King, or whoever he appoints for the purpose, shall open its proceedings with a speech, in which he shall inform it of the state of the Kingdom and of the issues to which he particularly desires to call the attention of the Storting. No deliberations may take place in the presence of the King.

When the proceedings of the Storting have been opened, the Prime Minister and the Members of the Council of State have the right to attend the Storting, as well as both of its divisions, and, like the members of the Storting, although without being entitled to vote, to take part in the current proceedings insofar as these are conducted in open session, while in the case of matters which are discussed in closed session only insofar as is permitted by the Ting concerned.

Sec. 75. The duties and prerogatives of the Storting are:

a) to enact and repeal laws; to impose taxes, duties, customs, and other public charges, which shall not, however, remain operative beyond 31 December of the following year, unless expressly renewed by a new ordinary Storting;

b) to float loans on the credit of the Kingdom;

c) to supervise the finances of the Kingdom;

d) to appropriate the sums of money necessary to meet government expenditure;

e) to decide how much shall be paid annually to the King for the Royal Household, and to determine the appanage of the Royal family, which may not, however, consist of real property;

f) to have submitted to it the records of the Council of State, and all public reports and documents;

g) to have communicated to it the conventions and treaties which the King, on behalf of the State, has concluded with foreign powers;

h) to have the power to summon anyone, the King and the Royal family excepted, to meet before it in matters of State; this exception does not, however, apply to the Royal Princes if they hold any public office;

i) to revise the lists of salaries and pensions temporarily granted, and to make therein such alterations as it deems necessary;

k) to appoint five auditors, who shall annually examine the accounts of the State and publish extracts of the same in print, for which purpose the accounts shall be delivered to the auditors within six months of the expiration of the year for which the appropriations of the Storting have been made, and to adopt provisions concerning the organization of an office to audit the accounts of the government accounting officials;

l) to naturalize aliens.

Sec. 76. Every Bill shall first be introduced in the Odelsting, either by one of its own members, or by the Government through a Member of the Council of State.

If the Bill is passed, it shall be sent to the Lagting, which either approves or rejects it, and in the latter case sends it back with comments appended. These are taken into consideration by the Odelsting, which either drops the Bill or again sends it to the Lagting, with or without alteration.

When a Bill from the Odelsting has twice been presented to the Lagting and has been a second time rejected by it, the Storting shall meet in plenary session, and the Bill is then decided by a majority of two thirds of the votes.

Between each such deliberation there shall be an interval of at least three days.

Sec. 77. When a Bill passed by the Odelsting has been approved by the Lagting or by the Storting in plenary session, it shall be sent to the King, with a request that it may receive the Royal Assent.

Sec. 78. If the King assents to the Bill, he shall attach to it his signature, whereby it becomes law.

If he does not assent to it, he shall return it to the Odelsting, with the statement that he does not for the time being find it expedient to give his Assent to it. In that case the Bill must not again be submitted to the King by the Storting then assembled.

Sec. 79. If a Bill has been passed unaltered by two ordinary sessions of the Storting, constituted after two separate successive elections and separated from each other by at least two intervening ordinary sessions of the Storting, without an amended Bill having been passed by any Storting in the period between the first and the last passing, and it is then submitted to the King with the petition that His Majesty shall not refuse his Assent to a Bill which, after the most mature deliberation, the Storting considers to be for the benefit of the country, it shall become law, even if the Royal Assent is not accorded before the Storting dissolves.

Sec. 80. The Storting shall remain in session as long as it deems this necessary. When, having concluded its business, it is prorogued by the King, he shall at the same time communicate his decision with regard to the Bills that have not already been decided (cf. Secs. 77–79), either by confirming or rejecting them. All those which he does not expressly approve are regarded as having been rejected by him.

Sec. 81. All Acts (with the exception of those mentioned in Sec. 79) shall be drawn up in the name of the King, under the seal of the Kingdom of Norway, and in the following terms: "We, X, make it publicly known that the decision of the Storting of the date stated has been laid before Us: (here follows the decision). In consequence whereof We have assented to and confirmed, as We hereby assent to and confirm the same as a Law under Our hand and the Seal of the Kingdom."

Sec. 82. (Repealed)

Sec. 83. The Storting may obtain the opinion of the Supreme Court on questions of law.

Sec. 84. The Storting shall meet in open session, and its proceedings shall be published in print, except in those cases in which a majority decides to the contrary.

Sec. 85. Any person who obeys an order, the purpose of which is to disturb the liberty and the security of the Storting, shall thereby be guilty of treason against the Country.

D. The judicial power.

Sec. 86. The Constitutional Court of the Realm shall pronounce judgment in the first and last instance in such proceedings as are brought by the Odelsting against Members of the Council of State, or of the Supreme Court of Justice or of the Storting for criminal offenses which they may have committed in the capacity of their office.

The particular rules concerning impeachment by the Odelsting, according to this Article, shall be determined by law. The period within which impeachment proceedings may be instituted in the Constitutional Court of the Realm shall not, however, be set at less than fifteen years.

The permanent members of the Lagting and the permanently appointed members of the Supreme Court shall be judges of the Constitutional Court of the Realm. The provisions contained in Sec. 87 shall apply to the composition of the Constitutional Court of the Realm in each particular case. In the Constitutional Court of the Realm the President of the Lagting shall take the chair.

A person sitting in the Constitutional Court of the Realm as a member of the Lagting shall not resign from the Court if the period for which he is elected as a representative to the Storting should expire before the Constitutional Court of the Realm has concluded the trial of the case. If he ceases for any other reason to be a member of the Storting, he shall resign as a judge of the Constitutional Court of the Realm. The same applies if a justice of the Supreme Court, who is a member of the Constitutional Court of the Realm, retires as a member of the Supreme Court.

Sec. 87. The accused and the person acting on behalf of the Odelsting in the proceedings have the right to challenge as many members of the Lagting and of the Supreme Court, as will leave remaining fourteen members of the Lagting and seven members of the Supreme Court as judges in the Constitutional Court of the Realm. Each party in the proceedings has the right to challenge an equal number of the members of the Lagting, the accused, however, having the preferential right of challenging one more, if the number permitted to be challenged is not divisible into two equal parts. The same shall apply to the challenging of the members of the Supreme Court. If there are several accused in such proceedings, they shall exercise the right of challenge collectively in accordance with rules prescribed by law. If the right of challenge is not exercised to the extent permitted, as many members of the Lagting and of the Supreme Court as are in excess of four-

teen and seven respectively shall retire following the drawing of lots.

When the case comes up for judgment, as many judges of the Constitutional Court of the Realm shall retire following the drawing of lots as to ensure that the Court due to render judgment is left with fifteen members, of whom at most ten are members of the Lagting and five justices of the Supreme Court.

The President of the Constitutional Court of the Realm and the President of the Supreme Court shall in no case retire following the drawing of lots.

If the Constitutional Court of the Realm cannot be composed of as many members of the Lagting or of the Supreme Court as prescribed above, the case may nevertheless be tried and judgment rendered provided that the Court numbers at least ten judges.

Specific provisions as to the procedure to be followed in the composition of the Constitutional Court of the Realm shall be laid down by law.

Sec. 88. The Supreme Court shall pronounce judgment in the final instance. Limitations on the right to bring a case before the Supreme Court may, however, be prescribed by law.

The Supreme Court shall consist of a President and at least four other members.

Sec. 89. (Repealed)

Sec. 90. The judgments of the Supreme Court may in no case be appealed.

Sec. 91. No one may be appointed a member of the Supreme Court before reaching 30 years of age.

E. General provisions.

Sec. 92. To senior official posts (embeter) in the State may be appointed only Norwegian citizens, men and women, who speak the language of the country, and who at the same time

a) either were born in the Kingdom of parents who at that time were subjects of the State;

b) or were born in a foreign country of Norwegian parents who were not at that time subjects of another State;

c) or hereafter have resided ten years in the Kingdom;

d) or have been naturalized by the Storting.

Others may, however, be appointed as teachers at the University and institutions of higher learning as physicians and as consuls in foreign places.

Sec. 93. In order to secure international peace and security or to promote international law and order and cooperation between nations, the Storting may, by a three-fourths majority, consent that an international organization of which Norway is or becomes a member, shall have the right, within a factually limited field, to exercise powers which in accordance with this Constitution are normally vested in the Norwegian authorities, exclusive of the power to alter this Constitution. For the

Storting to grant such consent, at least two thirds of the members of the Storting, as is required for proceedings on amendments to the Constitution, shall be present.

The provisions of this Article do not apply in cases of membership in an international organization, the decisions of which are not binding on Norway except as obligations under international law.

Sec. 94. The first, or if this is not possible, the second ordinary Storting, shall make provision for the publication of a new general civil and criminal code. However, the laws of the State now applicable shall remain in force, provided that they do not conflict with this Constitution or with such provisional ordinances as may be issued in the meantime.

The existing permanent taxes shall likewise remain operative until the next Storting.

Sec. 95. No dispensations, protections, moratoriums or redresses may be granted after the new general code has entered into force.

Sec. 96. No one may be convicted except according to law, or be punished except according to judicial sentence. Interrogation by torture must not take place.

Sec. 97. No law must be given retroactive effect.

Sec. 98. When special fees are paid to officials of the Courts of Justice, no further payment shall be made to the Treasury in respect of the same matter.

Sec. 99. No one may be taken into custody except in the cases determined by law and in the manner prescribed by law. For unwarranted arrest and illegal detention the officer concerned shall be responsible to the person imprisoned.

The Government is not entitled to employ military force against subjects of the State, except in accordance with the forms prescribed by law, unless any assembly should disturb the public peace and not immediately disperse after the articles of the Statute Book relating to riots have been read out aloud three times by the civil authority.

Sec. 100. There shall be liberty of the Press. No person may be punished for any writing, whatever its contents, which he has caused to be printed or published, unless he willfully and manifestly has either himself shown or incited others to disobedience to the laws, contempt of religion or morality or the constitutional powers, or resistance to their orders, or has advanced false and defamatory accusations against anyone. Everyone shall be free to speak his mind frankly on the administration of the State and on any other subject whatsoever.

Sec. 101. New and permanent privileges implying restrictions on the freedom of trade and industry must not in future be granted to anyone.

Sec. 102. Search of private homes shall not be made except in criminal cases.

Sec. 103. Asylum for the protection of debtors shall not be granted to such persons as hereafter become bankrupt.

Sec. 104. Forfeiture of lands and goods shall be abolished.

Sec. 105. If the welfare of the State requires that any person shall surrender his movable or immovable property for the public use, he shall receive full compensation from the Treasury.

Sec. 106. The purchase money, as well as the revenues of the landed property constituting ecclesiastical benefices, shall be applied solely to the benefit of the clergy and to the promotion of education. The property of charitable institutions shall be applied solely for their own benefit.

Sec. 107. Allodial right and the right of primogeniture shall not be abolished. The specific conditions under which these rights shall continue for the greatest benefit of the State and to the best advantage of the rural population shall be determined by the first or second subsequent Storting.

Sec. 108. No earldoms, baronies, entailed estates or fideicommissa may be created in the future.

Sec. 109. Every citizen of the State is as a general rule equally bound to defend the Country for a certain length of time, without any regard to birth or fortune.

The application of this principle, and the restrictions to which it shall be subject, shall be determined by law.

Sec. 110. It is incumbent on the authorities of the State to create conditions which make it possible for every person who is able to work to earn his living by work.

Sec. 111. The form and the colors of the Norwegian Flag shall be determined by law.

Sec. 112. If experience shows that any part of the Constitution of the Kingdom of Norway ought to be changed, a proposal to this effect shall be submitted to the first, second or third ordinary Storting after a General Election and be publicly announced in print. But it shall be left to the first, second and third ordinary Storting after the following General Election to decide whether or not the proposed amendment shall be adopted. Such amendment must never, however, contradict the principles embodied in this Constitution, but merely relate to modifications of particular provisions which do not alter the spirit of the Constitution, and such amendment requires that two thirds of the members of the Storting agree thereto.

An amendment of the Constitution adopted in the aforesaid manner shall be signed by the President and the Secretary of the Storting, and be sent to the King for public announcement in print, as an applicable provision of the Constitution of the Kingdom of Norway.

DECLARATION OF SENTIMENTS (1848)

In the United States the movement for women's rights generally, and for women's suffrage specifically, grew out of the antislavery movement of the 1830s and 1840s. Women working publicly for the abolition of slavery grew conscious of their own limited legal, civil, and social status; they were denied the right to vote and to hold public office, denied equal access to education, denied admittance to the legal profession and other professions, denied full rights to property, and denied many other rights and privileges enjoyed by men.

In 1848 two of the leading women's rights crusaders of the day—Lucretia Mott and Elizabeth Cady Stanton—organized the first convention devoted to the issue. Held at Seneca Falls, New York, July 19–20, the convention launched the modern women's rights movement. The Declaration of Sentiments, read to the delegates by Stanton, was modeled after the Declaration of Independence and was based on the notion of natural rights. It was a succinct indictment of the laws and customs of the time. The declaration was signed by sixty-eight women and thirty-two men in attendance.

The women's rights movement grew steadily in the decades following the Seneca Falls Convention. Similar conventions proliferated in the 1850s, and in 1869 two organizations were founded: the National Woman Suffrage Association, by Stanton and Susan B. Anthony; and the American Woman Suffrage Association, by Lucy Stone and Julia Ward Howe. The leaders of the movement focused primarily on obtaining for women the right to vote, believing that other forms of discrimination would be more easily overcome by wielding the power of the vote.

The suffrage movement met not only calculated resistance—from political parties and economic interests wary of how women's votes would affect them—but passive resistance from traditional customs and attitudes. In the United States, women's suffrage was not achieved until passage of the 19th Amendment to the Constitution, in the wake of World War I, in 1920. And, as the leaders of the movement had predicted, the power of the vote brought about a larger measure of equality in other aspects of life in the decades that followed.

When, in the course of human events, it becomes necessary for one portion of the family of man to assume among the people of the earth a position different from that which they have hitherto occupied, but one to which the laws of nature and of nature's God entitle them, a decent respect to the opinions of mankind requires that they should declare the causes that impel them to such a course.

We hold these truths to be self-evident; that all men and women are created equal; that they are endowed by their Creator with certain inalienable rights; that among these are life, liberty, and the pursuit of happiness; that to secure these rights governments are instituted, deriving their just powers from the consent of the governed. Whenever any form of Government becomes destructive of these ends, it is the right of those who suffer from it to refuse allegiance to it, and to insist upon the institution of a new government, laying its foundation on such principles, and organizing its powers in such form as to them shall seem most likely to effect their safety and happiness. Prudence, indeed, will dictate that governments long established should not be changed for light and transient causes; and accordingly, all experience hath shown that mankind are more disposed to suffer, while evils are sufferable, than to right themselves, by abolishing the forms to which they are accustomed. But when a long train of abuses and usurpations, pursuing invariably the same object, evinces a design to reduce them under absolute despotism, it is their duty to throw off such government, and to provide new guards for their future security. Such has been the patient sufferance of the women under this government, and such is now the necessity which constrains them to demand the equal station to which they are entitled.

The history of mankind is a history of repeated injuries and usurpations on the part of man toward woman, having in direct object the establishment of an absolute tyranny over her. To prove this, let facts be submitted to a candid world.

He has never permitted her to exercise her inalienable right to the elective franchise.

He has compelled her to submit to laws, in the formation of which she had no voice.

He has withheld from her rights which are given to the most ignorant and degraded men—both natives and foreigners.

Having deprived her of this first right of a citizen, the elective franchise, thereby leaving her without representation in the halls of legislation, he has oppressed her on all sides.

He has made her, if married, in the eye of the law, civilly dead.

He has taken from her all right in property, even to the wages she earns.

He has made her, morally, an irresponsible being, as she can commit many crimes with impunity, provided they be done in the presence of her husband. In the covenant of marriage, she is compelled to promise obedience to her husband, he becoming, to all intents and purposes, her master—the law giving him power to deprive her of her liberty, and to administer chastisement.

He has so framed the laws of divorce, as to what shall be the proper causes of divorce; in case of separation, to whom the guardianship of the children shall be given, as to be wholly regardless of the happiness of women—the law, in all cases, going upon the false supposition of the supremacy of man, and giving all power into his hands.

After depriving her of all rights as a married woman, if single and the owner of property, he has taxed her to support a government which recognizes her only when her property can be made profitable to it.

He has monopolized nearly all the profitable employments, and from those she is permitted to follow, she receives but a scanty remuneration.

He closes against her all the avenues to wealth and distinction, which he considers most honorable to himself. As a teacher of theology, medicine, or law, she is not known.

He has denied her the facilities for obtaining a thorough education—all colleges being closed against her.

He allows her in Church as well as State, but a subordinate position, claiming Apostolic authority for her exclusion from the ministry, and, with some exceptions, from any public participation in the affairs of the Church.

He has created a false public sentiment, by giving to the world a different code of morals for men and women, by which moral delinquencies which exclude women from society, are not only tolerated but deemed of little account in man.

He has usurped the prerogative of Jehovah himself, claiming it as his right to assign for her a sphere of action, when that belongs to her conscience and her God.

He has endeavored, in every way that he could to destroy her confidence in her own powers, to lessen her self-respect, and to make her willing to lead a dependent and abject life.

Now, in view of this entire disfranchisement of one-half the people of this country, their social and religious degradation,—in view of the unjust laws above mentioned, and because women do feel themselves aggrieved, oppressed, and fraudulently deprived of their most sacred rights, we insist that they have immediate admission to all the rights and privileges which belong to them as citizens of these United States.

In entering upon the great work before us, we anticipate no small amount of misconception, misrepresentation, and ridicule; but we shall use every instrumentality within our power to effect our object. We shall employ agents, circulate tracts, petition the State and national Legislatures, and endeavor to enlist the pulpit and the press in our behalf. We hope this Convention will be followed by a series of Conventions, embracing every part of the country.

Firmly relying upon the final triumph of the Right and the True, we do this day affix our signatures to this declaration.

Signers of the Declaration of Sentiments
Seneca Falls, New York, July 19–20, 1848

Barker, Caroline
Barker, Eunice
Barker, William G.
Bonnel, Rachel D. (Mitchell)
Bunker, Joel D.
Burroughs, William
Capron, E.W.
Chamberlain, Jacob P.
Conklin, Elizabeth
Conklin, Mary
Culvert, P.A.
Davis, Cynthia
Dell, Thomas
Dell, William S.
Doty, Elias J.
Doty, Susan R.
Douglass, Frederick
Drake, Julia Ann
Eaton, Harriet Cady
Foote, Elisha
Foote, Eunice Newton
Frink, Mary Ann
Fuller, Cynthia
Gibbs, Experience
Gilbert, Mary
Gild, Lydia
Hallowell, Sarah
Hallowell, Mary H.
Hatley, Henry
Hoffman, Sarah
Hoskins, Charles L.
Hunt, Jane C.
Hunt, Richard P.
Jenkins, Margaret
Jones, John
Jones, Lucy
King, Phebe
Latham, Hannah J.
Latham, Lovina
Leslie, Elizabeth
Martin, Eliza
Martin, Mary
Mathews, Delia
Mathews, Dorothy
Mathews, Jacob
McClintock, Elizabeth W.
McClintock, Mary
McClintock, Mary Ann
McClintock, Thomas
Metcalf, Jonathan

Milliken, Nathan J.
Mirror, Mary S.
Mosher, Pheobe
Mosher, Sarah A.
Mott, James
Mott, Lucretia
Mount, Lydia
Paine, Catharine C.
Palmer, Rhoda
Phillips, Saron
Pitcher, Sally
Plant, Hannah
Porter, Ann

Post, Amy
Pryor, George W.
Pryor, Margaret
Quinn, Susan
Race, Rebecca
Ridley, Martha
Schooley, Azaliah
Schooley, Margaret
Scott, Deborah
Segur, Antoinette E.
Seymour, Henry
Seymour, Henry W.
Seymour, Malvina

Shaw, Catharine
Shear, Stephen
Sisson, Sarah
Smallbridge, Robert
Smith, Elizabeth D.
Smith, Sarah
Spalding, David
Spalding, Lucy
Stanton, Elizabeth Cady
Stebbins, Catharine F.
Taylor, Sophronia
Tewksbury, Betsey
Tillman, Samuel D.

Underhill, Edward F.
Underhill, Martha
Vail, Mary E.
Van Tassel, Isaac
Whitney, Sarah
Wilbur, Maria E.
Williams, Justin
Woods, Sarah R.
Woodward, Charlotte
Woodworth, S.E.
Wright, Martha C.

CONSTITUTION OF ARGENTINA (1853)

Argentina emerged from 300 years of Spanish colonial rule on July 9, 1816, when representatives from several provinces meeting at Tucumán declared the independence of the United Provinces of the River Platte. The Congress of Tucumán drafted a constitution in 1819 creating a highly centralized state, but the provinces, under the rule of local chieftains called caudillos, rejected the constitution. Civil war among the caudillos flared intermittently for the next three decades.

Buenos Aires, the strongest of the provinces by virtue of its port facility and the revenue that the port generated, gradually gained effective control over the other provinces during the rule of Juan Manuel de Rosas. Elected governor of Buenos Aires in 1829 and reelected in 1835, Rosas was politically affiliated with the forces for provincial autonomy, but his economic policies served to tie Buenos Aires with the merchants, landowners, and herdsmen of the interior provinces. By the mid-1830s Buenos Aires had obtained the authority to represent the interior provinces in financial and foreign policy matters.

By 1851 the other Argentine coastal provinces were being squeezed economically by the dominance of Buenos Aires. The governor of Entre Ríos, Justo José de Urquiza, led a rebellion, in alliance with Brazil and Uruguay, that forced Rosas to flee the country in February 1852.

Urquiza called for a constituent assembly to draft a federal constitution for the Argentine state. The economic integration of the interior and coastal provinces had developed to such an extent that political integration was widely, though not universally, accepted. The constitution, modeled closely on that of the United States, was promulgated May 1, 1853. Buenos Aires, fearing that its predominant role would be eclipsed under the constitution, alone among the fourteen Argentine provinces refused to ratify it. Finally in 1862, after a long period of civil strife, Buenos Aires joined the state.

The federal character of the U.S. Constitution found favor in Argentina because the Argentine provinces shared with the U.S. states an aversion to strong central government. The separation of powers at the federal level among the executive, legislative, and judicial branches was also copied from the U.S. document with few alterations, as were the procedural aspects of their election and interaction.

The constitution of 1853 has proved resilient in the face of periodic domestic political instability. Amended in 1860, 1866, and 1898, it was supplanted in 1949 by a new constitution promulgated under President Juan Domingo Perón. After Perón's overthrow in 1955, the constitution of 1853 was reinstituted in 1957 with amendments. The constitution was further challenged by military coups and military juntas in 1962, 1966–1973, and 1976–1983. In all cases, however, the military selectively ignored rather than abolished the 1853 constitution, which remains in effect today.

Preamble

We, the representatives of the people of the Argentine Nation, assembled in General Constituent Congress by the will and election of the Provinces which compose it, in fulfillment of pre-existing pacts, with the object of constituting a national union, ensuring justice, preserving domestic peace, providing for the common defense, promoting the general welfare, and securing the blessings of liberty to ourselves, to our posterity, and to all men in the world who wish to dwell on Argentine soil: invoking the protection of God, source of all reason and justice, do ordain, decree, and establish this Constitution for the Argentine Nation.

First Part
DECLARATIONS, RIGHTS, AND GUARANTEES

ART. 1. The Argentine Nation adopts for its government the federal, republican, representative form, as established by the present Constitution.

ART. 2. The Federal Government supports the Roman Catholic Apostolic Faith.

ART. 3. The authorities who direct the Federal Government shall reside in the city that is declared the capital of the Republic by a special law of Congress, after cession made by one or more provincial legislatures of the territory to be federalized.

ART. 4. The Federal Government provides for the expenditures of the Nation with the funds of the National Treasury, formed with the proceeds of export and import duties; with those from the sale or lease of lands of national property; with the post office revenue; with whatever other taxes shall be equitable and proportionally imposed upon the population by the General Congress; and by whatever loans and credit operations shall be decreed by the same Congress for national emergencies or for undertakings of national utility.

ART. 5. Each Province shall adopt for itself a constitution under the republican, representative system, in accordance with the principles, declarations, and guarantees of the National Constitution, ensuring its administration of justice, municipal government, and elementary education. Under these conditions, the Federal Government guarantees to each Province the enjoyment and exercise of its institutions.

ART. 6. The Federal Government may intervene in the territory of a Province in order to guarantee the republican form of government or to repel foreign invasions, and at the request of its constituted authorities, to support or reestablish them, should they have been deposed by sedition or invasion from another Province.

ART. 7. The public acts and judicial proceedings of one Province enjoy full faith in the others; and Congress may, by general laws, determine what shall be the probative form of these acts and proceedings, and the legal effects which they shall produce.

ART. 8. The citizens of each Province enjoy all the rights, privileges, and immunities inherent in the status of citizens in the others. The extradition of criminals is a reciprocal obligation among all the Provinces.

ART. 9. Throughout the territory of the Nation there shall be no other custom house than the national ones, in which the tariffs sanctioned by the Congress shall be in force.

ART. 10. The circulation of goods of national production or manufacture is free from duties in the interior of the Republic, as is also that of goods and merchandise of all kinds dispatched through the national custom houses.

ART. 11. Articles of national or foreign production or manufacture, as well as livestock of all kinds, that may pass through the territory of one Province to another, shall be free from so-called transit duties, as likewise the vehicles, ships or beasts in or on which they are transported; and no other duty, whatever its name may be, shall be imposed on them by reason of their passing through the territory.

ART. 12. Ships bound from one Province to another shall not be obliged to enter, anchor, or pay duties by reason of transit; it being not allowed in any case whatsoever to grant preferences to any one port in respect to another, by means of trading laws or regulations.

ART. 13. New Provinces may be admitted into the Nation; but a Province cannot be established in the territory of another or others, nor one formed from several, without the consent of the legislatures of the interested Provinces and of the Congress.

ART. 14. All inhabitants of the Nation enjoy the following rights, in accordance with the laws that regulate their exercise, namely: working in and practicing any lawful industry; of navigating and trading; of petitioning the authorities; of entering, remaining in, travelling through, and leaving Argentine territory; of publishing their ideas through the press without previous censorship; of using and disposing of their property; of associating for useful purposes; of freely professing their religion; of teaching and learning.

Labor in its several forms shall enjoy the protection of the law, which shall ensure to workers: dignified and equitable working conditions; a limited working day; paid days of rest and vacations; fair remuneration; a flexible minimum essential wage; equal pay for equal work; a share in the earnings of enterprises, with control of production and collaboration in management; protection against arbitrary discharge; stability of public employment; free and democratic organization of labor unions, recognized by simple inscription in a special register.

Trade unions are hereby guaranteed: the right to conclude collective labor agreements; the right to resort to conciliation and arbitration; the right to strike. Union representatives shall enjoy the guarantees necessary for carrying out their union tasks and those relating to the stability of their employment.

The State shall grant the benefits of social security, which shall be complete and irrenounceable. In particular, the States shall establish: compulsory social security, which shall be in charge of national or provincial entities with financial and economic autonomy, administered by the interested parties with participation of the State, but there can be no overlapping of contributions; flexible retirement pay and pensions; full protection of the family; protection of the family welfare; economic compensation to families and access to decent housing.

ART. 15. In the Argentine Nation there are no slaves; the few that exist today are free from the promulgation of this Constitution; and a special law shall regulate whatever indemnifications this declaration may give rise to. Any contract for the purchase or sale of persons is a crime for which those committing it, and the notary or official authorizing it, shall be responsible. And slaves, by whatever manner they may be introduced, shall be free by the mere act of setting foot in the territory of the Republic.

ART. 16. The Argentine Nation does not admit prerogatives of blood or birth; in it there are no personal privileges, or titles of nobility. All its inhabitants are equal before the law, and admissible for employment without any other requisite than fitness. Equality is the basis of taxation and of the public burdens.

ART. 17. Property is inviolable, and no inhabitant of the Nation can be deprived thereof except by virtue of a sentence founded on law. Expropriation for reasons of public utility must be authorized by law and previously compensated. Congress alone imposes the taxes mentioned in Article 4. No personal service can be required except by virtue of a law or sentence based on law. All authors or inventors are exclusive proprietors of their work, invention, or discovery for the term granted them by law. The confiscation of property is stricken out forever from the Argentine Penal Code. No armed body may make requisitions, or demand assistance of any kind.

ART. 18. No inhabitant of the Nation may be punished without previous trial, based on an earlier law than the date of the offense, nor tried by special commissions, nor removed from the judges designated by law before the date of the offense. No one can be compelled to testify against himself, nor be arrested except by virtue of a written order from a competent authority. The defense, by trial, of the person and of rights is inviolable. The residence is inviolable, as are letters, correspondence and private papers; and a law shall determine in what cases and for what reasons their search and seizure shall be allowed. The penalty of death for political offenses, all kinds of torture, and flogging, are forever abolished. The prisons of the Nation shall be healthy and clean, for the security and not for the punishment of the prisoners confined therein; and any measure that under pretext of precaution inflicts on them punishment beyond the demands of security, shall render liable the judge who authorizes it.

ART. 19. The private actions of men that in no way offend public order or morality, nor injure a third party, are reserved only to God and are exempt from the authority of the magistrates. No inhabitant of the Nation shall be obliged to do what the law does not command nor be deprived of what it does not forbid.

ART. 20. Foreigners enjoy in the territory of the Nation all of the civil rights of a citizen; they may engage in their industry, commerce or profession; own real property, purchase it and alienate it; navigate the rivers and coasts; freely practice their religion; make wills and marry in accordance with the laws. They are not obliged to assume citizenship nor to pay forced extraordinary taxes. They may obtain naturalization by residing two continuous years in the Nation; but the authorities may shorten this term in favor of anyone so requesting, on asserting and proving services to the Republic.

ART. 21. Every Argentine citizen is obliged to bear arms in defense of his country and of this Constitution, in accordance with such laws as the Congress may enact for the purpose and with decrees of the National Executive. Citizens by naturalization are free to render this service or not for a period of ten years counting from the date on which they obtain their citizenship papers.

ART. 22. The people do not deliberate or govern except through their representatives and authorities created by this Constitution. Any armed force or meeting of persons assuming the rights of the people and petitioning in the latter's name, commits the crime of sedition.

ART. 23. In the event of internal disorder or foreign attack endangering the operation of this Constitution and of the authorities created thereby, the Province or territory in which the disturbance of order exists shall be declared in a state of siege and the constitutional guarantees shall be suspended therein. But during such suspension the President of the Republic shall not convict or apply punishment upon his own authority. His power shall be limited, in such a case, with respect to persons, to arresting them or transferring them from one point of the Nation to another, if they do not prefer to leave Argentine territory.

ART. 24. The Congress shall promote the improvement of existing legislation in all its branches, and the establishment of trials by juries.

ART. 25. The Federal Government shall encourage European immigration; and may not restrict, limit, or burden with any tax whatsoever, the entrance into Argentine territory of foreigners who arrive for the purpose of tilling the soil, improving industries, and introducing and teaching the arts and sciences.

ART. 26. Navigation of the inland rivers of the Nation is free to all flags, subject only to regulations that are enacted by the national authority.

ART. 27. The Federal Government is bound to strengthen its relations of peace and commerce with foreign powers, by means of treaties that are in conformity with the principles of public law laid down by this Constitution.

ART. 28. The principles, guarantees, and rights recognized in the foregoing articles may not be altered by the laws that regulate their exercise.

ART. 29. Congress may not confer on the National Executive, nor the provincial Legislatures on the provincial Governors extraordinary powers, nor the whole of the public authority, nor grant them acts of submission or supremacy whereby the lives, the honor, or the property of Argentinians will be at the mercy of governments or any person whatsoever. Acts of this nature shall be utterly void, and shall render those who formulate or consent to them or sign them liable to be called to account and to be punished as infamous traitors to their country.

ART. 30. The Constitution may be amended entirely or in any of its parts. The necessity of amendment must be declared by the Congress by a vote of at least two thirds of the members; but it shall not be effected except by a convention called for the purpose.

ART. 31. The Constitution, the laws of the Nation enacted by the Congress in pursuance thereof, and treaties with foreign powers are the supreme law of the Nation; and the authorities in every Province are bound thereby, notwithstanding any provision to the contrary which the provincial laws or constitutions may contain, excepting, for the Province of Buenos Aires, the treaties ratified following the Pact of November 11, 1859.

ART. 32. The Federal Congress shall not enact laws that restrict the freedom of the press or that establish federal jurisdiction over it.

ART. 33. The declarations, rights, and guarantees that the Constitution enumerates shall not be construed as a denial of other rights and guarantees not enumerated, but which rise from the principle of the sovereignty of the people and from the republican form of government.

ART. 34. The judges of the federal courts cannot at the same time hold an office in the provincial courts, nor does the federal service, whether civil or military, give a right of residence in the Province in which it is performed unless it is where the employee habitually resides, this provision being understood as pertaining to the right of obtaining employment in the Province in which he temporarily resides.

ART. 35. The designations successively adopted from 1810 up to the present, namely: "United Provinces of the River Platte," "Argentine Republic," "Argentine Confederation," shall henceforth be official names indiscriminately for the designation of the government and territory of the Provinces, the words "Argentine Nation" being used in the enactment and sanction of the laws.

Second Part

AUTHORITIES OF THE NATION

TITLE 1. Federal Government
FIRST SECTION. The Legislative Power

ART. 36. A Congress consisting of two Chambers, one of Deputies of the Nation and the other of Senators of the Provinces and of the Capital shall be vested with the Legislative Power of the Nation.

Chapter I. The Chamber of Deputies

ART. 37. The Chamber of Deputies shall consist of representatives elected directly by the people of the Provinces and of the Capital, which for this purpose are considered as electoral districts of a single State, and by a simple plurality of votes.

The number of representatives shall be one for every 33,000 inhabitants or fraction no smaller than 16,500. After the completion of each census the Congress shall determine the representation in accordance with the census referred to, being able to increase but not to decrease the basis indicated for each Deputy.

ART. 38. The Deputies for the first legislative session shall be appointed in the following proportion: for the Province of Buenos Aires, twelve; for that of Cordoba, six; for that of Catamarca, three; for that of Corrientes, four; for that of Entre Ríos, two; for that of Jujuy, two; for that of Mendoza, three; for that of La Rioja, two; for that of Salta, three; for that of Santiago, four; for that of San Juan, two; for that of Santa Fe, two; for that of San Luis, two; for that of Tucuman, three.

ART. 39. For the second legislative session a general census shall be taken and the number of Deputies shall then be arranged according thereto; but this census can be renewed only every ten years.

ART. 40. To be a Deputy it is necessary to have attained the age of twenty-five years, to have been four years a fully qualified citizen; and to be a native of the Province that elects him or to have had two years of immediately preceding residence therein.

ART. 41. For this time, the legislatures of the Provinces shall regulate the means by which the direct election of the Deputies of the Nation shall take place; for the future, the Congress shall enact a general law.

ART. 42. Deputies shall continue in office for four years and may be re-elected; but the Chamber shall be renewed by half every two years; to this end those named for the first Legislature, as soon as they meet, shall draw lots for those who must retire after the first period.

ART. 43. In case of vacancy, the Government of the Province or of the Capital shall order the legal election of a new member.

ART. 44. The initiative of laws relating to taxes and the recruiting of troops are exclusive functions of the Chamber of Deputies.

ART. 45. The Chamber of Deputies exclusively has the power to impeach before the Senate: The President, the Vice President, their Ministers, and the members of the Supreme Court and other lower courts of the Nation, in such cases of responsibility as are brought against them by reason of malfeasance or crime committed in exercise of their offices, or for common crimes, after a hearing and a declaration by two thirds of the members present that there are grounds for the proceeding.

Chapter II. The Senate

ART. 46. The Senate shall be composed of two Senators from each Province, elected by their legislatures by a plurality of votes; and two from the Capital, elected in the manner prescribed for the election of the President of the Nation. Each Senator shall have one vote.

ART. 47. The requirements to be elected Senator are: to have attained the age of thirty years, to have been six years a citizen of the Nation, to have an annual income of two thousand pesos or equivalent salary, and to be a native of the Province that elects him or to have had two years immediately preceding residence therein.

ART. 48. Senators serve for a term of nine years and may be re-elected indefinitely; but the Senate shall be renewed by thirds every three years, deciding by drawing lots, once assembled, those who must retire after the first and second three-year periods.

ART. 49. The Vice President of the Nation shall be President of the Senate, but shall have no vote except in the case of a tie in the balloting.

ART. 50. The Senate shall appoint a provisional president to preside in the event of absence of the Vice President, or when the latter exercises the functions of President of the Nation.

ART. 51. The Senate has the power to judge in public trial the persons impeached by the Chamber of Deputies, and when sitting for that purpose its members shall take an oath. If the person accused is the President of the Nation, the Senate shall be presided over by the President of the Supreme Court. No persons shall be declared guilty except by a majority of two thirds of the members present.

ART. 52. The judgment shall not go further than to remove the accused person from office, and disqualification to hold any office of honor, trust, or salary in the Nation. But the party convicted shall, nevertheless, be subject to indictment, trial, and punishment according to law before the ordinary courts.

ART. 53. It is also within the power of the Senate to authorize the President of the Nation to declare a state of siege in one or several districts of the Republic in case of foreign invasion.

ART. 54. When any vacancy occurs in the Senate through death, resignation or other cause, the government unit which the vacancy affects shall proceed immediately to the election of a new member.

Chapter III. Provisions Common to Both Chambers

ART. 55. Both Chambers shall assemble each year in regular sessions from May 1 until September 30. The President of the Nation may extend the regular sessions or convoke extraordinary sessions.

ART. 56. Each Chamber is the judge of the validity of the election, rights and titles of its members. Neither may meet without an absolute majority of its members; but a lesser number may compel the absent members to attend the sessions, under such terms and penalties as each Chamber may establish.

ART. 57. Both Chambers begin and conclude their sessions simultaneously. Neither of them during the session, shall, without the consent of the other, adjourn its sessions for more than three days.

ART. 58. Each Chamber shall determine the rules of its proceedings, and by a two-thirds vote may punish any one of its members for disorderly conduct in the performance of his duties, or can remove him for physical or moral disability occurring after his admission, and may even expel him from the body; but a majority of one more than half of those present shall be sufficient to decide on voluntary resignations from office.

ART. 59. Senators and Deputies, on assuming office, shall take an oath to faithfully discharge their duties, and to proceed in everything in conformity with the requirements of this Constitution.

ART. 60. No member of Congress may be indicted, judicially questioned, or molested for the opinions expressed or speeches made by him in the performance of his duties as a legislator.

ART. 61. No Senator or Deputy may be arrested, from the day of his election until he ceases in office, except when surprised *in flagrante* in the commission of a capital or other infamous or grave crime, in which case a summary report of the facts shall be made to the appropriate Chamber.

ART. 62. When a written charge is presented before the ordinary courts against any Senator or Deputy, each Chamber, examining the indictment in public trial, may by two thirds of its votes, suspend the accused from his office, and place him at the disposal of the proper court to be judged.

ART. 63. Either of the Chambers may summon the Ministers of the Executive Power to receive such explanations or reports as it may consider necessary.

ART. 64. No member of the Congress shall be appointed by the Executive to any employment or commission, without the previous authorization of the respective Chamber, except for promotions.

ART. 65. Regular members of the clergy cannot be members of Congress, nor may Governors for the Province that they head.

ART. 66. The services of the Senators and Deputies are paid for by the Treasury of the Nation, with the emoluments fixed by law.

Chapter IV. Powers of Congress

ART. 67. The Congress shall have power:

1. To legislate in regard to exterior custom houses and to establish import duties that shall be, as will be the valuations on which they are based, uniform throughout the Nation; it is understood that these and all national taxes may be paid with money that is current in the respective Provinces, at their fair equivalents. To establish also export duties.

2. To levy direct taxes for a specified time and proportionally equal throughout the national territory, whenever the defense, security and the general welfare of the State so require.

3. To borrow money on the credit of the Nation.

4. To provide for the use and disposition of the national lands.

5. To establish and regulate a National Bank in the capital, and its branches in the Provinces, with power to issue banknotes.

6. To arrange payment of the domestic and foreign debt of the Nation.

7. To fix annually the budget of expenditures for the administration of the Nation, and to approve or disapprove the accounts of disbursements.

8. To grant subsidies from the National Treasury to those Provinces whose revenues, according to their budgets, are insufficient to meet their ordinary expenses.

9. To regulate the free navigation of internal rivers, to open the ports it shall consider necessary, and to create or close custom houses, but never to close exterior custom houses already existing in each Province at the time of incorporation.

10. To coin money, to regulate its value and that of foreign moneys, and to adopt a uniform system of weights and measures for the whole Nation.

11. To enact the civil, commercial, penal, mining, labor, and social security codes, such codes not to alter jurisdictions, their execution belonging to the federal or provincial courts, depending on which jurisdiction the persons or things come under; and especially general laws of naturalization and citizenship for the whole Nation, based on the principle of citizenship by birth; as well as on bankruptcy, counterfeiting of current money and public documents of the States; and those that may be required to establish trial by jury.

12. To regulate maritime and land trade with foreign nations, and that of the Provinces among themselves.

13. To establish and regulate post offices and a general mail service for the Nation.

14. To settle permanently the boundaries of the national territory, to fix those of the Provinces, to create new ones, and to determine, by special legislation, the organization, administration, and government of the national territories remaining outside the boundaries assigned to the Provinces.

15. To provide for the security of the frontiers; to maintain peaceful relations with the Indians, and to promote their conversion to Catholicism.

16. To provide whatever is conducive to the prosperity of the country, to the progress and welfare of all the Provinces, and for the advancement of learning, enacting programs of general and university instruction, and promoting industry, immigration, the construction of railways and navigable canals, the settlement of government-owned lands, the introduction and establishment of new industries, the importation of foreign capital, and the exploration of the interior rivers, by protective laws and by temporary concessions of privileges and the offering of awards.

17. To establish courts inferior to the Supreme Court of Justice; to create and abolish offices, to fix the duties thereof, to grant pensions, to decree honors, and to grant general amnesties.

18. To accept or reject the reasons for the resignation of the President or Vice President of the Republic, and to declare the necessity for a new election.

19. To approve or reject treaties concluded with other nations and concordats with the Holy See; and to regulate the exercise of ecclesiastical appointments throughout the Nation.

20. To admit into the territory of the Nation other religious orders in addition to those already existing.

21. To authorize the Executive Power to declare war or to make peace.

22. To grant letters of marque and reprisal, and to make rules concerning prizes.

23. To fix the strength of land and naval forces in time of peace and war; and to provide regulations and rules for the government of such forces.

24. To authorize the summoning of the militia in all the Provinces or part of them, whenever the execution of the laws of the Nation may so require, and when necessary to suppress insurrection or repel invasion. To provide for the organization, equipment, and discipline of said militia, and the administration and government of such part of them as are employed in the service of the Nation, leaving to the Provinces the appointment of their respective chiefs and officers, and the duty of establishing in their respective militia the discipline prescribed by Congress.

25. To permit the entry of foreign troops into the territory of the Nation and to allow national troops to leave it.

26. To declare a state of siege in one or several parts of the Nation in case of internal disturbance, and to approve or suspend a state of siege declared by the Executive during a recess of the Congress.

27. To exercise exclusive legislation in the whole territory of the Capital of the Nation and over other places obtained by purchase or cession in any of the Provinces for the establishment of forts, arsenals, magazines, and other establishments of national utility.

28. To enact all laws and regulations that may be necessary to carry out the foregoing powers, and all others granted by the present Constitution to the Government of the Argentine Nation.

Chapter V. Enactment and Approval of Laws

ART. 68. Laws may be initiated in either of the Chambers of the Congress, by bills presented by their members or by the Executive Power, except those relating to the subjects considered in Article 44.

ART. 69. When a bill is approved by the Chamber in which it originated, it is passed on for discussion by the other Chamber. If approved by both, it is sent to the Executive of the Nation for his examination; and if it also obtains his approval, he promulgates it as law.

ART. 70. Every bill is considered approved by the Executive if it is not returned within a period of ten working days.

ART. 71. No bill wholly rejected by either Chamber shall be reintroduced in the sessions of the same year. But if it is only extended or amended by the revising Chamber, it shall be returned to the Chamber of origin; and if the additions or amendments are approved there by an absolute majority, it shall be sent to the Executive of the Nation. If the additions or amendments are rejected, the bill will be returned a second time to the revising Chamber, and if they are again sanctioned by a majority of two thirds of the members, the bill shall be sent to the other Chamber, where the additions and amendments are not considered to be rejected unless by a vote of two thirds of the members present.

ART. 72. A bill rejected wholly or in part by the Executive shall be returned with his objections to the Chamber of its origin; the latter shall discuss it anew and if it is confirmed by a majority of two thirds of the votes, it shall be sent again to the revising Chamber. If both Chambers approve it by such majority, the bill becomes law and is sent to the Executive for promulgation. In all such cases the voting in both Chambers shall be by roll call, by yeas and nays; and both the names and opinions of those voting as well as the objections of the Executive shall be immediately published in the press. If the Chambers disagree in regard to the objections, the bill cannot be reintroduced in the sessions of that year.

ART. 73. In the enactment of laws the following formula shall be used: "The Senate and Chamber of Deputies of the Argentine Nation, assembled in Congress, decree or sanction with the force of law . . ."

SECOND SECTION. The Executive Power

Chapter I. Its Nature and Duration

ART. 74. The Executive Power of the Nation shall be vested in a citizen with the title of "President of the Argentine Nation."

ART. 75. In case of illness, absence from the Capital, death, resignation, or removal of the President, the Executive Power shall be exercised by the Vice President of the Nation. In case of the removal, death, resignation, or disability of the President and the Vice President of the Nation, the Congress shall determine what public official shall act as President until the disability is removed or a new President is elected.

ART. 76. To be elected President or Vice President of the Nation, it is necessary to have been born in Argentine territory, or if born in a foreign country to be the son of a native-born citizen; to belong to the Roman Catholic Apostolic Church, and to possess the other qualifications to be elected a Senator.

ART. 77. The President and Vice President hold their offices for a term of six years; and they may not be re-elected except after an interval of one term.

ART. 78. The President of the Nation ceases in his authority on the same day on which his term of six years expires; no event that may have interrupted it shall be reason for completing the term later.

ART. 79. The President and Vice President receive for their services a compensation paid from the treasury of the Nation, which cannot be altered during their term of office. During their terms of office they may not hold any other office or receive any other emolument from the Nation or from a province.

ART. 80. On assuming office, the President and Vice President shall take the following oath administered by the President of the Senate (for the first time, the President of the Constituent Assembly), before the assembled Congress: "I, N.N., do swear before God, our Lord, and these Holy Gospels, to perform with loyalty and patriotism the office of President (or Vice President) of the Argentine Nation. Should I not do so, may God and the Nation call me to account."

Chapter II. Manner and Time of the Election of the President and Vice President of the Nation

ART. 81. The election of the President and Vice President of the Nation shall be made in the following manner: the Capital and each of the provinces shall choose by direct vote a board of electors equal to double the total of Senators and Deputies they send to Congress, with the same qualifications and under the same form prescribed for the election of Deputies.

Deputies, Senators, or salaried employees of the Federal Government may not be electors.

Four months before the expiration of the term of the retiring President, the electors for the Capital of the Nation and in the respective provinces shall meet and proceed to elect a President and Vice President of the Nation by signed ballots, stating on one the person for whom they vote for President and on another the one for whom they vote for Vice President.

Two lists shall be made of all persons named for President and two others of those named for Vice President, with the number of votes that each one of them has received. These lists shall be signed by the electors and two of them closed and sealed (one of each class) shall be sent to the president of the municipality, in whose registers they shall remain deposited and closed; and the other two to the President of the Senate (the first time, to the President of the Constituent Congress).

ART. 82. The President of the Senate (the first time, the President of the Constituent Congress), assembling all the lists, shall open them in the presence of both Chambers. The Secretaries, assisted by four members of Congress chosen by lot, shall proceed immediately with the count and announce the number of votes in favor of each candidate for the Presidency and Vice Presidency of the Nation. Whoever in each case receives an absolute majority of all the votes shall be proclaimed immediately President and Vice President.

ART. 83. In the event that by the division of the vote no absolute majority has been obtained, Congress shall choose between the two persons who have obtained the highest number of votes. Should the first majority have favored more than two persons, Congress shall choose from among all of them. Should the first majority pertain to only one person, and the second to two or more persons, Congress shall choose from among all persons who obtained the first and second majorities.

ART. 84. This election shall be made by an absolute majority and by signed ballots. If, after the first ballot, no person has an absolute majority, a vote shall be taken for the second time, limiting the balloting to the two persons who had obtained the highest number of votes on the first ballot. In case of a tie vote, the balloting shall be repeated, and in case of a new tie, the President of the Senate shall decide (the first time, the President of the Constituent Congress). The count cannot be taken nor the elections ratified unless three fourths of the total membership of Congress are present.

ART. 85. The election of President and Vice President of the Nation must be concluded at a single session of the Congress, and the results thereof, as well as the electoral proceedings, are to be made public through the press.

Chapter III. Powers of the Executive

ART. 86. The President of the Nation has the following powers:

1. He is the supreme Head of the Nation and has in his charge the general administration of the country.

2. He issues the instructions and regulations that may be necessary for the execution of the laws of the Nation, being careful not to alter their spirit by exceptions in the regulations.

3. He is the immediate and local Head of the Capital of the Nation.

4. He participates in the enactment of the laws according to the Constitution, and approves and promulgates them.

5. He appoints, with the consent of the Senate, the magistrates of the Supreme Court and of the other, lower federal courts.

6. He may grant pardons or commute punishment for crimes subject to the federal jurisdiction, based on a report by the appropriate court, except in cases of impeachment by the Chamber of Deputies.

7. He may grant pensions, retirements, leaves of absence, and enjoyment of death benefits in accordance with the laws of the Nation.

8. He exercises his rights of ecclesiastical appointments by selecting bishops for the cathedrals, from three names proposed by the Senate.

9. He approves or withholds applications of the decrees of the councils, bulls, briefs, and rescripts of the Supreme Pontiff of Rome, with the consent of the Supreme Court, a law being required if they contain general and permanent provisions.

10. He appoints and removes Ministers Plenipotentiary and chargés d'affaires, with the consent of the Senate; and by himself appoints and removes his Cabinet Ministers, the officials of their Departments, consular agents, and other employees of the administration whose appointment is not regulated otherwise by this Constitution.

11. He presides annually at the opening of the sessions of Congress, both Chambers being assembled for this purpose in the hall of the Senate, giving on this occasion a report on the state of the Nation to the Congress, on reforms promised by the Constitution, and recommending to their consideration the measures that he deems necessary and expedient.

12. He extends the regular sessions of Congress, or convokes it in extraordinary session, when some grave interest of order or progress requires it.

13. He causes the revenues of the Nation to be collected, and decrees their disbursement according to law or according to the budgets, of national expenditures.

14. He concludes and signs treaties of peace, of commerce, of navigation, of alliance, of boundaries, and of neutrality, concordats and other agreements required for the mainte-

nance of good relations with foreign powers; he receives their ministers and admits their consuls.

15. He is Commander-in-Chief of all the land and naval forces of the Nation.

16. He appoints the military officers of the Nation; with the consent of the Senate for the higher offices and ranks of the army and navy; and by himself, on the field of battle.

17. He disposes of the military and naval forces and attends to their organization and distribution, according to the necessities of the Nation.

18. He declares war and grants letters of marque and reprisal, with the authorization and approval of Congress.

19. He declares, with the consent of the Senate, one or more districts of the Nation in a state of siege for a limited period in the event of foreign attack. In the event of internal disorder, he has this power only when the Congress is in recess, since this is a power belonging to that body. The President exercises this power under the limitations prescribed in Article 23.

20. He may ask for whatever information he may consider proper from the chiefs of all branches and departments of the administration, and through them, from other employees, and they are required to give such information.

21. He cannot leave the territory of the Capital without the permission of Congress. During the recess of the latter, he may do so without permission only on serious grounds of public service.

22. The President shall have the power to fill vacancies in office that require the consent of the Senate, which occur while it is in recess, by means of temporary appointments to expire at the end of the next legislative session.

Chapter IV. Ministers of the Executive Branch

ART. 87. Eight Ministers, Secretaries of State, shall have in their charge the handling of the business of the Nation and shall legalize the acts of the President with their signatures, which requirement is necessary if they are to be valid. A special law shall delimit the business of the respective offices of the Ministers.

ART. 88. Each Minister is responsible for the acts he legalizes; and is jointly responsible for those in which he concurs with his colleagues.

ART. 89. Ministers may not, in any case, make decisions on their own account, except with regard to matters concerning the economic and administrative conduct of their respective departments.

ART. 90. Once the Congress has opened its sessions, the Ministers of the Cabinet shall submit a detailed report on the state of the Nation in connection with the business of their respective departments.

ART. 91. They may not be Senators or Deputies unless they resign their office as Minister.

ART. 92. The Ministers may attend the sessions of Congress and take part in their debates, but may not vote.

ART. 93. They shall receive for their services a salary established by law, which cannot be increased or diminished in favor of or to the detriment of the incumbents of office.

THIRD SECTION. The Judicial Power

Chapter I. Its Nature and Duration

ART. 94. The Judicial Power of the Nation shall be vested in a Supreme Court of Justice and in such lower courts as the Congress may establish in the territory of the Nation.

ART. 95. In no case may the President of the Nation exercise judicial functions, assume jurisdiction over pending cases, or reopen those decided.

ART. 96. The Justices of the Supreme Court and of the lower courts shall hold office during their good behavior, and shall receive for their services a compensation that shall be determined by law and that cannot be decreased in any way during their continuance in office.

ART. 97. No one may be a member of the Supreme Court of Justice unless he is a lawyer of the Nation, with eight years of practice, and possesses the qualifications required to be a Senator.

ART. 98. At the first organization of the Supreme Court, the persons appointed shall take an oath before the President of the Nation, to discharge their duties, administering justice well and faithfully and in conformity with the provisions of the Constitution. In the future they shall take it before the President of the Court itself.

ART. 99. The Supreme Court shall adopt its own internal and fiscal regulations and appoint all its subordinate employees.

Chapter II. Powers of the Judicial Branch

ART. 100. The Supreme Court of Justice and the lower courts of the Nation have jurisdiction over and decide all cases dealing with matters governed by the Constitution and the laws of the Nation, with the exception made in item 11, Article 67; and by treaties with foreign nations; all suits concerning Ambassadors, public Ministers, and foreign consuls; of cases in admiralty and maritime jurisdiction; of suits in which the Nation is a party: of suits between two or more provinces; between one province and the citizens of another; between the citizens of different provinces; and between one province and its citizens against a foreign State or citizen.

ART. 101. In these cases the Supreme Court shall exercise appellate jurisdiction, according to rules and exceptions prescribed by the Congress; but in all matters concerning Ambassadors, Ministers, and foreign consuls, and those in which any province shall be a party, the Court shall exercise original and exclusive jurisdiction.

ART. 102. All ordinary criminal trials, except cases of impeachment admitted by the Chamber of Deputies, shall be concluded by juries as soon as this institution is established in the Nation. The trial of such suits shall be held in the same Province where the crime has been committed; but when it was committed outside the boundaries of the Nation, against international law, the Congress shall determine, by a special law, the place where the trial is to be held.

ART. 103. Treason against the Nation shall consist only in taking up arms against it, or in adhering to its enemies, giving them aid and comfort. The Congress shall fix by a special law the punishment for this crime; but it shall not go beyond the person of the offender nor shall the infamy of the criminal be in any degree transmitted to his relatives of any degree.

TITLE II. Provincial Governments

ART. 104. The provinces retain all powers not delegated by the Constitution to the Federal Government and those expressly reserved by special covenants at the time of their incorporation.

ART. 105. Each province shall have its own local institutions and shall be governed by them. They elect their governors, legislators, and other provincial officials, without intervention of the Federal Government.

ART. 106. Each province enacts its own constitution, as provided in Article 5.

ART. 107. The provinces may, with the knowledge of the Federal Congress, enter into partial treaties for purposes of administration of justice, of economic interests, and works of common utility; and may promote their industry, immigration, railway and canal construction, settlement of lands owned by a province, introduction and establishment of new industries, importation of foreign capital, and exploration of rivers, by laws protecting these purposes and with their own funds.

ART. 108. The provinces do not exercise the power delegated to the Nation. They may not enter into partial treaties of a political character; nor enact laws dealing with commerce, internal or foreign navigation; nor establish provincial custom houses; nor coin money; nor establish banks having note-issuing powers, without authorization from the Federal Congress; nor enact civil, commercial, penal, or mining codes after the Congress shall have enacted them; nor enact special laws regarding citizenship and naturalization, bankruptcy, or counterfeiting of currency or State documents; nor impose tonnage dues; nor arm ships of war or raise armies except in case of foreign invasion or of such imminent danger as not to admit of delay, giving notice immediately to the Federal Government; nor appoint or receive foreign agents; nor admit new religious orders.

ART. 109. No province may declare or wage war against another province. Their claims must be submitted to and decided by the Supreme Court of Justice. Their actual hostilities are acts of civil war, considered as sedition or mutiny, which the Federal Government must suppress and punish in accordance with the law.

ART. 110. The governors of the provinces are the natural agents of the Federal Government for the enforcement of the Constitution and the laws of the Nation.

Done in the Hall of Sessions of the General Constituent Congress, in the City of Santa Fe, the 1st day of May in the year of our Lord 1853.

CONSTITUTION OF JAPAN (1947)

Constitutions generally, as bedrock documents of a political culture, are more than a dispassionate list of individual rights and governing bodies, relationships, and procedures; they are an expression of deeply felt principles derived gradually over centuries concerning the proper organization of society. It is remarkable, then, that the postwar Japanese constitution has proved so durable—having stood almost unchanged for nearly five decades—given that it was imposed by a victorious enemy and that its terms were somewhat foreign to Japanese society and culture.

In the aftermath of World War II, the victorious Allied powers, led principally by the United States, resolved that Japan should become a constitutional democracy. In October 1945 the supreme commander for the Allied powers, Gen. Douglas MacArthur, instructed the Japanese government to draft a new constitution to replace the Meiji Constitution of 1889, under which the emperor had been all-powerful. When the Japanese submitted a draft that was deemed unacceptable by the Far Eastern Commission—the eleven Allied powers' forum for supervising the occupation of Japan—MacArthur had his staff write a constitution. After review by the Far Eastern Commission, the "MacArthur constitution" was submitted to the Japanese emperor and government, who accepted it with only minor modifications. Nominally, the new constitution was promulgated November 3, 1946, as an imperial amendment to the Meiji Constitution and took effect May 3, 1947.

The postwar document was drafted largely on the lines of the British parliamentary system, toward which the Japanese had been gravitating since the 1890s. In fact, many of its features had been present superficially in the Meiji Constitution: both documents made provision for a bicameral legislature, a cabinet, national elections, and the emperor. But the power relationships among them were to change dramatically. The postwar cabinet would answer to the legislature (the Diet), rather than to the emperor; both houses of the legislature (the House of Representatives and the House of Councillors) would be popularly elected, whereas only the lower house had been under Meiji; all national elections would be based on the principle of universal suffrage, whereas prewar suffrage had been severely limited; and, most important, all sovereignty would reside in the people, and the emperor would be no more than a figurehead. Whereas the Meiji Constitution had been a grant from the emperor to the people, the postwar constitution adopted the Western notion of government by consent of the governed. Its specific terms were solidly grounded in the Western notions of democratic, representative government: separation of powers, representation, accountability, procedural stability, and openness.

We, the Japanese people, acting through our duly elected representatives in the National Diet, determined that we shall secure for ourselves and our posterity the fruits of peaceful cooperation with all nations and the blessings of liberty throughout this land, and resolved that never again shall we be visited with the horrors of war through the action of government, do proclaim that sovereign power resides with the people and do firmly establish this Constitution. Government is a sacred trust of the people, the authority for which is derived from the people, the powers of which are exercised by the representatives of the people, and the benefits of which are enjoyed by the people. This is a universal principle of mankind upon which this constitution is founded. We reject and revoke all constitutions, laws, ordinances, and rescripts in conflict herewith.

We, the Japanese people, desire peace for all time and are deeply conscious of the high ideals controlling human relationship, and we have determined to preserve our security and existence, trusting in the justice and faith of the peace-loving peoples of the world. We desire to occupy an honored place in an international society striving for the preservation of peace, and the banishment of tyranny and slavery, oppression and intolerance for all time from the earth. We recognize that all peoples of the world have the right to live in peace, free from fear and want.

We believe that no nation is responsible to itself alone, but that laws of political morality are universal; and that obedience to such laws is incumbent upon all nations who would sustain their own sovereignty and justify their sovereign relationship with other nations.

We, the Japanese people, pledge our national honor to accomplish these high ideals and purposes with all our resources.

Chapter I
THE EMPEROR

ARTICLE 1. The Emperor shall be the symbol of the State and of the unity of the people, deriving his position from the will of the people with whom resides sovereign power.

ARTICLE 2. The Imperial Throne shall be dynastic and succeeded to in accordance with the Imperial House Law passed by the Diet.

ARTICLE 3. The advice and approval of the Cabinet shall be required for all acts of the Emperor in matters of state, and the Cabinet shall be responsible therefor.

ARTICLE 4. The Emperor shall perform only such acts in matters of state as are provided for in this Constitution and he shall not have powers related to government.

The Emperor may delegate the performance of his acts in matters of state as may be provided by law.

ARTICLE 5. When, in accordance with the Imperial House Law, a Regency is established, the Regent shall perform his acts in matters of state in the Emperor's name. In this case, paragraph one of the preceding article will be applicable.

ARTICLE 6. The Emperor shall appoint the Prime Minister as designated by the Diet.

The Emperor shall appoint the Chief Judge of the Supreme Court as designated by the Cabinet.

ARTICLE 7. The Emperor, with the advice and approval of the Cabinet, shall perform the following acts in matters of state on behalf of the people:

Promulgation of amendments of the constitution, laws, cabinet orders and treaties.

Convocation of the Diet.

Dissolution of the House of Representatives.

Proclamation of general election of members of the Diet.

Attestation of the appointment and dismissal of Ministers of State and other officials as provided for by law, and of full powers and credentials of Ambassadors and Ministers.

Attestation of general and special amnesty, commutation of punishment, reprieve, and restoration of rights.

Awarding of honors.

Attestation of instruments of ratification and other diplomatic documents as provided for by law.

Receiving foreign ambassadors and ministers.

Performance of ceremonial functions.

ARTICLE 8. No property can be given to, or received by, the Imperial House, nor can any gifts be made therefrom, without the authorization of the Diet.

Chapter II
RENUNCIATION OF WAR

ARTICLE 9. Aspiring sincerely to an international peace based on justice and order, the Japanese people forever renounce war as a sovereign right of the nation and the threat or use of force as means of settling international disputes.

In order to accomplish the aim of the preceding paragraph, land, sea, and air forces, as well as other war potential, will never be maintained. The right of belligerency of the state will not be recognized.

Chapter III
RIGHTS AND DUTIES OF THE PEOPLE

ARTICLE 10. The conditions necessary for being a Japanese national shall be determined by law.

ARTICLE 11. The people shall not be prevented from enjoying any of the fundamental human rights. These fundamental human rights guaranteed to the people by this Constitution shall be conferred upon the people of this and future generations as eternal and inviolate rights.

ARTICLE 12. The freedoms and rights guaranteed to the people by this Constitution shall be maintained by the constant endeavor of the people, who shall refrain from any abuse of these freedoms and rights and shall always be responsible for utilizing them for the public welfare.

ARTICLE 13. All of the people shall be respected as individuals. Their right to life, liberty, and the pursuit of happiness shall, to the extent that it does not interfere with the public welfare, be the supreme consideration in legislation and in other governmental affairs.

ARTICLE 14. All of the people are equal under the law and there shall be no discrimination in political, economic or social relations because of race, creed, sex, social status or family origin.

Peers and peerage shall not be recognized.

No privilege shall accompany any award of honor, decoration or any distinction, nor shall any such award be valid beyond the lifetime of the individual who now holds or hereafter may receive it.

ARTICLE 15. The people have the inalienable right to choose their public officials and to dismiss them.

All public officials are servants of the whole community and not of any group thereof.

Universal adult suffrage is guaranteed with regard to the election of public officials.

In all elections, secrecy of the ballot shall not be violated. A voter shall not be answerable, publicly or privately, for the choice he has made.

ARTICLE 16. Every person shall have the right of peaceful petition for the redress of damage, for the removal of public officials, for the enactment, repeal or amendment of laws, ordinances or regulations and for other matters; nor shall any person be in any way discriminated against for sponsoring such a petition.

ARTICLE 17. Every person may sue for redress as provided by law from the State or a public entity, in case he has suffered damage through illegal act of any public official.

ARTICLE 18. No person shall be held in bondage of any kind. Involuntary servitude, except as punishment for crime, is prohibited.

ARTICLE 19. Freedom of thought and conscience shall not be violated.

ARTICLE 20. Freedom of religion is guaranteed to all. No religious organization shall receive any privileges from the State, nor exercise any political authority.

No person shall be compelled to take part in any religious act, celebration, rite or practice.

The State and its organs shall refrain from religious education or any other religious activity.

ARTICLE 21. Freedom of assembly and association as well as speech, press and all other forms of expression are guaranteed.

No censorship shall be maintained, nor shall the secrecy of any means of communication be violated.

ARTICLE 22. Every person shall have freedom to choose and change his residence and to choose his occupation to the extent that it does not interfere with the public welfare.

Freedom of all persons to move to a foreign country and to divest themselves of their nationality shall be inviolate.

ARTICLE 23. Academic freedom is guaranteed.

ARTICLE 24. Marriage shall be based only on the mutual consent of both sexes and it shall be maintained through mutual cooperation with the equal rights of husband and wife as a basis.

With regard to choice of spouse, property rights, inheritance, choice of domicile, divorce and other matters pertaining to marriage and the family, laws shall be enacted from the standpoint of individual dignity and the essential equality of the sexes.

ARTICLE 25. All people shall have the right to maintain the minimum standards of wholesome and cultured living.

In all spheres of life, the State shall use its endeavors for the promotion and extension of social welfare and security, and of public health.

ARTICLE 26. All people shall have the right to receive an equal education correspondent to their ability, as provided by law.

All people shall be obligated to have all boys and girls under their protection receive ordinary education as provided for by law. Such compulsory education shall be free.

ARTICLE 27. All people shall have the right and the obligation to work.

Standards for wages, hours, rest and other working conditions shall be fixed by law.

Children shall not be exploited.

ARTICLE 28. The right of workers to organize and to bargain and act collectively is guaranteed.

ARTICLE 29. The right to own or to hold property is inviolable.

Property rights shall be defined by law, in conformity with the public welfare.

Private property may be taken for public use upon just compensation therefor.

ARTICLE 30. The people shall be liable to taxation as provided by law.

ARTICLE 31. No person shall be deprived of life or liberty, nor shall any other criminal penalty be imposed, except according to procedure established by law.

ARTICLE 32. No person shall be denied the right of access to the courts.

ARTICLE 33. No person shall be apprehended except upon warrant issued by a competent judicial officer which specifies the offense with which the person is charged, unless he is apprehended, the offense being committed.

ARTICLE 34. No person shall be arrested or detained without being at once informed of the charges against him or without the immediate privilege of counsel; nor shall he be detained without adequate cause; and upon demand of any person such cause must be immediately shown in open court in his presence and the presence of his counsel.

ARTICLE 35. The right of all persons to be secure in their homes, papers and effects against entries, searches and seizures shall not be impaired except upon warrant issued for adequate cause and particularly describing the place to be searched and things to be seized, or except as provided by Article 33.

Each search or seizure shall be made upon separate warrant issued by a competent judicial officer.

ARTICLE 36. The infliction of torture by any public officer and cruel punishments are absolutely forbidden.

ARTICLE 37. In all criminal cases the accused shall enjoy the right to a speedy and public trial by an impartial tribunal.

He shall be permitted full opportunity to examine all witnesses, and he shall have the right of compulsory process for obtaining witnesses on his behalf at public expense.

At all times the accused shall have the assistance of competent counsel who shall, if the accused is unable to secure the same by his own efforts, be assigned to his use by the State.

ARTICLE 38. No person shall be compelled to testify against himself.

Confession made under compulsion, torture or threat, or after prolonged arrest or detention shall not be admitted in evidence.

No person shall be convicted or punished in cases where the only proof against him is his own confession.

ARTICLE 39. No person shall be held criminally liable for an act which was lawful at the time it was committed, or of which he has been acquitted, nor shall he be placed in double jeopardy.

ARTICLE 40. Any person, in case he is acquitted after he has been arrested or detained, may sue the State for redress as provided by law.

Chapter IV
THE DIET

ARTICLE 41. The Diet shall be the highest organ of state power, and shall be the sole law-making organ of the State.

ARTICLE 42. The Diet shall consist of two Houses, namely the House of Representatives and the House of Councillors.

ARTICLE 43. Both Houses shall consist of elected members, representative of all the people.

The number of the members of each House shall be fixed by law.

ARTICLE 44. The qualifications of members of both Houses and their electors shall be fixed by law. However, there shall be no discrimination because of race, creed, sex, social status, family origin, education, property or income.

ARTICLE 45. The term of office of members of the House of Representatives shall be four years. However, the term shall be terminated before the full term is up in case the House of Representatives is dissolved.

ARTICLE 46. The term of office of members of the House of Councillors shall be six years, and election for half the members shall take place every three years.

ARTICLE 47. Electoral districts, method of voting and other matters pertaining to the method of election of members of both Houses shall be fixed by law.

ARTICLE 48. No person shall be permitted to be a member of both Houses simultaneously.

ARTICLE 49. Members of both Houses shall receive appropriate annual payment from the national treasury in accordance with law.

ARTICLE 50. Except in cases provided by law, members of both Houses shall be exempt from apprehension while the Diet is in session, and any members apprehended before the opening of the session shall be freed during the term of the session upon demand of the House.

ARTICLE 51. Members of both Houses shall not be held liable outside the House for speeches, debates or votes cast inside the House.

ARTICLE 52. An ordinary session of the Diet shall be convoked once per year.

ARTICLE 53. The Cabinet may determine to convoke extraordinary sessions of the Diet. When a quarter or more of the total members of either House makes the demand, the Cabinet must determine on such convocation.

ARTICLE 54. When the House of Representatives is dissolved, there must be a general election of members of the House of Representatives within forty (40) days from the date of dissolution, and the Diet must be convoked within thirty (30) days from the date of the election.

When the House of Representatives is dissolved, the House of Councillors is closed at the same time. However, the Cabinet may in time of national emergency convoke the House of Councillors in emergency session.

Measures taken at such session as mentioned in the proviso of the preceding paragraph shall be provisional and shall become null and void unless agreed to by the House of Representatives within a period of ten (10) days after the opening of the next session of the Diet.

ARTICLE 55. Each House shall judge disputes related to qualifications of its members. However, in order to deny a seat to any member, it is necessary to pass a resolution by a majority of two-thirds or more of the members present.

ARTICLE 56. Business cannot be transacted in either House unless one-third or more of total membership is present.

All matters shall be decided, in each House, by a majority of those present, except as elsewhere provided in the Constitution, and in case of a tie, the presiding officer shall decide the issue.

ARTICLE 57. Deliberation in each House shall be public. However, a secret meeting may be held where a majority of two-thirds or more of those members present passes a resolution therefor.

Each House shall keep a record of proceedings. This record shall be published and given general circulation, excepting such parts of proceedings of secret session as may be deemed to require secrecy.

Upon demand of one-fifth or more of the members present, votes of the members on any matter shall be recorded in the minutes.

ARTICLE 58. Each House shall select its own president and other officials.

Each House shall establish its rules pertaining to meetings, proceedings and internal discipline, and may punish members for disorderly conduct. However, in order to expel a member, a majority of two-thirds or more of those members present must pass a resolution thereon.

ARTICLE 59. A bill becomes a law on passage by both Houses, except as otherwise provided by the Constitution.

A bill which is passed by the House of Representatives, and upon which the House of Councillors makes a decision different from that of the House of Representatives, becomes a law when passed a second time by the House of Representatives by a majority of two-thirds or more of the members present.

The provision of the preceding paragraph does not preclude the House of Representatives from calling for the meeting of a joint committee of both Houses, provided for by law.

Failure by the House of Councillors to take final action within sixty (60) days after receipt of a bill passed by the House of Representatives, time in recess excepted, may be determined by the House of Representatives to constitute a rejection of the said bill by the House of Councillors.

ARTICLE 60. The budget must first be submitted to the House of Representatives.

Upon consideration of the budget, when the House of Councillors makes a decision different from that of the House of Representatives, and when no agreement can be reached even through a joint committee of both Houses, provided for by law, or in the case of failure by the House of Councillors to take final action within thirty (30) days, the period of recess excluded, after the receipt of the budget passed by the House of Representatives, the decision of the House of Representatives shall be the decision of the Diet.

ARTICLE 61. The second paragraph of the preceding article applies also to the Diet approval required for the conclusion of treaties.

ARTICLE 62. Each House may conduct investigations in relation to government, and may demand the presence and testimony of witnesses, and the production of records.

ARTICLE 63. The Prime Minister and other Ministers of State may, at any time, appear in either House for the purpose of speaking on bills, regardless of whether they are members of the House or not. They must appear when their presence is required in order to give answers or explanations.

ARTICLE 64. The Diet shall set up an impeachment court from among the members of both Houses for the purpose of trying those judges against whom removal proceedings have been instituted.

Matters relating to impeachment shall be provided by law.

Chapter V
THE CABINET

ARTICLE 65. Executive power shall be vested in the Cabinet.

ARTICLE 66. The Cabinet shall consist of the Prime Minister, who shall be its head, and other Ministers of State, as provided for by law.

The Prime Minister and other Ministers of State must be civilians.

The Cabinet, in the exercise of executive power, shall be collectively responsible to the Diet.

ARTICLE 67. The Prime Minister shall be designated from among the members of the Diet by a resolution of the Diet. This designation shall precede all other business.

If the House of Representatives and the House of Councillors disagree and if no agreement can be reached even through a joint committee of both Houses, provided for by law, or the House of Councillors fails to make designation within ten (10) days, exclusive of the period of recess, after the House of Representatives has made designation, the decision of the House of Representatives shall be the decision of the Diet.

ARTICLE 68. The Prime Minister shall appoint the Ministers of State. However, a majority of their number must be chosen from among the members of the Diet.

The Prime Minister may remove the Ministers of State as he chooses.

ARTICLE 69. If the House of Representatives passes a non-confidence resolution, or rejects a confidence resolution, the Cabinet shall resign en masse, unless the House of Representatives is dissolved within ten (10) days.

ARTICLE 70. When there is a vacancy in the post of Prime Minister, or upon the first convocation of the Diet after a general election of members of the House of Representatives, the Cabinet shall resign en masse.

ARTICLE 71. In the cases mentioned in the two preceding articles, the Cabinet shall continue its functions until the time when a new Prime Minister is appointed.

ARTICLE 72. The Prime Minister, representing the Cabinet, submits bills, reports on general national affairs and foreign relations to the Diet and exercises control and supervision over various administrative branches.

ARTICLE 73. The Cabinet, in addition to other general administrative functions, shall perform the following functions:

Administer the law faithfully; conduct affairs of state.

Manage foreign affairs.

Conclude treaties. However, it shall obtain prior or, depending on circumstances, subsequent approval of the Diet.

Administer the civil service, in accordance with standards established by law.

Prepare the budget, and present it to the Diet.

Enact cabinet orders in order to execute the provisions of this Constitution and of the law. However, it cannot include penal provisions in such cabinet orders unless authorized by such law.

Decide on general amnesty, special amnesty, commutation of punishment, reprieve, and restoration of rights.

ARTICLE 74. All laws and cabinet orders shall be signed by the competent Minister of State and countersigned by the Prime Minister.

ARTICLE 75. The Ministers of State, during their tenure of office, shall not be subject to legal action without the consent of the Prime Minister. However, the right to take that action is not impaired hereby.

Chapter VI
JUDICIARY

ARTICLE 76. The whole judicial power is vested in a Supreme Court and in such inferior courts as are established by law.

No extraordinary tribunal shall be established, nor shall any organ or agency of the Executive be given final judicial power.

All judges shall be independent in the exercise of their conscience and shall be bound only by this Constitution and the laws.

ARTICLE 77. The Supreme Court is vested with the rule-making power under which it determines the rules of procedure and of practice, and of matters relating to attorneys, the internal discipline of the courts and the administration of judicial affairs.

Public procurators shall be subject to the rule-making power of the Supreme Court.

The Supreme Court may delegate the power to make rules for inferior courts to such courts.

ARTICLE 78. Judges shall not be removed except by public impeachment unless judicially declared mentally or physically incompetent to perform official duties. No disciplinary action against judges shall be administered by any executive organ or agency.

ARTICLE 79. The Supreme Court shall consist of a Chief Judge and such number of judges as may be determined by law; all such judges excepting the Chief Judge shall be appointed by the Cabinet.

The appointment of the judges of the Supreme Court shall be reviewed by the people at the first general election of members of the House of Representatives following their appointment, and shall be reviewed again at the first general election of members of the House of Representatives after a lapse of ten (10) years, and in the same manner thereafter.

In cases mentioned in the foregoing paragraph, when the majority of the voters favors the dismissal of a judge, he shall be dismissed.

Matters pertaining to review shall be prescribed by law.

The judges of the Supreme Court shall be retired upon the attainment of the age as fixed by law.

All such judges shall receive, at regular stated intervals, adequate compensation which shall not be decreased during their terms of office.

ARTICLE 80. The judges of the inferior courts shall be appointed by the Cabinet from a list of persons nominated by the Supreme Court. All such judges shall hold office for a term of ten (10) years with privilege of reappointment, provided that they shall be retired upon the attainment of the age as fixed by law.

The judges of the inferior courts shall receive, at regular stated intervals, adequate compensation which shall not be decreased during their terms of office.

ARTICLE 81. The Supreme Court is the court of last resort with power to determine the constitutionality of any law, order, regulation or official act.

ARTICLE 82. Trials shall be conducted and judgment declared publicly.

Where a court unanimously determines publicity to be dangerous to public order or morals, a trial may be conducted privately, but trials of political offenses, offenses involving the press or cases wherein the rights of people as guaranteed in Chapter III of this Constitution are in question shall always be conducted publicly.

Chapter VII
FINANCE

ARTICLE 83. The power to administer national finances shall be exercised as the Diet shall determine.

ARTICLE 84. No new taxes shall be imposed or existing ones modified except by law or under such conditions as law may prescribe.

ARTICLE 85. No money shall be expended, nor shall the State obligate itself, except as authorized by the Diet.

ARTICLE 86. The Cabinet shall prepare and submit to the Diet for its consideration and decision a budget for each fiscal year.

ARTICLE 87. In order to provide for unforeseen deficiencies in the budget, a reserve fund may be authorized by the Diet to be expended upon the responsibility of the Cabinet.

The Cabinet must get subsequent approval of the Diet for all payments from the reserve fund.

ARTICLE 88. All property of the Imperial Household shall belong to the State. All expenses of the Imperial Household shall be appropriated by the Diet in the budget.

ARTICLE 89. No public money or other property shall be expended or appropriated for the use, benefit, or maintenance of any religious institution or association, or for any charitable, educational or benevolent enterprises not under the control of public authority.

ARTICLE 90. Final accounts of the expenditures and revenues of the State shall be audited annually by a Board of Audit and submitted by the Cabinet to the Diet, together with the statement of audit, during the fiscal year immediately following the period covered.

The organization and competency of the Board of Audit shall be determined by law.

ARTICLE 91. At regular intervals and at least annually the Cabinet shall report to the Diet and the people on the state of national finances.

Chapter VIII
LOCAL SELF-GOVERNMENT

ARTICLE 92. Regulations concerning organization and operations of local public entities shall be fixed by law in accordance with the principle of local autonomy.

ARTICLE 93. The local public entities shall establish assemblies as their deliberative organs, in accordance with law.

The chief executive officers of all local public entities, the members of their assemblies, and such other local officials as may be determined by law shall be elected by direct popular vote within their several communities.

ARTICLE 94. Local public entities shall have the right to manage their property, affairs and administration and to enact their own regulations within law.

ARTICLE 95. A special law, applicable only to one local public entity, cannot be enacted by the Diet without the consent of the majority of the voters of the local public entity concerned, obtained in accordance with law.

Chapter IX
AMENDMENTS

ARTICLE 96. Amendments to this Constitution shall be initiated by the Diet, through a concurring vote of two-thirds or more of all the members of each House and shall thereupon be submitted to the people for ratification, which shall require the affirmative vote of a majority of all votes cast thereon, at a special referendum or at such election as the Diet shall specify.

Amendments when so ratified shall immediately be promulgated by the Emperor in the name of the people, as an integral part of this Constitution.

Chapter X
SUPREME LAW

ARTICLE 97. The fundamental human rights by this Constitution guaranteed to the people of Japan are fruits of the age-old struggle of man to be free; they have survived the many exacting tests for durability and are conferred upon this and future generations in trust, to be held for all time inviolate.

ARTICLE 98. This Constitution shall be the supreme law of the nation and no law, ordinance, imperial rescript or other act of government, or part thereof, contrary to the provisions hereof, shall have legal force or validity.

The treaties concluded by Japan and established laws of nations shall be faithfully observed.

ARTICLE 99. The Emperor or the Regent as well as Ministers of State, members of the Diet, judges, and all other public officials have the obligation to respect and uphold this Constitution.

Chapter XI
SUPPLEMENTARY PROVISIONS

ARTICLE 100. This Constitution shall be enforced as from the day when the period of six months will have elapsed counting from the day of its promulgation.

The enactment of laws necessary for the enforcement of this Constitution, the election of members of the House of Councillors and the procedure for the convocation of the Diet and other preparatory procedures necessary for the enforcement of this Constitution may be executed before the day prescribed in the preceding paragraph.

ARTICLE 101. If the House of Councillors is not constituted before the effective date of this Constitution, the House of Representatives shall function as the Diet until such time as the House of Councillors shall be constituted.

ARTICLE 102. The term of office for half the members of the House of Councillors serving in the first term under this Constitution shall be three years. Members falling under this category shall be determined in accordance with law.

ARTICLE 103. The Ministers of State, members of the House of Representatives and judges in office on the effective date of this Constitution, and all other public officials who occupy positions corresponding to such positions as are recognized by this Constitution shall not forfeit their positions automatically on account of the enforcement of this Constitution unless otherwise specified by law. When, however, successors are elected or appointed under the provisions of this Constitution, they shall forfeit their positions as a matter of course.

UNIVERSAL DECLARATION OF HUMAN RIGHTS (1948)

The rights of individuals became a concern of the international community only in the twentieth century. Prior to World War I (1914–1918), the political, civil, and human rights of citizens were considered properly to be the internal concerns of sovereign states. In the peace treaties concluded at the end of the war, some limited attempts were made for the first time to provide for the political and civil rights of certain minority groups. After the widespread horrors of World War II (1939–1945), the international community, as embodied in the United Nations, placed the extension and protection of individual rights at the forefront of the world agenda.

When the United Nations Charter was drafted in 1944–1945, a decision was made to defer a statement of fundamental human rights because of the cultural, political, and ideological difficulties involved in drafting such a document. In 1947 the UN Commission on Human Rights began working toward an international bill of human rights that would be acceptable to all member states: the long-established and the newly independent; the industrially developed and the underdeveloped; communist and noncommunist; colonial powers and noncolonial powers. The resolution was

adopted by a vote of 48–0 with eight abstentions by the UN General Assembly on December 10, 1948. (The six states of the Soviet bloc, Saudi Arabia, and the Union of South Africa abstained.)

The UN declaration includes the political and civil rights common to Western democratic constitutions: the rights to life, liberty, and equality; freedom from arbitrary arrest and the right to a public hearing by an impartial jury; freedom of conscience and religion; and freedom of assembly and association. It also addresses economic, social, and cultural issues not normally considered fundamental rights in the Western democratic tradition.

The Universal Declaration of Human Rights does not have the force of international law and hence places no obligations or restrictions on its signatory states. The declaration, however, provided the moral and intellectual underpinnings for subsequent covenants and conventions that do have the force of law. Among them are the International Covenant on Civil and Political Rights and the International Covenant on Economic, Social, and Cultural Rights, both of which were adopted in 1966 and entered into force in 1976.

Preamble

Whereas recognition of the inherent dignity and of the equal and inalienable rights of all members of the human family is the foundation of freedom, justice and peace in the world,

Whereas disregard and contempt for human rights have resulted in barbarous acts which have outraged the conscience of mankind, and the advent of a world in which human beings shall enjoy freedom of speech and belief and freedom from fear and want has been proclaimed as the highest aspiration of the common people,

Whereas it is essential, if man is not to be compelled to have recourse, as a last resort, to rebellion against tyranny and oppression, that human rights should be protected by the rule of law,

Whereas it is essential to promote the development of friendly relations between nations,

Whereas the peoples of the United Nations have in the Charter reaffirmed their faith in fundamental human rights, in the dignity and worth of the human person and in the equal rights of men and women and have determined to promote social progress and better standards of life in larger freedom,

Whereas Member States have pledged themselves to achieve, in co-operation with the United Nations, the promotion of universal respect for and observance of human rights and fundamental freedoms,

Whereas a common understanding of these rights and freedoms is of the greatest importance for the full realization of this pledge,

Now, therefore,

The General Assembly

Proclaims this Universal Declaration of Human Rights as a

common standard of achievement for all peoples and all nations, to the end that every individual and every organ of society, keeping this Declaration constantly in mind, shall strive by teaching and education to promote respect for these rights and freedoms and by progressive measures, national and international, to secure their universal and effective recognition and observance, both among the peoples of Member States themselves and among the peoples of territories under their jurisdiction.

ARTICLE 1

All human beings are born free and equal in dignity and rights. They are endowed with reason and conscience and should act towards one another in a spirit of brotherhood.

ARTICLE 2

Everyone is entitled to all the rights and freedoms set forth in this Declaration, without distinction of any kind, such as race, colour, sex, language, religion, political or other opinion, national or social origin, property, birth or other status.

Furthermore, no distinction shall be made on the basis of the political, jurisdictional or international status of the country or territory to which a person belongs, whether it be independent, trust, non-self-governing or under any other limitation of sovereignty.

ARTICLE 3

Everyone has the right to life, liberty and security of person.

ARTICLE 4

No one shall be held in slavery or servitude; slavery and the slave trade shall be prohibited in all their forms.

ARTICLE 5

No one shall be subjected to torture or to cruel, inhuman or degrading treatment or punishment.

ARTICLE 6

Everyone has the right to recognition everywhere as a person before the law.

ARTICLE 7

All are equal before the law and are entitled without any discrimination to equal protection of the law. All are entitled to equal protection against any discrimination in violation of this Declaration and against any incitement to such discrimination.

ARTICLE 8

Everyone has the right to an effective remedy by the competent national tribunals for acts violating the fundamental rights granted him by the constitution or by law.

ARTICLE 9

No one shall be subjected to arbitrary arrest, detention or exile.

ARTICLE 10

Everyone is entitled in full equality to a fair and public hearing by an independent and impartial tribunal, in the determination of his rights and obligations and of any criminal charge against him.

ARTICLE 11

(1) Everyone charged with a penal offence has the right to be presumed innocent until proved guilty according to law in a public trial at which he has had all the guarantees necessary for his defence.

(2) No one shall be held guilty of any penal offence on account of any act or omission which did not constitute a penal offence, under national or international law, at the time when it was committed. Nor shall a heavier penalty be imposed than the one that was applicable at the time the penal offence was committed.

ARTICLE 12

No one shall be subjected to arbitrary interference with his privacy, family, home or correspondence, nor to attacks upon his honour and reputation. Everyone has the right to the protection of the law against such interference or attacks.

ARTICLE 13

(1) Everyone has the right to freedom of movement and residence within the borders of each State.

(2) Everyone has the right to leave any country, including his own, and to return to his country.

ARTICLE 14

(1) Everyone has the right to seek and to enjoy in other countries asylum from persecution.

(2) This right may not be invoked in the case of prosecutions genuinely arising from non-political crimes or from acts contrary to the purposes and principles of the United Nations.

ARTICLE 15

(1) Everyone has the right to a nationality.

(2) No one shall be arbitrarily deprived of his nationality nor denied the right to change his nationality.

ARTICLE 16

(1) Men and women of full age, without any limitation due to race, nationality or religion, have the right to marry and to found a family. They are entitled to equal rights as to marriage, during marriage and at its dissolution.

(2) Marriage shall be entered into only with the free and full consent of the intending spouses.

(3) The family is the natural and fundamental group unit of society and is entitled to protection by society and the State.

ARTICLE 17

(1) Everyone has the right to own property alone as well as in association with others.

(2) No one shall be arbitrarily deprived of his property.

ARTICLE 18

Everyone has the right to freedom of thought, conscience and religion; this right includes freedom to change his religion or belief, and freedom, either alone or in community with others and in public or private, to manifest his religion or belief in teaching, practice, worship and observance.

ARTICLE 19

Everyone has the right to freedom of opinion and expression; this right includes freedom to hold opinions without interference and to seek, receive and impart information and ideas through any media and regardless of frontiers.

ARTICLE 20

(1) Everyone has the right to freedom of peaceful assembly and association.

(2) No one may be compelled to belong to an association.

ARTICLE 21

(1) Everyone has the right to take part in the government of his country, directly or through freely chosen representatives.

(2) Everyone has the right of equal access to public service in his country.

(3) The will of the people shall be the basis of the authority of the government; this will shall be expressed in periodic and genuine elections which shall be by universal and equal suffrage and shall be held by secret vote or by equivalent free voting procedures.

ARTICLE 22

Everyone, as a member of society, has the right to social security and is entitled to realization, through national effort and international co-operation and in accordance with the organization and resources of each State, of the economic, social and cultural rights indispensable for his dignity and the free development of his personality.

ARTICLE 23

(1) Everyone has the right to work, to free choice of employment, to just and favourable conditions of work and to protection against unemployment.

(2) Everyone, without any discrimination, has the right to equal pay for equal work.

(3) Everyone who works has the right to just and favourable remuneration ensuring for himself and his family an existence worthy of human dignity, and supplemented, if necessary, by other means of social protection.

(4) Everyone has the right to form and to join trade unions for the protection of his interests.

ARTICLE 24

Everyone has the right to rest and leisure, including reasonable limitation of working hours and periodic holidays with pay.

ARTICLE 25

(1) Everyone has the right to a standard of living adequate for the health and well-being of himself and of his family, including food, clothing, housing, and medical care and necessary social services, and the right to security in the event of unemployment, sickness, disability, widowhood, old age or other lack of livelihood in circumstances beyond his control.

(2) Motherhood and childhood are entitled to special care and assistance. All children, whether born in or out of wedlock, shall enjoy the same social protection.

ARTICLE 26

(1) Everyone has the right to education. Education shall be free, at least in the elementary and fundamental stages. Elementary education shall be compulsory. Technical and professional education shall be made generally available and higher education shall be equally accessible to all on the basis of merit.

(2) Education shall be directed to the full development of the human personality and to the strengthening of respect for human rights and fundamental freedoms. It shall promote understanding, tolerance and friendship among all nations, racial or religious groups, and shall further the activities of the United Nations for the maintenance of peace.

(3) Parents have a prior right to choose the kind of education that shall be given to their children.

ARTICLE 27

(1) Everyone has the right freely to participate in the cultural life of the community, to enjoy the arts and to share in scientific advancement and its benefits.

(2) Everyone has the right to the protection of the moral and material interests resulting from any scientific, literary or artistic production of which he is the author.

ARTICLE 28

Everyone is entitled to a social and international order in which the rights and freedoms set forth in this Declaration can be fully realized.

ARTICLE 29

(1) Everyone has duties to the community in which alone the free and full development of his personality is possible.

(2) In the exercise of his rights and freedoms, everyone shall be subject only to such limitations as are determined by law solely for the purpose of securing due recognition and respect for the rights and freedoms of others and of meeting the just requirements of morality, public order and the general welfare in a democratic society.

(3) These rights and freedoms may in no case be exercised contrary to the purposes and principles of the United Nations.

ARTICLE 30

Nothing in this Declaration may be interpreted as implying for any State, group or person any right to engage in any activity or to perform any act aimed at the destruction of any of the rights and freedoms set forth herein.

ISRAELI DECLARATION OF INDEPENDENCE (1948)

Modern nationalism—fealty to the common purpose of one's nation—emerged along with the eighteenth-century Enlightenment notion of representative democracy. Both concepts sprang from the decline of feudal loyalty to a local noble and the decline of provincial attitudes in the face of expanded commerce. But because the Jews were so widely dispersed, Zionism, the Jewish nationalist movement, was slow to develop.

For almost 2,000 years, since the temple in Jerusalem was destroyed in A.D. 70 and the Jewish people were exiled from Palestine, the Jews were a nation without a state. They shared a common language and literature, lore and history, and customs and culture. Those shared characteristics, which are the essence of nationhood, were grounded in the Jewish religion. Yet it was the development of the secular concept of nationalism, which gained momentum in the nineteenth and twentieth centuries, that led to the declaration of an independent Jewish nation-state.

The success of the Zionist movement, revived and inspired in the late nineteenth century by Hungarian-born Theodor Herzl, owed much to the cataclysms of World War I (1914–1918) and World War II (1939–1945). In 1917 Great Britain seized control of Palestine from the Ottoman Empire, ending four hundred years of Turkish rule, and issued the Balfour Declaration, which expressed support for the establishment of a Jewish "national home" in Palestine while simultaneously expressing support for the civil and religious rights of the non-Jewish population. The incompatibility of those two goals would vex British and international policy for thirty years.

British administration of Palestine, which was sanctioned by a 1922 mandate from the League of Nations, satisfied neither the Arabs nor the Jews. When Adolf Hitler came to power in Germany in 1933 and Jewish emigration from Europe to Palestine rose dramatically, tensions between Jews and non-Jews in Palestine escalated. The British could gain support neither for a unified Palestinian state to be run jointly by Jews and Arabs nor for a partition plan that would create two states. With no solution in sight, and with its occupation army taking casualties from both Jewish and Arab guerrilla movements, the British government turned the issue over to the United Nations and announced that it would relinquish its mandate.

After studying the issue, the United Nations voted on November 29, 1947, to partition Palestine. The Jews accepted the outcome, though they were unhappy with the borders; the Arab leaders of Egypt, Syria, Transjordan, Iraq, and Lebanon rejected the settlement. When the British mandate expired on May 14, 1948, and the last British troops left Palestine, the Jewish National Council proclaimed Israeli independence and open war broke out. Israel won the war a year later.

Issued at Tel Aviv on May 14, 1948 (5th of Iyar, 5708)

The Land of Israel was the birthplace of the Jewish people. Here their spiritual, religious and national identity was formed. Here they achieved independence and created a culture of national and universal significance. Here they wrote and gave the Bible to the world.

Exiled from Palestine, the Jewish people remained faithful to it in all the countries of their dispersion, never ceasing to pray and hope for their return and the restoration of their national freedom.

Impelled by this historic association, Jews strove throughout the centuries to go back to the land of their fathers and regain their statehood. In recent decades they returned in masses. They reclaimed the wilderness, revived their language, built cities and villages and established a vigorous and ever-growing community, with its own economic and cultural life. They sought peace yet were ever prepared to defend themselves. They brought the blessing of progress to all inhabitants of the country.

In the year 1897 the First Zionist Congress, inspired by Theodor Herzl's vision of the Jewish State, proclaimed the right of the Jewish people to national revival in their own country.

This right was acknowledged by the Balfour Declaration of November 2, 1917, and reaffirmed by the Mandate of the League of Nations, which gave explicit international recognition to the historic connection of the Jewish people with Palestine and their right to reconstitute their National Home.

The Nazi holocaust, which engulfed millions of Jews in Europe, proved anew the urgency of the re-establishment of the Jewish State, which would solve the problem of Jewish homelessness by opening the gates to all Jews and lifting the Jewish people to equality in the family of nations.

The survivors of the European catastrophe, as well as Jews from other lands, proclaiming their right to a life of dignity, freedom and labor, and undeterred by hazards, hardships and obstacles, have tried unceasingly to enter Palestine.

In the Second World War the Jewish people in Palestine made a full contribution in the struggle of the freedom-loving nations against the Nazi evil. The sacrifices of their soldiers and the efforts of their workers gained them title to rank with the peoples who founded the United Nations.

On November 29, 1947, the General Assembly of the United Nations adopted a Resolution for the establishment of an independent Jewish State in Palestine, and called upon the inhabitants of the country to take such steps as may be necessary on their part to put the plan into effect.

This recognition by the United Nations of the right of the Jewish people to establish their independent State may not be revoked. It is, moreover, the self-evident right of the Jewish people to be a nation, as all other nations, in its own sovereign State.

Accordingly, we, the members of the National Council, representing the Jewish people in Palestine and the Zionist movement of the world, met together in solemn assembly today, the day of termination of the British Mandate for Palestine, by virtue of the natural and historic right of the Jewish people and of the Resolution of the General Assembly of the United Nations.

Hereby proclaim the establishment of the Jewish State in Palestine, to be called *Israel.*

We hereby declare that as from the termination of the Mandate at midnight, this night of the 14th to 15th May, 1948, and until the setting up of the duly elected bodies of the State in accordance with a Constitution, to be drawn up by a Constituent Assembly not later than the first day of October, 1948, the present National Council shall act as the provisional administration, shall constitute the Provisional Government of the State of Israel.

The State of Israel will be open to the immigration of Jews from all countries of their dispersion; will promote the development of the country for the benefit of all its inhabitants; will be based on the precepts of liberty, justice and peace taught by the Hebrew Prophets; will uphold the full social and political equality of all its citizens, without distinction of race, creed or sex; will guarantee full freedom of conscience, worship, education and culture; will safeguard the sanctity and inviolability of the shrines and Holy Places of all religions; and will dedicate itself to the principles of the Charter of the United Nations.

The State of Israel will be ready to cooperate with the organs and representatives of the United Nations in the implementation of the Resolution of the Assembly of November 29, 1947, and will take steps to bring about the Economic Union over the whole of Palestine.

We appeal to the United Nations to assist the Jewish people in the building of its State and to admit Israel into the family of nations.

In the midst of wanton aggression, we yet call upon the Arab inhabitants of the State of Israel to return to the ways of peace and play their part in the development of the State, with full and equal citizenship and due representation in all its bodies and institutions—provisional or permanent.

We offer peace and unity to all the neighboring states and their peoples, and invite them to cooperate with the independent Jewish nation for the common good of all.

Our call goes out to the Jewish people all over the world to rally to our side in the task of immigration and development and to stand by us in the great struggle for the fulfillment of the dream of generations—the redemption of Israel.

With trust in Almighty God, we set our hand to this Declaration, at this Session of the Provisional State Council, in the city of Tel Aviv, on this Sabbath eve, the fifth of Iyar, 5708, the fourteenth day of May, 1948.

CONSTITUTION OF THE FEDERAL REPUBLIC OF GERMANY (1949)

The constitution of the Federal Republic of Germany (West Germany), like that of Japan, was drafted under the supervision of Allied occupation authorities in the aftermath of World War II. Known as the Basic Law, the German constitution represented an amalgam of German and non-German political traditions and philosophies. Its terms were both reactive to the perceived failures of the prewar constitutional order and proactive with respect to establishing the individual rights and governmental structures of a stable parliamentary democracy.

Germany under the Weimar constitution, drawn up in 1919 after Germany's defeat in World War I, was a democracy with serious political, economic, and social difficulties that undermined the stability of the constitutional order. An extremely liberal electoral law apportioned seats in the legislature proportionate to a party's share of the vote; consequently, the fragmentation of society—from communists on the extreme left to fascists on the extreme right—was replicated in the legislature, creating deadlock in government. By 1930, under the added pressure of the Great Depression and the increasing use of violence by anticonstitutional forces, a coalition could not be formed in the Reichstag, the parliament. The president dissolved the parliament and, together with the chancellor, governed under emergency powers and suspended civil rights. In this chaotic political environment, Adolf Hitler and the Nazi party came to power.

In June 1948 the Western Allies, in the face of cold war ac-

rimony with the Soviet Union, had given up hope of reunifying Germany. They authorized a constituent assembly to draft a constitution for the Federal Republic. The sixty-five delegates appointed to the assembly by the minister-presidents of the German states (Länder) met on September 1, 1948, and submitted a draft to the Länder and the occupation authorities two months later.

The draft constitution replaced proportional representation in the lower house of the legislature (Bundestag) with a system in which half the members were to be selected based on proportional representation and half based on single-member districts. Furthermore, a party that did not attract 5 percent of the vote could not be represented in the Bundestag, thus eliminating extremist parties and reducing the fragmentation that had paralyzed the Weimar government. The relationships between the chancellor, president, and legislature were revised in such a way as to prevent the executive from ruling under emergency powers or without the support of a majority of the legislature.

The constituent assembly made minor revisions to the draft in deference to the Länder and to the occupation authorities. The military governors approved the revised document on May 12, 1949, and the constitution was ratified by the Länder assemblies and formally adopted May 23. The document is reproduced below as amended through December 20, 1993.

Preamble

Conscious of their responsibility before God and humankind,

Animated by the resolve to serve world peace as an equal part of a united Europe,

The German people have adopted, by virtue of their constituent power, this Basic Law.

The Germans in the Länder of Baden-Württemberg, Bavaria, Berlin, Brandenburg, Bremen, Hamburg, Hesse, Lower Saxony, Mecklenburg-Western Pomerania, North-Rhine/Westphalia, Rhineland-Palatinate, Saarland, Saxony, Saxony-Anhalt, Schleswig-Holstein and Thuringia have achieved the unity and freedom of Germany in free self-determination. This Basic Law is thus valid for the whole German nation.

Chapter I. Basic Rights

ARTICLE 1 *(Protection of human dignity)*

(1) The dignity of man is inviolable. To respect and protect it shall be the duty of all public authority.

(2) The German people therefore uphold human rights as inviolable and inalienable and as the basis of every community, of peace and justice in the world.

(3) The following basic rights shall bind the legislature, the executive and the judiciary as directly enforceable law.

ARTICLE 2 *(Personal freedom)*

(1) Everybody has the right to self-fulfillment in so far as they do not violate the rights of others or offend against the constitutional order or morality.

(2) Everybody has the right to life and physical integrity. Personal freedom is inviolable. These rights may not be encroached upon save pursuant to a law.

ARTICLE 3 *(Equality before the law)*

(1) All people are equal before the law.

(2) Men and women have equal rights.

(3) Nobody shall be prejudiced or favored because of their sex, birth, race, language, national or social origin, faith, religion or political opinions.

ARTICLE 4 *(Freedom of faith, conscience and creed)*

(1) Freedom of faith and conscience as well as freedom of creed, religious or ideological, are inviolable.

(2) The undisturbed practice of religion shall be guaranteed.

(3) Nobody may be forced against their conscience into military service involving armed combat. Details shall be the subject of a federal law.

ARTICLE 5 *(Freedom of expression)*

(1) Everybody has the right freely to express and disseminate their opinions orally, in writing or visually and to obtain information from generally accessible sources without hindrance. Freedom of the press and freedom of reporting through audiovisual media shall be guaranteed. There shall be no censorship.

(2) These rights are subject to limitations embodied in the provisions of general legislation, statutory provisions for the protection of young persons and the citizen's right to personal respect.

(3) Art and scholarship, research and teaching shall be free. Freedom of teaching shall not absolve anybody from loyalty to the constitution.

ARTICLE 6 *(Marriage and family, children born outside marriage)*

(1) Marriage and family shall enjoy the special protection of the state.

(2) The care and upbringing of children are a natural right of parents and a duty primarily incumbent on them. It is the responsibility of the community to ensure that they perform this duty.

(3) Children may not be separated from their families against the will of their parents or guardians save in accordance with a law in cases where they fail in their duty or there is a danger of the children being seriously neglected for other reasons.

(4) Every mother is entitled to the protection and care of the community.

(5) Children born outside marriage shall be provided by law with the same opportunities for their physical and mental development and regarding their place in society as are enjoyed by those born in marriage.

ARTICLE 7 *(School education)*

(1) The entire school system shall be under the supervision of the state.

(2) Parents and guardians have the right to decide whether children receive religious instruction.

(3) Religious instruction shall form part of the curriculum in state schools except nondenominational schools. Without prejudice to the state's right of supervision, religious instruction shall be given in accordance with the doctrine of the religious community concerned. Teachers may not be obliged to give religious instruction against their will.

(4) The right to establish private schools shall be guaranteed. Private schools as alternatives to state schools shall require the approval of the state and be subject to Land legislation. Such approval shall be given where private schools are not inferior to state schools in terms of their educational aims, their facilities and the training of their teaching staff and where it does not encourage segregation of pupils according to the means of their parents. Approval shall be withheld where the economic and legal status of the teaching staff is not adequately secured.

(5) A private elementary school shall be approved only where the education authority finds that it meets a special educational need or where, at the request of parents or guardians, it is to be established as a nondenominational, denominational or alternative school and no state elementary school of that type exists locally.

(6) Preparatory schools shall remain abolished.

ARTICLE 8 *(Freedom of assembly)*

(1) All Germans have the right to assemble peacefully and unarmed without prior notification or permission.

(2) In the case of outdoor assemblies this right may be restricted by or pursuant to a law.

ARTICLE 9 *(Freedom of association)*

(1) All Germans have the right to form associations, partnerships and corporations.

(2) Associations whose aims or activities contravene criminal law or are directed against the constitutional order or the notion of international understanding shall be banned.

(3) The right to form associations in order to safeguard and improve working and economic conditions shall be guaranteed to every individual and all occupations and professions. Agreements restricting or intended to hamper the exercise of this right shall be null and void; measures to this end shall be illegal. Measures taken pursuant to Article 12a, paragraphs (2) and (3) of Article 35, paragraph (4) of Article 87a, or Article 91 may not be directed against industrial disputes engaged in by associations within the meaning of the first sentence of this paragraph in order to safeguard and improve working and economic conditions.

ARTICLE 10 *(Privacy of correspondence, posts and telecommunications)*

(1) Privacy of correspondence, posts and telecommunications is inviolable.

(2) Restrictions may only be ordered pursuant to a law. Where a restriction serves to protect the free democratic basic order or the existence or security of the Federation or a Land the law may stipulate that the person affected shall not be informed of such restriction and that recourse to the courts shall be replaced by a review of the case by bodies and subsidiary bodies appointed by parliament.

ARTICLE 11 *(Freedom of movement)*

(1) All Germans have the right to move freely throughout the federal territory.

(2) This right may be restricted only by or pursuant to a law and only where a person does not have a sufficient livelihood and his or her freedom of movement would be a considerable burden on the community or where such restriction is necessary to avert an imminent danger to the existence or the free democratic basic order of the Federation or a Land, or to prevent an epidemic, a natural disaster, grave accident or criminal act, or to protect young persons from serious neglect.

ARTICLE 12 *(Free choice of occupation or profession, prohibition of forced labor)*

(1) All Germans have the right freely to choose their occupation or profession, their place of work, study or training. The practice of an occupation or profession may be regulated by or pursuant to a law.

(2) Nobody may be forced to do work of a particular kind except as part of a traditional compulsory community service that applies generally and equally to all.

(3) Forced labor may only be imposed on people deprived of their liberty by court sentence.

ARTICLE 12a *(Compulsory military or alternative service)*

(1) Men who have reached the age of eighteen may be required to serve in the Armed Forces, the Federal Border Guard or a civil defense organization.

(2) Anybody who refuses military service involving armed combat on grounds of conscience may be assigned to alternative service. The period of alternative service shall not exceed that of military service. Details shall be the subject of a law which shall not impair the freedom to decide in accordance with the dictates of conscience and must also provide for the possibility of alternative service not connected with units of the Armed Forces or the Federal Border Guard.

(3) People liable to compulsory military service who are not assigned to service pursuant to paragraph (1) or (2) of this Article may, if the country is in a state of defense, be assigned by or pursuant to a law to employment involving civilian service for defense purposes, including protection of the civilian population; they may not be assigned to public employment except to carry out police or other responsibilities of public administration as can only be discharged by public servants. People may be assigned to employment of the kind referred to in the first sentence of this paragraph with the Armed Forces, including the supplying and servicing of the latter, or with public administrative authorities; assignments to employment connected with supplying and servicing the civilian population shall not be permissible except in order to meet their vital requirements or to ensure their safety.

(4) Where, if the country is in a state of defense, civilian service requirements in the civilian health system or in the stationary military hospital organization cannot be met on a voluntary basis women between eighteen and fifty-five years of age may be assigned to such service by or pursuant to a law. They may on no account be assigned to military service involving armed combat.

(5) Prior to a state of defense, assignments under paragraph (3) of this Article may only be made where the requirements of paragraph (1) of Article 80a are satisfied. Attendance at training courses in preparation for any service in accordance with paragraph (3) of this Article which demands spe-

cial knowledge or skills may be required by or pursuant to a law. To this extent the first sentence of this paragraph shall not apply.

(6) Where a state of defense exists and manpower requirements for the purposes referred to in the second sentence of paragraph (3) of this Article cannot be met on a voluntary basis the right of German citizens to give up their occupation, profession or employment may be restricted by or pursuant to a law in order to meet those requirements. The first sentence of paragraph (5) of this Article shall apply *mutatis mutandis* prior to a state of defense.

ARTICLE 13 *(Privacy of the home)*

(1) Privacy of the home is inviolable.

(2) Searches may be ordered only by a judge or, if there is a danger in delay, by other authorities as provided for by law and may be carried out only in the manner prescribed by the law.

(3) Intrusions and restrictions shall otherwise only be permissible to avert danger to the public or to the life of an individual or, pursuant to a law, an acute threat to public safety and order, in particular to relieve a housing shortage, to prevent an epidemic or to protect young persons at risk.

ARTICLE 14 *(Property, inheritance, expropriation)*

(1) Property and the right of inheritance shall be guaranteed. Their substance and limits shall be determined by law.

(2) Property entails obligations. Its use should also serve the public interest.

(3) Expropriation shall only be permissible in the public interest. It may only be ordered by or pursuant to a law which determines the nature and extent of compensation. Compensation shall reflect a fair balance between the public interest and the interests of those affected. In case of dispute regarding the amount of compensation recourse may be had to the ordinary courts.

ARTICLE 15 *(Public ownership)*

Land, natural resources and means of production may be transferred to public ownership or other forms of public enterprise by a law which determines the nature and extent of compensation. In respect of compensation the third and fourth sentences of paragraph (3) of Article 14 shall apply *mutatis mutandis*.

ARTICLE 16 *(Nationality, extradition)*

(1) Nobody may be deprived of their German citizenship. Loss of citizenship may only occur pursuant to a law, and against the will of those affected only if they do not thereby become stateless.

(2) No German may be extradited to another country.

ARTICLE 16a *(Asylum)*

(1) Anybody persecuted on political grounds has the right of asylum.

(2) Paragraph (1) may not be invoked by anybody who enters the country from a member state of the European Communities or another third country where the application of the Convention relating to the Status of Refugees and the Convention for the Protection of Human Rights and Fundamental Freedoms is assured. Countries outside the European Communities which fulfill the conditions of the first sentence of this paragraph shall be specified by legislation requiring the consent of the Bundesrat. In cases covered by the first sentence measures terminating a person's sojourn may be carried out irrespective of any remedy sought by that person.

(3) Legislation requiring the consent of the Bundesrat may be introduced to specify countries where the legal situation, the application of the law and the general political circumstances justify the assumption that neither political persecution nor inhumane or degrading punishment or treatment takes place there. It shall be presumed that a foreigner from such a country is not subject to persecution on political grounds so long as the person concerned does not present facts supporting the supposition that, contrary to that presumption, he or she is subject to political persecution.

(4) The implementation of measures terminating a person's sojourn shall, in the cases referred to in paragraph (3) and in other cases that are manifestly ill-founded or considered to be manifestly ill-founded, be suspended by the court only where serious doubt exists as to the legality of the measure; the scope of the investigation may be restricted and objections submitted after the prescribed time-limit may be disregarded. Details shall be the subject of a law.

(5) Paragraphs (1) to (4) do not conflict with international agreements of member states of the European Communities among themselves and with third countries which, with due regard for the obligations arising from the Convention relating to the Status of Refugees and the Convention for the Protection of Human Rights and Fundamental Freedoms, whose application must be assured in the contracting states, establish jurisdiction for the consideration of applications for asylum including the mutual recognition of decisions on asylum.

ARTICLE 17 *(Right of petition)*

Everybody has the right individually or jointly with others to address written requests or complaints to the appropriate authorities and to parliament.

ARTICLE 17a *(Restriction of certain basic rights by legislation on defense and alternative service)*

(1) Legislation on military and alternative service may restrict during their period of service the basic right of members

of the Armed Forces and of the alternative services freely to express and disseminate their opinions orally, in writing or visually (first half-sentence of paragraph (1) of Article 5), the freedom of assembly (Article 8), and the right of petition (Article 17) in so far as this right permits the submission of requests or complaints jointly with others.

(2) Legislation serving defense purposes including protection of the civilian population may provide for restriction of the basic rights of freedom of movement (Article 11) and privacy of the home (Article 13).

ARTICLE 18 (Forfeiture of basic rights)

Those who abuse their freedom of expression, in particular freedom of the press (paragraph (1) of Article 5), freedom of teaching (paragraph (3) of Article 5), freedom of assembly (Article 8), freedom of association (Article 9), privacy of correspondence, posts and telecommunications (Article 10), property (Article 14), or the right of asylum (Article 16a) in order to undermine the free democratic basic order shall forfeit these basic rights. Such forfeiture and its extent shall be determined by the Federal Constitutional Court.

ARTICLE 19 (Restriction of basic rights)

(1) In so far as a basic right may, under this Basic Law, be restricted by or pursuant to a law the law shall apply generally and not merely to one case. Furthermore, the law shall specify the basic right and relevant Article.

(2) In no case may the essence of a basic right be encroached upon.

(3) The basic rights shall also apply to domestic legal persons to the extent that the nature of such rights permits.

(4) Where rights are violated by public authority the person affected shall have recourse to law. In so far as no other jurisdiction has been established such recourse shall be to the ordinary courts. The second sentence of paragraph (2) of Article 10 shall not be affected by the provisions of this paragraph.

Chapter II. The Federation and the Länder

ARTICLE 20 (Political and social structure, defense of the constitutional order)

(1) The Federal Republic of Germany shall be a democratic and social federal state.

(2) All public authority emanates from the people. It shall be exercised by the people through elections and referendums and by specific legislative, executive and judicial bodies.

(3) The legislature shall be bound by the constitutional order, the executive and the judiciary by law and justice.

(4) All Germans have the right to resist anybody attempting to do away with this constitutional order, should no other remedy be possible.

ARTICLE 21 (Parties)

(1) The parties shall help form the political will of the people. They may be freely established. Their internal organization shall conform to democratic principles. They shall publicly account for the sources and use of their funds and for their assets.

(2) Parties which by reason of their aims or the conduct of their adherents seek to impair or do away with the free democratic basic order or threaten the existence of the Federal Republic of Germany shall be unconstitutional. The Federal Constitutional Court shall rule on the question of unconstitutionality.

(3) Details shall be the subject of federal laws.

ARTICLE 22 (The federal flag)

The federal flag shall be black, red and gold.

ARTICLE 23 (The European Union)

(1) With a view to establishing a united Europe the Federal Republic of Germany shall participate in the development of the European Union, which is committed to democratic, rule-of-law, social and federal principles as well as the principle of subsidiarity, and ensures protection of basic rights comparable in substance to that afforded by this Basic Law. To this end the Federation may transfer sovereign powers by law with the consent of the Bundesrat. The establishment of the European Union as well as amendments to its statutory foundations and comparable regulations which amend or supplement the content of this Basic Law or make such amendments or supplements possible shall be subject to the provisions of paragraphs (2) and (3) of Article 79.

(2) The Bundestag and, through the Bundesrat, the Länder shall be involved in matters concerning the European Union. The Federal Government shall inform the Bundestag and the Bundesrat comprehensively and as quickly as possible.

(3) The Federal Government shall give the Bundestag the opportunity to state its opinion before participating in the legislative process of the European Union. The Federal Government shall take account of the opinion of the Bundestag in the negotiations. Details shall be the subject of a law.

(4) The Bundesrat shall be involved in the decision-making process of the Federation in so far as it would have to be involved in a corresponding internal measure or in so far as the Länder would be internally responsible.

(5) Where in an area in which the Federation has exclusive legislative jurisdiction the interests of the Länder are affected or where in other respects the Federation has the right to legis-

late, the Federal Government shall take into account the opinion of the Bundesrat. Where essentially the legislative powers of the Länder, the establishment of their authorities or their administrative procedures are affected, the opinion of the Bundesrat shall in this respect prevail in the decision-making process of the Federation; in this connection the responsibility of the Federation for the country as a whole shall be maintained. In matters which may lead to expenditure increases or revenue cuts for the Federation, the approval of the Federal Government shall be necessary.

(6) Where essentially the exclusive legislative jurisdiction of the Länder is affected the exercise of the rights of the Federal Republic of Germany as a member state of the European Union shall be transferred by the Federation to a representative of the Länder designated by the Bundesrat. Those rights shall be exercised with the participation of and in agreement with the Federal Government; in this connection the responsibility of the Federation for the country as a whole shall be maintained.

(7) Details regarding paragraphs (4) to (6) shall be the subject of a law which shall require the consent of the Bundesrat.

ARTICLE 24 (International organizations)

(1) The Federation may by legislation transfer sovereign powers to international organizations.

(1a) Where the Länder have the right to exercise state powers and to discharge state functions they may with the consent of the Federal Government transfer sovereign powers to transfrontier institutions in neighboring regions.

(2) With a view to maintaining peace the Federation may become a party to a system of collective security; in doing so it shall consent to such limitations upon its sovereign powers as will bring about and secure a peaceful and lasting order in Europe and among the nations of the world.

(3) For the purpose of settling international disputes the Federation shall accede to agreements providing for general, comprehensive and obligatory international arbitration.

ARTICLE 25 (International law and federal law)

The general rules of international law shall be an integral part of federal law. They shall override laws and directly establish rights and obligations for the inhabitants of the federal territory.

ARTICLE 26 (Ban on preparations for military aggression)

(1) Any activities apt or intended to disturb peaceful international relations, especially preparations for military aggression, shall be unconstitutional. They shall be made a criminal offense.

(2) Weapons designed for warfare may not be manufac-

tured, transported or marketed except with the permission of the Federal Government. Details shall be the subject of a federal law.

ARTICLE 27 (The merchant fleet)

All German merchant vessels shall form one merchant fleet.

ARTICLE 28 (Federal guarantee of Land constitutions and local government)

(1) The constitutional order in the Länder shall conform to the principles of the republican, democratic and social state governed by the rule of law within the meaning of this Basic Law. In each of the Länder, counties and municipalities the people shall be represented by a body elected by general, direct, free, equal and secret ballot. In county and municipal elections persons who are nationals of member states of the European Community, too, may vote and shall be eligible for election in accordance with European Community law. In the municipalities the local council may take the place of an elected body.

(2) The municipalities shall be guaranteed the right to manage all the affairs of the local community on their own responsibility within the limits set by law. Within the framework of their statutory functions the associations of municipalities likewise have the right of self-government in accordance with the law.

(3) The Federation shall ensure that the constitutional order of the Länder conforms to the basic rights and the provisions of paragraphs (1) and (2) of this Article.

ARTICLE 29 (Modification of boundaries)

(1) Boundaries may be modified to ensure that the Länder, by virtue of their size and capacity, can effectively perform their functions. Due regard shall be given to regional, historical and cultural ties, economic expediency and the requirements of regional policy and planning.

(2) Boundary modifications shall be introduced by federal law which shall require confirmation by referendum. The affected Länder shall be consulted.

(3) A referendum shall be held in the Länder from whose territories or parts thereof a new Land or a Land with redefined boundaries is to be formed (affected Länder). The question to be voted on is whether the affected Länder are to remain within their existing boundaries or whether the new Land or Land with redefined boundaries should be formed. The vote shall be in favor of the formation of a new Land or of a Land with redefined boundaries if the modification is approved by a majority in the future territory of such Land and in the territories or parts thereof as a whole of an affected Land whose affiliation with a Land is to be changed according-

ly. The vote shall not be in favor where in the territory of one of the affected Länder a majority reject the change; such rejection shall, however, be of no consequence where in one part of the territory whose affiliation with the affected Land is to be changed a majority of two-thirds approve, unless in the entire territory of the affected Land a majority of two-thirds reject the change.

(4) Where in a clearly defined, homogeneous community and economic area whose parts lie in several Länder and which has a population of at least one million one-tenth of those entitled to vote in Bundestag elections submit a petition to the effect that the area in question belong to one Land, a federal law shall be enacted within two years which shall determine whether boundaries of the affected Länder are to be modified pursuant to paragraph (2) of this Article or that a referendum is to be held in the affected Länder.

(5) The referendum shall establish whether a boundary modification proposed in the law meets with approval. The law may contain different but not more than two proposals for the referendum. If a majority approve a proposed boundary modification a federal law shall be enacted within two years which shall determine whether such modification is to be introduced pursuant to paragraph (2) of this Article. If the referendum is approved in accordance with the third and fourth sentences of paragraph (3) of this Article a federal law providing for the formation of the proposed Land shall be enacted within two years of the referendum and shall not require any further confirmation by referendum.

(6) A majority in a referendum shall be a majority of the votes cast, provided that they amount to at least one-quarter of those entitled to vote in Bundestag elections. Detailed provisions concerning referendums and petitions shall be the subject of a federal law which may also provide that petitions may not be repeated within a period of five years.

(7) Other modifications of Land boundaries may be effected by agreement between the Länder concerned or by a federal law with the approval of the Bundesrat where the territory which is to be the subject of a boundary modification does not have more than 10,000 inhabitants. Details shall be the subject of a federal law requiring the approval of the Bundesrat and the majority of the Members of the Bundestag. It shall make provision for the affected municipalities and counties to be heard.

ARTICLE 30 *(Powers of the Federation and the Länder)*

Except as otherwise provided or permitted by this Basic Law the exercise of governmental powers and the discharge of governmental functions shall be incumbent on the Länder.

ARTICLE 31 *(Precedence of federal law)*

Federal law shall override Land law.

ARTICLE 32 *(Foreign relations)*

(1) Relations with other states shall be conducted by the Federation.

(2) Before a treaty which affects the specific circumstances of a German Land is concluded that Land shall be consulted in good time.

(3) In so far as the Länder have power to legislate they may, with the consent of the Federal Government, conclude treaties with other states.

ARTICLE 33 *(Equal civil status, professional civil service)*

(1) All Germans in every Land have the same civil rights and duties.

(2) All Germans are equally eligible for any public office according to their aptitude, qualifications and professional ability.

(3) The enjoyment of civil rights, eligibility for public office, and rights acquired in the public service shall not depend on a person's religious denomination. Nobody may suffer disadvantage by reason of their adherence or nonadherence to a denomination or their other convictions.

(4) The exercise of public authority as a permanent function shall, as a rule, be entrusted to members of the public service whose status, service and loyalty are governed by public law.

(5) Public service law shall be based on the traditional principles of the professional civil service.

ARTICLE 34 *(Liability for neglect of duty)*

Should anybody, in exercising a public office, neglect their duty towards a third party liability shall rest in principle with the state or the public body employing them. In the event of willful intent or gross negligence remedy may be sought against the person concerned. In respect of claims for compensation or remedy recourse to the ordinary courts shall not be precluded.

ARTICLE 35 *(Judicial and administrative assistance)*

(1) All federal and Land authorities shall render each other judicial and administrative assistance.

(2) In order to maintain or restore public safety or order a Land may in particularly serious cases call upon forces and facilities of the Federal Border Guard to assist its police where without such assistance the police could not, or only with considerable difficulty, carry out an assignment. In order to cope with a natural disaster or a particularly serious accident a Land may request the assistance of the police forces of other Länder or the forces and facilities of other administrative authorities or of the Federal Border Guard or the Armed Forces.

(3) Where the natural disaster or accident endangers a region larger than a Land the Federal Government may, in so far

as necessary to effectively combat such danger, instruct the Land governments to place their police forces at the disposal of other Länder and employ units of the Federal Border Guard or the Armed Forces in support of the police forces. Measures taken by the Federal Government pursuant to the first sentence of this paragraph shall be revoked at any time if requested by the Bundesrat, otherwise as soon as the danger has been removed.

ARTICLE 36 (Staff of federal authorities)

(1) Civil servants of supreme federal authorities shall be drawn from all Länder on a proportionate basis. People employed by other federal authorities should as a rule be drawn from the Land where those authorities are located.

(2) Military service laws shall, inter alia, take into account both the division of the Federation into Länder and the regional ties of their populations.

ARTICLE 37 (Exercise of federal authority over the Länder)

(1) Where a Land fails to comply with its federal obligations under this Basic Law or other federal law the Federal Government may, with the consent of the Bundesrat, take the necessary steps to enforce compliance.

(2) In exercising this authority the Federal Government or its representative may issue directives to all Länder and their authorities.

Chapter III. The Bundestag

ARTICLE 38 (Elections)

(1) The Members of the German Bundestag shall be elected in general, direct, free, equal and secret elections. They shall be representatives of the whole people; they shall not be bound by any instructions, only by their conscience.

(2) Anybody who has reached the age of eighteen is entitled to vote; anybody of majority age is eligible for election.

(3) Details shall be the subject of a federal law.

ARTICLE 39 (Electoral period and assembly of the Bundestag)

(1) The Bundestag shall be elected for four years. Its electoral period shall end with the assembly of a new Bundestag. The new election shall be held forty-five months at the earliest and forty-seven months at the latest after the beginning of the electoral period. Where the Bundestag is dissolved the new election shall be held within sixty days.

(2) The Bundestag shall assemble on the thirtieth day after the election at the latest.

(3) The Bundestag shall determine when its sittings are to end and be resumed. The President of the Bundestag may convene it earlier. The President shall be obliged to do so if one-third of the Members, the Federal President or the Federal Chancellor so demands.

ARTICLE 40 (President, rules of procedure)

(1) The Bundestag shall elect its President, Vice-Presidents and Secretaries. It shall draw up rules of procedure.

(2) The President shall exercise proprietary rights and police powers in the Bundestag building. No search or seizure may take place on the premises of the Bundestag without the President's permission.

ARTICLE 41 (Scrutiny of elections)

(1) Scrutiny of elections shall be the responsibility of the Bundestag. It shall also decide whether a Member's seat is forfeited.

(2) Complaints against such decisions of the Bundestag may be lodged with the Federal Constitutional Court.

(3) Details shall be the subject of a federal law.

ARTICLE 42 (Proceedings, voting)

(1) Sittings of the Bundestag shall be public. Upon a motion of one-tenth of the Members or the Federal Government the public may be excluded by a two-thirds majority. The vote on the motion shall be taken at a sitting not open to the public.

(2) Decisions of the Bundestag shall require a majority of the votes cast unless this Basic Law provides otherwise. The rules of procedure may provide for exceptions in respect of elections to be held by the Bundestag.

(3) True and accurate reports on public meetings of the Bundestag and its committees shall not give rise to any liability.

ARTICLE 43 (Attendance of members of the Federal Government and the Bundesrat)

(1) The Bundestag and its committees may demand the presence of any member of the Federal Government.

(2) The Members of the Bundesrat and the Federal Government as well as their representatives may attend any sittings of the Bundestag and its committees. They shall be heard at any time.

ARTICLE 44 (Committees of inquiry)

(1) The Bundestag has the right, and upon the motion of one-quarter of its Members the obligation, to set up committees of inquiry which shall hear evidence in public. The public may be excluded.

(2) The rules of criminal procedure shall apply *mutatis mutandis* to the hearing of evidence. The privacy of correspondence, posts and telecommunications shall remain unaffected.

(3) Courts and administrative authorities shall be bound to render judicial and administrative assistance.

(4) Decisions of committees of inquiry shall not be subject to judicial review. The courts shall be free to evaluate the facts on which the inquiry is based.

ARTICLE 45 *(The Committee on European Union)*

The Bundestag shall appoint a Committee on European Union. It may empower the Committee to exercise the Bundestag's rights in relation to the Federal Government in accordance with Article 23.

ARTICLE 45a *(The Foreign Affairs and Defense Committees)*

(1) The Bundestag shall appoint a Committee on Foreign Affairs and a Committee on Defense.

(2) The Committee on Defense also has the powers of a committee of inquiry. Upon the motion of one-quarter of its members it shall be obliged to investigate a specific matter.

(3) Paragraph (1) of Article 44 shall not apply to defense matters.

ARTICLE 45b *(The Parliamentary Commissioner for the Armed Forces)*

A Parliamentary Commissioner shall be appointed to safeguard the basic rights of members of the Armed Forces and to assist the Bundestag in exercising parliamentary control. Details shall be the subject of a federal law.

ARTICLE 45c *(The Petitions Committee)*

(1) The Bundestag shall appoint a Petitions Committee to deal with requests and complaints addressed to the Bundestag pursuant to Article 17.

(2) The powers of the Committee to consider complaints shall be the subject of a federal law.

ARTICLE 46 *(Indemnity and immunity)*

(1) A Member may at no time be subjected to court proceedings or disciplinary action or otherwise called to account outside the Bundestag for a vote cast or a statement made in the Bundestag or any of its committees. This shall not apply to defamatory insults.

(2) A Member may not be called to account or arrested for a punishable offense except by permission of the Bundestag, unless the person concerned is apprehended in the act of committing the offense or in the course of the following day.

(3) Permission of the Bundestag shall also be necessary for any other restriction of a Member's personal liberty or for the institution of proceedings against a Member under Article 18.

(4) Any criminal proceedings or proceedings under Article 18 against a Member and any detention or other restriction of the Member's personal liberty shall be suspended if the Bundestag so demands.

ARTICLE 47 *(Refusal to give evidence)*

Members may refuse to give evidence concerning persons who have confided information to them in their capacity as Members of the Bundestag or to whom they themselves have confided information in that capacity, as well as evidence concerning the information itself. To the extent that this right to refuse to give evidence applies, seizure of documents shall not be permissible.

ARTICLE 48 *(Entitlements of Members)*

(1) All candidates for election to the Bundestag are entitled to the leave necessary for their election campaign.

(2) Nobody may be prevented from assuming and exercising the office of Member of the Bundestag. Nobody may be given notice or dismissed from their employment on this ground.

(3) Members are entitled to adequate remuneration ensuring their independence. They are entitled to use all public transport free of charge. Details shall be the subject of a federal law.

ARTICLE 49 *(Repealed)*

Chapter IV. The Bundesrat

ARTICLE 50 *(Function)*

The Länder shall participate through the Bundesrat in the legislative process and administration of the Federation and in matters concerning the European Union.

ARTICLE 51 *(Composition)*

(1) The Bundesrat shall consist of members of the Land governments which appoint and recall them. Other members of their governments may serve as alternates.

(2) Each Land shall have at least three votes; Länder with more than two million inhabitants shall have four, Länder with more than six million inhabitants five, and Länder with more than seven million inhabitants six votes.

(3) Each Land may delegate as many members as it has votes. The votes of each Land may be cast only as a block vote and only by Members present or their alternates.

ARTICLE 52 *(President, rules of procedure)*

(1) The Bundesrat shall elect its President for one year.

(2) The President shall convene the Bundesrat. The President shall be obliged to do so where the delegates of at least two Länder or the Federal Government so demand.

(3) The Bundesrat shall take its decisions with at least the majority of its votes. It shall draw up rules of procedure. Its sittings shall be public. The public may be excluded.

(3a) For matters concerning the European Union the Bundesrat may form a Chamber for European Affairs whose decisions shall be considered decisions of the Bundesrat; paragraph (2) and paragraph (3), second sentence, of Article 51 shall apply *mutatis mutandis*.

(4) Other members or representatives of the Land governments may serve on the committees of the Bundesrat.

ARTICLE 53 (*Attendance of members of the Federal Government*)

The members of the Federal Government have the right, and upon demand a duty, to attend sittings of the Bundesrat and its committees. They shall be heard at any time. The Bundesrat shall be kept informed by the Federal Government about the conduct of business.

Chapter IVa. The Joint Committee

ARTICLE 53a (*Composition, rules of procedure*)

(1) Two-thirds of the Joint Committee shall be Members of the Bundestag and one-third Members of the Bundesrat. The Bundestag shall delegate Members in proportion to the strengths of its parliamentary groups; they may not be members of the Federal Government. Each Land shall be represented by a Bundesrat Member of its choice; these Members shall not be bound by instructions. The establishment of the Joint Committee and its procedures shall be governed by rules of procedure to be adopted by the Bundestag and requiring the consent of the Bundesrat.

(2) The Federal Government shall inform the Joint Committee about plans to be put into effect in the event of a state of defense. The right of the Bundestag and its committees under paragraph (1) of Article 43 shall remain unaffected.

Chapter V. The Federal President

ARTICLE 54 (*Election*)

(1) The Federal President shall be elected by the Federal Convention without debate. Every German entitled to vote in Bundestag elections and at least forty years old is eligible.

(2) The term of office of the Federal President shall be five years. Reelection for a consecutive term shall be permitted once only.

(3) The Federal Convention shall consist of the Members of the Bundestag and an equal number of members elected by the Land parliaments on the basis of proportional representation.

(4) The Federal Convention shall convene not later than thirty days before the expiration of the term of office of the Federal President or, in the event that it is prematurely terminated, not later than thirty days after that date. It shall be convened by the President of the Bundestag.

(5) After the expiration of a legislative term the period specified in the first sentence of paragraph (4) of this Article shall begin with the first meeting of the Bundestag.

(6) The candidate receiving the votes of the majority of the members of the Federal Convention is elected. If such majority is not obtained by any candidate in two ballots the one who receives most votes in the next ballot is elected.

(7) Details shall be the subject of a federal law.

ARTICLE 55 (*Debarment from other office*)

(1) The Federal President may not be a member of the government nor of a legislative body of the Federation or a Land.

(2) The Federal President may not hold any other salaried office nor practice a trade or profession nor belong to the management or supervisory board of an enterprise.

ARTICLE 56 (*Oath of office*)

On taking office the Federal President shall swear the following oath before the assembled Members of the Bundestag and the Bundesrat:

"I swear that I will dedicate my efforts to the well-being of the German people, enhance their benefits, save them from harm, uphold and defend the Basic Law and the laws of the Federation, perform my duties conscientiously, and do justice to all. So help me God."

The oath may be sworn without the religious affirmation.

ARTICLE 57 (*Deputization*)

Should the Federal President be prevented from performing the duties of office or should the office become vacant prematurely those duties shall be performed by the President of the Bundesrat.

ARTICLE 58 (*Countersignature*)

Orders and directives of the Federal President shall require for their validity the countersignature of the Federal Chancellor or the appropriate Federal Minister. This shall not apply to the appointment and dismissal of the Federal Chancellor, the dissolution of the Bundestag under Article 63, or a request made under paragraph (3) of Article 69.

ARTICLE 59 (*Representation of the Federation*)

(1) The Federal President represents the Federation in its international relations. He concludes treaties with other states on its behalf. He accredits and receives envoys.

(2) Treaties which regulate the political relations of the Federation or relate to matters of federal legislation shall require the approval or participation of the appropriate legislative

body in the form of a federal law. In the case of administrative agreements the provisions concerning federal administration shall apply *mutatis mutandis*.

ARTICLE 59a *(Repealed)*

ARTICLE 60 *(Appointment and dismissal of federal judges, federal civil servants and officers of the Armed Forces; prerogative of pardon)*

(1) The Federal President shall appoint and dismiss federal judges, federal civil servants and commissioned and noncommissioned officers of the Armed Forces unless otherwise provided for by law.

(2) The Federal President shall exercise the prerogative of pardon in individual cases on behalf of the Federation.

(3) These powers may be delegated to other authorities.

(4) Paragraphs (2) to (4) of Article 46 shall apply *mutatis mutandis* to the Federal President.

ARTICLE 61 *(Impeachment before the Federal Constitutional Court)*

(1) The Bundestag or the Bundesrat may impeach the Federal President before the Federal Constitutional Court for willful violation of the Basic Law or any other federal law. The motion for impeachment must have the support of at least one-quarter of the Members of the Bundestag or one-quarter of the votes of the Bundesrat. It must be carried by a majority of two-thirds of the Members of the Bundestag or two-thirds of the votes of the Bundesrat. The impeachment shall be pleaded by a representative of the impeaching body.

(2) Should the Federal Constitutional Court find the Federal President guilty of a willful violation of the Basic Law or any other federal law it may declare the office forfeited. After impeachment it may issue an injunction preventing the Federal President from performing the duties of office.

Chapter VI. The Federal Government

ARTICLE 62 *(Composition)*

The Federal Government shall consist of the Federal Chancellor and the Federal Ministers.

ARTICLE 63 *(Election and appointment of the Federal Chancellor)*

(1) The Federal Chancellor shall be elected by the Bundestag without debate upon the proposal of the Federal President.

(2) The candidate obtaining the votes of the majority of the Members of the Bundestag is elected. The person elected shall be appointed by the Federal President.

(3) If the candidate is not elected the Bundestag may, within fourteen days of the ballot, elect a Federal Chancellor with more than one-half of its Members.

(4) If no candidate has been elected within this period a new ballot shall be held without delay in which the person gaining most votes is elected. If the elected candidate has obtained the votes of the majority of the Members of the Bundestag the Federal President must make the appointment within seven days of the election. Failing that majority the Federal President shall either make the appointment or dissolve the Bundestag within seven days.

ARTICLE 64 *(Appointment of Federal Ministers)*

(1) The Federal Ministers shall be appointed and dismissed by the Federal President upon the proposal of the Federal Chancellor.

(2) On taking office the Federal Chancellor and the Federal Ministers shall swear before the Bundestag the oath provided for in Article 56.

ARTICLE 65 *(Powers within the Federal Government)*

The Federal Chancellor shall determine and be responsible for general policy guidelines. Within the limits set by these guidelines each Federal Minister shall run his department independently and on his own responsibility. The Federal Government shall settle differences of opinion between Federal Ministers. The Federal Chancellor shall preside over the conduct of Federal Government business in accordance with rules of procedure adopted by it and approved by the Federal President.

ARTICLE 65a *(Command of the Armed Forces)*

Command of the Armed Forces shall be vested in the Federal Minister of Defense.

ARTICLE 66 *(Debarment from other office)*

The Federal Chancellor and the Federal Ministers may not hold any other salaried office nor practice a trade or profession nor belong to the management or, without the consent of the Bundestag, the supervisory board of an enterprise.

ARTICLE 67 *(Constructive vote of no confidence)*

(1) The Bundestag may express its lack of confidence in the Federal Chancellor only by electing a successor with the majority of its Members and requesting the Federal President to dismiss the incumbent. The Federal President must comply with the request and appoint the person elected.

(2) Forty-eight hours must elapse between the motion and the vote.

ARTICLE 68 *(Vote of confidence, dissolution of the Bundestag)*

(1) Where a motion of the Federal Chancellor for a vote of confidence is not carried by the majority of the Members of the Bundestag the Federal President may, upon the proposal of the Federal Chancellor, dissolve the Bundestag within twenty-one days. As soon as the Bundestag elects another Federal Chancellor with the majority of its Members it may no longer be dissolved.

(2) Forty-eight hours must elapse between the motion and the vote.

ARTICLE 69 *(The Deputy Federal Chancellor and members of the Federal Government)*

(1) The Federal Chancellor shall appoint a Federal Minister as his deputy.

(2) The tenure of office of the Federal Chancellor or a Federal Minister shall end in any event when a new Bundestag convenes, that of a Federal Minister also where the Federal Chancellor's tenure ceases for any other reason.

(3) At the request of the Federal President the Federal Chancellor, or at the request of the Federal Chancellor or of the Federal President a Federal Minister, shall be obliged to continue in office until a successor has been appointed.

Chapter VII. Federal Legislation

ARTICLE 70 *(Legislative jurisdiction of the Federation and the Länder)*

(1) The Länder have the right to legislate in so far as this Basic Law does not confer legislative powers on the Federation.

(2) The legislative jurisdiction of the Federation and the Länder shall be governed by the provisions of this Basic Law concerning exclusive and concurrent legislation.

ARTICLE 71 *(Exclusive legislation of the Federation)*

In matters of exclusive federal legislation the Länder have the right to legislate only where and to the extent that they are explicitly empowered by federal law.

ARTICLE 72 *(Concurrent legislation of the Federation)*

(1) In matters of concurrent legislation the Länder have the right to legislate as long as and to the extent that the Federation does not exercise its legislative powers.

(2) The Federation has the right to legislate where

1. a matter cannot be effectively regulated by the legislation of individual Länder, or

2. regulation by a Land might prejudice the interests of other Länder or the country as a whole or

3. the maintenance of legal and economic unity, especially uniform living conditions beyond the territory of any one Land, calls for federal legislation.

ARTICLE 73 *(Areas of exclusive legislation)*

The Federation shall have exclusive legislative jurisdiction in respect of:

1. foreign affairs and defense including protection of the civilian population;

2. citizenship in the Federation;

3. freedom of movement, passports, immigration, emigration and extradition;

4. currency, money and coinage, weights and measures, as well as standard time;

5. unity of the customs and trading area, treaties of commerce and navigation, free movement of goods, as well as international trade and payments including customs and border protection;

6. air transport;

6a. the operation of railways wholly or majority-owned by the Federation (federal railways), the construction, maintenance and operation of tracks of the federal railways as well as rates charged for the use of tracks;

7. postal and telecommunications services;

8. the legal status of persons employed by the Federation and federal public corporations;

9. industrial property rights, copyright and publishing;

10. cooperation between the Federation and the Länder in

(a) criminal police work,

(b) safeguarding the free democratic basic order and existence of the Federation or a Land (protection of the constitution), and

(c) measures to counter activities in the federal territory which through preparations for or the use of force jeopardize the external interests of the Federal Republic of Germany, as well as the establishment of a Federal Criminal Police Office and international action to combat crime;

11. statistics for federal purposes.

ARTICLE 74 *(Areas of concurrent legislation)*

Concurrent legislative jurisdiction shall cover:

1. civil law, criminal law and penal measures, court organization and procedure, the legal profession, notarial and legal advice services;

2. registration of births, deaths and marriages;

3. association and assembly;

4. foreigners' residence and establishment;

4a. weapons and explosives;

5. measures to prevent the transfer of German cultural property abroad;

6. refugees and expellees;

7. public welfare;

8. citizenship in the Länder;

9. war damage and restitution;

10. pensions for war-disabled persons and dependents of war victims as well as assistance for former prisoners of war;

10a. war graves and graves of other victims of war and despotism;

11. economic affairs (mining, industry, energy, crafts and trades, commerce, banking, the stock exchange system and private insurance);

11a. production and utilization of nuclear energy for peaceful purposes, construction and operation of facilities serving such purposes, protection against hazards arising from the release of nuclear energy or from ionizing radiation, and disposal of radioactive substances;

12. labor relations including works constitution, industrial safety, labor placement, as well as social security including unemployment insurance;

13. educational and training grants and promotion of research;

14. expropriation where applicable to the matters enumerated in Articles 73 and 74;

15. transfer of land, natural resources and means of production to public ownership or other forms of public enterprise;

16. measures to prevent abuse of economic power;

17. promotion of agricultural production and forestry, food security, import and export of agricultural and forestry products, deep-sea and coastal fishing and coastal preservation;

18. real property transactions, land law and agricultural lease, as well as housing and land settlement;

19. measures to combat communicable human and animal diseases that constitute a danger to public health, admission to the medical or ancillary professions, as well as trade in drugs, medicines, narcotics and poisons;

19a. economic viability of hospitals and regulation of hospital charges;

20. protective measures in connection with the marketing of food, drink and tobacco, essential commodities, feedstuffs, agricultural and forest seed and seedlings, protection of plants against diseases and pests, as well as protection of animals;

21. ocean and coastal shipping, as well as sea-marks, inland navigation, meteorological services, sea routes and inland waterways used for general traffic;

22. road traffic, motor transport, construction and maintenance of roads for long-distance traffic as well as the collection of tolls for the use of public highways and allocation of the revenue;

23. nonfederal rail-bound systems, except mountain railways;

24. waste disposal, air pollution control and noise abatement.

ARTICLE 74a (*Concurrent legislation of the Federation, public service pay scales and pensions*)

(1) Concurrent legislation shall also extend to the pay scales and pensions of members of the public service whose status, service and loyalty are governed by public law in so far as the Federation does not have exclusive powers to legislate pursuant to Article 73 No. 8.

(2) Federal legislation pursuant to paragraph (1) of this Article shall require the consent of the Bundesrat.

(3) Federal legislation pursuant to Article 73 No. 8 shall likewise require the consent of the Bundesrat in so far as it envisages criteria for the structuring and computation of pay scales and pensions including appraisal of posts other than those provided for in federal legislation pursuant to paragraph (1) of this Article.

(4) Paragraphs (1) and (2) of this Article shall apply *mutatis mutandis* to the pay scales and pensions for Land judges. Paragraph (3) of this Article shall apply *mutatis mutandis* to legislation pursuant to paragraph (1) of Article 98.

ARTICLE 75 (*Areas of federal framework legislation*)

Subject to the conditions laid down in Article 72 the Federation has the right to enact framework legislation on:

1. the legal status of persons in the public service of the Länder, municipalities or other public corporations in so far as Article 74a does not provide otherwise;

1a. the general principles of higher education;

2. the general legal status of the press and the film industry;

3. hunting, nature conservation and landscape management;

4. land distribution, regional planning and water management;

5. registration of residence or domicile, as well as identity documents.

ARTICLE 76 (*Bills*)

(1) Bills shall be presented in the Bundestag by the Federal Government, Members of the Bundestag or the Bundesrat.

(2) Bills of the Federal Government shall first be submitted to the Bundesrat. The Bundesrat is entitled to comment upon them within six weeks. Where in exceptional cases the Federal Government declares a bill to be particularly urgent it may refer it to the Bundestag three weeks after its submission to the Bundesrat even though it may not yet have received the latter's comments: upon receiving such comments it shall transmit them to the Bundestag without delay.

(3) Bills of the Bundesrat shall be submitted to the Bundestag by the Federal Government within three months. The Federal Government shall state its own opinion on them.

ARTICLE 77 *(The legislative process)*

(1) Bills shall be adopted by the Bundestag. After their adoption they shall be transmitted to the Bundesrat by the President of the Bundestag without delay.

(2) The Bundesrat may within three weeks of receiving the adopted bill demand that it be referred to a committee composed of Members of the Bundestag and the Bundesrat. The composition and proceedings of this committee shall be governed by rules of procedure drawn up by the Bundestag and requiring the consent of the Bundesrat. The Members of the Bundesrat on this committee shall not be bound by instructions. Where the consent of the Bundesrat is required for a bill to become law the Bundestag and the Federal Government may likewise request that it be referred to such a committee. Should the committee propose an amendment to the bill the Bundestag shall vote on it a second time.

(3) In so far as its consent is not required for a bill to become law the Bundesrat may, when the procedure described in paragraph (2) of this Article is completed, object within two weeks to a bill adopted by the Bundestag. The period for objection shall begin, in the case of the last sentence of paragraph (2) of this Article, on receipt of the bill as passed again by the Bundestag and in all other cases on receipt of a communication from the chairman of the committee provided for in paragraph (2) of this Article to the effect that the committee's proceedings have been concluded.

(4) If the objection was adopted with a majority of the votes of the Bundesrat it may be rejected by a decision of the majority of the Members of the Bundestag. If the Bundesrat adopted the objection with a majority of at least two-thirds of its votes its rejection by the Bundestag shall require a majority of two-thirds of the votes or at least the majority of the Members of the Bundestag.

ARTICLE 78 *(Passage of federal laws)*

A bill adopted by the Bundestag shall become law if the Bundesrat consents, does not request a referral as provided for in paragraph (2) of Article 77, does not enter an objection within the period stipulated in paragraph (3) of Article 77 or withdraws its objection, or if the objection is overridden by the Bundestag.

ARTICLE 79 *(Amendments to the Basic Law)*

(1) This Basic Law may be amended only by a law expressly modifying or supplementing its text. In respect of international treaties concerning a peace settlement, the preparation of a peace settlement, or the phasing out of an occupation regime, or serving the defense of the Federal Republic, it shall be sufficient, in order to make clear that the provisions of this Basic Law do not preclude the conclusion and entry into force of such treaties, to supplement the text of this Basic Law and to confine the supplement to such clarification.

(2) Such law must be carried by two-thirds of the Members of the Bundestag and two-thirds of the votes of the Bundesrat.

(3) Amendments to this Basic Law affecting the division of the Federation into Länder, their participation in the legislative process, or the principles laid down in Articles 1 and 20 shall be prohibited.

ARTICLE 80 *(Delegated legislation)*

(1) The Federal Government, a Federal Minister or the Land governments may be empowered by law to issue statutory orders. The content, purpose and scope of that power shall be specified in the law. Statutory orders shall contain a reference to their legal basis. Where the law provides that the power to issue statutory orders may be further delegated another statutory order shall be required to that effect.

(2) Unless otherwise provided for by federal legislation the consent of the Bundesrat shall be required for statutory orders issued by the Federal Government or a Federal Minister concerning rules and rates governing the use of postal and telecommunications services, rules governing rates for the use of federal railways or concerning the construction and operation of railways, as well as for statutory orders issued pursuant to federal legislation requiring the consent of the Bundesrat or implemented by the Länder as agents of the Federation or in their own right.

ARTICLE 80a *(Application of legal provisions where a state of tension exists)*

(1) Where this Basic Law or a federal law on defense including protection of the civilian population stipulates that legal provisions may only be applied in accordance with this Article their application shall, except where the country is in a state of defense, be admissible only after the Bundestag has confirmed that a state of tension exists or where it has specifically approved such application. Confirmation of a state of tension and specific approval in the cases mentioned in the first sentence of paragraph (5) and the second sentence of paragraph (6) of Article 12a shall require a two-thirds majority of the votes cast.

(2) Any measures taken by virtue of legal provisions pursuant to paragraph (1) of this Article shall be revoked should the Bundestag so require.

(3) In derogation of paragraph (1) of this Article the application of such legal provisions shall also be admissible by virtue of and in accordance with a decision taken by an international organization within the framework of a treaty of alliance with the approval of the Federal Government. Any measures taken pursuant to this paragraph shall be re-

voked should the Bundestag with the majority of its Members so require.

ARTICLE 81 (Legislative emergency)

(1) Should in the circumstances provided for in Article 68 the Bundestag not be dissolved the Federal President may at the request of the Federal Government and with the consent of the Bundesrat declare a state of legislative emergency with respect to a bill which is rejected by the Bundestag although declared urgent by the Federal Government. The same shall apply where a bill has been rejected despite the Federal Chancellor having combined it with a motion under Article 68.

(2) Where after a state of legislative emergency has been declared the Bundestag again rejects the bill or adopts a version unacceptable to the Federal Government it shall be deemed to have become law if it receives the consent of the Bundesrat. The same shall apply where the bill is not passed by the Bundestag within four weeks of its reintroduction.

(3) During the term of office of a Federal Chancellor any other bill rejected by the Bundestag may become law in accordance with paragraphs (1) and (2) of this Article within a period of six months after the first declaration of a state of legislative emergency. After the expiration of this period no further declaration of a state of legislative emergency may be made during the term of office of the same Federal Chancellor.

(4) The Basic Law may not be amended nor repealed nor suspended in whole or in part by a law pursuant to paragraph (2) of this Article.

ARTICLE 82 (Signing, promulgation and entry into force)

(1) Laws enacted in accordance with the provisions of this Basic Law shall, after countersignature, be signed by the Federal President and promulgated in the Federal Law Gazette. Statutory orders shall be signed by the authority which issues them and, unless otherwise provided by law, promulgated in the Federal Law Gazette.

(2) Every law and statutory order should specify the day on which it enters into force. In the absence of such a provision it shall take effect on the fourteenth day after the day on which the Federal Law Gazette containing it was published.

Chapter VIII. Implementation of Federal Legislation, Federal Administration

ARTICLE 83 (Federal legislation)

The Länder shall implement federal legislation in their own right in so far as this Basic Law does not provide or permit otherwise.

ARTICLE 84 (Implementation by the Länder, supervision by the Federal Government)

(1) Where the Länder implement federal legislation in their own right they shall establish the authorities and administrative procedures in so far as federal legislation with Bundesrat consent does not provide otherwise.

(2) The Federal Government may, with the consent of the Bundesrat, issue general administrative rules.

(3) The Federal Government shall oversee the implementation of federal legislation by the Länder in accordance with applicable law. For this purpose the Federal Government may send commissioners to the supreme Land authorities and, with their approval or, where it is refused, with the consent of the Bundesrat, to subordinate authorities as well.

(4) Should any shortcomings in the implementation of federal legislation in the Länder which have been identified by the Federal Government not be rectified the Bundesrat shall decide, at the request of the Federal Government or the Land concerned, whether that Land is in breach of the law. The decision of the Bundesrat may be appealed in the Federal Constitutional Court.

(5) With a view to implementing federal legislation the Federal Government may be empowered by a federal law requiring the consent of the Bundesrat to issue directives in special cases. They shall be addressed to the supreme Land authorities unless the Federal Government deems the matter urgent.

ARTICLE 85 (Implementation by the Länder for the Federation)

(1) Where the Länder implement federal legislation for the Federation the establishment of authorities shall remain their concern except in so far as federal legislation with the consent of the Bundesrat provides otherwise.

(2) The Federal Government may, with the consent of the Bundesrat, issue general administrative rules. It may provide for the uniform training of civil servants and other public employees. The heads of intermediate authorities shall be appointed with its approval.

(3) The Land authorities shall comply with directives from the supreme federal authorities concerned. Such directives shall be addressed to the supreme Land authorities unless the Federal Government deems the matter urgent. Compliance with directives shall be ensured by the supreme Land authorities.

(4) Federal supervision shall relate to the legality and expediency of implementation. For this purpose the Federal Government may call for reports and the submission of files and send commissioners to any authority.

ARTICLE 86 *(Direct federal administration)*

Where the Federation implements laws through its own administration or through federal public corporations or institutions the Federal Government shall, in so far as the law in question does not contain any specific provision in this respect, issue the general administrative rules. It shall provide for the establishment of the necessary authorities unless the law provides otherwise.

ARTICLE 87 *(Areas of direct federal administration)*

(1) The Foreign Service, federal financial administration, posts and telecommunications administration and, in accordance with the provisions of Article 89, administration of federal waterways and shipping shall be under the direct responsibility of the Federation and have their own organizational substructures. Federal legislation may establish Federal Border Guard authorities and central offices for police information and communications, the criminal police and compilation of data for the purpose of protecting the constitution and countering activities on federal territory which, through the use of force or preparations for it, jeopardize the external interests of the Federal Republic of Germany.

(2) Social insurance institutions whose jurisdiction extends beyond the territory of one Land shall be administered as federal public corporations.

(3) Furthermore, independent higher federal authorities as well as new federal public corporations and institutions may be established by federal law for matters falling within the legislative jurisdiction of the Federation. Where new responsibilities arise for the Federation in areas where it has the power to legislate, intermediate and lower federal authorities may, in case of urgent need, be established with the consent of the Bundesrat and the majority of the Members of the Bundestag.

ARTICLE 87a *(Establishment and purpose of the Armed Forces)*

(1) The Federation shall establish Armed Forces for defense purposes. Their numerical strength and general organizational structure shall be shown in the budget.

(2) Other than for defense purposes the Armed Forces may only be employed to the extent explicitly permitted by this Basic Law.

(3) When a state of defense or tension exists the Armed Forces shall be authorized to protect civilian property and perform traffic control functions to the extent necessary to fulfill their defense mission. Moreover, they may, when a state of defense or tension exists, be assigned to protect civilian property, where necessary also in support of police measures; in this event the Armed Forces shall cooperate with the appropriate authorities.

(4) Where necessary to avert an imminent danger to the existence or free democratic basic order of the Federation or a Land the Federal Government may, should the conditions referred to in paragraph (2) of Article 91 prevail and the police forces and the Federal Border Guard be insufficient, employ Armed Forces to support the police and the Federal Border Guard in protecting civilian property and combating organized armed insurgents. Any such employment of Armed Forces shall be terminated if the Bundestag or the Bundesrat so requires.

ARTICLE 87b *(The Federal Defense Administration)*

(1) The Federal Defense Administration shall be the direct responsibility of the Federation and have its own organizational substructure. It shall be responsible for personnel and directly provide the equipment and facilities required by the Armed Forces. Responsibilities connected with the pensions of disabled persons or construction may not be assigned to the Federal Defense Administration except by federal legislation requiring the consent of the Bundesrat. Such consent shall also be required for any legislation authorizing the Federal Defense Administration to encroach upon rights of third parties; this shall, however, not apply in the case of legislation on personnel matters.

(2) Moreover, federal laws on defense including recruitment for military service and protection of the civilian population may, with the consent of the Bundesrat, provide that they shall be implemented wholly or in part either by the Federal Defense Administration direct or the Länder on behalf of the Federation. Where such laws are implemented by the Länder on behalf of the Federation they may, with the consent of the Bundesrat, provide that the powers vested in the Federal Government or the appropriate supreme federal authorities by virtue of Article 85 shall be transferred wholly or in part to higher federal authorities; in such an event they may provide that these authorities shall not require the consent of the Bundesrat in issuing general administrative rules in accordance with the first sentence of paragraph (2) of Article 85.

ARTICLE 87c *(Nuclear energy administration)*

Laws enacted under Article 74 No. 11a may with the consent of the Bundesrat provide that they shall be implemented by the Länder for the Federation.

ARTICLE 87d *(Air transport administration)*

(1) Air transport shall be under direct federal administration. The question of public or private status shall be determined by federal legislation.

(2) Air transport administration responsibilities may be

delegated to the Länder by means of federal legislation requiring the consent of the Bundesrat.

ARTICLE 87e (Privatization of federal railways)

(1) Federal rail transport shall be under direct federal administration. Rail transport administration responsibilities may be delegated to the Länder by means of federal legislation.

(2) The Federation shall discharge rail transport administration responsibilities assigned to it by federal legislation, over and above those concerning federal railways.

(3) Federal railways shall be operated as private enterprises. Such enterprises shall remain the property of the Federation to the extent that their operations include the construction, maintenance and operation of tracks. Any sale of federal shares in enterprises referred to in the second sentence shall be effected on the basis of a law; the Federation shall retain a majority holding. Details shall be the subject of federal legislation.

(4) The Federation shall ensure that in improving and maintaining tracks of the federal railways and in providing services other than local passenger rail services due account is taken of the interests and especially the transport requirements of the whole community. Details shall be the subject of federal legislation.

(5) Legislation pursuant to paragraphs (1) to (4) of this Article shall require the consent of the Bundesrat. Legislation governing the winding up, merging or splitting up of federal railway enterprises, the transfer of ownership of federal railway tracks to third parties or the closure of such tracks, or affecting local passenger rail services, shall likewise require the consent of the Bundesrat.

ARTICLE 88 (The Federal Bank)

The Federation shall establish a note-issuing and currency bank as the Federal Bank. Its responsibilities and powers may, within the framework of the European Union, be transferred to the European Central Bank, which is independent and whose primary aim is to safeguard price stability.

ARTICLE 89 (Federal waterways)

(1) The Federation shall be the owner of the former Reich waterways.

(2) The Federation shall manage the federal waterways through its own authorities. It shall discharge public responsibilities concerning inland navigation which extend beyond the territory of any single Land as well as those vested in it by law. Upon request the Federation may delegate the management of federal waterways, in so far as they lie within the territory of one Land, to that Land acting on its behalf. Where a waterway passes through the territory of several Länder the Federation may delegate responsibility to one Land at the request of the Länder concerned.

(3) In the management, development and construction of waterways account shall be taken of land improvement and water management requirements in agreement with the Länder.

ARTICLE 90 (Federal highways)

(1) The Federation shall be the owner of the former Reich motorways and Reich highways.

(2) The Länder or the local authorities with responsibility under Land law shall manage the motorways and other federal highways for the Federation.

(3) At the request of a Land the Federation may place motorways and other federal highways within the territory of that Land under its own administration.

ARTICLE 91 (Internal emergency)

(1) Where necessary to avert an imminent danger to the existence or free democratic basic order of the Federation or a Land, a Land may call upon the services of the police forces of other Länder or of the forces and facilities of other administrative authorities and of the Federal Border Guard.

(2) If the Land where such danger is imminent is not itself prepared or able to combat the danger the Federal Government may place the police in that Land and the police forces of other Länder under its own authority and employ units of the Federal Border Guard. The relevant order shall be canceled when the danger has been removed, otherwise at any time at the request of the Bundesrat. Where the danger extends to a region larger than a Land the Federal Government may, to the extent necessary to combat the danger effectively, issue directives to the Land governments; the first and second sentences of this paragraph shall not be affected by this provision.

Chapter VIIIa. Joint Responsibilities

ARTICLE 91a (Participation of the Federation)

(1) The Federation shall participate in discharging the responsibilities of the Länder in the following areas provided that they are relevant to the community as a whole and that its participation is necessary in order to improve living conditions (joint responsibilities):

1. building and extension of institutions of higher education including university clinics;

2. improvement of regional economic structures;

3. improvement of agricultural structure and coastal preservation.

(2) Joint responsibilities shall be specified by federal law requiring the consent of the Bundesrat. Such legislation should include general principles governing the discharge of responsibilities.

(3) The law shall provide for the procedure and institutions for joint overall planning. The inclusion of a project in overall planning shall require the consent of the Land in which it is to be carried out.

(4) In cases to which sub-paragraphs 1 and 2 of paragraph (1) of this Article apply the Federation shall meet one-half of the expenditure in each Land. In cases to which sub-paragraph 3 of paragraph (1) of this Article applies the Federation shall meet at least one-half of the expenditure; the proportion shall be the same for all Länder. Details shall be the subject of a law. Provision of funds shall be subject to appropriation in the budgets of the Federation and the Länder.

(5) The Federal Government and the Bundesrat shall, upon request, be informed about the discharge of joint responsibilities.

ARTICLE 91b *(Cooperation between the Federation and the Länder)*

The Federation and the Länder may, pursuant to agreements, cooperate in educational planning and in the promotion of research institutions and projects of supraregional importance. The apportionment of costs shall be regulated by the relevant agreements.

Chapter IX. Administration of Justice

ARTICLE 92 *(Judicial power)*

Judicial power shall be vested in the judges; it shall be exercised by the Federal Constitutional Court, the federal courts provided for in this Basic Law, and the courts of the Länder.

ARTICLE 93 *(The Federal Constitutional Court, jurisdiction)*

(1) The Federal Constitutional Court shall rule:

1. in the interpretation of this Basic Law in disputes concerning the extent of the rights and obligations of a supreme federal institution or other institutions concerned who have been vested with rights of their own by this Basic Law or by the rules of procedure of a supreme federal institution;

2. in case of disagreement or doubt as to the formal and material compatibility of federal or Land legislation with this Basic Law or as to the compatibility of Land legislation with other federal legislation at the request of the Federal Government, a Land government or one-third of the Members of the Bundestag;

3. in case of disagreement on the rights and obligations of the Federation and the Länder, particularly in the implementation of federal legislation by the Länder and in the exercise of federal supervision;

4. on other disputes involving public law between the Federation and the Länder, between Länder or within a Land, unless recourse to another court exists;

4a. on constitutional complaints which may be filed by anybody claiming that one of their basic rights or one of their rights under paragraph (4) of Article 20 or under Article 33, 38, 101, 103 or 104 has been violated by public authority;

4b. on constitutional complaints by municipalities or associations of municipalities alleging violation of their right of self-government under Article 28 by a (federal) law; in case of violation by a Land law, however, only where a complaint cannot be lodged with the Land constitutional court;

5. in the other cases provided for in this Basic Law.

(2) The Federal Constitutional Court shall also rule on any other cases referred to it by federal legislation.

ARTICLE 94 *(The Federal Constitutional Court, composition)*

(1) The Federal Constitutional Court shall be composed of federal judges and other members. Half of the members of the Federal Constitutional Court shall be elected by the Bundestag and half by the Bundesrat. They may not be members of the Bundestag, the Bundesrat, the Federal Government, nor of any of the corresponding institutions of a Land.

(2) The constitution and procedure of the Federal Constitutional Court shall be governed by a federal law which shall specify the cases in which its decisions have the force of law. Such law may make a complaint of unconstitutionality conditional upon the exhaustion of all other legal remedies and provide for a special admissibility procedure.

ARTICLE 95 *(Supreme federal courts, joint panel)*

(1) For the purposes of ordinary, administrative, financial, labor and social jurisdiction the Federation shall establish as supreme courts the Federal Court of Justice, the Federal Administrative Court, the Federal Finance Court, the Federal Labor Court and the Federal Social Court.

(2) The judges of each of these courts shall be selected jointly by the appropriate Federal Minister and a selection committee composed of the appropriate Land ministers and an equal number of members elected by the Bundestag.

(3) In order to ensure uniformity in the administration of justice a joint panel of the courts specified in paragraph (1) of this Article shall be formed. Details shall be the subject of a federal law.

ARTICLE 96 *(Other federal courts, exercise of federal jurisdiction by courts of the Länder)*

(1) The Federation may establish a federal court for matters concerning industrial property rights.

(2) The Federation may establish military criminal courts for the Armed Forces as federal courts. They may only exercise criminal jurisdiction while a state of defense exists and otherwise only over members of the Armed Forces serving abroad or on board warships. Details shall be the subject of a federal

law. Such courts shall be under the jurisdiction of the Federal Minister of Justice. Their full-time judges shall be people qualified to hold judicial office.

(3) The supreme court for appeals from the courts mentioned in paragraphs (1) and (2) of this Article shall be the Federal Court of Justice.

(4) The Federation may establish federal courts for disciplinary proceedings against, and for proceedings in pursuance of complaints by, members of the federal public service.

(5) In respect of criminal proceedings under paragraph (1) of Article 26 or concerning national security a federal law requiring the consent of the Bundesrat may make provision for Land courts to exercise federal jurisdiction.

ARTICLE 97 (*Independence of judges*)

(1) Judges shall be independent and subject only to the law.

(2) Judges appointed to full-time, permanent posts cannot, against their will, be dismissed or permanently or temporarily suspended or transferred or retired before the expiration of their term of office except by virtue of a judicial decision and only on the grounds and in the form provided for by law. Legislation may set age limits for the retirement of judges appointed for life. In the event of changes in the structure of courts or their districts judges may be transferred to another court or removed from office, but only on full salary.

ARTICLE 98 (*Status of federal and Land judges*)

(1) The status of federal judges shall be the subject of a special federal law.

(2) Where a federal judge, in an official capacity or unofficially, infringes the principles of this Basic Law or the constitutional order of a Land the Federal Constitutional Court may, upon the request of the Bundestag and with a two-thirds majority, order the judge's transfer or retirement. If the infringement was deliberate it may order dismissal.

(3) The status of Land judges shall be governed by specific Land legislation. The Federation may enact framework legislation in so far as paragraph (4) of Article 74a does not provide otherwise.

(4) The Länder may provide that the Land Minister of Justice together with a selection committee shall decide on the appointment of Land judges.

(5) In respect of Land judges the Länder may make provision corresponding to that described in paragraph (2) of this Article. Land constitutional law shall remain unaffected. The ruling in a case of impeachment of a judge shall rest with the Federal Constitutional Court.

ARTICLE 99 (*Rulings of the Federal Constitutional Court and the supreme federal courts in disputes concerning Land legislation*)

Rulings on constitutional disputes within a Land may be referred by Land legislation to the Federal Constitutional Court and rulings at last instance in matters involving the application of Land law to the supreme courts referred to in paragraph (1) of Article 95.

ARTICLE 100 (*Compatibility of legislation and constitutional law*)

(1) Where a court considers that a law on whose validity its ruling depends is unconstitutional it shall stay the proceedings and, if it holds the constitution of a Land to be violated, seek a ruling from the Land court with jurisdiction for constitutional disputes or, where it holds this Basic Law to be violated, from the Federal Constitutional Court. This shall also apply where this Basic Law is held to be violated by Land law or where a Land law is held to be incompatible with a federal law.

(2) Where in the course of litigation doubt exists whether a rule of international law is an integral part of federal law and whether such rule directly establishes rights and obligations for the individual (Article 25), the court shall seek a ruling from the Federal Constitutional Court.

(3) Where in interpreting this Basic Law the constitutional court of a Land proposes to deviate from a ruling of the Federal Constitutional Court or of the constitutional court of another Land it shall seek a ruling from the Federal Constitutional Court.

ARTICLE 101 (*Inadmissibility of courts with special jurisdiction*)

(1) Courts with special jurisdiction shall be inadmissible. Nobody may be removed from the jurisdiction of their lawful judge.

(2) Courts for specific matters may be established only by law.

ARTICLE 102 (*Abolition of capital punishment*)

Capital punishment is abolished.

ARTICLE 103 (*Court hearings, inadmissibility of retroactive criminal legislation and double jeopardy*)

(1) In court everybody is entitled to a hearing in accordance with the law.

(2) An act may be punished only if it constituted a criminal offense under the law before the act was committed.

(3) Nobody may be punished for the same act more than once under general criminal legislation.

ARTICLE 104 (*Legal guarantees in the event of detention*)

(1) Individual liberty may be restricted only pursuant to a formal law and only in the manner it prescribes. Detainees may not be subjected to mental or physical ill-treatment.

(2) Only a judge may decide on the admissibility or continuation of detention. Where such detention is not based on the order of a judge a judicial ruling shall be obtained without delay. The police may not hold anybody on their own authority longer than the end of the day after the arrest. Details shall be the subject of legislation.

(3) Anybody provisionally detained on suspicion of having committed a criminal offense shall be brought before a judge not later than the day after their detention; the judge shall inform them of the reasons for their detention, question them and allow them to plead. The judge shall forthwith either issue a warrant for their arrest containing the reasons or order their release.

(4) A relative or somebody enjoying the confidence of the detainee shall be notified without delay of any judicial ruling imposing or ordering the continuation of detention.

Chapter X. Finance

ARTICLE 104a (*Apportionment of expenditure between the Federation and the Länder*)

(1) The Federation and the Länder shall separately finance expenditure resulting from the discharge of their respective responsibilities in so far as this Basic Law does not provide otherwise.

(2) Where the Länder act for the Federation the latter shall finance the resulting expenditure.

(3) Federal laws to be implemented by the Länder and involving the disbursement of funds may provide that such funds shall be contributed wholly or in part by the Federation. Where the law provides that the Federation shall meet one-half of the expenditure or more the Länder shall implement it for the Federation. Where it provides that the Länder shall finance one-quarter of the expenditure or more it shall require the consent of the Bundesrat.

(4) The Federation may grant the Länder financial assistance for major investments by them and municipalities (associations of municipalities) provided they are necessary to avert a disturbance of overall economic equilibrium or to equalize differing economic capacities within the federal territory or promote economic growth. Details, especially concerning the kinds of investments to be promoted, shall be the subject of federal legislation requiring the consent of the Bundesrat or administrative arrangements under the Federal Budget Act.

(5) The Federation and the Länder shall finance the administrative expenditure incurred by their respective authorities and be responsible to each other for ensuring proper administration. Details shall be the subject of a federal law requiring the consent of the Bundesrat.

ARTICLE 105 (*Legislative powers*)

(1) The Federation shall have exclusive power to legislate on customs duties and fiscal monopolies.

(2) The Federation shall have concurrent power to legislate on all other taxes the revenue from which accrues to it wholly or in part or where the conditions provided for in paragraph (2) of Article 72 apply.

(2a) The Länder shall have power to legislate on local excise taxes as long and in so far as they are not identical with taxes imposed by federal legislation.

(3) Federal legislation on taxes the revenue from which accrues wholly or in part to the Länder or municipalities (associations of municipalities) shall require the consent of the Bundesrat.

ARTICLE 106 (*Apportionment of tax revenue*)

(1) The yield of fiscal monopolies and the revenue from the following taxes shall accrue to the Federation:

1. customs duties;

2. excise taxes in so far as they do not accrue to the Länder pursuant to paragraph (2) or jointly to the Federation and the Länder in accordance with paragraph (3) or to the municipalities in accordance with paragraph (6) of this Article;

3. road freight tax;

4. capital transaction taxes, insurance tax and tax on bills of exchange;

5. nonrecurrent levies on property and equalization of burdens levies;

6. income and corporation surtaxes;

7. levies within the framework of the European Communities.

(2) Revenue from the following taxes shall accrue to the Länder:

1. property (net worth) tax;

2. inheritance tax;

3. motor vehicle tax;

4. such taxes on transactions as do not accrue to the Federation pursuant to paragraph (1) of this Article or jointly to the Federation and the Länder pursuant to paragraph (3) of this Article;

5. beer tax;

6. tax on gambling establishments.

(3) Revenue from income tax, corporation tax and turnover tax shall accrue jointly to the Federation and the Länder (joint taxes) to the extent that the revenue from income tax is not al-

located to the municipalities pursuant to paragraph (5) of this Article. The Federation and the Länder shall share equally the revenue from income tax and corporation tax. The respective shares of the Federation and the Länder in the revenue from turnover tax shall be determined by federal legislation requiring the consent of the Bundesrat. Such determination shall be based on the following principles:

1. The Federation and the Länder shall have an equal claim to funds from current revenue to finance their necessary expenditure. The amount of such expenditure shall be determined on the basis of pluriennial financial planning.

2. The requirements of the Federation and the Länder shall be coordinated to establish a fair balance, to prevent excessive burdens on the taxpayer, and to ensure equal living conditions in the federal territory.

(4) The respective shares of the Federation and the Länder in turnover tax revenue shall be reapportioned whenever the ratio of revenue to expenditure differs substantially as between the Federation and the Länder. Where federal legislation imposes additional expenditure on or withdraws revenue from the Länder the additional burden may be compensated by federal grants pursuant to a federal law requiring the consent of the Bundesrat provided that burden is limited to a short period. The law shall lay down the principles for computing such grants and distributing them among the Länder.

(5) A share of the revenue from income tax shall accrue to the municipalities and shall be passed on by the Länder to their municipalities on the basis of the income tax paid by their population. Details shall be the subject of a federal law requiring the consent of the Bundesrat. The law may provide that the municipalities shall assess their respective proportions of this share.

(6) Revenue from tax on real property and trade shall accrue to the municipalities; revenue from local excise taxes shall accrue to the municipalities or, as may be provided for by Land legislation, to associations of municipalities. The municipalities shall be authorized to assess their real property and trade tax within the framework of existing legislation. Where a Land has no municipalities revenue from real property and trade tax as well as from local excise taxes shall accrue to the Land. The Federation and the Länder are entitled to a proportion of the revenue from trade tax in the form of an apportionment. Details regarding such apportionment shall be the subject of a federal law requiring the consent of the Bundesrat. In accordance with Land legislation real property and trade tax as well as the municipalities' share of revenue from income tax may be taken as a basis for computing the apportionment.

(7) An overall percentage, to be determined by Land legislation, of the Land share of total revenue from joint taxes shall accrue to the municipalities and associations of municipalities.

In all other respects Land legislation shall determine whether and to what extent revenue from Land taxes shall accrue to the municipalities (associations of municipalities).

(8) Where in individual Länder or municipalities (associations of municipalities) the Federation requires special facilities to be provided which directly result in increased expenditure or loss of revenue (extra burden) for those Länder or municipalities (associations of municipalities) the Federation shall grant the necessary compensation where and in so far as they cannot reasonably be expected to bear that burden. In granting such compensation due account shall be taken of indemnities of third parties and financial benefits accruing to the Länder or municipalities (associations of municipalities) concerned as a result of the provision of such facilities.

(9) For the purpose of this Article revenue and expenditure of municipalities (associations of municipalities) shall likewise be deemed Land revenue and expenditure.

ARTICLE 106a *(Tax allocation for local passenger transport services)*

As from 1 January 1996 the Länder shall be entitled to an allocation from federal tax revenue for public local passenger transport services. Details shall be the subject of federal legislation which shall require the consent of the Bundesrat. The allocation provided for in the first sentence of this Article shall not be taken into account in assessing financial capacity in accordance with paragraph (2) of Article 107.

ARTICLE 107 *(Financial equalization)*

(1) Revenue from Land tax and the Land share of revenue from income and corporation tax shall accrue to the Länder to the extent that the taxes are collected by the revenue authorities in their respective territories (local revenue). Federal legislation requiring the consent of the Bundesrat shall specify the breakdown of local revenue from corporation and wage tax as well as the method and extent of its allocation. Such legislation may also provide for the breakdown and allocation of local revenue from other taxes. The Land share of revenue from turnover tax shall accrue to the Länder on a per capita basis; federal legislation requiring the consent of the Bundesrat may provide for supplemental shares not exceeding one-quarter of a Land share to be granted to Länder whose per capita revenue from Land taxes and from income and corporation tax is below the average of all the Länder combined.

(2) Such legislation shall ensure a reasonable equalization of the financial disparity of the Länder, due account being taken of the financial capacity and requirements of the municipalities (associations of municipalities). The legislation shall specify the conditions governing the claims of Länder entitled to equalization payments and the liabilities of Länder required

to make such payments, as well as the criteria for determining the amounts. It may also provide for federal grants to be made to financially weak Länder in order to complement the coverage of their general financial requirements (complemental grants).

ARTICLE 108 (*Financial administration*)

(1) Customs duties, fiscal monopolies, excise taxes subject to federal legislation, including import turnover tax, and levies imposed within the framework of the European Communities shall be administered by federal revenue authorities. The organization of these authorities shall be regulated by federal legislation. The heads of intermediate authorities shall be appointed in consultation with the respective Land governments.

(2) All other taxes shall be administered by Land revenue authorities. The organization of these authorities and the uniform training of their civil servants may be regulated by federal legislation requiring the consent of the Bundesrat. The heads of intermediate authorities shall be appointed in agreement with the Federal Government.

(3) To the extent that taxes accruing wholly or in part to the Federation are administered by Land revenue authorities, the latter shall act on behalf of the Federation. Paragraphs (3) and (4) of Article 85 shall apply, the Federal Minister of Finance being substituted for the Federal Government.

(4) Federal legislation requiring the consent of the Bundesrat may provide for cooperation between federal and Land revenue authorities on matters of tax administration, in the case of taxes covered by paragraph (1) of this Article for administration by Land revenue authorities, and in the case of other taxes for administration by federal revenue authorities where and to the extent that this considerably improves or facilitates the implementation of tax laws. The administration of taxes the revenue from which accrues exclusively to the municipalities (associations of municipalities) may be delegated by the Land revenue authorities wholly or in part to the municipalities (associations of municipalities).

(5) The procedure to be applied by the federal revenue authorities shall be laid down by federal legislation. The procedure to be applied by Land revenue authorities or, as provided for in the second sentence of paragraph (4) of this Article, by the municipalities (associations of municipalities) may be laid down by federal legislation requiring the consent of the Bundesrat.

(6) Financial jurisdiction shall be uniformly regulated by federal legislation.

(7) The Federal Government may issue general administrative rules which, to the extent that administration is entrusted to Land revenue authorities or municipalities (associations of municipalities), shall require the consent of the Bundesrat.

ARTICLE 109 (*Budgets of the Federation and the Länder*)

(1) In their budget management the Federation and the Länder shall be autonomous and mutually independent.

(2) In their budget management the Federation and the Länder shall take account of the requirements of macroeconomic equilibrium.

(3) Through federal legislation requiring the consent of the Bundesrat principles applicable to both the Federation and the Länder may be established governing budgetary law, budget management reflecting the economic situation, and pluriennial financial planning.

(4) With a view to averting disturbances of macroeconomic equilibrium federal legislation requiring the consent of the Bundesrat may be enacted which:

1. provides for maximum amounts, terms and timing of loans raised by local authorities or joint authorities and

2. obliges the Federation and the Länder to maintain interest-free deposits at the German Federal Bank (anticyclical reserves).

Only the Federal Government may be empowered to issue statutory orders. Such orders shall require the consent of the Bundesrat. They shall be repealed if the Bundestag so requires; the details shall be contained in the legislation.

ARTICLE 110 (*Budget, Federal Budget Act*)

(1) All federal revenue and expenditure shall be included in the budget; in the case of federal enterprises and special funds only allocations to and revenue from them need be included. Budget revenue and expenditure shall be balanced.

(2) The budget shall be laid down in a bill covering one or several financial years separately before the beginning of the first year. Provision may be made for parts of the budget to apply to periods of different duration for different financial years.

(3) The bill provided for in the first sentence of paragraph (2) of this Article as well as bills amending the Budget Act and the budget shall be submitted simultaneously to the Bundesrat and the Bundestag; the Bundesrat shall be entitled to state its position on bills within six weeks or, in the case of amending bills, within three weeks.

(4) The Budget Act may contain only such provisions as apply to federal revenue and expenditure and to the period for which it is being enacted. The Budget Act may stipulate that such provisions shall cease to apply only upon the promulgation of the next Budget Act or, in the event of an empowerment pursuant to Article 115, at a later date.

ARTICLE 111 (*Provisional budget expenditure*)

(1) Where by the end of a financial year the budget estimates for the following year have not been determined by law

the Federal Government may, until such law comes into force, authorize all expenditure necessary:

(a) to maintain statutory institutions and implement statutory measures,

(b) to meet the legal obligations of the Federation,

(c) to continue building projects, procurements and other services or to continue to disburse funds for these purposes provided they have already been appropriated in the budget of a previous year.

(2) To the extent that revenue from taxes, duties and other sources based on specific legislation, or the working capital reserves, do not cover the expenditure referred to in paragraph (1) of this Article the Federal Government may borrow the funds needed to sustain budget management, up to a maximum of one-quarter of the total amount of the preceding budget estimates.

ARTICLE 112 *(Extrabudgetary expenditure)*

Extrabudgetary expenditure shall require the consent of the Federal Minister of Finance. Such consent may be given only in the case of an unforeseen and compelling necessity. Details may be provided by federal legislation.

ARTICLE 113 *(Expenditure increases, revenue cuts)*

(1) Bills which increase the budget expenditure proposed by the Federal Government or involve or will give rise to new expenditure shall require the consent of the Federal Government. This shall also apply to bills which involve or will give rise to cuts in revenue. The Federal Government may require the Bundestag to postpone the vote on such bills. In this case the Federal Government shall state its position within six weeks.

(2) Within four weeks after the Bundestag has adopted the bill the Federal Government may ask for another vote.

(3) Where the bill has become law pursuant to Article 78 the Federal Government may withhold its consent only within six weeks and only after having initiated the procedure provided for in the third and fourth sentences of paragraph (1) or in paragraph (2) of the present Article. Upon the expiry of this period such consent shall be deemed to have been given.

ARTICLE 114 *(Auditing)*

(1) The Federal Minister of Finance shall, on behalf of the Federal Government, submit to the Bundestag and the Bundesrat annual accounts for the preceding financial year covering all revenue and expenditure as well as assets and debts.

(2) The Federal Court of Audit, whose members enjoy the same independence as judges, shall audit the accounts and determine whether public finances have been properly and efficiently administered. The Federal Court of Audit shall submit

an annual report to the Federal Government as well as to the Bundestag and the Bundesrat direct. In all other respects the powers of the Federal Court of Audit shall be regulated by federal legislation.

ARTICLE 115 *(Borrowing)*

(1) The borrowing of funds and the assumption of sureties, guarantees or other commitments which may lead to expenditure in future financial years shall require an empowerment by federal law specifying or providing for the specification of the amounts involved. Revenue from borrowing shall not exceed the total expenditure for investment provided for in the budget estimates; exceptions shall be permissible only to avert a disturbance of macroeconomic equilibrium. Details shall be the subject of federal legislation.

(2) In respect of special federal funds exceptions to the provisions of paragraph (1) of this Article may be authorized by federal legislation.

Chapter Xa. State of Defense

ARTICLE 115a *(Definition and declaration of a state of defense)*

(1) Should federal territory be under armed attack or should such an attack be imminent the Bundestag shall declare a state of defense with the consent of the Bundesrat. Such declaration shall be made at the request of the Federal Government and shall require a two-thirds majority of the votes cast and at least the majority of the Members of the Bundestag.

(2) Where the situation calls for immediate action and insurmountable obstacles make it impossible for the Bundestag to be convened in time or it is not quorate, the Joint Committee shall make the declaration with a two-thirds majority of the votes cast and at least the majority of its members.

(3) The declaration shall be promulgated by the Federal President in the Federal Law Gazette pursuant to Article 82. If this cannot be done in time the promulgation shall be effected in another manner; it shall be published in the Federal Law Gazette as soon as circumstances permit.

(4) Where federal territory is under armed attack and the appropriate federal bodies are not immediately in a position to make the declaration provided for in the first sentence of paragraph (1) of this Article such declaration shall be deemed to have been made and promulgated at the time the attack began. The Federal President shall announce that time as soon as circumstances permit.

(5) Where the declaration of a state of defense has been promulgated and federal territory is under armed attack the

Federal President may with the consent of the Bundestag issue declarations under international law pertaining to the existence of a state of defense. Where the conditions mentioned in paragraph (2) of this Article apply the Joint Committee shall act in place of the Bundestag.

ARTICLE 115b *(Transfer of command to the Federal Chancellor)*

Upon the promulgation of a state of defense command over the Armed Forces shall pass to the Federal Chancellor.

ARTICLE 115c *(Extension of the legislative powers of the Federation)*

(1) The right of the Federation to legislate concurrently in respect of a state of defense shall also extend to matters within the legislative jurisdiction of the Länder. Such legislation shall require the consent of the Bundesrat.

(2) Where the conditions prevailing while the country is in a state of defense so require, federal legislation in respect of the state of defense may,

1. in derogation of the second sentence of paragraph (3) of Article 14, provide for provisional compensation in the event of expropriation,

2. with regard to detention, provide in cases where a judge has not been able to perform his functions within the time-limit applying in normal circumstances for a time-limit differing from that stipulated in the third sentence of paragraph (2) of Article 104 but not exceeding four days.

(3) Where necessary to repel an attack already in progress or imminent federal legislation for a state of defense may, subject to the consent of the Bundesrat, regulate the administration and finances of the Federation and the Länder in derogation of Chapters VIII, VIIIa and X, provided that the viability of the Länder, municipalities and associations of municipalities, especially in financial terms, is secured.

(4) Federal legislation pursuant to paragraph (1) or subparagraph 1 of paragraph (2) of this Article may for the purpose of preparing for its enforcement be applied even before a state of defense exists.

ARTICLE 115d *(Procedure in the case of urgent bills)*

(1) While a state of defense exists the provisions of paragraphs (2) and (3) of this Article shall apply in respect of federal legislation, in derogation of the provisions of paragraph (2) of Article 76, the second sentence of paragraph (1) and paragraphs (2) to (4) of Article 77, Article 78, and paragraph (1) of Article 82.

(2) Urgent bills submitted by the Federal Government shall be forwarded to the Bundesrat at the same time as they are presented in the Bundestag. The Bundestag and the Bundesrat shall debate the bill simultaneously without delay. In so far as the consent of the Bundesrat is necessary a majority shall be required for the bill to become law. Details shall be the subject of rules of procedure adopted by the Bundestag and requiring the consent of the Bundesrat.

(3) With regard to the promulgation of such legislation the second sentence of paragraph (3) of Article 115a shall apply *mutatis mutandis*.

ARTICLE 115e *(Powers of the Joint Committee)*

(1) Where, while a state of defense exists, the Joint Committee determines with a two-thirds majority of the votes cast and at least the majority of its members that insurmountable obstacles make it impossible for the Bundestag to be convened in time or that it is not quorate, the Committee shall have the status of both the Bundestag and the Bundesrat and exercise their rights as one body.

(2) The Joint Committee may not enact any legislation amending this Basic Law or rendering it ineffective or inapplicable either in whole or in part. The Joint Committee shall not be empowered to enact legislation pursuant to paragraph (1), second sentence, of Article 23, paragraph (1) of Article 24 or Article 29.

ARTICLE 115f *(Powers of the Federal Government)*

(1) While a state of defense exists the Federal Government may, to the extent necessitated by circumstances,

1. employ the Federal Border Guard throughout the federal territory;

2. issue directives not only to federal administrative authorities but also to Land governments and, where it deems the matter urgent, to Land authorities and may delegate this power to members of Land governments designated by it.

(2) The Bundestag, the Bundesrat and the Joint Committee shall be informed without delay of the measures taken in accordance with paragraph (1) of this Article.

ARTICLE 115g *(Status of the Federal Constitutional Court)*

The status and constitutional functions of the Federal Constitutional Court and its judges may not be impaired. The Federal Constitutional Court Act may not be amended by legislation enacted by the Joint Committee except where such amendment is deemed necessary to ensure that the Court can continue to function and the Court shares this opinion. Pending the enactment of such legislation the Federal Constitutional Court may take any measures necessary to continue functioning. Any decisions by the Federal Constitutional Court in pursuance of the second and third sentences of this Article shall require a majority of the judges present.

ARTICLE 115h (*Continued functioning of constitutional bodies*)

(1) Any legislative term of the Bundestag or of Land parliaments due to expire while a state of defense exists shall end six months after the termination of such state of defense. A term of office of the Federal President due to expire while a state of defense exists and the exercise of the powers of that office by the President of the Bundesrat should it prematurely become vacant shall end nine months after the termination of the state of defense. The term of office of a member of the Federal Constitutional Court due to expire while a state of defense exists shall end six months after the termination of the state of defense.

(2) Should it become necessary for the Joint Committee to elect a new Federal Chancellor it shall do so with the majority of its members; the Federal President shall propose a candidate to the Joint Committee. The Joint Committee may express its lack of confidence in the Federal Chancellor only by electing a successor with a two-thirds majority of its members.

(3) The Bundestag may not be dissolved while a state of defense exists.

ARTICLE 115i (*Powers of the Land governments*)

(1) Where the appropriate federal bodies are incapable of taking the measures necessary to avert the danger and the situation calls for immediate independent action in different parts of the federal territory the Land governments or the authorities or representatives designated by them shall be empowered to take within their area of jurisdiction the measures provided for in paragraph (1) of Article 115f.

(2) Any measures taken in accordance with paragraph (1) of this Article may be revoked at any time by the Federal Government or, in relation to Land authorities and subordinate federal authorities, by the Ministers President of the Länder.

ARTICLE 115k (*Extraordinary legislation*)

(1) Legislation in accordance with Articles 115c, 115e or 115g as well as statutory orders issued on the basis of that legislation shall, for the duration of their validity, suspend incompatible legislation. This shall not apply to earlier legislation enacted in accordance with Articles 115c, 115e or 115g.

(2) Legislation adopted by the Joint Committee as well as statutory orders issued on the basis of that legislation shall cease to have effect not later than six months after the termination of the state of defense.

(3) Legislation containing provisions that diverge from Articles 91a, 91b, 104a, 106 or 107 shall apply no longer than the end of the second financial year following the termination of the state of defense. After such termination they may with the consent of the Bundesrat be amended by federal legislation so as to revert to the provisions of Chapters VIIIa and X.

ARTICLE 115l (*Repeal of extraordinary legislation, termination of a state of defense, peace treaty*)

(1) The Bundestag, with the consent of the Bundesrat, may at any time repeal legislation enacted by the Joint Committee. The Bundesrat may require the Bundestag to adopt a resolution to this effect. Any measures taken by the Joint Committee or the Federal Government to avert danger shall be revoked if the Bundestag and the Bundesrat so resolve.

(2) The Bundestag, with the consent of the Bundesrat, may at any time declare a state of defense terminated in the form of a resolution to be promulgated by the Federal President. The Bundesrat may require the Bundestag to adopt such resolution. A state of defense shall be declared terminated without delay if the conditions which led to its being declared no longer exist.

(3) The conclusion of a peace treaty shall be the subject of federal legislation.

Chapter XI. Transitional and Concluding Provisions

ARTICLE 116 (*Definition of "a German," restoration of citizenship*)

(1) Unless otherwise provided by law a German within the meaning of this Basic Law is anybody who possesses German citizenship or who has been admitted to the territory of the German Reich within the frontiers of 31 December 1937 as a refugee or expellee of German ethnic origin or as their spouse or descendant.

(2) Former German citizens who between 30 January 1933 and 8 May 1945 were deprived of their citizenship on political, racial or religious grounds, and their descendants, shall have that citizenship restored on application. They shall be considered not to have been deprived of their citizenship if they have established their residence in Germany after 8 May 1945 and have not expressed a different intention.

ARTICLE 117 (*Temporary ruling for Article 3 (2) and Article 11*)

(1) Legislation which is inconsistent with paragraph (2) of Article 3 shall remain in force until adapted to that provision of the Basic Law but not beyond 31 March 1953.

(2) Legislation which restricts freedom of movement in view of the present housing shortage shall remain in force until repealed by federal legislation.

ARTICLE 118 (*Modification of Land boundaries in the south-west*)

Boundaries in the territory comprising the Länder Baden, Württemberg-Baden and Württemberg-Hohenzollern may in derogation of the provisions of Article 29 be modified by agreement between the Länder concerned. If no agreement is reached the modification shall be effected by federal legislation which shall provide for a referendum.

ARTICLE 119 (*Statutory orders relating to refugees and expellees*)

In matters relating to refugees and expellees, in particular as regards their distribution among the Länder, the Federal Government may, with the consent of the Bundesrat, issue statutory orders pending enactment of the appropriate federal legislation. The Federal Government may be empowered to issue directives for particular cases. Except where there is danger in delay, such directives shall be addressed to the supreme Land authorities.

ARTICLE 120 (*Occupation costs and war burdens*)

(1) The Federation shall meet occupation costs and other internal and external burdens resulting from the war as provided for by federal legislation. To the extent that such burdens have been covered by federal legislation on or before 1 October 1969 the Federation and the Länder shall meet such expenditure between them in accordance with that legislation. In so far as expenditure on war burdens as neither have been nor will be covered by federal legislation has been incurred on or before 1 October 1965 by Länder, municipalities (associations of municipalities) or other institutions performing Land or municipal functions the Federation shall not be obliged to meet such expenditure either before or after that date. The Federation shall make grants towards the cost of social security including unemployment insurance and unemployment benefit. The distribution of war burdens between the Federation and the Länder, as provided for in this paragraph, shall not affect any statutory regulation of claims for compensation in respect of consequences of the war.

(2) Revenue shall pass to the Federation at the same time as it assumes the expenditure referred to in this Article.

ARTICLE 120a (*Implementation of the equalization of burdens regime*)

(1) Legislation implementing the equalization of burdens regime may, with the consent of the Bundesrat, stipulate that with regard to equalization benefits it shall be implemented, partly by the Federation and partly by the Länder on behalf of the Federation and that the powers vested in the Federal Government and the appropriate supreme federal authorities by virtue of Article 85 shall be wholly or partly delegated to the Federal Equalization of Burdens Office. In exercising these powers the Federal Equalization of Burdens Office shall not require the consent of the Bundesrat; except in urgent cases its directives shall be addressed to the supreme Land authorities (equalization of burdens offices).

(2) The provisions of the second sentence of paragraph (3) of Article 87 shall not be affected.

ARTICLE 121 (*Definition of "majority of the Members"*)

Within the meaning of this Basic Law a majority of the Members of the Bundestag and a majority of the members of the Federal Convention shall be the majority of the statutory number of their members.

ARTICLE 122 (*Transference of legislative powers*)

(1) From the date of the first meeting of the Bundestag laws shall be enacted exclusively by the legislative bodies specified in this Basic Law.

(2) Legislative bodies as well as those institutions participating in legislation in an advisory capacity whose jurisdiction ends by virtue of paragraph (1) of this Article shall be dissolved with effect from that date.

ARTICLE 123 (*Continued validity of old law and treaties*)

(1) Law in force before the first meeting of the Bundestag shall remain in force in so far as it does not conflict with the Basic Law.

(2) Subject to all rights and objections of the interested parties the treaties concluded by the German Reich concerning matters which under this Basic Law fall within the legislative jurisdiction of the Länder shall remain in force, provided they are and continue to be valid in accordance with general principles of law, until new treaties are concluded by the authorities competent under this Basic Law or they are in any other way terminated pursuant to their provisions.

ARTICLE 124 (*Continued application of law as federal law within the sphere of exclusive legislation*)

Law affecting matters within the exclusive legislative powers of the Federation shall become federal law in the area in which it applies.

ARTICLE 125 (*Continued application of law as federal law within the sphere of concurrent legislation*)

Law affecting matters within the concurrent legislative power of the Federation shall become federal law in the area in which it applies:

1. in so far as it applies uniformly within one or more occupation zones;

2. in so far as it is legislation by which former Reich law has been amended since 8 May 1945.

ARTICLE 126 (*Disputes over the continued application of legislation as federal law*)

Disputes over the continued application of legislation as federal law shall be settled by the Federal Constitutional Court.

ARTICLE 127 *(Legislation of the Combined Economic Area)*

Within one year of the promulgation of this Basic Law the Federal Government may with the consent of the governments of the Länder concerned extend to the Länder Baden, Greater Berlin, Rhineland-Palatinate and Württemberg-Hohenzollern legislation introduced by the Administration of the Combined Economic Area in so far as it remains in force as federal law pursuant to Article 124 or Article 125.

ARTICLE 128 *(Continued validity of powers to issue directives)*

In so far as legislation continuing in force provides for powers to issue directives within the meaning of paragraph (5) of Article 84 those powers shall remain valid until otherwise provided by law.

ARTICLE 129 *(Continued validity of powers to issue statutory orders)*

(1) In so far as legal provisions which continue in force as federal law contain powers to issue statutory orders or general administrative rules or to perform administrative acts such powers shall pass to the henceforth appropriate authorities. In cases of doubt the Federal Government shall decide in agreement with the Bundesrat; such decisions shall be published.

(2) In so far as legal provisions which continue in force as Land legislation contain such powers they shall be acted upon by the authorities with jurisdiction under Land law.

(3) In so far as legal provisions within the meaning of paragraphs (1) and (2) of this Article contain powers for their amendment or supplementation or the issue of legal provisions in lieu of statutory law such powers shall be deemed to have expired.

(4) The provisions of paragraphs (1) and (2) of this Article shall apply *mutatis mutandis* where legal provisions refer to regulations no longer valid or to institutions no longer in existence.

ARTICLE 130 *(Control over existing institutions)*

(1) Administrative agencies and other institutions which serve the public administration or the administration of justice and are not governed by Land law or agreements between Länder, as well as the Administrative Union of South West German Railways and the Administrative Council for the Postal and Telecommunications Services of the French Occupation Zone, shall be placed under the control of the Federal Government. The latter shall provide, with the consent of the Bundesrat, for the transfer of control over or dissolution of such agencies.

(2) The supreme disciplinary authority for the staff of such agencies and institutions shall be the appropriate Federal Minister.

(3) Public corporations and institutions not directly subordinate to a Land and not governed by agreements between Länder shall be under the supervision of the appropriate supreme federal authority.

ARTICLE 131 *(Legal status of former public service staff)*

The legal status of people, including refugees and expellees, who on 8 May 1945 were employed in the public service, have left the service for reasons not covered by civil service regulations or collective agreements and have not until now been reinstated or are employed in positions which do not correspond to the ones they held previously shall be regulated by federal legislation. The same shall apply *mutatis mutandis* to people, including refugees and expellees, who, on 8 May 1945, were entitled to but no longer receive a pension or commensurate pension for reasons not covered by civil service regulations or collective agreements. Until the legislation comes into force no legal claims shall be admissible unless Land legislation provides otherwise.

ARTICLE 132 *(Temporary revocation of rights of public service staff)*

(1) Civil servants and judges who when this Basic Law comes into force are in permanent service may within six months after the first meeting of the Bundestag be permanently or temporarily retired or given other responsibilities in a lower salary group where they lack the personal or professional aptitude for their present office. This provision shall also apply *mutatis mutandis* to public employees other than civil servants or judges whose appointment has become permanent. In the case of public employees who do not hold a permanent appointment periods of notice in excess of those laid down in collective agreements may be revoked within the six months referred to above.

(2) The preceding provision shall not apply to members of the public service who are not affected by the legislation regarding "Liberation from National Socialism and Militarism" or are recognized victims of National Socialism, except on important grounds relating to them as individuals.

(3) Those affected may have recourse to the courts in accordance with paragraph (4) of Article 19.

(4) Details shall be the subject of a statutory order of the Federal Government requiring the consent of the Bundesrat.

ARTICLE 133 *(Administration of the Combined Economic Area)*

The Federation shall succeed to the rights and obligations of the Administration of the Combined Economic Area.

ARTICLE 134 *(Property of the Reich)*

(1) Reich property shall become federal property.

(2) In so far as such property was originally intended pre-

dominantly for administrative tasks which under this Basic Law do not come under the executive responsibility of the Federation, it shall be transferred without compensation to the authorities now responsible and to the Länder in so far as it is currently being used, not merely temporarily, for administrative tasks which under this Basic Law are now under the executive responsibility of the Länder. The Federation may also transfer other property to the Länder.

(3) Property which was placed at the disposal of the Reich by Länder or municipalities (associations of municipalities) without compensation shall revert to those Länder or municipalities (associations of municipalities) in so far as it is not required by the Federation for its own administrative tasks.

(4) Details shall be the subject of a federal law requiring the consent of the Bundesrat.

ARTICLE 135 (*Property of former Länder and public corporations*)

(1) Where after 8 May 1945 and before the coming into force of this Basic Law an area has passed from one Land to another, the Land to which the area now belongs shall be entitled to the property located there of the Land to which it belonged.

(2) Property of Länder, public corporations or institutions which no longer exist shall pass, in so far as it was originally intended predominantly for administrative tasks or is currently being used, not merely temporarily, primarily for administrative tasks, to the Land, public corporation or institution which now discharges these tasks.

(3) Real property of Länder which no longer exist, including appurtenances, shall pass to the Land within which it is located in so far as it does not belong to property within the meaning of paragraph (1) of this Article.

(4) Where an overriding interest of the Federation or the particular interest of an area so requires, a settlement other than that provided for in paragraphs (1) to (3) of this Article may be effected by federal legislation.

(5) In all other respects the succession in title and the settlement of the property, in so far as it has not been effected before 1 January 1952 by agreement between the Länder or public corporations or institutions concerned, shall be regulated by federal legislation requiring the consent of the Bundesrat.

(6) Holdings of the former Land of Prussia in private enterprises shall pass to the Federation. Details shall be the subject of a federal law, which may also diverge from this provision.

(7) In so far as property which on the coming into force of this Basic Law would devolve upon a Land, public corporation or institution pursuant to paragraphs (1) to (3) of this Article has been disposed of through or by virtue of a Land law or in any other manner by the party thus entitled, the transfer of the property shall be deemed to have taken place before such disposition.

ARTICLE 135a (*Old liabilities*)

(1) The legislation reserved to the Federation by virtue of paragraph (4) of Article 134 and paragraph (5) of Article 135 may also stipulate that the following liabilities shall not be discharged, or not to their full extent:

1. liabilities of the Reich and liabilities of the former Land of Prussia or public corporations and institutions which no longer exist;

2. such liabilities of the Federation or public corporations and institutions as are connected with the transfer of property pursuant to Article 89, 90, 134 or 135, and any liabilities of these corporations and institutions arising from measures taken by the corporations and institutions mentioned in subparagraph 1;

3. liabilities of Länder or municipalities (associations of municipalities) that have arisen from measures taken by them before 1 August 1945 within the scope of administrative tasks incumbent upon or delegated by the Reich in compliance with orders of the occupying powers or to terminate a state of emergency resulting from the war.

(2) Paragraph (1) above shall apply *mutatis mutandis* to liabilities of the German Democratic Republic or its institutions as well as to liabilities of the Federation or other public corporations and institutions which are connected with the transfer of property of the German Democratic Republic to the Federation, Länder and municipalities, and to liabilities arising from measures taken by the German Democratic Republic or its institutions.

ARTICLE 136 (*First assembly of the Bundesrat*)

(1) The Bundesrat shall convene for the first time on the day of the first assembly of the Bundestag.

(2) Until the election of the first Federal President the powers of that office shall be exercised by the President of the Bundesrat. The latter shall not have the right to dissolve the Bundestag.

ARTICLE 137 (*Eligibility of public servants for election*)

(1) The eligibility of civil servants, other salaried public employees, regular servicemen, temporary volunteer servicemen or judges for election in the Federation, Länder or municipalities may be restricted by legislation.

(2) The electoral bill to be adopted by the Parliamentary Council shall apply to the election of the first Bundestag, the first Federal Convention and the first President of the Federal Republic.

(3) The function of the Federal Constitutional Court pursuant to paragraph (2) of Article 41 shall, pending its establishment, be exercised by the German High Court for the Combined Economic Area, which shall decide in accordance with its rules of procedure.

ARTICLE 138 (*Notarial service in southern Germany*)

Changes in the notarial service as presently existing in the Länder Baden, Bavaria, Württemberg-Baden and Württemberg-Hohenzollern shall require the consent of the governments of these Länder.

ARTICLE 139 (*Continued validity of legislation on denazification*)

The legislation enacted for the "Liberation of the German People from National Socialism and Militarism" shall not be affected by the provisions of this Basic Law.

ARTICLE 140 (*Rights of religious communities*)

The provisions of Articles 136, 137, 138, 139 and 141 of the German Constitution of 11 August 1919 shall be an integral part of this Basic Law.

ARTICLE 141 (*"Bremen Clause"*)

The first sentence of paragraph (3) of Article 7 shall not apply in any Land in which different provisions of Land law were in force on 1 January 1949.

ARTICLE 142 (*Basic rights in Land constitutions*)

Notwithstanding the provision of Article 31, provisions of Land constitutions shall also remain in force where they guarantee basic rights in conformity with Articles 1 to 18 of this Basic Law.

ARTICLE 142a (*Repealed*)

ARTICLE 143 (*Derogations from the Basic Law*)

(1) Law in the territory specified in Article 3 of the Unification Treaty may derogate from provisions of this Basic Law for a period not extending beyond 31 December 1992 in so far and as long as it is not possible for that territory to comply fully with the requirements of the Basic Law on account of the different conditions existing there. Derogations must not violate paragraph (2) of Article 19 and must be compatible with the principles set out in paragraph (3) of Article 79.

(2) Derogations from Chapters II, VIII, VIIIa, IX, X and XI are permissible for a period not extending beyond 31 December 1995.

(3) Notwithstanding paragraphs (1) and (2) above, Article 41 of the Unification Treaty and implementing provisions shall remain valid in so far as they provide for the irreversibility of encroachments upon property in the territory specified in Article 3 of the said Treaty.

ARTICLE 143a (*Exclusive legislative jurisdiction for federal railways*)

(1) The Federation has the exclusive right to legislate on all matters resulting from the privatization of Federal Railways under its administration. Paragraph (5) of Article 87e shall apply *mutatis mutandis*. Officials of the Federal Railways may be assigned to a private federal railway whilst maintaining their legal status and continuing to be under the responsibility of their public employer.

(2) Legislation pursuant to paragraph (1) shall be executed by the Federation.

(3) Responsibility for local passenger rail services of the hitherto Federal Railways shall remain with the Federation until 31 December 1995. The same shall apply to corresponding responsibilities of the Rail Transport Administration. Details shall be the subject of federal legislation requiring the consent of the Bundesrat.

ARTICLE 144 (*Ratification of the Basic Law*)

(1) This Basic Law shall be subject to ratification by the parliaments of two-thirds of the German Länder in which it is temporarily to apply.

(2) In so far as the application of this Basic Law is subject to restrictions in any Land listed in Article 23 or in any part thereof, such Land or part thereof shall have the right to be represented in the Bundestag in accordance with Article 38 and in the Bundesrat in accordance with Article 50.

ARTICLE 145 (*Promulgation of the Basic Law*)

(1) The Parliamentary Council shall confirm in public session, with the participation of the members for Greater Berlin, the ratification of this Basic Law and shall sign and promulgate it.

(2) This Basic Law shall enter into force on the day after its promulgation.

(3) It shall be published in the Federal Law Gazette.

ARTICLE 146 (*Validity of the Basic Law*)

This Basic Law, which is valid for the entire German nation following the achievement of the unity and freedom of Germany, shall cease to have effect on the day on which a constitution adopted by a free decision of the German people enters into force.

Bonn on the Rhine, 23 May 1949

AFRICAN NATIONAL CONGRESS FREEDOM CHARTER (1955)

As late as the 1930s, European domination of Africa was virtually unchallenged across the continent. The African National Congress (ANC), which had been founded in 1912 under the name South African Native National Congress, had few members and sought only to improve some of the more odious aspects of colonial administration.

World War II (1939–1945) dramatically accelerated the urbanization and industrialization of South Africa, which had been developing slowly for several decades. As a result, the increasingly urbanized, educated, and sophisticated blacks of South Africa began to develop a sense of nationhood and nationalism and began to chafe under colonial rule.

Tensions between whites and blacks rose in the years following the war, and in 1948 the Afrikaner Nationalist Party was elected to power on a platform calling for rigid apartheid, or racial segregation, to guarantee white supremacy. The Nationalists immediately set about codifying the policy; they passed the Population Registration Act, the Group Areas Act, the Separate Representation of Voters Act, the Immorality of Mixed Marriages Act, and other discriminatory legislation.

The African National Congress, in turn, became more militant and began using boycotts, strikes, civil disobedience, and nationwide work stoppages, but it rigorously avoided violence. The ANC, in cooperation with other organizations representing Indians, coloreds, and liberal whites, called for a Congress of the People to draft a charter outlining a vision for the future of South Africa. Three thousand delegates to the congress met June 25–26, 1955, at Kliptown, near Johannesburg, and ratified the Freedom Charter, which subsequently was adopted as the official program of the ANC.

The charter expressed the liberal democratic ideals of political freedom and equality for all that had been resonating in Western political philosophy for two hundred years. It also encompassed the social and economic "rights" that had become common in post–World War II discourse. The charter's terms were moderate, and the ANC advocated a peaceful evolution. But to the Nationalist Party the document was radical because its goals could not be achieved without destroying the privileged economic and political status of whites.

The Freedom Charter evoked yet more government repression and, ironically, also fomented a schism within the black movement. In 1959 a faction withdrew from the ANC to form the Pan-Africanist Congress, a more militant organization that rejected the ANC's and the Freedom Charter's belief in cooperation with nonblack organizations. After being outlawed in 1961, the ANC, too, became more radical and began to advocate violence. But the ANC did not renounce its vision, as expressed in the Freedom Charter, of a democratic, nonracial South Africa.

Preamble

We, the people of South Africa, declare for all our country and the world to know:

That South Africa belongs to all who live in it, black and white, and that no government can justly claim authority unless it is based on the will of the people;

That our people have been robbed of their birthright to land, liberty and peace by a form of government founded on injustice and inequality;

That our country will never be prosperous or free until all our people live in brotherhood, enjoying equal rights and opportunities;

That only a democratic state, based on the will of the people, can secure to all their birthright without distinction of colour, race, sex or belief;

And therefore, we, the people of South Africa, black and white, together—equals, countrymen and brothers—adopt this Freedom Charter. And we pledge ourselves to strive together, sparing nothing of our strength and courage, until the democratic changes here set out have been won.

The people shall govern

Every man and woman shall have the right to vote for and stand as a candidate for all bodies which make laws;

All the people shall be entitled to take part in the administration of the country;

The rights of the people shall be the same regardless of race, colour or sex;

All bodies of minority rule, advisory boards, councils and authorities shall be replaced by democratic organs of self-government.

All national groups shall have equal rights

There shall be equal status in the bodies of state, in the courts and in the schools for all national groups and races;

All national groups shall be protected by law against insults to their race and national pride;

All people shall have equal rights to use their own language and to develop their own folk culture and customs;

All apartheid laws and practices shall be set aside.

The people shall share in the country's wealth

The national wealth of our country, the heritage of all South Africans, shall be restored to the people;

The mineral wealth beneath the soil, the banks and monopoly industry shall be transferred to the ownership of the people as a whole;

All other industries and trade shall be controlled to assist the well-being of the people;

All people shall have equal rights to trade where they choose, to manufacture and to enter all trades, crafts and professions.

The land shall be shared amongst those who work it

Restriction of land ownership on a racial basis shall be ended, and all the land redivided amongst those who work it, to banish famine and land hunger;

The state shall help the peasants with implements, seed, tractors and dams to save the soil and assist the tillers;

Freedom of movement shall be guaranteed to all who work on the land;

All shall have the right to occupy land wherever they choose;

People shall not be robbed of their cattle; forced labour and farm prisons shall be abolished.

All people shall be equal before the law

No one shall be imprisoned, deported or restricted without a fair trial;

No one shall be condemned by the order of any Government official;

The courts shall be representative of all the people;

Imprisonment shall be only for serious crimes against the people, and shall aim at re-education, not vengeance;

The police force and army shall be open to all on an equal basis and shall be the helpers and protectors of the people;

All laws which discriminate on grounds of race, colour or belief shall be repealed;

The preaching and practice of national, race or colour discrimination and contempt shall be a punishable crime.

All shall enjoy equal human rights

The law shall guarantee to all their right to speak, to organise, to meet together, to publish, to preach, to worship and to educate their children;

The privacy of the house from police raids shall be protected by law;

All shall be free to travel without restriction from countryside to town, from province to province, and from South Africa abroad;

Pass laws, permits and all other laws restricting these freedoms shall be abolished.

There shall be work and security

All who work shall be free to form trade unions, to elect their officers and to make wage agreements with their employers;

The state shall recognise the right and duty of all to work, and to draw full unemployment benefits;

Men and women of all races shall receive equal pay for equal work;

There shall be a forty-hour working week, a national minimum wage, paid annual leave, and sick leave for all workers, and maternity leave on full pay for all working mothers;

Miners, domestic workers, farm workers and civil servants shall have the same rights as all others who work;

Child labour, compound labour, the tot system and contract labour shall be abolished.

The doors of learning and of culture shall be opened

The government shall discover, develop and encourage national talent for the enhancement of our cultural life;

All the cultural treasures of mankind shall be open to all, by free exchange of books, ideas and contacts with other lands;

The aim of education shall be to teach the youth to love their people and their culture, to honour human brotherhood, liberty and peace;

Education shall be free, compulsory, universal and equal for all children;

Higher education and technical training shall be opened to all by means of state allowances and scholarships awarded on the basis of merit;

Adult illiteracy shall be ended by a mass state education plan;

Teachers shall have all the rights of other citizens;

The colour bar in cultural life, in sport and in education shall be abolished.

There shall be houses, security and comfort

All people shall have the right to live where they choose, to be decently housed, and to bring up their families in comfort and security;

Unused housing space shall be made available to the people;

Rent and prices shall be lowered, food plentiful and no one shall go hungry;

A preventive health scheme shall be run by the state;

Free medical care and hospitalisation shall be provided for all, with special care for mothers and young children;

Slums shall be demolished and new suburbs built where all have transport, roads, lighting, playing fields, creches and social centres;

The aged, the orphans, the disabled and the sick shall be cared for by the state;

Rest, leisure and recreation shall be the right of all;

Fenced locations and ghettoes shall be abolished, and laws which break up families shall be repealed.

There shall be peace and friendship

South Africa shall be a fully independent state, which respects the rights and sovereignty of all nations;

South Africa shall strive to maintain world peace and the settlement of all international disputes by negotiation—not war;

Peace and friendship amongst all our people shall be secured by upholding the equal rights, opportunities and status of all;

The people of the protectorates—Basutoland, Bechuanaland and Swaziland—shall be free to decide for themselves their own future;

The right of all the peoples of Africa to independence and self-government shall be recognised, and shall be the basis of close co-operation.

Let all who love their people and their country now say, as we say here; "These freedoms we will fight for, side by side, throughout our lives, until we have won our liberty."

AFRICAN CHARTER ON HUMAN AND PEOPLES' RIGHTS (1981)

Despite tremendous strides that had taken place since the end of World War II in 1945, the African continent was still wrestling in 1981 with the legacies of European colonialism and other difficulties of external and indigenous origin. The African Charter on Human and Peoples' Rights, adopted at the eighteenth meeting of the heads of state and government of the Organization of African Unity (OAU), was both a reaction to the continent's difficulties and a statement of hope for the future.

As the colonial powers withdrew from Africa they left behind independent states but few nations and even fewer functioning democracies. The populations, living within state boundaries that bore little relation to the ethnic, cultural, historical, or linguistic map of Africa, had by and large not been prepared by the colonial powers to function as political democracies. In many cases the populations lacked a sense of nationhood or nationalism, adequate educational institutions, experience in politics and administration, and industrial development, with its attendant social transformations.

By 1981 great progress had been made in ameliorating the colonial legacy, but old problems persisted and new ones had developed. In the 1970s Africa had become a cold war battleground; Soviet and U.S. proxies fought civil wars in a number of states, including Angola, Mozambique, and Ethiopia, which served to destabilize much of the continent. White-ruled South Africa remained a thorn in the side of its neighbors, and Libya under Muammar al-Qaddafi fo-

mented instability in Chad and Western Sahara. Domestic political instability remained the norm. In 1980 roughly a dozen coups were attempted across the continent; five of them were successful, including one in Liberia that destroyed the continent's oldest republic. And periodic famine and refugee migrations further eroded political and economic stability.

Against this backdrop the OAU met in Nairobi, Kenya, June 24–28, 1981, to adopt the African Charter on Human and Peoples' Rights, which had been drafted with great difficulty. As late as June 21 a working group of foreign ministers reported wide disagreement over the terms of the charter. Several nondemocratic nations with poor human rights records reportedly considered the document to be potentially embarrassing.

The gap between the charter's promise and practice in many African states is great. Furthermore, the Organization of African Unity, under its charter of May 25, 1963, lacks the authority or the means to intervene even in a limited way in the affairs of its member states. All OAU resolutions are strictly advisory. Past attempts to strengthen the organization so that it could protect the political, civil, and human rights of African citizens and the democratic order of African states foundered on the fear that the OAU would splinter. The weakness of the OAU as an organization rests largely on the underlying weakness of democracy in its member states, which in turn undermines the promise of fundamental human rights embodied in the charter.

Preamble

The African States members of the Organization of African Unity, parties to the present convention entitled "African Charter on Human and Peoples' Rights,"

Recalling Decision 115-XVI of the Assembly of Heads of State and Government at its Sixteenth Ordinary Session held in Monrovia, Liberia, from 17 to 20 July 1979 on the prepa-

ration of "a preliminary draft of an African Charter on Human and Peoples' Rights providing *inter alia* for the establishment of bodies to promote and protect human and peoples' rights";

Considering the Charter of the Organization of African Unity, which stipulates that "freedom, equality, justice and dignity are essential objectives for the achievement of the legitimate aspirations of the African peoples";

Reaffirming the pledge they solemnly made in Article 2 of the said Charter to eradicate all forms of colonialism from Africa, to coordinate and intensify their cooperation and efforts to achieve a better life for the peoples of Africa and to promote international cooperation having due regard to the Charter of the United Nations and the Universal Declaration of Human Rights;

Taking into consideration the virtues of their historical tradition and the values of African civilization which should inspire and characterize their reflection on the concept of human and peoples' rights;

Recognizing on the one hand, that fundamental human rights stem from the attributes of human beings, which justifies their international protection and on the other hand that the reality and respect of peoples' rights should necessarily guarantee human rights;

Considering that the enjoyment of rights and freedoms also implies the performance of duties on the part of everyone;

Convinced that it is henceforth essential to pay particular attention to the right to development and that civil and political rights cannot be dissociated from economic, social and cultural rights in their conception as well as universality and that the satisfaction of economic, social and cultural rights is a guarantee for the enjoyment of civil and political rights;

Conscious of their duty to achieve the total liberation of Africa, the peoples of which are still struggling for their dignity and genuine independence, and undertaking to eliminate colonialism, neocolonialism, apartheid, Zionism and to dismantle aggressive foreign military bases and all forms of discrimination, particularly those based on race, ethnic group, color, sex, language, religion or political opinions;

Reaffirming their adherence to the principles of human and peoples' rights and freedoms contained in the declarations, conventions and other instruments adopted by the Organization of African Unity, the Movement of Non-Aligned Countries and the United Nations;

Firmly convinced of their duty to promote and protect human and peoples' rights and freedoms taking into account the importance traditionally attached to these rights and freedoms in Africa;

Have agreed as follows:

Part I. Rights and Duties

Chapter 1. Human and Peoples' Rights

ARTICLE 1. The Member States of the Organization of African Unity, parties to the present Charter, shall recognize the rights, duties and freedoms enshrined in this Charter and shall undertake to adopt legislative or other measures to give effect to them.

ARTICLE 2. Every individual shall be entitled to the enjoyment of the rights and freedoms recognized and guaranteed in the present Charter without distinction of any kind such as race, ethnic group, color, sex, language, religion, political or any other opinion, national and social origin, fortune, birth or other status.

ARTICLE 3.
1. Every individual shall be equal before the law.
2. Every individual shall be entitled to equal protection of the law.

ARTICLE 4. Human beings are inviolable. Every human being shall be entitled to respect for his life and the integrity of his person. No one may be arbitrarily deprived of this right.

ARTICLE 5. Every individual shall have the right to respect for the dignity inherent in a human being and to the recognition of his legal status. All forms of exploitation and degradation of man, particularly slavery, slave trade, torture, cruel, inhuman or degrading punishment and treatment shall be prohibited.

ARTICLE 6. Every individual shall have the right to liberty and to the security of his person. No one may be deprived of his freedom except for reasons and conditions previously laid down by law. In particular, no one may be arbitrarily arrested or detained.

ARTICLE 7.
1. Every individual shall have the right to have his cause heard. This comprises:
a. the right to an appeal to competent national organs against acts violating his fundamental rights as recognized and guaranteed by conventions, laws, regulations and customs in force;
b. the right to be presumed innocent until proved guilty by a competent court or tribunal;
c. the right to defense, including the right to be defended by counsel of his choice;
d. the right to be tried within a reasonable time by an impartial court or tribunal.
2. No one may be condemned for an act or omission which did not constitute a legally punishable offense at the time it was committed. No penalty may be inflicted for an offense for which no provision was made at the time it was committed. Punishment is personal and can be imposed only on the offender.

ARTICLE 8. Freedom of conscience, the profession and free practice of religion shall be guaranteed. No one may, subject to law and order, be submitted to measures restricting the exercise of these freedoms.

ARTICLE 9.

1. Every individual shall have the right to receive information.

2. Every individual shall have the right to express and disseminate his opinions within the law.

ARTICLE 10.

1. Every individual shall have the right to free association provided that he abides by the law.

2. Subject to the obligation of solidarity provided for in Article 29 no one may be compelled to join an association.

ARTICLE 11. Every individual shall have the right to assemble freely with others. The exercise of this right shall be subject only to necessary restrictions provided for by law, in particular those enacted in the interest of national security, the safety, health, ethics and rights and freedoms of others.

ARTICLE 12.

1. Every individual shall have the right to freedom of movement and residence within the borders of a State provided he abides by the law.

2. Every individual shall have the right to leave any country including his own, and to return to his country. This right may only be subject to restrictions provided for by law for the protection of national security, law and order, public health or morality.

3. Every individual shall have the right, when persecuted, to seek and obtain asylum in other countries in accordance with the law of those countries and international conventions.

4. A non-national legally admitted in a territory of a State party to the present Charter may only be expelled from it by virtue of a decision taken in accordance with the law.

5. The mass expulsion of non-nationals shall be prohibited. Mass expulsion shall be that which is aimed at national, racial, ethnic or religious groups.

ARTICLE 13.

1. Every citizen shall have the right to participate freely in the government of his country, either directly or through freely chosen representatives in accordance with the provisions of the law.

2. Every citizen shall have the right of equal access to the public service of his country.

3. Every individual shall have the right of access to public property and services in strict equality of all persons before the law.

ARTICLE 14. The right to property shall be guaranteed. It may only be encroached upon in the interest of public need or in the general interest of the community and in accordance with the provisions of appropriate laws.

ARTICLE 15. Every individual shall have the right to work under equitable and satisfactory conditions, and shall receive equal pay for equal work.

ARTICLE 16.

1. Every individual shall have the right to enjoy the best attainable state of physical and mental health.

2. States parties to the present Charter shall take the necessary measures to protect the health of their people and to ensure that they receive medical attention when they are sick.

ARTICLE 17.

1. Every individual shall have the right to education.

2. Every individual may freely take part in the cultural life of his community.

3. The promotion and protection of morals and traditional values recognized by the community shall be the duty of the State.

ARTICLE 18.

1. The family shall be the natural unit and basis of society. It shall be protected by the State which shall take care of its physical and moral health.

2. The State shall have the duty to assist the family which is the custodian of morals and traditional values recognized by the community.

3. The State shall ensure the elimination of every discrimination against women and also ensure the protection of the rights of the woman and the child as stipulated in international declarations and conventions.

4. The aged and the disabled shall also have the right to special measures of protection in keeping with their physical or moral needs.

ARTICLE 19. All peoples shall be equal; they shall enjoy the same respect and shall have the same rights. Nothing shall justify the domination of a people by another.

ARTICLE 20.

1. All peoples shall have the right to existence. They shall have the unquestionable and inalienable right to self-determination. They shall freely determine their political status and

shall pursue their economic and social development according to the policy they have freely chosen.

2. Colonized or oppressed peoples shall have the right to free themselves from the bonds of domination by resorting to any means recognized by the international community.

3. All peoples shall have the right to the assistance of the States parties to the present Charter in their liberation struggle against foreign domination, be it political, economic or cultural.

ARTICLE 21.

1. All peoples shall freely dispose of their wealth and natural resources. This right shall be exercised in the exclusive interest of the people. In no case shall a people be deprived of it.

2. In case of spoliation the dispossessed people shall have the right to the lawful recovery of its property as well as to an adequate compensation.

3. The free disposal of wealth and natural resources shall be exercised without prejudice to the obligation of promoting international economic cooperation based on mutual respect, equitable exchange and the principles of international law.

4. States parties to the present Charter shall individually and collectively exercise the right to free disposal of their wealth and natural resources with a view to strengthening African unity and solidarity.

5. States parties to the present Charter shall undertake to eliminate all forms of foreign economic exploitation particularly that practiced by international monopolies so as to enable their peoples fully to benefit from the advantages derived from their national resources.

ARTICLE 22.

1. All peoples shall have the right to their economic, social and cultural development with due regard to their freedom and identity and to the equal enjoyment of the common heritage of mankind.

2. States shall have the duty, individually or collectively, to ensure the exercise of the right to development.

ARTICLE 23.

1. All peoples shall have the right to national and international peace and security. The principles of solidarity and friendly relations implicitly affirmed by the Charter of the United Nations and reaffirmed by that of the Organization of African Unity shall govern relations between States.

2. For the purpose of strengthening peace, solidarity and friendly relations, States parties to the present Charter shall ensure that:

a. any individual enjoying the right of asylum under Article 12 of the present Charter shall not engage in subversive activities against his country of origin or any other State party to the present Charter;

b. their territories shall not be used as bases for subversive or terrorist activities against the people of any other State party to the present Charter.

ARTICLE 24.
All peoples shall have the right to a general satisfactory environment favorable to their development.

ARTICLE 25.
States parties to the present Charter shall have the duty to promote and ensure, through teaching, education and publication, respect for the rights and freedoms contained in the present Charter and to see to it that these freedoms and rights as well as corresponding obligations and duties are understood.

ARTICLE 26.
States parties to the present Charter shall have the duty to guarantee the independence of the Courts and shall allow the establishment and improvement of appropriate national institutions entrusted with the promotion and protection of the rights and freedoms guaranteed by the present Charter.

Chapter 2. Duties

ARTICLE 27.

1. Every individual shall have duties towards his family and society, the State and other legally recognized communities and the international community.

2. The rights and freedoms of each individual shall be exercised with due regard to the rights of others, collective security, morality and common interest.

ARTICLE 28.
Every individual shall have the duty to respect and consider his fellow beings without discrimination, and to maintain relations aimed at promoting, safeguarding and reinforcing mutual respect and tolerance.

ARTICLE 29.
The individual shall also have the duty:

1. to preserve the harmonious development of the family and to work for the cohesion and respect of the family; to respect his parents at all times, to maintain them in case of need;

2. to serve his national community by placing his physical and intellectual abilities at its service;

3. not to compromise the security of the State whose national or resident he is;

4. to preserve and strengthen social and national solidarity, particularly when the latter is threatened;

5. to preserve and strengthen the national independence

and the territorial integrity of his country and to contribute to its defense in accordance with the law;

6. to work to the best of his abilities and competence, and to pay taxes imposed by law in the interest of society;

7. to preserve and strengthen positive African cultural values in his relations with other members of society, in the spirit of tolerance, dialogue and consultation and, in general, to contribute to the promotion of the moral well-being of society;

8. to contribute to the best of his abilities, at all times and at all levels, to the promotion and achievement of African unity.

Part II. Safeguarding Measures

Chapter 1. Establishment and Organization of the African Commission on Human and Peoples' Rights

ARTICLE 30. An African Commission on Human and Peoples' Rights, hereinafter called "the Commission," shall be established within the Organization of African Unity to promote human and peoples' rights and ensure their protection in Africa.

ARTICLE 31.

1. The Commission shall consist of eleven members chosen from among African personalities of the highest reputation, known for their high morality, integrity, impartiality and competence in matters of human and peoples' rights; particular consideration being given to persons having legal experience.

2. The members of the Commission shall serve in their personal capacity.

ARTICLE 32. The Commission shall not include more than one national of the same State.

ARTICLE 33. The members of the Commission shall be elected by secret ballot by the Assembly of Heads of State and Government, from a list of persons nominated by the States parties to the present Charter.

ARTICLE 34. Each State party to the present Charter may not nominate more than two candidates. The candidates must have the nationality of one of the States parties to the present Charter. When two candidates are nominated by a State, one of them may not be a national of that State.

ARTICLE 35.

1. The Secretary General of the Organization of African Unity shall invite States parties to the present Charter at least four months before the elections to nominate candidates;

2. The Secretary General of the Organization of African Unity shall make an alphabetical list of the persons thus nominated and communicate it to the Heads of State and Government at least one month before the elections.

ARTICLE 36. The Members of the Commission shall be elected for a six-year period and shall be eligible for re-election. However, the term of office of four of the members elected at the first election shall terminate after two years and the term of office of three others, at the end of four years.

ARTICLE 37. Immediately after the first election, the Chairman of the Assembly of Heads of State and Government of the Organization of African Unity shall draw lots to decide the names of those members referred to in Article 36.

ARTICLE 38. After their election, the members of the Commission shall make a solemn declaration to discharge their duties impartially and faithfully.

ARTICLE 39.

1. In case of death or resignation of a member of the Commission, the Chairman of the Commission shall immediately inform the Secretary General of the Organization of African Unity, who shall declare the seat vacant from the date of death or from the date on which the resignation takes effect.

2. If, in the unanimous opinion of other members of the Commission, a member has stopped discharging his duties for any reason other than a temporary absence, the Chairman of the Commission shall inform the Secretary General of the Organization of African Unity, who shall then declare the seat vacant.

3. In each of the cases anticipated above, the Assembly of Heads of State and Government shall replace the member whose seat became vacant for the remaining period of his term unless the period is less than six months.

ARTICLE 40. Every member of the Commission shall be in office until the date his successor assumes office.

ARTICLE 41. The Secretary General of the Organization of African Unity shall appoint the Secretary of the Commission. He shall also provide the staff and services necessary for the effective discharge of the duties of the Commission. The Organization of African Unity shall bear the cost of the staff and services.

ARTICLE 42.

1. The Commission shall elect its Chairman and Vice Chairman for a two-year period. They shall be eligible for re-election.

2. The Commission shall lay down its rules of procedure.

3. Seven members shall form the quorum.

4. In the case of an equality of votes, the Chairman shall have a casting vote.

5. The Secretary General may attend the meetings of the Commission. He shall neither participate in deliberations nor shall he be entitled to vote. The Chairman of the Commission may, however, invite him to speak.

ARTICLE 43. In discharging their duties, members of the Commission shall enjoy diplomatic privileges and immunities provided for in the General Convention on the Privileges and Immunities of the Organization of African Unity.

ARTICLE 44. Provision shall be made for the emoluments and allowances of the members of the Commission in the regular budget of the Organization of African Unity.

Chapter 2. Mandate of the Commission

ARTICLE 45. The functions of the Commission shall be:

1. To promote human and peoples' rights and in particular:

a. to collect documents, undertake studies and research on African problems in the field of human and peoples' rights, organize seminars, symposia and conferences, disseminate information, encourage national and local institutions concerned with human and peoples' rights, and should the case arise, give its views or make recommendations to Governments;

b. to formulate and lay down principles and rules aimed at solving legal problems relating to human and peoples' rights and fundamental freedoms upon which African Governments may base their legislations;

c. to cooperate with other African and international institutions concerned with the promotion and protection of human and peoples' rights.

2. To ensure the protection of human and peoples' rights under conditions laid down by the present Charter.

3. To interpret all the provisions of the present Charter at the request of a State party, an institution of the OAU or an African organization recognized by the OAU.

4. To perform any other tasks which may be entrusted to it by the Assembly of Heads of State and Government.

Chapter 3. Procedure of the Commission

ARTICLE 46. The Commission may resort to any appropriate method of investigation; it may hear from the Secretary General of the Organization of African Unity or any other person capable of enlightening it.

I. Communications from States

ARTICLE 47. If a State party to the present Charter has good reasons to believe that another State party to this Charter has violated the provisions of the Charter, it may draw, by written communication, the attention of that State to the matter. This communication shall also be addressed to the Secretary General of the OAU and to the Chairman of the Commission. Within three months of the receipt of the communication, the State to which the communication is addressed shall give the inquiring State a written explanation or statement elucidating the matter. This should include as much relevant information as possible relating to the laws and rules of procedure applied and applicable and the redress already given or course of action available.

ARTICLE 48. If within three months from the date on which the original communication is received by the State to which it is addressed, the issue is not settled to the satisfaction of the two States involved through bilateral negotiation or by any other peaceful procedure, either State shall have the right to submit the matter to the Commission through the Chairman and shall notify the other State involved.

ARTICLE 49. Notwithstanding the provisions of Article 47, if a State party to the present Charter considers that another State party has violated the provisions of the Charter, it may refer the matter directly to the Commission by addressing a communication to the Chairman, to the Secretary General of the Organization of African Unity and the State concerned.

ARTICLE 50. The Commission can only deal with a matter submitted to it after making sure that all local remedies, if they exist, have been exhausted, unless it is obvious to the Commission that the procedure of achieving these remedies would be unduly prolonged.

ARTICLE 51.

1. The Commission may ask the States concerned to provide it with all relevant information.

2. When the Commission is considering the matter, the States concerned may be represented before it and submit written or oral representations.

ARTICLE 52. After having obtained from the States concerned and from other sources all the information it deems necessary and after having tried all appropriate means to reach an amicable solution based on respect for human and peoples' rights, the Commission shall prepare, within a reasonable period of time from the notification referred to in Article 48, a report stating the facts and its findings. This report shall be sent to the States concerned and communicated to the Assembly of Heads of State and Government.

ARTICLE 53. While transmitting its report, the Commission may make to the Assembly of Heads of State and Government such recommendations as it deems useful.

ARTICLE 54. The Commission shall submit to each Ordinary Session of the Assembly of Heads of State and Government a report on its activities.

II. Other Communications

ARTICLE 55.

1. Before each Session, the Secretary of the Commission shall make a list of the communications other than those of States parties to the present Charter and transmit them to the members of the Commission, who shall indicate which communications should be considered by the Commission.

2. A communication shall be considered by the Commission if a simple majority of its members so decide.

ARTICLE 56. Communications relating to human and peoples' rights referred to in Article 55 received by the Commission shall be considered if they:

1. indicate their authors even if the latter request anonymity;

2. are compatible with the Charter of the Organization of African Unity or with the present Charter;

3. are not written in disparaging or insulting language directed against the State concerned and its institutions or the Organization of African Unity;

4. are not based exclusively on news disseminated through the mass media;

5. are sent after exhausting local remedies, if any, unless it is obvious that this procedure is unduly prolonged;

6. are submitted within a reasonable period from the time local remedies are exhausted or from the date the Commission is seized of the matter; and

7. do not deal with cases which have been settled by the States involved in accordance with the principles of the Charter of the United Nations or the Charter of the Organization of African Unity, or the provisions of the present Charter.

ARTICLE 57. Prior to any substantive consideration, all communications shall be brought to the knowledge of the State concerned by the Chairman of the Commission.

ARTICLE 58.

1. When it appears after deliberations of the Commission that one or more communications apparently relate to special cases which reveal the existence of a series of serious or massive violations of human and peoples' rights, the Commission shall draw the attention of the Assembly of Heads of State and Government to these special cases.

2. The Assembly of Heads of State and Government may then request the Commission to undertake an in-depth study of these cases and make a factual report, accompanied by its finding and recommendations.

3. A case of emergency duly noticed by the Commission shall be submitted by the latter to the Chairman of the Assembly of Heads of State and Government who may request an in-depth study.

ARTICLE 59.

1. All measures taken within the provisions of the present Charter shall remain confidential until such a time as the Assembly of Heads of State and Government shall otherwise decide.

2. However, the report shall be published by the Chairman of the Commission upon the decision of the Assembly of Heads of State and Government.

3. The report on the activities of the Commission shall be published by its Chairman after it has been considered by the Assembly of Heads of State and Government.

Chapter 4. Applicable Principles

ARTICLE 60. The Commission shall draw inspiration from international law on human and peoples' rights, particularly from the provisions of various African instruments on human and peoples' rights, the Charter of the United Nations, the Charter of the Organization of African Unity, the Universal Declaration of Human Rights, other instruments adopted by the United Nations and by African countries in the field of human and peoples' rights as well as from the provisions of various instruments adopted within the specialized agencies of the United Nations of which the parties to the present Charter are members.

ARTICLE 61. The Commission shall also take into consideration, as subsidiary measures to determine the principles of law, other general or special international conventions, laying down rules expressly recognized by member states of the Organization of African Unity, African practices consistent with international norms on human and peoples' rights, customs generally accepted as law, general principles of law recognized by African states as well as legal precedents and doctrine.

ARTICLE 62. Each State party shall undertake to submit every two years, from the date the present Charter comes into force, a report on the legislative or other measures taken with a view to giving effect to the rights and freedoms recognized and guaranteed by the present Charter.

ARTICLE 63.

1. The present Charter shall be open to signature, ratification or adherence of the member States of the Organization of African Unity.

2. The instruments of ratification or adherence to the present Charter shall be deposited with the Secretary General of the Organization of African Unity.

3. The present Charter shall come into force three months after the reception by the Secretary General of the instruments of ratification or adherence of a simple majority of the member States of the Organization of African Unity.

Part III. General Provisions

ARTICLE 64.

1. After the coming into force of the present Charter, members of the Commission shall be elected in accordance with the relevant Articles of the present Charter.

2. The Secretary General of the Organization of African Unity shall convene the first meeting of the Commission at the Headquarters of the Organization within three months of the constitution of the Commission. Thereafter, the Commission shall be convened by its Chairman whenever necessary but at least once a year.

ARTICLE 65. For each of the States that will ratify or adhere to the present Charter after its coming into force, the Charter shall take effect three months after the date of the deposit by that State of its instruments of ratification or adherence.

ARTICLE 66. Special protocols or agreements may, if necessary, supplement the provisions of the present Charter.

ARTICLE 67. The Secretary General of the Organization of African Unity shall inform member States of the Organization of the deposit of each instrument of ratification or adherence.

ARTICLE 68. The present Charter may be amended if a State party makes a written request to that effect to the Secretary General of the Organization of African Unity. The Assembly of Heads of State and Government may only consider the draft amendment after all the States parties have been duly informed of it and the Commission has given its opinion on it at the request of the sponsoring State. The amendment shall be approved by a simple majority of the States parties. It shall come into force for each State which has accepted it in accordance with its constitutional procedure three months after the Secretary General has received notice of the acceptance.

CANADIAN CHARTER OF RIGHTS AND FREEDOMS (1982)

The complexity of a bill of rights is directly proportional to the complexity of the society that gives rise to it. In a simple, culturally homogeneous, agrarian society such as the United States in the eighteenth century, reaching consensus on a definition of fundamental rights is comparatively easy. In a modern, culturally diverse, industrialized society the definition is more contentious.

Canada, though an independent and self-governing state in practice, was in a legal and technical sense a colony of Great Britain until 1982. The Canadian federation had been founded and governed under the British North America Act of 1867. In the late 1970s a movement arose in Canada, led by Prime Minister Pierre Elliott Trudeau, to transform that British legislation into a truly Canadian constitution. As a prerequisite, however, a bill of rights had to be drafted for inclusion in the constitution.

The bill of rights that Trudeau submitted to the Canadian Parliament on November 18, 1981, was the result of months of negotiation and compromise among the nine English-speaking provinces and the French-speaking province of Quebec. Still, the document was widely criticized throughout Canada on several grounds; in the Quebec provincial assembly, it was rejected entirely.

A vocal and politically active minority in Quebec sought outright independence from a federal Canada dominated by the English-speaking provinces. Although a majority of citizens of Quebec opposed independence in a May 1980 referendum, there was strong support for obtaining the greatest possible constitutional protections for their linguistic, cultural, and historical heritage. The provincial assembly objected particularly to a clause in the bill of rights that would guarantee the right of a minority population to be educated in its native language; that clause would require Quebec to provide English-language instruction to the many English-speaking citizens of the province, thus hindering Quebec's ability to protect the province's majority French language and culture.

Other provinces had objected to guarantees of rights for native peoples, and consequently those guarantees had been weakened in the compromise draft submitted to Parliament. Native groups protested that the protections were inadequate, while the governments of Quebec, British Columbia, Alberta, and Manitoba worried about the financial and legal implications if aboriginal groups were to sue the provinces over old treaty provisions under their newly recognized constitutional rights.

All disputes became the subject of litigation. Quebec filed suit in the provincial supreme court, arguing that it could not be forced to accept a federal constitution in which it did not consent. Quebec lost, as did native peoples who sued in British courts on the grounds that the British government was still liable as the colonial power for treaties it had signed.

Ultimately, the bill of rights passed by majority vote of both houses of the Canadian Parliament and of the British Parliament, and it survived all court challenges. The Charter of Rights and Freedoms was incorporated into the Constitution Act of 1982. Queen Elizabeth II proclaimed the new constitution the law of Canada in a formal ceremony on April 17, 1982, making Canada a sovereign state.

Whereas Canada is founded upon principles that recognize the supremacy of God and the rule of law:

Guarantee of Rights and Freedoms

1. The Canadian Charter of Rights and Freedoms guarantees the rights and freedoms set out in it subject only to such reasonable limits prescribed by law as can be demonstrably justified in a free and democratic society.

Fundamental Freedoms

2. Everyone has the following fundamental freedoms:
   (a) freedom of conscience and religion;
   (b) freedom of thought, belief, opinion and expression, including freedom of the press and other media of communication;
   (c) freedom of peaceful assembly; and
   (d) freedom of association.

Democratic Rights

3. Every citizen of Canada has the right to vote in an election of members of the House of Commons or of a legislative assembly and to be qualified for membership therein.

4.—(1) No House of Commons and no legislative assembly shall continue for longer than five years from the date fixed for the return of the writs at a general election of its members.
   (2) In time of real or apprehended war, invasion or insurrection, a House of Commons may be continued by Parliament and a legislative assembly may be continued by the legislature beyond five years if such continuation is not opposed by the votes of more than one-third of the members of the House of Commons or the legislative assembly, as the case may be.

5. There shall be a sitting of Parliament and of each legislature at least once every twelve months.

Mobility Rights

6.—(1) Every citizen of Canada has the right to enter, remain in and leave Canada.
   (2) Every citizen of Canada and every person who has the status of a permanent resident of Canada has the right
   (a) to move to and take up residence in any province; and
   (b) to pursue the gaining of a livelihood in any province.
   (3) The rights specified in subsection (2) are subject to
   (a) any laws or practices of general application in force in a province other than those that discriminate among persons primarily on the basis of province of present or previous residence; and
   (b) any laws providing for reasonable residency requirements as a qualification for the receipt of publicly provided social services.
   (4) Subsections (2) and (3) do not preclude any law, program or activity that has as its object the amelioration in a province of conditions of individuals in that province who are socially or economically disadvantaged if the rate of employment in that province is below the rate of employment in Canada.

Legal Rights

7. Everyone has the right to life, liberty and security of the person and the right not to be deprived thereof except in accordance with the principles of fundamental justice.

8. Everyone has the right to be secure against unreasonable search or seizure.

9. Everyone has the right not to be arbitrarily detained or imprisoned.

10. Everyone has the right on arrest or detention
   (a) to be informed promptly of the reasons therefor;
   (b) to retain and instruct counsel without delay and to be informed of that right; and
   (c) to have the validity of the detention determined by way of habeas corpus and to be released if the detention is not lawful.

11. Any person charged with an offence has the right
   (a) to be informed without unreasonable delay of the specific offence;
   (b) to be tried within a reasonable time;
   (c) not to be compelled to be a witness in proceedings against that person in respect of the offence;
   (d) to be presumed innocent until proven guilty according to law in a fair and public hearing by an independent and impartial tribunal;
   (e) not to be denied reasonable bail without just cause;
   (f) except in the case of an offence under military law tried before a military tribunal, to the benefit of trial by jury where the maximum punishment for the offence is imprisonment for five years or a more severe punishment;
   (g) not to be found guilty on account of any act or omission unless, at the time of the act or omission, it constituted an offence under Canadian or international law or was criminal according to the general principles of law recognized by the community of nations;

(h) if finally acquitted of the offence, not to be tried for it again and, if finally found guilty and punished for the offence, not to be tried or punished for it again; and

(i) if found guilty of the offence and if the punishment for the offence has been varied between the time of commission and the time of sentencing, to the benefit of the lesser punishment.

12. Everyone has the right not to be subjected to any cruel and unusual treatment or punishment.

13. A witness who testifies in any proceedings has the right not to have any incriminating evidence so given used to incriminate that witness in any other proceedings, except in a prosecution for perjury or for the giving of contradictory evidence.

14. A party or witness in any proceedings who does not understand or speak the language in which the proceedings are conducted or who is deaf has the right to the assistance of an interpreter.

Equality Rights

15.—(1) Every individual is equal before and under the law and has the right to the equal protection and equal benefit of the law without discrimination and, in particular, without discrimination based on race, national or ethnic origin, colour, religion, sex, age or mental or physical disability.

(2) Subsection (1) does not preclude any law, program or activity that has as its object the amelioration of conditions of disadvantaged individuals or groups including those that are disadvantaged because of race, national or ethnic origin, colour, religion, sex, age or mental or physical disability.

Official Languages of Canada

16.—(1) English and French are the official languages of Canada and have equality of status and equal rights and privileges as to their use in all institutions of the Parliament and government of Canada.

(2) English and French are the official languages of New Brunswick and have equality of status and equal rights and privileges as to their use in all institutions of the legislature and government of New Brunswick.

(3) Nothing in this Charter limits the authority of Parliament or a legislature to advance the equality of status or use of English and French.

17.—(1) Everyone has the right to use English or French in any debates and other proceedings of Parliament.

(2) Everyone has the right to use English or French in any debates and other proceedings of the legislature of New Brunswick.

18.—(1) The statutes, records and journals of Parliament shall be printed and published in English and French and both language versions are equally authoritative.

(2) The statutes, records and journals of the legislature of New Brunswick shall be printed and published in English and French and both language versions are equally authoritative.

19.—(1) Either English or French may be used by any person in, or in any pleading in or process issuing from, any court established by Parliament.

(2) Either English or French may be used by any person in, or in any pleading in or process issuing from, any court of New Brunswick.

20.—(1) Any member of the public in Canada has the right to communicate with, and to receive available services from, any head or central office of an institution of the Parliament or government of Canada in English or French, and has the same right with respect to any other office of any such institution where

(a) there is a significant demand for communications with and services from that office in such language; or

(b) due to the nature of the office, it is reasonable that communications with and services from that office be available in both English and French.

(2) Any member of the public in New Brunswick has the right to communicate with, and to receive available services from, any office of an institution of the legislature or government of New Brunswick in English or French.

21. Nothing in sections 16 to 20 abrogates or derogates from any right, privilege or obligation with respect to the English and French languages, or either of them, that exists or is continued by virtue of any other provision of the Constitution of Canada.

22. Nothing in sections 16 to 20 abrogates or derogates from any legal or customary right or privilege acquired or enjoyed either before or after the coming into force of this Charter with respect to any language that is not English or French.

Minority Language Educational Rights

23.—(1) Citizens of Canada

(a) whose first language learned and still understood is

that of the English or French linguistic minority population of the province in which they reside; or

(b) who have received their primary school instruction in Canada in English or French and reside in a province where the language in which they received that instruction is the language of the English or French linguistic minority population of the province, have the right to have their children receive primary and secondary school instruction in that language in that province.

(2) Citizens of Canada of whom any child has received or is receiving primary or secondary school instruction in English or French in Canada, have the right to have all their children receive primary and secondary school instruction in the same language.

(3) The right of citizens of Canada under subsections (1) and (2) to have their children receive primary and secondary school instruction in the language of the English or French linguistic minority population of a province

(a) applies wherever in the province the number of children of citizens who have such a right is sufficient to warrant the provision to them out of public funds of minority language instruction; and

(b) includes, where the number of those children so warrants, the right to have them receive that instruction in minority language educational facilities provided out of public funds.

Enforcement

24.—(1) Anyone whose rights or freedoms, as guaranteed by this Charter, have been infringed or denied may apply to a court of competent jurisdiction to obtain such remedy as the court considers appropriate and just in the circumstances.

(2) Where, in proceedings under subsection (1), a court concludes that evidence was obtained in a manner that infringed or denied any rights or freedoms guaranteed by this Charter, the evidence shall be excluded if it is established that, having regard to all the circumstances, the admission of it in the proceedings would bring the administration of justice into disrepute.

General

25. The guarantee in this Charter of certain rights and freedoms shall not be construed so as to abrogate or derogate from any aboriginal treaty or other rights or freedoms that pertain to the aboriginal peoples of Canada including

(a) any rights or freedoms that have been recognized by the Royal Proclamation of October 7, 1763; and

(b) any rights or freedoms that may be acquired by the aboriginal peoples of Canada by way of land claims settlement.

26. The guarantee in this Charter of certain rights and freedoms shall not be construed as denying the existence of any other rights or freedoms that exist in Canada.

27. This Charter shall be interpreted in a manner consistent with the preservation and enhancement of the multicultural heritage of Canadians.

28. Notwithstanding anything in this Charter, the rights and freedoms referred to in it are guaranteed equally to male and female persons.

29. Nothing in this Charter abrogates or derogates from any rights or privileges guaranteed by or under the Constitution of Canada in respect of denominational, separate or dissentient schools.

30. A reference in this Charter to a province or to the legislative assembly or legislature of a province shall be deemed to include a reference to the Yukon Territory and the Northwest Territories, or to the appropriate legislative authority thereof, as the case may be.

31. Nothing in this Charter extends the legislative powers of any body or authority.

Application of Charter

32.—(1) This Charter applies

(a) to the Parliament and government of Canada in respect of all matters within the authority of Parliament including all matters relating to the Yukon Territory and Northwest Territories; and

(b) to the legislature and government of each province in respect of all matters within the authority of the legislature of each province.

(2) Notwithstanding subsection (1), section 15 shall not have effect until three years after this section comes into force.

33.—(1) Parliament or the legislature of a province may expressly declare in an Act of Parliament or of the legislature, as the case may be, that the Act or a provision thereof shall operate notwithstanding a provision included in section 2 or sections 7 to 15 of this Charter.

(2) An Act or a provision of an Act in respect of which a declaration made under this section is in effect shall have such

operation as it would have but for the provision of this Charter referred to in the declaration.

(3) A declaration made under subsection (1) shall cease to have effect five years after it comes into force or on such earlier date as may be specified in the declaration.

(4) Parliament or the legislature of a province may re-enact a declaration made under subsection (1).

(5) Subsection (3) applies in respect of a re-enactment made under subsection (4).

Citation

34. This Part may be cited as the Canadian Charter of Rights and Freedoms.

CHARTER OF PARIS FOR A NEW EUROPE (1990)

The Conference on Security and Cooperation in Europe (CSCE), a loose-knit association of member nations, including Canada, the United States, and every European state except Albania, was created in 1975 by what came to be known as the Helsinki Accords. In return for tacit recognition of the European boundaries determined by World War II, the Soviet Union and its Warsaw Pact partners promised greater respect for human rights in their countries. The accords placed fundamental human rights at the forefront of international politics and lent moral support to dissidents when their governments sought to evade the promises they had made in Helsinki. Subsequently, U.S. presidents made the accords, and human rights in general, a keystone of their foreign policy. In the late 1980s, as Soviet general secretary Mikhail Gorbachev sought cooperation rather than confrontation with the West, the CSCE provided the basic framework and process for bringing about evolutionary political change in Europe.

On November 21, 1990, at a summit in Paris, the CSCE member states signed the Charter of Paris for a New Europe, a lengthy agreement proclaiming a new order of peaceful relations. The charter established a permanent secretariat in Prague, a center in Vienna for conflict prevention, and an office in Warsaw for monitoring elections. It also called for the creation of a CSCE parliamentary assembly.

"The cold war is over," said U.S. president George Bush. "In signing the Charter of Paris we have closed a chapter of history." President François Mitterrand of France ended the conference by declaring that all members "share a common vision of the world and a common set of values." The hyperbole masked serious threats to human rights and to peace, as became apparent a year later when Yugoslavia dissolved into war and chaos. Nonetheless, the document is a powerful statement of the ultimate goal of achieving fundamental human rights.

A New Era of Democracy, Peace and Unity

We, the Heads of State or Government of the States participating in the Conference on Security and Co-operation in Europe, have assembled in Paris at a time of profound change and historic expectations. The era of confrontation and division of Europe has ended. We declare that henceforth our relations will be founded on respect and co-operation.

Europe is liberating itself from the legacy of the past. The courage of men and women, the strength of will of the peoples and the power of the ideas of the Helsinki Final Act have opened a new era of democracy, peace and unity in Europe.

Ours is a time for fulfilling the hopes and expectations our peoples have cherished for decades: steadfast commitment to democracy based on human rights and fundamental freedoms; prosperity through economic liberty and social justice; and equal security for all our countries.

The Ten Principles of the Final Act will guide us towards this ambitious future, just as they have lighted our way towards better relations for the past fifteen years. Full implementation of all CSCE commitments must form the basis for the initiatives we are now taking to enable our nations to live in accordance with their aspirations.

Human Rights, Democracy and Rule of Law

We undertake to build, consolidate and strengthen democracy as the only system of government of our nations. In this endeavor, we will abide by the following:

Human rights and fundamental freedoms are the birthright of all human beings, are inalienable and are guaranteed by law. Their protection and promotion is the first responsibility of government. Respect for them is an essential safeguard against an over-mighty State. Their observance and full exercise are the foundation of freedom, justice and peace.

Democratic government is based on the will of the people, expressed regularly through free and fair elections. Democracy has as its foundation respect for the human person and the rule of law. Democracy is the best safeguard of freedom of expression, tolerance of all groups of society, and equality of opportunity for each person.

Democracy, with its representative and pluralist character, entails accountability to the electorate, the obligation of public authorities to comply with the law and justice administered impartially. No one will be above the law.

We affirm that, without discrimination, every individual has the right to:

freedom of thought, conscience and religion or belief,
freedom of expression,
freedom of association and peaceful assembly,
freedom of movement;

no one will be:

subject to arbitrary arrest or detention,
subject to torture or other cruel, inhuman or degrading treatment or punishment;

everyone also has the right:

to know and act upon his rights,
to participate in free and fair elections,
to fair and public trial if charged with an offence,
to own property alone or in association and to exercise individual enterprise,
to enjoy his economic, social and cultural rights.

We affirm that the ethnic, cultural, linguistic and religious identity of national minorities will be protected and that persons belonging to national minorities have the right freely to express, preserve and develop that identity without any discrimination and in full equality before the law.

We will ensure that everyone will enjoy recourse to effective remedies, national or international, against any violation of his rights.

Full respect for these precepts is the bedrock on which we will seek to construct the new Europe.

Our States will co-operate and support each other with the aim of making democratic gains irreversible.

Economic Liberty and Responsibility

Economic liberty, social justice and environmental responsibility are indispensable for prosperity.

The free will of the individual, exercised in democracy and protected by the rule of law, forms the necessary basis for successful economic and social development. We will promote economic activity which respects and upholds human dignity.

Freedom and political pluralism are necessary elements in our common objective of developing market economies towards sustainable economic growth, prosperity, social justice,

expanding employment and efficient use of economic resources. The success of the transition to a market economy by countries making efforts to this effect is important and in the interest of us all. It will enable us to share a higher level of prosperity which is our common objective. We will co-operate to this end.

Preservation of the environment is a shared responsibility of all our nations. While supporting national and regional efforts in this field, we must also look to the pressing need for joint action on a wider scale.

Friendly Relations among Participating States

Now that a new era is dawning in Europe, we are determined to expand and strengthen friendly relations and co-operation among the States of Europe, the United States of America and Canada, and to promote friendship among our peoples.

To uphold and promote democracy, peace and unity in Europe, we solemnly pledge our full commitment to the Ten Principles of the Helsinki Final Act. We affirm the continuing validity of the Ten Principles and our determination to put them into practice. All the Principles apply equally and unreservedly, each of them being interpreted taking into account the others. They form the basis for our relations.

In accordance with our obligations under the Charter of the United Nations and commitments under the Helsinki Final Act, we renew our pledge to refrain from the threat or use of force against the territorial integrity or political independence of any State, or from acting in any other manner inconsistent with the principles or purposes of those documents. We recall that non-compliance with obligations under the Charter of the United Nations constitutes a violation of international law.

We reaffirm our commitment to settle disputes by peaceful means. We decide to develop mechanisms for the prevention and resolution of conflicts among the participating States.

With the ending of the division of Europe, we will strive for a new quality in our security relations while fully respecting each other's freedom of choice in that respect. Security is indivisible and the security of every participating State is inseparably linked to that of all the others. We therefore pledge to co-operate in strengthening confidence and security among us and in promoting arms control and disarmament.

We welcome the Joint Declaration of Twenty-Two States on the improvement of their relations.

Our relations will rest on our common adherence to democratic values and to human rights and fundamental freedoms. We are convinced that in order to strengthen peace and security among our States, the advancement of democracy, and respect for and effective exercise of human rights, are indispensable. We reaffirm the equal rights of peoples and their right to self-determination in conformity with the Charter of the United Nations and with the relevant norms of international law, including those relating to territorial integrity of States.

We are determined to enhance political consultation and to widen co-operation to solve economic, social, environmental, cultural and humanitarian problems. This common resolve and our growing interdependence will help to overcome the mistrust of decades, to increase stability and to build a united Europe.

We want Europe to be a source of peace, open to dialogue and to co-operation with other countries, welcoming exchanges and involved in the search for common responses to the challenges of the future.

Security

Friendly relations among us will benefit from the consolidation of democracy and improved security.

We welcome the signature of the treaty on Conventional Armed Forces in Europe by twenty-two participating States, which will lead to lower levels of armed forces. We endorse the adoption of a substantial new set of Confidence- and Security-building Measures which will lead to increased transparency and confidence among all participating States. These are important steps towards enhanced stability and security in Europe.

The unprecedented reduction in armed forces resulting from the Treaty on Conventional Armed Forces in Europe, together with new approaches to security and co-operation within the CSCE process, will lead to a new perception of security in Europe and a new dimension in our relations. In this context we fully recognize the freedom of States to choose their own security arrangements.

Unity

Europe whole and free is calling for a new beginning. We invite our peoples to join in this great endeavour.

We note with great satisfaction the Treaty on the Final Settlement with respect to Germany signed in Moscow on 12 September 1990 and sincerely welcome the fact that the German people have united to become one State in accordance with the principles of the Final Act of the Conference on Security and Co-operation in Europe and in full accord with their neighbours. The establishment of the national unity of Germany is an important contribution to a just and lasting order of peace for a united, democratic Europe aware of its responsibility for stability, peace and co-operation.

The participation of both North American and European States is a fundamental characteristic of the CSCE: it underlies its past achievements and is essential to the future of the CSCE

process. An abiding adherence to shared values and our common heritage are the ties which bind us together. With all the rich diversity of our nations, we are united in our commitment to expand our co-operation in all fields. The challenges confronting us can only be met by common action, co-operation and solidarity.

The CSCE and the World

The destiny of our nations is linked to that of all other nations. We support fully the United Nations and the enhancement of its role in promoting international peace, security and justice. We reaffirm our commitment to the principles and purposes of the United Nations as enshrined in the Charter and condemn all violations of these principles. We recognize with satisfaction the growing role of the United Nations in world affairs and its increasing effectiveness, fostered by the improvement in relations among our States.

Aware of the dire needs of a great part of the world, we commit ourselves to solidarity with all other countries. Therefore, we issue a call from Paris today to all the nations of the world. We stand ready to join with any and all States in common efforts to protect and advance the community of fundamental human values.

Guidelines for the Future

Proceeding from our firm commitment to the full implementation of all CSCE principles and provisions, we now resolve to give a new impetus to a balanced and comprehensive development of our co-operation in order to address the needs and aspirations of our peoples.

Human Dimension

We declare our respect for human rights and fundamental freedoms to be irrevocable. We will fully implement and build upon the provisions relating to the human dimension of the CSCE.

Proceeding from the Document of the Copenhagen Meeting of the Conference on the Human Dimension, we will co-operate to strengthen democratic institutions and to promote the application of the rule of law. To that end, we decide to convene a seminar of experts in Oslo from 4 to 15 November 1991.

Determined to foster the rich contribution of national minorities to the life of our societies, we undertake further to improve their situation. We reaffirm our deep conviction that friendly relations among our peoples, as well as peace, justice, stability and democracy, require that the ethnic, cultural, linguistic and religious identity of national minorities be protected and conditions for the promotion of that identity be created. We declare that questions related to national minorities can only be satisfactorily resolved in a democratic political framework. We further acknowledge that the rights of persons belonging to national minorities must be fully respected as part of universal human rights. Being aware of the urgent need for increased co-operation on, as well as better protection of, national minorities, we decide to convene a meeting of experts on national minorities to be held in Geneva from 1 to 19 July 1991.

We express our determination to combat all forms of racial and ethnic hatred, antisemitism, xenophobia and discrimination against anyone as well as persecution on religious and ideological grounds.

In accordance with our CSCE commitments, we stress that free movement and contacts among our citizens as well as the free flow of information and ideas are crucial for the maintenance and development of free societies and flourishing cultures. We welcome increased tourism and visits among our countries.

The human dimension mechanism has proved its usefulness, and we are consequently determined to expand it to include new procedures involving, *inter alia,* the services of experts or a roster of eminent persons experienced in human rights issues which could be raised under the mechanism. We shall provide, in the context of the mechanism, for individuals to be involved in the protection of their rights. Therefore, we undertake to develop further our commitments in this respect, in particular at the Moscow Meeting of the Conference on the Human Dimension, without prejudice to obligations under existing international instruments to which our States may be parties.

We recognize the important contribution of the Council of Europe to the promotion of human rights and the principles of democracy and the rule of law as well as to the development of cultural co-operation. We welcome moves by several participating States to join the Council of Europe and adhere to its European Convention on Human Rights. We welcome as well the readiness of the Council of Europe to make its experience available to the CSCE.

Security

The changing political and military environment in Europe opens new possibilities for common efforts in the field of military security. We will build on the important achievements attained in the Treaty on Conventional Armed Forces in Europe and in the Negotiations on Confidence- and Security-building Measures. We undertake to continue the CSBM negotiations under the same mandate, and to seek to conclude them no later than the Follow-up Meeting of the CSCE to be held in Helsinki in 1992. We also welcome the decision of the participating States concerned to continue the CFE negotiation under the same mandate and to seek to conclude it no later than the Helsinki Follow-up Meeting. Following a period for national preparations, we look forward to a more structured co-operation among all participating States on security matters, and to discussions and consultations among the thirty-four participating States aimed at establishing by 1992, from the conclusion of the Helsinki Follow-up Meeting, new negotiations on disarmament and confidence and security building open to all participating States.

We call for the earliest possible conclusion of the Convention on an effectively verifiable, global and comprehensive ban on chemical weapons, and we intend to be original signatories to it.

We reaffirm the importance of the Open Skies initiative and call for the successful conclusion of the negotiations as soon as possible.

Although the threat of conflict in Europe has diminished, other dangers threaten the stability of our societies. We are determined to co-operate in defending democratic institutions against activities which violate the independence, sovereign equality or territorial integrity of the participating States. These include illegal activities involving outside pressure, coercion and subversion.

We unreservedly condemn, as criminal, all acts, methods and practices of terrorism and express our determination to work for its eradication both bilaterally and through multilateral co-operation. We will also join together in combating illicit trafficking in drugs.

Being aware that an essential complement to the duty of States to refrain from the threat or use of force is the peaceful settlement of disputes both being essential factors for the maintenance and consolidation of international peace and security, we will not only seek effective ways of preventing, through political means, conflicts which may yet emerge, but also define, in conformity with international law, appropriate mechanisms for the peaceful resolution of any disputes which may arise. Accordingly, we undertake to seek new forms of co-operation in this area, in particular a range of methods for the peaceful settlement of disputes, including mandatory, third-party involvement. We stress that full use should be made in this context of the opportunity of the Meeting on the peaceful settlement of disputes which will be convened in Valletta at the beginning of 1991. The Council of Ministers for Foreign Affairs will take into account the Report of the Valletta Meeting.

Economic Co-operation

We stress that economic co-operation based on market economy constitutes an essential element of our relations and will be instrumental in the construction of a prosperous and united Europe. Democratic institutions and economic liberty foster economic and social progress, as recognized in the Document of the Bonn Conference on Economic Co-operation, the results of which we strongly support.

We underline that co-operation in the economic field, science and technology is now an important pillar of the CSCE. The participating States should periodically review progress and give new impulses in these fields.

We are convinced that our overall economic co-operation should be expanded, free enterprise encouraged and trade increased and diversified according to GATT rules. We will promote social justice and progress and further the welfare of our peoples. We recognize in this context the importance of effective policies to address the problem of unemployment.

We reaffirm the need to continue to support democratic countries in transition towards the establishment of market economy and the creation of the basis for self-sustained economic and social growth, as already undertaken by the Group of twenty-four countries. We further underline the necessity of their increased integration, involving the acceptance of disciplines as well as benefits, into the international economic and financial system.

We consider that increased emphasis on economic co-operation within the CSCE process should take into account the interests of developing participating States.

We recall the link between respect for and promotion of human rights and fundamental freedoms and scientific progress. Co-operation in the field of science and technology will play an essential role in economic and social development. Therefore, it must evolve towards a greater sharing of appropriate scientific and technological information and knowledge with a view to overcoming the technological gap which exists among the participating States. We further encourage the participating States to work together in order to develop human potential and the spirit of free enterprise.

We are determined to give the necessary impetus to co-operation among our States in the fields of energy, transport and tourism for economic and social development. We welcome, in particular, practical steps to create optimal conditions for the economic and rational development of energy resources, with due regard for environmental considerations.

We recognize the important role of the European Community in the political and economic development of Europe. International economic organizations such as the United Nations Economic Commission for Europe (ECE), the Bretton Woods institutions, the Organisation for Economic Co-operation and Development (OECD), the European Free Trade Association (EFTA) and the International Chamber of Commerce (ICC) also have a significant task in promoting economic co-operation, which will be further enhanced by the es-

tablishment of the European Bank for Reconstruction and Development (EBRD). In order to pursue our objectives, we stress the necessity for effective co-ordination of the activities of these organizations and emphasize the need to find methods for all our States to take part in these activities.

Environment

We recognize the urgent need to tackle the problems of the environment and the importance of individual and co-operative efforts in this area. We pledge to intensify our endeavours to protect and improve our environment in order to restore and maintain a sound ecological balance in air, water and soil. Therefore, we are determined to make full use of the CSCE as a framework for the formulation of common environmental commitments and objectives, and thus to pursue the work reflected in the Report of the Sofia Meeting on the Protection of the Environment.

We emphasize the significant role of a well-informed society in enabling the public and individuals to take initiatives to improve the environment. To this end, we commit ourselves to promoting public awareness and education on the environment as well as the public reporting of the environmental impact of policies, projects and programmes.

We attach priority to the introduction of clean and low-waste technology, being aware of the need to support countries which do not yet have their own means for appropriate measures.

We underline that environmental policies should be supported by appropriate legislative measures and administrative structures to ensure their effective implementation.

We stress the need for new measures providing for the systematic evaluation of compliance with the existing commitments and moreover, for the development of more ambitious commitments with regard to notification and exchange of information about the state of the environment and potential environmental hazards. We also welcome the creation of the European Environment Agency (EEA).

We welcome the operational activities, problem-oriented studies and policy reviews in various existing international organizations engaged in the protection of the environment, such as the United Nations Environment Programme (UNEP), the United Nations Economic Commission for Europe (ECE) and the Organisation for Economic Co-operation and Development (OECD). We emphasize the need for strengthening their co-operation and for their efficient co-ordination.

Culture

We recognize the essential contribution of our common European culture and our shared values in overcoming the division of the continent. Therefore, we underline our attachment to creative freedom and to the protection and promotion of our cultural and spiritual heritage, in all its richness and diversity.

In view of the recent changes in Europe, we stress the increased importance of the Cracow Symposium and we look forward to its consideration of guidelines for intensified co-operation in the field of culture. We invite the Council of Europe to contribute to this Symposium.

In order to promote greater familiarity amongst our peoples, we favour the establishment of cultural centres in cities of other participating States as well as increased co-operation in the audio-visual field and wider exchange in music, theatre, literature and the arts.

We resolve to make special efforts in our national policies to promote better understanding, in particular among young people, through cultural exchanges, co-operation in all fields of education and, more specifically, through teaching and training in the languages of other participating States. We intend to consider first results of this action at the Helsinki Follow-up Meeting in 1992.

Migrant Workers

We recognize that the issues of migrant workers and their families legally residing in host countries have economic, cultural and social aspects as well as their human dimension. We reaffirm that the protection and promotion of their rights, as well as the implementation of relevant international obligations, is our common concern.

Mediterranean

We consider that the fundamental political changes that have occurred in Europe have a positive relevance to the Mediterranean region. Thus, we will continue efforts to strengthen security and co-operation in the Mediterranean as an important factor for stability in Europe. We welcome the Report of the Palma de Mallorca Meeting on the Mediterranean, the results of which we all support.

We are concerned with the continuing tensions in the region, and renew our determination to intensify efforts towards finding just, viable and lasting solutions, through peaceful means, to outstanding crucial problems, based on respect for the principles of the Final Act.

We wish to promote favourable conditions for a harmonious development and diversification of relations with the non-participating Mediterranean States. Enhanced co-operation with these States will be pursued with the aim of promoting economic and social development and thereby enhancing stability in the region. To this end, we will strive together with these countries towards a substantial narrowing of the prosperity gap between Europe and its Mediterranean neighbours.

Non-governmental Organizations

We recall the major role that non-governmental organizations, religious and other groups and individuals have played in the achievement of the objectives of the CSCE and will further facilitate their activities for the implementation of the CSCE commitments by the participating States. These organizations, groups and individuals must be involved in an appropriate way in the activities and new structures of the CSCE in order to fulfill their important tasks.

New Structures and Institutions of the CSCE Process

Our common efforts to consolidate respect for human rights, democracy and the rule of law, to strengthen peace and to promote unity in Europe require a new quality of political dialogue and co-operation and thus development of the structures of the CSCE.

The intensification of our consultations at all levels is of prime importance in shaping our future relations. To this end, we decide on the following:

We, the Heads of State or Government, shall meet next time in Helsinki on the occasion of the CSCE Follow-up Meeting 1992. Thereafter, we will meet on the occasion of subsequent follow-up meetings.

Our Ministers for Foreign Affairs will meet, as a Council, regularly and at least once a year. These meetings will provide the central forum for political consultations within the CSCE process. The Council will consider issues relevant to the Conference on Security and Co-operation in Europe and take appropriate decisions.

The first meeting of the Council will take place in Berlin.

A Committee of Senior Officials will prepare the meetings of the Council and carry out its decisions. The Committee will review current issues and may take appropriate decisions, including in the form of recommendations to the Council.

Additional meetings of the representatives of the participating States may be agreed upon to discuss questions of urgent concern.

The Council will examine the development of provisions for convening meetings of the Committee of Senior Officials in emergency situations.

Meetings of other Ministers may also be agreed by the participating States.

In order to provide administrative support for these consultations we establish a Secretariat in Prague.

Follow-up meetings of the participating States will be held, as a rule, every two years to allow the participating States to take stock of developments, review the implementation of their commitments and consider further steps in the CSCE process.

We decide to create a Conflict Prevention Centre in Vienna to assist the Council in reducing the risk of conflict.

We decide to establish an Office for Free Elections in Warsaw to facilitate contacts and the exchange of information on elections within participating States.

Recognizing the important role parliamentarians can play in the CSCE process, we call for greater parliamentary involvement in the CSCE, in particular through the creation of a CSCE parliamentary assembly, involving members of parliaments from all participating States. To this end, we urge that contacts be pursued at the parliamentary level to discuss the field of activities, working methods and rules of procedure of such a CSCE parliamentary structure, drawing on existing experience and work already undertaken in this field.

We ask our Ministers for Foreign Affairs to review this matter on the occasion of their first meeting as a Council.

Procedural and organizational modalities relating to certain provisions contained in the Charter of Paris for a New Europe are set out in the Supplementary Document which is adopted together with the Charter of Paris.

We entrust to the Council the further steps which may be required to ensure the implementation of decisions contained in the present document, as well as in the Supplementary Document, and to consider further efforts for the strengthening of security and co-operation in Europe. The Council may adopt any amendment to the supplementary document which it may deem appropriate.

The original of the Charter of Paris for a New Europe, drawn up in English, French, German, Italian, Russian and Spanish, will be transmitted to the Government of the French Republic, which will retain it in its archives. Each of the participating States will receive from the Government of the French Republic a true copy of the Charter of Paris.

The text of the Charter of Paris will be published in each participating State, which will disseminate it and make it known as widely as possible.

The Government of the French Republic is requested to transmit to the Secretary-General of the United Nations the text of the Charter of Paris for a New Europe which is not eligible for registration under Article 102 of the Charter of the United Nations, with a view to its circulation to all the members of the Organization as an official document of the United Nations.

The Government of the French Republic is also requested to transmit the text of the Charter of Paris to all the other international organizations mentioned in the text.

Wherefore, we, the undersigned High Representatives of the participating States, mindful of the high political significance we attach to the results of the Summit meeting, and declaring our determination to act in accordance with the provisions we have adopted, have subscribed our signatures below.

SANTIAGO COMMITMENT TO DEMOCRACY AND THE RENEWAL OF THE INTER-AMERICAN SYSTEM (1991)

When the European powers, primarily Spain and Portugal, began to relinquish control of their colonies in the Americas in the early nineteenth century, democracy sank wide but shallow roots in the newly independent states. Most people of the region accepted democracy as the most desirable and legitimate system of government, and many states adopted seemingly democratic institutions. But the social, economic, and intellectual underpinnings that had nurtured democracy in North America and Western Europe were largely absent from Latin America.

In practice, most Latin American states in the years following independence were ruled by oligarchies of the wealthiest citizens or by the military. Politics in many states was characterized by instability and violence, revolution and counterrevolution, and dictatorships of the left followed by dictatorships of the right. But, remarkably, belief in democracy as the destiny of Latin America remained strong.

Democracy gained strength as economic development progressed. It was also promoted by international cooperation among the states of the Western Hemisphere. In April 1948 the United States and a score of Latin American and Caribbean countries formed the Organization of American States (OAS) to institutionalize hemispheric cooperation. The OAS was established to address a number of issues, including regional security, peaceful settlement of regional disputes, democracy and human rights, and economic, social, and cultural development.

Democracy and human rights emerged as major issues in the OAS in the late 1970s as democracy took hold in more and more states. By 1991 every OAS member state (except

Cuba, which had been suspended in 1962) had a democratically elected government, and the OAS began to focus on protecting the fledgling democratic regimes. At the twenty-first annual general assembly meeting, in Santiago, Chile, in June 1991, the member states signed the Santiago Commitment to Democracy and the Renewal of the Inter-American System. The document pledged the signatories to "ensure the promotion and defense of representative democracy. . . ."

The member states also adopted enforcement procedures to effect the principles embodied in the declaration. In the event a democratically elected government was overthrown or constitutional rule interrupted, the OAS secretary general would call the Permanent Council into session. Within ten days the council would organize an emergency meeting of all members' foreign ministers. The foreign ministers would determine the collective actions to be taken in the name of the OAS to restore democratic rule.

Unlike the Organization of African Unity, which lacks the authority and will to enforce the principles embodied in the African Charter on Human and Peoples' Rights, the OAS is a robust organization. The enforcement procedures adopted in Santiago have been invoked on several occasions to restore constitutional rule: in Haiti in September 1991, when President Jean-Bertrand Aristide was overthrown; in Peru in April 1992, when President Alberto Fujimori suspended constitutional government; and in Guatemala in May 1993, when President Jorge Serrano suspended the constitution and dissolved the congress.

The Ministers of Foreign Affairs and Heads of Delegation of the member states of the Organization of American States, meeting in Santiago, Chile, as the representatives of their democratically elected governments to the twenty-first regular session of the General Assembly of the OAS;

Aware that profound international political and economic changes and the end of the cold war open up new opportunities and responsibilities for concerted action by all countries through global and regional organizations, as well as in their bilateral relationships;

Bearing in mind that the changes towards a more open and democratic international system are not completely established, and that therefore, cooperation must be encouraged and strengthened so that those favorable trends may continue;

Recognizing the need to advance decisively towards a just and democratic order based on full respect for international law, the peaceful settlement of disputes, solidarity, and the revitalization of multilateral diplomacy and of international organizations;

Mindful that representative democracy is the form of government of the region and that its effective exercise, consolidation, and improvement are shared priorities;

Reaffirming that the principles enshrined in the OAS Charter and the ideals of peace, democracy, social justice, comprehensive development and solidarity are the permanent foundation of the inter-American system;

Recognizing that cooperation to guarantee the peace and security of the hemisphere is one of the essential purposes consecrated in the Charter of the Organization of American States (OAS), and that the proliferation of arms adversely affects international security and takes resources away from the economic and social development of the peoples of the member states;

Resolved to work for the intensification of the struggle against extreme poverty and the elimination of the economic and social inequalities in each nation and among the nations of the hemisphere;

Noting with interest the report of the consultation group on the renewal of the inter-American system; and

Convinced that the OAS is the political forum for dialogue, understanding, and cooperation among all the countries of the hemisphere, whose potential, enhanced by the admission of new member states, must be increased to make it an effective voice in the world for the decisions of its members,

DECLARE:

Their inescapable commitment to the defense and promotion of representative democracy and human rights in the region, within the framework of respect for the principles of self-determination and non-intervention;

Their firm resolve to stimulate the process of renewal of the Organization of American States, to make it more effective and useful in the application of its guiding principles and for the attainment of its objectives;

Their determination to continue to prepare and develop a relevant agenda for the Organization, in order to respond appropriately to the new challenges and demands in the world and in the region, and their decision to assign special priority on that agenda, during the present decade, to the following actions:

a. Intensifying the common struggle and cooperative action against extreme poverty to help reduce economic and social inequalities in the hemisphere, and thereby strengthen the promotion and consolidation of democracy in the region;

b. Strengthening representative democracy as an expression of the legitimate and free manifestation of the will of the people, always respecting the sovereignty and independence of member states;

c. Promoting the observance and defense of human rights in accordance with the inter-American instruments in force and through the specific existing agencies; and ensuring that no form of discrimination becomes an obstacle to political participation by undervalued or minority ethnic groups;

d. Promoting the progressive liberalization of trade and the expansion of investments, access to scientific and technological knowledge, and the reduction of the foreign debt of the countries of the region and, from this perspective, support for the "Enterprise for the Americas Initiative" and the Uruguay Round of the GATT negotiations;

e. Contributing to the protection of our environment by all for the benefit of present and future generations, thus assuring sustainable development in the region;

f. Encouraging the adoption and execution of appropriate measures to prevent and combat the illicit use and production of narcotic drugs and psychotropic substances, and traffic therein, chemical precursors and money laundering, and related clandestine traffic in arms, ammunitions, and explosives;

g. Favoring integration processes in the region and, to this end, adopting a program of work designed, *inter alia,* to harmonize legislation in the region, particularly that of the civil and common law systems;

h. Promoting and intensifying cultural, educational, scientific, and technological exchanges as instruments for integration, with full respect for the cultural heritage of each of the member states;

i. Increasing technical cooperation and encouraging a transfer of technology to enhance the capabilities for economic growth of the countries in the region.

Their decision to initiate a process of consultation on hemispheric security in light of the new conditions in the region and the world, from an updated and comprehensive perspective of security and disarmament, including the subject of all forms of proliferation of weapons and instruments of mass destruction, so that the largest possible volume of resources may be devoted to the economic and social development of the member states; and an appeal to other competent organizations in the world to join in the efforts of the OAS.

Their decision to adopt efficacious, timely, and expeditious procedures to ensure the promotion and defense of representative democracy, in keeping with the Charter of the Organization of American States.

Consequently, the Ministers of Foreign Affairs and the Heads of Delegation of the member states of the OAS, in the name of their peoples, declare their firm political commitment to the promotion and protection of human rights and representative democracy, as indispensable conditions for the stability, peace, and development of the region, and for the success of the changes and renewal that the inter-American system will require at the threshold of the twenty-first century.

CONSTITUTION OF THE CZECH REPUBLIC (1993)

The Czechs and Slovaks had little in common when in the waning days of World War I (1914–1918) a small group of émigré Czech and Slovak intellectuals lobbied Allied leaders to create a Czechoslovak state. The Czechs, who had been incorporated into the Austrian empire in the sixteenth and seventeenth centuries, and the Slovaks, who had been under Hungarian rule for nearly one thousand years, combined to form the most stable and prosperous democracy in Central Europe. Despite economic depression, extremist ideologies, and ethnic turmoil—factors that gutted other Central European democracies in the interwar period—Czechoslovakia adopted a model Western-style constitution. The constitution embodied representative legislative institutions, universal suffrage, due process of law, a guarantee of individual liberties, and other democratic features. However, the stability of the constitutional order belied longstanding resentments and disaffection between Czechs and Slovaks.

Czechoslovakia's short-lived democratic republic was crushed during World War II (1939–1945) by Nazi Germany, and after the war the Soviet Union imposed a communist regime on the country. The Czech Communist Party began to crumble in 1988–1989, along with the governments of the other Soviet satellite states in Eastern Europe, when its legitimacy and support were undercut by liberalizing reforms taking place in the Soviet Union under Mikhail Gorbachev. In the face of increasingly large street demonstrations in February, May, August, and October 1989, the communist government of Czechoslovakia resigned in December.

The transition to democracy was exceptionally smooth, in large part because of the constitutional traditions established in the interwar period. Legislative elections were held in June 1990 in which 97 percent of eligible voters participated. And in July, Václav Havel, a leading intellectual and dissident during the communist era, was elected president.

Efforts to draft a new constitution for the Czech and Slovak Federative Republic, as Czechoslovakia was renamed in April 1990, proved impossible, however. Nationalism was growing in intensity, particularly among Slovaks, who resented (and had resented since the 1920s) the predominance of ethnic Czechs in government and the economy, a status derived from the more extensive economic development of the Czech lands under the Austro-Hungarian Empire. Legislative elections held in June 1992 dramatically strengthened the parties that supported separation. By July it was clear that a federal constitution acceptable to all parties could not be drafted. Separation was inevitable even though opinion polls indicated that a majority of Czechs and Slovaks favored maintaining the federal republic.

In the closing months of 1992 legislation was passed and arrangements made to dissolve the state effective January 1, 1993. The Czech National Council adopted on December 16 the Constitution of the Czech Republic, which was similar in many respects to the interwar constitution of Czechoslovakia. The new constitution, like the old one, established a bicameral parliament elected by universal suffrage; the parliament elects the president, who in turn appoints the prime minister and cabinet.

Preamble

We, the citizens of the Czech Republic in Bohemia, Moravia and Silesia,

at the time of the renewal of an independent Czech state,

loyal to all good traditions of the ancient statehood of the Lands of the Czech Crown and the Czechoslovak statehood,

resolved to build, protect and develop the Czech Republic in the spirit of the inviolable values of human dignity and freedom,

as the home of equal and free citizens who are conscious of their duties towards others and their responsibility towards the whole, as a free and democratic state based on the respect for human rights and the principles of civic society,

as part of the family of European and world democracies,

resolved to jointly protect and develop the inherited natural and cultural, material and spiritual wealth,

resolved to abide by all time-tried principles of a law-observing state,

through our freely elected representatives, adopt this Constitution of the Czech Republic.

Chapter One. Basic Provisions

ARTICLE 1

The Czech Republic is a sovereign, unified and democratic law-observing state, based on the respect for the rights and freedoms of the individual and citizen.

ARTICLE 2

(1) All state power derives from the people; they exercise this power by means of their legislative, executive and judicial bodies.

(2) A constitutional law may stipulate the cases when the people exercise state power directly.

(3) The state power serves all citizens and can be exercised only in cases and within the scope stipulated by law, and by means specified by law.

(4) Every citizen may do whatever is not forbidden by law, and no one may be forced to do what the law does not enjoin.

ARTICLE 3

Part of the constitutional order of the Czech Republic is the Charter of Fundamental Rights and Freedoms.

ARTICLE 4

The fundamental rights and freedoms enjoy the protection of the judiciary.

ARTICLE 5

The political system is based on the free and voluntary foundation and free competition of political parties respecting fundamental democratic principles and rejecting force as a means for asserting their interests.

ARTICLE 6

Political decisions shall derive from the will of the majority expressed through free voting. Minorities shall be protected by the majority in decision-making.

ARTICLE 7

The state shall see to it that natural resources are used economically and natural wealth is protected.

ARTICLE 8

The autonomy of units of territorial self-administration shall be guaranteed.

ARTICLE 9

(1) The Constitution may be amended or altered solely by constitutional laws.

(2) Any change of fundamental attributes of the democratic law-observing state is inadmissible.

(3) Legal norms cannot be interpreted as warranting the removal or threatening of the foundations of the democratic state.

ARTICLE 10

Ratified and promulgated international accords on human rights and fundamental freedoms, to which the Czech Republic has committed itself, are immediately binding and are superior to law.

ARTICLE 11

The territory of the Czech Republic encompasses an indivisible whole whose state border may be altered exclusively by constitutional legislation.

ARTICLE 12

(1) Procedures binding for the acquisition and loss of Czech citizenship are stipulated by law.

(2) No one can be stripped of his or her citizenship against his or her will.

ARTICLE 13

The capital of the Czech Republic is Prague.

ARTICLE 14

(1) The state symbols of the Czech Republic are the large and small state emblems, the state colors, the state flag, the banner of the president of the republic, the state seal and the state anthem.

(2) The state symbols and their use are determined by law.

Chapter Two. Legislative Power

ARTICLE 15

(1) Legislative power in the Czech Republic shall be vested in Parliament.

(2) Parliament is composed of two chambers, the Chamber of Deputies and the Senate.

ARTICLE 16

(1) The Chamber of Deputies has 200 deputies, elected for a term of four years.

(2) The Senate has 81 senators, elected for a term of six years. One third of the senators is elected every second year.

ARTICLE 17

(1) Elections to both chambers shall be held in a period of time starting the thirtieth day before the expiration of the electoral term and ending on the day of its expiration.

(2) If the Chamber of Deputies is dissolved, elections shall take place within sixty days of its dissolution.

ARTICLE 18

(1) Elections to the Chamber of Deputies shall be held on the basis of universal, equal and direct suffrage by secret ballot, according to the principles of proportional representation.

(2) Elections to the Senate shall take place on the basis of universal, equal and direct suffrage by secret ballot, on the basis of the majority system.

(3) Every citizen of the Czech Republic on reaching the age of 18 has the right to vote.

ARTICLE 19

(1) Every citizen of the Czech Republic who is eligible to vote and has reached the age of 21 may be elected to the Chamber of Deputies.

(2) Every citizen who is eligible to vote and has reached the age of 40 may be elected to the Senate.

(3) The mandate of a deputy or a senator shall be effective upon his or her election.

ARTICLE 20

Additional conditions for the exercise of suffrage, the organization of elections and the scope of judicial review are stipulated by law.

ARTICLE 21

No one may simultaneously be a member of both chambers of Parliament.

ARTICLE 22

(1) The exercise of the office of the president of the republic, the office of judges and other functions, set forth by law, are incompatible with the post of deputy or senator.

(2) A deputy's or a senator's mandate expires the day he or she enters upon the office of the president of the republic, or the day he or she assumes a judgeship or another post incompatible with the post of deputy or senator.

ARTICLE 23

(1) A deputy shall take the oath at the first session of the Chamber of Deputies which he or she attends.

(2) A senator shall take the oath at the first session of the Senate which he or she attends.

(3) The oath of a deputy or a senator is worded as follows: "I pledge allegiance to the Czech Republic. I pledge to uphold its Constitution and laws. I pledge on my honor to exercise my mandate in the interest of the people and in accordance with my best conviction and conscience."

ARTICLE 24

A deputy or a senator may surrender his or her mandate by a declaration made personally at a session of the chamber of which he or she is a member. If he or she is prevented from doing so by serious circumstances, he or she may do so by a method set forth by law.

ARTICLE 25

A deputy's or a senator's mandate expires upon

a) refusing to take the oath or taking the oath with reservations,

b) the expiration of the term of office,

c) the surrender of the mandate,

d) the loss of eligibility,

e) the dissolution of the Chamber of Deputies, in the case of deputies,

f) the incompatibility of the functions specified in Article 22.

ARTICLE 26

(1) Deputies and senators shall exercise their mandates personally in accordance with their oath and shall not be bound by any directions.

ARTICLE 27

(1) A deputy or a senator may not be prosecuted for voting in the Chamber of Deputies or the Senate or their bodies.

(2) A deputy or a senator may not be prosecuted for statements made in the Chamber of Deputies or the Senate or their bodies. A deputy or a senator is only accountable to the disciplinary authority of the chamber of which he or she is a member.

(3) A deputy or a senator shall be accountable for his or her misdemeanor only to the disciplinary authority of the chamber of which he or she is a member, unless determined by law otherwise.

(4) A deputy or a senator may not be criminally prosecuted without consent of the chamber of which he or she is a member. If the respective chamber declines its consent, criminal proceedings are rendered impossible forever.

(5) A deputy or a senator may be taken into custody only if caught while committing a criminal offense or immediately thereafter. The responsible body is obliged to immediately notify of the detention the chairman of the chamber of which the detainee is a member; if the chamber's chairman fails to give his or her consent to handing the detainee over to court within 24 hours of the detention, the responsible body is obliged to set him or her free. The chamber shall decide with final authority about the admissibility of the prosecution at its first following session.

ARTICLE 28

A deputy or a senator is entitled to withhold testimony about matters of which he or she learned in connection with the exercise of his or her mandate, even after he or she ceased to be a deputy or a senator.

ARTICLE 29

(1) The Chamber of Deputies elects and dismisses the chairman and vice chairmen of the Chamber of Deputies.

(2) The Senate elects and dismisses the chairman and vice chairmen of the Senate.

ARTICLE 30

(1) The Chamber of Deputies may set up an investigatory commission for the investigation of an affair of public interest, if this is suggested by at least one fifth of the deputies.

(2) Proceedings before the commission shall be determined by law.

ARTICLE 31

(1) The chambers establish committees and commissions as their bodies.

(2) The activities of committees and commissions shall be determined by law.

ARTICLE 32

A deputy or a senator who is a member of the government may not be the chairman or vice chairman of the Chamber of Deputies or the Senate, or a member of parliamentary committees, investigatory commission or commissions.

ARTICLE 33

(1) If the Chamber of Deputies is dissolved, the Senate shall be responsible for adopting legislative measures in matters which cannot be postponed and which would otherwise require the adoption of a law.

(2) The Senate, however, cannot adopt legislative measures on matters of the Constitution, the state budget, the state annual account, the election law and international agreements according to Article 10.

(3) Only the government may propose legislative measures to the Senate.

(4) The chairman of the Senate, the president of the republic and the premier shall sign legislative measures of the Senate; these measures are promulgated like laws.

(5) A legislative measure of the Senate must be approved by the Chamber of Deputies at its first session. If the Chamber of Deputies does not approve it, the measure loses further validity.

ARTICLE 34

(1) The chambers are continually in session. A session of the Chamber of Deputies is called by the president of the republic so that it be started no later than the thirtieth day after the election day. If he fails to do so, the Chamber of Deputies shall meet on the thirtieth day after the election day.

(2) A session of a chamber may be adjourned by resolution. The total period for which a session may be adjourned shall not exceed 120 days in one year.

(3) During the period of adjournment, the chairman of the Chamber of Deputies or of the Senate may convene a session of the respective chamber before the scheduled date. He shall always do so if requested by the president of the republic, the government or at least one fifth of deputies of the respective chamber.

(4) A session of the Chamber of Deputies ends with the expiration of its election term or with its dissolution.

ARTICLE 35

(1) The president of the republic can dissolve the Chamber of Deputies if:

a) the Chamber of Deputies passes a vote of non-confidence in a newly appointed government, whose premier was appointed by the president of the republic on the suggestion of the chairman of the Chamber of Deputies,

b) the Chamber of Deputies fails to decide within three months on a government bill with the discussion of which the government links the question of confidence,

c) a session of the Chamber of Deputies is adjourned for a longer period than admissible,

d) the Chamber of Deputies has not reached a quorum for a period longer than three months, although its session was not adjourned and although it was repeatedly called to session during this period.

(2) The Chamber of Deputies cannot be dissolved three months before the expiration of its election term.

ARTICLE 36

Sessions of both chambers are open to the public. The public can be excluded solely under conditions stipulated by law.

ARTICLE 37

(1) A joint session of both chambers is called by the chairman of the Chamber of Deputies.

(2) The proceedings of a joint session of both chambers are governed by the rules of procedure of the Chamber of Deputies.

ARTICLE 38

(1) A member of the government has the right to attend sessions of both chambers, their committees and commissions. He shall be given the floor any time he requests for it.

(2) A member of the government is obliged to attend personally a session of the Chamber of Deputies upon the basis of its resolution. This also applies to a session of a committee, commission or investigatory commission, where, however, a member of the government may have himself be represented by his deputy or any other member of the cabinet, if his or her personal presence is not expressly requested.

ARTICLE 39

(1) The chambers constitute a quorum if at least one third of their members are present.

(2) The passage of a resolution of the respective chamber requires consent of an absolute majority of deputies or senators present, if not prescribed otherwise by the Constitution.

(3) The passage of a resolution on the declaration of the state of war and a resolution approving the presence of foreign troops on the territory of the Czech Republic requires consent of an absolute majority of all deputies and of all senators.

(4) The passage of a constitutional law and the approval of an international agreement under Article 10 shall require consent of a three fifths majority of all deputies and a three fifths majority of all senators present.

ARTICLE 40

The passage of an election law and the legislation on the principles of deliberations and contacts between both chambers, as well as external contacts, and the law on the rules of procedure of the Senate shall necessitate its approval by both the Chamber of Deputies and the Senate.

ARTICLE 41

(1) Draft laws shall be submitted to the Chamber of Deputies.

(2) A draft law may be submitted by deputies, groups of deputies, the Senate, the government and representatives of a higher territorial self-governing entity.

ARTICLE 42

(1) A draft law on the state budget and a draft state annual account are presented by the government.

(2) These draft proposals are discussed and decided on only by the Chamber of Deputies at a public session.

ARTICLE 43

(1) Parliament decides on a declaration of the state of war in the event that the Czech Republic is attacked or if it is necessary to meet international treaty obligations concerning joint defense against aggression.

(2) Armed forces can be sent outside the territory of the Czech Republic only with the consent of both chambers.

ARTICLE 44

(1) The government has the right to comment on all draft laws.

(2) If the government fails to express its opinion within thirty days of the receipt of a draft law, it is assumed that it has expressed itself positively.

(3) The government has the right to demand that the Chamber of Deputies complete discussing a government draft law within three months of its submission, as long as the government links with it a request for a vote of confidence.

ARTICLE 45

The Chamber of Deputies shall advance a draft law with which it expressed its approval to the Senate without unnecessary delay.

ARTICLE 46

(1) The Senate shall discuss a draft law and decide upon it within a period of thirty days of its advancement.

(2) With its resolution, the Senate approves the draft law or turns it down, or returns it to the Chamber of Deputies with draft amendments, or expresses its intention not to concern itself with it.

(3) If the Senate fails to express its resolution in a time limit given in Paragraph 1, it is assumed that the draft law was passed.

ARTICLE 47

(1) If the Senate rejects a draft law, the Chamber of Deputies shall vote on it again. A draft law is passed if it is approved by an absolute majority of all deputies.

(2) If the Senate returns a draft law to the Chamber of Deputies with draft amendments, the Chamber of Deputies shall vote on the wording approved by the Senate. With its resolution, the draft law is passed.

(3) If the Chamber of Deputies fails to pass a draft law in the wording approved by the Senate, it shall vote once again on the

version of the draft law advanced to the Senate. A draft law is passed if it is approved by an absolute majority of all deputies.

(4) In discussion of a rejected or returned draft law in the Chamber of Deputies draft amendments are inadmissible.

ARTICLE 48

If the Senate expresses its intention not to concern itself with a draft law, it is passed with this resolution.

ARTICLE 49

(1) International accords requiring consent from Parliament are passed by Parliament in the same way as draft laws.

(2) Accords on human rights and fundamental freedoms, political agreements and economic agreements of a general nature, as well as agreements on the implementation of which a law must be passed, require consent from Parliament.

ARTICLE 50

(1) The president of the republic has the right to return an adopted law except a constitutional law, giving explanation within fifteen days of the day of its advancement.

(2) The Chamber of Deputies shall vote on the rejected law once again. Draft amendments are inadmissible. If the Chamber of Deputies re-approves the returned law by an absolute majority of all deputies, the law is promulgated. Otherwise it is assumed that the law was not passed.

ARTICLE 51

Adopted laws are signed by the chairman of the Chamber of Deputies, the president of the republic and the premier.

ARTICLE 52

A law becomes effective upon its promulgation. The method of promulgation is stipulated by law. The same applies to international treaties approved by Parliament.

ARTICLE 53

(1) Every deputy has the right to interpellate the government or its members in matters falling under their jurisdiction.

(2) Interpellated members of government shall be obliged to respond to the interpellation within a period of thirty days from the day of its notification.

Chapter Three. Executive Power

The President of the Republic

ARTICLE 54

(1) The president of the republic is the head of state.

(2) The president of the republic is elected by Parliament at a joint session of both chambers.

(3) The president of the republic is not accountable for the discharge of his office.

ARTICLE 55

The president of the republic enters upon his office by taking an oath. The term of office of the president of the republic is five years and begins on the day of taking the oath.

ARTICLE 56

The election takes place within the last thirty days of the term of office of the incumbent president of the republic. If the office of the president of the republic becomes vacant, the election takes place within thirty days.

ARTICLE 57

(1) A citizen eligible to the Senate may be elected the president of the republic.

(2) No one can be elected for more than two consecutive terms of office.

ARTICLE 58

(1) No less than ten deputies or ten senators are entitled to nominate a candidate.

(2) A candidate who received an absolute majority of votes of all deputies and an absolute majority of votes of all senators is elected the president of the republic.

(3) If no candidate succeeds in receiving an absolute majority of votes of all deputies and of all senators, the second round of election shall be held within fourteen days.

(4) The candidate with the highest number of votes in the Chamber of Deputies and the candidate with the highest number of votes in the Senate advances to the second round.

(5) If there are more candidates who receive the same highest number of votes in the Chamber of Deputies or if there are more candidates who receive the same highest number of votes in the Senate, votes they received in both chambers are summed up, and a candidate who in this way receives the highest number of votes advances to the second round.

(6) A candidate who received an absolute majority of votes of deputies present as well as an absolute majority of votes of senators present is elected.

(7) If a president of the republic is not elected in the second round, the third round of election takes place within fourteen days, in which that candidate from the second round is elected who receives an absolute majority of votes of deputies and senators present.

(8) If a president of the republic is not elected in the third round, new elections take place.

ARTICLE 59

(1) The president of the republic takes the oath before the chairman of the Chamber of Deputies at a joint session of both chambers.

(2) The president's oath has the following wording: "I pledge allegiance to the Czech Republic. I pledge to uphold its Constitution and laws. I pledge on my honor to discharge my office in the interest of the people and in accordance with my best conviction and conscience."

ARTICLE 60

If the president of the republic refuses to take the oath or if he takes it with reservations, he is considered not to have been elected.

ARTICLE 61

The president of the republic may surrender his office into the hands of the chairman of the Chamber of Deputies.

ARTICLE 62

The president of the republic:

a) appoints and dismisses the premier and other members of the government and accepts their resignation, dismisses the government and accepts its resignation,

b) convenes sessions of the Chamber of Deputies,

c) dissolves the Chamber of Deputies,

d) entrusts the government whose resignation he has accepted or which he has dismissed with discharging its functions temporarily until a new government is appointed,

e) appoints judges of the Constitutional Court, its chairman and deputy chairmen,

f) appoints from judges the chairman and deputy chairmen of the Supreme Court,

g) pardons and mitigates penalties imposed by penal courts, orders that criminal proceedings be not opened, and if they have been, orders their discontinuation, and expunges previous sentences,

h) has the right to return to Parliament adopted laws with the exception of constitutional laws,

i) signs laws,

j) appoints the president and vice president of the Supreme Inspection Office,

k) appoints members of the Bank Council of the Czech National Bank.

ARTICLE 63

(1) The president of the republic further:

a) represents the state in external affairs,

b) negotiates and ratifies international treaties; he may transfer the negotiation of international agreements to the government or, with its approval, to its individual members,

c) is commander-in-chief of the armed forces,

d) receives heads of diplomatic missions,

e) accredits and recalls heads of diplomatic missions,

f) calls elections to the Chamber of Deputies and to the Senate,

g) appoints and promotes generals,

h) confers and awards state distinctions, unless he authorizes another body to do so,

i) appoints judges,

j) has the right to grant amnesty.

(2) The president of the republic is also entitled to exercise powers which are not expressly specified in the constitutional law, if it is stipulated so by law.

(3) Decisions of the president of the republic issued in accordance with Paragraphs 1 and 2 require a signature of the premier, or a member of the government entrusted by the premier, to come into effect.

(4) The government is responsible for decisions of the president of the republic which require the signature of the premier or a member of the government authorized by the premier.

ARTICLE 64

(1) The president of the republic has the right to take part in sessions of both chambers of Parliament, their committees and commissions. He shall be given the floor any time he requests it.

(2) The president of the republic has the right to take part in sessions of the government, request reports from the government and its members and discuss with the government or with its members issues falling under their jurisdiction.

ARTICLE 65

(1) The president of the republic cannot be detained, exposed to criminal prosecution, or prosecuted for a misdemeanor or other administrative offense.

(2) The president of the republic can be prosecuted for high treason before the Constitutional Court on the basis of an indictment by the Senate. Punishment can be the loss of presidential office and of the qualification to hold it again.

(3) Criminal prosecution for criminal acts committed while discharging the office of the president of the republic is rendered impossible forever.

ARTICLE 66

If the office of the president of the republic becomes vacant and a new president of the republic is not yet elected or has not yet been sworn in, and also if the president of the republic is unable to discharge his office for serious reasons and the Chamber of Deputies and the Senate resolves so, the exercise of functions specified in Article 63, Paragraph 1, Subparagraphs a), b), c), d), e), h), i), and j), and Article 63, Paragraph 2 falls to the premier. During the period in which the premier is discharging the specified functions of the president of the republic, the exercise of functions of the president of the republic according to Article 62, Subparagraphs a), b), c), d), e), and k) falls to the chairman of the Chamber of Deputies; if the office of the president of the republic becomes vacant at the time when the Chamber of Deputies is dissolved, the exercise of these functions falls to the chairman of the Senate.

The Government

ARTICLE 67

(1) The government is the supreme body of executive power.

(2) The government is composed of the premier, the deputy premiers and ministers.

ARTICLE 68

(1) The government is accountable to the Chamber of Deputies.

(2) The president of the republic appoints the premier and, on his suggestion, appoints other members of the government and entrusts them with managing the ministries or other bodies.

(3) The government shall appear before the Chamber of Deputies within thirty days of its appointment and request of it a vote of confidence.

(4) If the newly appointed government fails to obtain the confidence of the Chamber of Deputies, the procedure advances in accordance with Paragraphs 2 and 3. If even the government, appointed in this way, fails to obtain the confidence of the Chamber of Deputies, the president of the republic shall appoint the premier upon the suggestion of the chairman of the Chamber of Deputies.

(5) In other cases, the president of the republic appoints and dismisses, upon the suggestion of the premier, other members of the cabinet and entrusts them with managing the ministries or other bodies.

ARTICLE 69

(1) A member of the government is sworn in before the president of the republic.

(2) The oath of a member of the government has the following wording: "I pledge allegiance to the Czech Republic. I pledge to uphold its Constitution and laws and introduce them into life. I pledge on my honor that I will conscientiously hold my office and will not abuse my position."

ARTICLE 70

A member of the government must not pursue activities whose nature is in conflict with the exercise of his function. Details are stipulated by law.

ARTICLE 71

The government is entitled to submit to the Chamber of Deputies a request for a vote of confidence.

ARTICLE 72

(1) The Chamber of Deputies may pass a vote of non-confidence in the government.

(2) The Chamber of Deputies shall discuss a proposal for a vote of non-confidence in the government only if it is submitted in writing by no less than 50 deputies. Passing the proposal requires the consent of an absolute majority of all deputies.

ARTICLE 73

(1) The premier offers his resignation to the president of the republic. Other members of the government offer their resignations to the president of the republic through the premier.

(2) The government shall offer its resignation if the Chamber of Deputies rejects its request for a vote of confidence or if it passes a vote of non-confidence in it. The government shall always offer its resignation after the constituent session of a newly elected Chamber of Deputies.

(3) If the government offers its resignation according to Paragraph 2, the president of the republic shall accept it.

ARTICLE 74

The president of the republic shall dismiss a member of the government, if this is proposed by the premier.

ARTICLE 75

The president of the republic shall dismiss a government which did not offer its resignation although it was obliged to offer it.

ARTICLE 76

(1) The government makes decisions as a body.

(2) The passage of a resolution of the government requires the consent of an absolute majority of all its members.

ARTICLE 77

(1) The premier organizes the activities of the government, chairs its meetings, acts in its name, and executes further activities entrusted to him by the Constitution or by other laws.

(2) The premier is represented by a deputy premier or another authorized member of the government.

ARTICLE 78

For the execution of a law and within its limits, the government is entitled to issue decrees. Decrees are signed by the premier and a respective member of the government.

ARTICLE 79

(1) Ministries and other administrative bodies can be established and their powers defined only by law.

(2) The legal relations of state employees in the ministries and other administrative bodies are determined by law.

(3) The ministries, other administrative offices, and bodies of territorial self-administration may issue legal regulations on the basis of and within the limits of law, if authorized so by law.

ARTICLE 80

(1) A public prosecutor's office represents public prosecution in criminal proceedings: it also executes other tasks, if law so stipulates.

(2) The status and jurisdiction of the public prosecutor's office are defined by law.

Chapter Four. Judicial Power

ARTICLE 81

Judicial power is exercised by independent courts on behalf of the republic.

ARTICLE 82

(1) Judges are independent in the execution of their function. Their impartiality must not be threatened by anyone.

(2) A judge cannot be dismissed or transferred to another court against his or her will; exceptions stemming predominantly from disciplinary responsibility are stipulated by law.

(3) The discharge of the function of a judge is incompatible with the office of the president of the republic, member of parliament, or any other function in public administration; other activities incompatible with the discharge of the function of a judge are determined by law.

Constitutional Court

ARTICLE 83

The Constitutional Court is a judicial body for the protection of constitutionality.

ARTICLE 84

(1) The Constitutional Court is composed of 15 judges appointed for a term of ten years.

(2) The judges of the Constitutional Court are appointed by the president of the republic with the consent of the Senate.

(3) Any citizen of integrity, eligible for election to the Senate, having a university education in law and at least ten years of experience in legal profession may be appointed a judge of the Constitutional Court.

ARTICLE 85

(1) A judge of the Constitutional Court assumes his or her function upon taking an oath before the president of the republic.

(2) A judge of the Constitutional Court takes the following oath: "I pledge on my honor and conscience that I will protect the inviolability of the natural rights of the individual and the rights of any citizen, abide by constitutional laws, and make decisions according to my best conviction, independently and impartially."

(3) If a judge refuses to take the oath or if he or she takes it with reservations, he or she is regarded as if not appointed.

ARTICLE 86

(1) A judge of the Constitutional Court cannot be criminally prosecuted without the consent of the Senate. If the Senate declines to give its consent, criminal prosecution is rendered impossible forever.

(2) A judge of the Constitutional Court may be detained only if caught while committing a criminal act or immediately thereafter. The respective authority is obliged to immediately notify the chairman of the Senate of the detention. If the chairman of the Senate fails to give his consent to passing the detainee to court within 24 hours, the respective authority is obliged to release him. The Senate shall make a definitive decision about whether criminal prosecution is admissible or not at its first following session.

(3) A judge of the Constitutional Court has the right to deny testimony on matters about which he or she learnt while discharging his or her function, and, as well, after he or she ceased to be a judge of the Constitutional Court.

ARTICLE 87

(1) The Constitutional Court resolves:

a) the nullification of laws or their individual provisions if they are in contradiction with a constitutional law or an international agreement under Article 10,

b) the nullification of other legal regulations or their individual provisions if they are in contradiction with a constitutional law, legislation or international agreement under Article 10,

c) constitutional complaints by bodies of territorial self-administration against unlawful interference by the state,

d) constitutional complaints against authorized decisions and other interference by bodies of public power with fundamental rights and freedoms guaranteed by the Constitution,

e) legal remedies against decisions on matters of the verification of election of a deputy or a senator,

f) doubts concerning a loss of eligibility of a deputy or a senator and incompatibility of the discharge of his or her function according to Article 25,

g) a constitutional indictment by the Senate against the president of the republic according to Article 65, Paragraph 2,

h) a proposal by the president of the republic to repeal a resolution by the Chamber of Deputies and the Senate according to Article 66,

i) measures necessary to effect a decision by an international court which is binding for the Czech Republic, if it cannot be effected otherwise,

j) the congruency of a decision to dissolve a political party or other decisions concerning the activities of a political party with constitutional laws and other acts,

k) controversies on the scope of powers of state bodies and bodies of territorial self-administration, if, according to law, these do not fall under jurisdiction of another body.

(2) The law may stipulate that instead of the Constitutional Court the Supreme Administrative Court shall pass decisions on:

a) the annulment of legal regulations or their individual provisions, if they are at variance with law,

b) controversies concerning the scope of powers of state bodies and bodies of territorial self-administration, if, according to law, these do not come within jurisdiction of another body.

ARTICLE 88

(1) The law specifies who and under what conditions is entitled to table a proposal to initiate proceedings and other rules on proceedings before the Constitutional Court.

(2) In decision-making, judges of the Constitutional Court are bound only by constitutional laws and international agreements under Article 10 and by laws under Paragraph 1.

ARTICLE 89

(1) A decision of the Constitutional Court becomes executable as soon as it is promulgated in the manner determined by law, if the Constitutional Court did not decide about its execution otherwise.

(2) Executable decisions of the Constitutional Court are binding for all bodies and persons.

Courts

ARTICLE 90

The task of courts is above all to provide protection to rights in the manner determined by law. Only a court can decide on the guilt and penalty for criminal acts.

ARTICLE 91

(1) The judiciary consists of the Supreme Court, the Supreme Administrative Court, high, regional and district courts. Legislation may determine other terms for them.

(2) The jurisdiction and organization of courts is stipulated by law.

ARTICLE 92

The Supreme Court is the highest judicial body in matters falling under the jurisdiction of courts with the exception of matters decided by the Constitutional Court or the Supreme Administrative Court.

ARTICLE 93

(1) Judges are appointed by the president of the republic for an unlimited term. They assume the office on taking an oath.

(2) Any citizen of integrity, having a university education in law can be appointed judge. Other requirements and procedures are stipulated by law.

ARTICLE 94

(1) The law stipulates cases in which judges decide as a bench and the composition of the bench. In other cases they decide as single judges.

(2) The law may stipulate in which matters and in what manner also other citizens, in addition to judges, participate in court decision-making.

ARTICLE 95

(1) In decision-making judges are bound by law; they are entitled to judge congruency of another legal regulation with the law.

(2) If a court arrives at the conclusion that a law which is to be applied in decision-making is in contradiction with a constitutional act, it shall pass the matter to the Constitutional Court.

ARTICLE 96

(1) All parties in legal proceedings have equal rights before the court.

(2) Proceedings in the court are verbal and open to the public; exceptions are specified by law. The verdict of the court is always publicly declared.

Chapter Five. The Supreme Inspection Office

ARTICLE 97

(1) The Supreme Inspection Office is an independent body. It executes inspection of the management of state property and the fulfillment of the state budget.

(2) The president and vice president of the Supreme Inspection Office are appointed by the president of the republic upon the suggestion of the Chamber of Deputies.

(3) The status, jurisdiction, organizational structure and other details are set down by law.

Chapter Six. The Czech National Bank

ARTICLE 98

(1) The Czech National Bank is the central bank of the state. Its activities are primarily oriented towards currency stability; it is possible to interfere with its activities exclusively on the basis of law.

(2) The status, jurisdiction and other details are set down by law.

Chapter Seven. Territorial Self-Administration

ARTICLE 99

The Czech Republic is divided into municipalities which are the basic units of territorial self-administration. Higher units of territorial self-administration are lands or regions.

ARTICLE 100

(1) The units of territorial self-administration are territorial communities of citizens, which have the right to self-administration. The law determines when they are administrative districts.

(2) A municipality is always part of a higher unit of territorial self-administration.

(3) A higher unit of territorial self-administration may be established or dissolved solely by a constitutional law.

ARTICLE 101

(1) A municipality is independently administered by a board of representatives.

(2) A higher unit of territorial self-administration is independently administered by a board of representatives.

(3) Units of territorial self-administration are public corporations which may have their own property and may engage in management according to their own budgets.

(4) The state may interfere in the activities of units of territorial self-administration only if it is necessary for the protection of law and solely by means specified by law.

ARTICLE 102

(1) Members of the board of representatives are elected by secret ballot on the basis of universal, equal, and direct suffrage.

(2) The term of office of the board of representatives is four years. The law stipulates under what conditions new elections to the board of representatives shall be called before the expiration of its term of office.

ARTICLE 103

The name of a higher unit of territorial self-administration shall be decided by its board.

ARTICLE 104

(1) The powers of the board of representatives may be set down solely by law.

(2) The board of representatives resolves matters of self-administration, unless these are entrusted by law to the board of representatives of a higher unit of territorial self-administration.

(3) Boards of representatives may issue generally binding decrees within the limits of their jurisdiction.

ARTICLE 105

The exercise of state administration may be entrusted to bodies of self-administration only when determined so by law.

Chapter Eight. Temporary and Final Provisions

ARTICLE 106

(1) On the day this Constitution comes into effect the Czech National Council becomes the Chamber of Deputies whose election term expires on June 6, 1996.

(2) Until the Senate is elected according to the Constitution, the functions of the Senate shall be discharged by the Provisional Senate. The Provisional Senate shall be constituted in the manner determined by constitutional law. The Chamber of Deputies shall execute the functions of the Senate until this law becomes effective.

(3) The Chamber of Deputies cannot be dissolved as long as it discharges the function of the Senate according to Paragraph 2.

(4) Until laws on the rules of procedure of the chambers are passed, the individual chambers shall proceed according to the rules of procedure of the Czech National Council.

ARTICLE 107

(1) The law on elections to the Senate sets down the way in which one third of senators whose election term will be two years, and one third of senators whose election term will be four years will be determined in the first elections to the Senate.

(2) The president of the republic shall call a session of the Senate so that it may begin no later than the thirtieth day after the election day; if he fails to do so, the Senate shall meet on the thirtieth day after the election day.

ARTICLE 108

The government of the Czech Republic appointed after the 1992 elections and executing its function on the day when the

Constitution comes into effect is considered a government appointed according to this Constitution.

ARTICLE 109

Until the State Prosecutor's Office is established, its functions shall be exercised by the Prosecutor's Office of the Czech Republic.

ARTICLE 110

Until December 31, 1993, the judiciary shall also include military courts.

ARTICLE 111

Judges of all courts of the Czech Republic, exercising the function of judge on the day on which this Constitution comes into effect are considered judges appointed according to the Constitution of the Czech Republic.

ARTICLE 112

(1) The constitutional order of the Czech Republic comprises this Constitution, the Charter of Fundamental Rights and Freedoms, constitutional laws adopted in accordance with this Constitution and constitutional laws of the National Assembly of the Czechoslovak Republic, the Federal Assembly of the Czechoslovak Socialist Republic, and the Czech National Council, which define the state borders of the Czech Republic, and constitutional laws of the Czech National Council adopted after June 6, 1992.

(2) Annulled are the present constitution, the Constitutional Act on the Czechoslovak Federation, constitutional laws which amended them, and the Constitutional Act of the Czech National Council No. 67/1990 Digest of Laws, on the state symbols of the Czech Republic.

(3) Other constitutional laws valid on the territory of the Czech Republic shall have the power of a law on the day this Constitution comes into effect.

ARTICLE 113

This Constitution takes effect as of January 1, 1993.

SUMMIT OF THE AMERICAS DECLARATION OF PRINCIPLES (1994)

Democracy is often conceived of in narrowly political terms: rule of law, representation, voting rights, constitutional prescriptions, separation of powers, and the philosophical notions underpinning these practical issues of process and institutions. But political relationships and philosophies cannot be considered in isolation. They influence and are influenced by the economic and social conditions of a society. Whereas rising economic power contributed to the Dutch and American independence movements of the sixteenth and eighteenth centuries, respectively, economic chaos and the social strife it engendered contributed to the post–World War I breakdown of German government under the Weimar constitution.

The correlation between a healthy economy and stable, representative democracy is strong. In the late twentieth century the wealthy nations of North America and Western Europe began to promote the spread of democracy by promoting world trade and international investment. Their motives were a combination of altruism and self-interest. Democracy, Western leaders believed, is intrinsically "good" and its spread laudable, and the economic and political stability that it engenders is beneficial economically to the industrialized nations.

In April 1967 the leaders of seventeen Western Hemisphere nations met in Uruguay to discuss political and economic development in the hemisphere. The leaders approved a plan to create a common market by 1985. But, in part because many of the nations of Central and South America were dictatorships and had economies dominated by state-run enterprises, nothing came of the summit.

By 1994 all Western Hemisphere nations except Cuba had elected civilian governments that were fighting tough economic problems and seeking to improve living standards for their people. On December 9–11, U.S. president Bill Clinton hosted the first hemispheric summit since 1967, at which the participants pledged their support for the principles of democratic government. In recognition of the importance of economic development for the consolidation of democratic rule, they agreed to negotiate a free trade agreement by 2005. All thirty-four leaders in attendance supported the goal, but some chafed at the long time-frame: "It would be a tragic mistake to engage in a prolonged process where struggling nations with fragile democracies must wait ten, fifteen, maybe twenty years in economic purgatory," said Bolivian president Gonzalo Sánchez de Lozada. "The cost could be nothing less than the democratic foundations of our countries."

Partnership for Development and Prosperity: Democracy, Free Trade, and Sustainable Development in the Americas

The elected Heads of State and Government of the Americas are committed to advance the prosperity, democratic values and institutions, and security of our Hemisphere. For the first time in history, the Americas are a community of democratic societies. Although faced with differing development challenges, the Americas are united in pursuing prosperity through open markets, hemispheric integration, and sustainable development. We are determined to consolidate and advance closer bonds of cooperation and to transform our aspirations into concrete realities.

We reiterate our firm adherence to the principles of international law and the purposes and principles enshrined in the United Nations Charter and in the Charter of the Organization of American States (OAS), including the principles of the sovereign equality of states, non-intervention, self-determination, and the peaceful resolution of disputes. We recognize the heterogeneity and diversity of our resources and cultures, just as we are convinced that we can advance our shared interests and values by building strong partnerships.

To Preserve and Strengthen the Community of Democracies of the Americas

The Charter of the OAS establishes that representative democracy is indispensable for the stability, peace and development of the region. It is the sole political system which guarantees respect for human rights and the rule of law; it safeguards cultural diversity, pluralism, respect for the rights of minorities, and peace within and among nations. Democracy is based, among other fundamentals, on free and transparent elections and includes the right of all citizens to participate in government. Democracy and development reinforce one another.

We reaffirm our commitment to preserve and strengthen our democratic systems for the benefit of all people of the Hemisphere. We will work through the appropriate bodies of the OAS to strengthen democratic institutions and promote and defend constitutional democratic rule, in accordance with the OAS Charter. We endorse OAS efforts to enhance peace and the democratic, social, and economic stability of the region.

We recognize that our people earnestly seek greater responsiveness and efficiency from our respective governments. Democracy is strengthened by the modernization of the state, including reforms that streamline operations, reduce and simplify government rules and procedures, and make democratic institutions more transparent and accountable. Deeming it essential that justice should be accessible in an efficient and expeditious way to all sectors of society, we affirm that an independent judiciary is a critical element of an effective legal system and lasting democracy. Our ultimate goal is to better meet the needs of the population, especially the needs of women and the most vulnerable groups, including indigenous people, the disabled, children, the aged, and minorities.

Effective democracy requires a comprehensive attack on corruption as a factor of social disintegration and distortion of the economic system that undermines the legitimacy of political institutions.

Recognizing the pernicious effects of organized crime and illegal narcotics on our economies, ethical values, public health, and the social fabric, we will join the battle against the consumption, production, trafficking and distribution of illegal drugs, as well as against money laundering and the illicit trafficking in arms and chemical precursors. We will also co-operate to create viable alternative development strategies in those countries in which illicit crops are grown. Cooperation should be extended to international and national programs aimed at curbing the production, use and trafficking of illicit drugs and the rehabilitation of addicts.

We condemn terrorism in all its forms, and we will, using all legal means, combat terrorist acts anywhere in the Americas with unity and vigor.

Recognizing the important contribution of individuals and associations in effective democratic government and in the enhancement of cooperation among the people of the Hemisphere, we will facilitate fuller participation of our people in political, economic and social activity, in accordance with national legislation.

To Promote Prosperity Through Economic Integration and Free Trade

Our continued economic progress depends on sound economic policies, sustainable development, and dynamic private sectors. A key to prosperity is trade without barriers, without subsidies, without unfair practices, and with an increasing stream of productive investments. Eliminating impediments to market access for goods and services among our countries will foster our economic growth. A growing world economy will also enhance our domestic prosperity. Free trade and increased economic integration are key factors for raising standards of living, improving the working conditions of people in the Americas and better protecting the environment.

We, therefore, resolve to begin immediately to construct the "Free Trade Area of the Americas" (FTAA), in which barriers to trade and investment will be progressively eliminated. We further resolve to conclude the negotiation of the "Free Trade Area of the Americas" no later than 2005, and agree that concrete progress toward the attainment of this objective will be made by the end of this century. We recognize the progress that already has been realized through the unilateral undertakings of each of our nations and the sub-regional trade arrangements in our Hemisphere. We will build on existing sub-regional and bilateral arrangements in order to broaden and deepen hemispheric economic integration and to bring the agreements together.

Aware that investment is the main engine for growth in the Hemisphere, we will encourage such investment by cooperating to build more open, transparent and integrated markets. In this regard, we are committed to create strengthened mechanisms that promote and protect the flow of productive investment in the Hemisphere, and to promote the development and progressive integration of capital markets.

To advance economic integration and free trade, we will work, with cooperation and financing from the private sector and international financial institutions, to create a hemispheric infrastructure. This process requires a cooperative effort in fields such as telecommunications, energy and transportation, which will permit the efficient movement of the goods, services, capital, information and technology that are the foundations of prosperity.

We recognize that despite the substantial progress in dealing with debt problems in the Hemisphere, high foreign-debt burdens still hinder the development of some of our countries.

We recognize that economic integration and the creation of a free trade area will be complex endeavors, particularly in view of the wide differences in the levels of development and size of economies existing in our Hemisphere. We will remain cognizant of these differences as we work toward economic integration in the Hemisphere. We look to our own resources, ingenuity, and individual capacities as well as to the international community to help us achieve our goals.

To Eradicate Poverty and Discrimination in Our Hemisphere

It is politically intolerable and morally unacceptable that some segments of our populations are marginalized and do not share fully in the benefits of growth. With an aim of attaining greater social justice for all our people, we pledge to work individually and collectively to improve access to quality education and primary health care and to eradicate extreme poverty and illiteracy. The fruits of democratic stability and economic growth must be accessible to all, without discrimination by race, gender, national origin or religious affiliation.

In observance of the International Decade of the World's Indigenous People, we will focus our energies on improving the exercise of democratic rights and the access to social services by indigenous people and their communities.

Aware that widely shared prosperity contributes to hemispheric stability, lasting peace and democracy, we acknowledge our common interest in creating employment opportunities that improve the incomes, wages and working conditions of all our people. We will invest in people so that individuals throughout the Hemisphere have the opportunity to realize their full potential.

Strengthening the role of women in all aspects of political, social and economic life in our countries is essential to reduce poverty and social inequalities and to enhance democracy and sustainable development.

To Guarantee Sustainable Development and Conserve Our Natural Environment for Future Generations

Social progress and economic prosperity can be sustained only if our people live in a healthy environment and our ecosystems and natural resources are managed carefully and responsibly. To advance and implement the commitments made at the 1992 United Nations Conference on Environment and Development, held in Rio de Janeiro, and the 1994 Global Conference on the Sustainable Development of Small Island Developing States, held in Barbados, we will create cooperative partnerships to strengthen our capacity to prevent and control pollution, to protect ecosystems and use our biological resources on a sustainable basis, and to encourage clean, efficient and sustainable energy production and use. To benefit future generations through environmental conservation, including the rational use of our ecosystems, natural resources and biological heritage, we will continue to pursue technological, financial and other forms of cooperation.

We will advance our social well-being and economic prosperity in ways that are fully cognizant of our impact on the environment. We agree to support the Central American Alliance for Sustainable Development, which seeks to strengthen those democracies by promoting regional economic and social prosperity and sound environmental management. In this context, we support the convening of other regional meetings on sustainable development.

Our Declaration constitutes a comprehensive and mutually reinforcing set of commitments for concrete results. In accord with the appended Plan of Action, and recognizing our different national capabilities and our different legal systems, we pledge to implement them without delay.

We call upon the OAS and the Inter-American Development Bank to assist countries in implementing our pledges, drawing significantly upon the Pan American Health Organization and the United Nations Economic Commission for Latin America and the Caribbean as well as sub-regional organizations for integration.

To give continuity to efforts fostering national political involvement, we will convene specific high-level meetings to address, among others, topics such as trade and commerce, capital markets, labor, energy, education, transportation, telecommunications, counter-narcotics and other anti-crime initiatives, sustainable development, health, and science and technology.

To assure public engagement and commitment, we invite the cooperation and participation of the private sector, labor, political parties, academic institutions and other non-governmental actors and organizations in both our national and regional efforts, thus strengthening the partnership between governments and society.

Our thirty-four nations share a fervent commitment to democratic practices, economic integration, and social justice. Our people are better able than ever to express their aspirations and to learn from one another. The conditions for hemispheric cooperation are propitious. Therefore, on behalf of all our people, in whose name we affix our signatures to this Declaration, we seize this historic opportunity to create a Partnership for Development and Prosperity in the Americas.

CREDITS FOR PHOTOGRAPHS AND OTHER IMAGES

A

Abdul Rahman, Tunku / *Library of Congress*
Adams, John / *Library of Congress*
Adenauer, Konrad / *Library of Congress*
Aid policy/ *American Red Cross*
Almond, Gabriel / *Yale University Archives*
Althusius, Johannes / *no credit*
Anthony, Susan B. / *Library of Congress*
Arias Sánchez, Oscar / *UPI/Bettmann*
Aristotle / *The Bettmann Archive*
Aron, Raymond / *Library of Congress*
Atatürk, Kemal / *Library of Congress*
Aung San Suu Kyi / *Reuters/Bettmann*
Aylwin, Patricio / *Embassy of Chile*
Azikiwe, Nnamdi / *National Archives*

B

Bagehot, Walter / *The Bettmann Archive*
Batlle y Ordóñez, José / *Organization of American States*
Berlin, Isaiah / *CBS Television Network*
Bernstein, Eduard / *AP/Worldwide Photos*
Betancourt, Rómulo / *Organization of American States*
Biko, Bantu Stephen / *Reuters/Bettmann*
Bolívar, Simón / *Library of Congress*
Bryce, James / *Library of Congress*
Buddhism / *The Bettmann Archive*
Burke, Edmund / *Library of Congress*
Bustamante, Alexander / *Embassy of Jamaica*

C

Catholicism, Roman / *The Bettmann Archive*
Censorship / *Reuters/Bettmann*
China
   Mao Zedong / *UPI/Bettmann*
   Tiananmen Square / *Reuters/Bettmann*
   People voting / *Courtesy of International Republican Institute*
Churchill, Winston / *Library of Congress*
Cicero, Marcus Tullius / *The Bettmann Archive*
City-states, communes, and republics / *Courtesy Archivio di State di Firenze*
Civil disobedience / *UPI/Bettmann*
Classical Greece and Rome / *National Museum of American History*
Confucianism / *National Archives*

D

Dahl, Robert A. / *Yale University*

De Gasperi, Alcide / *Harry S. Truman Library*
de Gaulle, Charles / *Library of Congress*
de Klerk, Frederik Willem / *Michael Jenkins, Congressional Quarterly*
Dewey, John / *Library of Congress*
Disraeli, Benjamin / *UPI/Bettmann*
Districting / *The Bettmann Archive*
Downs, Anthony / *Brookings Institution*
Duverger, Maurice / *Embassy of France*

E

Election campaigns / *Library of Congress*
Engels, Friedrich / *Library of Congress*
Enlightenment, Scottish / *Library of Congress*
Environmentalism / *Bush Presidential Materials Project*
Europe, East Central / *National Archives*
Existentialism / *Library of Congress*

F

Fascism / *Library of Congress*
Figueres Ferrer, José / *UPI/Bettmann*
Freedom of speech / *The British Tourist Authority*
Frei, Eduardo / *UPI/Bettmann*

G

Gambetta, Léon-Michel / *Library of Congress*
Gandhi, Mohandas Karamachand / *Library of Congress*
Gladstone, William E. / *Library of Congress*
Gorbachev, Mikhail Sergeyevich / *APN*
Gramsci, Antonio / *no credit*

H

Hamilton, Alexander / *Library of Congress*
Havel, Václav / *Michael Jenkins, Congressional Quarterly*
Hegel, Georg Wilhelm Friedrich / *Library of Congress*
Hermens, Ferdinand A. / *University of Notre Dame Archives*
Hobbes, Thomas / *Library of Congress*
Hook, Sidney / *New York University*

I

Idealism, German / *Library of Congress*
Industrial relations / *National Archives*
Islam / *Library of Congress*

J

Jackson, Andrew / *Library of Congress*
James, William / *by permission of the Houghton Library, Harvard University*

Jefferson, Thomas / *Library of Congress*
Jinnah, Mohammad Ali / *Embassy of Pakistan*

K

Kant, Immanuel / *Library of Congress*
Karamanlis, Constantine / *Embassy of Greece*
Kelsen, Hans / *The Bancroft Library, University of California, Berkeley*
Kennedy, John F. / *John F. Kennedy Library*
Kenyatta, Jomo / *Library of Congress*
Kerensky, Alexander Fedorovich / *The Bettmann Archive*
Key, V. O., Jr. / *Yale University Library*
Khama, Seretse / *UPI/Bettmann*
King, Martin Luther, Jr. / *Flip Schulke*
Kirchheimer, Otto / *no credit*
Koirala, Bishweshar Prasad / *UPI/Bettmann*

L

Laissez-faire economic theory / *Library of Congress*
Laski, Harold / *The Bettmann Archive*
Lasswell, Harold D. / *Yale University*
Legislatures and parliaments / *London Pictures Service*
Leninism / *Library of Congress*
Lincoln, Abraham / *Library of Congress*
Lippmann, Walter / *National Archives/Harris & Ewing*
Lipset, Seymour Martin / *Gunilla Wisén*
Locke, John / *Library of Congress*
Luxemburg, Rosa / *Hoover Institution Archives*

M

Machiavelli, Niccolò / *Library of Congress*
Macpherson, C. B. / *University of Toronto*
Madison, James / *Library of Congress*
Magsaysay, Ramón / *Library of Congress*
Mandela, Nelson / *Reuters/Bettmann*
Maritain, Jacques / *Embassy of France*
Marshall, John / *Collection of the Supreme Court of the United States*
Marx, Karl / *Library of Congress*
Masaryk, Tomáš Garrigue / *Library of Congress*
Mill, John Stuart / *Library of Congress*
Monarchy, Constitutional / *Reuters/Bettmann*
Monnet, Jean / *Library of Congress*
Montesquieu, Charles-Louis de Secondat / *no credit*
Mosca, Gaetano / *Biblioteca Central della Regione Siciliana*

N

Nehru, Jawaharlal / *Library of Congress*
Nietzsche, Friedrich / *Library of Congress*
Nkrumah, Kwame / *National Archives*
Nyerere, Julius / *Library of Congress*

O

Ortega y Gasset, José / *Library of Congress*

P

Paine, Thomas / *Library of Congress*
Pankhurst, Emmeline / *UPI/Bettmann*

Pareto, Vilfredo / *no credit*
Plato / *The Bettmann Archive*
Popper, Karl / *Open Court Publishing Company, Chicago and La Salle*
Psychoanalysis / *AP/Wide World Photos*

R

Reformation / *Library of Congress*
Revolution, French / *The Bettmann Archive*
Rhetoric / *National Archives*
Roh Tae Woo / *Embassy of the Republic of South Korea*
Roosevelt, Franklin D. / *Franklin Roosevelt Library*
Roosevelt, Theodore / *Library of Congress*
Rousseau, Jean-Jacques / *Library of Congress*
Russia, Post-Soviet / *Reuters/Bettmann*
Russia, Pre-Soviet / *Library of Congress*

S

Sakharov, Andrei Dmitrievich / *AP/Wide World Photos*
Sanguinetti, Julio María / *no credit*
Schumpeter, Joseph / *Harvard University Archives*
Senghor, Léopold Sédar / *UPI/Bettmann*
Sieyès, Emmanuel-Joseph / *Library of Congress*
Slavery / *Library of Congress*
Sobukwe, Robert / *UPI/Bettmann*
South Africa
    Nelson Mandela / *AP/Wide World Photos*
    Johannesburg residents / *Bettmann*
Spinoza, Benedict de / *Library of Congress*
Stanton, Elizabeth Cady / *Library of Congress*
Suárez González, Adolfo / *Library of Congress*
Sukarno / *National Archives*
Sun Yat-sen / *Library of Congress*
Switzerland / *Swiss National Tourist Office*

T

Thatcher, Margaret / *British Tourist Authority*
Theory, African American / *Library of Congress*
Thiers, Louis-Adolphe / *Library of Congress*
Tocqueville, Alexis de / *The Bettmann Archive*

V

Voting rights / *AP/Wide World Photos*

W

Walesa, Lech / *Embassy of Poland*
Washington, George / *Library of Congress*
Weber, Max / *Library of Congress*
Williams, Eric / *Organization of American States*
Wilson, Woodrow / *Library of Congress*
Wollstonecraft, Mary / *The Bettmann Archive*
Women and democracy / *Reuters/Bettmann*
Women's suffrage in the United States / *Library of Congress*

Y

Yeltsin, Boris Nikolayevich / *Dennis Brack/Black Star*
Yoshida, Shigeru / *Library of Congress*

INDEX

INDEX

Duns Scotus, 879
Duplessis, Maurice, 159
Durán Ballén, Sixto, 67
Durham, Earl of, 268
Durham report, 268
Durkheim, Emile, 93
Dutch East Indies, 510, 1397
Dutra, Eurico, 135
Duvalier, Jean-Claude "Baby Doc," 104
Duverger, Maurice, 324, 327, 380–382, 1256
Dwellers in the Land (Sale), 440
Dworkin, Ronald, 1140
Dzyuba, Ivan, 362

E
East Africa, 37, 41, 855, 1234
East Germany, 526, 528, 1310, 1365, 1397
    See also Germany
East India Company, 599–600
East Timor, 86
Eastern Europe. *See* Europe, East Central;
    specific countries
Easton, David, 961, 962, 964
Ebert, Friedrich, 525
Ecevit, Bülent, 1274, 1275
Eckersley, Robyn, 441
Ecologism, 439
    See also Environmentalism
Economic and Social Council, 465
"Economic Contradictions of Democracy, The"
    (Brittain), 1252
Economic democracy, 803
    political democracy distinguished, 495, 802,
    1311
Economic development
    Central America, 195
    democratic legitimacy and, 750–751
    democratization and, 350–356, 388, 508, 1221,
        1223, 1237
    dictatorships as hindering, 802
    dominant party democracies and, 375–376
    Eastern Europe, 445–448, 450–451
    education relationship, 804
    egalitarianism affected by, 395, 396
    elite consolidation and, 425
    English Caribbean, 173–174
    Latin America debt crisis, 66, 73
    Malaysia, 793–795
    Middle East, 835–436
    Philippines, 945–946
    Puerto Rico, 179–180
    Southeast Asia, 87–88
    Soviet Union, 1297, 1298
    Thailand, 1227–1228
    Ukraine, 1292–1293
    voting behavior affected by, 404–405, 1351
    Western Europe, 452–453
Economic policies
    aid policies contingent on, 48–50
    Catholicism and Christian democrats, 183,
        185, 214
    corporatism and, 309
    Costa Rica, 315
    Czechoslovakia, 329
    economic planning, 383–387, 448, 654,
        802–805
    elitism, 616, 1252
    fascism regulation, 472
    globalization and, 532–538
    government formation and policy making,

459–460
    international organizations, 622–623
    Mexico, 827, 829
    Soviet Union, 1295, 1296, 1298, 1300
    state growth and intervention, 1185–1189
    Sun Yat-sen ideas, 1264
    Thatcherism, 597, 772, 1048, 1230–1231,
        1307–1309
Economic power, and foreign policy, 496–497
Economic science, 560
    commercial republics, 1061–1065
    existentialism indifference to, 468
    pragmatism and, 994–995
    Scottish Enlightenment contributions,
        435–436
Economic theories
    ultra-individualism, 125
    See also Laissez-faire economic theory
Economic Theory of Democracy, An (Downs),
    378–380
Ecuador, 62–67, 259, 381, 826, 1226
Eden, Anthony, 1306–1307
Education, 460, 1065
    bilingual, 792
    Canada, 160, 161
    communitarianism view, 278
    democratization and, 353, 355, 387–392
    civic, 111, 392–395, 408, 587–589, 672, 777, 850,
        923, 1260, 1280, 1345
    economic development relationship, 804
    France, 1070
    government spending, 1373
    intellectuals, 613–616
    Ireland, 637
    Mannheim sociology of knowledge, 798
    political knowledge and, 1030
    political socialization, 1153–1158
    prayer in public schools, 824
    racial balance in schools, 1038
    right to, 1375
    Rousseau theory, 1087, 1089, 1344
    technological innovation and, 1224
    United States, land-grant colleges, 1191
    voter turnout and, 918
    Western Europe, 453
Education of Cyrus (Xenophon), 357
Egalitarianism, 773
    Africa, precolonial societies, 1232
    arithmetic versus proportionate equality, 395,
        398
    belief defined, 395
    conservatism view, 294
    economic equality, 396–397, 692
    equality of opportunity, 397, 685
    equality of spirit, 397–398
    existentialism and, 468–469
    fascism, 473
    liberty and, 144, 722–723, 1258
    mass society, 814–815
    political equality, 278
    political inequalities, 395–396
    relativism and, 396, 1050
    right-wing criticism, 1255
    Rousseau view, 397–398, 1085–1089
    social inequality, 1253
    technological innovation and, 1221–1225
    women's rights. *See* Women's rights; Wom-
        en's suffrage
Egypt, 831, 1272, 1277, 1365
    dissidents, 367

economic privatization, 836
Islam, and political practice, 508, 509, 639,
    640, 643–645
    political history, 38, 103, 227–228, 270,
        398–402, 735
    populism, 986
    regional politics, 641, 649, 713, 1194–1196, 1412,
        1480
    Suez Canal politics, 272, 1306–1307
    women's suffrage, 1383
Ehrlichman, John D., 1367
Eichmann, Adolf, 225–226
Eighty Years and More: Reminiscences, 1815–1897
    (Stanton), 1185
Eisenhower, Dwight D., 700, 765, 875, 1397
Eisenstadt, S. N., 1073
Ekpu, Ray, 366
El Salvador, 75, 168, 192, 194–197, 214, 352, 354, 683,
    1313
Elazar, Daniel, 1193
Elchibey, Abulfaz, 187
Election campaigns, 402–406
    electoral college effect on strategy, 410
    finance reform, 1368
    machine politics, 969–973
    media coverage, 402, 405, 822, 823
    monitoring of, 408
    public opinion polling, 974, 1033
    United States, 454, 661
    and voting behavior, 1347, 1350, 1351
    Western Europe, 454
Election platforms, 926, 936
Elections
    Aristotle view, 726
    at-large elections, 368
    ballots, 112–115
    Canada, 160
    candidate selection and recruitment, 163–166
    Catholic Church endorsement, 183
    direct, 1354
    Greek concept, 1056
    indirect, 406–407, 1354
    institutional role, 777, 985, 1353
    as measure of democracy, 167, 818–819
    monitoring of, 22, 49, 404, 407–409, 620,
        621–622, 626, 1313, 1527
    private organizations, 1001
    United States, 1323
Electoral college, 406, 409–410, 911, 1354
    France, 500
    United States, 113, 199, 406, 409–412, 481, 485,
        660, 996, 1273
Electoral systems
    Baltic states, 115, 118
    candidate selection and recruitment, 163–166
    cube law, 327–328
    dimensions analyzed, 412–422
    districting and, 367–372
    Duverger's rule, 380–382
    Eastern Europe, 450
    election campaigns shaped by, 402
    Germany, Weimar Republic, 420, 561
    Israel, 647
    Italy, 652
    Japan, 665–667, 669
    party numbers determined by, 935–936
    tactical voting, 1350
    Turkey, 1273
    Uruguay, 1331, 1332
    Western Europe, 456–457

Peirce, Charles S., 993
Peisistratus, 252
Peloponnesian War, 188, 251, 253, 394, 981, 1241, 1419
Peloponnesian War (Thucydides), 320, 1221, 1241
Peña Gómez, José Francisco, 377, 378
Pendergast, Tom, 970, 972
Pendleton Act of 1883, 972
Pennsylvania, 6, 57, 410, 970, 971, 1022, 1177
Penrose, Boies, 970
Peonage Abolition Act of 1867, 231
People's Action Party, 373, 374, 1125–1126
People's democracy, 1283–1284
People's Liberation Front, 1181–1183
People's Liberation Movement, 1196, 1197
People's National Congress, 175
People's National Movement, 174, 1376
People's National Party
    Ghana, 530
    Jamaica, 152, 153, 174
People's Party, 985–986
People's Party for Freedom and Democracy, 778
People's Progressive Party, 175
Peoples Redemption Party, 888
People's Republic of China. *See* China, People's Republic of
Peres, Shimon, 649
Perestroika, 116, 122, 1298, 1381
Pérez, Carlos Andrés, 594, 1339, 1340
Pérez de Cuéllar, Javier, 621, 859
Pérez Jiménez, Marcos, 128, 214, 492, 1338
Pericles, 188, 252, 253, 320, 394, 981, 1241, 1243
    funeral oration, text, 1419–1422
Perlman, Selig, 611
Perón, Eva, 1385
Perón, Juan Domingo, 72, 103, 105, 838, 911, 987, 1310, 1458
Perón, María Estela (Isabel) Martínez de, 72, 911
Peronism, 72, 838–839, 987, 988
Perot, Ross, 410, 825, 912, 964, 1031, 1350
Perpetual Peace (Kant), 575
Perry, Matthew, 663
Persia (modern). *See* Iran
Persian empire, 253, 1244
Persian Gulf war, 255, 391, 533, 634, 832, 834, 1029, 1274
Persians (Aeschylus), 253
Personality
    authoritarian, 942–943
    democratic, 941–942
    political culture and, 965–969
    psychoanalysis and, 317, 724, 764–765, 1025–1027
Peru, 826
    colonial experience, 263
    democratization, 347, 424, 511, 626, 725, 838, 1534
    electoral politics, 381, 413
    military rule, 129, 838
    political history, 62–67, 103, 105
    political structures, 1123
    populism, 987
    women's suffrage and other rights, 1384
Pétain, Philippe, 103, 343, 344, 474
Peter (king of Yugoslavia), 1396
Peter (prince regent of Serbia), 1391
Peter (saint), 181
Peter the Great (czar of Russia), 898, 899, 1097
Petlyura, Simon, 1289

Petroleum. *See* oil entries
Phaedrus (Plato), 1079
Phalanxes, 1148
Phenomenology, 1256
Phenomenology of Mind (Hegel), 559, 589
Philip II (king of Spain), 1429
Philip of Macedon, 76, 252
Philippines, 86, 511, 1057
    aid policies and, 48
    authoritarian dictatorship, 104, 357
    Christian democracy, 215
    colonial experience, 86, 263–265, 943–944
    dissidents, 365
    economic decline, 350, 352, 374–375, 945
    education levels, 354
    elections monitoring, 409
    electoral system, 412
    elite consolidation, 424
    Magsaysay leadership, 787
    political history, 86–88, 90, 943–947
    polyarchy, 977
    terms of office, 1225, 1226
    women's suffrage and other rights, 1383, 1385, 1386
    World War II, 1397
Phillips, Anne, 1253
Philosopher-kings, 1244, 1246
Philosophers, 321
Philosophic radicals, 1334
Philosophy of Democratic Government, The (Simon), 183
Philosophy of Right (Hegel), 322, 559, 590, 1259
Physics and Politics (Bagehot), 112
Picado, Teodoro, 314
Pierce, Franklin, 1190
Pilgrims, 1022
Pillarization, 778–779
Pilsudski, Marshal Józef, 227, 447, 949
Pinochet, Augusto, 103, 108, 201–202, 348, 366, 507, 803, 938
Pirandello, Luigi, 325, 326
Pisa, Italy, 222
Pistoia, Italy, 222
Pius IX (pope), 182, 212
Pius XI (pope), 212–213
Pius XII (pope), 183
Plan for the Prince, A (Huang), 286
Planinc, Milka, 1385
Plato, 76, 247, 776, 947, 977, 1049, 1111, 1240, 1281, 1369
    Arab thinkers influenced by, 642, 643
    on censorship, 189
    on democracy, 253, 320, 690, 947, 981, 1120, 1241, 1242, 1246, 1279, 1281
    on freedom of speech, 504
    influence of, 148, 217, 254, 586, 813, 1052
    on justice, 686, 1369
    on natural law, 878
    on obedience to laws, 593
    postmodernism and, 992, 993
    on reasoning power, 397
    on rhetoric, 1079, 1080
    on rule by philosopher-kings, 615, 616, 1244
    on slavery, 1128
    on tyranny, 357
Platt, Thomas C., 970
Platt amendment, 177, 179
Plea bargaining, 684
Plebiscites, 254, 278, 514, 825, 984, 987, 1284, 1371
Plekhanov, Georgy, 752

Plessy v. Ferguson (1896), 232
Plural agency, 300
Plural voting, 842
Pluralism
    collective bargaining, 610–613
    federalism and, 480
    Furnivall theory of plural society, 510–511
    institutional role, 756, 761
    interest politics, 459, 460
    justification for democracy, 692
    Laski views, 722–723
    Lebanon experience, 732–736
    local government, 770
    polyarchy and, 334, 976
    Popper open society, 978, 979
    religious fundamentalism rejection of, 507–510
    socialism and, 1152–1153
    See also Multiethnic democracy
Plurality, 1278
Plyushch, Leonid, 362
Pocock, J. G. A., 254–255
Podrabinik, Alexander, 362
Poetry, and civic education, 393
Pohnpei, 1137
Pol Pot, 89, 90, 357, 1313
Poland, 730, 780, 1096, 1297
    Catholic Church, 181, 184, 185
    civil-military relations, 227, 230
    democratization, 348, 354–355, 424, 426, 839
    dissident movement, 363, 364, 1260
    electoral system, 118, 381, 413
    European Union assistance, 624
    liberum veto, 1340–1341
    market-oriented reforms, 802
    political history, 525, 443, 444, 446–450, 947–953, 1393, 1398
    political structures and practice, 738, 933, 1123
    Solidarity, 1158–1160
    Walesa leadership, 1359–1360
    women's suffrage, 1383
    World War II, 526, 870, 1394, 1395, 1397
Polanyi, Karl, 167
Police power, 103, 954–957
Policy communities, 282
Policy implementation, 957–961
Policy networks, 282
Policy sciences, 723–725
Polignac, Auguste-Jules-Armand-Marie de, 1262
Polisario Front, 851
Polish Peasants' Party, 950
Politica methodice digesta (Althusius), 55, 479
Political action committees, 404, 619, 972
Political advertising, 404, 405, 822
Political alienation, 323, 961–965
    industrial democracy, 608–610
    political culture, 965–969
Political clubs, 1069–1070
Political communication, 1080
Political correctness, 190, 992
Political culture, 53–55, 965–969
    Antifederalist view, 69–70
    Baltic states, 117–120
    Belarus, 122
    Botswana, 133
    Costa Rica, 315–316
    and democratic legitimacy, 747–751
    democratization and, 354–355
    and dominant party democracy, 374
    Mexico, 827